AFFIRMATIVE ACTION

AFFIRMATIVE ACTION

An Encyclopedia   Volume II: J–Z

Edited by **James A. Beckman**

Advisory Editors
Maria D. Beckman and Paulina X. Ruf

Greenwood Press
Westport, Connecticut • London

Library of Congress Cataloging-in-Publication Data

Affirmative action : an encyclopedia / edited by James A. Beckman.
    p. cm.
   Includes bibliographical references and index.
   ISBN 1–57356–519–9 (set : alk. paper)—ISBN 0–313–33023–9 (vol. 1 : alk. paper)—
ISBN 0–313–33024–7 (vol. 2 : alk. paper)
    1. Affirmative action programs—United States—Encyclopedias.   I. Beckman, James A.
HF5549.5.A34A426   2004
331.13'3'097303—dc22   2003064257

British Library Cataloguing in Publication Data is available.

Library of Congress Catalog Card Number: 2003064257
ISBN: 1–57356–519–9 (set)
    0–313–33023–9 (vol. I)
    0–313–33024–7 (vol. II)

First published in 2004

Greenwood Press, 88 Post Road West, Westport, CT 06881
An imprint of Greenwood Publishing Group, Inc.
www.greenwood.com

Printed in the United States of America

The paper used in this book complies with the
Permanent Paper Standard issued by the National
Information Standards Organization (Z39.48–1984).

10   9   8   7   6   5   4   3   2   1

This work is dedicated to my parents, Robert and Jean Beckman, who have been a great source of inspiration and strength to me all of my life. They taught me the value of education, scholarship, and hard work without having to forsake the simple joys of life. Sadly, my father passed away while the first draft of the book was being finalized in June 2003. While he never had the chance to see the book in print or to comment on the content, his work ethic in life was contagious, and so, in a sense, he has contributed to the worthy endeavor of this book by serving as a role model and a source of inspiration for me.

CONTENTS

LIST OF EDITORS AND CONTRIBUTORS

Editor

James A. Beckman, B.A., J.D., LL.M.
Assistant Professor, University of Tampa
Tampa, Florida

Advisory Editors

Maria D. Beckman, B.A., J.D.*
Practicing Attorney, Federal Government
Tampa, Florida

Paulina X. Ruf, B.A., M.A., M.D.A., Ph.D.
Assistant Professor, University of Tampa
Tampa, Florida

Contributors

Thomas A. Adamich, B.A., M.L.S.
Librarian, Ohio Public School System
Cuyahoga Falls, Ohio

Adalberto Aguirre Jr., B.A., M.A., Ph.D.
Professor, University of California at
   Riverside
Riverside, California

Mohammed B. Alam, B.A., M.A., M.Phil.,
   Ph.D.
Professor, Miyazaki International College
Miyazaki, Japan

Gayle Avant, B.A., M.A., Ph.D.
Associate Professor, Baylor University
Waco, Texas

Maya Alexandra Beasley, B.A., M.A., Ph.D.
Postdoctorate Fellowship
Harvard University
Cambridge, Massachusetts

James A. Beckman, B.A., J.D., LL.M.
Assistant Professor, University of Tampa
Tampa, Florida

Maria D. Beckman, B.A., J.D.*
Practicing Attorney, Federal Government
Tampa, Florida

Mirza Asmer Beg, B.A., M.A., M.Phil., Ph.D.
Associate Professor, Aligarh Muslim
   University
Aligarh, India

Richard J. Bennett, B.S., J.D.
Practicing Attorney, Private Practice
Adjunct Faculty, John Carroll University
Cleveland, Ohio

Ann Marie Bissessar, B.A., LL.B., M.S.,
   Ph.D.
Lecturer, University of the West Indies
St. Augustine, Trinidad

*The views expressed by these contributors are their own and do not necessarily reflect those of the federal government or of the particular federal agency with which the contributor is affiliated.

Sheila Bluhm, B.A., M.A., Ph.D.
Lecturer, University of Michigan
Ann Arbor, Michigan

Rachel Bowen, B.A., J.D., (Ph.D. candidate)
Georgetown University
Washington, D.C.

Scott S. Brenneman, B.A., J.D.*
Assistant Professor, U.S. Military Academy
West Point, New York

Susan F. Brinkley, B.A., M.A., Ph.D.
Associate Professor, University of Tampa
Tampa, Florida

F. Erik Brooks, B.A., M.S., M.P.A., M.Ed.,
 Ph.D.
Assistant Professor, Georgia Southern
 University
Statesboro, Georgia

Christopher R. Capsambelis, B.S., M.A.,
 Ph.D.
Chair, Criminology Department
Associate Professor, University of Tampa
Tampa, Florida

Pamela C. Corley, B.A., M.A., J.D., (Ph.D.
 candidate)
Georgia State University
Atlanta, Georgia

Jack A. Covarrubias, B.A., M.S.
University of Southern Mississippi
Long Beach, Mississippi

John W. Dietrich, B.A., M.A., Ph.D.
Assistant Professor, Bryant College
Smithfield, Rhode Island

Paulette Patterson Dilworth, B.A., M.A.,
 Ph.D.
Assistant Professor, Indiana University
Bloomington, Indiana

Marc Dollinger, B.A., M.A., Ph.D.
Professor and Richard Goldman Chair in
 Jewish Studies, San Francisco State
 University
San Francisco, California

Gregory M. Duhl, B.A., J.D., LL.M.
Lecturer, Temple University
Philadelphia, Pennsylvania

Lisa A. Ennis, B.A., M.A., M.S.
Assistant Professor, Austin Peay State
 University
Clarksville, Tennessee

Abby L. Ferber, B.A., M.A., Ph.D.
Director of Women's Studies
Associate Professor, University of Colorado
Colorado Springs, Colorado

Christopher Flannery, B.A., M.A., Ph.D.
Chair, Department of History and Political
 Science
Professor, Azusa Pacific University
Azusa, California

Jayson J. Funke, B.A., M.A.
Wrentham, Massachusetts

Robert Don Gifford II, B.A., J.D.*
Practicing Attorney, Federal Government
Reno, Nevada

Denise O'Neil Green, B.A., M.P.A., Ph.D.
Assistant Professor, University of Illinois
Champaign, Illinois

Kyra R. Greene, B.A., M.A., (Ph.D.
 candidate)
Stanford University
Stanford, California

Paul M. Haridakis, B.A., J.D., Ph.D.
Assistant Professor, Kent State University
Kent, Ohio

Thomas J. Hickey, B.A., M.A., J.D., Ph.D.
Professor, University of Tampa
Tampa, Florida

Arthur M. Holst, B.S., M.P.A., Ph.D.
Government Affairs Manager, City of
 Philadelphia
Philadelphia, Pennsylvania

Paul M. Hughes, B.A., M.A., Ph.D.
Chair, Department of Humanities
Associate Professor, University of Michigan
 at Dearborn
Dearborn, Michigan

Eileen Husselbaugh, B.A., J.D.*
Practicing Attorney, Federal Government
Adjunct Faculty, University of Tampa
Tampa, Florida

Janis Judson, B.A., M.A., Ph.D.
Professor, Hood College
Frederick, Maryland

Jeffrey Kraus, B.A., M.A., M.Phil., Ph.D.
Professor, Wagner College
Staten Island, New York

Tom Lansford, B.A., M.A., Ph.D.
Assistant Professor, University of Southern
   Mississippi
Long Beach, Mississippi

Michael K. Lee, B.S., J.D.
Practicing Attorney, Private Practice
Southfield, Michigan

Sharon Meyers, B.A., (M.S. candidate)
University of Southern Mississippi
Long Beach, Mississippi

Carlton Morse, B.A.
Azusa, California

Rae W. Newstad, B.A., M.A., Ph.D.
Blanchard, Oklahoma

Paul Obiyo Mbanaso Njemanze, B.A., M.A.,
   Ph.D.
Professor, University of Lagos
Yaba, Lagos, Nigeria

Betty Nyangoni, B.A., M.A., Ph.D.
Educational Consultant
Washington, D.C.

Kingsley Ufuoma Omoyibo, B.S., M.S.,
   Ph.D.
Lecturer, University of Benin
Benin, Nigeria

Peter L. Platteborze, B.S., Ph.D.*
Major, U.S. Army
Frederick, Maryland

Michael D. Quigley, B.A., M.A., J.D., Ph.D.
Lecturer, California State University at
   Pomona
Pomona, California

Aimée Hobby Rhodes, B.A., J.D.*
Assistant Professor, U.S. Military Academy
West Point, New York

Sean Richey, B.A., M.A., Ph.D.
Adjunct Faculty, City University of New York
New York, New York

Naomi Robertson, B.A., B.S., M.P.A., Ph.D.
Assistant Professor, Macon State College
Macon, Georgia

Paulina X. Ruf, B.A., M.A., M.D.A., Ph.D.
Assistant Professor, University of Tampa
Tampa, Florida

Robert A. Russ, B.A., M.A., Ph.D.
Assistant Professor, Elon University
Elon, North Carolina

James P. Scanlan, B.A., J.D.
Practicing Attorney, Private Practice
Washington, D.C.

Mark J. Senediak, B.A., M.S.
Financial Risk Analyst
Mount Lebanon, Pennsylvania

Maria Jose Sotelo, B.A., M.A., Ph.D.
Professor, Universidad de Santiago de
   Compostela
A Caruna, Spain

Glenn L. Starks, B.S., M.S., Ph.D.*
Chief, Planning and Requirements, Defense
   Supply, U.S. Defense Department
Richmond, Virginia

Arthur K. Steinberg, B.A., J.D., Ph.D.
Professor, Catawba College
Salisbury, North Carolina

Nicole M. Stephens, B.A., M.A., Ph.D., Ed.S.
Assistant Professor, St. Louis University
St. Louis, Missouri

Mfanya D. Tryman, A.A., B.A., M.S., Ph.D.
Dean, College of Liberal Arts
Professor, Mississippi State University
Starkville, Mississippi

Ronnie B. Tucker Sr., B.A., M.A., Th.D.,
  Ph.D.
Assistant Professor, Shippensburg University
Shippensburg, Pennsylvania

La Trice M. Washington, B.A., M.A.,
  Ph.D.
Assistant Professor, Otterbein College
Westerville, Ohio

David L. Weeks, B.A., M.A., Ph.D.
Dean, College of Liberal Arts and Sciences
Professor, Azusa Pacific University
Azusa, California

LIST OF ENTRIES

GUIDE TO RELATED TOPICS

Affirmative Action–Related Laws

Alaska Native Claims Settlement Act
Busing
Civil Rights Act of 1866
Civil Rights Act of 1875
Civil Rights Act of 1957
Civil Rights Act of 1960
Civil Rights Act of 1964
Civil Rights Act of 1968
Civil Rights Act of 1991
Civil Rights Restoration Act of 1988
Civil Service Reform Act of 1978
Civil War (Reconstruction) Amendments and
   Civil Rights Acts
Equal Employment Opportunity Act of 1972
Equal Opportunity Act of 1995
Equal Pay Act of 1963
Fair Housing Amendments Act of 1988
GI Bill
Head Start
Housing and Urban Development Act of
   1968
Immigration Act of 1965
National Labor Relations Act of 1935 (Wag-
   ner Act)
One Florida Initiative
Percentage Plans
Proposition 209
Public Works Employment Act of 1977
Rehabilitation Act of 1973
Title VI of the Civil Rights Act of 1964
Title VII of the Civil Rights Act of 1964

Title IX of the Education Amendments of
   1972
Voting Rights Act of 1965
Washington Initiative 200

Alternatives to Traditional Affirmative Action

Affirmative Access
Affirmative Action, Arguments for
Affirmative Action, Criticisms of
Affirmative Action, Decline in Usage of
Affirmative Action, Myths and Misconcep-
   tions of
Class-Based Affirmative Action
Color-Blind Constitution
Economically Disadvantaged
Head Start
Majority-Group Resentment
Merit Selections
Meritocracy
One Florida Initiative
Percentage Plans
Performance-Based Selections
Proposition 209
Race-Neutral Criteria
Scapegoating/Displaced-Aggression Theories
Washington Initiative 200

Beneficiaries of Affirmative Action

African Americans
Alaskan Natives

Mott, Lucretia Coffin
Moynihan, Daniel Patrick
Nixon, Richard Milhous
Powell, Adam Clayton, Jr.
Randolph, Asa Philip
Roosevelt, Eleanor
Roosevelt, Franklin Delano
Stanton, Elizabeth Cady
Stone, Harlan Fiske
Stone, Lucy
Truman, Harry
Washington, Booker T.

Housing and Land Issues

Alaska Native Claims Settlement Act
Busing
Civil Rights Act of 1866
Civil Rights Act of 1875
Civil Rights Act of 1968
Department of Housing and Urban Development
Environmental Racism
Fair Housing Amendments Act of 1988
Gentrification
Housing
Housing and Urban Development Act of 1968
Lending Practices and Affirmative Action
Zoning and Affirmative Action

Implementation Issues and Alternatives to Affirmative Action

Affirmative Access
Affirmative Action, Arguments for
Affirmative Action, Criticisms of
Affirmative Action, Decline in Usage of
Affirmative Action, Myths and Misconceptions of
Affirmative Action Plan/Program
Census Classifications, Ethnic and Racial
Class-Based Affirmative Action
Diversity
Diversity Management
Good-Old-Boy Factor
Majority-Group Resentment
Merit Selections

Narrowly Tailored Affirmative Action Plans
Percentage Plans
Performance-Based Selections
Quotas
Race-Neutral Criteria
Role Model Theory
Scapegoating/Displaced-Aggression Theories
Standardized Testing
Statistical Proof of Discrimination
Supreme Court and Affirmative Action

Legal Theories/Concepts

All Deliberate Speed
Benign Discrimination
Color-Blind Constitution
Compelling Governmental Interest
De Facto and De Jure Segregation
Disability Classifications under the Fifth and Fourteenth Amendments
Discrete and Insular Minority
Disparate Treatment and Disparate Impact
Equal Protection Clause
Intermediate Scrutiny
Invidious Discrimination
Manifest Imbalance Standard
Narrowly Tailored Affirmative Action Plans
Rational Basis Scrutiny
Reverse Discrimination
Strict Scrutiny
Suspect Classification

Media and Affirmative Action

Federal Communications Commission
First Amendment
Licensing and Affirmative Action
Lutheran Church–Missouri Synod v. FCC
Media and Affirmative Action
Metro Broadcasting, Inc. v. FCC
Red Lion Broadcasting Co. v. FCC

Military and Veterans

Executive Order 8802
GI Bill
Military and Affirmative Action
Powell, Colin

Veterans' Preferences
Vietnam Era Veterans' Readjustment Assistance Act of 1974

Organizations (Nongovernmental)

American Association for Affirmative Action
American Association of University Professors
American Bar Association
American Civil Liberties Union
American Civil Rights Institute
American Jewish Committee
American Jewish Congress
Americans for Democratic Action
Americans United for Affirmative Action
Anti-Defamation League
Black Panther Party
Brotherhood of Sleeping Car Porters
Center for Equal Opportunity
Center for Individual Rights
Chronicle of Higher Education
Citizens' Commission on Civil Rights
Citizens' Initiative on Race and Ethnicity
Coalition to Defend Affirmative Action, Integration, and Fight for Equality by Any Means Necessary
Congress of Racial Equality
Congressional Black Caucus
Democratic Party and Affirmative Action
Ku Klux Klan
Leadership Conference on Civil Rights
League of Women Voters
National Association for the Advancement of Colored People
National Education Association
National Organization for Women
Rainbow PUSH Coalition
Republican Party and Affirmative Action
Southern Christian Leadership Conference
Urban League

Political Leaders, Events, and Concepts

Abolitionists
Affirmative Access
Afrocentrism
Alaska Native Claims Settlement Act
American Civil War
Anthony, Susan Brownell

Articles of Confederation
Baker v. Carr
Bill of Rights
Black Panther Party
Brooke, Edward W.
Brotherhood of Sleeping Car Porters
Bush, George Herbert Walker
Bush, George W.
Busing
Carmichael, Stokely
Carter, James "Jimmy" Earl, Jr.
Caste System
Census Classifications, Ethnic and Racial
Chavez, Linda
Chisholm, Shirley
Civil Rights Act of 1866
Civil Rights Act of 1875
Civil Rights Act of 1957
Civil Rights Act of 1960
Civil Rights Act of 1964
Civil Rights Act of 1968
Civil Rights Act of 1991
Civil Rights Restoration Act of 1988
Civil Service Reform Act of 1978
Civil War (Reconstruction) Amendments and Civil Rights Acts
Clinton, William Jefferson
Congress of Racial Equality
Congressional Black Caucus
Constitution, Civil Rights, and Equality
Darwinism
Declaration of Independence and Equality
Democratic Party and Affirmative Action
Douglass, Frederick
E Pluribus Unum
Eisenhower, Dwight David
Federalism
Ford, Gerald Rudolph
Jackson, Jesse
Jim Crow Laws
Johnson, Lyndon Baines
Jordan, Barbara Charline
Kennedy, John Fitzgerald
Kerner Commission
King, Martin Luther, Jr.
Leadership Conference on Civil Rights
League of Women Voters
Level Playing Field

Marshall, Thurgood
McGovern Commission
Moynihan, Daniel Patrick
Nixon, Richard Milhous
Norton, Eleanor Holmes
Paternalistic Race Relations Theory
Pluralism
Powell, Adam Clayton, Jr.
Powell, Colin
Proposition 209
Public Works Employment Act of 1977
Radicalism
Randolph, Asa Philip
Rangel, Charles
Reagan, Ronald
Reparations
Republican Party and Affirmative Action
Riots, Economically and Racially Motivated
Roosevelt, Eleanor
Roosevelt, Franklin Delano
Slavery
Slavery and the Founding Fathers
Social Contract
Social Engineering
Split Labor Market Theory
Supreme Court and Affirmative Action
Voting Rights Act of 1965
White Primary

Presidents and Supreme Court Justices

Blackmun, Harry Andrew
Brennan, William Joseph
Breyer, Stephen Gerald
Burger Court and Affirmative Action
Bush, George Herbert Walker
Bush, George W.
Carter, James "Jimmy" Earl, Jr.
Clinton, William Jefferson
Eisenhower, Dwight David
Ford, Gerald Rudolph
Ginsburg, Ruth Bader
Johnson, Lyndon Baines
Kennedy, Anthony McLeod
Kennedy, John Fitzgerald
Marshall, Thurgood
Nixon, Richard Milhous
O'Connor, Sandra Day

Powell, Lewis Franklin, Jr.
Reagan, Ronald
Rehnquist, William Hobbs
Roosevelt, Franklin Delano
Scalia, Antonin
Souter, David Hackett
Stevens, John Paul
Stone, Harlan Fiske
Thomas, Clarence
Truman, Harry
Warren Court and Affirmative Action
White, Byron Raymond

Race-Based Programs, Concepts, and Miscellaneous Issues

Census Classifications, Ethnic and Racial
Chicanismo
A Common Destiny: Blacks and American Society
Criminal Justice System and Affirmative Action
Double Consciousness
Hate Crimes
Japanese Internment and World War II
Jury Selection and Affirmative Action
Race in Colonial America
Race-Based Affirmative Action
Race-Neutral Criteria
Racial and Ethnic Stratification
Racial Discrimination
Racial Privacy Initiative
Racial Profiling
Racial Stereotyping
Reparations
Slavery
Slavery and the Founding Fathers
Uncle Tom

Sociological Theories and Concepts

Afrocentrism
Amalgamation
Assimilation Theory
The Bell Curve
Bigotry
Caste System
Class Identification
Color Consciousness

Critical Race Theory
Darwinism
Deracialization
Discrimination
Double Consciousness
Ethnocentrism
Eugenics
Eurocentrism
Ideological Racism/Racist Ideology
Institutional Discrimination
Integration
Majority-Group Resentment
Marxist Theory and Affirmative Action
Meritocracy
Multiculturalism
Multiple-Jeopardy Hypothesis
Multiracialism
Occupational Prestige
Overt Racism
Paternalistic Race Relations Theory
Plantation System
Pluralism
Preferences
Prejudice
Relative Deprivation Theory
Rigid Competitive Race Relations Theory
Scapegoating/Displaced-Aggression Theories
Scientific Racism
Social Engineering

Socialization Theory of Equality
Talented Tenth
Uncle Tom
WASP (White Anglo-Saxon Protestant)
Weber, Max
White Supremacy
Xenophobia

Writers, Scholars, and Activists

Bell, Derrick A., Jr.
Bolick, Clint
Carter, Stephen L.
Chavez, Linda
Clark, Kenneth Bancroft
Connerly, Ward
D'Souza, Dinesh
Edley, Christopher F.
Gates, Henry Louis, Jr.
Glazer, Nathan
Guinier, Lani
Jackson, Jesse
Loury, Glenn C.
Morrison, Toni
Skocpol, Theda
Sowell, Thomas
Steele, Shelby
Thernstrom, Stephan, and Thernstrom, Abigail
West, Cornel

TIMELINE OF MAJOR EVENTS IMPACTING AFFIRMATIVE ACTION

See individual entries for an in-depth description of these events.

Major Historical Events Relating to Affirmative Action
1865

End of American Civil War.

Ratification of the Thirteenth Amendment, constitutionally abolishing the institution of slavery.

Freedmen's Bureau Act is passed by Congress; the Freedmen's Bureau is later described by Justice Thurgood Marshall as one of the country's earliest affirmative action programs.

1866

Civil Rights Act of 1866 enacted by Congress; act identifies certain basic civil rights that shall not be abridged on account of race.

1868

Ratification of the Fourteenth Amendment, which in part provides that states shall not deprive an individual of due process of law or the equal protection of the laws.

1870

Ratification of the Fifteenth Amendment, prohibiting states from depriving an individual of the right to vote on account of race or previous condition of involuntary servitude.

1875

Congress enacts the Civil Rights Act of 1875, which provides sweeping civil rights in the area of public accommodations; however, most of the act is held unconstitutional eight years later in the *Civil Rights Cases*.

1876

Reconstruction ends in the South; beginning of segregationist and discriminatory Jim Crow laws throughout the South.

1883

The Supreme Court decides the *Civil Rights Cases*, declaring the Civil Rights Act of 1875 unconstitutional and declaring that Congress lacks the authority to regulate private conduct under the Fourteenth Amendment; the *Civil Rights Cases* decision represents a colossal setback for civil rights in the South.

1896

The Supreme Court decides *Plessy v. Ferguson*, ratifying the state practice of "Jim Crow" and segregation and creating the separate-but-equal doctrine.

1920

Ratification of the Nineteenth Amendment, granting women the right to vote.

1935

The first usage of the term "affirmative action" is found in Section 10c of the National Labor Relations Act of 1935, which states that the National Labor Relations Board (in a case involving unfair labor practices) might "take such affirmative action, including reinstatement of employees with or without back pay."

1941

President Franklin Roosevelt issues Executive Order 8802, requiring nondiscrimination practices by defense contractors.

1945

Congress enacts the GI Bill, providing special benefits to veterans and arguably becoming the largest affirmative action program in U.S. history.

1954

The Supreme Court decides *Brown v. Board of Education*, holding "separate-but-equal" racial segregation in public schools to be a violation of the Fourteenth Amendment.

Major Current Events Relating to Affirmative Action
1961

President John Kennedy issues Executive Order 10925, making the first modern reference to "affirmative action" in federal government policy by mandating that federal contractors "take affirmative action" to ensure that no discrimination is employed against minorities.

1964

Congress enacts the Civil Rights Act of 1964, a sweeping piece of legislation that bars discrimination based upon race, color, sex, religion, or national origin in public accommodations, in employment, and in federally funded educational programs.

1965

President Lyndon B. Johnson gives his famous Howard University speech, in which he argues that civil rights laws alone are not adequate to remedy discrimination and inequality; Johnson uses the "chained-runner" metaphor during the speech.

President Johnson issues Executive Order 11246, expanding on President Kennedy's Executive Order 10925 and ordering "affirmative action" to ensure no discrimination by contractors and federal employees on account of race, creed, color, or national origin in the hiring and employment of minority employees; E.O. 11246 also requires contractors to document their compliance with the executive order.

Congress enacts the Voting Rights Act of 1965, which ensures that the rights of citizens to vote will not be denied or impaired because of racial or language discrimination.

1967

President Lyndon B. Johnson amends Executive Order 11246 to cover gender discrimination, as does Executive Order 11375.

1969

President Richard M. Nixon promotes race-conscious affirmative action in his Philadelphia Plan, the most forceful race-conscious/preferential program for minorities up to that time; the Philadelphia Plan calls for timetables and goals by which the construction industry is obligated to increase minority employment.

Executive Order 11478 is promulgated. Executive Order 11478 supersedes Executive Order 11246 in part and prohibits discrimination on the basis of race, color, religion, sex, or national origin (and is later amended to prohibit discrimination on the basis of handicap, age, sexual orientation, and status as a parent). The order requires most federal government employers to take affirmative action to ensure equal employment opportunities.

1972

Congress enacts the Equal Employment Opportunity Act, which amends and strengthens Title VII of the Civil Rights Act of 1964, which had made it illegal for employers to discriminate against any individual because of race, color, religion, sex, or national origin; the 1972 act expands the groups covered by Title VII and gives the Equal Employment Opportunity Commission (EEOC) new enforcement powers.

Congress enacts the Education Amendments (Title IX), which prohibit gender-based discrimination by public and private institutions receiving public funds.

1973

Congress enacts the Vocational Rehabilitation Act, which includes qualified individuals with disabilities in affirmative action requirements for federal contractors.

1974

The Supreme Court decides *DeFunis v. Odegaard,* the first Supreme Court case dealing with the constitutionality of affirmative action as the central issue in the case. The Court rules that a white student's challenge of "reverse discrimination" in a university affirmative action admission plan is moot (and not reviewable on the merits) because the student was subsequently admitted to the school. The Court will not take another case dealing with this topic until the seminal *Regents of the University of California v. Bakke* case in 1978.

Congress enacts the Vietnam Era Veterans' Readjustment Assistance Act, which includes veterans with disabilities and Vietnam veterans in the then-typical affirmative action requirements for federal contractors.

1975

The Supreme Court decides *Albemarle Paper Co. v. Moody*, stating that the goals of antidiscrimination laws are twofold, to bar "like discrimination in the future" and "eliminate the discriminatory effects of the past"; the goal of eliminating the discriminatory effects of the past becomes the chief compelling government interest for affirmative action plans.

1976

The Supreme Court decides *Franks v. Bowman*, in part holding that affirmative action may be appropriate to eliminate discriminatory effects of the past.

1978

The Supreme Court decides *Regents of the University of California v. Bakke*, a landmark affirmative action case that rejects fixed racial quotas in the educational context as unconstitutional while allowing for the use of race as one factor in admissions policies.

1979

The Supreme Court decides *United Steelworkers of America v. Weber*, holding that a voluntary affirmative action plan by a private employer is permissible under Title VII provided that a "manifest racial imbalance" exists in the job at issue, the job is historically one that was segregated by race, and the plan does not "unnecessarily trammel" the rights of nonminority employees and is temporary.

1980

The Supreme Court decides *Fullilove v. Klutznick*, allowing flexible modest quotas/set-asides (10 percent set-aside for minority contractors) in the federal contracting context for minority contractors in response to prior institutional discrimination.

1984

The Supreme Court decides *Firefighters Local Union No. 1784 v. Stotts*, holding that white employees with more seniority on the job cannot be laid off in lieu of newer minority employees on the job, regardless of the existence of affirmative action plans; that is, a bona fide seniority system is a legitimate and protected practice under Title VII of the 1964 Civil Rights Act.

1986

The Supreme Court decides *Wygant v. Jackson Board of Education*, declaring that affirmative action plans that lay off nonminority teachers on account of race are not legally permissible; the Court also rejects the "role model theory" and concern for diversity in the general population as legitimate justifications for imposing an affirmative action plan upon employees and holds that affirmative action cannot be lawfully used in the context of reduction-in-force layoffs where race is a factor.

The Supreme Court decides *Local 93, International Association of Firefighters v. City of Cleveland* and *Local 28 of the Sheet Metal Workers' International Association v. EEOC*, upholding in both cases court-ordered (i.e., not voluntary) racially conscious hiring and promotion affirmative action plans after past discrimination has been documented.

1987

The Supreme Court decides *Johnson v. Transportation Agency, Santa Clara County*, upholding a gender-based affirmative action plan and holding that a severe underrepresentation of women and minorities when compared to the qualified labor force is sufficient justification for maintaining a gender-conscious affirmative action plan, so long as the use of race and/or gender is only "one factor" in choosing candidates.

The Supreme Court decides *United States v. Paradise*, upholding a lower federal court's imposition of strict racial quotas in the employment hiring context as an appropriate remedial measure in response to four decades of overt and defiant racism by the State of Alabama Department of Public Safety.

1989

The Supreme Court decides *City of Richmond v. J.A. Croson Co.*, holding that the use of state/local racial quotas/set-asides (30 percent set-asides for minority contractors) in the contracting arena is impermissible; the *Croson* decision rejects a contracting set-aside scheme similar to the one the Court had approved in *Fullilove* in the 1980s; in *Croson*, the Court states for the first time that affirmative action is a "highly suspect tool," a decision that marks the beginning of the current era, where the Court views affirmative action with suspicion. Before *Croson*, the Supreme Court was generally considered to be supportive of affirmative action.

1990

The Supreme Court decides *Metro Broadcasting, Inc. v. FCC*, ultimately holding that the Federal Communications Commission's minority preference policies do not violate the Equal Protection Clause because they are consistent with legitimate congressional objectives of increasing program diversity.

President George H.W. Bush refuses to sign the Civil Rights Act of 1990, which Bush believes will inevitably lead to rigid racial quotas in affirmative action plans in employment.

1991

Congress enacts the Civil Rights Act of 1991, containing many of the same provisions as the failed Civil Rights Act of 1990; the 1991 measure contains many provisions meant to reverse Supreme Court decisions of 1988–1989, which were deemed too draconian, onerous, or unfavorable to the employee in the Title VII and affirmative action contexts.

1992

The U.S. Circuit Court of Appeals for the Fourth Circuit holds in *Podberesky v. Kirwin* that race-based scholarship programs do not satisfy a "compelling governmental interest" as is required for race-conscious plans under the Fourteenth Amendment unless there is a finding of a need for the program to remedy the present effects of past discrimination.

1995

The Supreme Court decides *Adarand Constructors, Inc. v. Peña*, holding that the use of federal race-based preferences in the contracting context is impermissible except in the most exceptional circumstances; the Court imposes the strict scrutiny standard on federal racial classifications, holding that use of a racial classification must be narrowly tailored to fulfill a "compelling governmental interest"; this decision explicitly overrules the *Metro Broadcasting* and *Fullilove* decisions to the extent that those decisions applied a less onerous test than strict scrutiny.

In a speech after the *Adarand* decision, President Bill Clinton states that affirmative action is still needed by society, but should be restructured to ensure that the plan does not reversely discriminate, a speech (and proposal) that becomes known as "Mend It, Don't End It"; on the same day as the speech, Clinton releases a White House memorandum that calls for the elimination of any affirmative action program that (1) uses fixed racial quotas; (2) creates preferences for the unqualified; (3) reversely discriminates; or (4) is not temporary in nature (i.e., no permanent programs).

1996

The Federal Fifth Circuit Court decides *Hopwood v. Texas*, rejecting the University of Texas's affirmative action program under the Fourteenth Amendment and rejecting Justice Lewis Powell's assertion in the *Bakke* case that diversity in higher education could be a compelling state interest; the *Hopwood* decision is the first of several important and conflicting federal circuit court cases on this subject, ultimately leading to Supreme Court review of the *Gratz v. Bollinger/Grutter v. Bollinger* cases in 2003.

1997

California's Proposition 209 goes into effect, essentially abolishing affirmative action in the state; Proposition 209 prohibits affirmative action (granting any preferential treatment to any individual or group based upon race, sex, color, or ethnicity) in the areas of public employment, contracting, or education.

In response to the *Hopwood* decision, Texas adopts its "10 Percent" percentage plan as a race-neutral alternative to affirmative action in higher education, requiring all public colleges and universities in the state to admit the top 10 percent of the graduating high-school classes in the state; Florida follows Texas's lead several years later, becoming the second state to adopt a percentage plan in lieu of affirmative action.

The U.S. Court of Appeals for the Ninth Circuit upholds the constitutionality of California Proposition 209 in *Coalition for Economic Equity v. Wilson*; the Supreme Court refuses review of the case.

A lawsuit is filed in federal district court in Michigan challenging the University of Michigan's admissions program as providing unjust preferences to minorities; this lawsuit culminates in 2003 in the landmark decisions by the Supreme Court on affirmative action in *Gratz v. Bollinger* and *Grutter v. Bollinger*.

1998

Washington State adopts Initiative 200, which, like Proposition 209 in California, abolishes affirmative action in the state.

2000

Florida adopts the educational component of Governor Jeb Bush's One Florida Plan, ending the use of affirmative action in the state.

A federal district court judge upholds the use of race as constitutional and as a permissible factor to consider in admissions at the University of Michigan in *Gratz v. Bollinger*; the case is appealed.

2001

A federal district court judge rejects an affirmative action plan used at the University of Michigan law school in *Grutter v. Bollinger*; the case is appealed.

2002

The federal Sixth Circuit in the University of Michigan law school case (*Grutter*) holds that the affirmative action program being used is unconstitutional; however, before the Sixth Circuit can issue an opinion in the undergraduate case (*Gratz*), the Supreme Court announces that it will consolidate and review both cases.

2003

The Supreme Court decides the *Gratz v. Bollinger* and *Grutter v. Bollinger* cases, heralded as the "Alamo for affirmative action" and as landmark cases even before the Court issues its decisions. In *Gratz*, the Court declares the University of Michigan undergraduate admissions process unconstitutional in violation of the Fourteenth Amendment because the plan uses race-conscious preferences that, according to the Court, make race the determining factor for many applicants and interfere with the individualized consideration of each applicant. In *Grutter*, the Court upholds the affirmative action plan utilized at the University of Michigan Law School, holding that the plan is narrowly tailored to achieve a compelling governmental interest because it does allow for individual consideration of each applicant. In so holding, the Court declares that diversity in higher education is a compelling government interest, adopting Justice Powell's diversity rationale announced twenty-five years earlier in *Regents of the University of California v. Bakke*. However, the majority opinion also states that affirmative action in higher education should no longer be needed in twenty-five years (i.e., 2028).

AFFIRMATIVE ACTION

J

Jackson, Jesse (1941–   )

Jesse Louis Jackson Sr. has been one of the most prominent, popular, charismatic, and controversial African American civil rights activists for more than thirty-five years in the United States. In 1984 and 1988, Jackson became the first serious African American candidate in history to run for the office of president of the United States. Although African American congresswoman Shirley Chisholm had sought the Democratic nomination some twelve years earlier, her candidacy was largely symbolic, while Jackson's campaign has been described as impacting the actual election. Jackson is a leading advocate of race-conscious affirmative action and stated in March 2003 that its potential termination is "the most significant threat to civil rights in our lifetime." In a speech at a rally in favor of affirmative action on the University of Michigan campus in April 2001, Jackson claimed that terminating affirmative action would be akin to reversing civil rights laws. Jackson stated, "You must not let them turn back the clock. Ann Arbor, it's your day. Don't let these Confederates turn back the clock. This is an American flag, not a Confederate flag" (*Black Issues in Higher Education* 2001, 19).

In addition to his strong support of affirmative action, Jackson is currently involved in many other civil rights activities and is the founder of the National Rainbow Coalition and Operation PUSH (People United to Serve Humanity). The National Rainbow Coalition is a political organization that is headquartered in Chicago, Illinois. The purpose of this organization is to work on political agendas involving poor people and people of color throughout the United States. Jackson founded Operation PUSH shortly after his resignation from the Southern Christian Leadership Conference (SCLC) in 1971, an organization founded by Dr. Martin Luther King Jr. His whole agenda for both organizations was to help people of all races, but particularly people of color, to push for greater economic and political equality in the United States. He is currently active in the effort to keep affirmative action programs in place in schools, colleges, and workplaces. He is known throughout the world for using his most famous quote: I AM SOMEBODY!

Jackson was born in Greenville, South Carolina, on October 8, 1941. He attended the University of Illinois in Chicago for a short period, but found the environment during the late 1950s to the early 1960s to be very insensitive to African American students. He transferred to North Carolina Agricultural and Technical State University (A&T) in Greensboro. He was very active as a student, was elected student body president, and became involved in civil rights issues even before he graduated in 1964 with a degree in political science. Jackson later completed his master's of divinity from Chicago Theological Seminary in 2000. Shortly after obtaining his bachelor's degree, Jackson joined the SCLC, led by King. In 1966, as a member of SCLC, Jackson helped to found a branch of Operation Breadbasket in Chicago. He was in Memphis with King when King was assassinated in 1968. Jackson was catapulted into national prominence, especially among African Americans who wanted a leader, because of the death of King.

In 1971, Jackson was suspended from the SCLC and resigned because some in the organization accused him of looking out for his own personal interests and not for the good of the organization. Jackson founded Operation PUSH shortly after his dismissal from SCLC. Because Jackson is such a stirring orator, he won many ears, particularly in the African American community, as he spoke about civil rights, economic problems, and racism throughout Chicago and the United States. Jackson was also very concerned about the nihilism within the African American community, which Jackson perceived as being due to years of oppression within the United States. This nihilism consisted of a high teenage pregnancy rate, hopelessness, high school dropout rates, and rampant crime within black communities. He would often speak to crowds of young people about self-worth and self-love. One of the young men whom he encouraged and mentored was the popular judge Greg Mathis from Chicago, Illinois. Judge Mathis has become one of the most popular judges on television. Mathis often speaks about his encouragement from Jackson, and, in March 2003, Mathis and Jackson oversaw a rally at the U.S. Supreme Court on the eve of the decisions in the affirmative action cases *Gratz v. Bollinger*, 123 S. Ct. 2411, 2003 U.S. LEXIS 4801 (2003), and *Grutter v. Bollinger*, 123 S. Ct. 2325, 2003 U.S. LEXIS 4800 (2003).

Perhaps one of Jackson's most important accomplishments was encouraging young African American people to register and vote in national and local elections. Because Jackson was well respected and supported in the African American community, he was able to influence many elections. He was able to stir a crowd and to get many young people motivated and interested in politics and the government. Jackson accomplished many things, such as helping to negotiate the release of American hostages from Middle Eastern countries during times of unrest. He was also active in rallying against apartheid in South Africa.

However, arguably his most important accomplishment was his run in the 1984 and 1988 elections for the presidency of the United States on the Democratic ticket. Although Jackson did not win the Democratic nomination, he received millions of votes. Particularly in the 1984 election, the majority of his votes came from newly registered voters, mostly African Americans, minorities, and the poor. This showed that his run was not in vain, but had stirred hope in those who might have never voted before or who felt disenfranchised within the United States. Jackson has also influenced his son Jesse Jackson Jr., who is a Democratic congressman from Illinois. Jackson is still actively involved in the political scene as he works with the Rainbow Coalition and continues to fight for civil rights, women's rights, economic independence and help for the poor, and affirmative action. He has six children and has been married to his wife Jacqueline for forty years.

See also African Americans; Chisholm, Shirley; *Gratz v. Bollinger/Grutter v. Bollinger*; King, Martin Luther, Jr.; Rainbow PUSH Coalition; Southern Christian Leadership Conference.

FURTHER READING: Frady, Marshall, 1996, *Jesse Jackson: A Biography*, New York: Random House; Hamill, Sean D., 2003, "Rev. Jesse Jackson Organizes March for Affirmative Action on April 1," *Knight Ridder/Tribune Business News*, March 20, 1; Jackson, Jesse, 1997, "Civil Rights Gone Wrong," *Nation*, June 9, L5; Jackson, Jesse, Sr., 2000, "Race and Racism in America," *National Forum* 80, no. 2 (spring): 9–13; "Jesse Jackson Urges Students to Fight University of Michigan Ruling," 2001, *Black Issues in Higher Education* 18, no. 5 (April 26): 19; Timmerman, Kenneth R., 2002, *Shakedown: Exposing the Real Jesse Jackson*, Washington, DC: Regnery Publishing.

NICOLE M. STEPHENS

Japan and Affirmative Action

Japan is viewed as a very homogenously populated country, yet behind this homogeneity lurk the remnants of a centuries-old caste system, as well as a strong practice of sex discrimination and gender segregation. In recent years, Japan has attempted to rectify the problem of caste and gender discrimination through several antidiscrimination laws, notably the Equal Employment Opportunity Law of 1985 and the Revised Equal Employment Opportunity Law of 1998, and "positive action" initiatives meant to improve the plight of members of discriminated-against castes (e.g., the *buraku* group). "Positive action" initiatives are analogous to affirmative action programs or plans in the United States. These positive action initiatives are often described as "special measures laws." To understand modern efforts by the Japanese government to employ antidiscrimination laws and positive action laws, one must have an understanding of the centuries-old caste distinction in Japan, as well as the historical practice of gender segregation and discrimination.

The class system in Japan originated during the Edo period that lasted from 1603 to 1867. During this long phase of more than 250 years, Japan was secluded from the rest of the world, and the country sustained itself through a class-based system known as *shinoukousyon*. The Tokugawa shogunate perpetuated this class system to keep its tight grip on power in all of Japan. Through a careful and deliberate scheme of control and domain, the Tokugawa rulers maintained their dominance over various classes by adopting a policy of "divide and rule" among competing class groups. The class system known as *shinoukousyon* was divided into four classes: *shi* (warriors), *nou* (farmers), *kou* (artisans), and *syou* (tradesmen). Finally, outside of the class system existed the lowest echelon of people, similar to the "untouchables" in India (i.e., *eta* and *hinin*), who lived on the outskirts of towns and were the victims of significant discrimination. Today, these groups, under the name of *buraku*, still suffer significant discrimination.

The class system during the Edo period was based on people's occupations as well as on family lineage. There were distinct sets of rules for each class, and each class had its own style of living. Members of the *shi* group were charged to guard and keep an eye on the day-to-day operations of the government and the castle. They collected annual tribute from the farmers. The warriors used the farmers as a tool for paying the annual tribute that eventually went to the shoguns. The warriors were rulers in the overall class system. They also had certain privileges in accordance with their enhanced status. For example, they could wear a sword on their waist, they could use a surname, and they were authorized to kill anyone in the farmers' and merchants' classes for perceived impolite and improper behavior.

Farmers belonged to the second-tier class and had to pay annual tribute to their shoguns and other warlords. This was particularly severe for the farmers because the tax rate imposed on them was quite heavy. Farmers could not be extravagant even if they wished to because of the stringent rules imposed upon them by the Tokugawa shogunate. The Tokugawa shoguns thought that if the farmers were extravagant, they would not work and as a result would default on paying their annual tribute. There were also other rules. For example, farmers could not produce alcohol or tobacco products, could not wear the clothes of their choice, and could not drink any alcohol in public. There were also severe restrictions on the movements of people belonging to the farmers' class.

The *kou* artisans were one class lower than the farmers. Although they did not have to pay annual tribute to the shoguns, their movements and activities were severely restricted. They also could not change their residence or place of domicile freely without the consent of the shoguns. The *syou*, or merchants or tradesman, belonged to the fourth class. Although, like the artisan class, they did not pay annual tribute to the shogun, members of the merchant class could not practice their profession freely by trading with the community they wanted to serve. Also, the Tokugawa shoguns specifically required the merchant class not to deviate from their occupations and try learning new ones.

However, the persons who suffered the most under the Japanese class system were those at the very bottom, the *eta* and *hinin*. The *eta* class of people lived in the least livable area around a village or a city. Their jobs were to produce articles made of leather, and they worked as animal executioners and operated the leather tanneries. People belonging to the *eta* class could not interact with persons from the higher classes. Persons born in the *eta* class, like the untouchables in India, remained in that status from birth to death, and this status pervaded all aspects of these persons' lives, resulting in a life of secondary status in society. Like the *eta* class, people of the *hinin* class also lived at the edge of a city or a village on a narrow strip of land. Originally, the Tokugawa shoguns assigned the *hinin* class to those who were convicted as criminals or who were beggars and panhandlers. Later, the children of these categories of people were also required to remain in the *hinin* status, although the second or third generation had nothing to do with criminal activity and had clearly moved ahead in the social order. Persons belonging to the *hinin* class faced discrimination firsthand because they were completely marginalized in terms of jobs, living places, and even marriage. On many occasions, people of the *hinin* class had to face false charges and were ordered to be killed by persons of the upper class under a system known as *goningumi seido*.

Although discrimination was abolished as a matter of law in 1871 at the end of the Edo period and the beginning of the Meiji period in Japanese society, an abundance of overt and covert discrimination continued and still exists against a class denoted by a separate term, *buraku*, which today is considered the largest discriminated-against class in Japan. In response to persistent demands made by an organization known as the Buraku Liberation League, the Japanese government has enacted several "special measures laws" for the benefit of members of the *buraku* class. While these special measures laws were envisioned to lend specific assistance to the *buraku* class, they were criticized as giving broad authority for the government to act, but mandating no specific cause of action or giving *buraku* individuals no new legally enforceable rights.

Three specific special measures laws are worthy of note. First, the 1969 Law on Special Measures for Assimilation (*Dowa*) Projects allows local bodies to give scholarships to minority members, give tax benefits for *buraku* businesses, offer loans at better rates, and improve roads and infrastructure in *buraku* areas. Second, the 1982 Law on Special Fiscal Measures for Regional Improvement, while not expressly mentioning the *buraku*, authorized area improvements in *buraku*-inhabited areas. The 1982 law remained in effect for five years, until March 31, 1987. Finally, the third law is a similar law dealing with internal improvement of *buraku* areas, the 1987 Law for Special Fiscal Measures for Area Improvement Projects. Its original five-year term expired on March 31, 1992, but it was subsequently extended until March 1997 and again until 2002. No further extensions to the special programs for the Buraku are expected in the future.

It should also be noted that in addition to the *buraku* group, there are several indigenous peoples who have suffered discrimination. The Ainus, the indigenous people of the island region of Hokkaido, have long complained of bias against and disregard of their tribes by the Japanese power elite. Forced into assimilation into the mainstream Japanese society, the small minority of identifiable Ainus, who constitute less than 0.02 percent of the total population of Japan, are struggling for survival. In the last 100 years, nothing substantive has been done to alleviate the sufferings of Ainus except enacting a new Ainu Culture Protection Law in 1997 for developing a society where the pride of Ainus as a people is respected, and a commitment is made to contribute to the development of cultural diversity by promoting Ainu culture.

Similarly, people living in Okinawa, which is not among the four central islands, have complained of invasion into their cultural domain by forcing them to integrate with the mainstream Japanese culture, most notably with Honshu islanders, who include the populations of megacities such as Tokyo and Osaka. For their part, in spite of intense pressures brought upon them, people of Okinawa and the greater Ryukyu Islands see themselves as a distinct race (Uchinancho) with Pacific and Chinese cultural traditions and not as a typical Japanese mainland culture (Yamatonchu). This is supported by the fact that Okinawa's history in a cultural sense is more tied to China, Taiwan, and Korea because of geographical and ethnic proximity.

Longtime residents of Korean descent, known as Zainichi, who comprise 1 percent of the population in Japanese society, too, complain bitterly of discrimination against them in areas such as education, housing, employment, and pensions, as well as being forced to work in pachinko parlors, *mizu shobai* (night entertainment), and restaurants (especially *yaki nikku*). Most permanent, special-status foreign residents came from the Korean Peninsula under Japanese colonial rule in the early twentieth century and also lost their Japanese citizenship after the San Francisco Peace Treaty went into effect in 1952. Although in recent times, governing coalition partners New Komeito and Hishuto (New Conservative Party) have voiced support for granting these special groups of Koreans and other foreigners with permanent residency status the right to vote in local elections, the process of naturalization in Japan is too complicated and time consuming. Furthermore, the Korean residents in Japan demand a legal framework in which Korean identity, including names, language, and culture, can be inherited and fully respected by the Japanese government and the Japanese people.

Finally, in addition to the class and caste issues, Japan has had a particular problem among industrialized nations in regard to the issue of gender discrimination and gender segregation in the workforce. To remedy this problem, the Japanese Diet (parliament) passed the Equal Employment Opportunity Law of 1985, which mandates equal participation of men and women in the workforce. The Diet was forced to pass this law (as implementing legislation) as a result of Japan signing the Convention on the Elimination of All Forms of Discrimination against Women. The 1985 law and its 1998 revisions are best described as antidiscrimination measures that prohibit gender discrimination in training, benefits, and retirement. However, the legislation only mandates good-faith attempts, or "endeavors," at eliminating gender discrimination in the areas of recruitment, hiring, job assignment, and promotion. Hence the law is criticized as being more of a recommendation than a mandate. Furthermore, critics argue that the law's weak enforcement measures (reporting and public disclosure) make it ineffective at combating gender discrimination and segregation in the workplace. In the last few years, more and more women have been rallying for an affirmative action plan for women. In the words of one Japanese woman interviewed in the *Washington Post* in 1996, "Men do not understand women's segregated condition; women have to change their own condition" (Jordan 1996, A1).

See also Caste System; China and Affirmative Action; Convention on the Elimination of All Forms of Discrimination against Women; Gender Norms; Gender Segregation in Employment; India and Affirmative Action.

FURTHER READING: DeVos, George A., and Hiroshi Wagatsuma, 1967, *Japan's Invisible Race/Caste in Culture and Personality*, Berkeley: University of California Press; Hall, John Whitney, 1971, *Japan: From Pre-history to Modern Times*, Tokyo: C.E. Tuttle; Jordan, Mary, 1996, "Japan's Rising Women Pursue Political Power; More Balance Home and Career to Gain Voice in Male-Run Society," *Washington Post*, October 16, A1; Neary, Ian, 2003, "Burakumin at the End of History," *Social Research* 70, no. 1:269–280; Reber, Emily A. Su-lan, 1999, "Buraku Mondai in Japan: Historical and Modern Perspectives and Directions for the Future," *Harvard Human Rights Journal* 12 (spring): 297–327; Yokoyama, Kazuko, 1999, "Affirmative Action Programs in the United States and Their Application in Japan," http://www.toyogakuen-u.ac.jp/kiyo/k7/yokoyama1999-1.htm.

MOHAMMED B. ALAM

Japanese Internment and World War II

The internment of Japanese Americans in relocation camps during World War II was one of the few openly discriminatory practices of the United States that has survived "strict scrutiny" analysis by the U.S. Supreme Court. In *Korematsu v. United States*, 323 U.S. 214 (1944), one of two cases to reach the Supreme Court dealing with the constitutionality of the Japanese internment camps, the Supreme Court held that federal statutes classifying individuals on account of race should receive strict scrutiny review by the courts. The Supreme Court went on to uphold the racial classification allowing internments as constitutional. Today, the *Korematsu* decision is often referenced in affirmative action and racial profiling debates and was discussed by the Supreme Court in the affirmative action case *Adarand Constructors, Inc. v. Peña*, 515 U.S. 200 (1995). Therefore, the historical chapter of U.S. history on the World War II Japanese internment camps has become linked to such topics as affirmative action, racial profiling, *Adarand,* and the use of strict scrutiny analysis by the Supreme Court.

The history leading up to the internment of Japanese Americans in World War II was extensive. The atmosphere culminating in the internment of Japanese Americans was colored by historical experiences between the United States and the empire of Japan going back many years. The extralegal excesses of Executive Order 9066, which ultimately called for the internment of Japanese Americans, derived from precedents that caused the two peoples to view the other as economic and political competitors in their struggle for markets throughout Asia. In conjunction with the economic war, the West's lack of appreciation of Japanese character caused many non–Japanese Americans to view their Asian counterparts as alien to American customs and traditions. Animus and fear were nurtured and evolved, beginning with the initial encounter of Admiral Matthew Perry with the Japanese shogunate in 1853. Quite significant was American insensitivity to the intrusion of Christian missionaries and racial stereotyping that exacerbated the relationship leading to Pearl Harbor. Japanese expansion into Manchuko for material resources and the constant pressure to annex portions of the Chinese mainland, violating agreements for spheres of influence, including Formosa, caused concern on both sides of the Pacific. The recognition of growing Japanese military prowess made matters worse for the two countries' diplomatic relations.

Tokyo's awareness about the conditions of Japanese American citizens, immigrants, and guest workers helped convince the Yamato dynasty and the American government of their intractable relationship. At the same time that the United States was attempting to establish a *cordon sanitaire* in portions of Asia, people of Japanese ethnic ancestry were being subjected to treatment violative of American law. Japanese contributions colored the entire spectrum of life in the West, but many were the targets of hostile actions. The San Francisco school board initiated segregated schools in 1908, the United States insulted Japan by the signing of the "Gentlemen's Agreement" by which Tokyo agreed to limit the number of Japanese immigrants coming to the United States, and 1913 California legislation prohibited aliens from owning property. All these actions were viewed negatively by Tokyo. Federal legislation designed to exclude non–Western Europeans was passed in 1921, and in 1924 the number of immigrants was greatly reduced.

The distrust engendered by American attitudes compelled President Franklin D. Roosevelt to initiate a study in November 1941 about Japanese American patriotism to the United States. Roosevelt selected Curtis B. Munson, a special representative from the U.S. Department of State, to lead the study. Munson's government report found no evidence of disloyalty among the Japanese Americans. However, on December 7, 1941, after Pearl Harbor, the atmosphere within the United States changed. Washington began to arrest Japanese and began clas-

Evacuees of Japanese descent among a contingent of 664, the first to be removed from San Francisco, awaiting buses to transport them to the Santa Anita reception center at Arcadia, to be transported later to war relocation centers for the duration of the war. Courtesy of Library of Congress.

sifying them as aliens. Japanese west coast residents were ordered to surrender all personal items to the authorities that the government considered potentially dangerous for American security. Dissemination of information about the Rape of Nanking reinforced American fears of the plausible consequences of Pearl Harbor; American shipping losses along the coast after Pearl Harbor, radio transmissions, and the many Japanese American dual-national residents on the west coast provided justification for extralegal governmental actions. General John L. DeWitt expressed the prevailing views about the Japanese Americans: "The Japanese race is an enemy race and while many second and third generations of Japanese born on United States soil possessed of U.S. citizenship have become Americanized the racial strain is undiluted" (Dewitt 1942).

On February 19, 1942, Roosevelt signed Executive Order 9066, covering potential threats to national security posed by Japanese Americans. Although two-thirds of the 120,000 detainees were American citizens, apprehension governed, and no thought was given to the executive's legal authority to publish the order. The secretary of state was empowered to define dangerous persons and create regions from which the detainees were excluded even though no evidence of sabotage by the Japanese had been presented to the federal government. Under the secretary of war's mandate, General DeWitt was empowered to create the military districts from which Japanese could be excluded. General DeWitt issued Proclamation One establishing areas of exclusion on the west coast and authorizing the eviction of Japanese ethnic people from the proscribed areas. Executive Order 9066 was only applied to the Japanese population. The Department of the Treasury took possession of farms and equipment owned by Japanese Americans. General DeWitt issued a second proclamation informing the Japanese American population of their pending deportation to camps for the duration of the war. Order Two described what they could take and the rules governing their expected behavior in the internment camps.

The first camp, which opened on March 18, 1942, housed more than 10,000 people. Conditions were poor; homeowning families now occupied small apartments. Camp residents were not provided with the same food consumed prior to detention. The government's camps were located in low-population-density areas; public services were not as plentiful; the camps were situated in harsh climates. While an infrastructure of normalcy was the goal, camp residents were not allowed to leave; most lost all of their property located outside of the camps, real and personal, sustaining great financial loss for which the United States, in 1980, provided some restitution and acknowledged that the Japanese had been victims of discrimination. Five thousand, seven hundred sixty-six Japanese detainees eventually renounced their American citizenship, while other nisei Americans formed the 442nd Regiment and served in the European theater. They volunteered partly because it was the only way the detainees could legally leave the internment camps.

Following the fear and chaos caused by Pearl Harbor, Roosevelt instituted several executive extralegal actions; his executive order 9066 and its consequences indicated his course of action. The Supreme Court case *Hirabayashi v. United States*, 320 U.S. 81 (1943), was the first appeal against Japanese interment policy. The *Hirabayashi* and *Korematsu* cases both dealt with whether or not the Japanese American detainees were victims of Fifth Amendment violations by the federal government based upon clear racial discrimination. The Supreme Court ruled for the government in both cases. In the *Korematsu* case, the Court held that while racial classifications should be subject to the strictest judicial scrutiny possible ("strict scrutiny"), Executive Order 9066 was permissible racial discrimination by the government, as the discrimination dealt with a compelling state interest, that of national security.

In *Hirabayashi*, the Court ruled the executive order constitutional, averring that President Roosevelt's powers fell within constitutional provisions that mandated that he pursue the war to a successful conclusion as commander in chief. General DeWitt had instituted Expulsion Order 34, barring persons of Japanese descent from entering military areas. The appellant, Hirabayashi, refused to relocate and used his rights as a citizen to appeal the expulsion order. The Supreme Court ruled President Roosevelt's action constitutional and declared that his policies were not motivated by purely racial discrimination desires, but rather preservation of the nation during time of war. The Court stated that other means might be found to protect the nation, but did not specify what those other means might have been. The Court stated, "Peacetime procedures do not necessarily fit wartime needs."

In *Korematsu v. United States*, 323 U.S. 214 (1944), the Court acknowledged that approximately 112,000 Japanese lived along the west coast, of whom 70,000 were American citizens. However, the Court recognized that many people of Japanese origin had emotional ties to Japan; they sent their children to school in Japan, had relatives throughout the country, and pursued a deeper understanding of the culture than they deemed possible in the United States. Some had returned to Japan to assist it in the war against China. From this premise, the Court went on to conclude that it was therefore within the president's powers during wartime to order the relocation of "suspect" citizens. The case still stands today as precedent in affirmative action and racial profiling cases.

See also Adarand Constructors, Inc. v. Peña; Asian Americans; *Korematsu v. United States;* Racial Profiling; Reparations; Roosevelt, Franklin Delano; Strict Scrutiny.

FURTHER READING: Dewitt, John L., 1942, *Final Report: Japanese Evacuation from the West Coast*, Washington, DC: U.S. Government Printing Office; Grossman, Joel B., 1997, "The Japanese American Cases and the Vagaries of Constitutional Adjudication in Wartime: An Institutional Perspective," *Hawaii Law Review* 19:649–695; *Hirabayashi v. United States*, 320 U.S. 81 (1943); *Hohri v. United States*, 782 F.2d 227 (1986); Irons, Peter, 1999, *A People's History of the Supreme Court*, New York: Viking Press; *Korematsu v. United States*, 323 U.S. 214 (1944); Oh, Reggie, and Frank Wu, 1996, "The Evolution of Race in the Law: The Supreme Court Moves from Approving Internment of Japanese Americans to Disapproving Affirmative Action for African Americans," *Michigan Journal of Race and Law* 1:165–193; Rehnquist, William H., 1998, *All the Laws but One: Civil Liberties in Wartime*, New York: Alfred A. Knopf.

ARTHUR K. STEINBERG

Jews

See Anti-Semitism, Jews, and Affirmative Action.

Jim Crow Laws

The term "Jim Crow laws" connotes segregationist laws enacted by various southern states to circumvent the attempted reconstruction of the South and return the liberated slaves to "their place," that is, their subordinate position, in the South. Jim Crow laws formed the backbone for the enthronement of racial segregation and poor treatment of African Americans in the South and constituted a body of laws that ensured racial segregation in America until the modern civil rights movement. Jim Crow laws are part of the historic explanation of inequality between races today. Therefore, one purpose of affirmative action has been said to be the remuneration or compensation of past wrongs inflicted upon historically discriminated-against classes under Jim Crow laws.

The term "Jim Crow" had its origins in the minstrels of the early nineteenth century and was made popular by the minstrel Thomas "Daddy" Rice in the 1820s. Using burned cork to blacken his face, attired in ill-fitting, tattered garments, and smiling broadly and profusely, Thomas Rice imitated the dancing, singing, and demeanor that he (and many other white Americans at the time) generally ascribed to African Americans. Rice called his routine "jumping jim crow" and said that he based it on an act he had seen in 1828 by an elderly and crippled Louisville stableman belonging to a Mr. Crow.

Thus even before the Civil War, the term became popular as a label for a distorted view of the demeanor and behavior of African Americans. In the 1840s, abolitionists picked up the term as a way to describe unfair separate railroad cars for the different races. After the Civil War, the term "Jim Crow" was used increasingly to describe an array of different segregationist statutes and laws. These included laws that discriminated against African Americans in regard to attendance in public schools, the use of means of public transportation (trains, ships, buses, and so on), and the use of other public facilities such as restaurants, theaters, hotels, cinemas, and public baths. In 1896, Jim Crow laws were tested by Homer Plessy in the now-infamous case *Plessy v. Ferguson*, 163 U.S. 537 (1896), in which the Supreme Court ultimately held that Jim Crow laws were not constitutionally impermissible under the Fourteenth Amendment's Equal Protection Clause. The

Supreme Court held that "separate-but-equal" facilities were constitutional.

It is important to note that with the action of the Supreme Court in the *Plessy* case, putting forth the separate-but-equal doctrine, racial segregation assumed monumental dimensions for years to come. As a complementary discriminatory force to literacy tests, grandfather clauses, and other subtle and blatant means aimed at undermining the social elevation of African Americans in the voting rights context, Jim Crow laws unleashed havoc on African American communities, compelling many to resort to various means of survival such as emigrationism (back-to-Africa migration) and immigration to northern states. This phenomenon has been described by Kenneth Stampp as "a kind of twilight zone between slavery and freedom" (Stampp 1965, 80). Alphonso Pinkney dubbed it a "virtual re-enslavement of blacks" (Pinkney 1976, 27). It has also been de-

An African American man, Eddie Mitchell, approaching the entrance to the movie theater's "colored balcony," probably in Birmingham, Alabama. Courtesy of Library of Congress.

scribed as "subordinate categorisation" (Williams 1975, 45), "involuntary servitude" (McFeely 1971, 8), and "the depth below the depth" (Scruggs 1971, 70).

Seen as an evil, Jim Crowism spawned ill will in many individuals, white and black, resulting in a number of civil rights protests and race riots, the latter of which led to destruction of lives and property. Ultimately, Jim Crow laws, as a body of discriminatory laws that caused much pain to the citizens of the United States of America, were repealed in large part by the Civil Rights Act of 1964 and modern Supreme Court adjudication of the Equal Protection Clause in the Fourteenth Amendment and the Due Process Clause of the Fifth and Fourteenth Amendments.

See also Civil Rights Act of 1964; Constitution, Civil Rights, and Equality; Equal Protection Clause; Fifth Amendment; Fourteenth Amendment; *Plessy v. Ferguson*; Segregation.

FURTHER READING: McFeely, William S., 1971, "Unfinished Business: The Freedmen's Bureau and Federal Action in Race Relations," in *Key Issues in the Afro-American Experience*, vol. 2, edited by Nathan I. Huggins, Martin Kilson, Daniel M. Fox, John Merton Blum, New York: Harcourt Brace Jovanovich; Pinkney, Alphonso, 1976, *Red, Black, and Green: Black Nationalism in the United States*, Cambridge: Cambridge University Press; Scruggs, Otey M.,

1971, "The Economic and Racial Components of Jim Crow," in *Key Issues in the Afro-American Experience*, vol. 2, edited by Nathan I. Huggins, New York: Harcourt Brace Jovanovich; Spartacus Educational, 2001, "Jim Crow Laws," http://www.spartacus.schoolnet.co.uk/USAjimcrow.htm; Stampp, Kenneth, 1965, *The Era of Reconstruction, 1865–1877*, New York: Alfred A. Knopf; Williams, Loretta J., 1975, "Black Subordination in Colonies and Nation, 1619–1976," in *Politics of Race: Comparative Studies*, edited by Donald G. Baker, London: Saxon House/Lexington Books; Worthman, Paul B., and James R. Green, 1971, "Black Workers in the New South, 1865–1915," in *Key Issues in the Afro-American Experience*, vol. 2, edited by Nathan I. Huggins, New York: Harcourt Brace Jovanovich.

PAUL OBIYO MBANASO NJEMANZE

Johnson, Lyndon Baines (1908–1973)

Lyndon B. Johnson assumed the presidency of the United States after President John F. Kennedy was murdered by an assassin in Dallas, Texas, on November 22, 1963. Martin Luther King Jr., the renowned civil rights leader, and Robert F. Kennedy, a presidential candidate himself in 1968, were both assassinated during Johnson's presidency. Despite these terrible tragedies and the Vietnam War, the thirty-sixth president made an indelible imprint on domestic affairs through his myriad legislative initiatives. He continued and expanded on President Kennedy's "War on Poverty" to create his own "Great Society." Among other things, Johnson signed into law the Civil Rights Act of 1964 and the Voting Rights Act of 1965. Additionally, in his famous 1965 commencement address at Howard University, Johnson promoted the need for affirmative action as a means to rectify previous incidents of discrimination and unfair treatment. Finally, Johnson issued Executive Order 11246, which promoted equal opportunity in federal employment and promised continued affirmative action programs in each department and agency of the federal government.

Johnson's congressional experience before he arrived in the White House uniquely prepared him to serve as a facilitator between the executive and legislative branches of government. He was able to break the legislative quagmire that had held up some congressional bills for a long time. As Kennedy's vice president, among other duties, Johnson was selected as the chairman of the new President's Committee on Equal Employment Opportunity. This committee, established by Executive Order 10925, was vested with ending discrimination in public contracting. It was Executive Order 10925 that first utilized the term "affirmative action," requiring government contractors to take "affirmative action" to ensure that applicants for positions were treated fairly and did not suffer from discrimination.

After Kennedy's assassination, Johnson not only vowed to continue Kennedy's legislative agenda (including Kennedy's support of civil rights), but also promised to build "a Great Society." Such a society, according to Johnson, "demands an end to poverty and racial injustice, to which we are totally committed in our time." In 1964, under Johnson's leadership, Congress passed the Tax Reduction Act, which reflected an economic theory that at times the federal government must spend more than it takes in to foster economic growth. Also, it passed broad civil rights laws geared toward ending segregation, banning discrimination in public facilities, and widening job opportunities. Minorities were the target recipients of this sweeping social and economic legislation. The Civil Rights Act of 1964 is perhaps the most expansive of these sweeping pieces of legislation. Johnson also signed the Economic Opportunity Act, which established an office of economic opportunity to conduct his "war on poverty."

The first session of the Eighty-Seventh Congress enacted additional bills that changed the lives of many. Again, President Johnson led in establishing Medicare and getting the Voting Rights Act of 1965 passed. He created the Department of Transportation and the Department of Housing and Urban Development. Funding was substantially increased for K–12 education. Legislation that enhanced unemployment payments, expanded the food stamp program, and extended employment for youth were all the result of President Johnson's agenda. On the domestic front, President Johnson and his administration were responsible for a broad set of laws that ushered in a new era in the midst of tumultuous social upheavals occurring at that time.

In 1965, Johnson gave a now-famous commencement address at Howard University in which he advocated affirmative action. Johnson remarked:

President Johnson signing the Civil Rights Act of 1964 into law in a ceremony in the East Room of the White House. Courtesy of Library of Congress.

> You do not take a person who for years has been hobbled by chains and liberate him, bring him up to the starting line of a race and then say, "You're free to compete with all the others," and still justly believe that you have been completely fair. Thus it is not enough just to open the gates of opportunity. All our citizens must have the ability to walk through those gates. . . . We seek not . . . just equality as a right and a theory but equality as a fact and equality as a result. (Public Papers of the President 1966, 635–636)

Johnson's race metaphor has been cited often since 1965 in the affirmative action debate. Several months after his Howard University speech, Johnson signed Executive Order 11246, which set forth the policy of the federal government in providing equal opportunities in federal employment, prohibited discrimination in hiring, and promised the "full realization of equal employment opportunity through a positive, continuing program in each department and agency." This executive order was amended in 1967 to prohibit discrimination on the basis of sex as well. Despite Johnson's support of affirmative action–type programs, Johnson considered his best accomplishment the passage (and signing) of the Voting Rights Act of 1965, which prohibited racial discrimination in voting and assisted African Americans in registering. Johnson also nominated the first African American to the U.S. Supreme Court, Thurgood Marshall, in 1968.

Foreign policy proved to be a challenge for President Johnson. The Soviet Union, the People's Republic of China, and the Dominican Republic all occupied Johnson's attention during his tenure in the White House. Each presented unique problems for the administration. But by far the looming hot spot was Vietnam. Previously, President Johnson had supported President Harry Truman's foreign policy of containment. He deeply believed that the containment policy applied to South Vietnam. In his reasoning, the United States had to honor its commitments to South Vietnam by helping it resist the spread of communism onto its land. By the end of 1965, more than 180,000 American troops had been deployed to Vietnam by the commander in chief in the hope of stemming the tide of encroaching communism. Resistance was strong, so by 1966, 360,000 troops had been dispatched to win the war. But there was no win in sight. Fighting escalated. Vietnam became an albatross around the presidency. Within the country, there was great division. Massive antiwar demonstrations, marches, sit-ins, teach-ins, draft card burnings, and increasing numbers of draft dodgers were regular occurrences. By the end of the war, at least 536,000 soldiers were sent to fight in Vietnam, and nearly 30,610 perished. Vietnam was the most unpopular military involvement in the history of the United States. Protesters trailed the president nearly everywhere he went. To make a bad situation worse, riots, fires, and destruction erupted in the inner cities, mostly in the North.

All of this exacted a heavy toll on President Johnson. Even so, it was still a shock to many when the president announced to the nation that he would not be a candidate in the 1968 elections, thus ending the political career of a complex yet accomplished leader in the twentieth century. When the president started out in Gillespie County, Texas, it was not expected that he would rise to attain the highest political office in the country. He was born on August 27, 1908 to Sam Ealy Johnson Jr. and Rebekah Baines Johnson. His father moved the family to Johnson City, Texas, a town that was named for earlier Johnson family members. Johnson spent his childhood in Johnson City and graduated from high school there.

In 1927, he enrolled in Southwest Texas State Teachers College in San Marcos, Texas. After college he briefly taught young Hispanic students in Cotulla, Texas, and at a high school in Houston. His grandfather, Joseph William Baines, was Texas secretary of state, and Johnson's father served for five years in the Texas legislature. He followed them into politics. His earliest foray into politics was serving as secretary to Congressman Richard Kleberg in Washington. He made friends with Congressman Sam Rayburn and others who were part of the New Deal. At the young age of twenty-seven, Johnson became Texas administrator of the National Youth Administration. In 1937, campaigning as a New Deal Democrat, he won handily the Tenth Congressional District seat in Texas. His friends and mentors in Washington made sure that Johnson received desirable committee assignments. From there, in 1948, he sought and obtained a seat in the U.S. Senate. He quickly became a member of the Senate Armed Services Committee. His climb to the top of political power gained momentum. In 1951, he became party whip. In 1952, he became leader of the Democrats in the Senate as minority leader and after 1954 as majority leader. By most accounts, Johnson was skillful and effective in this role. Johnson rallied a unanimous vote to censure Senator Joseph McCarthy, a Republican from Wisconsin, who was notorious for his anti-Communist stance.

While hoping for the presidency, Johnson ended up as vice president under John F. Kennedy. He was not a traditional vice president because he was particularly active, probably because of his background, skills, and experiences. With the untimely death of President Kennedy, Vice President Johnson was sworn into office as president of the United States on Air Force One at Dallas's Love Field. He assured a shocked and grieving nation that he would continue Kennedy's policies. Lyndon Baines Johnson was married to Claudia Alta "Lady Bird" Johnson on November 17, 1934. She too made her mark on Washington with her beautification efforts. Two daughters were born to the couple, Lynda and Luci. The Johnson presidency ended officially on January 20, 1969. He died of heart complications at his ranch near Johnson City, Texas, on January 22, 1973.

See also Civil Rights Act of 1964; Department of Housing and Urban Development; Executive Order 10925; Executive Order 11246; Kennedy, John Fitzgerald; Marshall, Thurgood; President's Committee on Equal Employment Opportunity; Voting Rights Act of 1965.

FURTHER READING: Bornet, Vaughn, 1983, *The Presidency of Lyndon B. Johnson*, Lawrence: University Press of Kansas; Califano, Joseph, 2000, *The Triumph and Tragedy of Lyndon Johnson: The White House Years, a Personal Memoir*, Joseph and Holly Hughes Series in the Presidency and Leadership Studies, College Station: Texas A&M University Press; Goodwin, Doris Kearns, 1991, *Lyndon Johnson and the American Dream*, New York: St. Martin's Press; Johnson, Lyndon B., 1971, *The Vantage Point: Perspectives of the Presidency, 1963–1969*, New York: Holt; *Public Papers of the Presidents of the United States: Lyndon B. Johnson (1965)*, 1966, vol. 2, entry 301, 635–640, Washington, DC: U.S. Government Printing Office; White, Theodore H., 1964, *The Making of the President*, New York: New American Library.

BETTY NYANGONI

Johnson v. Board of Regents of the University of Georgia, 263 F.3d 1234 (11th Cir. 2001)

Johnson v. Board of Regents of the University of Georgia is an opinion of the U.S. Court of Appeals for the Eleventh Circuit that struck down an affirmative action policy of a state university concerning university admissions as a violation of the Equal Protection Clause of the Fourteenth Amendment to the U.S. Constitution. The University of Georgia maintained an admissions policy for freshman applicants that gave preferential treatment to minority candidates and to males by giving additional points to minority student applications in the admissions application evaluation process. Three white female applicants challenged this affirmative action policy under federal statutes and under the Equal Protection Clause of the Fourteenth Amendment. The U.S. district court ruled that the preferential admissions policy was unlawful. The university appealed the district court's ruling to the Eleventh Circuit Court of Appeals inasmuch as it declared the minority preference invalid, but did not appeal the invalidation of the policy's preference for males.

The parties agreed that the policy should be subjected to strict scrutiny constitutional review. This meant that to be held to be constitutional, the policy's race-based preference had to be narrowly tailored to fulfill a compelling governmental interest. The university argued that the purpose of the racial preference, which was to promote "the educational benefits of student body diversity in higher education," was a compelling governmental interest. The circuit court did not decide the question of whether such diversity could be a compelling governmental interest because it found that even if it was, the preference was unconstitutional because it was not narrowly tailored. The racial preference was not narrowly tailored to achieve the goal of a diverse student body, the Court concluded, because it was too inflexible. It awarded a fixed number of bonus points to every minority applicant being evaluated at a "decisive state" in the admissions process "regardless of that applicant's potential overall contribution to diversity" while also limiting the other factors that might earn bonus points for contributing to diversity at the same stage of the process. The court stated: "[I]f UGA wants to ensure diversity through its admission decisions, and wants race to be a part of that calculus, then it must be prepared to shoulder the burden of fully and fairly analyzing applicants as individuals and not merely as members of groups when deciding their likely contribution to student body diversity."

See also Compelling Governmental Interest; Diversity; Education and Affirmative Action; Equal Protection Clause; Fourteenth Amendment; *Hopwood v. Texas; Local 28 of the Sheet Metal Workers' International Association v. EEOC; Regents of the University of California v. Bakke;* Title VII of the Civil Rights Act of 1964; *United Steelworkers of America v. Weber.*

FURTHER READING: Hebel, Sara, 2001, "U. of Georgia Won't Appeal Affirmative Action Case to Supreme Court," *Chronicle of Higher Education,* November 23, A23.

MARIA D. BECKMAN

Johnson v. Transportation Agency, Santa Clara County, 480 U.S. 616 (1987)

The Supreme Court case *Johnson v. Transportation Agency, Santa Clara County,* attempted to settle one of the most controversial issues in modern civil rights—affirmative action—and is considered one of a handful of the most significant affirmative action/reverse-discrimination cases since *Regents of the University of California v. Bakke,* 438 U.S. 265 (1978). In a 6–3 opinion authored by Justice William Brennan, the Court explicitly held that it was permissible to take gender and race into consideration in employment decisions. In essence, the Court said that women, blacks, and other minorities can be given preferential treatment in hiring, which is clearly a violation of the language and spirit of Title VII of the 1964 Civil Rights Act, which mandated a color-blind approach to the workplace.

This case was filed by Paul Johnson, a white male and an employee of the Santa Clara County, California, Transportation Agency for thirteen years. Johnson brought suit when he lost a promotion to road dispatcher to a woman, Diane Joyce, who ranked two points lower than he did on an oral interview. Johnson joined the agency in 1967 and spent the next twelve years working toward becoming a road dispatcher. He applied for the position in 1974, but ranked second on the promotion list. He then took a demotion and became a road maintenance worker to gain experience and to increase his chances for promotion. Johnson again applied for the position in 1979, but lost the position to the only woman in the agency who applied. The previous year, the agency had adopted an affirmative action plan.

Diane Joyce joined the roads division in 1972 as a senior accounts clerk. She was the first female ever to work in the yard. In 1974, Joyce applied for the road dispatcher job, but was told that she did not have the necessary qualifications. To remedy the situation, Joyce applied for and became the first female to work on a county road crew. After five years of filling potholes, she again applied for the dispatcher job, as did Johnson. After the first round of interviews, Johnson ranked second and Joyce ranked third out of nine applicants. Following the second round of interviews, the panel recommended Johnson for the job. Joyce complained to the county's affirmative action officials and was awarded the job by the agency's director, James Graebner. Her promotion was based on a voluntary affirmative action plan adopted by the county to bring women into positions traditionally held by males. The plan stated that race or sex could be taken into consideration to correct underrepresentation. Johnson sued in federal court, claiming that the agency had violated Title VII of the 1964 Civil Rights Act. The Justice Department joined in on his behalf and filed an amicus curiae brief. Johnson won at the district court level. In 1983, he was awarded a dispatcher job and back pay of $6,800. The federal court of appeals reversed the decision, and Johnson appealed to the Supreme Court.

This was the Supreme Court's first ruling involving a voluntary affirmative action plan that favored women. Not only did the Court reject the reverse-discrimination claim of Paul Johnson, a white male, but Brennan's opinion marked the first time that the Court said that "without any proof of past discrimination" against women or minorities, an employer may use preferences based on race and sex in hiring and promotion to reflect the demographics of the surrounding community. In his opinion, Brennan stated:

> In determining whether an imbalance exists that would justify taking sex or race into account, a comparison of the percentage in the area labor market or general population is appropriate in analyzing jobs that require no special expertise or training programs to provide expertise. . . . Where a job requires special training, however, the comparison should be with those in the labor force who possess the relevant qualifications.

Brennan further stated that if there is a "manifest imbalance" in a "traditionally segregated job category," then sex or race can be taken into consideration to eliminate the effects of discrimination. In applying this manifest imbalance standard to the facts of the case, the Court found that in the Transportation Agency of Santa Clara County, there were no women filling the 238 positions in the skilled craft job category, and there was only one woman, Joyce, who was a crew member of the 110 road maintenance workers. The agency's plan recognized that women were tremendously underrepresented in certain job classifications and wanted to correct the manifest imbalance.

Concurring with Justice Brennan in full were Justices Thurgood Marshall, Harry Blackmun, and Lewis Powell and, in part, Justices John Paul Stevens and Sandra Day O'Connor, who both wrote separate opinions. Dissenting was Justice Antonin Scalia, joined in full by Chief Justice William Rehnquist and in part by Justice Byron White, who wrote a separate dissent. The dissenters believed that the majority had gone too far in broadening the decision in *United Steelworkers of America v. Weber*, 443 U.S. 193 (1979), which upheld a "voluntary" and "temporary" affirmative action plan devised by the Kaiser Aluminum and Chemical Corporation and the United Steelworkers of America for the Gramercy, Louisiana, plant to remedy previous past discrimination. In a separate strong dissent, White argued that the *Johnson* decision now gave employers, both public and private, the license to intentionally discriminate on the basis of race and sex. He was especially critical of the majority's decision to permit a statistical imbalance to justify an affirmative action plan, rather than proof of past discrimination.

In *Johnson*, the Court held that Title VII of the 1964 Civil Rights Act permits the employer to institute an affirmative action program to correct a manifest imbalance in the workforce without proof of past discrimination. The Court did not, however, overrule the decisions in previous discrimination cases of *Bakke* (1978), *Firefighters Local Union No. 1784 v. Stotts*, 467 U.S. 561 (1984) (reduction in force), and *Wygant v. Jackson Board of Education*, 476 U.S. 267 (1986). The *Bakke* case dealt with affirmative action in admissions selection decisions, while the *Stotts* and *Wygant* cases dealt with affirmative action in workforce reduction, where the court struck down affirmative action plans that favored one class over another as a violation of Title VII and the Fourteenth Amendment.

The facts in *Johnson* and *Weber* were similar, except that the affirmative action plan in *Weber* was temporary and Kaiser was a private company. The plan in *Johnson* was permanent and allowed the exclusion of better-qualified whites. The decision in *Johnson* resulted in a serious blow to reverse discrimination—thus laying the groundwork for future litigation—and eventually a narrowing of the permissibility of affirmative action plans under Title VII.

See also Blackmun, Harry Andrew; Brennan, William Joseph; Civil Rights Act of 1964; *Firefighters Local Union No. 1784 v. Stotts*; Manifest Imbalance Standard; Marshall, Thurgood; O'Connor, Sandra Day; Powell, Lewis Franklin, Jr.; *Regents of the University of California v. Bakke*; Rehnquist, William Hobbs; Scalia, Antonin; Stevens, John Paul; Title VII of the Civil Rights Act of 1964; *United Steelworkers of America v. Weber*; White, Byron Raymond; *Wygant v. Jackson Board of Education*.

FURTHER READING: Abraham, Henry J., and Barbara A. Perry, 1994, *Freedom and the Court: Civil Rights and Liberties in the United States*, 6th ed., New York: Oxford University Press; Hall, Kermit L., William M. Wiecek, and Paul Finkelman, 1991, *American Legal History: Cases and Materials*, New York: Oxford University Press; Sovereign, Kenneth L., 1994, *Personnel Law*, 3d ed., Englewood Cliffs, NJ: Prentice Hall.

NAOMI ROBERTSON

Jordan, Barbara Charline (1936–1996)

Barbara C. Jordan was a prominent lawyer, politician, and university professor who was strongly in favor of affirmative action. Jordan, a three-term congressional representative from Texas (1973–1979), was the first African American woman to be elected to Congress from a Deep South state. Prior to her service in Congress, she served in the Texas Senate from 1966 until 1972, being the first African American member of that body since 1883 and the first woman ever to be elected to the Texas Senate. She gained national recognition when she gave her famous "We the People" speech when the House Judiciary Committee was considering impeachment articles against President Richard Nixon. In 1999, the *Journal of*

Blacks in Higher Education conducted a survey listing the most important African Americans of the twentieth century. In this study, Jordan was ranked first of all African American elected officials who made the greatest contributions to American society in the twentieth century (Adam Clayton Powell was ranked second). Shortly before her death in 1996, Jordan commented that she believed that the United States was seeing "a re-segregation into the two societies" of black and white, in large part due to opposition to affirmative action programs and opposition to the use of busing to achieve school integration.

Born in Houston, Texas, on February 21, 1936, Barbara Jordan was the youngest of three daughters of a Baptist minister. She graduated from Phillis Wheatley High School in 1952 and from Texas Southern University with a bachelor's degree in government. She then earned a law degree from Boston University, where she competed in a desegregated setting for the first time. She was one of two black women in a class of 128. She passed both the Texas and Massachusetts bar exams, but opted to open a practice in Texas.

Jordan was very articulate and spoke with force and conviction. She never married, but instead dedicated her life to politics. When she could not get enough legal work, she served as a volunteer for the Kennedy-Johnson campaign during the 1960 presidential election. She was able to successfully organize a black-worker program in several black precincts of Harris County and managed to get an 80 percent voter turnout. She ran unsuccessfully for the Texas House of Representatives in 1962 and 1964. When Harris County reapportioned in 1965, creating the new Eleventh State Senatorial District, Jordan ran and won this seat by a 2–1 margin over a popular liberal candidate, becoming the first black state senator in Texas history. She spent six years in the Texas Senate, where she sponsored most of the state's environmental bills and authored Texas's first minimum-wage law. She also pushed through the first package of urban legislation and forced the state to place antidiscrimination clauses in all of its contracts.

In 1972, she ran for Congress and became the first southern black elected to Congress since Reconstruction. On the advice of President Lyndon Johnson, she served on the House Judiciary Committee. During the impeachment proceedings against Richard Nixon, she gave her eloquent "We the People" speech. In the speech, she remarked in part as follows:

> Earlier today we heard the beginning of the preamble to the Constitution of the United States. "We the People." It is a very eloquent beginning. But when the document was completed on the 17th of September in 1787, I was not included in that "We the People." I felt somehow for many years that George Washington and Alexander Hamilton left me out by mistake. But through the process of amendment, interpretation and court decisions, I have finally been included in "We the People." (Rhodes 1987, 707)

In 1976, Jordan gave another famous and resounding speech at the Democratic National Convention in the keynote address of the convention. However, Jordan decided against running for a fourth term in Congress and, after six years in Washington, retired from Congress in 1979 and returned to Texas. In 1979, she published an autobiographical book titled *Barbara Jordan, a Self-Portrait*. She also accepted a professorship at the Lyndon Baines Johnson School of Public Affairs, University of Texas, in Austin, where she remained as a teacher until her death in 1996.

In 1992, candidate Bill Clinton asked her to be a keynote speaker at the Democratic Convention. In 1994, Clinton created a task force to address the issue of illegal immigrants and appointed her chairperson. The task force that she chaired ultimately recommended restricting access at U.S. borders and cutting legal immigration by one-third. While her plan proposed limited benefits and an employment register to monitor immigrants, she believed that increased immigration led to competition among the poorer U.S. citizens for jobs and benefits. Her recommendations were subsequently endorsed by President Clinton.

Jordan was diagnosed with multiple sclerosis and spent her last years in a wheelchair. On January 17, 1996, she died at the age of fifty-nine from complications of viral pneumonia and leukemia. She was the first and only black woman to be buried in the Texas State Cemetery. Approximately a year before her death, in 1994, she received the Presidential Medal of Freedom.

See also Busing; Clinton, William Jefferson; Immigration Act of 1965; Johnson, Lyndon Baines; Nixon, Richard Milhous; Powell, Adam Clayton, Jr.

FURTHER READING: Duckworth, James, 2001, "Barbara Jordan," in *Black Heroes*, edited by Jessie C. Smith, Canton, MI: Visible Ink Press; Gates, Henry Louis, Jr., and Cornel West, 2000, *The African-American Century: How Black Americans Have Shaped Our Country*, New York: Free Press; Rhodes, Paula, 1987, "An Afro-American Perspective: We the People and the Struggle for a New World," *Howard Law Journal*, 705–731.

NAOMI ROBERTSON

Jury Selection and Affirmative Action

An underlying principle of the American justice system is the idea that before one can be held criminally culpable for a criminal act, one has the right to be tried before an impartial jury of one's peers. However, questions abound as to the exact meaning of that relatively simple statement. For example, does the right to an impartial trial by a jury of one's peers mean that a black defendant should have jurors who themselves are black? Does it mean that a female defendant should have jurors who are all female? While the simple answer to each of these questions is a resounding "no," the question remains as to how diversified the composition of a jury should be. Additionally, to the extent that one wishes not to have an all-white jury, should affirmative action play a part in jury selection in America (to achieve racially mixed juries)? The idea of jury selection and affirmative action has been the source of many scholarly articles in law reviews and the subject of several Supreme Court cases, as well as the subject of federal statutes, primarily the Federal Jury Selection and Service Act of 1968. Ensuring diversity in jury composition through the means of affirmative action has been recently described as "balancing the box" or "jurymandering."

Traditionally, juries in the United States have consisted of white males. Early in the history of the jury system, the jurors had to own land, thus having a stake in the community. Another qualifier for jury duty historically has been the voting lists, which kept the jury pool largely white in light of the fact that many blacks throughout the South were not registered to vote prior to the Voting Rights Act of 1965. Unfortunately, the application of all-white juries in the South often led to miscarriages of justice in the criminal justice system. For example, in 1931, all-white juries in Alabama led to multiple capital convictions (in multiple trials) for rape for nine black teenagers in the "Scottsboro Boys" case, despite the fact that the evidence clearly supported that the "victims" were not raped by the teenagers. In 1955, a fourteen-year-old African American named Emmett Till was murdered for speaking to a white woman in a local store. The all-white jury acquitted the white defendants and discounted the damning testimony of an African American in the case. After the case, one of the defendants admitted to killing Till. Such cases were unfortunately not the exception. Gunnar Myrdal, in his book *An American Dilemma: The Negro Problem and Modern Democracy,* summed it up when he stated: "It is notorious that practically never have white lynching mobs been brought to court in the South, even when the killers are known to all the community and are mentioned by name in the local press" (Myrdal, 552–553).

Miscarriages of justice continued into the late twentieth century by all-white juries. Most famously, in 1992, a jury with no black members (although one Asian American and one Latino did serve on the jury) acquitted four Los Angeles police officers for assaulting Rodney King, despite the fact that the jury was shown a videotape showing the police officers hitting and kicking King while he was on the ground. Thus the specter of an all-white jury has caused angst, distrust, and skepticism among minorities. It is no wonder that many have been concerned about the fundamental fairness of the legal system that denied blacks (and to a lesser extent, other minorities) an opportunity to participate in the administration of justice.

There have been many proposals in recent years to achieve diversity on juries through the use of affirmative action–type measures. Some have suggested the use of actual racial quotas (although this approach would be of doubtful constitutionality under a strict scrutiny analysis by the courts). Under quotas, the jury would be composed in a representative percentage/proportional manner, representing the exact demographics of the location at issue. Thus if blacks constituted 9 percent of the county, there must be that percentage of blacks in the jury pool. Others have suggested creating separate jury pools for each ethnicity/racial background and drawing jurors from each subset of the jury pool to make up an actual jury in any given case. Finally, some have argued that judges should be encouraged to affirmatively strike down any potential jury that is not representative of the community as a whole.

On the federal level, there exists a statute that mandates that jury pools be diversified. Specifically, in the Federal Jury Selection and Service Act of 1968, 28 U.S.C. §§ 1861–1878, discrimination in the selection of jury pools is expressly prohibited. Furthermore, for federal jury trials, the act requires that the actual jury pools be drawn from voter registration or voting lists. However, the act further specifies that if the voting list results in a substantial underrepresentation of minorities in the jury pool, then federal courts are required to supplement the list with minority names to achieve a fair cross section of the community (if the voting list alone did not accomplish this).

The U.S. Supreme Court first began to address the need for diversity on juries in the case of *Strauder v. West Virginia,* 100 U.S. 303 (1879). In *Strauder,* the Court held that a state cannot systematically exclude blacks from serving on a jury under the Equal Protection Clause of the Fourteenth Amendment. It struck down all such state laws that denied people of color the right to serve on a jury. However, the Court in *Strauder* only invalidated laws that on their face preclude people of color from serving on juries and did not address the exclusion of minorities in fact or in practice. Thus for many years following the *Strauder* decisions, all-white juries presided throughout the country. In 1935, as part of several U.S. Supreme Court–ordered reviews of how Alabama handled the "Scottsboro Boys" case, the U.S. Supreme Court again heard a case dealing with the exclusion of blacks from juries in *Norris v. Alabama*, 294 U.S. 587 (1935). In *Norris*, the Court held that because no blacks had ever served on juries within the state, and because the state had attempted to fraudulently falsify the jury records to list blacks when none in fact had served, the defendant was denied equal protection under the law in his case.

When a state based jury rolls upon voter registration, the likely outcome was that few black individuals would be found on those rolls. For example, in the late 1950s in Carroll County, Mississippi, a black defendant was convicted of murder by an all-white jury. No one could remember the last time a black had served on a jury in that county even though the county was 57 percent black, and the last two blacks to appear on the voter lists had died in the early 1950s. In many parts of America, certainly before the Voting Rights Act of 1965, blacks did not participate in the voting process because of historical discrimination and threats of violence and reprisals. Thus discrimination in voting translated into discrimination in the jury and criminal justice system. As Charles Morgan Jr. wrote in a *Newsweek* article in 1965, "The jury system stands behind the power to vote. How easy is it to cast a ballot when you're afraid someone, from the sheriff on down, might shoot you and nobody will do anything about it?"

A similar issue of fundamental fairness concerning the racial makeup of juries was litigated in the U.S. Court of Appeals for the Fifth Circuit in *Whitus v. Balkcom*, 333 F.2d 496 (5th Cir. 1964). Previous court decisions had required the defendant to raise the lack of black representation on the jury at the time of trial. The fear was that if this issue were raised at trial, the defendant would alienate the mostly or totally white jury and thus prejudice his or her case. The court held that the right to a jury selected without discrimination was a fundamental constitutional right that could only be waived by an informed defendant. Additionally, the Fifth Circuit ruled that it was unconstitutional for a state to force a black defendant to choose between prejudicing the jury by raising the issue or accepting a jury that systematically excluded black jurors.

One area where it appears that the makeup of a jury is still not representative is in death penalty cases. Death cases have historically been seen as unfair by some, especially when one examines the racial makeup of the death row population in the United States. Some scholars have referred to this as nothing short of institutional racism. The courts have been willing to address institutional racism in other areas such as public accommodations, employment, and even jury selection, but have failed to recognize the existence of institutional racism when looking at the race of defendants in death cases. In the case *McCleskey v. Kemp*, 481 U.S. 279 (1987), the U.S. Supreme Court did look at the issue of race of defendant and race of victim via social science research. The "Baldus study," as the research has become known (named after Professor David Baldus), showed that in Georgia there was racial discrimination in the handling of death cases and in juries. The study concluded that the death penalty was more likely to be applied where the defendant was black and the victim was white. Also clear from the study was that prosecutors were more likely to ask for the death penalty when the suspect was black and the victim was white. However, the Court did not ultimately accept the statistical analysis in the Baldus study and determined that race when applied to the defendant and victim were qualitatively different than racial issues relating to the makeup of juries, thus denying relief in this case. In other words, the defendant could not establish that in his case, race was used in a discriminatory fashion that adversely impacted him at trial (by virtue only of the fact that he was black and the victim white). In essence, the Court expected the defendant to make some actual connection, or put forward some concrete facts, to suggest that the jury in his case was racially biased. Some scholars have found the decision interesting in that the Baldus study employed the same type of statistical analysis that has been accepted by the Court in cases ranging from housing to employment as proof of institutional racism.

See also Criminal Justice System and Affirmative Action; Fourteenth Amendment; Institutional Discrimination; Scottsboro Boys; *Strauder v. West Virginia*; Strict Scrutiny; Voting Rights Act of 1965.

FURTHER READING: Alschuler, Albert W., 1995, "Racial Quotas and the Jury," *Duke Law Journal* 44 (February): 704–743; Cohn, Avern, and David R. Sherwood, 1999, "The Rise and Fall of Affirmative Action in Jury Selection," *University of Michigan Journal of Legal Reform* 32:323–333; King, Nancy J., 1993, "Racial Jurymandering: Cancer or Cure? A Contemporary Review of Affirmative Action in Jury Selection," *New York University Law Review* 68:707; Myrdal, Gunnar, 1944, *An American Dilemma: The Negro Problem and Modern Democracy*, New York: Harper and Row.

SUSAN F. BRINKLEY

K

Kennedy, Anthony McLeod (1936–   )

Anthony McLeod Kennedy, an associate justice of the U.S. Supreme Court, while occasionally centrist in his jurisprudence, usually aligns well within the conservative bloc on most issues the Court addresses. In the area of affirmative action, Kennedy joins his conservative colleagues in viewing affirmative action in a negative light and voting to nullify affirmative action plans at issue in cases. As Georgetown University law professor Girardeau Spann has explained, "A five-justice conservative voting bloc has formed on the present Court consisting of justices who have almost never voted to uphold an affirmative action plan in a constitutional case. The members of this conservative bloc are Chief Justice Rehnquist, and Justices O'Connor, Scalia, Kennedy, and Thomas" (Spann 2000, 160).

Kennedy was born into a middle-class family in Sacramento, California, on July 23, 1936. He attended Stanford University, earning a B.A. in 1958. He then went on to Harvard University Law School, where he graduated with a law degree in 1961, and returned to California to practice law in the private sector. Kennedy also taught constitutional law at the McGeorge School of Law (University of the Pacific) during this time. He practiced in the private sector for approximately thirteen years, until President Gerald Ford appointed him to the federal Court of Appeals for the Ninth Circuit, where he distinguished himself as a productive and industrious jurist, authoring more than 400 opinions between 1975 and 1988.

In 1988, President Ronald Reagan nominated Kennedy for a seat on the high court to replace retiring Justice Lewis Powell, but only after seeing two of his other selections not make it to the Supreme Court (Reagan's first choice, Robert Bork, was rejected by the Senate; Reagan's second choice, Douglas Ginsburg, withdrew his name from consideration when it was revealed that he had smoked marijuana with his students at Harvard). Once on the Court, Kennedy immediately joined the conservative bloc of the Court. During his first term on the Court, 1988–1989, he aligned himself with William Rehnquist in 90 percent of all the cases he heard, and with Justice Antonin Scalia in 89 percent of the cases. Since that time, Kennedy has consistently and uniformly aligned himself with Scalia and Rehnquist in opposition to affirmative action in 100 percent of all the cases that have come before him. As of January 2004, Kennedy also has not authored any majority opinion for the Court in any affirmative action case.

See also Affirmative Action Plan Program; Nixon, Richard Milhous; O'Connor, Sandra Day; Powell, Lewis Franklin, Jr.; Reagan, Ronald; Rehnquist, William Hobbs; Scalia, Antonin; Thomas, Clarence.

FURTHER READING: Spann, Girardeau A., 2000, *The Law of Affirmative Action: Twenty-five Years of Supreme Court Decisions on Race and Remedies*, New York: New York University Press.

JAMES A. BECKMAN

Kennedy, John Fitzgerald (1917–1963)

Any timeline discussing modern affirmative action will find President John Fitzgerald Kennedy near the beginning of its trajectory. President Kennedy is credited with being the first president to use the term "affirmative action." He did so in 1961 in Executive Order (E.O.) 10925. This order required federal contractors to take affirmative action to ensure that they treated potential and existing workers equally without regard to race, color, or national origin. This executive order also created the President's Committee on Equal Employment Opportunity. President Kennedy's influence on affirmative action was expanded further with his subsequent appointees to the Federal Communications Commission, who brought affirmative action changes to television programming and overall television station operations, as well as his appointment of Archibald Cox as solicitor general, who would later argue on behalf of the Regents of the University of California in *Regents of the University of California v. Bakke*, 438 U.S. 265 (1978), the "racial preference" case nearly two decades later. Finally, President Kennedy influenced affirmative action for decades to come with his appointment of Byron White to the U.S. Supreme Court in 1962, as Justice White became a long-term supporter of affirmative action while on the Court.

President Kennedy's Executive Order 10925 required government agencies and executive departments to recommend "positive measures for the elimination of any discrimination, direct or indirect, which now exists." It also called for government contractors to "take affirmative action to ensure that applicants are employed, and that employees are treated during employment, without regard to their race, creed, color, or national origin." E.O. 10925 also invested the President's Committee on Equal Employment Opportunity, chaired by Vice President Lyndon B. Johnson, with broad powers to obtain pledges of nondiscrimination and affirmative cooperation from labor unions associated with government contract work. The Committee on Equal Employment Opportunity grew out of President Dwight Eisenhower's Committee on Government Contracts and has since evolved into the Equal Employment Opportunity Commission. While Eisenhower required that his policy of nondiscrimination be posted in conspicuous places, Kennedy made contractors state in solicitations and advertisements that all qualified applicants, without regard to race, would be considered. This same concept reappeared later in Title VII of the Civil Rights Act of 1964. The committee was to report annually on detailed and specific actions taken by each and every agency, as well as these agencies' respective results. The committee's analysis would also

NAACP delegation visits President Kennedy at the White House to promote civil rights legislation. Courtesy of Library of Congress.

make recommendations to executive departments to assist them in meeting the goals of the new national nondiscrimination policy. The committee also included in its efforts outside agencies such as state and local officials, contractors and their agencies, and any other instrumentality to compel labor unions and recruiting agencies to comply with the order by hiring more minority workers.

President Kennedy's order can trace its foundations to an earlier President Franklin D. Roosevelt executive order executed during World War II instituting a policy of nondiscrimination for workers in defense industries or government. The progression of presidential regulation continued with President Lyndon Johnson when he expanded upon Kennedy's framework in 1965 with Executive Order 11246, which provided equal opportunity in federal employment. Johnson's order was initially limited to discrimination based on race, color, religion, or national origin but was later amended to address the issue of gender discrimination as well.

Kennedy extended the coverage of Executive Order 10925 in 1963 with Executive Order 11114 to include contractors who received federal assistance, for example, those businesses (e.g., construction) that were supported by federal funds. Executive Order 10925's affirmative action provisions remained unchanged by E.O. 11114, but now a contractor had to certify that it would take affirmative action. What were missing from the language adopted in the new order were specific measures to accomplish this task of taking affirmative action. The potential for affirmative action at that time was unrecognized. Thus the government looked to volunteerism rather than enforcement. Large companies voluntarily created affirmative action plans committing them to "antidiscrimination in all phases of their personnel policies" or to "plans for progress" (Jones 1988, 396). Kennedy clearly believed in affirmative action to achieve equality. He remarked in 1963 that "the cruel disease of discrimination knows no sectional or state boundaries. The continuing attack on this problem must be equally broad. It must be both private and public—it must be conducted at national, state and local levels—and it must include both legislative and executive action" (Public Papers, 222).

Volumes have been written about this World War II veteran decorated for bravery in a PT-boat rescue in the Pacific, who later served as a senator from Massachusetts and became the thirty-fifth, the youngest, and the first Roman Catholic president of the United States. President John Fitzgerald Kennedy's vision of challenge and change ended in midpassage when it was halted on November 22, 1963, by assassination. Whether he is viewed as a mere rhetorician or a patriotic visionary, Kennedy set up the pillars of change in a decade to be filled with turmoil. The Peace Corps, the Alliance for Progress, and the challenge for putting a man on the moon all were initiatives of Kennedy's short-lived administration, but a legacy of future legislation like the Civil Rights Act of 1964 and the early foundations of modern affirmative action also arose from his tenure. What else may have been achieved by Kennedy if he were not assassinated has now been left to the hypothetical and to myth, as well as endless discussions on what might have been in America's Camelot, but the image of President John F. Kennedy burns eternally and stands nobly for the best and the brightest of a generation.

See also Civil Rights Act of 1964; Eisenhower, Dwight David; Executive Order 10925; Executive Order 11246; Federal Communications Commission; Johnson, Lyndon Baines; President's Committee for Equal Employment Opportunity; Roosevelt, Franklin Delano; *Regents of the University of California v. Bakke*; Title VII of the Civil Rights Act of 1964; White, Byron Raymond.

FURTHER READING: Anderson, Corinne E., 1999, "A Current Perspective: The Erosion of Affirmative Action in University Admissions," *Akron Law Review* 32:181–232; Ashe, Bernard F., 2001, "Government Efforts to Erase Employment Discrimination," *Experience—American Bar Association* 11 (winter): 14; Jones, James E., Jr., 1982, "Twenty-One Years of Affirmative Action: The Maturation of the Administrative Enforcement Process under the Executive Order 11,246 as Amended," *Chicago Kent Law Review* 59:67; Jones, James E., Jr., 1988, "The Origins of Affirmative Action," *University of California Davis Law Review* 21:383–410; President's Special Message to the Congress on Civil Rights, 1963, *Public Papers* 82 (February 28): 222, Washington, DC: U.S. Government Printing Office; Schlesinger, Arthur, Jr., 1965, *A Thousand Days: John F. Kennedy in the White House*, Boston: Houghton Mifflin Co.

ROBERT DON GIFFORD II

Kerner Commission

Officially known as the National Advisory Commission on Civil Disorders, the Kerner Commission was established by President Lyndon Johnson to analyze the urban race riots of the mid-1960s. Named after its chairperson, Otto Kerner, a former governor of Illinois, the Kerner Commission included prominent white and African American political leaders such as New York mayor John Lindsay, Roy Wilkins of the National Association for the Advancement of Colored People, and

Oklahoma senator Fred Harris. The commission produced a 426-page report on the status of race relations in the United States.

Separate and unequal were the key concepts in the Kerner Commission report. The existence of a "white society" of affluence and control and a separate "black society" of poverty and subservience was a recurring theme as the commission identified the causes and effects of racial inequality in America. According to the report, the causes of racial inequality were as follows: first, pervasive discrimination and segregation in employment, education, and housing were found to exist, thereby preventing black participation in the economic process; second, black in-migration and white exodus from urban areas existed, creating urban blight, economic stagnation, and social decay; and third, black ghettos and their disabling physical and psychological barriers to health and prosperity were found to exist.

Other concepts discussed in the Kerner Commission report were the existence of racial bias in the media and law enforcement and the emergence of a new African American concept of self-worth and attitude, which resulted in the rise of the Black Power movement. This movement was noted for its use of violence and protest as a means of creating socioeconomic equality and solving related problems. Leaders in the Black Power movement included Malcolm X, Stokely Carmichael, James Meredith, and H. Rap Brown. These individuals were often also associated with other key national African American organizations at the time, including the National Association for the Advancement of Colored People (NAACP), the Southern Christian Leadership Conference (SCLC), and the Congress of Racial Equality (CORE).

See also Black Nationalism; Carmichael, Stokely; A Common Destiny: Blacks and American Society; Congress of Racial Equality; Johnson, Lyndon Baines; Media and Affirmative Action; National Association for the Advancement of Colored People; Relative Deprivation Theory; Riots, Economically and Racially Motivated; Segregation.

FURTHER READING: Carmichael, Stokely, 1976, Black Power: The Politics of Liberation in America, New York: Vintage Books; Harris, Fred R., and Roger W. Wilkins, eds., 1988, Quiet Riots: Race and Poverty in the United States, New York: Pantheon Books; Mereanto, Phillip J., ed., 1970, The Kerner Report Revisited: Final Report and Background Papers, Urbana: Institute of Government and Public Affairs, University of Illinois; Report of the National Advisory Commission on Civil Disorders, New York: Bantam Books, 1968.

THOMAS A. ADAMICH

King, Martin Luther, Jr. (1929–1968)

Martin Luther King Jr. was one of the most prominent and best-known civil rights leaders of the twentieth century. He spent the last few years of his life leading mass civil rights movements against the practice of segregation and inequality in the South. He organized marches, gave speeches, and conferred with politicians on key civil rights legislation (e.g., the Civil Rights Act of 1964 and the Voting Rights Act of 1965). Contrary to some other minority leaders of the time (e.g., Malcolm X and Stokely Carmichael), King preached nonviolent integration and assimilation. King's means were peaceful, based in part upon Mahatma Gandhi's nonviolent protests in India, and King did not adhere to notions of separatism or employ militant means in protest to segregation. At the pinnacle of the civil rights movement, King delivered his famous "I Have a Dream" speech in Washington, D.C. King's speech, which today is frequently cited in affirmative action debates, set out his vision of an integrated color-blind society, wherein he stated that people would not be judged "on the color of their skin, but the content of their character." King was also one of the first individuals in the modern era to address the need for affirmative action in the United States. King, in his book *Why We Can't Wait* (1964), argued for the creation of "some sort of compensatory consideration for the handicaps [the black individual] has inherited from the past" (King, 146). King also first put forth the fair-race metaphor that for blacks to compete with whites in a meaningful way, they must both start out at the same point on the starting line.

Martin Luther King Jr. was born on January 15, 1929, in Atlanta, Georgia. He was one of three children born to the Reverend Martin Luther King Sr. and Mrs. Alberta Williams King. He attended high school in the Atlanta area. In 1944, he began his higher-education studies at a historically black college, Morehouse College in Atlanta, Georgia. While King was an undergraduate student at Morehouse College, the school's president, the Reverend Benjamin E. Mays, mentored him. Some scholars believe that the influence of Mays assisted King's decision to enter the ministry. After receiving his bachelor of arts degree in 1948, he studied at Crozer Theological Seminary in Chester, Pennsylvania. On June 18, 1953, Martin Luther King married Coretta Scott.

In 1955, King received a doctorate in systematic theology from Boston University. While completing his dissertation, King accepted the pastorate of Dexter Avenue Baptist Church in Montgomery, Alabama. In fact, King was from a royal preaching pedigree. His grandfather was the Reverend A.D. Williams, pastor of Ebenezer Baptist Church in Atlanta, who was succeeded by King's father, the Reverend Martin Luther King Sr., at that church. King's grandfather and father were social activists in the African American community and were a major influence in Martin Luther King's social activism.

Martin Luther King Jr. rose to national prominence and became the undeniable leader of the civil rights movement in 1955. On December 1, 1955, Rosa Parks refused to comply with a city ordinance that mandated segregation of the city of Montgomery's public bus system. Soon after the Rosa Parks incident, the African American citizens of Montgomery organized a bus boycott that lasted an entire year. While the bus boycott unfolded, King endured many hardships, unwarranted arrests, death threats, and the bombing of his home. As a result of the bus boycott, King gained national notoriety as the boycott garnered national media attention, and the country witnessed his charismatic leadership ability. The nation was captivated by King's integrity and dynamic oratorical skills. In December 1956, the U.S. Supreme Court declared the city of Montgomery's segregated public transit system unconstitutional.

In 1957, King and several other ministers founded the Southern Christian Leadership Conference (SCLC) to assist in the mobilization of various communities in protest initiatives against discrimination and other social ills. Among the organization's many aims was to gain voting rights for African Americans. In 1959, King moved from Montgomery back to Atlanta to be closer to the SCLC headquarters. King also led several protests in several southern states. In 1963, King guided mass

Dr. Martin Luther King Jr. delivering his famous "I Have a Dream" speech in Washington, D.C., in August 1963. Courtesy of Photofest.

demonstrations in Birmingham, Alabama, protesting segregated department stores and restaurants. Media news footage of the Birmingham clashes and the massive resistance efforts of staunch segregationists, most notably Alabama governor George C. Wallace, were aired nationwide and allegedly compelled President John F. Kennedy to submit civil rights legislation to Congress. King was arrested after this protest, and while incarcerated, he wrote his famous "Letter from a Birmingham Jail."

In August 1963, King was at the apex of the civil rights movement when a mass demonstration was held in Washington, D.C., where he delivered the "I Have a Dream" speech. Ironically, today, King's speech is often utilized by opponents of affirmative action in arguing that the United States should be a truly color-blind society based upon a color-blind constitution and should not employ racial preferences (based on color of skin) as a substitute for promotion and/or selection based upon merit (content of character). For example, in 1995, Dinesh D'Souza argued that modern affirmative action programs are a contradiction to Martin Luther King's civil rights beliefs. In 1997, Stephan and Abigail Thernstrom argued that it is essential to abide by King's famous "color-blind" quotation as a country if we are going to get beyond a negative racial climate and to a point where "blacks and whites can come together" (Thernstrom and Thernstrom 1997, 539). Shelby Steele, in his widely publicized book criticizing affirmative action, reflects his belief in affirmative action being contrary to King's message by the very title of his book, *The Content of Our Character*. Finally, Ward Connerly, in announcing the creation of a new anti–affirmative action organization on King's birthday, stated, "Dr. King personifies the quest for a color-blind society and I felt that it would be a great symbol to give birth to an organization that wants the nation to resume that journey on the birthday of the man who symbolizes it" (White, 46).

Supporters of affirmative action (and the prediction that King would have favored modern affirmative action programs) stress that King repeatedly talked about an unpaid debt that America owed to blacks and that the "content of character" quote is taken out of context. Specifically, supporters argue that an earlier passage in the speech is more telling as to King's views for societal compensation for blacks:

> When the architects of our Republic wrote the magnificent words of the Constitution and the Declaration of Independence, they were signing a promissory note to which every American was to fall heir. This note was the promise that all men, yes, black men as well as white men, would be guaranteed the unalienable rights of life, liberty, and the pursuit of happiness. . . . Instead of honoring this sacred obligation, America

has given the Negro people a bad check; a check which has come back marked "insufficient funds." (White 1997, 2)

Furthermore, supporters point to language in King's 1964 book *Why We Can't Wait*. In this book, King argued for the creation of some societal program to compensate blacks for the evils of slavery and segregation. King also put forth the race metaphor, expressing it as follows in his book: "It is obvious that if a man is entered at the starting line in a race three hundred years after another man, the first would have to perform some impossible feat to catch up with his fellow runner" (King 1964, 147). King also remarked that "whenever the issue of compensatory or preferential treatment for the Negro is raised, some of our friends recoil in horror. The Negro should be granted equality, they agree, but he should ask for nothing more" (King 1964, 147).

King received several significant awards. Notably, King was named as *Time* magazine's "Man of the Year" for 1963. In 1964, he became the recipient of the Nobel Peace Prize, which was presented to him in Oslo, Norway. Once King returned from Norway, the battle for voting rights was heating up in the South. In Selma, Alabama, African Americans organized a march from Selma to the state capital in Montgomery to highlight African American voting registration activities. On the first attempt, the marchers were beaten and turned back by Alabama state troopers, an event that has become known as "Bloody Sunday." King entered this battle and successfully led a second march from Selma to Montgomery.

After the passage of the 1964 Civil Rights Act, King found a new battleground, the war in Vietnam. King focused his efforts on the war in Southeast Asia and became a staunch opponent of the nation's foreign policy practices. In a speech titled "Beyond Vietnam" that was given in 1967, King called the United States "the greatest purveyor of violence in the world." During this time, King expanded his focus to include human rights for the poor. In the last months of King's life, he organized the Poor People's Campaign, which consisted of a group of people of various races and cultures who would march on Washington to address their needs to a Congress that he believed demonstrated apathy for the poor. The Poor People's Campaign was designed to bring attention to the economic problems that had not been addressed through the original civil rights movement.

On the evening of April 4, 1968, while helping striking sanitation workers in Memphis, Tennessee, King was shot as he stood on the balcony of the Lorraine Motel. King's assassination caused turmoil in several major cities across the country. The third Monday in January is now recognized as a national holiday in honor of the birthday of Martin Luther King Jr., a holiday initially opposed by Ronald Reagan.

See also African Americans; Assimilation Theory; Carmichael, Stokely; Civil Rights Act of 1964; Civil Rights Movement; Color-Blind Constitution; D'Souza, Dinesh; Historically Black Colleges and Universities; Integration; Kennedy, John Fitzgerald; Malcolm X; Reagan, Ronald; Segregation; Southern Christian Leadership Conference; Thernstrom, Stephan, and Thernstrom, Abigail; Voting Rights Act of 1965.

FURTHER READING: Byrnes, Erin E., 1999, "Therapeutic Jurisprudence: Unmasking White Privilege to Expose the Fallacy of White Innocence: Using a Theory of Moral Correlativity to Make the Case for Affirmative Action Programs in Education," *Arizona Law Review* 41:

535–572; Carson, Clayborne, ed., 1998, *The Autobiography of Martin Luther King*, New York: Warner Books; Dyson, Eric Michael, 2000, *I May Not Get There with You: The True Martin Luther King, Jr.*, New York: Simon and Schuster/Free Press; "If Martin Luther King Jr. Were Alive Today," 1997, *Pittsburgh Business Times* 149, no. 5 (January 20): 2; "Jesse Jackson Leads Protest of California's Affirmative Action Ban on 34th Anniversary of King's 'Dream' Speech," 1997, *Jet* 92, no. 17 (September 15): 4–8; King, Martin Luther, Jr., 1964, *Why We Can't Wait?* New York: Harper and Row; King, Martin Luther, Jr., 1967, *Where Do We Go from Here: Chaos or Community?* Boston: Beacon Press; "Martin Luther King, Jr.: Morehouse Years," 2001, *Footsteps* 3, no. 5 (November/December); Moses, Greg, 1998, "To Begin Where We Have Not Yet Reached: Affirmative Action in the Philosophy of Martin Luther King, Jr.," *NWSA Journal* 10, no. 3 (fall): 54–93; Steele, Shelby, 1990, *The Content of Our Character: A New Vision of Race in America*, New York: St. Martin's Press; Thernstrom, Stephan, and Abigail Thernstrom, 1997, *America in Black and White: One Nation, Indivisible: Race in Modern America*, New York: Simon and Schuster; Trounstine, Philip J., 1996, "GOP to Use Martin Luther King's Speech to Promote California Anti–Affirmative Action Proposal," Knight Ridder/Tribune Service, October 21; White, Jack E., 1997, "I Have a Scheme: Ward Connerly's Effort to Hijack Dr. King's Legacy Is Full of Black Humor," *Time* 149, no. 5 (February 3): 46.

F. ERIK BROOKS

Knight v. Alabama, 787 F. Supp. 1030 (N.D. Ala. 1991)

The federal district court ruling in *Knight v. Alabama* illustrates the problems of truly integrating educational institutions in the southern states in the modern era. The decision in the case ultimately held that vestiges of de jure segregation still existed in institutions of higher learning in Alabama and that the state of Alabama needed to take steps to rectify the situation. The court ruling mandated that the state of Alabama engage in affirmative efforts to break down the remaining vestiges of discrimination and segregation, including such affirmative actions as actively recruiting more African American students and faculty in the historically white state schools, ensuring that the historically black colleges and universities (HBCUs) within the state receive appropriate resources and funding, and ensuring that white students are recruited for HBCUs and that diversity is promoted at the state's HBCUs.

The case *Knight v. Alabama* originated from a Title VI compliance investigation of Alabama's public higher education by the Office of Civil Rights, U.S. Department of Health, Education, and Welfare, which now operates under the title of the Department of Education. In 1981, Governor Fob James and the presidents of the state's public higher-education institutions received letters from the Department of Education alleging that vestiges of the former de jure segregated system remained in the state's universities and colleges, which charges if true, were a violation of Title VI. Alabama was directed to submit a plan that would ensure that all remaining vestiges of segregation would be removed. Nineteen other southern and border states were ordered to prepare plans as well.

After months of unsuccessful negotiations between the governor's office and the Office of Civil Rights, the assistant secretary for the Office of Civil Rights sent a letter to the governor stating that within ten days of receipt of the letter, Alabama must submit a plan or the matter would be referred to the U.S. Justice Department for litigation. Alabama did not submit a plan. On January 15, 1981, John F. Knight and nineteen other alumni, students, and faculty members from historically black Alabama State University filed suit in federal court. Knight was designated as the lead plaintiff, and thus the suit became known as *Knight v. James.* The plaintiffs alleged that duplicative programs and services at the branch campuses in Montgomery of historically white Auburn University and historically white Troy State University were impeding desegregation at Alabama State University. They specifically stated that segregation was part of an official state policy of white supremacy that enforced, among other things, discrimination in allocation of resources to the state's HBCUs, noncompliance in fulfilling the promise that HBCUs' roles, mission, and scope would be equal to those of the state's flagship universities, the University of Alabama and Auburn University, and last, denying federal funds to the HBCUs within the state.

The district court granted a motion of the governor and the Alabama Commission of Higher Education to stay all further action in the suit until a pending resolution of a Title VI administrative proceeding between the state and the U.S. Department of Education. However, no resolution was reached at the administrative proceeding. The Justice Department filed its own suit, alleging that Alabama was maintaining vestiges of de jure segregation. The cases were then merged together when the district court granted the motion of Knight and the other parties to intervene in *United States v. Alabama* on the ground that its outcome would be determinative of the issues in *Knight v. James.*

Judge U.W. Clemon, the first of seven judges assigned to the case, presided in the first trial, which began on July 1, 1985, and concluded on August 2, 1985. Judge Clemon ruled that Alabama had not dismantled the vestiges of its prior de jure system. He then ordered the state to submit a plan to eliminate all vestiges of the dual system. He approved consent decrees between the United States and Jacksonville State University, the University of West Alabama (then Livingston University), the University of South Alabama, and the University of Montevallo. The consent decrees required an increase of African Americans in relation to governing boards, student admissions, and employment opportunities within the state institutions.

In 1986, Auburn University and the University of Alabama filed a motion in the Eleventh Circuit Court of Appeals to stay Judge Clemon's ruling, and the stay was granted. A year later, the Eleventh Circuit Court reversed and remanded Judge Clemon's ruling. The court held that the Justice Department's case should be dismissed, the Knight plaintiffs' Title VI claim should be dismissed, Judge Clemon should be removed, and a new trial should be conducted if the Justice Department and the *Knight* plaintiffs refiled their claims. The court of appeals did affirm the plaintiffs' right to sue under the Fourteenth Amendment, but specified that the action must be refiled.

In 1989, after six other judges recused themselves or were removed by the Eleventh Circuit Court of Appeals, the court assigned Judge Harold Murphy of Rome, Georgia, to preside in the case. He reaffirmed the consent decrees with the previously mentioned universities. He disposed of all pending motions to dismiss the statewide Title VI claims of the *Knight* plaintiffs. Judge Murphy also approved consent decrees of the State Board of Education, Athens State College, Calhoun State Community College, and Troy State University at Montgomery. The trial began on October 29, 1990, and concluded on April 16, 1991. On December 30, 1991, Judge Murphy also ruled that there were vestiges of de jure segregation in Alabama's higher education system. He specifically ruled that vestiges of segregation had impeded and restricted the two historically black universities, and the Fourteenth Amendment required the state to eliminate all vestiges of segregation. In light of this decision, the court further ordered the following: first, that Alabama's two historically black universities, Alabama State University and Alabama A&M University, increase their endowments and establish new academic programs and other race scholarships at their institutions; second, that the land-grant extension services at Alabama A&M University and Auburn University be consolidated into a unitary system and a committee be established to monitor desegregation in the state; third, that Auburn University, Calhoun State Community College, the University of West Alabama, Troy State University, and the University of Montevallo hire more African American faculty members; fourth, that Auburn University, Jackson State University, the University of Alabama, the University of Alabama at Huntsville, and the University of North Alabama employ more African American administrators; fifth, that Alabama State University be awarded $15 million and Alabama A&M University be awarded $16 million for capital improvements; sixth, that the Alabama Commission of Higher Education be ordered to change the higher-education funding formula; seventh, that the historically black universities be ordered to develop and implement recruitment policies targeting white students and establish a diversity scholarship, for which the state would reimburse the two schools up to $1 million a year for ten years ending in 2005; and eighth, that a trust fund for educational excellence be established to help the historically black institutions' endowments. Finally, both Alabama State University and Alabama A&M University were awarded $1 million annually for ten years ending in 2005, and the state was required to match these annual contributions up to $1 million for each university's endowment.

See also African Americans; *Brown v. Board of Education*; De Facto and De Jure Segregation; Department of Education; Department of Justice; Fourteenth Amendment; Historically Black Colleges and Universities; Title VI of the Civil Rights Act of 1964; *United States v. Fordice; United States v. Louisiana.*

FURTHER READING: Brown, Christopher M., 1999, *The Quest to Define Collegiate Desegregation: Black Colleges, Title VI Compliance, and Post-Adams Litigation*, Westport, CT: Bergin and Garvey; Evelyn, Jamilah, 1998, "Beneath the Veneer," *Black Issues in Higher Education* 15, no. 20:35; Preer, Jean L., 1982, *Lawyers v. Educators: Black Colleges and Desegregation in Public Higher Education*, Westport, CT: Greenwood Press; Watkins, Levi, 1987, *Fighting Hard: The Alabama State Experience*, Detroit: Harlo Press.

F. ERIK BROOKS

Korematsu v. United States, 323 U.S. 214 (1944)

The U.S. Supreme Court decided in *Korematsu v. United States* that all federal statutes classifying individuals on account of race should receive strict scrutiny review by the courts. Even today, the decision is often referenced in affirmative action and racial profiling debates and was discussed by the Supreme Court in the affirmative action case *Adarand Constructors, Inc. v. Peña*, 515 U.S. 200 (1995). The decision affirmed the conviction of Toyosaburo ("Fred") Korematsu, a native-born citizen of the United States, for being in an area from which those of Japanese ancestry were barred during World War II. It has been roundly criticized as the culmination of one of the bleaker examples of the failure of the federal courts to protect U.S. citizens from disparate treatment on the basis of their national origin.

The events leading to the case occurred during an extraordinary period in the nation's history. Following Japan's military attack on Pearl Harbor on December 7, 1941, state and federal government officials began calling for the removal of persons of Japanese ancestry from the west coast and their relocation to more interior geographic locations. Apparently this clamor became more pronounced after the Roberts Commission (which President Franklin Roosevelt appointed to investigate the facts related to the Japanese attack on Pearl Harbor) issued its findings. The Roberts Commission report noted, in part, that Japanese spies in Hawaii had provided information to Japan. In addition to such findings, there were a few sporadic instances of Japanese attacks (aircraft strikes, shelling) on the coasts of Oregon, California, and Alaska in 1942.

The report heightened military concerns that persons of Japanese ancestry disloyal to the United States could engage in activity aimed at assisting Japan in conducting attacks on the west coast. On February 19, 1942, President Roosevelt issued Executive Order 9066. It authorized the exclusion of persons of Japanese origin from the west coast of the United States to protect against feared espionage and sabotage. Congress then enacted a law that imposed criminal penalties for violation of the executive order or regulations implementing it. Several steps aimed at Japanese Americans were taken. A curfew was imposed. They were required to report to relocation centers, and ultimately, many were relocated to internment facilities. The constitutionality of this program was widely criticized. However, once it was in place, it was up to the courts to handle challenges to these government actions.

Relying on the government's position that the actions were justified by military necessity, in *Hirabayashi v. United States,* 320 U.S. 81 (1943), the U.S. Supreme Court ruled that the curfew was constitutional and sustained Hirabayashi's conviction for violating it. In response to the argument that distinctions based on race are unconstitutional, the Court held that the fact that the United States was at war with Japan justified differentiating those of Japanese origin from other groups in the United States. In deciding only the curfew issue, the Court avoided deciding the more difficult question of the constitutionality of the forced relocation and internment of Japanese Americans.

The Supreme Court addressed this issue in *Korematsu v. United States.* Again relying on the government's argument of military necessity, and on its own decision in *Hirabayashi,* the Court held that the exclusion of Japanese Americans from areas on the west coast designated by the government and their relocation were constitutional. Specifically, Civilian Exclusion Order 34 was promulgated by the commanding general of the Western Defense Command under authority of Executive Order 9066. The order directed the exclusion after May 9, 1942, from a described west coast military area of all persons of Japanese ancestry. The intent was to protect the United States during the war with Japan against espionage and sabotage. Therefore, in a six-justice majority opinion authored by Justice Hugo Black, the Court stressed that Korematsu was relocated because the United States

A group arriving by train in May 1942 from Elk Grove, and boarding a bus for Manzanar, a war relocation authority center where evacuees of Japanese ancestry from certain West Coast areas stayed for the duration of the war. Courtesy of Library of Congress.

was at war with Japan and the military danger that posed, rather than because of hostility toward him on the basis of his race.

However, three justices (Owen Roberts, Frank Murphy, and Robert Jackson) dissented. The former two specifically condemned the racist nature of the exclusion program. They agreed with the decision to uphold the curfew found to be constitutional in *Hirabayashi*, but disagreed with the decision to uphold the relocation requirement. Justice Murphy wrote in dissent that the exclusion of Japanese Americans from their homes "falls into the ugly abyss of racism" and that the government position was "largely an accumulation of much of the misinformation, half-truths and insinuations that for years have been directed against Japanese Americans by people with racial and economic prejudices." Murphy concluded by saying that he dissented from the "legalization of racism." Justice Jackson, also in dissent, characterized the majority's opinion in the *Korematsu* case as "a loaded weapon ready for the hand of any authority that can bring forward a plausible claim of an urgent need."

Approximately forty years later, the federal District Court for the Northern District of California revisited this issue when it vacated Fred Korematsu's conviction on the grounds of government misconduct. However, much had changed in the forty years separating the two decisions. For example, in 1954, the Supreme Court ruled that segregating students on the basis of race violated the Equal Protection Clause of the Fourteenth Amendment. Ten years later, the Civil Rights Act of 1964 was enacted. In 1965, President Johnson issued Executive Order 11246 establishing affirmative action obligations for federal contractors and organizations receiving federal funds. Had such laws been in place in 1944, it is likely that arguments relied upon by the Court would not have been deemed sufficient to justify such disparate treatment of Japanese Americans during World War II.

The most immediately relevant event impacting the district court's decision was the 1982 report of the Commission on Wartime Relocation and Internment of Civilians. Congress appointed the commission in 1980 to investigate the facts and circumstances surrounding the relocation and internment of Japanese Americans during World War II. The commission's report indicated that the government knew at the time of the *Hirabayashi* and *Korematsu* cases that there was no military necessity justifying the relocation and internment program. Relying, in large part, on its finding of the trustworthiness of the report, the district court found that the government knowingly concealed evidence from the Supreme Court that contradicted the military necessity justification for the relocation of persons of Japanese ancestry. Finding that relevant evidence was withheld, the court set aside Korematsu's conviction.

By focusing on the government's misconduct in concealing relevant evidence from the courts, the district court avoided a detailed discussion of the propriety of the racial classification used to relocate and intern Japanese American citizens. Perhaps the most valid criticism of the Supreme Court's 1944 decision in *Korematsu* was that the Court affirmed a program that was based clearly on a racial classification. Not only Japanese resident aliens, but also U.S. citizens born in the United States were displaced because they were Japanese. Thus they were treated differently than other U.S. citizens because of their race.

The Supreme Court's decision in *Korematsu v. United States* has had an important impact on civil rights. In *Korematsu*, the Supreme Court made it clear that governmental racial classifications are "immediately suspect" and that the most "rigid scrutiny" (i.e., strict scrutiny) is the proper standard for reviewing the constitutionality of racial classifications. Unfortunately, despite articulating this rigorous test for judging such classifications, the Court upheld the race-based internment of Japanese Americans. Application of that test in later cases, however, has made it difficult for such classifications to withstand constitutional scrutiny. Today, the *Korematsu* case remains one of the rare instances in which the Court has utilized a strict scrutiny analysis while still upholding the government's racial classification actions and/or plans.

In addition, several steps in ensuing years have been taken in the United States to acknowledge or otherwise address the past wrongs perpetrated on Japanese Americans in World War II and upheld by the Supreme Court in the *Korematsu* and *Hirabayashi* cases. For example, the Evacuation Claims Act of 1948, the later Japanese-American Evacuations Claims Act of 1982, the Civil Liberties Act of 1988, the U.S. district court's decision in *Korematsu v. United States* (1984), and the use of the 1982 commission report findings to toll the statute of limitations and permit Japanese Americans to maintain Takings Clause claims all evidence efforts at some redress for those interned on the basis of their race.

Calling it a national mistake, President Gerald Ford rescinded Executive Order 9066 in 1976. The Civil Liberties Act of 1988 contained a national apology, and President Ronald Reagan signed the apology that accompanied the redress checks of $20,000 for each of the living survivors. Three years after Korematsu's conviction was vacated, the Ninth Circuit Court of Appeals in 1987 finally reversed Hirabayashi's curfew conviction. In January 1998, President Bill Clinton awarded Fred Korematsu the Presidential Medal of Freedom in a ceremony at the White House. President Clinton described Fred Korematsu as a man of "quiet bravery" and deserving of "our respect and thanks for his patient pursuit to preserve the civil liberties we hold so dear" (Irons 1999, 364).

Although the Supreme Court itself never specifically overruled its *Korematsu* and *Hirabayashi* decisions, individual Supreme Court justices have denounced the decisions and the racism that led to the internment of Japanese Americans. For example, in 1995, the Court decided *Adarand Constructors, Inc. v. Peña.* In *Adarand,* the Court established unequivocally that strict scrutiny is to be applied when testing the constitutionality of race-based affirmative action programs in government employment. Justice Sandra Day O'Connor, writing for the majority, and Justice Ruth Bader Ginsburg, in her dissent, each used the opportunity to criticize the Court's reasoning in *Korematsu.*

O'Connor stressed that the Court's failure to apply strict scrutiny in *Hirabayashi* led to "unfortunate results." Calling the order upheld in *Korematsu* "racially discriminatory," she cautioned that *Korematsu* demonstrates that strict scrutiny does not always "detect an illegitimate racial classification," and that failure to apply strict scrutiny rigorously "can only increase the risk of another such error occurring in the future." In her dissent, Justice Ginsburg called the discrimination upheld in *Korematsu* "invidious" and suggested that such a classification would not again survive strict scrutiny. Accordingly, the *Adarand* decision confirms that the courts must view any racial or ethnic classifications as suspect, thereby triggering strict scrutiny analysis. However, the Supreme Court's *Korematsu* decision remains a relevant reminder that the real test is making sure that strict scrutiny is not just articulated, but used rigorously. Otherwise, the injustice upheld in *Korematsu* can recur.

See also Adarand Constructors, Inc. v. Peña; Brown v. Board of Education; Civil Rights Act of 1964; Clinton, William Jefferson; Equal Protection Clause; Executive Order 11246; Fourteenth Amendment; Ginsburg, Ruth Bader; Japanese Internment and World War II; O'Connor, Sandra Day; Racial Profiling; Reparations; Strict Scrutiny; Suspect Classification.

FURTHER READING: Grossman, Joel B. 1997, "The Japanese American Cases and the Vagaries of Constitutional Adjudication in Wartime: An Institutional Perspective," *Hawaii Law Review* 19:649–695; Irons, Peter, 1999, *A People's History of the Supreme Court,* New York: Viking Press; Oh, Reggie, and Frank Wu, 1996, "The Evolution of Race in the Law: The Supreme Court Moves from Approving Internment of Japanese Americans to Disapproving Affirmative Action for African Americans," *Michigan Journal of Race and Law* 1:165–193; Rehnquist, William H., 1998, *All the Laws but One: Civil Liberties in Wartime,* New York: Alfred A. Knopf.

PAUL M. HARIDAKIS

Ku Klux Klan

The Ku Klux Klan (KKK) is a collection of loosely affiliated white supremacist groups in the United States. The KKK has a history of using violence and intimidation to suppress or oppose civil rights for ethnic and religious minorities. Since the American Civil War, the KKK has gone through several periods of rise and decline. Today, the group attempts to recruit among white Christian males who harbor hatred and resentment for modern civil rights programs and initiatives, such as affirmative action programs.

The Klan was initially formed in 1866 in Tennessee by former Confederate soldiers. The organization was a secret society that undertook a variety of efforts to intimidate the newly freed African Americans and to weaken the Reconstruction governments in southern states. The level of violence prompted Congress to pass legislation to suppress the KKK. The organization was officially disbanded in 1869, but it continued to operate in many localities. The KKK was revived on a national basis in 1915. During the 1920s, the organization spread beyond the South and reached a membership of 4 million.

During the civil rights movement of the 1950s and 1960s, the KKK launched a new wave of violence throughout the South, including lynchings and bombings. As various affirmative action policies were implemented, the KKK sought to intimidate minorities and block programs. However, the extreme tactics and racism of the KKK alienated the organization from all but a handful of Americans. By the 1990s, membership in the KKK had declined to under 6,000.

See also Civil War (Reconstruction) Amendments and Civil Rights Acts; Fourteenth Amendment; Hate Crimes; Majority-Group Resentment; Scapegoating/Displaced-Aggression Theories.

FURTHER READING: Quarles, Chester L., 1999, *The Ku Klux Klan and Related American Racialist and Antisemitic Organizations: A History and Analysis,* Jefferson, NC: McFarland; Ruiz, Jim, 1998, *The Black Hood of the Ku Klux Klan,* San Francisco: Austin and Winfield.

TOM LANSFORD

L

Laidlaw, Harriet Burton (1873–1949)

Harriet Burton Laidlaw was one of the leading women critics and social thinkers in the early 1900s on the issue of political and social rights for women. While her life and work predate modern affirmative action programs, Laidlaw's beliefs and dedication to the suffrage movement and equality of women have relevancy to the affirmative action debate today, if for no other reason than as an illustration of the struggle for gender equality in the United States. Laidlaw spent her life dedicated to promoting the suffrage movement, abolishing white slavery, and supporting America's entry into the League of Nations. From 1893 until the ratification of the Nineteenth Amendment in 1920, Laidlaw worked tirelessly for women's suffrage. She served in Carrie Chapman Catt's New York Woman Suffrage Party, as the chairman for the Manhattan borough of the party (1909–1916), and as auditor for the National American Woman Suffrage Association (1911–1913). In 1911 and 1914, she and her husband traveled to the American West together on a speech campaign. Laidlaw also produced a handbook for suffragists in 1914 titled *Organizing to Win*. The handbook encouraged suffragists to attend meetings, meet with legislators, work on voter education, and stress publicity. Laidlaw was also involved in abolishing white slavery and served on the boards of the Florence Crittenton League and the American Social Hygiene Association. She even made a point of attending women's night court.

Once the Nineteenth Amendment was ratified, Laidlaw dedicated her energies toward developing and encouraging international peace. She was a founder of the League of Nations Non-Partisan Association and served in a number of organizations such as the Women's Pro-League Council, the American Association for the United Nations, and the League of Nations Association. Always active and concerned about reform, Laidlaw was an active member and held a number of different offices in the League for Civil Service Reform, the New York State Food Conservation Committee, the Children's Aid Society, the Municipal Art League, and then New York State Prohibition Society, among others. Her commitment to reform was boundless even when she was caring for her husband, who suffered from Parkinson's disease. In 1932, Laidlaw became the first female member of the board of directors of the financial and statistical firm Standard and Poor's.

Laidlaw was born in Albany, New York, in 1874. Laidlaw's father, a bank cashier, died when she was six, and the family moved in with her father's parents. She attended the public schools in Albany, New York, and completed a bachelor of pedagogy in 1895 and a master's of pedagogy in 1896 from Albany Normal College. Continuing her education, Laidlaw moved to New York, attended Barnard College, and taught English in New York public high schools. Laidlaw was exceptionally pretty, possessing beautiful eyes and a charming smile. She was raised Presbyterian but practiced some Hinduism, which influenced her to become a strict vegetarian. She enjoyed a number of activities, including golf. She also attended a number of summer programs at Oxford, Harvard, Columbia, and the University of Chicago. In New York, Laidlaw took advantage of the cultural events offered by the city. She indulged interests in the opera and Hinduism as well as in the suffragist movement. On October 25, 1905, she married James Lee Laidlaw, a successful banker and strong advocate of women's rights. In 1930, Harriet Laidlaw was awarded an honorary LL.D. from Rollins College. She died in New York on January 25, 1949, from a heart condition.

See also Nineteenth Amendment; Suffrage Movement.

FURTHER READING: James, Edward T., 1971, *Notable American Women, 1607–1950: A Biographical Dictionary*, Cambridge, MA: Harvard University Press.

LISA A. ENNIS

Latinos

See Hispanic Americans.

Lau v. Nichols, 414 U.S. 563 (1974)

In *Lau v. Nichols*, the U.S. Supreme Court held that a school district that received federal funds violated Title VI of the Civil Rights Act of 1964 by failing to provide English-language instruction to students of Chinese ancestry who did not speak English. This failure denied these students a "meaningful opportunity to participate in the public educational program" and thus had a discriminatory effect upon the students. The school district was required to "take affirmative steps" to ensure that non-English-speaking students could effectively participate in the school system's educational program even though the school district did not intentionally discriminate against the students. Although *Lau v. Nichols* was never expressly overruled, its "effects-only" test may not have survived *Regents of the University of California v. Bakke*, 438 U.S. 265 (1978), a question that divided the Court in *Guardians Association v. Civil Service Commission*, 463 U.S. 582 (1983).

In *Lau*, non-English-speaking Chinese students brought a class-action suit against the San Francisco school district for failure to provide English-language instruction. The plaintiff class claimed that their rights had been violated under Title VI of the Civil Rights Act and under the Equal Protection Clause of the Fourteenth Amendment. The Supreme Court did not reach the constitutional claim, finding that the school district violated section 601 of the Civil Rights Act, which bans discrimination "on the ground of race, color, or national origin" in "any program or activity receiving Federal financial assistance."

The Department of Health, Education, and Welfare (HEW) (now the Department of Education and the Department of Health and Human Services) promulgated specific guidelines under Title VI, one of which required school districts to "take affirmative steps to rectify [any] language deficiency." The Court found that it was not sufficient to simply provide the same "facilities, textbooks, teachers, and curriculum" to the non-English-speaking students. Because students who do not understand English are "effectively foreclosed from any meaningful education," the Court reasoned that non-English-speaking students would find their education "wholly incomprehensible." Thus there was a discriminatory effect upon these students by failing to provide English-language instruction "even though no purposeful design is present." Therefore, the Court found that a disparate impact could constitute a violation of Title VI.

Justice Potter Stewart's concurrence was joined by Chief Justice Warren Burger and Justice Harry Blackmun. The concurrence pointed out that section 601, standing alone, arguably would not warrant withholding federal funds from these schools. According to Stewart, the language of section 601 seemed to prohibit intentional discrimination, and there was no allegation that the schools were intentionally discriminating against non-English-speaking students. Thus the question was whether the guidelines promulgated by HEW went beyond the authority of section 601. Stewart found that the promulgations were within the authority of section 601 because the guidelines were "reasonably related to the purposes of the enabling legislation."

See also Blackmun, Harry Andrew; Civil Rights Act of 1964; Disparate Treatment and Disparate Impact; Equal Protection Clause; Fourteenth Amendment; *Regents of the University of California v. Bakke*; Title VI of the Civil Rights Act of 1964; Warren Court and Affirmative Action.

FURTHER READING: *Guardians Association v. Civil Service Commission*, 463 U.S. 582 (1983); *Lau v. Nichols*, 414 U.S. 563 (1974); McPherson, Stephanie S., 2000, *Lau v. Nichols: Bilingual Education in Public Schools*, Berkeley Heights, NJ: Enslow Publishers, Inc.

PAMELA C. CORLEY

Leadership Conference on Civil Rights

The Leadership Conference on Civil Rights (LCCR) involves more than 180 organizations on the national level concerned with congressional legislation on a number of issues that include not only civil rights, but social program expenditures and related issues that affect the well-being of American citizens. Specifically, the LCCR includes organizations representing not only African Americans and other people of color, but also women, the elderly, and the economically disadvantaged. The LCCR evaluates the performance and voting behavior of members of Congress based upon roll-call votes and the extent to which individuals support policies that have been advocated by the conference. Some of the bills considered in the voting are only peripheral to civil rights, but the index measure used by the LCCR has still been shown to be a reliable feature of congressional voting behavior. The LCCR issued its first report of roll-call voting on civil rights issues in the Ninety-First Congress (1969–1970).

Significantly, as the civil rights movement gained momentum during the 1950s and 1960s, the potential of the LCCR expanded with regard to its base clientele outside as well as in the federal government. The Congress of Racial Equality (CORE), the Southern Christian Leadership Conference (SCLC), the Student Nonviolent Coordinating Committee (SNCC), the Urban League (UL), and the National Association for the Advancement of Colored People (NAACP) represented the traditional black civil rights organizations outside of government that became increasingly active during this time period. But the LCCR's base increased inside government as well as regulatory and monitoring agencies were created to implement and measure the success of the various civil rights initiatives. These included the U.S. Commission on Civil Rights and the Civil Rights Division of the Justice Department, both agencies spawned by the Civil Rights Act of 1957. The Equal Employment Opportunity Commission originated as the result of the Civil Rights Act of 1964, in which it was charged with the enforcement of Title VII in the private sector. Eventually, in time, the Office of Civil Rights in the Department of Health, Education, and Welfare (now in the Department of Education) and the Office of Federal Contract Compliance Programs in the Departments of Labor, Defense, Housing and Urban Development, and Transportation would also soon be elevated to cabinet-level status. The Nixon administration created the Office of Minority Business Enterprise (OMBE) as well as a new section addressing voting in the Justice Department. These various federal subagencies, in turn, reached out to similar entities in state and local governments, fully taking advantage of American federalism built into the U.S. Constitution. The LCCR was clearly developing strong constituencies inside these governmental agencies as well as outside government.

Over the years, the LCCR has played a critical role on a number of important votes, including, but not limited to, civil rights restoration acts, civil rights legislation, reparations to the Japanese for their internment during World War II, hate-crime legislation, redlining, racial justice amendments, race-based sentencing amendments, gun control, school integration, busing, gays in the military, balanced budget amendments, voting rights amendments, housing, the Americans with Disabilities Act, welfare reform, and a number of other areas affecting the constituencies mentioned earlier. The LCCR continues to be a major force in policy initiatives and development.

See also African Americans; Civil Rights Act of 1957; Civil Rights Act of 1964; Civil Rights Movement; Congress of Racial Equality; Department of Education; Department of Justice; Department of Labor; Disadvantaged Business Enterprises; Economically Disadvantaged; Equal Employment Opportunity Commission; Hate Crimes; Japanese Internment and World War II; National Association for the Advancement of Colored People; Office of Federal Contract Compliance Programs; Southern Christian Leadership Conference; Title VII of the Civil Rights Act of 1964; U.S. Commission on Civil Rights; Urban League.

FURTHER READING: Graham, Hugh Davis, 1992, *Civil Rights and the Presidency: Race and Gender in American Politics, 1960–1972*, New York: Oxford University Press; Whitby, Kenny J., 2000, *The Color of Representation: Congressional Behavior and Black Interests*, Ann Arbor: University of Michigan Press.

MFANYA D. TRYMAN

League of Women Voters

Carrie Chapman Catt of the National American Woman Suffrage Association (NAWSA) proposed the organization of a League of Women Voters more than a year prior to the winning of suffrage. The thrust behind the formation of the league was the idea that for women's votes to be effective, women needed to be trained in the basics of voting and be well informed about a variety of issues of interest, including women's rights. On August 26, 1920, the fight for suffrage was ended when Tennessee's ratification of the Nineteenth Amendment was signed and made official by the U.S. secretary of state. During the NAWSA's last convention in Chicago in February 1920, the League of Women Voters became a reality, and Maud Wood Park was chosen its first president. Carrie Chapman Catt was the honorary president until 1947. Today, the bylaws of the organization reflect its early history and state its purpose as follows: " 'To promote political responsibility through informed and active participation of citizens in government' and to 'take action on governmental measures and policies in the public interest' " (Young 1989, 3).

The League of Women Voters has been supportive of affirmative action programs since their inception. In fact, the league has filed amicus briefs in several affirmative action lawsuits, including *Kaiser Aluminum and Chemical Corp. v. Weber*, 444 U.S. 889 (1979), *Boston Firefighters Union, Local 718 v. Boston Chapter NAACP*, 468 U.S. 1206 (1984), *Firefighters Local Union No. 1784 v. Stotts*, 467 U.S. 561 (1984), and *Patterson v. McLean Credit Union*, 491 U.S. 164 (1988), among others. In addition, the league urged Congress to pass the Civil Rights Restoration Act of 1988 that restored antidiscrimination laws previously narrowed by the Supreme Court's decision in *Grove City College v. Bell*, 465 U.S. 555 (1984). The league also supported the civil rights bill that would have reversed a series of 1989 Supreme Court decisions that threatened federal employment discrimination laws. This bill passed both houses of Congress in 1990, but was later vetoed by President George H.W. Bush. In 1991, a compromise bill was passed by Congress and signed by the president. However, the League of Women Voters did not actively support the bill because it placed monetary limits on damages for sex discrimination, including sexual harassment. In 1992, the league joined supporters of the Equal Remedies Act that would remove the monetary limit on damages in civil rights laws and provide women greater opportunity to gain compensation for employment discrimination. The proposed act has been introduced several times in the House and Senate but, as of January 2004, the proposed act has not become law. The League of Women Voters is also responsible for promulgating several studies and policy papers on race and affirmative action, as well as serving as a facilitator for public debates on issues impacting governance and public policy.

See also Civil Rights Restoration Act of 1988; *Firefighters Local Union No. 1784 v. Stotts*; *Grove City College v. Bell*; *Patterson v. McLean Credit Union*; Sex Discrimination.

FURTHER READING: League of Women Voters, 2002, "Impact on Issues, 2000–2002: A Guide to Public Policy Positions," www.lwv.org; Stuhler, Barbara, 2000, *For the Public Record: A Documentary History of the League of Women Voters*, Westport, CT: Greenwood Press; Young, Louise M., 1989, *In the Public Interest: The League of Women Voters, 1920–1970*, New York: Greenwood Press.

PAULINA X. RUF

Legacy Admissions Policy

As the U.S. Supreme Court considered arguments about racial preferences and the use of affirmative action in college admissions in 2002–2003, another form of preference was cited in the debates, that of "legacies." The term "legacy preferences" in college admissions refers to the policies of most colleges and universities to grant preference to children (and sometimes other relatives) of alumni. The students gaining admittance through this type of preference are often referred to as legacies or legacy applicants. Legacy admissions policies in higher-education institutions were first introduced in the early twentieth century, along with quotas, to keep Jews out of elite institutions. It was believed at the time that if college admission was solely based on merit, the number of Jewish students would rapidly increase and they would be disproportionately represented among the student body.

Higher-education institutions give preference to the children of alumni for a variety of reasons, most notably loyalty and funding. Proponents of legacy preferences argue that outlawing these practices may have negative financial consequences for many colleges and universities that depend on the generosity of alumni. However, opponents argue that they are racist practices, given the fact that past college graduates are disproportionately white. Also, legacy preferences benefit students who had the most advantages to begin with, having well-educated parents who were able to provide them a secure and comfortable upbringing. According to William Bowen and Derek Bok's 1998 book *The Shape of the River: Long-Term Consequences of Considering Race in College and University Admissions*, the overall admission rate for legacy applicants was almost twice that for all other applicants and roughly the same as the admission rate for black candidates (Bowen and Bok 1998, 28).

See also Anti-Semitism, Jews, and Affirmative Action; Education and Affirmative Action; Merit Selections; Meritocracy; Performance-Based Selections; *The Shape of the River;* Standardized Testing.

FURTHER READING: American Association of Collegiate Registrars and Admissions Officers and the College Board, 1980, *Undergraduate Admissions: The Realities of Institutional Policies, Practices, and Procedures: A Report on a Survey Conducted by the American Association of Collegiate Registrars and Admissions Officers and the College Board,* New York: College Entrance Examination Board; Bowen, William G., and Derek Bok, 1998, *The Shape of the River: Long-Term Consequences of Considering Race in College and University Admissions,* Princeton, NJ: Princeton University Press; Orfield, Gary, and Edward Miller, eds., 1998, *Chilling Admissions: The Affirmative Action Crisis and the Search for Alternatives,* Cambridge, MA: Harvard Education Publishing Group; Thomas, Debra, and Terry Shepard, 2003, "Legacy Admissions Are Defensible, Because the Process Can't Be 'Fair,' " *Chronicle of Higher Education,* March 14, B15.

PAULINA X. RUF

Lending Practices and Affirmative Action

Affirmative action in lending refers to class-based programs that reduce the direct and indirect market costs associated with lending instruments to disadvantaged individuals or businesses through access enhancements, underwriting treatments, and direct loans or subsidies. Programs are sponsored by depository institutions complying with the Community Reinvestment Act (CRA), by federal agencies such as the U.S. Department of Housing and Urban Development (HUD), the Small Business Administration (SBA), and the Department of Transportation (DOT), and by state and local governments.

Disadvantaged individuals and businesses, including vastly disproportionate percentages of minorities and women, often face disproportionately high direct and indirect cost barriers to lending instruments and other credit opportunities driven by de facto segregation and market forces. De facto segregation, which is segregation in fact as opposed to segregation sanctioned by law, concentrates a high proportion of minority individuals into disadvantaged communities that are often poor and isolated. These communities do not create optimal lending markets for depository institutions like commercial banks, which generate most of their profit from wealthy businesses and individuals that have long and strong credit histories, that borrow and save in large volumes, and that purchase multiple investment products. Bank branches in disadvantaged communities often operate at a loss because they do not generate enough deposit, loan, or investment instrument volume to cover overhead branch expenses and loss rates that exceed those of branches in wealthier areas. Branches in disadvantaged communities that can cover their overhead expenses usually cannot generate a high-enough return on equity to justify their existence when capital could instead be invested into more profitable branches in wealthier areas. As a consequence, in a practice referred to as "redlining," banks and other lending institutions often refused to approve loans for disadvantaged neighborhoods, neighborhoods that had very large African American and/or Hispanic American concentrations.

Under market conditions alone, banks and other lending institutions have very few profit incentives to provide, tailor, or subsidize lending and investment services to borrowers in disadvantaged communities. In these communities, bank branch offices, which sell retail investments and loans to businesses and individuals for a profit, would be scarce, would have limited hours and services, and would impose high-minimum-balance loan and investment requirements. These access restrictions would increase transportation and transaction costs of prospective customers by forcing them either to travel long distances to full-service banks with extended hours or to limit their investment options. Branches that need high-volume lending and savings to cover variable overhead expenses would require high minimum account balances or loan amounts that restrict access or would charge fees to customers with lower incomes and smaller financing needs. Bank underwriting policies that maximize profit and minimize the risk of default by penalizing applicants with short credit histories, previous delinquencies, and low collateral market values that borrowers in disadvantaged communities often present would either increase loan interest rates above prime to cost-prohibitive levels or result in outright denials of credit. This would increase costs to these borrowers by forcing them to either accept high interest rates from primary banks or to go to nontraditional lenders with even higher interest rates. The result of all these factors would be low amounts of private community residential or business investment and deterioration in disadvantaged areas. Therefore, to keep private residential and business credit available to prevent community deterioration, the government intervenes in the lending market to ensure that the credit needs of disadvantaged communities are met.

The CRA was enacted in 1977 to compel banks to take affirmative action to meet the credit needs of businesses and individuals in the disadvantaged communities within their charters by withholding approval of applications for deposit facilities from those that do not. Every depository institution that receives the benefit of deposit insurance through the Federal Deposit Insurance Corporation (FDIC) is required to comply with CRA and other "fair-play" regulations. Periodically, federal banking regulators from FDIC, the Office of the Comptroller of the Currency (OCC), or the Office of Thrift Supervision (OTS) review and rate each institution's efforts to comply with CRA. Institutions receive one of four ratings, from "outstanding record of meeting community credit needs" to "substantial noncompliance in meeting community credit needs." If an institution receives a poor rating, federal agencies reviewing any applications for mergers, acquisitions, or branch openings for that bank may deny the applications. CRA does not require banks to make loans or investments or to provide services that do not earn a profit or that are inconsistent with safe or sound operations in theory, but it does require that banks serve disadvantaged communities, even if this requires less-than-optimum utilization of capital and higher risk of loss, if they want FDIC insurance.

A bank's CRA rating is based on its service to disadvantaged communities estimated by a lending test, an investment test, and a service test. For the lending test, the examiner reviews the institution's consumer loan portfolio to assess the proportion of loans in number and amount that the bank originates and holds and in some circumstances buys within the low- and moderate-income geographies of its assessment area. In practice, banks seeking a good rating often adjust underwriting standards, lower minimum loan or account balance amounts, create specialized marketing plans, and take other actions to lend money in disadvantaged communities even though this does not represent the most profitable use of capital. This reduces the cost of loans to members of disadvantaged communities beyond what market conditions would provide. As the proportion of loans that are made in low- and moderate-income areas increases, so does the rating. For the investment test, the examiner reviews the bank's investments in low- and moderate-income geographies in number, innovativeness, consistency, and responsiveness. Donating, selling on favorable terms, or renting, rent-free, a branch in a minority community to a minority- or women-owned depository institution and investment in community development projects are considered for this test. In practice, large institutions subsidize women- and minority-owned banks and invest capital in marginally profitable or unprofitable projects that they would not otherwise invest in. For the service test, the examiner reviews the availability and effectiveness of a bank's system for delivering banking services by reviewing the distribution of branches, branch openings, the availability of ATMs, and the degree to which available services are tailored to meet the needs of each bank's assessment area. To comply, banks often keep unprofitable, full-service branches operating in low- and moderate-income areas. Limited-purpose and wholesale banks are exempted from many of these provisions, but they remain subject to a community development test, which reviews their community development investment, lending practices, and services. Small banks do not have to meet the same levels of participation as large banks do to receive a good rating under CRA.

The federal government has provided lending assistance to disadvantaged businesses, individuals, and communities in the form of direct loans and indirect credit enhancements through the Small Business Administration (SBA), the Department of Transportation (DOT), and the Department of Housing and Urban Development (HUD). The SBA has administered lending assistance to small businesses that could not otherwise obtain credit since its creation by the 1958 Small Business Investment Act. The SBA's first program specifically targeted to assist disadvantaged, minority-owned businesses was the 1964 "6-by-6" program, which was expanded and rolled up into the Small Business Act in 1966 as the Economic Opportunity Loan (EOL) program. The 6-by-6 and EOL programs provided direct loans to inner-city businesses that would not otherwise qualify for credit from private lenders. Currently, the SBA provides direct low-interest loans and loan packaging, facilitates indirect "mentor program" loans, and provides access to SBA small business loan credit enhancements to socially and economically disadvantaged businesses through the section 8(a) Business Development Program. To become a certified participant in the 8(a) program, a business must be at least 51 percent owned by a person who is economically disadvantaged because of a social disadvantage. Members of minority groups, including African Americans, Asian Americans, Hispanic Americans, and Native Americans, are presumed to be socially disadvantaged, while nonminorities must prove that they have a distinctive feature not common to general society and that they have experienced substantially disadvantaged social treatment within the United States because of that feature. Then a business owner must prove that his or her social disadvantage has made him or her economically disadvantaged by restricting his or her access to capital or credit resources.

The DOT provides assistance to disadvantaged businesses through its Office of Small and Disadvantaged Business Utilization (OSDBU). OSDBU's assistance includes direct short-term working-capital loans given to section 8(a)–certified and women-owned businesses bidding on construction contracts through its Short Term Lending Program (STLP) that they would not otherwise qualify for from a private bank. HUD has provided indirect lending assistance to disadvantaged individuals and businesses through redevelopment programs, mortgage insurance for low- and moderate-income home buyers, property insurance support, and Community Development Block Grant (CDBG) funds. Since its inception, HUD has administered and funded programs to improve the general financial situation in disadvantaged urban communities to make conditions more favorable for private lenders. Since banks require property insurance for any item used as collateral for a loan and since the cost of that insurance is included in the calculation determining the borrower's ability to pay, HUD subsidized property insurance rates for urban disadvantaged individuals and businesses by reinsuring private insurers against loss from urban unrest through the Federal Insurance Administration (FIA), which now resides within the Federal Emergency Management Agency (FEMA). Currently, HUD's mortgage insurance program provides affordable credit enhancements targeted for low- and moderate-income home buyers to give banks incentive to originate small mortgages with low down payments in deteriorating areas. HUD provides CDBG funds to local governments, which they can use to provide or subsidize loans for businesses and individuals in disadvantaged communities.

In addition to federally funded programs, state and local governments and authorities use federal CDBG funds and local funds to provide lending services to disadvantaged businesses, individuals, and communities through direct and indirect lending, credit enhancements, and cost and interest write-downs. Direct lending programs include interest-rate write-downs on home mortgages, home rehabilitation loans, and home construction loans. Indirect lending programs include lease-purchase programs that get around buyer credit problems by purchasing the prospective property through a governmental authority and leasing it back to its prospective buyer, whose lease payments eventually give him or her ownership of the property. Credit enhancement programs provide letters of credit and other guarantees to lenders as collateral for loans given to disadvantaged individuals and businesses in distressed communities. Cost write-down programs allow the government to purchase the property only to use governmental powers to improve the property and then sell it to an individual or business as equity for their loans.

See also African Americans; Asian Americans; De Facto and De Jure Segregation; Department of Housing and Urban Development; Disadvantaged Business Enterprises; Gentrification; Hispanic Americans; Housing; Housing and Urban Development Act of 1968; Native Americans; Zoning and Affirmative Action.

FURTHER READING: Bernotas, Bob, 1991, *Know Your Government: The Department of Housing and Urban Development*, New York: Chelsea House; Code of Federal Regulations, 1997, *Banks and Banking: Federal Reserve System: Community Reinvestment, Title 12, Chapter 2, Part 228 (revised as of July 1, 1997)*, Washington, DC: U.S. Government Printing Office; Code of Federal Regulations, 2001, *Business Credit and Assistance: Small Business Administration: 8(a) Business Development/Small Disadvantaged Business Status Determinations, Title 13, Chapter 1, Part 124 (revised as of January 1, 2001)*, Washington, DC: U.S. Government Printing Office; Comptroller of the Currency, Administrator of National Banks, 2002, "Community Reinvestment Act Information," http://www.occ.treas.gov/crainfo.htm; Dwyer, Christopher, 1991, *Know Your Government: The Small Business Administration*, New York: Chelsea House; Federal Reserve Board, 2002, "The Community Reinvestment Act," http://www.federalreserve.gov/DCCA/CRA/; Schroder, Oliver, Jr., and David T. Smith, 1965, *De Facto Segregation and Civil Rights*, Buffalo, NY: William S. Hein and Co.; Thakor, Anjan V., and Jess Beltz, 1994, "A 'Barter' Theory of Bank Regulation and Credit Allocation," *Journal of Money, Credit, and Banking* 26, no. 3:679–705; U.S. Department of Housing and Urban Development, 2002, "Mortgage Insurance for Low- and Moderate-Income Buyers (Section 221(d)(2))," http://www.hud.gov/funds/singlefamily.cfm; U.S. Department of Housing and Urban Development, 2002, "Mortgage Insurance for Older, Declining Areas (Section 223(e))," http://www.hud.gov/funds/singlefamily.cfm; U.S. Department of Transportation, 2002, "Office of Small and Disadvantaged Business Utilization," http://osdbuweb.dot.gov/business/mp/miphtml2.html#TOC9.

MARK J. SENEDIAK

Level Playing Field

The term "level playing field" is now a popular metaphor utilized in affirmative action debates to refer to fair competition and the need for affirmative action programs. It is a reference to an athletic field, where neither side has the advantage of running downhill while the opponents run uphill. The analogy of fair athletic competition and affirmative action was famously made by President Lyndon B. Johnson in his speech "To Fulfill These Rights" given as a commencement address at Howard University on June 4, 1965. President Johnson spoke of the need for a fair race as follows:

> You do not take a person who for years has been hobbled by chains and liberate him, bring him to the starting line of the race and then say, "You're free to compete with all the others," and still justly believe that you have been completely fair. Thus it is not enough just to open the gates of opportunity. All our citizens must have the ability to walk through those gates. This is the next and the more profound stage of the battle for civil rights. We seek not just freedom but opportunity. We seek not just legal equity but human ability, not just equality as a right and a theory but equality as a fact and equality as a result. (Public Papers 1966, 635–636)

President Johnson thus justified affirmative action efforts by calling for a fair race, where racial injustices in the United States would be attacked via jobs, better education, and social programs that would allow all Americans to compete on fair grounds.

Other advocates of affirmative action have employed the sports metaphors of the "chained runner," "fair race," or "level playing field" to illustrate the need for affirmative action in society. The "chained-runner" metaphor states that you cannot take a runner who has been chained for much of the race, undo the chain, and declare the race fair. You must advance the disadvantaged runner up to the runners who were not previously chained or hindered and then recommence the race. Martin Luther King Jr. put forward the fair-race metaphor in his 1964 book *Why We Can't Wait*, stating that "it is obvious that if a man is entered at the starting line in a race three hundred years after another man, the first would have to perform some impossible feat in order to catch up with his fellow runner" (King 1964, 147). Yet under both metaphors, the "level playing field" and the "chained runner," the measures meant to ensure equity were temporary in nature and would be terminated once the participants had an equal chance of success. Thus in the affirmative action context, it is argued also that preferential programs should be temporary measures and should end once there is a "level playing field" and equal chance for all Americans.

See also Johnson, Lyndon Baines; King, Martin Luther, Jr.

FURTHER READING: Beckwith, Francis J., and Todd E. Jones, eds., 1997, *Affirmative Action: Social Justice or Reverse Discrimination?* Amherst, NY: Prometheus Books; King, Martin Luther, Jr., 1964, *Why We Can't Wait?* New York: Harper and Row; Pauley, Garth E., 2001, *The Modern Presidency and Civil Rights: Rhetoric on Race from Roosevelt to Nixon*, College Station: Texas A&M University Press; *Public Papers of the President of the United States: Lyndon B. Johnson (1965)*, 1966, vol. 2, entry 301, 635–640, Washington, DC: U.S. Government Printing Office; Stern, Mark, 1992, *Calculating Visions: Kennedy, Johnson, and Civil Rights*, New Brunswick, NJ: Rutgers University Press.

PAULINA X. RUF

Levels of Scrutiny

See Intermediate Scrutiny; Rational Basis Scrutiny; Strict Scrutiny.

Licensing and Affirmative Action

Affirmative action is used in the practice of licensing in two chief ways. First, programs that grant members of disadvantaged social groups admission preferences for training programs required for occupational licensing constitute affirmative action in licensing. Second, programs that grant members of disadvantaged social groups the usage of a limited governmental resource (e.g., the use of an airwave frequency in the broadcast media) needed for business also constitute affirmative action in licensing. Historically, minorities were kept out of well-paid professional and skilled technical occupations by segregation, which excluded them from the training programs required for licensing. Alternatively, those attempting to practice their trade in certain areas (e.g., broadcast media) were denied licenses to utilize scarce governmental resources (e.g., airwave frequencies) needed to engage in business. These exclusions reduced the number of licensed minority practitioners, retarding upward economic mobility and public service effectiveness for minorities.

To remedy these situations as they related to occupational licensing, affirmative action programs were established for training facilities to increase the number of minority candidates enrolled and thereby potentially increase the number of licensed practitioners in the marketplace. While these programs provide preferential access to training programs for minorities, most do not provide preferential treatment in consideration of licensing competency exams. Many occupations that provide important services to the general public and/or have a direct impact on public health, order, and safety require practitioners to be licensed before they can enter the service marketplace. This requirement is meant to ensure that only competent individuals practice and to provide competent practitioners with a monopoly over service delivery markets. To obtain a license, candidates are often required to complete a certified training program and/or an apprenticeship and pass a relevant competency exam.

Examples of licensed professionals include physicians, psychologists, pharmacists, lawyers, pilots, and teachers. To obtain a professional license, candidates are often required to obtain a degree from a certified professional school and pass a proficiency exam. Professional schools vary on their requirements for admission, but most require that candidates compete for a fixed number of openings on the basis of entrance exams and their academic record. Some professions, especially in medical fields, also require candidates to participate in an apprenticeship program before they can become licensed to practice on their own. After they complete their training, these candidates must pass a special competency exam such as the bar exam or the medical boards to become licensed and must intermittently continue their training to remain licensed. Most licenses are granted at the state level and are recognized only in that state. Those wishing to practice in another state may have to take an additional exam to become licensed there. Professional license holders monopolize service markets because unlicensed individuals are precluded from them. For instance, lawyers have the sole ability to advocate for others in a court of law, and physicians have the sole ability to provide medical services, including the prescription of medications and the oversight of certain types of medical research.

Examples of licensed skilled technical practitioners include boilermakers, plumbers, contractors, and electricians. Practitioners in these fields require specific and unique expertise necessary to prevent bodily harm to customers or the general public from their work. To obtain a skilled technical license, candidates must demonstrate competency over time by completing an accredited apprenticeship program. Practitioners without a license must practice under the supervision of a licensed practitioner until they complete their program.

During much of the twentieth century, segregated training programs curtailed adequate minority participation in these occupations. Up to 1964, many colleges and apprenticeship programs were segregated de jure. Those that were not segregated by law were often segregated de facto through exorbitantly high educational expenses. Some states did not have any training programs that would admit black students, forcing candidates to seek out-of-state training programs. This was a special hindrance for occupations with state-specific competency exams such as the bar exam for lawyer candidates. Black medical school graduates, who had attended one of a handful of schools that would accept them, were often limited to a few specified "black" hospitals from which they could complete their required residency apprenticeship. Minorities were also denied the opportunity to apply for licenses for skilled technical occupations by craft unions, which often excluded them from apprenticeship training programs. They were able to exclude minorities because they were considered private clubs, which are not subject to equal protection laws, throughout much of the twentieth century.

The effects of these discriminatory and segregation policies have remained long after de jure segregation was declared unconstitutional and unions were opened up to everyone. Qualified minorities were forced into jobs with fewer opportunities for upward economic and social mobility. Furthermore, the hereditary nature of many professional and skilled technical occupations has continued the racial imbalance in the makeup of these workforces because the children of professional and skilled technical practitioners often receive education, socialization, inspiration, and financial and legacy support helpful to future candidates for these occupations that other children do not.

When racial, ethnic, or gender groups are not to some degree proportionally represented within professional and skilled technical occupations that hold a monopoly over important public services, deficient communities face a more difficult path to economic prosperity and less effective professional service availability. They miss out on the economic growth and social standing that accompany the high incomes and the entrepreneurial self-employment culture engendered by these practitioners in their communities. The professional services that they do receive can often be inadequate because the ratio of minority patients to minority practitioners becomes too high to allow for adequate interaction. Additionally, several research efforts on client/practitioner interaction have concluded that social distance can affect the quality of the services rendered, especially by medical and legal practitioners. It affects communication between practitioner and client, where a practitioner locates his or her place of business, the quality of the diagnoses, research topics and funding, treatment within the judicial system, and the articulation and implementation of political priorities. For instance, psychologists with less social distance between themselves and their clients often use fewer stereotypes in their client's diagnoses and come closer to diagnoses obtained when race and gender are unknown (Loring and Powell 1988, 17; Kadushin 1962, 520), and physicians, with incomplete clinical and historical client information and under intense time pressure, often rely more on negative stereotypical "priors" when assessing treatment options for minority patients than a minority physician would (Smedley, Stith and Nelson 2002, 9).

The second chief type of licensing has to do with the governmental allocation of scarce resources to minority groups via licensing schemes. The best example of this type of licensing is in the area of the broadcast media. The resources of the airwaves have always been viewed as a scarce and limited resource. Therefore, those wishing to broadcast over the airwaves must apply to the Federal Communications Commission (FCC) for a license to enable usage of a particular frequency on the airwaves. Traditionally, groups obtaining these licenses have been wealthy nonminority groups.

During the last quarter of the twentieth century, the federal government has put forth a policy of granting these airwave licenses based upon a broad array of factors, including divergent points of views of the applicant, social background, and racial components. The chief goal of this licensing approach is to ensure diversity over the airwaves and thus increase the diversity of information available to the American public in their homes. In the Supreme Court cases *Red Lion Broadcasting Co. v. FCC*, 395 U.S. 367 (1969), and *Metro Broadcasting v. FCC*, 497 U.S. 547 (1990), the Court upheld this FCC licensing scheme based upon what the Court described as fairness and diversity arguments. That is, according to the Court, the FCC is entitled to grant licenses to promote diversity and ensure fair distribution of the government resource across a broad array of different groups. Furthermore, Congress has the power to authorize such licensing schemes pursuant to its powers under the Authorization Clause (section 5) of the Fourteenth Amendment and its power to regulate interstate commerce pursuant to Article I of the Constitution. Broadcasting frequencies are viewed as a scarce resource that should be distributed to a broad array of persons/groups, who will serve as fiduciaries for the public in disseminating information over the airwaves. The *Red Lion* and *Metro Broadcasting* cases represent two of the few instances in which the Supreme Court has upheld the government's usage of an affirmative action scheme not based upon specific past instances of racial discrimination. *Metro Broadcasting* was the last significant case during the Rehnquist Court in which the Court was supportive of affirmative action schemes.

See also De Facto and De Jure Segregation; Education and Affirmative Action; Federal Communications Commission; *Metro Broadcasting, Inc. v. FCC*; Minority Professionals and Affirmative Action; *Red Lion Broadcasting Co. v. FCC*; Rehnquist, William Hobbs.

FURTHER READING: Bianco, David P., 1993, *Professional and Occupational Licensing Directory*, Washington, DC: Gale Research; Callis, H.A., 1935, "The Need and Training of Negro Physicians," *Journal of Negro Education* 4, no. 1:32–41; Colombotos, John, 1969, "Social Origins and Ideology of Physicians: A Study of the Effects of Early Socialization," *Journal of Health and Social Behavior* 10, no. 1:16–29; Darlin, Damon, 1994, "Quota Queen: Esther Renteria May Have Figured a Way to Reap Profit from Affirmative Action Guidelines," *Forbes* 153, no. 13 (June 20): 42; Elesh, David, and Paul T. Schollaert, 1972, "Race and Urban Medicine: Factors Affecting the Distribution of Physicians in Chicago," *Journal of Health and Social Behavior* 13, no. 3:236–250; Ferris, Charles D., and James A. Kirkland, 1985,

"Fairness: The Broadcaster's Hippocratic Oath," *Catholic University Law Review* 34:605–622; Fields, 1987, "Licensing Preferences to Women, Minorities: What Do They Achieve?" *Television/Radio Age* 34 (May 11): 89–90; Gregory, Charles O., and Harold A. Katz, 1979, *Labor and the Law*, New York: W.W. Norton; Johnson, Joseph L., 1949, "The Supply of Negro Health Personnel—Physicians," *Journal of Negro Education* 18, no. 3:346–356; Kadushin, Charles, 1962, "Social Distance between Client and Professional," *American Journal of Sociology* 67, no. 5:517–531; Loring, Marti, and Brian Powell, 1988, "Gender, Race, and DSM-III: A Study of the Objectivity of Psychiatric Diagnostic Behavior," *Journal of Health and Social Behavior* 29, no. 1:1–22; Rumble, Wilfrid C., 1994, "Comment: The FCC's Reliance on Market Incentives to Provide Diverse Viewpoints on Issues of Public Importance Violates the First Amendment Right to Receive Critical Information," *University of San Francisco Law Review* 28:793–857; Smedley, Brian D., Adrienne Y. Stith, and Alan R. Nelson, eds., 2002, *Unequal Treatment: Confronting Racial and Ethnic Disparities in Health Care*, Washington, DC: National Academy Press.

MARK J. SENEDIAK

Local 28 of the Sheet Metal Workers' International Association v. EEOC, 478 U.S. 421 (1986)

In *Local 28 of the Sheet Metal Workers' International Association v. EEOC*, the U.S. Supreme Court affirmed a federal district court's authority to order and enforce preferential race-conscious remedies for discriminatory practices even when the relief would benefit individuals who were not victims of the discrimination. On June 2, 1986, the Supreme Court upheld the district court's assignment of a percentage nonwhite membership goal to the union and its imposition of fines and other fees on the union to coerce compliance with the court's order and to fund remedial programs. Justice William Brennan, writing in part for a majority and in part for a plurality, argued that Title VII of the Civil Rights Act of 1964 authorized such remedies, and that the remedies did not violate the Equal Protection Clause of the Fourteenth Amendment, claiming thereby both statutory and constitutional validity for the decision.

In 1975, the district court had found the union and its apprenticeship committee guilty of violating Title VII by discriminating against nonwhite workers in recruiting, selection, training, and admission policies. The court appointed an administrator who drafted an affirmative action plan for the union. This plan, which the court adopted, mandated a nonwhite membership goal of 29 percent (subsequently revised to 29.23 percent) to be achieved by 1981. After twice finding the union in contempt of its orders (in 1982 and 1983), the court reaffirmed its goal, imposed a new deadline (August 31, 1987) for its attainment, and levied a civil contempt fine of $150,000. This amount, to be supplemented by additional collections of $0.02 per hour for each hour worked by a journeyman or apprentice, was designated the Employment, Training, Education, and Recruitment Fund. This fund would underwrite such remedial programs as publicity campaigns directed at minorities, part-time and summer sheet-metal jobs for nonwhite youth, and counseling, tutorial, and financial assistance to nonwhite apprentices. The fund would remain operational until the district court determined that it was no longer needed.

In its review, the U.S. Court of Appeals for the Second Circuit had affirmed the following: (1) that Local 28 had a long-standing history of egregious racial discrimination; (2) that the contempt remedies prescribed by the district court, including its appointment of an administrator with broad supervisory powers and the fund and its maintenance, were appropriate; and (3) that the nonwhite membership goal was proper and not violative of either Title VII or the U.S. Constitution. Although similar court-ordered quotas in the public sector had been employed by federal district court judges for more than fifteen years prior to this case, the Supreme Court had heretofore avoided ruling on them.

Local 28 challenged the appeals court findings in arguments before the Supreme Court in February 1986. Justice Brennan, announcing the Court's plurality decision later that year, reckoned that the key issue before the Court was whether or not the remedial provision of Title VII "empowers a district court to order race-conscious relief that may benefit individuals who are not identified victims of unlawful discrimination." The Court found in the affirmative: Justices Harry Blackmun, John Paul Stevens, and Thurgood Marshall joined Brennan, with Justice Lewis Powell concurring in the judgment and Justice Byron White, in dissent, agreeing that this proposition might be valid in some instances. Justice Brennan's written opinion included a brief recounting of certain legislative arguments both for and against passage of the Civil Rights Act of 1964. He focused specifically on debate over section 706(g), which addresses remedies for violations of Title VII of the act. Counsel for Local 28, he asserted, had misread the significance of prior decisions (for example, *Ford Motor Co. v. EEOC*, 458 U.S. 219 [1982], and *Connecticut v. Teal*, 457 U.S. 440 [1982]) that provided "make-whole" remedies available to actual victims of discrimination. Brennan argued that while this limited option was open to courts under section 706(g), even the decisions cited did not hold that such relief was the only remedy allowable. In fact, Brennan claimed to discover in House debates no indication that Congress intended in any way to limit benefits under the statute solely to identifiable victims. The question, he asserted, "simply did not arise"; therefore, since section 706(g) did not directly prohibit court-ordered remedies that benefited nonvictims, it could thus be read to allow them.

What the plurality opinion, with Justice Powell's concurrence, did insist was that Congress had intended affirmative action to be the means by which the judiciary might extirpate past patterns of racial discrimination: "Congress gave the lower courts broad power under section 706(g) to fashion 'the most complete relief possible' to remedy past discrimination." Brennan cited an example from House debate that read in part: " 'If his firm is not "racially balanced", [the employer] has no choice, he must employ the person of that race which, by ratio, is next up, even though he is certain in his own mind that the [prospective job seeker] he is not allowed to employ would be a superior employee.' "

The Court also addressed the constitutional validity of the district court's decisions under the Equal Protection Clause. Acknowledging that the Court had been unable to agree upon "the proper test to be applied in analyzing the constitutionality of race-conscious remedial measures," Justice Brennan circumvented the issue by insisting that "the relief ordered in this case passes even the most rigorous test—it is narrowly tailored to further the Government's compelling interest in remedying past discrimination." Both the percentage nonwhite membership goal and the monetary fund were "necessary to combat the lingering effects of past discrimination." In fact, the Court was merely approving in the public sector the same sort of agreement it had affirmed in the private sector in *United Steelworkers of America v. Weber*, 443 U.S. 193 (1979).

In a concurring opinion, Justice Powell, a consistent advocate of strict scrutiny, argued that such race-conscious remedies answered the government's "compelling interest" in eradicating discrimination. The fund order itself, in Powell's opinion, had been "carefully structured to vindicate the compelling governmental interest"—as well as society's broader interests—"present in the case." The nonwhite membership goal likewise passed the test: "[I]t is doubtful, given the petitioners' history in this legislation, that the District Court had available to it any other effective remedy."

Throughout their opinions, both Brennan and Powell denied having legitimized racial quotas and mandatory racial balancing as tools of affirmative action. Addressing this dimension of the case was inescapable, given the legislative history of the act, potential interpretations of the Court's judgment, and the social divisiveness of the issues involved. Many of the bill's original supporters had publicly renounced both outcomes in plain language. Senator Hubert Humphrey, Democratic floor manager for H.R. 7152, in congressional debate, had pledged that " '[contrary] to the allegations of some opponents of this title [VII], there is nothing in it that will give any power to . . . any court to require hiring, firing, or promotion of employees in order to meet a racial 'quota' or to achieve a certain racial balance.' " Hence the Court majority's resolute insistence that the nonwhite percentage was a "goal" only, despite the district court's edict: " '[If] the goal is not attained by [August 31, 1987], defendants will face fines that will threaten their very existence.' " Commenting on this decree, Justice Powell claimed that it "cannot be taken as evidence that the goal will be applied as an inflexible quota." With regard to racial balancing in either a place of employment or labor-union membership, Justice Brennan argued that while Congress in 1964 had "opposed the use of quotas or preferences merely to maintain racial balance," it had given no guidance as to the acceptability of such measures "as remedies for Title VII violations."

Justice Sandra Day O'Connor concurred in part and dissented in part. With regard to the "membership 'goal' and the Fund order," she would have reversed the court of appeals judgment on statutory grounds, but she would not have reached the union's constitutional claims. She agreed with Justice White that the "membership 'goal' in this case operates as a rigid racial quota." Furthermore, the wording of the 1964 Civil Rights Act itself, she wrote, "preclude[s] courts from ordering racial quotas" such as the "membership 'goal' and the Fund order" had clearly established. The legislative history of the Civil Rights Act, she wrote, in no way lent itself to Brennan and Powell's interpretation—an interpretation, in her words, that "defies common sense." "Fairly read," this history rendered racial quotas impermissible, both because they harmed "innocent nonminority workers" and because they restricted employer freedoms. She therefore dissented from the Court's judgment affirming, as it did, the use of "mandatory quotas."

Justices White and William Rehnquist also filed brief dissents arguing that the court order was subject to section 706(g), requiring that relief generally be limited to victims of past discrimination. White acknowledged the possibility that in unusual instances, nonvictims might benefit, but claimed that the strict racial quota in this case was inequitable. Rehnquist, joined by Chief Justice Warren Burger, referenced his dissenting opinion in *Local No. 93, International Association of Firefighters v. City of Cleveland*, 478 U.S. 501 (1986), also decided on July 2, 1986, in which he contended that beneficiaries must have been victims. His position, similar to O'Connor's, was based on section 706(g): "[No] order of the court shall require the . . . promotion of an individual . . . if such individual was refused . . . advancement for any reason other than discrimination on account of race, color, religion, sex or national origin." This language, Rehnquist insisted, required a finding that those who "receive preferential promotions were victims of racial discrimination" before any court order, including a consent decree. He insisted that this was the position of the Court in *Firefighters Local Union No. 1784 v. Stotts*, 467 U.S. 561 (1984), and that his fellow justices in the current case had sidestepped both principle and precedent.

See also Affirmative Action Plan/Program; Brennan, William Joseph; Burger Court and Affirmative Action; Civil Rights Act of 1964; Compelling Governmental Interest; Equal Protection Clause; *Firefighters Local Union No. 1784 v. Stotts*; Fourteenth Amendment; *Local No. 93, International Association of Firefighters v. City of Cleveland*; Marshall, Thurgood; O'Connor, Sandra Day; Powell, Lewis Franklin, Jr.; Quotas; Rehnquist, William Hobbs; Stevens, John Paul; Strict Scrutiny; Supreme Court and Affirmative Action; *United Steelworkers of America v. Weber*; White, Byron Raymond.

FURTHER READING: Belz, Herman, 1991, *Equality Transformed: A Quarter-Century of Affirmative Action*, New Brunswick, NJ: Social Philosophy and Policy Center and Transaction Publishers; Schwartz, Herman, 1987, "The 1986 and 1987 Affirmative Action Cases: It's All Over but the Shouting," *Michigan Law Review* 86:524–576; Spann, Girardeau A., 2000, *The Law of Affirmative Action: Twenty-five Years of Supreme Court Decisions on Race and Remedies*, New York: New York University Press.

RAE W. NEWSTAD and DAVID L. WEEKS

Local No. 93, International Association of Firefighters v. City of Cleveland, 478 U.S. 501 (1986)

The U.S. Supreme Court announced in its decision in *Local No. 93, International Association of Firefighters v. City of Cleveland* that consent decrees that include racial preferences are not invalid under Title VII of the Civil Rights Act of 1964 merely because the racial preference may benefit persons who are not victims of discrimination as long as the terms of the decree do not themselves violate federal nondiscrimination law. A group of African American and Hispanic firefighters called the Vanguard sued the city of Cleveland, alleging that the city engaged in systematic race and national-origin discrimination with respect to its employment practices, including its promotion practices. Before the Vanguard's complaint was filed, Cleveland lost two race discrimination cases, one against its police department and one against its fire department. Therefore, the city sought to settle the Vanguard's lawsuit. A union representing employees in the fire department intervened in the case and opposed the proposed consent decree because it reserved a certain number of planned promotions for minority firefighters and required minority promotion goals for the succeeding four years.

The union argued that section 706 of Title VII prohibited a court from approving a voluntary consent decree between litigants in a Title VII case when the consent decree used racial preferences that might benefit persons who had not suffered race discrimination. Section 706(g) of Title VII provides in pertinent part: "[No] order of the court shall require the hiring, reinstatement, or promotion of an individual as an employee . . . if such individual was refused employment or advancement for any reason other than discrimination on account of race, color, religion, sex or national origin." The Court rejected the union's argument. It reasoned that because the consent decree was a voluntary agreement and not a coercive order of the court, and because Title VII encourages voluntary action to eliminate discrimination, section 706 did not apply. Therefore, even if section 706(g) did limit the relief a court could order after trial, it was not a limitation on consent decrees. The Court also noted that the terms of consent decrees must not themselves violate federal nondiscrimination law, but recognized that the Court had previously found that reasonable, voluntary race-conscious affirmative action measures to eliminate the effects of discrimination are not illegal under Title VII even though the measures might benefit persons who were not subject to discrimination (*United Steelworkers v. Weber*, 443 U.S. 193 [1979]). The Court also noted that on the same day it decided *Local No. 93*, it also decided *Local 28 of the Sheet Metal Workers' International Association v. EEOC*, 478 U.S. 421 (1986), which held that even court orders, after finding that an employer engaged in discrimination, can include affirmative action measures in certain circumstances without violating section 706 even where the measures benefit persons who were not actual victims of the discrimination.

See also Affirmative Action Plan/Program; Discrimination; *Local 28 of the Sheet Metal Workers' International Association v. EEOC*; Racial Discrimination; Title VII of the Civil Rights Act of 1964; *United Steelworkers of America v. Weber*.

FURTHER READING: *Local No. 93, International Association of Firefighters v. City of Cleveland*, 478 U.S. 501 (1986); Sullivan, Kathleen, M., 1986, "The Supreme Court, 1985 Term: Comment: Sins of Discrimination: Last Term's Affirmative Action Cases," *Harvard Law Review* 100 (November): 78–98.

MARIA D. BECKMAN

Lorance v. AT&T Technologies, Inc., 490 U.S. 900 (1989)

The U.S. Supreme Court case *Lorance v. AT&T Technologies, Inc.* reaffirmed that in cases of alleged discrimination under seniority systems, a plaintiff must show that the system was intentionally discriminatory and held that the statute of limitations begins to run at the time the seniority system is adopted. This second holding by the Court in this case was subsequently overturned by Congress in the Civil Rights Act of 1991, which provided that when a seniority system is adopted by an employer for intentionally discriminatory purposes, the time period for filing a complaint with the Equal Employment Opportunity Commission (EEOC) starts either when the employee first becomes subject to the seniority system at issue, or when the employee first suffers personal injury as a result of the seniority system.

The petitioners (Patricia Lorance, Janice King, and Carol Bueschen) were female hourly wage employees for AT&T Technologies who began work for AT&T

in the early 1970s. According to a company policy that was in place until 1979, all hourly wage earners accrued competitive seniority exclusively on the basis of years spent in the plant. A worker promoted to the highly skilled and better-paid "tester" positions retained plantwide seniority. However, a collective-bargaining agreement enacted in July 1979 changed the method of calculating tester seniority. The new method determined seniority by time actually spent as a tester.

When the seniority system was implemented, one plaintiff was working as a tester, but subsequently received a demotion four years later due to the new seniority system. The other plaintiffs became testers several months after the implementation of the new seniority system. These other plaintiffs were not affected by the restructured seniority system until 1982. Under the original plantwide seniority system, the plaintiffs would not have been demoted. However, because of the new seniority system, the plaintiffs felt that they had been the victims of discrimination and filed charges with the EEOC in 1983. Upon receiving the right-to-sue letters, the plaintiffs filed legal action in the federal District Court for the Northern District of Illinois, alleging discrimination and violations of Title VII of the Civil Rights Act of 1964. The allegation was that the new seniority system's purpose and effect resulted in the "protection of incumbent testers" (men) from female employees who had greater plantwide seniority and constituted increasing numbers of testers. The seniority system at issue was a "competitive seniority" one designed to allocate entitlement to limited benefits such as promotion and nondemotion.

The district court granted judgment in favor of AT&T on the procedural grounds that the women had failed to file their complaints with the EEOC within the applicable period of limitations. The district court used the time frame then outlined in 42 U.S.C. § 2000e-5(e), which provided that "a charge must be filed with EEOC within 180 days of the alleged unfair employment practice unless the complainant has first instituted proceedings with a state or local agency, in which case the period is extended to a maximum of 300 days." The Court of Appeals for the Seventh Circuit affirmed the ruling, "noting that the relevant discriminatory act that triggered the period of limitations occurred at the time an employee was subject to a facially neutral but discriminatory seniority system that the employee knew, or reasonably had known, was discriminatory." The Supreme Court granted certiorari to resolve the legal conflict regarding the statute of limitations.

Justice Antonin Scalia wrote for the majority of the Court in the 5–3 decision. He noted that the Civil Rights Act of 1964 mandated that discrimination charges be filed with the EEOC within an applicable period after the alleged unlawful employment practice occurred. In assessing timeliness, Scalia noted that the Court must "identify precisely the unlawful employment practice of which [the plaintiff] complains."

First, the Court reaffirmed its earlier ruling that under the terms of Title VII, "absent a discriminatory purpose, the operation of a seniority system cannot be an unlawful employment practice even if the system had some discriminatory consequences." The Court reasoned that "for the liability to be incurred, there must be a finding of actual intent to discriminate on statutorily prohibited grounds on the part of those who negotiated or maintained the seniority system." The Court indicated that the existence of a seniority system containing discriminatory impact was not sufficient in and of itself to invalidate the system. The Court then noted that the plaintiffs did not dispute that the seniority system was not discriminatory on its face and that it was applied in a nondiscriminatory manner. The plaintiffs' only claim of intentional discrimination was that the employer decided to adopt the new seniority system, which unfavorably changed female employees' seniority rights, to discriminate against female employees. Therefore, the Court reasoned that any intentional discrimination that occurred, occurred at the time the new seniority system was adopted—before the limitations period. According to the Court's reasoning, the plaintiffs' claim "depended on proof of intentional discrimination occurring outside the period of limitations." It was the viewpoint of the Court that the plaintiffs' claims were "wholly dependent on discriminatory conduct occurring well outside the period of limitations" and therefore, did not constitute "a continuing violation." The Court held that the signing date of the contract governed the limitation period. It was "the alleged discriminatory adoption that triggered the limitations period."

Justice Thurgood Marshall wrote the dissenting opinion, with Justices William Brennan and Harry Blackmun joining. Justice Sandra Day O'Connor took no part in the consideration or decision of the case. Marshall expressed failure to comprehend how the Court concluded that a seniority system designed to discriminate, which was a violation of Title VII, 42 U.S.C. § 2000e-5(e), began immediately upon the adoption of the system. It was Marshall's contention that to adhere to the criteria set forth by the Court, one had to know in advance that discrimination was a possibility. Justice Marshall complained in his dissent that the majority position created the "harsh reality" that employees must "sue anticipatorily or forever hold their peace." Marshall suggested that the view of the Court was that the plaintiffs were denied legal action because they failed to anticipate discriminatory practices within the first 300 days of the new system's adoption.

The U.S. Congress ultimately followed the logic of Justice Marshall's dissent when it overturned the majority's opinion in *Lorance* in the Civil Rights Act of 1991. In this statute, Congress provided that when a seniority system is adopted by an employer for intentionally discriminatory purposes, the time period for filing a complaint with the EEOC starts either when the employee first becomes subject to the seniority system at issue or when the employee first suffers personal injury as a result of the seniority system. The *Lorance* decision was one of several Supreme Court decisions in this area overturned by Congress in passing the Civil Rights Act of 1991.

See also Blackmun, Harry Andrew; Brennan, William Joseph; Civil Rights Act of 1964; Civil Rights Act of 1991; Disparate Treatment and Disparate Impact; Equal Employment Opportunity Commission; Marshall, Thurgood; O'Connor, Sandra Day; Scalia, Antonin; Title VII of the Civil Rights Act of 1964.

FURTHER READING: Bell, Derrick, 1992, *Race, Racism, and American Law*, Boston: Little, Brown and Company; Farber, Daniel A., William N. Eskridge Jr., and Philip P. Frickey, 1993, *Constitutional Law: Themes for the Constitution's Third Century*, St. Paul, MN: West Publishing Co.; Tucker, Ronnie B., 2000, *Affirmative Action, the Supreme Court, and Political Power in the Old Confederacy*, Lanham, MD: University Press of America.

RONNIE B. TUCKER SR.

Loury, Glenn C. (1949–   )

Glenn C. Loury earned a national reputation in the 1980s and early 1990s as a prominent conservative black intellectual who wrote extensively on issues of race and economics and was very critical of social programs such as affirmative action. During this period, Loury preached a message of self-help and claimed that problems afflicting minorities could not "simply be laid at the door of white racism" (Shatz 2002, 20). Loury adhered to a belief that the laws should truly be "color blind" and not give preferences to minority classes. He gained national prominence by aligning with the Reagan administration and a host of conservative critics of affirmative action, such as Clarence Thomas, Shelby Steele, and Dinesh D'Souza. Because of his conservative alignment and lack of support for affirmative action, he was "persona non grata in liberal black circles. He was called an Uncle Tom, a 'black David Stockman' and a 'pathetic mascot of the right.' " (Shatz 2002, 21).

However, in the mid-1990s, Loury was alleged to have made a metamorphosis, casting off his ultraconservative ideology. Loury terminated ties with many of his once close conservative colleagues, like Clarence Thomas and Shelby Steele, and began to backtrack on his previous mantra of self-help as the best route for blacks in society. In 1994, he publicly opposed Charles Murray and Richard Herrnstein's conservative book *The Bell Curve.* In 1995, he publicly opposed D'Souza's conservative book *The End of Racism.* In 1996, Loury resigned from a conservative think tank (the Center for New Black Leadership) with which he had been affiliated when that organization went on record as supporting Ward Connerly's Proposition 209, which ended racial preferences in public contracting, employment, and education in California. By the late 1990s and early 2000s, Loury appeared to have come full circle from his views in the 1980s and now seems to indicate that affirmative action is permissible to remedy certain ailments. In 1999, Loury began criticizing conservatives for their efforts at allegedly attempting to undo the advances of civil rights and equality, calling these efforts a conservative "crusade." Specifically on affirmative action, Loury now claims that the anti–affirmative action "reform movement" has turned into an "abolitionist crusade" (*Journal of Blacks in Higher Education,* 49).

Finally, on March 29, 2003, on the eve of Supreme Court oral arguments in the Michigan affirmative action cases *Gratz v. Bollinger,* 123 S. Ct. 2411, 2003 U.S. LEXIS 4801 (2003), and *Grutter v. Bollinger,* 123 S. Ct. 2325, 2003 U.S. LEXIS 4800 (2003), Loury admitted in a *New York Times* editorial that he had changed his views on race and affirmative action, stating that "opponents of affirmative action hold that justice in matters of race requires strict adherence to a policy of 'colorblindness.' Many Americans share this view: I know because I used to be one of them." Loury also renounced his previous view of a color-blind constitution, stating that "colorblindness is a false ideal." Paraphrasing Justice Lewis Powell's famous statement in *Regents of University of California v. Bakke,* 438 U.S. 265 (1978), Loury wrote that "[b]ecause we use race to articulate our self-understandings, we must sometimes be mindful of race as we conduct our public affairs." Last, Loury reconciled his recent support for affirmative action with his long-held beliefs in individualism and personal responsibility:

> Taking race into account, in university admissions or in other aspects of life, does not require abandoning a commitment to individualism. One can hold that race is irrelevant to a person's moral worth—that people, not groups, are the bearers of rights—and still affirm that to deal effectively with individuals, we must consider the categories of thoughts in which they understand themselves. (Loury 2003, 11)

Thus Loury's ideology is in flux, and it is correct to speak of his old positions and new positions on affirmative action and race relations. In Loury's own words in a comprehensive 2002 *New York Times Magazine* interview on his life and political transformation, "Friends of mine sometimes have joked to me that the old Loury and the new Loury should have a conversation" (Shatz, 27).

Loury was born into a lower-middle-class family in the South Side of Chicago in 1949. As a teenager, Loury had two children out of wedlock and was forced to drop out of school in order to work, obtaining a job at a local plant. However, before the work day, Loury took classes at a local community college (Southeast Junior College) and did sufficiently well to earn a scholarship to Northwestern University. He then went on to graduate school at the Massachusetts Institute of Technology, working under the faculty supervision of a Nobel laureate. By 1982, Loury was a tenured professor at Harvard University in the economics department. In 1984, he transferred to Harvard's John F. Kennedy School of Government. For several years, he was a darling of conservative circles because of his conservative writings and speeches. In March 1987, he was even offered a position in the Reagan administration as the under secretary of education to William Bennett.

However, starting at about the time the position was offered in the Reagan administration, Loury experienced several serious setbacks. The culmination of these setbacks in 1987 (being arrested for cocaine possession) would ultimately be the catalyst for a change in Loury's ideology. In June 1987, Loury was forced to withdraw his name from consideration for a position as the under secretary of education when a clandestine relationship with a young graduate student was revealed, and the student leveled assault charges against Loury. While the charges were dropped, Loury received very bad publicity over the incident, especially when it was revealed that the student had been living at his expense in Boston. At the same time, Loury admitted in the 2002 *New York Times* interview, he was spending time in "some really rough spaces," using illicit substances, and spending an inordinate amount of time in the public housing areas of Boston, often picking up women. Again, in the words of Loury, "It was pathological. . . . I was castigating the moral failings of African American life even as I was deeply caught up in it." In November 1987, Loury was arrested and judicially punished for cocaine possession (Shatz, 22).

After recuperating in a hospital and in a halfway house, Loury began to reconstruct his life. He had several children with his wife. In 1991, Loury accepted a tenured professorship position at Boston University, anxious to leave his reputation at Harvard behind. Loury has remained at Boston University since that time and founded (and is the director of) Boston University's Institute on Race and Social Division. However, once he was at Boston, his politics began to change, and he would arguably achieve his full ideological metamorphosis by the mid-1990s.

The "old" Loury's position on affirmative action was relatively clear. He was an outspoken critic of affirmative action and often spoke of the need for self-help in the African American community. In the words of Loury, he advocated a "just straighten up, for crying out loud" attitude. He believed that the "greatest threat to racial equality was no longer the 'enemy without'—white racism—but rather the 'enemy within:' problems inherent in the black community" (Shatz 2002, 20). He rejected the use of strict quotas and held that affirmative action programs could have only a very limited role in remedying racial inequality. Loury said that affirmative action was poorly suited to address some of the most enduring effects of historical discrimination: lower skill levels among African Americans, family dissolution, and declining communities. Rather, he held that these programs usually helped the most advantaged members of the African American community. Loury thought of affirmative action as largely an excuse or crutch for the weak. He stated that "to me, affirmative action has taken the place of focusing on the development of effective performance capacity among blacks, and it's a kind of cover for the absence of that capacity" (Megalli, 73).

Loury also supported (and still supports today) programs that provide outreach and special training for women and minorities as a way to increase minority representation. However, unlike his current position, he argued that the solution to many of the problems of the black community lay within the black community. He called for a greater emphasis on self-help and contended that the African American poor must accept greater responsibility for their own advancement. In addition, Loury argued that the black middle class and white elites were abdicating their responsibility when they failed to hold disadvantaged African Americans to high moral and ethical standards. The "old" Loury also rejected affirmative action in part because he thought that it caused his colleagues at Harvard to wonder whether he was there on his own merits or merely because of affirmative action. This is a criticism of affirmative action that is held by African American Supreme Court justice Clarence Thomas.

Some of Loury's historical opposition to race-based programs arises from his attempt to focus on pragmatic rather than political solutions. For example, Loury opposed mandatory busing to desegregate public schools on the grounds that busing could not be effectively enforced. According to Loury, the legal system could not require white parents to send their children to public schools, nor, as demonstrated by white flight from urban school districts since the enactment of busing programs, could parents be forced to remain in districts that were being forced to desegregate. Loury believed that the data showed that segregation had actually increased in many urban school districts since the busing began. In addition, Loury argued that the belief that desegregation necessarily led to improvements was rooted in beliefs that African Americans and Latinos were inferior to whites. Loury argued that the logic of desegregation was that being educated in a predominantly black or Latino setting was by definition inferior to attending classes with white students. Loury acknowledged that African American and Latino students in inner-city schools often attended low-quality institutions, but he argued that improving the quality of minority education would be better met by decreasing classroom sizes, increasing school hours, and encouraging minority youth to invest in educational achievement.

As alluded to earlier, the "new" Loury emerged in the mid-1990s. While he still advocates personal and individual responsibility, he has become a supporter of affirmative action. Despite agreeing with conservatives in many of their critiques of affirmative action in the past, Loury has now disagreed publicly with some of the most prominent conservative thinkers of the past decade. Loury has terminated his relationships with and no longer speaks to once close personal friends like Shelby Steele and Clarence Thomas. He became one of the more outspoken critics of Richard J. Herrnstein and Charles Murray's 1994 book *The Bell Curve: Intelligence and Class Structure in American Life*, which alleged that black problems were caused by lower intellects. In addition, Loury has criticized Dinesh D'Souza for espousing a view that suggests that African Americans are culturally inferior to whites. Loury now believes that many conservatives lack compassion for the disadvantaged and have abandoned attempts to find real solutions to inequality. He now thinks that conservatives are obsessed with their "crusade" to end affirmative action.

Perhaps most relevant to affirmative action, Loury has switched his position from advocating a color-blind constitution to declaring in 2003 that "colorblindness is a false ideal." He now also advocates affirmative action in higher education. His new ideology was best described by his interviewer in the 2002 *New York Times Magazine* interview:

> Despite his new appreciation of racial solidarity, Loury remains fiercely independent. His outlook today is an unclassifiable, pragmatic blend of entrepreneurialism, black nationalism, Christian faith and social egalitarianism. Though he has relaxed his opposition to affirmative action, he quibbles with the way it is practiced, recommending instead what he calls developmental affirmative action—programs intended to improve minority performance while upholding standards of evaluation. (Shatz, 28)

Thus Loury remains enigmatic today on the issue of affirmative action: not completely liberal and not completely conservative. However, in light of his historical position on the subject, his ideology has changed significantly. His most recent publication is *The Anatomy of Racial Inequality*, 2002, which embodies his new ideology. In this book, Loury no longer places the blame for racial problems squarely on the shoulders of black individuals. Rather, Loury now focuses on how racial discrimination and racial stigma contribute to enduring racial inequality, so much so that "the entire nation bears a responsibility."

Currently, Loury is professor of economics and director of the Institute on Race and Social Division at Boston University. He has also served on the faculties of Harvard University, the University of Michigan, and Northwestern University. In addition to his responsibilities as a writer, professor, and researcher of economics, he is a social critic and frequent contributor to national radio and television programs. In 1995, Loury ended his relationship with the American Enterprise Institute to protest D'Souza's position as a research fellow. In 1996, he won the American Book Award for his collection of essays published under the title *One by One, from the Inside Out: Essays and Reviews on Race and Responsibility in America*.

See also African Americans; *The Bell Curve;* Busing; Color-Blind Constitution; Connerly, Ward; D'Souza, Dinesh; Education and Affirmative Action; *Gratz v. Bollinger/Grutter v. Bollinger*; Powell, Lewis Franklin, Jr.; Proposition 209; Reagan, Ronald; *Regents of the University of California v. Bakke*; Steele, Shelby; Thomas, Clarence; Uncle Tom.

FURTHER READING: Loury, Glenn C., 1995, *One by One, from the Inside Out: Essays and Reviews on Race and Responsibility in America*, New York: Free Press; Loury, Glenn C., 1997, "Integration Has Had Its Day," *New York Times*, Op-Ed, April 23, A23; Loury, Glenn C., 2003, "Affirmative Action—and Reaction: Admissions (and Denials) of Responsibility," *New York Times*, March 29, A11; Megalli, Mark, 1995, "The High Priests of the Black Academic Right," *Journal of Blacks in Higher Education*, autumn, 71–77; "Racial Preferences: Five Influential Conservatives Signal a Possible Change of Views," *Journal of Blacks in Higher Education*, no.

38 (January 31): 49; Shatz, Adam, 2002, "Glenn Loury's About Face," *New York Times Magazine*, January 20, 18–28.

KYRA R. GREENE

Lutheran Church–Missouri Synod v. FCC, 141 F.3d 487 (D.C. Cir. 1998)

In *Lutheran Church–Missouri Synod v. FCC*, the U.S. Court of Appeals for the District of Columbia Circuit held that a Federal Communications Commission (FCC) regulation that required radio stations to maintain an affirmative action program to benefit minorities was unconstitutional. This case is important because (1) it imposes an onerous standard of review upon an affirmative action program of the federal government even though it did not require race-based decision, (2) it holds that the FCC did not have a compelling interest in promoting a diversity of viewpoint of radio stations that would justify the plan's intention to increase employment of minorities in radio, and (3) the D.C. Circuit's opinions concerning federal government action are especially influential.

The church appealed an FCC order finding that it violated FCC regulations by inadequately recruiting minorities for employment on the grounds that the FCC regulations violated the equal protection guarantee of the Fifth Amendment to the U.S. Constitution. The regulations not only required stations to make special efforts to recruit minorities for employment, but also required stations to evaluate whether underrepresentation for any racial group or for women existed in their workforce, and if so, to closely examine their employment practices to ensure that they were not barriers to minority and women hiring. In evaluating the sufficiency of a station's program, the FCC used the fact that a station had not met minority and women employment goals as an indication that further FCC review was required. Because the Court concluded that this scheme encouraged race-based hiring decisions (even though it did not require them), it held that the FCC's affirmative action program was subject to strict scrutiny review.

To survive strict scrutiny constitutional review, the challenged race-based action must be narrowly tailored to achieve a compelling governmental interest. This standard has been historically difficult to meet. Few governmental actions have survived such review. The D.C. Circuit Court concluded that the FCC's articulated interest for the minority affirmative action program—fostering a "diverse programming content"—was not a compelling interest sufficient to justify racial classifications in employment. The Court criticized the FCC's assumption that members of minority racial groups would have race-based viewpoints. The Court also concluded that even if the interest in diversity of programming was compelling, the affirmative action program was not narrowly tailored to achieve diversity of programming. The Court reasoned that the program applied to low-level employees and that there was no proof that the viewpoints of low-level employees affect what viewpoints are broadcast by the station.

See also Affirmative Action Plan/Program; Compelling Governmental Interest; Diversity; Federal Communications Commission; Fifth Amendment; Licensing and Affirmative Action; *Metro Broadcasting, Inc. v. FCC*; Narrowly Tailored Affirmative Action Plans; *Red Lion Broadcasting Co. v. FCC*; Strict Scrutiny; Supreme Court and Affirmative Action.

FURTHER READING: Holder, Pamela, 1999, "Note: A Square Peg Trying to Fit into a Round Hole: The Federal Communication Commission's Equal Employment Opportunity Regulations in *Lutheran Church v. FCC*," *Akron Law Review* 32:351.

MARIA D. BECKMAN

M

Majority-Group Resentment

Majority-group resentment is considered a significant impediment in the serious implementation of affirmative action programs. A serious commitment to an affirmative action program frequently proves to be disruptive to a company's workforce because individuals at the workplace within the majority group resent the disruption and potential loss of individual opportunity they believe results from affirmative action. The resentment often has to do with perceptions, correct or not, that the individuals within majority groups will not be fairly promoted or earn their just rewards because of affirmative action. Additionally, due to this resentment, these individuals are in a position to oppose implementation of the affirmative action plans at the workplace.

The great majority of studies about affirmative action and majority-group resentment have focused on white males as the majority group at issue. Research suggests that white men are likely to resent their company's affirmative action programs because they believe that these programs will have a negative impact on their career opportunities and that these programs produce a reverse-discrimination result among the majority group.

To understand majority-group opposition to affirmative action, it is important to take into account the distinction between different types of affirmative action policies. These policies can range from "soft" to "hard" affirmative action plans. On the hard end of the continuum, minority-group membership is the exclusive criterion in decision making. Conversely, on the soft end of the continuum, the primary criterion is individual merit and competency, and minority-group membership constitutes only one of a diverse array of factors to be considered. The harder the affirmative action policy on the continuum, the more likely it is to increase the majority-group resentment and the perception of unfairness. Research on reactions to different affirmative action policies lends support to this idea: soft forms of affirmative action result in more favorable reactions among majority-group members than hard ones.

A credible conclusion regarding the negative attitudes of majority-group members toward affirmative action is that these attitudes are determined by the perception of unfairness in the selection process and the allocation of goods and resources. One of the frameworks within which these perceptions of unfairness may be examined is organizational justice theories. Organizational justice theories include concepts of distributive justice (i.e., fairness of allocated organizational outcomes/results) and procedural justice (i.e., fairness of the process used to allocate these outcomes).

The first model of distributive justice is equity theory. In a 1987 study, David Taylor and Fathali Moghaddam summarized this theory by stating that the "fundamental assumption of [equity theory] is that individuals strive to maximize rewards for themselves. However, in pursuit of this end, individuals learn they must conform to certain norms of justice in their dealings with others" (Taylor and Moghaddam 1987, 85). The basic justice principle underlying equity theory is a balance between the contributions two people make and the rewards those people receive. The perception of fair distribution of outcomes (equity) occurs when people feel that they receive rewards that are consistent with their contributions relative to a reference comparison. In the preferential affirmative action program, nonbeneficiaries of such programs perceive that in the selection decision, beneficiaries have lesser inputs (competence) and get greater rewards (selection) as compared with themselves. This feeling of inequity produces perceptions of unfairness and resentment.

However, perceptions of unfairness by the majority group also seem likely to be affected by procedural justice considerations. That is, opposition to affirmative action by the majority group could be explained in two ways: first, resentment is due to the unfairness of considering group membership criteria at the expense of individual merits; or second, resentment is due to changes introduced in the evaluation process undermining individual feelings of control. The first explanation of majority-group attitudes incorporates beliefs in meritocracy. Therefore, majority-group attitudes toward affirmative action depend on the extent to which the program procedures evaluate each individual in terms of competency and merit, rather than as a function of group membership. Research on affirmative action shows that majority-group resentment is lower when group membership variables are eliminated from procedural selection. The second explanation postulates that opposition to affirmative action reduces individual control of the situation because it changes expectations about the criteria to be evaluated. There are other factors at play in majority-group opposition to affirmative action programs as well. First, feelings of self-interest and preservation are often involved. Several studies have shown that individuals present more positive attitudes toward affirmative action when they feel that their personal interests are not disadvantaged or threatened by the plan or program. Second, racism and sexism are also clearly associated with opposition to affirmative action policies. Finally, beliefs about the existence of organizational discrimination (past or present) and the need for affirmative action to remedy past incidents of discrimination are involved. Many majority-group members do not believe that discrimination and its effects persist and therefore see no just purpose for affirmative action.

See also Affirmative Action Plan/Program; Merit Selections; Meritocracy; Performance-Based Selections; Racial Discrimination; Reverse Discrimination; Scapegoating/Displaced-Aggression Theories; Sexism.

FURTHER READING: Adams, Stacey J., 1965, "Inequity in Social Exchange," in *Advances in Experimental Social Psychology*, vol. 2, edited by L. Berkowitz, New York: Academic Press; Matheson, Kimberly J., Krista L. Warren, Mindi D. Foster, and Chris Painter, 2000, "Reactions to Affirmative Action: Seeking the Bases for Resistance," *Journal of Applied Social Psychology* 30, no. 5:1013–1038; Nacoste, Rupert B., 1985, "Selection Procedures and Response to Affirmative Action: The Case of Favorable Treatment," *Law and Human Behavior* 9:225–242; Nacoste, Rupert B., 1994, "If Empowerment Is the Goal . . .: Affirmative Action and Social Interaction," *Basic and Applied Social Psychology*, 15:87–112; Seligman, Dan, 1973, "How 'Equal Opportunity' Turned into Employment Quotas," *Fortune*, March 1973, 158–168; Taylor, David M., and Fathali M. Moghaddam, 1987, *Theories of Intergroup Relations: International Social Psychological Perspectives*, New York: Praeger; Walster, Ellen, William G. Walster, and Ellen Berscheid, 1978, *Equity: Theory and Research*, Boston: Allyn and Bacon.

MARIA JOSE SOTELO

Malaysia and Affirmative Action

Affirmative action was implemented in Malaysia in 1971 under the title the New Economic Policy (NEP). The NEP was implemented following violent racial incidents between Malays (known as the Bumiputra), Indians, and Chinese groups. Further, the NEP was not only an economic program, but also a sociopolitical agenda aimed at equitable distribution among groups with the expectation that it would promote national unity and maintain political stability. Specifically, the policy was aimed at helping the indigenous people of Malaysia (i.e., the Malays), the majority of the population, improve their economic position. Although the Chinese population of Malaysia was the numerical minority, it had enjoyed substantial economic power since its large-scale immigration to Malaysia started during the second half of the nineteenth century.

The NEP contained a two-part development program. The first part was directed at reducing and eventually eradicating poverty by raising income levels and increasing employment opportunities for all Malaysians. The second part was "aimed at accelerating the process of restructuring Malaysian society to correct economic imbalances, so as to reduce and eventually eliminate the identification of race with economic functions" (Abdullah 1997, 201–202). The Malaysian government set a timetable that within twenty years from the inception of the New Economic Policy, certain targets would be achieved. The government set these "restructuring targets" under the Second Malaysia Plan (1971–1975). For instance, one of the restructuring targets called for Malays and other indigenous people to manage and own at least 30 percent of all commercial and industrial activities in all categories and scales of operation. To achieve these targets, the Malaysian government was committed to play a significant role, particularly in education and business arenas. For instance, from 1971 until June 2003, when quotas in higher education were formally abandoned by Malaysia, the government reserved up to 55 percent of college places every year for Malay applicants.

The New Economic Policy, with some assistance from the rapid economic growth experienced in the region, has been very successful in achieving its goals. However, the policy has come under more intensive attack in recent years. Opponents of the policy argue that it has served its purpose and, if left unchanged, could become counterproductive and undermine achievement based on merit, fairness, and hard work. Criticisms of the three-decade-plus practice of affirmative action have become widespread, and many have become disillusioned. In light of this disillusionment, the Malaysian government finally abandoned the practice of affirmative action, or "positive discrimination," at all of the country's seventeen public universities. While the use of affirmative action in the higher education system has generally been regarded as successful (today, 70 percent of all undergraduates are of Malay descent, compared with 30 percent in the early 1970s), many see the goals of the program as completed. As such, many advocate returning to a society based solely on merit. As one disillusioned student remarked in 2003 in explaining why she was hoping to attend a university in the United States or Australia, "they don't use quotas, students aren't spoon-fed on account of their background, and you're judged on the merits of your work" (Cohen 2004, A42).

See also Australia and Affirmative Action; Brazil and Affirmative Action; Canada and Affirmative Action; China and Affirmative Action; European Union and Affirmative Action; Global Implementation of Affirmative Action Programs; Great Britain and Affirmative Action; India and Affirmative Action; Japan and Affirmative Action; Meritocracy; South Africa and Affirmative Action.

FURTHER READING: Abdullah, Firdaus H., 1997, "Affirmative Action Policy in Malaysia: To Restructure Society, to Eradicate Poverty," *Ethnic Studies Report* 15, no. 2 (July): 189–221; Andersson, Martin, and Christer Gunnarsson, eds., 2003, *Development and Structural Change in Asia-Pacific: Globalising Miracles or End of a Model?* London and New York: Routledge-Curzon; Cohen, David, 2004, "In Malaysia, the End of Quotas," *Chronicle of Higher Education* 50, no. 23 (February 13): A42; Drabble, John H., 2000, *An Economic History of Malaysia, c. 1800–1990: The Transition to Modern Economic Growth*, New York: St. Martin's Press.

PAULINA X. RUF

Malcolm X (1925–1965)

Malcolm X, born Malcolm Little in 1925 in Omaha, Nebraska, is best known for his radical and discriminatory views against white Americans and as a leading spokesman and member of the Nation of Islam. Contrary to Martin Luther King Jr.'s beliefs that racial equality could be achieved through integration and nonviolent resistance, Malcolm X believed that African Americans were purposely suppressed by whites and should exist in their own separate state. Malcolm X advocated black pride, black self-dependence, and separatism. He outright rejected integration and equality in the United States, calling instead for separatism and a "nation within a nation." Malcolm X also coined the phrase "by any means necessary" to fight for black independence, and the slogan often appeared alongside a picture of Malcolm X pointing a firearm, implying that violence was permissible. Ironically, one group that has been formed to lobby for affirmative action and claims to be guided in part by the teachings of Martin Luther King Jr. has adopted the phrase as part of its group name, the Coalition to Defend Affirmative Action, Integration, and Fight for Equality by Any Means Necessary.

Malcolm X's initial views were partly a result of a turbulent early life. By the time he was fifteen, his father was allegedly murdered by a white supremacist group and his mother was committed to a mental institution for twenty-six years. He dropped out of school after being told by his favorite teacher that his dream of becoming a lawyer was "no realistic goal for a nigger." After living in various foster homes until adulthood, he worked various jobs for short periods of time and engaged in numerous crimes involving narcotics, running prostitution rings, stealing, breaking and entering, and carrying firearms while living in Harlem, Boston, and Michigan. It was while he was serving an eight- to ten-year sentence in prison (beginning in 1946) that he was introduced to the teachings of Elijah Muhammad. He gained notoriety as a speaker for the Nation of Islam and his extreme views against white Americans, but soon became concerned over the prominent media attention focused on him rather than Elijah Muhammad. Malcolm X was even the focus of a weeklong television special with Mike Wallace in 1959 titled "The Hate That Hate Produced." He was constantly under surveillance by the FBI.

Malcolm was silenced by Elijah Muhammad in 1963 for his comments that John F. Kennedy "never saw the chickens would come home to roost so soon" in response to Kennedy's assassination, meaning that poor treatment of minorities in the United States had led to Kennedy's assassination. Tension continued to escalate between Malcolm X and Eli-

Malcolm X during a Harlem, New York, rally in 1963. Courtesy of Library of Congress.

jah Muhammad until Malcolm left the Nation of Islam in 1964 after hearing rumors of Muhammad's adultery with numerous Muslim women. He formed the Muslim Mosque, met Martin Luther King Jr. for the first and only time, and began working on his autobiography with Alex Haley in that same year. He then changed his name to El-Hajj Malik El-Shabazz. After making a pilgrimage to Mecca, Saudi Arabia, Malcolm X returned to the United States with an allegedly new outlook on racial equality and integration. In Mecca, he stated that he met "blonde-haired, blue-eyed men I could call my brother." He renounced Elijah Muhammad, and several attempts were subsequently made on his life. He was shot to death on February 21, 1965, while giving a speech in New York. The three convicted assassins were all members of the Nation of Islam. He left behind his wife, Betty Shabazz, and six daughters. Members of the Nation of Islam who were convicted of assassinating Malcolm X committed the act because of his changed views on integration and his renouncing of the Nation of Islam's leader, Elijah Muhammad.

See also Black Nationalism; Civil Rights Movement; Coalition to Defend Affirmative Action and Fight for Equality by Any Means Necessary; Farrakhan, Louis; Integration; Kennedy, John Fitzgerald; King, Martin Luther, Jr.; Racial Discrimination.

FURTHER READING: Goldman, Peter, 1979, *The Death and Life of Malcolm X*, 2d ed., Urbana: University of Illinois Press; Malcolm X, 1965, *The Autobiography of Malcolm X*, New York: Grove Books.

GLENN L. STARKS

Mandela, Nelson

See South Africa and Affirmative Action.

Manifest Imbalance Standard

The manifest imbalance standard refers to the U.S. Supreme Court test that has been utilized to assess whether voluntary affirmative action plans by employers violate Title VII of the Civil Rights Act of 1964. According to the Supreme Court, an employer does not need a finding of intentional discrimination to justify an affirmative action plan. Rather, under the manifest imbalance standard, the Court has indicated its willingness to permit affirmative action plans under Title VII that are promulgated to eliminate manifest racial or gender imbalances in the workplace. A manifest imbalance in the workforce has been defined by the Court to mean the existence of a significant statistical racial or gender disparity in a workforce or job category as compared to the relevant segment of the general labor force.

The overall purpose of Title VII of the Civil Rights Act of 1964 is to promote and protect equal employment opportunities. Title VII, as amended by Congress, applies to the actions of both public and private employers. Consequently, voluntary affirmative action plans adopted by public employers to cure perceived racial imbalances in the workplace are subject to scrutiny under the Fifth (federal employers) and Fourteenth (state and local employers) Amendments' equal protection guarantee and also under Title VII.

These well-intentioned plans are often challenged by white males who are typically disadvantaged by the affirmative action plans. The resolution of these challenges under Title VII has hinged, in part, upon the interpretation of the Court's manifest imbalance standard. In interpreting the Civil Rights Act of 1964, in *McDonald v. Santa Fe Trail Transportation Co.*, 427 U.S. 273 (1976), the Supreme Court unanimously held that Title VII of the Civil Rights Act of 1964 prohibited private employers from discriminating against white employees. Three years later, in *United Steelworkers of America v. Weber*, 443 U.S. 193 (1979), the Court ruled that, notwithstanding *McDonald*, Title VII does not prohibit private, race-conscious affirmative action plans "designed to eliminate conspicuous racial imbalances in traditionally segregated job categories." Alternatively referring to the pattern whereby blacks were represented in the employer's workforce at rates far below their representation in the local labor force as a "manifest imbalance," the Court did not further elaborate on the meaning of the phrase. According to the concurring opinion of Associate Justice Harry Blackmun, however, the Court had found that a manifest imbalance could be something less than would be necessary to establish an arguable violation of Title VII.

Eight years later, reaffirming the *Weber* precedent in *Johnson v. Transportation*

Agency, Santa Clara County, 480 U.S. 616 (1987), the Court indicated that while for unskilled jobs identification of a manifest imbalance rests on comparisons between an employer's workforce and the general labor force, for more skilled jobs "the comparison should be with those in the labor force who possess the requisite qualifications." Otherwise, however, as observed in the concurrence of Associate Justice Sandra Day O'Connor, apart from denying that a manifest imbalance must be such as to make out a prima facie case of discrimination, the Court gave little guidance on what sort of imbalance would be necessary to support an affirmative action plan. At a minimum, however, the Court's decision in *Johnson v. Transportation Agency* provided that employers were permitted to adopt affirmative action plans when the employer could demonstrate that the plan was promulgated to cure a manifest racial or gender imbalance in the workforce without violating Title VII.

In the years that have followed, the Court has not provided further guidance on the meaning of manifest imbalance. Additionally, the Court has not explained how this more lenient "manifest imbalance" under Title VII relates to the strict scrutiny test under the equal protection guarantees of the Fifth and Fourteenth Amendments. Finally, the lower courts have also failed to meaningfully elucidate the exact meaning of the standard. A concurrence in one appellate decision suggested that the phrase was limited to situations where jobs might be deemed actually to be segregated, presumably meaning an extremely limited representation of group in a particular job following total or near total exclusion (*Hammon v. Barry,* 862 F.2d 73 [D.C. Cir. 1987] [Silberman, J., concurring]). On the other hand, another appellate court accepted that a manifest imbalance in pay could justify race- or gender-conscious pay decisions, an interpretation entirely at odds with notions of job segregation (*Smith v. Virginia Commonwealth University,* 84 F.3d 672 [4th Cir. 1996]). However, although appearing to demand that the manifest imbalance sufficient to justify implementing a gender-conscious pay plan would be akin to a prima facie showing of discrimination, the court gave no guidance on how large the disparity would have to be to justify such a plan.

In attempting to provide internal guidance for determining when to implement race- or gender-conscious affirmative action plans for their own employees, some federal agencies have attempted to define manifest imbalances numerically (e.g., where a group's representation in a job is "less than 50 percent" or "from 26 to 75 percent" of the group's representation in the civilian labor force). It is not possible to predict how reliance on benchmarks such as these will be regarded by the courts in future cases.

See also Affirmative Action Plan/Program; Blackmun, Harry Andrew; Civil Rights Act of 1964; Disparate Treatment and Disparate Impact; Equal Protection Clause; Fifth Amendment; Fourteenth Amendment; *Johnson v. Transportation Agency, Santa Clara County;* O'Connor, Sandra Day; Strict Scrutiny; Supreme Court and Affirmative Action; Title VII of the Civil Rights Act of 1964; *United Steelworkers of America v. Weber; Wygant v. Jackson Board of Education.*

FURTHER READING: Adelman, Ronald, 1987, "Note: Voluntary Affirmative Action Plans by Public Employers: The Disparity in Standards between Title VII and the Equal Protection Clause," *Fordham Law Review* 56:403–430; "Note: The Constitutionality of Proposition 209 as Applied," 1998, *Harvard Law Review* 111 (May): 2081–2093; Selig, Joel, 1987, "Affirmative Action in Employment: The Legacy of a Supreme Court Majority," *Indiana Law Journal* 63 (spring): 301–368.

JAMES P. SCANLAN

Marshall, Thurgood (1908–1993)

Thurgood Marshall, the first African American solicitor general of the United States and the first African American appointed to the U.S. Supreme Court, was a staunch defender of equal rights for African Americans and a defender of affirmative action policies for African Americans and women. Marshall believed that governmental practices such as preferential treatment, set-asides, and other race-conscious policies were valid remedies in response to historical discrimination. While he was on the Supreme Court, Marshall voted in favor of affirmative action plans for African Americans or women in every case that was granted certiorari and was the subject of an official opinion of the Court.

Marshall's primary motivation as a lawyer and Supreme Court justice was his belief that integration was the solution to the attainment of equal rights under the law. Marshall's conviction of equal treatment under the law provided him with the necessary drive to become successful in achieving victories as a litigator for the National Association for the Advancement of Colored People (NAACP) in a series of desegregation cases throughout the South in the 1930s, 1940s, and early 1950s. Marshall also played a key role in the pivotal 1954 Supreme Court case *Brown v. Board of Education*, 347 U.S. 483 (1954). Prior to his appointment as solicitor general of the United States and as a justice of the U.S. Supreme Court, Marshall had served as the chief counsel for the NAACP Legal Defense and Educational Fund and as a judge on the Court of Appeals for the Second Circuit.

Marshall was born on July 2, 1908, in Baltimore, Maryland, and died on January 24, 1993. He was the son of a Pullman porter and a schoolteacher, and great-grandson of a slave. Marshall was a graduate of Lincoln University, a historically black college located in Chester, Pennsylvania, and of Howard University Law School in Washington, D.C. Marshall's attendance at Lincoln University served as an indicator of the barriers confronting African Americans in the field of education. Marshall was not allowed to attend the University of Maryland Law School because he was African American. It was this fact of life that provided him with the motivation for opposing all forms of racial segregation and the denial of equal opportunities for African American citizens.

During his public primary and secondary education, which also was all at segregated schools, Marshall was considered to be a rebellious student. To punish Marshall for his misbehavior, he was required by his teachers to memorize different parts of the Constitution. As a result, Marshall came to know the Constitution by heart at an early age. This would be advantageous in his later years. Furthermore, as a result of Marshall's personal experience with segregated schools, he began to develop plans to fight segregation in education.

After graduating from Lincoln University, Marshall enrolled in Howard University Law School. While there, he met Charles Hamilton Houston, the dean of the school. Houston eventually became the NAACP's first chief counsel, a position that Marshall would later occupy. Houston hired Marshall as an assistant legal counsel for the NAACP. In 1936, Marshall and Houston teamed up as cocounsel in *Murray v. Maryland*, 169 Md. 478 (1936), successfully challenging the University of Maryland Law School's discriminatory admissions practice against African Americans in front of the Maryland Supreme Court. The case also provided Marshall with a personal victory in that he had once been denied admission to that very school on account of his race.

In 1940, Marshall became director of the NAACP Legal Defense and Educational Fund and remained in this position until 1961. In this position, Marshall masterminded the legal strategy to utilize the federal court system to challenge racial oppression and discrimination in education, housing, transportation, and the criminal justice system. During his tenure as director of the NAACP Legal Defense Fund, Marshall achieved impressive legal victories in the area of racial integration and desegregation. Early on, Marshall successfully argued such landmark cases as *Smith v. Allwright*, 321 U.S. 649 (1944) (dealing with the unconstitutionality of white primary elections) and *Shelley v. Kraemer*, 334 U.S. 1 (1948) (dealing with racially restrictive covenants).

Marshall then began a nationwide campaign to integrate institutions of higher education by attacking the lack of equal educational facilities for African Americans as mandated by the Supreme Court's then-standing interpretation of the Fourteenth Amendment's Equal Protection Clause. In 1950, in the cases of *Sweatt v. Painter*, 339 U.S. 629 (1950), and *McLaurin v. Oklahoma State Board of Regents*, 339 U.S. 637 (1950), Marshall used this tactic of arguing the lack of equal facilities as a way to attack the separate-but-equal doctrine as established in *Plessy v. Ferguson*, 163 U.S. 537 (1896), but without directly challenging the doctrine. Marshall argued that racial classifications were per se unreasonable and that the law school established by Texas in the *Sweatt* case was unequal to the white facilities and therefore violated the protections of the Fourteenth Amendment. In *McLaurin*, the point of emphasis was that admission on segregated bases into a white facility also violated the principles set forth in the Fourteenth Amendment. In both cases, Marshall successfully demonstrated that "separate-but-equal" facilities for African American professional and graduate students in state universities were not in fact "equal" and were, therefore, unconstitutional under then Supreme Court Fourteenth Amendment jurisprudence. Finally, in *Brown v. Board of Education* (1954), Marshall gained national recognition for his role as one of the key lawyers arguing the *Brown* case before the U.S. Supreme Court, a case that led to the Supreme Court declaring the doctrine of separate but equal unconstitutional under the Fourteenth Amendment. Marshall argued, and the Court found, that separate facilities for different races in the educational context were inherently unequal.

President John Kennedy appointed Marshall in 1961 as a judge on the U.S. Court of Appeals for the Second Circuit. While serving on the Second Circuit, from 1961 to 1965, he wrote 112 opinions, none of which were overturned on appeal. In 1965, President Lyndon Johnson appointed Marshall to serve as the first African American solicitor general of the United States, a position he held until his elevation to the Supreme Court in 1967. During his career, both with the NAACP Legal Defense Fund and as U.S. Solicitor General, he argued thirty-two cases before the Supreme Court, winning twenty-nine of the thirty-two cases.

George E. Hayes, Thurgood Marshall, and James M. Nabrit congratulating each other, following the Supreme Court's *Brown v. Board of Education* decision declaring segregation unconstitutional. Courtesy of Library of Congress.

In 1967, President Lyndon Johnson appointed Marshall to the U.S. Supreme Court to succeed Justice Tom Clark, thereby making Marshall the first African American appointed to the high court. Marshall served on the Supreme Court from 1967 to 1991. As a member of the Supreme Court, Marshall continued to enforce his liberal judicial philosophy and was considered a key member of the liberal bloc on the Court. In affirmative action, Marshall was always aligned with Justices Harry Blackmun and William Brennan. In fact, from the Supreme Court's decision in *Regents of the University of California v. Bakke*, 438 U.S. 265 (1978), until the decision in *City of Richmond v. J.A. Croson Co.*, 488 U.S. 469 (1989), Marshall, Blackmun, and Brennan always voted in favor of affirmative action plans for African Americans and women. In these cases, Marshall illustrated his apparent belief that affirmative action plans were logical extensions of the civil rights movement and that such plans did not violate the Equal Protection Clause of the Fourteenth Amendment.

See also Blackmun, Harry Andrew; Brennan, William Joseph; *Brown v. Board of Education*; *City of Richmond v. J.A. Croson Co.*; Equal Protection Clause; Fifteenth Amendment; Fourteenth Amendment; Johnson, Lyndon Baines; Kennedy, John Fitzgerald; National Association for the Advancement of Colored People; *Plessy v. Ferguson*; *Regents of the University of California v. Bakke*; *Sweatt v. Painter*.

FURTHER READING: Davis, Michael D., and Hunter R. Clark, 1992, *Thurgood Marshall: Warrior at the Bar, Rebel on the Bench*, New York: Carol Publishing Company; Gates, Henry Louis, Jr., and Cornel West, 2000, *The African-American Century: How Black Americans Have Shaped Our Country*, New York: Free Press; Irons, Peter, 1999, *A People's History of the Supreme Court*, New York: Viking Press; Tushnet, Mark V., 1997, *Making Constitutional Law: Thurgood Marshall and the Supreme Court, 1961–1991*, New York: Oxford University Press; Williams, Juan, 1998, *Thurgood Marshall: American Revolutionary*, New York: Times Books.

RONNIE B. TUCKER SR.

Marxist Theory and Affirmative Action

Marxism refers to the body of theory or system of thought associated with the work of Karl Marx (1818–1883) and Friedrich Engels (1820–1895). Marxism is concerned with political economy and the power of capitalism in shaping social life, particularly the power struggle between the classes. Marxist theorists study social relations to uncover the inequalities and injustices created by capitalist economic relations so that these can be changed. In this light, it is considered the organizing principle behind revolutionary movements around the world, most notably in Russia. Marx's ideas and work provide significant support for affirmative action programs that attempt to level the field, so to speak, for groups of people who have historically been subordinate to and exploited by the dominant class. Marxist theories are also occasionally cited in affirmative action literature.

Marx's early work reflects his interest in alienation, particularly that produced by working conditions. In his later work, Marx turned his attention to the connection between economics and social life. According to Marx, people are born into societies where property relations have already been determined. These relations in turn give rise to different social classes, which express different views of the world. These views reflect existing class relations and tend to either reinforce or undermine the power and authority of the dominant class. Marx was particularly interested in explaining how capitalism shaped society. The most significant consequence of capitalism, according to him, was the creation and endurance of a social class system where dominant classes (i.e., the bourgeoisie) obtain wealth that is produced by subordinate classes (i.e., the proletariat). Marx believed that this economic organization of society was the most significant influence on the thoughts and behavior of people. Because the capitalist class owns not only the means of production, but also the production of ideas, Marx found that the beliefs of the subordinate classes tended to support the interests of the capitalist system. He believed that eventually the workers would become class conscious and create a society without class divisions and, hence, without class exploitation.

Karl Heinrich Marx was born into a comfortable middle-class home on May 5, 1818, in Trier in the German Rhineland. He studied law at the University of Bonn and later studied philosophy at the University of Berlin. In Berlin, he joined a group of radical intellectuals, who become known as the Young Hegelians, and studied philosophy. In 1841, he finished his studies and became a journalist, editing a radical newspaper called the *Rheinische Zeitung*. In 1843, Marx married his childhood sweetheart, Jenny von Westphalen, and moved to Paris. During his stay in Paris, Marx met Friedrich Engels, who would become his lifelong friend, collaborator, and benefactor. Marx was expelled from Paris in 1845 and moved to Brussels, Belgium, for a time. He later returned to Paris but in 1849 was expelled again and moved to London, where he strengthened his friendship with Engels, who collaborated with Marx and helped him and his family through very trying economic periods. Marx spent the rest of his life studying economics and its impact on every aspect of social life. He died in London on March 14, 1883. He outlived his wife and all but two of his six children. The influence of Marx's ideas has been enormous. Although he stressed economic issues in his writings, his major impact was and continues to be in the fields of sociology and history.

See also Class-Based Affirmative Action; Economically Disadvantaged; Weber, Max.

FURTHER READING: Coser, Lewis A., 1977, *Masters of Sociological Thought: Ideas in Historical and Social Context*, 2d ed., New York: Harcourt Brace Jovanovich College Publishers; McLellan, David, 1973, *Karl Marx: His Life and Thought*, New York: Harper and Row; McLellan, David, 1983, *Marx: The First Hundred Years*, New York: St. Martin's Press; Mills, C. Wright, 1962, *The Marxists*, New York: Dell Publishing.

PAULINA X. RUF

Maryland Troopers Association v. Evans, 993 F.2d 1072 (4th Cir. 1993)

Maryland Troopers Association v. Evans is one of the significant employment affirmative action cases handed down at the federal court of appeals level. The ultimate ruling in the case illustrates how critically the federal circuit courts and the Supreme Court have viewed claims of racial discrimination based upon statistical disparities alone in the workforce. The decision also illustrates how closely the justifications for affirmative action plans are scrutinized by the courts, even when the affirmative action plans are based upon judicial consent decrees.

In *Maryland Troopers Association v. Evans*, the U.S. Court of Appeals for the Fourth Circuit reversed the decision by the U.S. District Court for the District of Maryland that allowed the state of Maryland to adopt an affirmative action plan with numerical employment goals based upon race. The Maryland Troopers Association challenged a judicially approved consent decree between the Coalition of Black Maryland State Troopers and the Maryland State Police under which the state police agreed to hire and promote a certain percentage of black troopers at each state trooper rank. The Maryland Troopers Association contended that the numerical goals set forth in the consent decree violated the Equal Protection Clause of the Fourteenth Amendment and Title VII of the Civil Rights Act of 1964.

This dispute began in 1974 when the United States sued the state of Maryland for racial discrimination in hiring state troopers. The parties settled the litigation by entering into a consent decree under which the Maryland State Police agreed to hire black applicants at a rate that would achieve an overall percentage of 16 percent black troopers within five years. In 1979, the consent decree was reviewed and modified to reduce the overall goal to 14 percent black troopers, but additionally required the Maryland State Police to achieve 33 percent black troopers among its entry-level troopers a figure that by 1980 was slightly under 10 percent.

In 1982, when cronyism and rigged examinations in the Maryland State Police's promotional system were alleged, the attorney general of Maryland issued a critical report on promotional practices in the agency. The report concluded that high-ranking officers within the agency were tampering with promotional examination scores in an attempt to favor their chosen candidates and that the low representation of blacks in upper ranks of the Maryland State Police suggested that the promotional system was to blame.

In response to the attorney general's report, the Maryland State Police adopted an affirmative action promotional plan for law-enforcement personnel that set specific numerical goals for the percentage of black troopers within the lower ranks of the agency. Additionally, the agency contracted with an outside consulting firm to develop and administer a promotional evaluation for the ranks of corporal through captain. At the same time, the Coalition of Black Maryland State Troopers sued the Maryland State Police in the U.S. district court, alleging ongoing racial discrimination by the agency in the hiring and promotion process.

Within three years of the installation of the new promotional examination process, black troopers were being promoted at rates that actually exceeded the percentage of blacks in the eligible ranks below. For example, in 1989, of the 81 troopers promoted from trooper to corporal, 23 percent were black; of the 212 troopers promoted from corporal to sergeant, 21 percent were black; and of the 5 troopers promoted from sergeant to sergeant first class, 1 was black. Despite these rates of promotion of black troopers, the coalition and the Maryland State Police settled the lawsuit by entering into a consent decree requiring the agency to meet specific numerical goals within each rank until an overall goal of 22 percent was met.

The Maryland Troopers Association challenged the consent decree in district court, but the court rejected the challenge, ruling that enough evidence of racial discrimination did exist to warrant the race-conscious remedy. The court based its rejection on two grounds, the findings of the 1982 attorney general's report and a pair of statistical compositions between the black proportion of the Maryland State Police and the black proportion of what was referred to as the "relevant qualified labor pool." The first statistical comparison was between the percentage of blacks in each rank of the agency and the percentage of black Maryland residents working in jobs allegedly requiring equivalent skills. The second comparison was between the average percentage of blacks employed as troopers and the percentage of blacks who met the basic criteria to become a Maryland state trooper. The Court found that because approximately 22 percent of black Maryland residents were high-school graduates between the ages of twenty-one and twenty-nine—the most likely age for applicants to be hired—the parties should be permitted to use the 22 percent baseline "to assess underrepresentativeness" in all ranks of the agency. The court therefore concluded that black officers had been victims of past discrimination in promotion. The Maryland Troopers Association unsuccessfully argued that more than simply a high-school graduation and meeting an age requirement were needed to become a trooper and appealed to the U.S. court of appeals.

The court of appeals cited the Supreme Court case *Wygant v. Jackson Board of Education*, 476 U.S. 267 (1986), which stated that "racial and ethnic distinctions of any sort are inherently suspect and thus call for the most exacting judicial examination." The court stated that the Fourteenth Amendment forbids states to classify persons on the basis of race except as a "last-resort remedy for well-defined instances of racial discrimination." Citing another Supreme Court case, *City of Richmond v. J.A. Croson Co.*, 488 U.S. 469 (1989), the court further stated that a two-step analysis for evaluating a race-conscious remedy must include a "strong basis in evidence for its conclusion that remedial action is necessary" and that the remedy must be "narrowly tailored."

The court rejected several arguments made by the district court and ruled the consent decree to be invalid. First, the court could not find any evidence of racial discrimination in hiring or promoting of black troopers and regarded the issue of suspected cronyism as unfair and "no way to run a police department," but not evidence of discrimination. Second, with regard to the use of the two statistical comparisons, the court called the inference that minorities would choose a vocation in a similar proportion to their representation in the local population "most dubious" and unrealistic. The court went further, stating that it found no "gross statistical disparity" and that the 22 percent figure failed to establish any "gross disparity" between the number of blacks in the Maryland State Police and the composition of the qualified labor pool. The court actually applauded the agency for taking action by instituting its own affirmative action promotional plan in an attempt to eliminate cronyism without any judicial order to do so. As a result of the findings of the court of appeals, the judgment of the district court was reversed, and the objections to the hiring and promotional goals of the consent decree made by the Maryland Troopers Associations were upheld.

See also Affirmative Action Plan/Program; *City of Richmond v. J.A. Croson Co.*; Civil Rights Act of 1964; Disparate Treatment and Disparate Impact; Equal Protection Clause; Fourteenth Amendment; Manifest Imbalance Standard; Narrowly Tailored Affirmative Action Plans; Statistical Proof of Discrimination; Title VII of the Civil Rights Act of 1964; *Wygant v. Jackson Board of Education.*

FURTHER READING: Joseph, David H., 1994, "Statistical Evidence of Discrimination and Affirmative Action: The Numbers Game and *Maryland Troopers v. Evans*," *Temple Law Review* 67:451–472; *Maryland Troopers Association v. Evans*, 993 F.2d 1072 (4th Cir. 1993).

CHRISTOPHER R. CAPSAMBELIS

McGovern Commission

For more than a century, the Democratic and Republican Parties have nominated presidential candidates at national conventions. The McGovern Commission was assigned to solve a problem concerning these presidential nominations: the exclusion of certain populations—African Americans, women, youth, and antiwar activists—from the Democratic convention process. At the root of the problem were the systems used to select delegates for the national party conventions and the way in which delegate votes were counted at the national level. It has been alleged that the McGovern Commission was a type of affirmative action in the political party context, and that the McGovern Commission "urged quotas at the Democratic National Convention to 'overcome the effects of past discrimination' " (Kahlenberg 1996, 29).

Prior to the McGovern Commission, national party conventions were markedly dominated by those already in power, that is, elected officials and local party leaders. Much of this was due to the way in which states selected delegates for the national conventions. While some states held primaries, others used the caucus method. The primary method was criticized for allowing candidates to concentrate on only a few of the primaries (i.e., those with the largest electoral votes), while the caucus method, which chooses national party convention delegates through a series of local political meetings and elections, was criticized for its exclusion of participants based on its time-consuming and elitist nature. Critics of these systems argued that they were undemocratic since they allowed for little input or attention to ordinary party members and voters.

The specific stimulus for convention reform and the McGovern Commission came from the presidential nomination of Vice President Hubert Humphrey in the 1968 Democratic Convention. In 1968, the anti–Vietnam War candidates, Eugene McCarthy and Robert Kennedy, sought the Democratic nomination by running in every Democratic primary and challenging each party caucus. Vice President Hubert Humphrey, on the other hand, chose the traditional strategy of relying on party leaders to manage delegations for him at caucuses; he did not enter any primaries. As a result, Humphrey did not win any popular votes, while McCarthy and Kennedy won approximately 6 million popular votes combined. Peace activists registered significant protest against Humphrey winning the presidential nomination without participating in any primaries and asserted that party bosses held too much power in the election process. Because the Democratic Party needed the support of antiwar activists to win the general election, they made a concession to the protesters: a reform commission chaired by Senator George McGovern of South Dakota, a politician known for his antiwar stance.

The McGovern Commission revised the Democratic candidate selection process in several ways. Perhaps most important, the commission required the party caucuses, which had been controlled by party leaders, to open up to regular party members. It required that each delegation represent the popular strength of the candidates in the state, as well as the racial, gender, and age composition of the state. Initially, this specified African Americans, youth, and women. The Democratic Party later amended this to include Hispanics, Native Americans, and homosexuals. This requirement made operating caucuses so logistically difficult that many states eventually began to use primaries. The McGovern Commission also pressed to award national convention delegates to candidates in proportion to their popular voting strength in each respective state rather than the former system in which the candidate who won the most votes in a caucus or primary was awarded all of the state's delegates in the national convention. Since the McGovern reforms went into effect in the 1972 election year, no candidate of either party has won his party's nomination without running in every primary.

See also Baker v. Carr; Democratic Party and Affirmative Action; Quotas; *Shaw v. Reno.*

FURTHER READING: Democratic National Committee (U.S.), 1968, 1972, *Mandate for Reform: A Report,* Washington, DC: Commission on Party and Delegate Selection; Kahlenberg, Richard D., 1996, *The Remedy: Class, Race, and Affirmative Action,* New York: Basic Books.

MAYA ALEXANDRA BEASLEY

Media and Affirmative Action

The subject of affirmative action is likely to engender considerable debate in any political or social setting. Media communication experts maintain that no other issue, with the exception of abortion, is as divisive among policy makers, political analysts, and the American public. As a topic of political dialogue and public conversations in print, television, and radio, affirmative action tends to result in a conflict-laden discussion between opponents and proponents. To some extent, public opinion is shaped by what is heard, seen, and read via the media relating to affirmative action.

In the United States, the media are viewed as a powerful institution in shaping the way citizens come to understand and view current public issues. Furthermore, citizens depend on broadcast radio, television, and print media for their news. Media communication analysts maintain that for citizens to make informed and reasoned decisions about public policy issues, the media have a responsibility to present information in a fair and unbiased manner. Yet prominent individuals in the affirmative action debate, such as Harvard law professor Christopher Edley, have claimed that the media do not adequately and meaningfully cover the myriad of issues germane to affirmative action and needed to reach an educated conclusion on the efficacy of affirmative action, which ultimately results in a misguided or uninformed public on this important topic. Edley commented in 1998 that in covering affirmative action, many journalists do not adequately prepare as they would for other topics and, through this lack of preparation, propagate misconceptions. According to Edley, in the area of affirmative action, "many journalists think that shooting from the hip should suffice. This is not rocket science; this is harder than rocket science" (Roach 1998, 26). The theory of "agenda setting" has been used since the early 1920s to explain how the media shape public opinion. This theory proposes that the media do not tell the public what to think, but instead what to think about. First introduced by Walter Lippman, the agenda-setting hypothesis suggests that the media can control public opinion by focusing attention on selected issues while ignoring others.

Conservatives have charged that television and print media are dominated by liberal ideology and use their influence to promote the liberal agenda, including affirmative action. Liberals have made similar claims that radio media are biased toward conservative causes. In a 1980 study of the media elite, S. Robert Lichter provided evidence of the degree to which journalists, in their reporting, lean to the left. Lichter's findings were later confirmed by results from American Society of Newspaper Editors (ASNE) surveys conducted in 1988 and 1997. In the 1997 ASNE study, 1,037 newspaper reporters were surveyed. Results showed that 61 percent identified themselves as liberal/Democratic compared to only 15 percent who identified themselves as conservative/Republican. After the 1997 ASNE study was made public, members of the media argued that although they tended to express personal preference for liberal ideals, they were still able to maintain their professional neutrality. Some media professionals argued that their opinions do not matter because as professional journalists and reporters, they report what they observe without letting their opinions affect their judgment. Media communication experts counter that journalists and reporters routinely make subjective decisions about news content. As decision makers, journalists choose "what to cover and what not to cover, which sources are most credible and which are not, which quotes to use in a story and which to toss out" (Schmitz 2002). Consequently, liberal and conservative bias in the news media is a reality in U.S. society. Author John Leo, in a 1998 *U.S. News and World Report* article addressing the issue of media coverage on affirmative action in Texas, described it this way: "Many people now understand that the selection and treatment of news stories often reflect the social views of the reporters and editors rather than any nonpartisan or objective standard. Our newsroom culture is so strongly committed to affirmative action that a lot of reporting on the subject is simply unreliable" (Leo, 12).

William McGowan in his book titled *Coloring the News* examined several newsrooms, including *USA Today*, the *New York Times*, the *Washington Post*, and other giants of the mainstream press. McGowan's research illustrates the tension-filled relationship between liberal and conservative bias in the media and the extent to which the media have been significantly affected by the U.S. struggle to resolve the diversity dilemma. In his study, McGowan focused on media coverage of diversity issues including affirmative action, immigration, race, gay rights, and feminism. The results of McGowan's research provide a compelling analysis of what stories get reported and how information is conveyed during news reports. For example, McGowan examined the manner in which the press misrepresented information in stories involving figures like Kara Hultgren (the navy fighter pilot who died after missing a carrier landing), Kelly Flinn (the air force officer who had an affair with a married man), and Patrick Chavis (the black physician who was once held up as illustrative of the success of affirmative action programs and then had his license taken away because of medical malpractice).

Interestingly, more examples of how the media affect the national affirmative action debate continue to emerge, as in the case of the 2003 *New York Times* scandal involving Jayson Blair, a twenty-seven-year-old African American reporter at the *New York Times* who committed plagiary and made up a substantial number of his *New York Times* articles. According to some affirmative action critics, Blair is the new example illustrating the alleged need to repeal affirmative action. The Jayson Blair scandal was made public in early May 2003, and arguments continue in the industry over whether affirmative action played a part in keeping Blair on the fast track despite character flaws, plagiarized articles, and questionable professional behavior. At a minimum, it is argued that Blair was hired as a result of the *New York Times* affirmative action employment practices (which it follows in part based upon the 1978 ASNE statement on diversity and minority employment), whereby newspaper organizations agree to recruit and retain minority reporters and staff in the same proportion as those minority groups appear in the local community. Regardless of the particular merits of the Blair case, it is a good example of how the media continue to fuel and feed the debate by focusing on the exceptional cases, as opposed to all of the other writers and staff members who may be succeeding in the organization pursuant to the same affirmative action plans.

In his analysis titled "The Color Game: How the Media Play the Race Card in Affirmative Action Coverage and Stack the Deck against Rational Debate," media expert Robert Entman focuses on the way in which the media use race to colorize the news and maintains that affirmative action coverage consistently misleads Americans by posing the issue "in black and white terms that contradict reality." Entman writes, "In truth, conflicts of interest over these policies do not arise mainly between whites and African Americans. There is far more common ground than the folks who craft the news have suggested." According to Entman, "such coverage might have contributed to opposition to affirmative action" (SFSU Public Affairs 1999).

Indeed, the simplification of the debate into a "black" versus "white" issue, it is argued, is another reoccurring problem of media coverage. This misplaced emphasis gives viewers or readers the false impression that affirmative action only benefits African Americans and that African Americans can only get ahead with help. Arguably, much of America's workforce has benefited from affirmative action programs at one point or another. There are affirmative action programs that benefit women, veterans, persons with disabilities, and many ethnic and racial groups. Nevertheless, whenever the topic is discussed in the media in terms of unqualified persons displacing qualified white males, the background pictures or anecdotes usually deal with African Americans.

The opponents of affirmative action have long been aware of this, which is why conservative pollster and strategist Frank Luntz advised congressional Republicans in an October 12, 1997, *New York Times* article to redefine affirmative action to mean government-sponsored quotas and preferential treatment for African Americans. Indeed, the saturated media coverage was important in ensuring the ultimate success of anti–affirmative action ballot initiatives in California (Proposition 209) and Washington (Initiative 200). Yet even after the California and Washington ballot initiatives demonstrated how language makes a difference in characterizing affirmative action, and despite ample proof in polls of the prejudicial effect that calling affirmative action "rigid preferences" or "quotas" has on the American public (especially whites), the mainstream media continue to equate quotas and rigid preferences with affirmative action and to use the two terms interchangeably. Mainstream media also largely fail to discuss the historical events and issues leading up to modern affirmative action programs, a historical progression that is essential to fully understand the various merits in affirmative action debates.

In recent years, conservatives have also attempted to use the media to refocus and neutralize the African American community on issues relating to affirmative action. For example, conservative politicians have sought to promote African Americans as spokespersons against affirmative action. The result has been conservatives engaging in a form of tokenism that is inconsistent with their purported belief in a color-blind society.

Not only do the media affect the affirmative action debate directly by manipulating the way they present the issue, but some charge that the media affect the debate indirectly by shaping the public view of African Americans. According to media expert Robert Entman, television news programs, particularly local television newscasts, consciously or unconsciously tend to show African Americans in a much worse light than whites. For example, a substantial number of blacks accused of crimes are shown without name identification, while whites accused of crimes are almost always identified, implying that black criminals are more plentiful (therefore, no name identification) and white criminals are the exception (therefore, worthy of name identification as a rare exception). According to Entman's research, far more stories about crimes involving black defendants appear on local newscasts than do stories about white defendants. Far fewer black than white "good Samaritans" are the subjects of stories. African American politicians are often shown as posturing on behalf of the black community, and these same politicians are often shown as being demanding. Stories about poverty are often set in black neighborhoods, even though statistics indicate that substantially more whites live in poverty in the United States. At the highest levels, there are few African American government officials who are in positions where they might be shown regularly on the media as experts; rather, when senior black officials appear, it is often because they have gotten into trouble in some way. Entman contends that the pattern of these stories allows viewers to assume that African Americans are poor, uneducated, strident, demanding, selfish, and corrupt, citing as evidence studies that indicate that Americans who get their news primarily from television are more likely to express racist opinions about African Americans than are those who do not.

Finally, any discussion of the media and affirmative action should also include a brief discussion of the role of the Federal Communications Commission (FCC). Historically, the Supreme Court has upheld the FCC's broad authority to regulate the airwaves. Additionally, as the Supreme Court pointed out in *Red Lion Broadcasting Co. v. FCC*, 395 U.S. 367 (1969), "because of the scarcity of electromagnetic frequencies, the Government is permitted to put restraints on licensees in favor of others whose views should be expressed on this unique medium." Thus this broad FCC authority allows the FCC to require that as a condition to receiving a federal broadcast license, broadcasters agree not to engage in discrimination against designated minorities and are required to maintain affirmative action plans. The broad FCC authority recognized in *Red Lion* was also used by the U.S. Supreme Court in *Metro Broadcasting, Inc. v. FCC*, 497 U.S. 547 (1990), to uphold the FCC's authority to utilize preferences in ensuring that federal broadcast licenses are issued to minority-owned enterprises. This affirmative action program was designed to increase diversity of viewpoints on the airwaves. The FCC's minority hiring programs were addressed in two opinions of the U.S. Court of Appeals for the District of Columbia Circuit. In *Lutheran Church–Missouri Synod v. Federal Communications Commission*, 154 F.3d 487 (D.C. Cir. 1998), the District of Columbia Circuit Court of Appeals rejected the FCC's argument that "diversity of programming" was a compelling interest sufficient to withstand strict scrutiny for its licensing preference. Accordingly, the court declared the FCC's practice unconstitutional in the confines of that specific case. Similarly, in *DC/MD/DE Broadcasters Association v. FCC*, 253 F.3d 732 (D.C. Cir. 2001), the District of Columbia Circuit Court of Appeals held that the FCC's rule of promoting diversity through programming was also unconstitutional. The court reasoned that the outreach requirements of the rule did not survive strict scrutiny. The FCC continues to revise its affirmative action policies in an attempt to implement a plan that would satisfy strict scrutiny review.

Finally, as part of individual affirmative action plans, broadcasters agree to make good-faith efforts to recruit and hire minorities, as well as to bring their minority representation within their organization up to the proportional representation of those minority groups in the local community. Increased representation of minorities in the media may assist in resolving some of the issues noted earlier. New voices from different backgrounds and experiences and increasingly diverse perspectives may bring to the public's attention the nuances and depth of affirmative action issues and help dispel the notion that the debate is a black versus white issue. Moreover, if the media do tend to overreport negative news stories featuring African Americans, increased minority participation in the media may result in a correction of this trend.

See also African Americans; Federal Communications Commission; First Amendment; *Lutheran Church–Missouri Synod v. FCC*; *Metro Broadcasting, Inc. v. FCC*; Persons with Disabilities and Affirmative Action; Preferences; Proposition 209; Quotas; *Red Lion Broadcasting Co. v. FCC*; Veterans' Preferences; Washington Initiative 200.

FURTHER READING: Childs, Kelvin, 1998, "Media Affirmative Action Pact," *Editor and Publisher* 131, no. 32 (August 8): 11; Cook, Timothy E., 1998, *Governing with the News: The News Media as a Political Institution*, Chicago: University of Chicago Press; Diamond, Edwin, 1993, *Behind the Times: Inside the New York Times*, Chicago: University of Chicago Press; Entman, Robert S., and Andrew Rojecki, 2000, *The Black Image in the White Mind: Media and Race in America*, Chicago: University of Chicago Press; Gilens, Martin, 1999, *Why Americans Hate Welfare: Race, Media, and the Politics of Antipoverty Policy*, Chicago: University of Chicago Press; Leo, John, 1998, "Hold the 'Wrong' Story," *U.S. News and World Report* 125, no. 6 (August 10): 12; Lichter, Robert S., Stanley Rothman, and Linda S. Lichter, 1990, *The Media Elite: America's New Powerbroker*, New York: Hastings House; McGowan, William, 2001, *Coloring the News*, San Francisco: Encounter Books; Roach, Ronald, 1998, "More Rigorous Reporting Needed," *Black Issues in Higher Education* 15, no. 13 (August 20): 26–27; San Francisco State University Public Affairs, 1999, "The Affirmative Action Debate—Is the Media Getting It Right?" Press Release 99.

PAULETTE PATTERSON DILWORTH

Mend It, Don't End It

See Clinton, William Jefferson.

Merit Selections

The concept of merit selections refers to the selection of individuals for jobs, education, or other societal benefits based upon qualifications and meritorious characteristics. It is referred to as a theory of justice and fairness in the selection process. In theory, merit selections involve a social process entailing procedures, standards, and mechanisms that are fair in selecting candidates for limited available positions. Merit selection has even been equated to justice, equity, and democracy. Nevertheless, such processes result in outcomes that some consider unjust and unfair. Depending on the program at issue, there are contentions over what constitutes "merit" as a concept or what its attributes are in a wide range of disciplines and fields. Arguably in scholarly circles, merit selection is largely influenced by "biosocial factors" such as race, skin color, education, background, economic strength, religion, income, occupation, environment, social status, and so on.

However, merit selection is intended to enable individuals to compete for opportunities or positions on equal terms regardless of biosocial differences like social background, race, and early disadvantages or advantages. It is a social process based on who has the necessary ability and potential. However, ability and how it can be measured have raised a number of contentions between psychologists and other humanistic experts. Historically, the development of intelligence tests provided the answer to this question. Today, there is a reliance on either performance-based factors or standardized tests as the chief means of measuring merit and potential. Advocates of merit selection hold that the process can be a more effective instrument of social justice in pluralistic societies only if a level playing ground is prepared for all candidates to compete, such as a distribution of resources among all individuals by way of improvement in the social level and background of all individuals, the enhancement of the ability of individuals to participate in competitions despite economic difficulties, and improvement in the material standards and environment of all persons.

See also Level Playing Field; Meritocracy; Performance-Based Selections; Standardized Testing.

FURTHER READING: Nisbet, John, 1953, "Family Environment and Intelligence," *Eugenics Review* 45:31–42; Ottaway, A.K.C. 1966, *Education and Society: An Introduction to the Sociology of Education*, London: Routledge and Kegan Paul.

KINGSLEY UFUOMA OMOYIBO

Meritocracy

Meritocracy can be defined as the selection of persons based on open competition and merit. Meritocracy embodies the notion that only those who have the requisite skills and drive or desire to succeed should be elevated in society. It is therefore ironic that one of the first mechanisms that were introduced to prevent interference by politicians in the recruitment of public servants, the idea of merit-based selections, has now come under attack. Merit in the civil services of many countries was largely based on the implementation of general, standardized, nonpolitical entrance examinations. These examinations generally served two broad functions. First, candidates were selected on the basis of an impartial examination irrespective of their racial, class, or religious origins. Second, they allowed a large number of qualified persons to be selected to fill existing vacancies in the civil services.

To ensure neutrality and impartiality in the recruitment, selection, and promotion process, it was felt that all personnel decisions should be made by one agency or institution that was supposedly impartial, independent, and nonpolitical. In the United Kingdom, an agency referred to as the Civil Service Commission was established in 1855. It was set up specifically to prevent politicians from interfering in the recruitment of public servants and to prevent abuses in the system of personnel administration. Similarly, in the United States, the Civil Service Commission had its origin in the Pendleton Act of 1883 and was established for the purpose of eliminating preference, particularly with respect to political patronage, and to allow for the entry of qualified professionals into the civil service. It was thought that the maintenance of merit principles would ensure orderly, standardized, nonpolitical, and efficient personnel administration. Therefore, a reliance on the application of open competitive examinations for testing applicants for appointment to what were described as "competitive services" became the norm. These examinations were to be practical in character and as far as possible related to matters that fairly tested the relative capacity and fitness of the applicants (Quaintance 1980, 128). In the United States, the Civil Service Reform Act of 1978 reinforced the merit principle by insisting that selection and advancement in the federal service should be determined solely on the basis of relative ability, knowledge, and skills and after fair and open competition that assured that all applicants received an equal chance. This adherence to the merit principle was supported in many countries, so that today most government employees have been selected primarily on the basis of merit. This principle allowed many governments to obtain and retain qualified individuals for public service employment, while at the same time it tended to protect the integrity of the appointment process.

Yet increasingly public agencies are confronting the challenge for equal opportunity from a number of other subgroups (ethnic, religious, and gender groups, veterans, and the handicapped), and they are now expected to engage in fair employment practices that satisfy multiple objectives. Among their many objectives are concerns to avoid discriminatory treatment against any individual or group; to redress the effects of historical occupational exclusion; and to build a workforce that mirrors the society—in other words, to establish a more representative bureaucracy. However, in trying to adhere to the merit principle while at the same time trying to achieve a more representative type of bureaucracy, both private and public employers have recognized that they have become vulnerable to legal attacks by various groups.

One growing and important area of concern is that of "reverse discrimination." The concept of reverse discrimination is based on the argument that majority-group members are being illegally disadvantaged in employment opportunities because of affirmative action programs that were established to improve opportunities for traditionally underrepresented groups such as women and racial minorities. It is, therefore, ironic that the legal underpinnings for affirmative action programs also formed the basis for attacks upon them. For example, in the public sector, the primary justification for remedial employment policies came from Title VII of the Civil Rights Act of 1964 and the Equal Protection Clause of the Fourteenth Amendment to the Constitution of the United States. The basic contradiction in these provisions was that while both the statute and the constitutional amendment were recognized by the courts as grounds for affirmative action, both have also been ruled as constituting prohibitions against preferential employment by the U.S. Supreme Court.

See also Civil Rights Act of 1964; Civil Service Commission; Civil Service Reform Act of 1978; Darwinism; Equal Protection Clause; Fourteenth Amendment; Merit Selections; Reverse Discrimination; Standardized Testing; Title VII of the Civil Rights Act of 1964.

FURTHER READING: Coleman, Major G., 1999, "Merit, Cost and the Affirmative Action Policy Debate," *Review of Black Political Economy* 27, no. 1:99–128; Greene, Lawrence D., 1982, "Federal Merit Requirements: A Retrospective Look," *Public Personnel Management* 11, no. 1: 39–54; Gullet, Carlos Ray, 2000, "Reverse Discrimination and Remedial Affirmative Action in Employment," *Public Personnel Management* 29, no. 1 (spring): 107–119; Quaintance, Marilyn Koch, 1980, "The Impact of the Uniform Selection Guidelines on Public Merit Systems," *Public Personnel Management* 9, no. 3:125–133.

ANN MARIE BISSESSAR

Messer v. Meno, 130 F.3d 130 (5th Cir. 1997)

Messer v. Meno was a case in the U.S. Court of Appeals for the Fifth Circuit that held that diversity programs are not legal "absent a specific showing of prior discrimination." Phrased another way, the Fifth Circuit held that the diversity rationale as a justification for affirmative action programs is not a compelling governmental interest that would allow employers to discriminate or classify by race. The appellate court overturned a lower court decision that denied the plaintiff's claim. *Messer v. Meno* was one of a number of court cases from the 1990s that limited the scope of affirmative action programs on a regional basis and brought into question the future of affirmative action in the workplace. The *Messer* decision is analogous to the Fifth Circuit's decision in *Hopwood v. Texas*, 78 F.3d 932 (5th Cir. 1996), in the educational context. In *Hopwood*, a year earlier than Messer, the Fifth Circuit held that the diversity rationale was not a legitimate justification for affirmative action plans in higher education under the Fourteenth Amendment's Equal Protection Clause.

Karen Messer worked for the Texas Education Agency as the senior director of the Budget Management Division from 1978 to 1996, when she resigned. Messer claimed that affirmative action programs at the agency caused her to be passed over for promotion and underpaid and that she was retaliated against when she complained. Messer alleged that she was denied two promotions because one African American candidate was "reclassified" into a new position, and the other position was given to a white male. She also asserted that four senior directors, two African American females and two Hispanic males, performed comparable work to hers but were paid higher wages based solely on their affiliation with underrepresented groups. Messer specifically asserted that hiring, promotion, and salary decisions were based on race and gender instead of merit. During her employment, the agency was tasked by the state of Texas to pursue a "balanced" workforce that matched the general population. To achieve this goal, the state monitored hiring and promotion by compiling statistics and issuing monthly utilization reports that traced the diversity of the workplace in relation to the state's general population. However, since women comprised 60 percent of the agency's workforce, her superiors undertook steps to reduce the number of women employed. In addition, since minorities were underrepresented in some branches of the bureau, Messer claimed that she was discriminated against because of her race. In short, Messer asserted that she was doubly discriminated against because she was both female and Caucasian.

Messer filed a complaint with the Equal Employment Opportunity Commission (EEOC). After receiving notification from the EEOC that she had a right to sue, Messer filed suit against Lionel R. Meno, the former Texas commissioner of education during her tenure at the Education Agency, and against the Texas Education Agency. Her suit contended that the state had violated Title VII of the 1964 Civil Rights Act, which forbade discrimination based on "race, color, religion, sex, or national origin" in hiring, dismissal, promotion, and salary. She also sued under 42 U.S.C. §§ 1981 and 1982, which, among other things, forbade racial discrimination in contracts. Messer also asserted that the state violated the Equal Protection Clause of the Constitution. The defendants claimed that since the agency was considered a federal contractor, under Executive Order 11246 (September 24, 1965) they were required to put an affirmative action plan in place. Also, they contended that their affirmative action programs did not require any remedial action to address underrepresentation of men.

The original trial court, the U.S. District Court for the Western District of Texas (Austin Division), dismissed Messer's claims on July 8, 1996. One reason for the court's decision was that under law Messer had 180 days to file a complaint from the time of the discrimination. Messer did not file her complaint until 300 days after the incident. However, Messer contended that her complaint was part of ongoing Title VII violations. Furthermore, the trial court concluded that although the agency had used race and gender in employment decisions, there was no evidence that these were the exclusive factors in such decisions. On appeal, the Fifth Circuit overturned the part of the lower court's decision that held that "racial preferences are constitutional in the absence of remedial action." The appellate court held that consideration of race is unconstitutional without evidence of past discrimination and that "good intentions alone are not enough to sustain a supposedly benign racial classification."

See also Benign Discrimination; Civil Rights Act of 1964; Compelling Governmental Interest; Equal Employment Opportunity Commission; Equal Protection Clause; Executive Order 11246; Fourteenth Amendment; *Hopwood v. Texas*; Strict Scrutiny; Title VII of the Civil Rights Act of 1964.

FURTHER READING: Broadnax, Walter D., 2000, *Diversity and Affirmative Action in Public Service*, Boulder, CO: Westview.

TOM LANSFORD and SHARON MEYERS

Metro Broadcasting, Inc. v. FCC, 497 U.S. 547 (1990)

Metro Broadcasting, Inc. v. FCC was the U.S. Supreme Court case that dealt with minority licensing and preferences in the field of broadcast media. The Supreme Court's decision in this case ultimately held that the Federal Communications Commission's minority preference policies did not violate the Equal Protection Clause because they provided appropriate remedies for the victims of discrimination and were consistent with legitimate congressional objectives of program diversity. The case is the leading Supreme Court decision in the area of federal licensing and affirmative action.

The case constituted a challenge, based on the Equal Protection Clause, to the Federal Communications Commission's (FCC) minority preference policies. Congress, through the Communications Act of 1934, authorized the FCC to grant broadcast licenses based on "public convenience, interest, or necessity." Over the years, the FCC had attempted to encourage program diversity through other means. In the late 1960s, a commission found that television stations were not providing services to their minority audiences. The FCC itself conducted evaluations of the broadcast media's service to minority audiences in 1960 and 1971. In response, the FCC adopted equal employment opportunity requirements for station owners and new guidelines for licensees to devote a significant proportion of their programming to the concerns of minorities and ethnic groups.

In 1978, the FCC acknowledged that its policies had not increased the diversity of broadcast content and that the views of minorities had been inadequately represented. As a result, the FCC adopted the two minority ownership policies challenged before the Supreme Court. The purpose of these policies was to increase the number of broadcast licenses (over the air by television and radio) held by members of minority groups and minority-owned businesses. The goal of the policies was to provide a diversity of opinions, especially those of minorities, on the broadcast spectrum. One policy established by the FCC, challenged by Metro Broadcasting, gave minority applicants for broadcast licenses preference if all other relevant factors were equal. In *Metro*, the FCC had awarded an applicant, Rainbow Broadcasting, "substantial credit" on its review of license applications because the applicant was 90 percent Hispanic owned.

The second policy, challenged by Shurberg Broadcasting of Hartford, allowed broadcasters who were in danger of losing their licenses to sell their stations to FCC-approved minority buyers before the FCC held a revocation hearing. In *Astroline Communications v. Shurberg Broadcasting*, which the Supreme Court decided with *Metro Broadcasting*, Shurberg challenged the "distress sale" of a television station by Faith Center to Astroline, a minority-owned firm. Shurberg had asked the commission to deny the distress sale and to set up a comparative hearing to examine its application for a television station.

Justice William Brennan delivered the opinion of the Court, in which Byron White, Thurgood Marshall, Harry Blackman, and John Paul Stevens joined. A sharply divided Supreme Court (5–4) held that the FCC's minority preferences did not violate the Equal Protection Clause because they provided appropriate remedies for the victims of discrimination and were consistent with legitimate congressional objectives of program diversity. As the majority noted, it was of overriding significance in these cases that the FCC's minority ownership programs had been specifically approved—indeed, mandated—by Congress. The Court found that a nexus existed between minority ownership and diversity of viewpoint. The Court held that the availability of program diversity served the entire broadcast audience, not just the members of minority groups, and was an important governmental objective. The Court pointed out that minority groups constituted at least 20 percent of the U.S. population during the two decades leading up to its decision. However, in 1971, minorities owned 10 of the approximately 7,500 radio stations and none of the 1,000 television stations. The Court also noted that the FCC's minority preference policies did not unduly burden nonminorities. Describing the FCC's racial classification system as "benign," the Court's majority wrote:

> Benign race-conscious measures mandated by Congress—even if those measures are not "remedial" in the sense of being designed to compensate victims of past governmental or societal discrimination—are constitutionally permissible to the extent that they serve important governmental objectives within the power of Congress and are substantially related to the achievement of those objectives.

Stevens filed a concurring opinion. Sandra Day O'Connor filed a dissenting opinion, which Chief Justice William Rehnquist, Antonin Scalia, and Anthony Kennedy joined. Kennedy also filed a dissenting opinion, which Scalia joined.

In *Adarand Constructors, Inc. v. Peña*, 515 U.S. 200 (1995), the Court overruled *Metro* (the four dissenting justices in *Metro* being part of the majority in *Adarand*) by applying strict equal protection scrutiny to what amounted to racial preferences in the government business contracting area. In doing so, the Court eliminated the distinction between "invidious" classifications and "benign" classifications, deciding instead that all racial classifications must meet the strictures of the strict scrutiny standard.

See also Adarand Constructors, Inc. v. Peña; Benign Discrimination; Blackmun, Harry Andrew; Contracting and Affirmative Action; Equal Protection Clause; Fourteenth Amendment; Invidious Discrimination; Kennedy, Anthony McLeod; Licensing and Affirmative Action; Marshall, Thurgood; O'Connor, Sandra Day; *Red*

Lion Broadcasting Co. v. FCC; Rehnquist, William Hobbs; Scalia, Antonin; Stevens, John Paul; Strict Scrutiny; White, Byron Raymond.

FURTHER READING: Gahr, Evan, 1993, "FCC Preferences: Affirmative Action for the Wealthy," *Insight on the News* 9, no. 8 (February 22): 6–9; Rohde, Gregory Lewis, 2002, *Minority Broadcast Ownership*, New York: Novinka Books; Williams, Patricia, 1990, "*Metro Broadcasting, Inc. v. FCC*: Regrouping in Singular Times," *Harvard Law Review* 104:525–546.

JEFFREY KRAUS

Military and Affirmative Action

The U.S. armed forces have led the country throughout its history in regard to integration and desegregation, as well as the successful utilization of affirmative action plans. As a result of its desegregation and then affirmative action efforts, the military has been described as "one of the most integrated institutions in America" (*Amici Curiae* Brief 2003, 12). The U.S. military was the first major institution to desegregate after World War II pursuant to President Harry Truman's Executive Order 9981 in 1948. After several decades of difficulty with integration, minority participation in the chain of command and officer ranks has dramatically increased since the 1980s to include even an African American chairman of the Joint Chiefs of Staff in the 1990s, largely as a result of affirmative action. As one military leader was quoted as saying as part of the Clinton administration's 1995 *Review of Federal Affirmative Action Programs: Report to the President* (hereafter the Clinton report on affirmative action), "Doing affirmative action the right way is deadly serious for us—people's lives depend on it" (Department of Justice 1995, § 7.1). Proponents of affirmative action often point to the military as a kind of "social laboratory" in which affirmative action has been successful in improving true equality for all races and ethnicities in the ranks, promoting diversity, and serving as a model for how affirmative action programs might work throughout American society.

In 2003, a group of highly prominent former military leaders (including former secretaries of defense, chairmen of the Joint Chiefs of Staff, leading commanding generals in regions of the world, and generals and admirals who had served as superintendents of the service academies) submitted an amicus curiae (friend-of-the-court) brief to the Supreme Court in *Gratz v. Bollinger*, 123 S. Ct. 2411, 2003 U.S. LEXIS 4801 (2003), and *Grutter v. Bollinger*, 123 S. Ct. 2325, 2003 U.S. LEXIS 4800 (2003). In the brief, the group concluded that "a highly qualified, racially diverse officer corps educated and trained to command our nation's racially diverse enlisted ranks is essential to the military's ability to fulfill its principal mission to provide national security." The group of distinguished leaders also claimed that affirmative action in the military is indispensable to the operation of the military. The group argued that "at present, the military cannot achieve an officer corps that is both highly qualified and racially diverse unless the service academies and the ROTC use limited race-conscious recruiting and admissions policies." The group also strongly asserted that affirmative action must be utilized in the military, and "the military must be permitted to train and educate a diverse officer corps to further our compelling government interest in an effective military." Thus the compelling governmental interest in the continuation of affirmative action in the military is said to be nothing less than the national security of the United States (Amicus Curie Brief, 5).

The history of desegregation and integration of the armed forces goes back much further than Truman's executive order in 1948. In fact, the full and meritorious participation of minorities in the armed forces goes back to the very beginning of the American experience. During the Revolutionary War, it is reported that as many as 5,000 African Americans served in the Continental army and in state militias fighting to win independence from the British. There were also famous women such as Molly Pitcher and Margaret Corbin who served during the Revolution. During the Lewis and Clark expeditions of 1803–1805 (a military expedition), two of the expedition members were York, the black slave of Captain William Clark, and Sacagawea, a Shoshone Indian who, joining the expedition in midstride, is said to have single-handedly saved the expedition from destruction. During the Civil War, approximately 200,000 African Americans served in the Union army and navy by 1865. The rallying cry (and song) embodying this epic black struggle against the Confederacy was "We are coming, Father Abraham, with three hundred thousand more." During the Indian Wars of the 1870s, the Buffalo Cavalry (Tenth Cavalry) served with great distinction. During the Spanish-American War (1898), the black Tenth Cavalry led the charge to seize San Juan Hill, and Theodore Roosevelt and the much-praised "Rough Riders" "panted on foot up Kettle Hill, roughly six hundred yards from San Juan Hill, behind the 10th Cavalry" (Perret 1989, 286). "Black Jack" Pershing and his American Expeditionary Force included more than 200,000 black soldiers in its midst in World War I, and black troops served with valor in World War II. These are just a few examples of meritorious service by nonwhites in the military prior to the official legal desegregation of the armed forces in 1948.

Yet despite this strong history of service to the country in the U.S. armed forces, the black soldier returned to segregation, discrimination, and mistreatment at home in the United States. Due to strong lobbying by Eleanor Roosevelt, in World War II, President Franklin Roosevelt revised and made more just some of the rules pertaining to minorities in the military. However, he never ordered the full and complete integration of the armed forces. The order to integrate the military did not come until roughly three years after President Roosevelt's death, in the Truman administration. On July 26, 1948, President Truman issued Executive Order 9981, which commanded the integration of the armed forces. Initially, the military resisted Truman's order of integration; however, the Korean War (and the need for manpower) ultimately overcame the military's reluctance to integrate. By October 1954, military leadership announced that the integration of the last military unit was complete.

Even though the enlisted ranks were completely integrated, minorities were woefully underrepresented in the officer ranks during the 1960s and 1970s. Thus while minorities were overrepresented after Truman's integration order in the enlisted ranks, the officer corps still remained largely segregated. In 1962, for all branches of the armed forces, only 1.6 percent of the officer corps was African American. By 1973, the number of minority officers had risen only to 2.8 percent. This de facto segregation in the leadership of the military, in conjunction with the racial strife occurring at home in the United States during the 1960s and early 1970s, caused monumental problems in morale, unit cohesion, and chain-of-command communications and even diminished the fighting ability of the military. Furthermore, black soldiers in combat units in Vietnam "were taking 21 percent of the casualties" (Perret 1989, 526). Geoffrey Perret reports that "by 1970, black radicalism was hampering combat operations in the air force and navy. Army commanders were reluctant to issue weapons to black troops" (Perret 1989, 527). Fortunately, the military noted the deleterious effect of the lack of diversity, and "the military of the 1970s recognized that its race problem was so critical that it was on the verge of self-destruction." As the Clinton report on affirmative action pointed out, "racial conflict within the military during the Vietnam era was a blaring wakeup call to the fact that equal opportunity is absolutely indispensable to unit cohesion, and therefore critical to military effectiveness and our national security" (Department of Justice 1995, § 7.5.1).

Since the mid-1970s, the military has instituted aggressive programs not only to prevent discrimination, but also to actively promote equal opportunity and diversity. A 1995 Department of Defense Directive (DoD Directive 1350.2) has even described affirmative action programs as a "military necessity," essential to the nation's "combat readiness and mission accomplishments." Today, as a result, the military is considered one of the best-integrated institutions in the United States. According to the Department of Defense, as of March 2002, minority members in the military constituted almost 40 percent of the entire armed forces. In the Persian Gulf War against Iraq in 1990–1991, for example, approximately 30 percent of all army ground forces in the theater of operations were African American. As of March 2002, the specific breakdown of races in the military was as follows: 61.7 percent white; 21.7 percent African American; 9.6 percent Hispanic American; 4 percent Asian American; 1.2 percent Native American; and 1.8 percent who classified themselves as "others." While minorities are still underrepresented in the officer ranks, according to the Department of Defense, improvements have been made. The Department of Defense reported, again as of March 2002, that approximately 19 percent of the officer corps was minority, with approximately 8.8 percent being comprised of African Americans. The number of minority officers increased 6 percent in roughly seven years, from 13 percent in 1995 to 19 percent in 2002.

In terms of implementation, the Department of Defense gives general guidelines about affirmative action, and then implementation is up to each of the individual armed service branches (i.e., U.S. Air Force, Army, Navy, and Marine Corps). Although each service implements affirmative action in different ways, all military affirmative action plans address the following areas: recruiting and training, selection and promotion procedures, and management requirements and procedures. Recruiting and training in the affirmative action context involve using race-conscious efforts to recruit new officers through race-conscious admissions program or through other programs meant to bolster minority representation. For example, as a way to gain admittance to the U.S. Military Academy at West Point, New York, candidates who are not academically qualified may opt to attend the U.S. Military Academy preparatory school in New Jersey first. According to the 1995 Clinton report on affirmative action, "The enrollees are disproportionately but not exclusively minority" (Department of Justice 1995, § 7.2). The preparatory schools of the various services have been described as "truly an affirmative action success story" (*Amici Curiae* Brief 2003, 24). The service academies have also historically created targets and goals for the number of minority students in each regular entering class. As Colin Powell remarked in a 1996 speech in Bowie, Maryland, "In the military, we . . . used affirmative action to reach out to those who were qualified, but who were often overlooked or ignored as a result of indifference or inertia" (Powell, S9312).

The services also incorporate affirmative action in the selection and promotion of officers. According to the 1995 Clinton report on affirmative action, army promotion board members are instructed to be sensitive to "past personal or institutional discrimination" and to encourage the promotion of minorities and women (as a goal) at a rate at least equal to the promotion rate of the general applicant pool. To use an example from the Clinton report on affirmative action, "If, for example, a selection board has a general guideline that 44 percent of eligible lieutenant colonels be promoted to colonel, the flexible goal is that promotions of minorities and women be at that same rate" (Department of Justice 1995, § 7.2). However, according to the Clinton report, the notion of promotion of minorities and females at the same rate as the general population is not a quota, but rather only a "flexible goal," as evidenced by the fact that "the minority and women promotion rates often diverge considerably from the goal." This specific usage of affirmative action in promotions by the army was subsequently held in 2002 to be a violation of employment laws by a federal judge, and the army has discontinued its specific usage at centralized selection and promotion boards.

Last, in terms of implementation, the Department of Defense (as well as the subordinate services) employs management devices to ensure the successful implementation of affirmative action. First, the Department of Defense requires each service to maintain an affirmative action plan, as well as to review the affirmative action plan periodically. The Department of Defense also requires that each service annually complete a "Military Equal Opportunity Assessment," which delineates whether the various affirmative action/equal opportunity goals were met and identifies existing problems to be worked on during the next year. Finally, as a management tool, the Department of Defense trains personnel on equal opportunity and affirmative action, as well as conducting studies and surveys on race relations and integration in the armed forces.

As explained at the beginning of this entry, proponents of affirmative action often point to the military as a kind of "social laboratory" in which affirmative action has been successful in improving true equality for all races and ethnicities in the ranks, promoting diversity, and serving as a model for how affirmative action programs might work in the rest of American society. Phrased another way, if affirmative action works in the military, advocates of affirmative action ask, why should it not work in corporate America, the legal profession, or higher education? However, those critical of affirmative action might argue in response that the military is a unique institution, and its lesson of desegregation and integration is not transferable to the rest of American society. Specifically, the following factors make the military unique: First, the military is a disciplined system, and the military hierarchy can force change from the top down, with little internal opposition. Those who are opposed to these integration measures will simply exit the military, but certainly will not protest the orders from above in a visible fashion.

Second, the military is largely an autonomous institution and has discretion to train, promote, and handle personnel in a manner much different than in the civilian sector. Even the Supreme Court has deferred to military judgment in many cases that have reached the high court, refusing to substitute judicial judgment for that of the military leadership that is in the best position to make decisions dealing with the operation of the military and the security of the nation. Finally, the military is a closed system, which means that competition for promotions is from a closed group, and the military can eventually promote minorities to a higher level simply by recruiting more minorities into the service. Regardless of the applicability of the "lessons" of the military to the civilian sector, the military's success in desegregation and its improvement of diversity and minority representation in all ranks of the armed forces are worthy of study.

See also Affirmative Action Plan/Program; African Americans; Clinton, William Jefferson; Compelling Governmental Interest; *Gratz v. Bollinger/Grutter v. Bollinger*; Powell, Colin; Roosevelt, Eleanor; Roosevelt, Franklin Delano; Truman, Harry.

FURTHER READING: *Amici Curiae* Brief, 2003, *Gratz/Grutter v. Bollinger*, No. 02-241, 02-516, Washington, DC: Supreme Court of the United States; Clymer, A., 2003, "Service Academies Defend Use of Race in Their Admissions Policies," *New York Times*, January 28, A17; Cook, Holly O'Grady, 1996, "Affirmative Action: Should the Army Mend It or End It?" *Military Law Review* 151 (Winter): 113–201; Department of Justice, 1995, *Review of Federal Affirmative Action Programs: Report to the President*, Washington, DC: U.S. Government Printing Office; Killian, Lewis M., 1999, "Generals, the Talented Tenth, and Affirmative Action," *Society* 36, no. 6 (September): 33–46; Perret, Geoffrey, 1989, *A Country Made by War: From the Revolution to Vietnam: The Story of America's Rise to Power*, New York: Random House; Powell, Colin, 1996, "Commencement Address," Bowie State University, reprinted in 142 Cong. Rec. S9311–S9312; Schmidt, Peter, 2003, "Hundreds of Groups Back University of Michigan on Affirmative Action," *Chronicle of Higher Education*, February 28, A25; Tucker, Neely, 2002, "Judge Halts an Army Policy on Promotion; Ruling Says Gender, Race Overly Stressed," *Washington Post*, March 5, A01.

JAMES A. BECKMAN

Minor v. Happersett, 88 U.S. (21 Wall.) 162 (1874)

The U.S. Supreme Court decision in *Minor v. Happersett* was significant in the historical struggle for suffrage rights and equality for women. At the time of the *Minor* case, the political status of women in American life was one of exclusion and discrimination. Men and women were acknowledged as residing in wholly separate spheres—men in the public space of work and civic participation and women in the private sphere of home and family. Furthermore, these separate spheres were specifically sanctioned by the Supreme Court in *Bradwell v. Illinois*, 83 U.S. (16 Wall.) 130 (1873), in which the Supreme Court refused to allow Myra Bradwell the chance to secure a license to practice law. As the Court wrote, "[T]he natural and proper timidity and delicacy which belongs to the female sex evidently unfits it for many occupations of civil life." The notion that women were "unfit" for employment in the public sphere was joined by the idea that women were also ill equipped for the civic responsibilities of voting and political participation. Finally, as illustrated by such infamous cases as *Bradwell* and *Minor*, the Court offered women scant protections under the Fourteenth Amendment, much like the Court's treatment of minorities during the same time period. Today, the case is relevant in understanding the historical background to discrimination and the historical interpretation of the Fourteenth Amendment by the Supreme Court.

Virginia Minor, one of the leaders of the National Woman Suffrage Association (NWSA), attempted to vote in the general presidential election on October 15, 1872, in St. Louis, Missouri. The NWSA was an organization that opposed the passage of the Fifteenth Amendment, which in 1870 had extended voting rights to African American men. Minor and others in the NWSA criticized the Fifteenth Amendment for excluding women from those same franchise privileges. The NWSA believed that the word "sex" should have been added to the amendment, which read, "The right of citizens of the United States to vote shall not be denied or abridged by the United States or by any State on account of race, color, or previous condition of servitude." This rift in feminist ideology led to a break with the American Woman Suffrage Association (AWSA) headed by Lucy Stone, a more conservative group that supported the passage of the Fifteenth Amendment. The AWSA believed that when the abolitionist movement completed its work on slavery, the demand for women's rights could then be addressed. Virginia Minor and other suffrage activists, including Elizabeth Cady Stanton and Susan B. Anthony, had little patience for the AWSA's incremental strategy.

When Virginia Minor did try to vote in St. Louis, Reese Happersett, a voter registrar in the state, refused to permit her registration on the basis of a Missouri law that barred women from voter participation. Minor, together with her husband Francis, who was an attorney, filed suit claiming that the denial to register and vote violated Minor's rights as a citizen under the Privileges and Immunities Clause of the Fourteenth Amendment. This use of the Fourteenth Amendment was a new legal tactic in the struggle for equality. (Francis Minor actually filed the appeal for his wife because women could not sue in their own name.) As the Minors insisted, those state constitutions that excluded women from the franchise on account of sex were in violation of the "spirit and letter of the federal Constitution." The suffrage guarantee, argued the Minors, was one of those compelling and fundamental privileges of citizenship.

Elizabeth Cady Stanton and Susan B. Anthony published the Minors' interpretation of the Fourteenth Amendment's Privileges and Immunities Clause in their newspaper, the *Revolution*. Stanton and Anthony also used the Minors' thesis to encourage a pattern of nationwide disobedience on voting and called for women to demand the right to vote in opposition to state laws. Women in more than ten states followed this defiant call to exercise the franchise, but most were repudiated and turned away from the polls. Anthony did manage to cast a ballot in Rochester, New York, for Ulysses Grant as president. Several weeks after casting her vote, though, Anthony was arrested, tried, and convicted for voter fraud.

Although Virginia Minor was not arrested and did not face criminal charges as Anthony had, the Minors sought an appeal in Missouri courts for the state's refusal to allow women the right to vote. When the Missouri Supreme Court decided against them on the grounds that states were free to "limit the right of suffrage to male inhabitants," the Minors took their appeal to the U.S. Supreme Court. The *Minor* case was actually one of three test cases brought by the NWSA that received a plenary review (full consideration) by the Court.

In October 1874, a unanimous Court upheld the lower court's ruling. Chief Justice Morrison R. Waite wrote that suffrage was not a guarantee of citizenship under the Fourteenth Amendment and that individual states' enfranchisement of males only was constitutionally permissible. This defeat at the hands of the federal judiciary forced the suffragists to move the battle to achieve affirmative voting rights to a different arena. Women's rights advocates now focused on initiatives in individual states that would revise state constitutions to allow women the opportunity to vote. Their efforts were partially successful in the West when Wyoming, Colorado, Utah, and Idaho all began to permit universal suffrage. Suffragists also sought a separate amendment to the U.S. Constitution that was eventually submitted to Congress in 1878. Although the Nineteenth Amendment giving all women the unfettered right to vote was not ratified until 1920, the *Minor* case was clearly a milestone in the protracted and contentious quest for political equality.

See also Anthony, Susan Brownell; *Bradwell v. Illinois*; Equal Protection Clause; Fifteenth Amendment; Fourteenth Amendment; Gender Norms; Nineteenth Amendment; Stanton, Elizabeth Cady; Stereotypes, Gender; Suffrage Movement.

FURTHER READING: McGlen, Nancy E., Karen O'Connor, Laura van Assendelft, and Wendy Gunther-Canada, 2002, *Women, Politics, and American Society*, 3d ed., New York: Longman.

JANIS JUDSON

Minority

See Census Classifications, Ethnic and Racial.

Minority Business Enterprises

See Disadvantaged Business Enterprises.

Minority Professionals and Affirmative Action

One of the chief justifications put forth for affirmative action programs in higher education is to increase the number of minority professionals. That is, one of the chief goals of the use of racial preferences in affirmative action programs is to create opportunities for advanced training of minority-group members who would otherwise not be able to achieve professional occupational status. As more minority members enter the professional occupation ranks, these individuals theoretically serve as role models for others who aspire to achieve the same professional occupational standing. Additionally, encouraging minority-group members to become professionals may also allow for the spread of professional services (e.g., medicine and law) into traditionally underrepresented areas in society. According to this theory, a minority member who came from an inner-city urban environment might be more inclined to return to this environment to practice his or her profession, thereby ensuring the greater distribution of professional services in underrepresented areas.

Broadly speaking, a profession is an occupation that requires unique and advanced education and training. Professionals include such occupations as lawyers, doctors, college professors, school administrators, accountants, and engineers. Even after years of affirmative action programs during the 1970s and 1980s, minority-group members as a whole are grossly underrepresented in a wide array of professions. For example, while African Americans constitute approximately 12.5 percent of the U.S. population, they constitute less than 5 percent of the total number of physicians, engineers, and lawyers in the country.

As advanced education and training are prerequisites to entrance into the professional ranks, any discussion of affirmative action and minority professionals should begin with a review of affirmative action programs in higher education. After all, there can be no minority professionals until there are minorities in higher education. The use of affirmative action in higher education was in a state of flux in the 1990s. Several federal circuit courts of appeals were in disagreement with each other over the permissible use of race and ethnicity in admissions decisions. The consideration of race and ethnicity was prohibited in the Fifth and Eleventh Circuits by the decisions in *Hopwood v. Texas*, 78 F.3d 932 (5th Cir. 1996), and *Johnson v. Board of Regents of the University of Georgia*, 263 F.3d 1234 (11th Cir. 2001), respectively. The Sixth Circuit, however, in *Grutter v. Bollinger*, 288 F.3d 732 (6th Cir. 2002), affirmed the use of affirmative action programs in the law school admissions context. The Ninth Circuit also affirmed the use of affirmative action programs in the law school admissions context in *Smith v. University of Washington Law School*, 233 F.3d 1188 (9th Cir. 2000), holding that the government has a compelling interest in promoting racial diversity on campus.

However, after twenty-five years of silence from the high court on the issue of the constitutionality of affirmative action in higher education, the Supreme Court in 2003 broke its silence and offered guidance in using race as a factor in the higher-education admissions process in the cases *Gratz v. Bollinger*, 123 S. Ct. 2411, 2003 U.S. LEXIS 4801 (2003), and *Grutter v. Bollinger*, 123 S. Ct. 2325, 2003 U.S. LEXIS 4800 (2003). In these two landmark cases, the Court sanctioned the use of affirmative action in higher education for at least twenty-five years following the date of its decisions in *Gratz* and *Grutter* in June 2003. The *Grutter* decision is especially germane to the topic of minority professionals. Historically, many proponents of race-based affirmative action argued that affirmative action was needed, among other reasons, to increase minority participation in professional occupations. By increasing minority participation in law schools and medical schools, for example, a diverse cadre of practitioners develops to serve the needs of a diverse society. In reaffirming diversity in higher education as a compelling governmental interest, the Supreme Court upheld the University of Michigan Law School's affirmative action plan (*Grutter* case) and acknowledged the particular need for diversity in graduate and professional schools. Thus in the *Grutter* decision, the Court held that affirmative action was still needed to ensure minority professionals. In the majority decision, Justice O'Connor noted that "universities, and in particular, law schools, represent the training ground for a large number of our Nation's leaders," and "[i]n order to cultivate a set of leaders with legitimacy in the eyes of the citizenry, it is necessary that the path to leadership be visibly open to talented and qualified individuals of every race and ethnicity."

However, the Court also warned in the *Gratz* decision that fixed racial quotas and mechanized formulas (which have the effect of operating as a quota) would not be tolerated. In the *Gratz* decision, the Court struck down the University of Michigan's undergraduate admissions affirmative plan that gave extra points for race alone. The plan struck down by the Court had awarded African American,

Hispanic, and Native American applicants an automatic 20 points on a 150-point undergraduate admissions scale. This, the Court held, was akin to racial quotas, which violate the Fourteenth Amendment.

While the *Gratz* and *Grutter* decisions clarify the conflicting federal circuit court views on affirmative action, they do nothing to change state initiatives that have banned or prohibited the use of affirmative action in higher education. Specifically, several states, such as California, Texas, Washington, and Florida, have disavowed the use of racial preferences in college and university admissions decisions through state initiatives, referenda, or the normal state legislative process. In the states of California (Proposition 209) and Washington (Washington Initiative 200), there have been ballot initiatives in which the general population voted to end the use of race and ethnicity in higher education. Texas and Florida have done away with their respective affirmative action programs and have instituted percentage-plan approaches in the place of the old affirmative action plans.

In those places where affirmative action has been outlawed, institutions of higher education have taken alternative actions to encourage diversity. For example, the University of Texas took several steps to continue to recruit minority students. One of these was the creation by private individuals of the Texas Leaders Scholarship. Since this is a private foundation, it is legally permitted to use ethnicity in granting scholarships. These scholarships can be used to attract minority students since they will make higher education more affordable. In addition, the University of Texas began using essays in which students could describe how they overcame special forms of adversity. Some of these forms of adversity could include economic, racial, and ethnic discrimination. The university also created several new criteria to examine each applicant's social and economic background. These can include information on household income, parents' level of education, whether the applicant is the first in his or her family to attend college, whether the applicant's household speaks primarily English, and a description of the applicant's household or other responsibilities while attending high school. Finally, the university made personal interviews a larger part of the picture. From 1992 to 1998, the University of Texas ranked third among major law schools in the number of African Americans who were admitted.

In *The Shape of the River: Long-Term Consequences of Considering Race in College and University Admissions*, former Ivy League university presidents William Bowen and Derek Bok found that African Americans who entered elite institutions achieved notable success after graduation. For example, they earned advanced degrees at rates identical to those of their white classmates. When Bowen and Bok examined African American students and white students at the same institutions, they found that the African American students were slightly more likely than the white students to obtain professional degrees after graduation in areas such as law, business, and medicine. Further, Bowen and Bok found that African Americans were more active in civic and community organizations than their white classmates. Bowen and Bok began to accumulate information in 1994. Their studies were based on students who entered college in the years 1976 and 1989. Bowen and Bok examined students from twenty-eight different institutions. Most if not all of these individuals were in some form or fashion beneficiaries of affirmative action. If it were not for affirmative action, they would not for the most part have had the opportunity to attend these elite institutions and go on, in many cases, to professional careers.

See also African Americans; *Gratz v. Bollinger/Grutter v. Bollinger; Hopwood v. Texas; Johnson v. Board of Regents of the University of Georgia;* One Florida Initiative; Percentage Plans; Preferences; Proposition 209; Role Model Theory; *The Shape of the River;* Washington Initiative 200.

FURTHER READING: Bowen, William, and Derek Bok, 1998, *The Shape of the River: Long-Term Consequences of Considering Race in College and University Admissions,* Princeton, NJ: Princeton University Press; Carter, Stephen L., 1991, *Reflections of an Affirmative Action Baby,* New York: Basic Books; Darity, William, Jr., "Give Affirmative Action Time to Act;" *Chronicle of Higher Education,* December 1.

MICHAEL K. LEE

Mississippi University for Women v. Hogan, 458 U.S. 718 (1982)

The constitutionality of single-sex education and equal educational opportunity was directly addressed in the Supreme Court decision in *Mississippi University for Women v. Hogan* in 1982. In 1884, the Mississippi Industrial Institute and College for the Education of White Girls of the State of Mississippi was created, and it held the distinction of being the oldest state-supported all-female college in the nation. The institution changed its name in 1974 to Mississippi University for Women (MUW) and, consistent with the original school charter, only enrolled women. The university established a School of Nursing in 1971, and this case originated when Joe Hogan, a registered male nurse, applied for admission to the MUW School of Nursing baccalaureate program in 1979. Hogan, who was academically qualified, was denied admission solely on the basis of sex. He subsequently filed an action in the U.S. District Court for the Northern District of Mississippi arguing that the single-sex policy violated his Fourteenth Amendment guarantee of equal protection of the laws. The district court denied Hogan's request for injunctive relief. When the Court of Appeals for the Fifth Circuit reversed the lower court and ordered Hogan's admission to the school, MUW sought an appeal to the U.S. Supreme Court.

In *Mississippi University for Women v. Hogan,* the Supreme Court was faced with the unique challenge of weighing the commitment to single-sex education for women against a claim of a denial of equal opportunity for men. The Court began its majority opinion by recalling how the Equal Protection Clause of the Fourteenth Amendment prohibits discrimination on the basis of sex or gender. The Court further explained that the state carried the responsibility of "showing an exceedingly persuasive justification" for the classification—in this case, why MUW should maintain its single-sex admission of women only. As in other cases of gender classifications, the state must follow the middle-tier standard of proving how the particular classification (women only) served important governmental objectives and was substantially related to the achievement of these objectives. One of the historical objectives that Mississippi intended with the single-sex policy was to provide women with a variety of choices as to the type of institution they would be able to attend. In effect, the Mississippi policy at MUW amounted to educational affirmative action for women.

In writing for the Court majority, Justice Sandra Day O'Connor argued that while the Mississippi classification discriminated against men rather than women, that fact alone did not automatically mean the program was unconstitutional, and such a program might be constitutional if the state had sufficiently strong reasons for the program's discrimination. The single-sex admission policy, the Court argued, was discrimination nonetheless. The Court also rejected the argument that women lacked opportunities to receive training in the area of nursing and therefore insisted that the state objective of providing additional choices to women was not substantially related to the policy of single-sex admissions. Since women were not denied opportunities in nursing in the first place, it made no sense for the state to provide a compensatory program for them on that basis. The Court further insisted that by limiting the School of Nursing to women, Mississippi was actually reinforcing old and archaic stereotypes that nursing was uniquely a field for women only. The Court proposed that this educational affirmative action would prove to be a self-fulfilling prophecy that only women were meant for the vocation of nursing.

The Court also concluded that the presence of men in a nursing school environment would not impact the teaching patterns of instructors and would not adversely affect the performance of female students and finally asserted that co-education would not result in men dominating the classroom experience. The totality of these observational arguments, along with the constitutional claim that the gender-based classification was not defensible, led the Court to conclude that the policy of excluding males from MUW's School of Nursing violated the Equal Protection Clause of the Fourteenth Amendment. In ruling against the state, the Court upheld the decision of the court of appeals that had decided in Hogan's favor.

The Court, however, was clearly not unanimous in its decision. Several dissents were written by Justices Warren Burger, Harry Blackmun, Lewis Powell, and William Rehnquist, and each of these dissents sharply criticized the Court's majority opinion in invalidating MUW's single-sex admissions policy. Justice Blackmun chastised the majority for ruling only on the basis of providing convenience for Hogan, who could have applied for admission to baccalaureate programs in nursing in Jackson and Hattiesburg, Mississippi. The other justices agreed that the Court's sweeping decision that states were prohibited from providing single-sex institutions for higher learning was precipitated by the appeal of one man "who represents no class and whose primary concern is personal convenience." Finally, the dissenters spoke to the benefits of single-sex education as a form of educational diversity and as a time-honored tradition of America's democratic system. The decision in *Mississippi University for Women v. Hogan* was clearly a controversial one for the substantive issues of educational affirmative action, equal opportunity, and the requirements of the Fourteenth Amendment's Equal Protection Clause.

See also Blackmun, Harry Andrew; Burger Court and Affirmative Action; Equal Protection Clause; Fourteenth Amendment; Gender-Based Affirmative Action; Intermediate Scrutiny; O'Connor, Sandra Day; Powell, Lewis Franklin, Jr.; Rehnquist, William Hobbs; Strict Scrutiny; Warren Court and Affirmative Action.

FURTHER READING: Lee, Allison Herron, 1997, "Title IX, Equal Protection, and the Richter Scale: Will VMI's Vibrations Topple Single-Sex Education?" *Texas Journal of Women and*

Law 7 (fall): 37–88; Safterstein, Bennett L., 1993, "Revisiting *Plessy* at the Virginia Military Institute: Reconciling Single-Sex Education with Equal Protection," *University of Pittsburgh Law Review* 54 (winter): 637–683.

JANIS JUDSON

Model Minorities (Stereotyping Asian Americans)

Repeatedly depicted by the American press as a "model" minority, Asian Americans are stereotyped first and perhaps foremost as a monolithic body, both racially and culturally, even though there are in fact many distinct groups of Asian Americans (as well as individual Asian Americans) who do not conform to the stereotype. Historically, some of the more negative kinds of stereotyping of Asians include their depiction as inarticulate individuals who have only excelled at the laundry business. They are sometimes depicted as duplicitous and untrustworthy—the inscrutable Asian mind, capable of committing and predisposed to commit infamous acts such as Pearl Harbor. It was the belief in this particular stereotype that caused the massive racial segregation of individuals of Japanese descent in internment camps during World War II and led to the infamous Supreme Court decision in *Korematsu v. United States*, 323 U.S. 214 (1944). Even more generally, Asians have been depicted at times as less than completely human. During the Vietnam War, for example, General George Patton III asserted that Asians do not value human life, at least in the most elevated sense that westerners value it. Others noted with distaste that the North Vietnamese soldier ate rat meat. The more recent and predominant stereotype of Asian Americans, however, is quite positive, at least on its face.

This new stereotype is based on the model of the Horatio Alger myth that America is a land of unlimited opportunity for an industrious, self-reliant entrepreneur (or, in the case of Asian Americans, a group of individual entrepreneurs). Reputedly, Asian Americans are the most successful ethnic minority economically and socially because they work hard, they are self-reliant, and they recognize that education is key to upward mobility in America. Supporters of the model minority image point to the fact that the median family income of Asian Americans is higher than that of any other ethnic minority and, more pointedly, even higher than that of white American families. Critics of the model minority image assert that the facts about Asian Americans are at best half-truths.

The median family income of many Asian American families is in fact higher than that of white American families. Critics point out, however, that this is due primarily to the additional fact that typically there is more than one and sometimes there are more than two wage earners in an Asian American family. The individual income of the typical Asian American is in fact not higher than that of individual white wage earners or even significantly higher than that of individual members of other ethnic minorities, such as blacks and Hispanics. Additionally, the majority of Asian Americans live in major urban areas in three states, Hawaii, New York, and California, where incomes as well as living costs are significantly higher than in most other areas of the country. In short, the generalization that Asian Americans are more successful than other minorities is suspect. This is especially true for the more recent Asian American immigrants, who have come to America in greater and greater numbers from Southeast Asia.

Very few of the CEOs of major American companies are Asian Americans, and typically the Asian Americans who are CEOs own the company. There are also relatively few Asian Americans in positions of middle management except in companies owned by Asian Americans. Most new Asian American immigrants either open their own small businesses or labor in low-level, nonmanagement positions for low wages. It has been argued that the primary reason so many Asian American immigrants open their own businesses is that the management opportunities in traditional American, white-owned companies are not typically open to Asian Americans and other nonwhite immigrants.

Another aspect of the myth of the model minority is that Asian Americans place a premium on the value of education, so the children of Asian Americans excel in school. Many Asian Americans do in fact do well in school, especially in math and science, where the language difficulties of first-generation, nonnative Asian Americans are less pronounced. Asian Americans do have the highest high-school graduation rate of any ethnic minority, and a large percentage of Asian American graduates do go on to college. Such accomplishments are more typical of the children of more affluent groups of Asian Americans, especially Japanese and Chinese. The accomplishments of other groups of Asian Americans, especially more recent immigrants from Southeast Asia, are less impressive. The problems that nonnative-speaking Asian Americans encounter are rarely mentioned or even recognized.

Notably, there are very few Asian Americans serving in public office, especially at the state and national levels. There are relatively few Asian American legislators or judges. Nor do many Asian Americans draw on government to solve their problems, especially with respect to so-called entitlements, such as welfare. Asian Americans are less likely than other ethnic minorities to apply for welfare or even unemployment benefits. At least, this is one of the claims made by proponents of the idea that Asian Americans are the model minority. Reputedly, most Asian Americans are more willing to work than are other ethnic minorities, such as blacks and Hispanics, and they are less likely to look to government to solve their problems. This is what makes them a model minority: their self-reliance and their work ethic.

Arguably, Asian Americans are characterized monolithically as a model minority to deflect any and all criticism by other ethnic minorities with respect to racial discrimination. Blacks and Hispanics have in fact been far more vocal about racial discrimination. The white establishment, in turn, and the American press in particular, have lauded the material success of Asian Americans. Some critics of this characterization of a model minority, however, claim that the model minority is in fact a myth, and that it is inaccurate as well as unfair to generalize about Asian Americans as if they were one, monolithic population. Moreover, the claims about the economic success of Asian Americans are at best half-truths. Typically, a stereotype of a racial or ethnic minority is employed to denigrate the minority. Arguably, in the case of Asian Americans, although the stereotype is on its face quite laudatory, the purpose of the stereotype is the same: to maintain a racial pecking order both politically and economically.

See also Asian Americans; *Korematsu v. United States*; Stereotyping and Minority Classes.

FURTHER READING: Archdeacon, Thomas J., 1983, *Becoming American: An Ethnic History*, New York: Macmillan; Daniels, Roger, 1988, *Asian America: Chinese and Japanese in the United States since 1850*, Seattle: University of Washington Press; Fong, Timothy, 1998, *The Contemporary Asian American Experience: Beyond the Model Minority*, Upper Saddle River, NJ: Prentice Hall; Hsia, Jayjia, 1988, *Asian Americans in Higher Education and at Work*, Hillsdale, NJ: Lawrence Erlbaum Associates; Lee, Stacey J., 1996, *Unraveling the "Model Minority" Stereotype: Listening to Asian American Youth*, New York: Teachers College Press; Liu, Eric, 1998, *The Accidental Asian: Notes of a Native Speaker*, New York: Random House; Takaki, Ronald, 1989, *Strangers from a Different Shore: A History of Asian Americans*, Boston: Little, Brown and Co.

MICHAEL D. QUIGLEY

Morrison, Toni (1931–   )

"As a black and a woman, I have had access to a range of emotions and perceptions that were unavailable to people who were neither" (Calwell, 1). This is the passionate voice of Toni Morrison, novelist, social critic, and winner of the Nobel Prize for literature in 1993, who writes with eloquence and power about the African American experience within a dominant white culture. Along with Cornel West, Henry Louis Gates Jr., and Derrick Bell, Morrison signed a national advertisement in 1996 advocating the continuation of affirmative action in the United States. Toni Morrison, born in 1931, received a B.A. from Howard University in 1953 and an M.A. from Cornell University and has taught fiction and writing at numerous institutions, including Howard University, the State University of New York at Albany, and Yale University.

In 1987, Morrison was named the Robert F. Goheen Professor in the Council of the Humanities at Princeton University—the first black woman writer to hold a chair at an Ivy League university. In addition to the Nobel Prize, Morrison won the Pulitzer Prize in 1988 for *Beloved*, the National Book Critics Circle Award and the American Academy and Institute of Arts and Letters Award in 1997 for *Song of Solomon*, and the Robert F. Kennedy Award in 1988. From *The Bluest Eye* (1970), which portrayed a victimized black teenager who dreams of looking white, to *Beloved* (1987), which chronicled the story of a runaway slave who must kill her own daughter to spare her a life of slavery, to *Jazz* (1992), an account of violence in Harlem, Toni Morrison has depicted the struggle that black Americans face in a world where they are almost always relegated to the "lowest level of the racial hierarchy." Her other works of fiction—*Sula* (1973), *Song of Solomon* (1977), *Tar Baby* (1981), *Paradise* (1998), and the play *Dreaming Emmett*—are all poignant narratives of how race, sex, and class discrimination impact the lives and voices of its victims.

Morrison's many works of nonfiction also address how racial identity is defined and shaped by the dominant culture. Morrison wrote *Playing in the Dark: Whiteness and the Literary Imagination* (1992); she edited a collection of works for *Race-ing Justice, En-gendering Power: Essays on Anita Hill, Clarence Thomas, and the Construction of Social Reality* (1992) and another anthology called *Birth of a Nation'hood: Gaze, Script, and Spectacle in the O.J. Simpson Case* (1997). In these accounts, Morrison details the complex ways in which race and racism continue to "infect" American culture and the various ways in which African Americans are affected by this insidious racism. In an interview, Morrison commented, "There is nothing of any consequence in education, in the economy, in city planning, in social policy that does not concern black people," and certainly affirmative action is one such policy that will remain a topic of contemporary urgency (Angelo, 121). Morrison's eloquent prose and her analyses of contemporary issues make her one of the most important social critics of our time. She remains a powerful voice in the advocacy of affirmative action on the national stage.

See also African Americans; Bell, Derrick A., Jr.; Double Consciousness; Gates, Henry Louis, Jr., Racism; West, Cornel.

FURTHER READING: Angelo, Bonnie, 1989, "The Pain of Being Black: An Interview with Toni Morrison," *Time*, May 22, 120–123; Caldwell, Gail, 1993, "Morrison Awarded Nobel Writer's 'Visionary Force' Cited," *Boston Globe*, October 8, 1; Morrison, Toni, 1993, "On the Backs of Blacks," *Time*, December 2, 10; Rhodes, Lisa Renee, 2000, *Toni Morrison: Great American Writer*, New York: Franklin Watts.

JANIS JUDSON

Morton v. Mancari, 417 U.S. 535 (1974)

In *Morton v. Mancari*, the U.S. Supreme Court held that certain kinds of congressionally mandated employment preferences for Native Americans do not constitute invalid racial classifications because the preference is given to persons holding the political status of being members of federally recognized tribes rather than to persons who are racially or ethnically Indian. According to the Court, employment preferences for Native Americans contained in the Indian Reorganization Act of 1934 were not a racial classification and therefore did not run afoul of the Fifth Amendment (and the implied "equal protection" clause the Court says is implicit in the Fifth Amendment). The classification was instead based on political status.

The Indian Reorganization Act of 1934 (IRA or Wheeler-Howard Act) created an employment preference within the Bureau of Indian Affairs (BIA) for "Indians," defined as individuals who are enrolled members of federally recognized tribes who possess at least one-quarter Indian blood quantum. In 1972, the commissioner of Indian affairs issued a directive revising this policy to give preference to Indians not only in hiring but also in job promotions. A district court invalidated the rule on the grounds that it violated the Equal Employment Opportunity Act Amendments of 1972 as well as the Fifth Amendment to the Constitution, which prohibit the federal government from engaging in racial discrimination. The Supreme Court, in a unanimous opinion by Justice Harry Blackmun, reversed the lower court's decision.

The respondents had brought a class-action suit in the District of New Mexico, alleging that the Indian preference policy was an invalid form of racial discrimination. The respondents were a group of non-Indian BIA employees who now faced a significantly more difficult challenge in getting promoted. They argued that the policy violated the Fifth Amendment and that the provisions of the IRA creating the preference had been revoked by implication by the 1972 Equal Employment Opportunity Act Amendments, which prohibited racial discrimination in hiring by the federal government. The petitioner was Rogers Morton, secretary of the interior under Presidents Richard Nixon and Gerald Ford. He argued that the policy was constitutional because it was not a racial classification.

The Court ruled in favor of the government. The Court held that the status of "Indian" is political rather than racial. According to the Court, because the preference was rationally related to furthering the government's goal of increasing tribal self-governance, the policy was valid. The Court discussed the history of this practice at some length. The federal government had engaged in the practice of preferring to employ Indians in the administration of Indian affairs since as early as 1824. The IRA simply renewed this preference and codified it. The 1972 directive from the commissioner of Indian affairs simply extended this practice as part of the broader self-determination policy pursued by the Nixon administration. Congress had not revoked the relevant provisions of the IRA because those provisions were extended later the same year.

Some commentators have argued that the Court's analysis is somewhat disingenuous. The preference did have a clear racial component: an applicant had to have a certain quantum of Indian blood in addition to being an enrolled member. Furthermore, BIA commissioner John Collier's 1934 comments on this provision indicate that he may have intended that each tribe would ultimately provide the people whom the BIA would employ to administer programs and trust assets for that tribe. Nonetheless, even alongside the Nixon administration's self-determination policy toward Indian tribes, there were no provisions for tribes to actually be administered by their own members as a part of the employment preference policy. Although the Supreme Court has not overruled *Mancari*, it and lower federal courts have had trouble squaring that decision with its later decisions on affirmative action (e.g., *Adarand Constructors, Inc. v. Peña*, 515 U.S. 200 [1995]), given the partially racial nature of the classification.

The distinction drawn in *Mancari* that makes this employment preference different from others is the question of Native American tribal sovereignty and congressional plenary power over Indian affairs. During the colonial era and into the nineteenth century, Indian tribes were considered to have a degree of sovereignty, although the extent of that sovereignty has often been a source of conflict. The core of this sovereignty includes the right for tribes to govern their internal affairs. Given that many of the internal affairs of tribes are in fact controlled by the Bureau of Indian Affairs through its administration of trust property and federal programs on behalf of the Native Americans, Commissioner Collier felt that an important component of this sovereignty was control or at least influence over decisions made at the BIA. The Nixon administration's extension of this employment preference was part of a broader program of reversing the termination policies of the 1950s and reinvigorating tribal sovereignty.

Employment preferences are not limited to the BIA, but are practiced in a number of other federal programs intended to aid Indians or administer Indian affairs. The Indian Health Service, the Bureau of Land Management, and the military, among other agencies, all have policies of giving preference in employment and contracts to Native Americans on projects performed on or around reservations or other tribal lands. Many of these policies come from the Indian Self-Determination and Education Assistance Act.

While affirmative action programs have been eliminated in nearly every case that has come before the Supreme Court, *Mancari* stands alone as case law in favor of a particular kind of affirmative action. In addition to the sovereignty argument for the employment preference policy, this unusual case may be possible because of the recognition granted by the Court to Congress's plenary power over Indian affairs. The plenary power doctrine gives Congress immense freedom in designing Indian policy. As a consequence, the Court allows Congress to provide and revoke rights based in tribal sovereignty such as the one at issue here with relatively little intervention.

While *Mancari* has not been overruled, the strong statement at its core has been weakened. In recent years, the Court has begun to encroach on tribal sovereignty where it meets nontribal communities. There have been decisions restricting the jurisdiction of tribal courts and enforcing due process standards that had previously existed and have not been imposed by Congress. In *Rice v. Cayetano*, 528 U.S. 495 (2000), the Court struck down as racial discrimination a voting restriction in Hawaii that only allowed Native Hawaiians to vote for the board members of the Office of Hawaiian Affairs, the state body that administers Native Hawaiian lands. While this decision did not overturn *Mancari* because it was decided on the basis of the Fifteenth Amendment right to vote, the Court explicitly declined to follow *Mancari*.

See also Adarand Constructors, Inc. v. Peña; Blackmun, Harry Andrew; Equal Employment Opportunity Act of 1972; Fifteenth Amendment; Fifth Amendment; Ford, Gerald Rudolph; Indian; Native Americans; Native Hawaiians; Nixon, Richard Milhous; One-Drop Rule; Preferences; *Rice v. Cayetano*.

FURTHER READING: *Morton v. Mancari*, 417 U.S. 535 (1974); Frank Shockey, 2001, " 'Invidious' American Indian Tribal Sovereignty: *Morton v. Mancari* contra *Adarand Constructors, Inc. v. Peña, Rice v. Cayetano*, and Other Recent Cases," *American Indian Law Review* 25:275–313.

RACHEL BOWEN

Mott, Lucretia Coffin (1793–1880)

Lucretia Mott, a notable abolitionist of the nineteenth century, is known for her contributions to the antislavery and women's rights movements in America. She is also known for her eloquent speeches against slavery. She formed the Philadelphia Female Anti-Slavery Society in 1833 after being denied membership in the all-male American Anti-Slavery Society. When the American Anti-Slavery Society relinquished its ban on women, Mott became an active member on the national level, as well as serving on the executive committee of the Pennsylvania chapter of the organization.

In 1840, she was selected to be the delegate to the World Anti-Slavery Conference in London, England. She and her husband, James Mott, sailed for England on May 5, 1840, in what would be her only trip abroad. On June 12, she and the five other American women delegates, as well as all the British women delegates, were denied seating at the conference, because of their sex. Lucretia Mott met her fellow American abolitionist Elizabeth Cady Stanton, and they were relegated to a gallery where they could only view the proceedings of the World Anti-Slavery Conference, but not participate in it. They both were shaken by the irony that they were being discriminated against because of their sex while trying to eradicate prejudicial and discriminatory practices and policies that were based on race. They vowed that from that moment forth they would not only campaign against slavery, but also promote the rights of women. They discussed the need for a national convention at which the rights of women could be discussed. It took eight years before their vision became a reality, but on July 19, 1848, the Seneca Falls Convention was held for just that purpose. At this convention, Lucretia's husband, James Mott, presided. The Declaration of Sentiments demanding equal rights for women was written, mostly by Mott and Stanton, and Lucretia Mott was the first to sign it. It intentionally paralleled the Declaration of Independence, stating "We hold these truths to be self-evident, that all men and women are created equal."

Mott was a key organizer of the women's rights convention held in Rochester, New York, in 1850 at the Unitarian Church. In that same year, she published a book titled *Discourse on Women*, which covered the American and western European restrictions on women. She worked with other antislavery leaders, including William Lloyd Garrison, Lucy Stone, and Frederick Douglass. After the Civil War, she continued to advocate for the rights of African Americans, and in 1864 she was instrumental in the founding of Swarthmore College.

Suffragists continued to struggle with the dual commitment of abolishing slavery and fortifying the rights of women. This dualism of purpose posed a threat of division that Mott, among others, wished to avoid. To that end, the American Equal Rights Association was founded in 1866 to work for the rights of both former slaves and women in America. Lucretia Mott was the president of this organization, with Susan B. Anthony acting as secretary and Elizabeth Cady Stanton taking on the position of vice president. Feminists within the organization, however, were outraged when women's voting rights were not included in the Fifteenth Amendment. The National Woman Suffrage Association was formed in 1869 by Susan B. Anthony and Elizabeth Cady Stanton, claiming many former members of the American Equal Rights Association, including Lucretia Mott.

Lucretia Coffin Mott was born on January 3, 1793, into a Quaker community in the seaport town of Nantucket, Massachusetts. At age thirteen, she was sent to Poughkeepsie, New York, to attend a Quaker boarding school named Nine Partners, which was run by the Society of Friends. From 1808 to 1810, she served as an assistant teacher at this school. It was here that she began her interest in women's rights after learning that male employees earned twice as much as female employees. It was also at this school that she met fellow teacher James Mott. He, too, was active in opposing the slave trade, and they married in 1811. During this time, her family moved to Philadelphia, which became Mott's home for the rest of her life. Mott had six children between 1812 and 1828, with one child dying at age five and the five other children surviving into adulthood. Lucretia and James Mott refused to use cotton cloth, cane sugar, or any other goods that were produced by slave labor. They organized "free stores" throughout Philadelphia that sold only those products that were manufactured or produced by nonslave labor. They often hid runaway slaves in their home and were threatened with physical violence. In 1818, she began speaking at Quaker meetings and in 1821 became a minister in the Philadelphia Society of Friends. She spoke out against the clergy who proclaimed and preached that women were created as inferior creatures to men.

Lucretia Mott remained a feminist and antislavery nonviolent activist throughout her life. She was active in the women's right movement into her seventies. At age eighty-five, she delivered her last public speech on the thirtieth anniversary of the Seneca Falls convention in Rochester. She died on November 11, 1880, following her husband, who had died twelve years earlier.

See also Abolitionists; Anthony, Susan Brownell; Declaration of Sentiments; Douglass, Frederick; Seneca Falls Convention; Stanton, Elizabeth Cady; Stone, Lucy; Suffrage Movement.

FURTHER READING: Gurko, Miriam, 1974, *The Ladies of Seneca Falls: The Birth of the Woman's Rights Movement,* New York: Schocken Books; Hymowitz, Carol, and Michaele Weissman, 1978, *A History of Women in America,* New York: Bantam Books; Lunardini, Christine, 1994, *What Every American Should Know about Women's History,* Holbrook, MA: Bob Adams.

SHEILA BLUHM

Moynihan, Daniel Patrick (1927–2003)

As politician, presidential advisor, intellectual, and author of the Moynihan Report, Daniel Patrick Moynihan helped mold the affirmative action debate during the 1960s and early 1970s. Politician, ambassador, senator, university professor, social scientist, and author are titles that describe Daniel Patrick Moynihan during the span of his lifetime. He contributed to society in several areas and served in the Kennedy, Johnson, and Nixon presidential administrations. His career was one of impressive successes, and he was viewed as a consummate intellectual with multiple books and articles published to respectable acclaim. Moynihan also was a professor at Harvard and Syracuse Universities and served for nearly twenty-five years in the U.S. Senate, representing the state of New York.

In 1963, he teamed up with Nathan Glazer to write *Beyond the Melting Pot,* a book that addressed problems facing ethnic groups in New York. Some of the many books he authored or coauthored are *Ethnicity and Experience* (1976), *Family and Nation* (1986), *Came the Revolution* (1988), *On the Law of Nations* (1990), *The South Americans* (1994), *Miles to Go* (1996), and *The American Secrecy* (1998). However, in 1965, the U.S. Department of Labor released by far the most controversial publication that Moynihan wrote as President Lyndon Johnson's assistant secretary of labor. The report was formally titled *The Negro Family: The Case for National Action,* but was more popularly known as the "Moynihan Report." The core of the report was that chronic poverty among urban African Americans could be traced to the absence of a strong nuclear family structure. Moynihan followed up the report with several policy recommendations such as more jobs programs and a family assistance plan to supplement earned income.

President Lyndon Johnson used the report to develop his landmark speech at graduation ceremonies in June 1965 at Howard University. In the speech, he acknowledged that African Americans indeed had made some progress in the past few years; however, more needed to be done. He stated that "we seek [for blacks] not just equality as a right and a theory but equality as a fact and equality as a result." Then he announced that there would be a White House conference to explore ways to attain this equality. Johnson's speech received widespread support from the civil rights community.

Despite the general support for Johnson's speech, there was a huge, vitriolic backlash from many African American leaders and academicians regarding the Moynihan Report. They rejected the basic premise of the Moynihan Report and believed that African Americans were not responsible for the breakdown of the black family and the resulting poverty. According to these skeptics, to focus on family instability, as the report did, was to divert attention away from the real villains, racism, job discrimination, insufficient enforcement of civil rights laws, and the lack of a national imperative to eradicate poverty. Critics of his report assailed Moynihan for "blaming the victim." Quietly, the administration retreated from further publicizing of the views regarding the black family. Moynihan left the U.S. Department of Labor to return to Harvard University. While he had been considered a liberal, it is widely believed that this incident led him to rethink some of his liberal assumptions. When the 1966 Coleman Report on Education was published, Moynihan seized upon it because it removed him further from his liberal policies. Liberals heretofore had believed that economic inequality between blacks and whites was the result of unequal access to educational opportunities, which ultimately determined life chances. The argument was that if government intervened with more money provided for minority education, then the economic gap between the races would close. The Coleman Report challenged these previously held beliefs. One of its most startling conclusions was that the most important factor affecting student achievement by race was family background and not the funding levels for schools in minority communities nor the school curricula. Moynihan welcomed this report.

After teaching at Harvard, Moynihan took a two-year leave of absence and returned to work in the Republican administration of Richard Nixon. He prepared a report for the president giving "a general assessment of the position of Negroes." He reported that blacks in America had made great economic and social progress despite unfavorable trends in crime and family instability. In the report, he used the term "benign neglect," referring to a recommendation that the administration step back from racial rhetoric. Again, as before, with the Moynihan Report, there was a groundswell of opposition to Moynihan and the Nixon administration. While the Nixon White House did not seem too concerned over the leak of this report to the *New York Times*, Moynihan believed that the term was unfairly taken out of context. He returned to Harvard, but upon President Nixon's reelection in 1972, he was appointed by the president to represent the United States as ambassador to India. On May 1975, Moynihan was given another appointment by a Republican president, Gerald Ford, as the U.S. representative to the United Nations. Generally, he believed that third-world nations and their interests were overshadowing the United States. He was a staunch supporter of Israel.

In 1976, he defeated the well-known feminist Bella Abzug in the Democratic primary for the U.S. Senate from New York. He was reelected three times. He chaired the Senate Finance Committee from 1993 to 1995. Moynihan ultimately served in the Senate until 2001. On domestic issues as a senator, Moynihan made sure that his New York constituents received their share of government spending. He worked to reform the tax system for low-income people and to preserve Social Security. He remained focused on the family, particularly illegitimacy and single mothers on welfare. Moynihan died at the age of seventy-six on March 26, 2003. Upon Moynihan's death, he left a conflicting record regarding his views on affirmative action. While he authored Moynihan Report and assisted President Johnson in Johnson's formulation of affirmative action, Moynihan also served in the Nixon administration where he suggested that the race problem in America could benefit from "benign neglect." Furthermore, in 1995, Moynihan intimated to then President Clinton that perhaps the idea of affirmative action had served its purposes in society. Moynihan remarked in 1995, "I think what began as an effort to redress the legitimate concerns and needs of African Americans has expanded to other things entirely unexpected" (Wiessler, A5).

See also Department of Labor; Glazer, Nathan; Johnson, Lyndon Baines; Kennedy, John Fitzgerald; Nixon, Richard Milhous.

FURTHER READING: Clymder, Adam, "Daniel Patrick Moynihan Is Dead; Senator from Academia Was 76," *New York Times*, March 27, A1; Hodgson, Godfrey, 2000, *The Gentleman from New York: Daniel Patrick Moynihan, a Biography*, Boston: Houghton Mifflin; Katzman, Robert, ed., 1998, *Daniel Patrick Moynihan: The Intellectual in Public Life*, Baltimore: Johns Hopkins University Press; Moynihan, Daniel Patrick, 1996, *Miles to Go: A Personal History of Social Policy*, Cambridge, MA: Harvard University Press; Skrentny, John David, 1996, *The Ironies of Affirmative Action*, Chicago: University of Chicago Press; Turner, Douglas, 2000, "Senator Unpredictable Summing Up a Career That Has Run Both Wide and Deep," *Buffalo News*, December 31, A1; Wiessler, Judy, 1995, "Armey Wants to End Affirmative Action," *Houston Chronicle*, February 27, A5.

BETTY NYANGONI

Multiculturalism

The contemporary migrant movements mean that almost all contemporary nations are multicultural. Multiculturalism can be defined as "a social-intellectual movement that promotes the value of diversity as a core principle and insists that all cultural groups be treated with respect and as equals" (Fowers and Richardson 1996, 609). These authors suggest that multiculturalism is "a moral movement that is intended to enhance the dignity, rights, and recognized worth of marginalized groups."

John Berry and his colleagues in Canada studied several attitudes related to multiculturalism. One set of studies examined the attitude of ethnic tolerance, defined as "one's willingness to accept individuals or groups that are culturally or racially different from oneself" (Berry and Kalin 1995, 306), concluding that "tolerant individuals show little differential preference for various groups" (Berry and Kalin 1995, 315). Another set of studies corresponded to the two-dimensional typology of orientations toward ethnic acculturation. They distinguished attitudes toward the maintenance of one's own ethnic traditions from attitudes toward interethnic contact and found that the latter support movement across group lines, creating the potential for positive intergroup relations.

In a 1984 article on the psychology of segregation and cross-cultural relations, John Berry has further argued that there are four different forms of interethnic relations in a multicultural society, depending on how members of distinct ethnic groups relate to their own ethnic identity and to members of the host society: integration (ethnic groups maintain their original cultural identity and at the same time want to interact with host community members), separation (ethnic groups maintain their original cultural identity and do not want relationships to members of the host society), assimilation (ethnic groups reject their original cultural identity and seek contact with members of the host society), and marginalization (ethnic groups reject both their original cultural identity and contact with members of the host society). It seems that integration is the most adaptive form of inter-ethnic relations, as it relates to the peaceful coexistence and harmonization of both the host society and individual ethnic groups.

Affirmative action programs are viewed as a means to achieve a multicultural society. Affirmative action programs are said to encourage integration of minority-group members into mainstream culture. Berry and Kalin (1995) have recommended the following set of strategies to achieve a multicultural society: first, facilitating intergroup contacts and socialization; second, creating common goals for both minority- and majority-group members in society, as intergroup conflict may decrease if groups and their members pursue a common goal; third, implementing integrative language policies; fourth, making one overriding identity (e.g., Americans, as opposed to Italian Americans, German Americans, African Americans, and so on), with the goal of uniting members of different groups under a common identity; fifth, avoiding extremes of wealth and poverty between different groups; and sixth, enhancing perceptions of procedural justice and educational resources.

See also Assimilation Theory; Integration; Pluralism; Segregation.

FURTHER READING: Berry, John W., 1984, "Cultural Relations in Plural Societies: Alternatives to Segregation and Their Socio-Psychological Implications," in *Groups in Contact: The Psychology of Desegregation,* edited by Norman Miller and Marilynn B. Brewer, New York: Academic Press; Berry, John W., and Rudolph Kalin, 1995, "Multicultural and Ethnic Attitudes in Canada: An Overview of the 1991 National Survey," *Canadian Journal of Behavioral Science* 27:301–320; Fowers, Blaine J., and Frank C. Richardson, 1996, "Why Is Multiculturalism Good?" *American Psychologist* 51:609–621.

MARIA JOSE SOTELO

Multiple-Jeopardy Hypothesis

The multiple-jeopardy hypothesis contends that older African Americans, as well as other minorities, are doubly jeopardized relative to their white counterparts. A lifetime of economic and racial discrimination has resulted in adverse living conditions in later life for many minorities. In particular, older African Americans' lower economic status is at least partly due to their disadvantaged position in the labor force over the years. A lifetime of discrimination in higher education and the job market has kept them from jobs that offer higher pay and benefits, both at the time of employment and during retirement.

Researchers have also looked at older women using the double-jeopardy hypothesis. Their argument is that since gender and age are significant sources of inequality in our society, the cumulative effects of their interaction cannot be ignored. Older women experience double jeopardy because they are likely to experience discrimination both because they are female and because they are old. In fact, older women's economic vulnerability in later life is largely due to the fact that women are largely concentrated in low-paying jobs that offer no or few benefits, and from which they often take time off to care for their families. In old age, this means that nearly 75 percent of the elderly whose incomes are below the poverty line and depend on Supplemental Security Income (SSI) to survive are female. For older women of color, the experience is that of triple or multiple jeopardy. For instance, the median income of African American women over sixty-five is 66 percent of that of their white counterparts.

The implications of the double- or multiple-jeopardy hypothesis are closely related to the controversies surrounding affirmative action. Do gender and racial/ethnic differences support arguments for policies and programs that advocate differential treatment? Many argue that the differences are so significant that they require policies and programs that directly address these issues.

See also African Americans; Gender Stratification; Gendered Racism; Glass Ceilings.

FURTHER READING: Jackson, J.J., 1971, "Negro Aged: Toward Needed Research in Social Gerontology," *Gerontologist*, 11:52–57; National Council on Aging, 1971, *Triple Jeopardy: Myth or Reality?* Washington, DC: National Council on Aging; National Urban League, 1964, *Double Jeopardy: The Older Negro in America Today*, New York: National Urban League.

PAULINA X. RUF

Multiracialism

Affirmative action and a host of other programs depend upon racial classifications for their implementation. However, the U.S. population is increasingly multiracial. It is estimated that between 75 and 90 percent of African Americans have some white ancestry. The large majority of people in the United States are the product of intermixture. Thus the concept of multiracialism reveals the problems inherent in racial classification schemes. Where to draw the boundaries between races is arbitrary and is tied to access to power and privilege. Most people are of mixed ancestry, yet many seem unfamiliar with their heritage.

Historically, racially mixed people have been defined as mixed throughout the world, except in the United States. Throughout the 1980s and 1990s, a growing grassroots movement fought for recognition of mixed-race identities, arguing for the creation of multiracial categories or the option to check multiple categories on the census and other governmental forms. These organizations have argued that it is offensive and inaccurate for multiracial people to have to select one racial or ethnic identity. The 2000 census was the first to allow individuals to check more than one box in describing their race, and nearly 7 million people chose to do so.

U.S. racial classifications have assumed that groups are racially pure; however, widespread intermixture has occurred throughout history. Miscegenation between blacks and whites began at the same time as slavery, and defining who was white and who was not became a concern. As early as the early 1700s, the one-drop rule, defining anyone with a drop of black blood as black, was accepted in parts of the South. In this way, slave masters could coerce slave women and reproduce a source of free labor without worrying about the children having any claim to their property. In the first decades of the twentieth century, the one-drop rule became increasingly accepted across the nation. For white Americans, this rule was essential to maintain segregation and white supremacy. For black Americans, on the other hand, this rule contributed to greater unity and sense of identity in dealing with increasing racism and inequality. While laws against interracial marriage were struck down by the Supreme Court in 1967, the one-drop rule has remained largely entrenched.

The definitions of race and multiracial people have been intertwined with historical and political imperatives, and so there is little attempt by the government to define children who are the product of mixtures between nonwhite groups. The primary concern has been with protecting white purity. Yet racial purity is a myth, and the color lines are blurring further with each generation.

See also Bureau of the Census; Census Classifications, Ethnic and Racial; One-Drop Rule; Racial Privacy Initiative.

FURTHER READING: Ferber, Abby L., 1998, *White Man Falling: Race, Gender, and White Supremacy*, Lanham, MD: Rowman and Littlefield; Spickard, Paul R., 1992, *Mixed Blood: Intermarriage and Ethnic Identity in Twentieth-Century America*, Madison: University of Wisconsin Press; Zack, Naomi, 1993, *Race and Mixed Race*, Philadelphia: Temple University Press; Zack, Naomi, ed., 1995, *American Mixed Race: The Culture of Microdiversity*, Lanham, MD: Rowman and Littlefield.

ABBY L. FERBER

Murray, Charles

See The Bell Curve.

Myths and Misconceptions of Affirmative Action

See Affirmative Action, Myths and Misconceptions of.

NAACP Legal Defense and Educational Fund

See National Association for the Advancement of Colored People.

Narrowly Tailored Affirmative Action Plans

The term "narrowly tailored affirmative action plans," in essence, means that an affirmative action practice using race can only be instituted in a specific workplace, not generalized to other work sites or places, and can be used to adversely affect only those persons necessary to achieve a particular goal to remedy discrimination. If the program is not narrowly tailored, it runs the risk of failing judicial scrutiny under the levels of scrutiny the courts employ in interpreting the plan in conjunction with the Equal Protection Clause of the Fourteenth Amendment.

Affirmative action policies are designed to remove the past and continuing effects of discrimination against constitutionally protected groups of people, who historically have been the victims of racially invidious practices. These policies take the form of plans and programs covering a wide range of remedies, but all designed to eliminate discrimination primarily in the workplace and in public education. In the past, these have included everything from public advertisements for jobs to preferential treatment and hiring of workers based upon their race or gender. Preferential hiring has created a great deal of controversy in the public and private sectors because women and persons of color have been able to obtain jobs and positions over equally or better-qualified whites in some instances. This has led to charges of "reverse discrimination" and "reverse racism." These charges became part of President Ronald Reagan's rhetoric in attacking all affirmative action programs as discriminatory in nature.

Affirmative action plans developed as the result of Title VI and Title VII of the 1964 Civil Rights Act. Title VI authorizes the federal government to cut off federal funding to educational institutions and other agencies that discriminate on the basis of race. Title VI, along with Title IV of the 1964 Civil Rights Act, empowers the U.S. attorney general to investigate complaints of discrimination in educational institutions and prosecute those entities that continue to practice racial segregation. Specifically, Title VI covers the nineteen state systems of public colleges and universities that operated separate-but-equal educational institutions prior to the monumental case *Brown v. Board of Education*, 347 U.S. 483 (1954). Title VI is considered the cousin of Title VII. Title VII addresses employment discrimination based upon race, color, religion, sex, or national origin and allows the courts to order affirmative action programs to remedy the effects of past discrimination in employment. As a result, numerical goals, recruitment of persons of color, and job-related testing became valid instruments to remedy past discrimination.

Related to Title VI and Title VII, Executive Order 11242 stipulates that institutions of higher education must take affirmative action to increase the employment of women and people of color in work areas in which there is underutilization of this segment of the workforce. Similarly, Executive Order 11246 mandates that government contractors not engage in discriminatory practices and that such contractors set affirmative action goals and timetables.

The Supreme Court has generally been tolerant of affirmative action programs that were implemented by state and local governments or when they were court ordered and instituted preferential hiring and promotion policies to remedy the effects of past discriminatory practices, but in *Regents of the University of California v. Bakke*, 438 U.S. 265 (1978), the Court made an important distinction between goals and quotas, ruling the latter unconstitutional. Such plans, nevertheless, had to meet the test of "strict scrutiny." That is, such plans had to show a "compelling governmental interest" acceptable in meeting the constitutional restriction on racial classifications. Strict scrutiny also meant that such programs had to be "narrowly tailored" to meet the specific discriminatory practice. Narrowly tailored meant that affirmative action programs and practices could not be generalized to other companies or state and local governments.

The strict scrutiny test involving narrowly tailored plans was operationalized in *City of Richmond v. J.A. Croson Co.*, 488 U.S. 469 (1989), in which the U.S. Supreme Court struck down Richmond, Virginia's set-aside program because the city had no data, such as a disparity study, showing systemic discrimination against minorities. Because minority businesses had received less than 1 percent of city contracts, it was assumed that racial discrimination existed, and an arbitrary figure of 30 percent was arrived at as the right percentage of contracts that should go to minority vendors. The Court found that the plan at issue was clearly not narrowly tailored as the city employed no study to verify the existence of racial disparities in contracting or to consider the impact on nonminority vendors. Furthermore, the city arbitrarily selected a very high set-aside percentage, again without any evidence of the actual race disparities (if any).

See also Affirmative Action Plan/Program; *Brown v. Board of Education*; *City of Richmond v. J.A. Croson Co.*; Civil Rights Act of 1964; Compelling Governmental Interest; Discrimination; Education and Affirmative Action; Employment (Private) and Affirmative Action; Employment (Public) and Affirmative Action; Equal Protection Clause; Executive Order 11246; Fourteenth Amendment; Invidious Discrimination; Preferences; Quotas; Reagan, Ronald; *Regents of the University of California v. Bakke*; Reverse Discrimination; Strict Scrutiny; Title VI of the Civil Rights Act of 1964; Title VII of the Civil Rights Act of 1964.

FURTHER READING: Eastland, Terry, 1996, *Ending Affirmative Action: The Case for Colorblind Justice*, New York: Basic Books; *Regents of the University of California v. Bakke*, 438 U.S. 265 (1978); Rice, Mitchell, 1991, "Government Set-Asides, Minority Business Enterprises, and the Supreme Court," *Public Administration Review* 51, no. 2:114–122; Sullivan, Harold J., 2001, *Civil Rights and Liberties: Provocative Questions and Evolving Answers*, Upper Saddle River, NJ: Prentice Hall; Williams, John B., 1997, *Race Discrimination in Higher Education: Interpreting Federal Civil Rights Enforcement, 1964–1996*, Westport, CT: Praeger.

MFANYA D. TRYMAN

National Association for the Advancement of Colored People

The National Association for the Advancement of Colored People (NAACP) was founded in 1909 by a group of multiracial individuals who believed in the struggle for equality of black people and men and women of all races. While the organization spent much of its existence fighting for basic civil rights, today the group is a lobbying and protest group on issues that impact the African American community. The group today describes itself on its web page as "premier advocates for social justice and equal opportunity in their communities." The organization strongly supports affirmative action initiatives and programs, as illustrated by the amicus curiae (friend-of-the-court) brief filed by the NAACP on behalf of the University of Michigan's affirmative action program in *Gratz v. Bollinger*, 123 S. Ct. 2411, 2003 U.S. LEXIS 4801 (2003), and *Grutter v. Bollinger*, 123 S. Ct. 2325, 2003 U.S. LEXIS 4800 (2003). The NAACP lobbies for affirmative action and protests against individuals who are spearheading campaigns to end affirmative action. For example, in 2000, the NAACP mobilized to help combat Ward Connerly's proposal to have a ballot initiative in Florida similar to Proposition 209 in California.

The cofounders of the NAACP in 1909 were W.E.B. Du Bois, Henry Moscowitz, Oswald Garrison Villard, and William English Walling, as well as Mary White Ovington and Ida Wells-Barnett, the two women in the founding group. The NAACP has a long history of fighting against injustices and particularly of fighting for greater African American representation in areas of education on various levels. It also fought against other injustices early in its inception, for example, inflammatory media such as the silent film *Birth of a Nation*, the practice of lynching, and Ku Klux Klan attacks against blacks, especially in the southern states. The NAACP, and more particularly the NAACP Legal Defense and Educational Fund, headed the battle to desegregate the schools in the South during the 1930s to the 1950s. The culmination of their work came with the landmark case *Brown v. Board of Education*, 347 U.S. 483 (1954). Thurgood Marshall, the lead counsel in the *Brown* case and in charge of the NAACP Legal Defense and Educational Fund at the time of *Brown*, was later named the first African American to serve on the U.S. Supreme Court.

Another triumphant moment in the civil rights movement was the Montgomery bus boycott that lasted nearly a year in Alabama. Rosa Parks, an active member and officer in the Montgomery branch of the NAACP at the time, refused to move from a bus seat that was designated for whites only. She was arrested, and this act of protest became one of the important and symbolic moments in the civil rights movement and the catalyst for many later protests. Another historical event that was spearheaded by NAACP members in the NAACP youth council branch oc-

People marching with signs protesting segregation in education at the college and secondary school levels. Courtesy of Library of Congress.

curred when a group of students from North Carolina A&T State University ignited a series of sit-ins in which they refused to leave their seats at a segregated lunch counter in Greensboro, North Carolina. This and subsequent protests led to a series of sit-in cases that culminated in Supreme Court decisions ordering desegregation. For example, during the 1963 term of the Supreme Court alone, the Warren Court reviewed six sit-in cases: *Peterson v. Greenville*, 373 U.S. 244, *Avent v. North Carolina*, 373 U.S. 375, *Gober v. Birmingham*, 373 U.S. 374, *Lombard v. Louisiana*, 373 U.S. 267, *Shuttlesworth v. Birmingham*, 373 U.S. 262, and *Griffin v. Maryland*, 373 U.S. 920. The NAACP was also important in registering black voters in the South. After the Voting Rights Act of 1965 was passed, the NAACP registered more than 80,000 new voters in the South.

In regard to affirmative action, the NAACP supports candidates who are favorable to race-conscious programs and vigorously lobbies for the continuation of affirmative action. The NAACP also launched the Economic Reciprocity Program in 1997, a program that encouraged blacks to start their own businesses and boycott organizations and companies that did not have a fair representation of people of color in their organizations and institutions. Since that time, the NAACP has launched many boycotts and has threatened boycotts against organizations that have either discriminated against people of color or do not have a fair number of minorities from the various racial/ethnic groups. The president of the organization since 1996 has been Kweisi Mfume. Mfume, along with the NAACP, supported the University of Michigan case that has special considerations for those who have historically been underrepresented within the United States for many years in higher education and schooling.

See also African Americans; *Brown v. Board of Education;* Civil Rights Movement; Connerly, Ward; Du Bois, William Edward Burghardt; *Gratz v. Bollinger/Grutter v. Bollinger;* Marshall, Thurgood; Proposition 209.

FURTHER READING: Kellogg, Charles Flint, 1973, *NAACP: A History of the National Association for the Advancement of Colored People,* Baltimore, MD: Johns Hopkins University Press; NAACP, web site: http://www.naacp.org.

NICOLE M. STEPHENS

National Education Association

A leading organization on education in America, the National Education Association (NEA) was founded in 1857 in Philadelphia under the original name of the National Teachers' Association. The National Education Association is a nonprofit volunteer-based organization that is supported at the national, state, and local levels mainly by public schools, public educational institutions, public colleges and universities, and other state-supported educational affiliates. Today, the NEA has more than 2.7 million members, and its headquarters is located in Washington, D.C. NEA members are active in numerous activities on the local, state, and national levels, including professional workshops, raising funds for scholarships, lobbying legislators to help support the many needs of public school education, and working with and promoting projects that will help public school educators. Other activities include ongoing dialogue with politicians to protect academic freedom and rights of employees. The NEA has been a strong supporter of race- and gender-conscious affirmative action programs in education and was one of the sixty organizations that filed amicus curiae (friend-of-the-court) briefs defending the University of Michigan's affirmative action program in *Gratz v. Bollinger,* 123 S. Ct. 2411, 2003 U.S. LEXIS 4801 (2003), and *Grutter v. Bollinger,* 123 S. Ct. 2325, 2003 U.S. LEXIS 4800 (2003). The NEA also filed an amicus brief in favor of affirmative action in the famous case *Regents of the University of California v. Bakke,* 438 U.S. 265 (1978).

The NEA is deeply rooted in civil rights activities. Robert Campbell, a black man born in Jamaica who also taught in Philadelphia, was one of the founding members of the NEA. Two women were signers of the first NEA (formerly NTA) constitution, H.D. Conrad and A.W. Beecher, both teachers from Dayton, Ohio. The NEA formally admitted women into the organization in 1866. Booker T. Washington, founder of Tuskegee Institute, was the keynote speaker at the 1884 and 1904 NEA Conventions. The NEA created a department devoted to women in 1908 and endorsed the women's suffrage movement in 1912. The NEA also inspired the formation of other teaching organizations, particularly for black educators. In 1861, black educators from Ohio formed the Ohio Colored Teachers' Association, the first recognized and organized group of black teachers.

See also Education and Affirmative Action; *Gratz v. Bollinger/Grutter v. Bollinger; Regents of the University of California v. Bakke;* Washington, Booker T.

FURTHER READING: National Education Association, web site: http://www.nea.org.

NICOLE M. STEPHENS

National Labor Relations Act of 1935 (Wagner Act)

The National Labor Relations Act of 1935, named after Senator Robert F. Wagner and popularly known as the Wagner Act, was legislation created during the New Deal aimed at establishing and protecting workers' rights. The New Deal is the collective name for President Franklin Delano Roosevelt's various programs of relief, recovery, and reform in the years from 1933 to 1939, aimed in general at solving the economic problems caused by the Great Depression of the 1930s. Wagner's purpose in introducing the National Labor Relations Act (NLRA) was to help protect trade unionists from their employers. More specifically, Wagner was aware of unfair practices engaged in by employers designed to keep workers economically weak by preventing collective bargaining and unionization. These practices were an outgrowth of the tense relationship between employers and employees that dated back to the earliest days of the nation. The term "affirmative action" also first appears in the labor context as part of the National Labor Relations Act of 1935, although not in the context in which it is used today. This legislation specified that employers should employ "affirmative action" to restore workers who were victims of discrimination to their prediscrimination employment status.

The history of employer-employee relations in the United States is one of ongoing struggle between relatively powerless employees and powerful employers. In colonial times, slavery and indentured servitude were legal, and any activity to establish a labor union for any class of workers was regarded in law as a "conspiracy" against the public good. Until the 1930s, the judicial branch of federal and state governments was primarily concerned with protecting employers, routinely issuing injunctions to prevent labor strikes or other efforts to collectively negotiate with employers. Post–World War I relations between employers and employees were especially hostile, and this climate prevailed until the Great Depression of the 1930s, motivating Congress to implement policies to effect more peaceful relations between labor and management. This is the context in which the NLRA was conceived and enacted into law. The act may thus be seen as essentially an effort to require employers to recognize workers' rights to bargain collectively and to unionize. The legal basis for the act was the argument that employers' refusal to recognize the right of workers to unionize and to bargain collectively adversely affected interstate commerce. The constitutional rationale for the act was the Commerce Clause of the U.S. Constitution, which empowers Congress to regulate commerce among the states. Notwithstanding the NLRA's broad sweep, it did not protect all workers. For example, agricultural workers and domestic servants, occupations more likely to be filled by members of minorities, were excluded from the act. Moreover, the act covered employers and employees in the private sector only, thus creating the need for legislation at the state level to articulate and protect the rights of such public employees as those who worked for state or local governments or public universities.

The most significant entitlements established by the Wagner Act were workers' rights to bargain collectively with employers over the terms of employment and to join unions of their choice without coercion or other interference from employers. The act also mandated that employers could not require workers to join company unions, and it prohibited employers from engaging in "unfair labor practices" such as interfering with employees in the selection of a union or coercing them in their rights to bargain collectively. The original act construed unfair labor practices as exclusive to employers, and only later with the passage of the Taft-Hartley Act in 1947 were labor unions made subject to unfair labor practices. The passage in 1959 of the Landrum-Griffin Act protected employees' union membership rights from such unfair practices by unions as misappropriation of union dues and collusion with employer management. The National Labor Relations Act also created the National Labor Relations Board (NLRB) to enforce its provisions.

Though the NLRA has no formal link to affirmative action, its role in generating and enforcing people's rights to self-determination in the workplace is at least indirectly related to affirmative action and other federal and state agencies and policies intended to establish a society of greater inclusion and equality. As noted, the history of employer-employee relations in the United States is a tale of conflict between powerful employers and relatively weak employees. Prior to the Wagner Act, employers were free to hire, interrogate, transfer, demote, discipline, and discharge employees for any reason whatsoever, including racial or ethnic bias. The NLRA's definitions of what count as unfair labor practices by employers anticipate in broad outline some of the more recent advances in equality and justice accomplished during the civil rights era. An obvious example is the Equal Employment Opportunity Commission (EEOC), which was created to enforce Title VII of the Civil Rights Act of 1964. Though the original mandate of the EEOC was to enforce equal opportunity in employment, it evolved from a reactive organization to stop discriminatory practices in employment to an advocacy agency intent on eradicating the continuing effects of past discrimination via such measures as minority employment recruitment plans. In this way, the National Labor Relations Act is of a piece with many initiatives, including affirmative action, to create a more just and humane society.

See also Civil Rights Act of 1964; Equal Employment Opportunity Commission; National Labor Relations Board; Roosevelt, Franklin Delano.

FURTHER READING: Anglim, Christopher Thomas, 1997, *Labor, Employment, and the Law: A Dictionary*, Santa Barbara, CA: ABC-CLIO; Irons, Peter H., 1982, *The New Deal Lawyers*, Princeton, NJ: Princeton University Press; Jasper, Margaret C., 2002, *Labor Law*, 2d ed., Dobbs Ferry, NY: Oceana Publications; The National Labor Relations Act of 1935 (the "Wagner Act"), web site: http://www.nlrb.gov/facts/html; Terkel, Studs, 1970, *Hard Times: An Oral History of the Great Depression*, New York: Pantheon Books.

PAUL M. HUGHES

National Labor Relations Board

As part of the depression New Deal legislation, the National Labor Relations Board (NLRB) was created by Congress in 1935 as an independent federal agency whose purpose was to administer the National Labor Relations Act (Wagner Act). The object of the Wagner Act was to function as the primary law governing relations between unions and employers in the private sector. That law ensures the right of employees to unionize and to bargain collectively with their employers if they so desire. The law applies, in general, to employees involved in interstate commerce, with the exception of airlines, railroads, agriculture, government, and several other professions. Politically, the Wagner Act was viewed as the key national labor policy for guaranteeing free choice and encouraging collective bargaining as a means of maintaining industrial peace at a time of great tension in the United States between labor and management. Over the years, Congress amended the act, creating new exceptions, and the NLRB and the courts have developed a body of law interpreting and implementing its provisions. Indeed, Thomas Sowell, a conservative black critic of affirmative action, has argued that the NLRB and the Wagner Act of 1935 were the first instances of modern affirmative action, preferential treatment toward mistreated labor groups.

The relationship between the NLRB and affirmative action is indirect. The scope of the NLRB is restricted to private employment practices, while mandatory affirmative action programs, insofar as they govern employment relations, generally cover management and employee relations in such public employment as publicly funded universities and state and federal governments. This is not to say, however, that affirmative action has not influenced private employment practices. Affirmative action programs and policies are an outgrowth of the civil rights struggle in the 1960s and, as such, developed alongside other civil rights measures that changed the legal landscape, including labor law. The scope of affirmative action programs and policies is much broader than employment practices alone, covering such issues as access to education and health care and equal legal rights. But there is no denying the important role of the NLRB as one among various agencies like the Equal Employment Opportunity Commission (EEOC) in establishing and ensuring justice in the workplace. Since the NLRB is concerned with labor relations in general, and not matters of race per se, its mandate differs from that of affirmative action programs. Nevertheless, since the main purpose of the NLRB, like that of the EEOC, is to oversee the creation and maintenance of fairness and greater equality in labor relations, it is, like affirmative action, one element in the evolution of social justice in the United States.

The NLRB has a twofold purpose: first, to ascertain by vote the free democratic choices of employees regarding their desire, if any, for union representation, as well as for the specific union they wish to have serve in this capacity; second, to deter and correct the illegal acts (i.e., unfair labor practices) of employers or unions. It functions, in essence, as a referee between labor (and its representatives) and management. To achieve these objectives, the NLRB was given broad enforcement powers, including the right to issue cease-and-desist orders and the power to issue subpoenas. The NLRB was also empowered to order corrective measures in response to violations of the National Labor Relations Act, including employee reinstatement, back pay, and good-faith bargaining.

There are two major components to the structure of the NLRB. The first is a five-member board appointed by the president for five-year terms, the term of one member expiring each year. These appointees are subject to Senate approval. This group is similar to a judicial body and is responsible for conducting formal administrative hearings of cases of alleged unfair labor practices. The other element of the NLRB is its general counsel. The general counsel is appointed for a four-year term, also with Senate consent, but is independent of the five-member NLRB board. The general counsel is responsible for investigating and prosecuting cases of unfair labor practices and for supervising the regional NLRB field offices in processing cases within the geographical area they serve.

See also Civil Rights Movement; Equal Employment Opportunity Commission; National Labor Relations Act; Sowell, Thomas.

FURTHER READING: Boyce, Timothy J., 1978, *Fair Representation, the NLRB, and the Courts*, Philadelphia: University of Pennsylvania Press; Gould, William B., 2000, *Labored Relations: Law, Politics, and the NLRB: A Memoir*, Cambridge, MA: MIT Press; Gross, James A., 1974, *The Making of the National Labor Relations Board*, Albany: State University of New York Press; McCulloch, Frank W., and Tim Bornstein, 1974, *The National Labor Relations Board*, New York: Praeger; Miscimarra, Phillip A., 1983, *The NLRB and Managerial Discretion: Plant Closings, Relocations, Subcontracting, and Automation*, Philadelphia: University of Pennsylvania Press.

PAUL M. HUGHES

National Organization for Women

The National Organization for Women (NOW) is the largest U.S. organization for feminist activists. The organization began with a conversation between Betty Friedan, author of *The Feminine Mystique*, and Pauli Murray, an African American feminist. At a women's conference, Murray mentioned to Friedan that women needed an organization to work for them as the NAACP worked for African Americans. Friedan scribbled some notes on a napkin that became the organization's official purpose statement. The official creation date for NOW is June 30, 1966, by Friedan, Murray, twenty-five other women, and one man at the Third National Conference of the Commission on the Status of Women in Washington, D.C. The group gathered in Friedan's motel room, continued the meeting at lunch the next day, each person gave five dollars, and NOW was launched. Friedan was the first president. NOW's primary goal, which Friedan scribbled on the napkin, was "to take action to bring women into the full participation in the mainstream of American society now, exercising all privileges and responsibilities thereof in truly equal partnership with men."

NOW's earliest priority was to foster the recognition of women's work. With its slogan "Every Mother Is a Working Mother," NOW lobbied and picketed newspapers that printed sex-segregated want ads and launched lawsuits against workplace sex discrimination. NOW also conducted a nationwide campaign in support of the Equal Rights Amendment (ERA). NOW's work on the ERA provided the organization with a vast network of grassroots groups and a multimillion-dollar budget. Although the ERA failed to pass, NOW's efforts provided the organization with the foundation and infrastructure to support and help elect feminist politicians.

NOW also focuses on sexual harassment, ending violence against women, promoting diversity, and supporting abortion and reproductive rights, as well as advocating rights for lesbians and gays. NOW developed the first "Take Back the Night" marches, created shelters and hot lines for battered women, and won passage of the 1994 Violence against Women Act. NOW was also the first major national women's organization to support the rights of lesbians.

To accomplish its goals, NOW employs both traditional and non-traditional tactics. NOW members conduct extensive political lobbying and bring lawsuits. NOW also sponsors and organizes rallies, picketing projects, nonviolent civil disobedience demonstrations, and marches. NOW organized a march for the ERA in 1995 that drew more than 100,000 people. NOW's efforts have helped more women achieve political posts, have increased educational, business, and employment opportunities for women, and have spearheaded tougher laws against violence, discrimination, and harassment. NOW is organized into a forty-two-member national board, nine regions, an official state organization in each state, and more than 600 local chapters where most of the organizing and action take place.

See also Equal Rights Amendment; *The Feminine Mystique.*

FURTHER READING: National Organization for Women, 1995–2002, web site: http:// www.now.org; Singleton, Carl, ed., 1999, *The Sixties in America,* Pasadena: Salem Press.

LISA A. ENNIS

National Origin

The term "national origin" is not specifically defined in Title VII of the Civil Rights Act of 1964. However, the legislative history of Title VII, the Equal Employment Opportunity Commission (EEOC), and the courts over the years have made it clear that national origin refers to the nation/country from which a person or his/her ancestors originate. Although similar, national origin is distinct from citizenship, alienage, and race. Some courts have considered ethnic characteristics when determining a person's national origin. Still other courts have determined that subgroups within a nation (e.g., Ukrainians before the dissolution of the Soviet Union) can constitute a national origin group. The EEOC has taken the position that Title VII's prohibition against national-origin discrimination makes it unlawful to discriminate on the basis of a person's ancestry, culture, language, accent, customs, or marriage to a person of another national origin. It also is illegal to discriminate against someone because he or she associates with a person of another national origin.

Various other federal laws and regulations, in addition to Title VII, prohibit discrimination on the basis of a person's national origin. These include affirmative action regulations promulgated by the Office of Federal Contract Compliance Programs (OFCCP), the Immigration Reform and Control Act (IRCA), the Civil Rights Act of 1871 (42 U.S.C. § 1983), and, at times, the Civil Rights Act of 1866 (42 U.S.C. § 1981). In addition, various state fair employment practice laws and affirmative action requirements prohibit national origin discrimination. As in the case of discrimination on the basis of other protected categories (e.g., sex and race), intentional disparate treatment on the basis of national origin and practices that are neutral on their face but have a disparate (adverse) impact on a national-origin group are both illegal employment practices under Title VII. Such practices also violate OFCCP affirmative action regulations promulgated pursuant to Executive Order 11246.

There are some limited exceptions to the general Title VII prohibitions. One of these is a "bona fide occupational qualification" exception. A bona fide occupational qualification may exist if being a member of a particular national origin is a business necessity for the job. For example, this exception may in limited circumstances allow an Italian restaurant to hire only Italian waiters. However, such preferences are permitted only in rare instances. The burden is on the employer to prove that only members of a particular national origin can fulfill the qualifications for the position, and the argument that national origin may be a bona fide occupational qualification is strictly construed. Thus using national origin as a bona fide occupational qualification often fails.

Another controversial employment issue that has received considerable attention in recent years is the application of English-only rules. The EEOC has taken the position that such rules may violate Title VII unless the employer can establish a legitimate business necessity for such a rule, and the employees are fully notified of the rule and the consequences for violating it.

See also Civil Rights Act of 1866; Civil Rights Act of 1964; *Diaz v. Pan American World Airways*; Employment (Private) and Affirmative Action; Employment (Public) and Affirmative Action; Equal Employment Opportunity Commission; Equal Employment Opportunity Commission's Affirmative Employment Management Directives; Executive Order 11246; Office of Federal Contract Compliance Programs; Title VII of the Civil Rights Act of 1964.

FURTHER READING: Lindemann, Barbara, and Paul Grossman, 1996, *Employment Discrimination Law*, 3d ed., vols. 1 and 2, Chicago: American Bar Association.

PAUL M. HARIDAKIS

Native Alaskans

See Alaskan Natives.

Native Americans

Native Americans are the original inhabitants of the Americas and are typically a type of minority group provided for in affirmative action programs and plans. This term can be used to refer to either the Native Peoples of the entire Western Hemisphere or only the Native Peoples of the United States. The term "Native American" generally refers to an individual's cultural or ethnic identity, whereas the term "Indian" is more often used in the legal or historical context. As such, a Native American is generally self-identified. A person may assert his Native American heritage although he has no ongoing relationship with any tribal community. Furthermore, Native American can also refer to culture in a broader sense. There is today a relatively large amount of Native American art and literature that reflects the historical and contemporary experiences and beliefs of Native Americans.

Historically, being Native American has often been considered a racial category. In *United States v. Rogers*, 45 U.S. (4 How.) 567 (1846), Chief Justice Roger B. Taney declared that the government would not consider an individual to be a member of a Native American tribe unless that person possessed a blood quantum of at least 25 percent. In his view, it was impossible to imagine a nation that was not also a race. Segregationist Jim Crow laws throughout much of the South also treated Native Americans as "colored." In Virginia, Native Americans were denied access to publicly funded education for many years in the first half of the twentieth century through the operation of these laws.

Legally, the ethnic status Native American continues to be used alongside other racial groups in a variety of laws. For the purposes of antidiscrimination law or hate-crime laws, Native American ethnicity is considered a form of racial or ethnic category. Affirmative action programs generally include Native Americans as a disadvantaged minority for purposes of determining disadvantaged business enterprise status or racial classification for admissions programs. The U.S. census has had many problems with accounting for Native Americans either as a race or as an ethnicity. Because the census is entirely self-reported, the proportion of people indicating Native American heritage fluctuates with social and political attitudes toward Native Americans.

Native American communities are very diverse. In the United States, there are more than 500 federally recognized tribal communities and Native Alaskan villages, in addition to numerous communities that have been unable to produce the necessary documentation of their Native American history. The Navajo of the Southwest desert, the Mohawk of the Northeast, the whaling Makah of Washington State, and the Alaskan Yup'iq have little in common other than a shared status as Native Americans and the similar historical struggles that status has produced. Thanks to government programs that moved Native Americans off reservations and into cities, these diverse communities have developed ties and a sense of solidarity.

The term "Native American" can also refer to the indigenous populations in the rest of the hemisphere. Canada has a relatively large First Nation population and created a majority Inuit province in the Arctic in the late 1990s. The Chiapas rebellion of New Year's Day 1994 brought the indigenous population of Mexico into the spotlight. Similarly, Native American or Indian communities have become increasingly active politically in most countries of Latin America, from the Maya of Guatemala to the Guarani of Paraguay. These communities are all Native Americans and in the past thirty years have begun to coordinate with each other.

Long discriminated against, Native American communities throughout the hemisphere have been gaining prominence and respect through political and social action designed to protect their environments and safeguard human rights during the past thirty years and longer. The Nobel Peace Prize was awarded in 1992 to Rigoberta Menchú, a Maya woman from Guatemala. The United Nations and the Organization of American States both have draft declarations on the rights of Native Americans, although neither has been formalized. The United Nations, under pressure from international organizations of native peoples such as the International Indian Treaty Council, sponsored an International Decade of the World's Indigenous People that began December 10, 1994.

See also Indian; Jim Crow Laws; Segregation.

FURTHER READING: Nagel, Joane, 1996, *American Indian Ethnic Renewal: Red Power and the Resurgence of Identity and Culture*, New York: Oxford University Press; Pritzker, Barry M., 1999, *Native America Today: A Guide to Community Politics and Culture*, Santa Barbara, CA: ABC-CLIO.

RACHEL BOWEN

Native Hawaiians

The term "Native Hawaiian" refers to people who trace their origins to the aboriginal people of Hawaii. The first inhabitants of Hawaii were Polynesian seafarers who migrated in two waves. The first wave came from the Marquesas Islands about AD 400, and the second from Tahiti around the ninth or tenth century. By the time the British sea captain James Cook arrived in 1778, there were about 300,000 Hawaiians thriving in the islands. In 2000, the de facto population of Hawaii was about 1,334,000, of which 22.1 percent reported being Hawaiian or part Hawaiian. Individuals classified as Native Hawaiians are a type of minority group occasionally provided for in affirmative action programs and plans.

See also Census Classifications, Ethnic and Racial; Native Americans.

FURTHER READING: Craig, Robert D., 1998, *Historical Dictionary of Honolulu and Hawaii*, Lanham, MD: Scarecrow Press; Kuykendall, Ralph S., 1926, *A History of Hawaii* (prepared under the direction of the Historical Commission of the Territory of Hawaii), New York: Macmillan; Kuykendall, Ralph S., and A. Grove Day, 1961, *Hawaii: A History, from Polynesian Kingdom to American State*, Englewood Cliffs, NJ: Prentice-Hall.

PAULINA X. RUF

Nineteenth Amendment

The Nineteenth Amendment to the U.S. Constitution, ratified in 1920, enfranchised female citizens, guaranteed the federal right to vote for women for the first time, and allowed for fuller participation of females in the body politic. At the 1848 Seneca Falls Convention, women's right to vote was considered too contro-

At the time of the photo, Tennessee had just ratified the Nineteenth Amendment, sometimes called the "Susan B. Anthony amendment," giving suffrage to women. Alice Paul is seen raising the suffrage flag over headquarters in Washington, D.C. Courtesy of Library of Congress.

versial to be voted on for selection as a resolution of the first women's movement meeting. It took from that date until 1920 for the vote for women to be established in America through the seventy-year-long fight for passage of the Nineteenth Amendment to the U.S. Constitution.

Women felt the pain of the passage of the Fifteenth Amendment to the Constitution in 1870, which provided that no state shall deprive any person of the right to vote on account of race while still excluding women's voting privileges in its coverage. Many early feminists had worked diligently for the rights of African Americans and were outraged when protection of the right to vote was won for black men, but denied to them. In 1875, Susan B. Anthony wrote the first woman suffrage amendment, based on the wording of the Fifteenth Amendment. The amendment consisted of only these words: "The right of citizens of the United States to vote shall not be denied or abridged by the United States or by any State on account of sex. Congress shall have the power, by appropriate legislation, to enforce the provisions of this article."

It took three years to convince Senator Arlen A. Sargent of California to submit the amendment to Congress, but it was introduced for the first time in the U.S. Senate on January 10, 1878. It was reintroduced in Congress each year until it finally passed more than forty years later, in 1919.

The amendment passed with the exact wording it had when it was first introduced in 1878.

See also Anthony, Susan Brownell; Fifteenth Amendment; Fourteenth Amendment; Seneca Falls Convention; Suffrage Movement.

FURTHER READING: Foner, Eric, and John A. Garraty, eds., 1991, *The Reader's Companion to American History*, 1043–1047, Boston: Houghton Mifflin; Gurko, Miriam, 1974, *The Ladies of Seneca Falls*, New York: Schocken Books; Hymowitz, Carol, and Michaele Weissman, 1978, *A History of Women in America*, New York: Bantam Books; Lunardini, Christine, 1994, *What Every American Should Know about Women's History*, Holbrook, MA: Bob Adams.

SHEILA BLUHM

Nixon, Richard Milhous (1913–1994)

Described as the "greatest irony of all in the story of affirmative action" (Skrentny 1996, 177), conservative president Richard M. Nixon was responsible, more so than John F. Kennedy or Lyndon Johnson, for putting forward and supporting the most race-conscious affirmative action plan, the Philadelphia Plan. James Farmer, a great civil rights leader, once similarly remarked that Nixon was "the strongest president on affirmative action—up to that point." The Philadelphia Plan, part of Nixon's broader "southern strategy," involved a race-conscious affirmative action plan for the construction industry. Specifically, the Philadelphia Plan (a plan first drafted in the Johnson administration) mandated that those contractors bidding for government business must meet the government-determined numerical amount of minority workers in the firm. Phrased another way, the government mandated an explicit number or quota of minority workers that was needed to successfully bid on government contracts. Thus the Philadelphia Plan has been described as the first federal use of "racial quotas," even though the Nixon administration defended the plan as stipulating "goals" and not "racial quotas" (which would presumably be a violation of Executive Order 11246 and Title VII of the Civil Rights Act of 1964).

Prior to the Nixon administration, the notion of modern affirmative action was an amorphous one. President Kennedy, in Executive Order 10925, ordered that contractors were not permitted to discriminate and that contractors should take "affirmative action" in ensuring that considerations of race, color, or national origin did not enter the decision to hire minorities. Hence affirmative action was meant in the negative sense, to take affirmative action to ensure that there was no special treatment on account of race. Furthermore, Title VII of the Civil Rights Act of 1964 prohibits discrimination in employment against persons based on their race, color, religion, sex, or national origin. Finally, President Johnson, in Executive Order 11246, also prohibited employment discrimination based on race, color, religion, or national origin by executive branch agencies and federal contractors and subcontractors. Thus prior to the Nixon administration, the stance of the Kennedy and Johnson administrations can best be described as color blind. As John David Skrentny has remarked in his book *The Ironies of Affirmative Action*, "While suggested in various parts and practices of civil rights enforcement and crisis management, affirmative action was not completely institutionalized in any specific policy" (Skrentny 1996, 177).

However, in proposing the Philadelphia Plan and ensuring its passage through Congress, Nixon was responsible for creating the first modern usage of racial preferences or set-asides as part of an affirmative action plan. Again in the words of Skrentny, "Whereas President Johnson and his fellow Democrats had struggled mightily both to help blacks and to avoid giving this help a racial label, Nixon, for a time, rather proudly marched under a race-conscious [affirmative action] banner" (Skrentny 1996, 177).

Richard Milhous Nixon, the eventual thirty-seventh president of the United States, was born on January 9, 1913, in Yorba Linda, California, to Francis Anthony Nixon and Hannah Milhous Nixon. Nixon had four siblings, all brothers. Nixon's family moved from Yorba Linda to Whittier, California, when he was nine. He attended public school and entered Whittier College, a small Quaker college. In 1934, he received a bachelor of arts degree from Whittier College and won a scholarship to Duke University Law School. At Duke University, Nixon ranked third in his graduating class and was elected president of the Duke University Bar Association. In 1937, Nixon received a juris doctorate (law degree) from Duke University. After graduation, he returned to Whittier, where he joined the town's most prestigious law firm and gained litigation experience working with corporation and tax cases. He married Catherine Patricia Ryan in 1940.

In 1942, at the onset of World War II, Nixon moved to Washington, where he worked in the Office of Price Administration's tire-rationing division. Later in 1942, Nixon joined the navy as a lieutenant. While Nixon was serving in the navy, a group of California Republicans courted him to run for California's Twelfth Congressional District seat. In 1946, Nixon began to actively campaign for the seat and won the Republican primary election. In the general election, he defeated the Democratic incumbent. This campaign spotlighted Nixon's penchant for politics.

By 1950, Nixon had gained national attention and, after two terms in the House, sought the Republican nomination for the U.S. Senate. In the general election, his opponent for the Senate seat was Democratic congresswoman Helen Gahagan Douglas. Nixon's campaign was heated and centered on two hot-button issues of the time, communism and socialism. Nixon was relentless in his campaigning and used hardball smear tactics and name-calling during this campaign. He branded his opponent as "the pink lady" to illuminate her perceived lukewarm support of the United States. The tactics used in this campaign would come back to haunt Nixon and provide the Democrats with inflammatory campaign materials in future elections. Nixon won the Senate seat in November 1950 and attracted more national recognition.

After approximately six years of public service combined in the House and Senate, and at the age of thirty-nine, Nixon was selected as the vice presidential running mate of Dwight Eisenhower on the Republican ticket. Eisenhower and Nixon were victorious over the Democratic nominees, Adlai E. Stevenson of Illinois and John J. Sparkman of Alabama. Nixon became the second-youngest vice president in U.S. history. Due to several illnesses of President Eisenhower, Nixon gained valuable presidential experience by carrying out some of the office's executive and ceremonial duties.

During Eisenhower's second term in office, Nixon became the overwhelming choice to be named the Republican nominee for president. He staved off a challenge from Nelson Rockefeller, but his first attempt at the nation's highest office ended in defeat by John F. Kennedy in the 1960 presidential election. After the defeat, Nixon returned to California and began work at a Los Angeles law firm. In 1962, Nixon sought to become governor of California. The rationale for the gubernatorial run in 1962 was to secure more political support for future political campaigns and national elections. Nixon lost the election to Edmund G. Brown, the incumbent governor. Nixon was bitter after this crushing defeat, as evidenced by his lashing out at reporters at a press conference the morning after his election defeat and claiming that no one would have Richard Nixon to "kick around" any longer.

By the mid-1960s, Nixon had recovered from his California gubernatorial defeat and had begun to revive his political career by assisting Republican candidates' campaigns in various elections across the United States. He spoke at several fundraising events and, after assisting the party in such yeoman's tasks for elections, regained his popularity within the Republican Party. He became the favorite within the party for the nomination for the presidential race of 1968. He chose Spiro Agnew, the governor of Maryland, as his running mate, which shocked many at the time. Choosing Agnew as his running mate was a strategic attempt of Nixon to broaden the Republican Party base and his voting base.

In 1968, Nixon was elected president of the United States at a critical time in American history. He inherited the social concerns of the nation, the Vietnam War, and government programs from President John F. Kennedy and President Lyndon Johnson's Great Society. Shortly after the election, Arthur Fletcher, an assistant secretary of labor in the Nixon administration, began working on revising the Philadelphia Plan. The Philadelphia Plan, named after a model plan in the city of Philadelphia, had been designed during the Johnson administration, but shelved after the Comptroller General's Office issued an opinion indicating that the plan was illegal because it did not give bidding parties sufficient guidelines as to the governmental bidding requirements. Fletcher believed in the plan and pushed it to his supervisor, Department of Labor secretary George Shultz, who was also supportive of the plan. Fletcher explained:

> I decided to go ahead with the Philadelphia Plan of putting specifications of minority employment goals in all contracts. I did this because my study and experience had convinced me that such targets were essential if we are to measure results in terms of increased minority employment. Without such targets, the paper compliance, and the interminable ineffectiveness of the government programs would go on. I had not come to Washington to preside over a continuation of the ineffective programs of the past. (Skrentny, 139)

Nixon agreed with the plan, but probably not out of a primary concern for the equality of black workers. Rather, Nixon saw the Philadelphia Plan as part of his "southern strategy," whereby he could politically divide the labor organizations (who would oppose the Philadelphia Plan) and civil rights organizations (who would support the plan), thereby "producing discontent and factional rivalry in two of the liberal establishment's major supporters" (Skrentny 1996, 182).

Nixon's revised Philadelphia (affirmative action) Plan called for the use of time-tables and goals that contractors must make a good-faith effort to comply with. In the words of Arthur Fletcher, in a 1969 statement:

> Affirmative action means that Government contractors must pledge themselves to establish goals and timetables for employing minority personnel. They must make an honest and good faith effort to hire a percentage or number of qualified workers. Percentages or numbers are used because industrial progress itself is measured in numerical standards. (Skrentny, 144)

After heavy lobbying by the Nixon administration, the plan was passed by Congress and became federal law in 1969. The Nixon plan was defended as not being inconsistent with Title VII or Executive Order 11246, as the plan called for goals and not quotas.

However, while the Philadelphia Plan divided organized labor and the National Association for the Advancement of Colored People, it failed to substantially change Nixon's low reputation in the area of civil rights. In 1969, the Department of Justice began serious enforcement of desegregation laws. While Nixon was generally supportive of the Supreme Court's ruling in *Brown v. Board of Education*, 347 U.S. 483 (1954), he was not overly anxious to aggressively implement integration in the schools. In 1971, the Supreme Court upheld the practice of busing to achieve racial balance in schools, but Nixon publicly stated that he wanted only to minimally enforce the busing mandate. Nixon was adamant that his civil rights enforcers in the Justice Department rein in the zeal that they had displayed in the Kennedy and Johnson administrations. Nixon's commitment to aggressively pursuing integration was tepid, and, in the Justice Department, "the crucial topic to shut up about was school integration" (Skrentny 1996, 189). In the early 1970s, the Nixon administration faced opposition on many different fronts. On many college and university campuses, there were student protests of the country's continued involvement in the Vietnam War. Both radical African American and Caucasian groups used terrorist techniques to protest the Nixon administration. However, Nixon viewed these groups as fringe elements of America and believed that the "silent majority" was in support of his policies.

The Nixon administration could boast of many accomplishments. Notably, on the domestic front, Nixon created the Environmental Protection Agency and expanded Social Security. In foreign affairs, he opened dialogue with the People's Republic of China and negotiated modest cutbacks in the arms race with the the then Soviet Union. However, this record was tempered by Nixon's perceived disregard for civil rights at home (the Philadelphia Plan notwithstanding), his brief expansion of the Vietnam War (sending troops into Cambodia), and the scandals that engulfed his second term as president.

In 1972, Nixon defeated Democratic presidential nominee George McGovern and was elected to a second term. His second inauguration took place on January 20, 1973. Shortly thereafter Vice President Spiro Agnew resigned after pleading no contest to income tax evasion. On June 17, 1972, at the Watergate complex in Washington, D.C., a special investigation unit commissioned by Nixon was involved in wiretapping of the Democratic National Committee headquarters, as well as breaking and entering. Nixon and his aides attempted to cover up the White House's involvement in the fiasco. A few days later, Nixon approved a plan to pay those arrested in exchange for their silence about the covert wiretapping operation. An inquiry by the Federal Bureau of Investigation exposed the illegal acts perpetrated at the Watergate complex. In 1974, a grand jury named Nixon a coconspirator in the Watergate cover-up. The House Judiciary Committee recommended that he be impeached for abusing his presidential power and for refusing to comply with subpoenas. After Nixon realized that he would be impeached and removed from office, he resigned on August 9, 1974, and Gerald Ford was sworn in as president. One month later, Ford granted Nixon a full pardon for his involvement in the Watergate scandal.

Upon his resignation, Nixon moved into seclusion. He spent many of the waning years after Watergate writing books, but was always overshadowed by his involvement in the scandal and resignation. On April 22, 1994, Richard Milhous Nixon, the thirty-seventh president of the United States, died in New York.

See also Brown v. Board of Education; Busing; Civil Rights Act of 1964; Department of Justice; Department of Labor; Eisenhower, Dwight David; Executive Order 10925; Executive Order 11246; Farmer, James; Ford, Gerald Rudolph; Johnson, Lyndon Baines; Kennedy, John Fitzgerald; Quotas; Republican Party and Affirmative Action; Title VII of the Civil Rights Act of 1964.

FURTHER READING: Kotlowski, Dean J., 2001, *Nixon's Civil Rights: Politics, Principle, and Policy*, Cambridge, MA: Harvard University Press; Rubio, Philip F., 2001, *A History of Affirmative Action, 1619–2000*, Jackson: University Press of Mississippi; Skrentny, John David, 1996, *The Ironies of Affirmative Action: Politics, Culture, and Justice in America*, Chicago: University of Chicago Press.

F. ERIK BROOKS

Norton, Eleanor Holmes (1938–)

A delegate in the House of Representatives from the District of Columbia for well over a decade and a tenured law professor at Georgetown University, Eleanor Holmes Norton has been a lifelong advocate of affirmative action. In 2002, Norton commented that she believed that "affirmative action in education is the key to every other opportunity in this society" (Edney 2002). Furthermore, Norton believes that the termination of affirmative action programs would wreak havoc upon black communities, commenting, "If you want to cut the legs out from under the minority community, you take back their right to become qualified for jobs by making it difficult to attend colleges and universities" (Edney 2002). Prior to her service in Congress, Norton had established herself as a champion of women and minorities and gained national prominence when she was appointed by President Jimmy Carter to serve as the first woman chair of the Equal Employment Opportunity Commission. Earlier in her career, she was also the first woman to head the New York City Commission on Human Rights.

Her experience growing up in a racially inhospitable Washington, D.C., served as the impetus for her lifelong achievements. Norton commented in 2003, "It's as a child growing up in D.C. going to segregated schools. . . . It's witnessing my black cousins going to fight in WWII—a war on racism. It's any notion of irony, that puts a fire in your soul" (Guevarra 2003, 1). She attended Antioch College, earning a bachelor of arts degree in 1960 and a master's degree in 1963 and a law degree from Yale Law School in 1964. While she was a tenured professor at Georgetown University in 1990, she was elected to the House of Representatives.

See also Carter, James "Jimmy" Earl, Jr.; Equal Employment Opportunity Commission.

FURTHER READING: Edney, Hazel Trice, 2002, "Affirmative Action Cases before Supreme Court Could Limit Opportunity," http://www.greaterdiversity.com/education-resources; Guevarra, Lolita, 2003, "Activist Shares New Book," *Weekly: Mills College*, April 3, 1; House of Representatives, Committee on the Judiciary, Subcommittee on the Constitution, 1997, "Testimony of U.S. Delegate Eleanor Holmes Norton," http://www.house.gov/judiciary/22303.htm.

JAMES A. BECKMAN

Occupational Prestige

Occupational prestige is defined as the subjective evaluation or deference individuals give to occupations. Thus the social standing of individuals derives, at least in part, from the jobs they hold. Vocational counselors were the first to systematically study occupational prestige in an effort to identify the social standing associated with different occupations. It is usually measured by asking a random sample of individuals to rank a set of occupations according to what they believe is their standing in society. In general, there is consensus on the relative placement of most occupations, both within countries and between different ones. The concept of occupational prestige is significant because it is a major avenue through which people in modern societies obtain access to valuable resources (e.g., high incomes and power). Affirmative action policies and programs have afforded many racial/ethnic minorities and women the opportunity to pursue occupations with higher levels of prestige. In turn, these higher-ranking occupations have provided them greater access to valuable societal resources and improved prospects of achieving the American dream.

Explanations of the reasons behind the amount of prestige associated with each occupation vary. Some social scientists argue that the functional necessities found in societies lead to the development of occupational prestige hierarchies. Others argue that the level of prestige associated with occupations is related to the quality and quantity of skills required by each occupation. Yet others argue that in modern societies, occupations with high prestige also tend to require high levels of formal education or specialized training.

Because occupational prestige hierarchies are part of the traditional culture of a society and are thus passed from one generation to the next, they also reflect the patterns of inequality found in society. Although significant variation exists today, both racial/ethnic minorities and women tend to have lower-ranking jobs than other groups. Historically, racial/ethnic minorities and women have faced many obstacles in their attempts to secure higher-ranking jobs. The most significant obstacle these groups have faced is discrimination.

See also Discrimination; Gender Stratification; Minority Professionals and Affirmative Action; Racial and Ethnic Stratification; Segregation.

FURTHER READING: Davis, Kingsley, and Wilbert Moore, 1945, "Some Principles of Stratification," *American Sociological Review* 10:242–249; Glick, Peter, 1995, "Images of Occupations: Components of Gender and Status in Occupational Stereotypes," *Sex Roles* 32:565–583; MacKinnon, Neil J., and Tom Langford, 1994, "The Meaning of Occupational Prestige Scores," *Sociological Quarterly* 35:215–245; Nakao, Keiko, and Judith Treas, 1994, "Updating Occupational Prestige and Socioeconomic Scores: How the New Measures Measure Up," in *Sociological Methodology*, edited by Peter Marsden, 1–72, Washington, DC: American Sociological Association; Parsons, Talcott, 1951, *The Social System*, New York: Free Press; Treiman, Donald J., 1997, *Occupational Prestige in Comparative Perspective*, New York: Academic Press; Treiman, Donald J., and Harry B.G. Ganzeboom, 1990, "Cross-National Status Attainment Research," *Research in Social Stratification and Mobility* 9:105–130; Wu, Xu, and Ann Leffler, 1992, "Gender and Race Effects on Occupational Prestige, Segregation, and Earnings," *Gender and Society* 6:376–392.

PAULINA X. RUF

O'Connor, Sandra Day (1930–   )

Sandra Day O'Connor, the first female U.S. Supreme Court justice, authored the decisions in two of the Supreme Court's most significant affirmative action cases: *Grutter v. Bollinger*, 123 S. Ct. 2325, 2003 U.S. LEXIS 4800 (2003), and *Adarand Constructors, Inc. v. Peña*, 515 U.S. 200 (1995). O'Connor is known for her centrist role on the Court on many issues, but had generally taken a conservative stance on affirmative action until she authored the *Grutter* opinion in 2003. According to Georgetown University law professor Girardeau A. Spann, prior to 2000, "Justice O'Connor participated in thirteen affirmative action cases that were decided on constitutional grounds. She voted against affirmative action in twelve of these cases" (Spann 2000, 268). O'Connor has consistently held the viewpoint in a series of cases that race-conscious affirmative action plans should be held to the highest judicial scrutiny (strict scrutiny). O'Connor has insisted that affirmative action plans be promulgated by the government only to achieve a compelling governmental interest, and that they be narrowly tailored to achieve that interest, earning her the title of "the champion of the narrowness requirement" (Spann 2000, 30). She has "rejected the role model and general societal discrimination justifications for affirmative action; insisted on a very tight fit between the state interest and the nature of the remedy; and disfavored layoffs of innocent whites" (Spann 2000, 30). On the other hand, she has opposed the most conservative anti–affirmative action position taken by Justices Antonin Scalia and Clarence Thomas, who appear opposed to race-based affirmative action ·in all contexts. For instance, she has maintained that race-conscious affirmative action programs may be justified to remedy past racial discrimination by the user of the program and has insisted that strict scrutiny review of race-based affirmative action plans is not "strict in theory, but fatal in fact."

In the landmark decisions in *Grutter v. Bollinger* and *Gratz v. Bollinger*, 123 S. Ct. 2411, 2003 U.S. LEXIS 4801 (2003), O'Connor illustrated her centrist role on the Court in serving as the swing vote on the issue of affirmative action while appearing to move away from her traditionally conservative stance on the issue of affirmative action. In *Grutter*, the Court, in a decision authored by Justice O'Connor, reaffirmed the diversity rationale that Justice Lewis Powell that had enunciated twenty-five years earlier in *Regents of the University of California v. Bakke*, 438 U.S. 265 (1978). In reaffirming diversity in higher education as a compelling governmental interest needed to satisfy the Court's strict scrutiny analysis, the Supreme Court upheld the University of Michigan Law School's affirmative action plan and endorsed affirmative action plans that utilize race as one factor or ingredient (among many) in the overall evaluation of candidates so long as the consideration of race allows for the individualized assessment of applicants. Although her opinion stated that it was applying the strict scrutiny review standard, she gave a degree of deference to the University of Michigan Law School's justification for the racial preferences in the plan that is atypical of previous strict scrutiny cases. For example, she wrote: "The Law School's educational judgment that such diversity is essential to its educational mission is one to which we defer," and " 'good faith' on the part of a university is 'presumed' absent 'a showing to the contrary.' " Traditional strict scrutiny review presumes the race-based classification to be invalid unless shown otherwise. O'Connor also wrote that the law school affirmative action program "bears the hallmarks of a narrowly tailored plan" and that "[n]arrow tailoring does not require exhaustion of every conceivable race-neutral alternative." However, O'Connor also indicated that affirmative action "must have a logical end point," and "25 years from now, the use of racial preferences will no longer be necessary to further the interest approved today." O'Connor also illustrated her centrist position on the Court by voting with the majority in *Gratz* in striking down the affirmative action admissions plan at the University of Michigan undergraduate level. In the *Gratz* decision, the Court warned that fixed racial quotas and mechanized formulas (which have the effect of operating as a quota) would not be tolerated.

In the other landmark Supreme Court affirmative action case O'Connor authored, *Adarand Constructors, Inc. v. Peña*, the Court held that strict scrutiny analysis should be applied to race-conscious affirmative action plans of the federal government. This opinion reversed a previous Supreme Court opinion holding that such plans were subject to a more lenient standard of review that allowed the federal government more leeway in how it used racial preferences in its affirmative action programs.

O'Connor was born in El Paso, Texas, on March 26, 1930. She attended Stanford University, graduating in 1950, and Stanford University Law School, graduating in 1952 along with fellow classmate and future colleague William Rehnquist. O'Connor married John Jay O'Connor III, another Stanford classmate, and went into private practice in Maryville, Arizona. O'Connor earned a solid legal reputation in Arizona and in 1965 was named an assistant attorney general for Arizona. She then went on to serve as a member of the Arizona Senate from 1969 until 1974, eventually becoming Republican majority leader of the Senate, the first female to hold this position. In 1974, O'Connor was elected to serve as an Arizona superior court judge, a position she held until she was appointed to the Arizona Court of Appeals in 1979. When U.S. Supreme Court Justice Potter Stewart retired, President Ronald Reagan nominated O'Connor on July 7, 1981, to fill the vacant seat. She was sworn in on September 25, 1981.

See also Adarand Constructors, Inc. v. Peña; Affirmative Action Plan/Program; Compelling Governmental Interest; Employment (Public) and Affirmative Action; *Gratz v. Bollinger/Grutter v. Bollinger;* Narrowly Tailored Affirmative Action Plans; Reagan, Ronald; Rehnquist, William Hobbs; Role Model Theory; Strict Scrutiny; Suspect Classification.

FURTHER READING: O'Connor, Sandra Day, 2003, *The Majesty of the Law: Reflections of a Supreme Court Justice,* New York: Random House; Schmidt, Peter, 2003, "Affirmative Action Survives, and So Does the Debate: The Supreme Court Upholds Race-Conscious Admissions in Principle, but Not Always as Practiced," *Chronicle of Higher Education,* July 4, S1; Spann, Girardeau A., 2000, *The Law of Affirmative Action: Twenty-five Years of Supreme Court Decisions on Race and Remedies,* New York: New York University Press.

JAMES A. BECKMAN

Office of Federal Contract Compliance Programs

The Office of Federal Contract Compliance Programs (OFCCP) was created as part of the U.S. Department of Labor pursuant to Executive Order 11246, as amended. The OFCCP's principal duties are to oversee compliance with Executive Order 11246 by government contractors and subcontractors. The OFCCP's authority was later expanded to include oversight of compliance with the Rehabilitation Act of 1973 and document compliance with the Immigration Reform and Control Act of 1986.

In large measure, the OFCCP carries out its duties by conducting audits and investigations to ensure that contractors and subcontractors are in compliance with the extensive regulations created to bring the purposes of the Executive Order 11246 into effect. The OFCCP is authorized to initiate investigations and audits of government contractors and subcontractors. Which employers are selected for audit is determined in large part by computer analysis of annual compliance report data regarding an employer's affirmative action efforts. Occasionally audits may be undertaken at the discretion of an OFCCP district director based upon information other than the computer analysis.

The OFCCP also receives and investigates complaints by employees or prospective employees of a government contractor or subcontractor that allege discrimination contrary to the requirements of Executive Order 11246. The OFCCP is also authorized to receive and investigate complaints alleging violation of the Rehabilitation Act of 1973. The OFCCP is not authorized to receive and investigate complaints under other employment rights legislation, but may refer complainants to the appropriate enforcement agency. Audits may take the form of a "desk audit" or an "on-site audit." A desk audit consists of an employer providing extensive documentation to the OFCCP for more detailed analysis than that allowed by the information contained in annual compliance reports. An on-site audit involves OFCCP compliance officers visiting an employer's facility and over a period of several days touring the facility, reviewing documentation (including, in part, review of completed I-9 forms required by the Immigration Reform and Control Act), and conducting interviews of employees.

Under the OFCCP, all contractors and subcontractors with fifty or more employees and contracts of $50,000 or more must take a series of steps to ensure a good-faith effort in following/implementing the affirmative action mandate of E.O. 11246. The contractor must file a report on its equal employment and affirmative action programs. The contractor must also have an affirmative action plan, which includes a utilization analysis of women and minorities in the contractor's firms, and a statement of goals and timetables to repair any deficiencies in its employee population. Finally, the government contractor must report the total number of minority and female workers in each of the contractor's respective job titles/series. The OFCCP monitors these reports.

If as a result of an audit or investigation the OFCCP finds evidence that a government contractor or subcontractor is not in compliance with Executive Order 11246 and/or the Rehabilitation Act of 1973, the OFCCP issues a "show-cause" notice to the employer. The employer has thirty days within which to provide evidence that it is in compliance and that enforcement proceedings are not warranted. During this thirty-day period, the OFCCP is required to attempt to conciliate its claims with the employer. If the employer fails to show cause or if conciliation fails, the OFCCP may refer the matter to the secretary of labor for administrative enforcement proceedings.

Enforcement proceedings are quasi-judicial, involving a formal hearing before an administrative law judge (ALJ). The ALJ takes evidence and renders a written opinion that is subject to review by the secretary of labor. The secretary's decision may then be subjected to judicial review in federal court. Employers found to be in violation may be subjected to injunctive relief, including hiring, reinstatement, back pay, and benefits for victims of discrimination. Employers found to be in gross violation of Executive Order 11246 may have their existing government contracts suspended or canceled and, in the most extreme circumstances, may be barred from participating in future government contracts until the director of the OFCCP determines that the contractor is in compliance.

See also Contracting and Affirmative Action; Department of Labor; Executive Order 11246; Rehabilitation Act of 1973.

FURTHER READING: Office of Federal Contract Compliance Programs, 41 Code of Federal Regulations (C.F.R.) Chapter 60; OFCCP, web site: http://www.dol.gov/esa/ofcp org.htm.

RICHARD J. BENNETT

Office of Management and Budget

See Census Classifications, Ethnic and Racial.

Office of Management and Budget (OMB) Statistical Policy Directive 15

See Census Classifications, Ethnic and Racial.

One Florida Initiative

Diversity among those individuals admitted as students into the nation's colleges and universities has been an important goal of the U.S. system of higher education. In the past, institutions of higher education have given preference to individuals based on race and ethnicity to achieve a fair balance of diverse groups within the student population. In recent years, these race-based policies have come under attack across the United States. Voters in both California and Washington, for example, have rejected the use of affirmative action in the applicant selection process. In 2001, the U.S. Circuit Court of Appeals for the Eleventh Circuit struck down the University of Georgia's policy that gave preference to racial minorities in admissions, saying that admission decisions cannot be based on race alone. As part of this climate, in 1999, Governor Jeb Bush of Florida proposed the One Florida Initiative that was intended to eliminate the use of race, ethnicity, and gender as considerations in the admissions process at Florida's ten public universities. To achieve this goal, a two-part strategy has been enacted.

The first part of the One Florida Initiative attempts to deliver opportunity for success to minority and low-income students who are attending Florida's primary and secondary public schools. It is believed that tremendous gaps in performance among schools across the state have led to dramatic differences in student test scores, rates of suspension of students, graduation rates, attendance rates, and college readiness. By use of a standardized test referred to as the Florida Comprehensive Assessment Test (FCAT) given to all students in grades three through ten, public schools are now graded based on student results. Early results following implementation of the use of the FCAT indicated that successful schools had predominantly white student populations, while the poorer-performing schools had large populations of African American and Hispanic students. The inequity is not considered one of race or ethnicity, but the failure of school districts to equitably offer educational opportunities and resources to low-performing and high-performing schools alike.

To equalize the opportunities in low-performing schools, several plans of action have been proposed. First, the A+ Plan for Education has been implemented. The plan calls for increased attention to be given to low-performing schools, including an end to social promotion, stringent accountability for failure of schools, incentives and rewards for improvement, opportunity scholarships for students attending failing schools, and resources for schools to succeed. Second, the Preliminary Scholastic Aptitude Test (PSAT) will be made available to all tenth-grade students throughout Florida. Third, a partnership will be formed with the College Board to assist both students and faculty in the low-performing high schools. Fourth, advanced placement course opportunities in high schools will be expanded. Fifth, access to college preparatory courses through Florida's Online High School will be expanded. Sixth, opportunity alliances will be created between Florida's public schools and its public and private colleges and universities to provide mentoring, tutoring, advanced courses, and recruitment programs to encourage students to strive for higher achievement. Seventh, a statewide student mentoring initiative will be developed in low-performing schools in an effort to increase the use of community resources for improving academic performance. Eighth, an Equity in Education Opportunity Task Force charged with evaluating inequities in opportunity among schools and proposing changes to close the equality gap will be appointed. Finally, efforts will be made to expand the number of students earning associate degrees and transferring to baccalaureate programs.

The second part of the One Florida Initiative replaces race- and ethnic-based admissions policies in the state's university system with achievement-based admissions policies while still improving and enlarging diversity within the system. The revised alternative admissions policy will eliminate the use of race and ethnicity as factors but will allow for other avenues of admission for students not meeting all criteria to enter the system. Universities will be able to consider such things as special talents in arts and athletics, socioeconomic factors, geographic location, Americans with Disabilities Act (ADA) criteria, and first-generation college students.

Additionally, the One Florida Initiative will guarantee admission to the state's ten public universities to students in the top 20 percent of every graduating class from every public high school in Florida who have completed the nineteen required credits that provide the academic base for a rigorous university experience. The plan, referred to as the Talented 20 program, is intended to benefit poor and minority students because it does not require a particular score on tests such as the SAT (Scholastic Assessment Test) or ACT (American College Test) on which these student populations have traditionally scored lower. By creating the Talented 20 program and the elimination of using race and ethnicity in admissions, the pool of eligible minority and low-income students will expand. By improving the low-performing public schools, ensuring that minority students graduate at the same rates as nonminority students, and preparing minority students for a successful college experience, the One Florida Initiative hopes to eliminate race- and ethnicity-based admissions policies while maintaining diversity within the state's university system. The success of Bush's One Florida Initiative is still being debated in Florida. Since the revocation of affirmative action and the implementation of One Florida, the number of minority students has continued to incrementally increase by a very small margin. Governor Bush has touted the increase as proof that affirmative action is not needed to maintain strong minority enrollment in colleges and universities across the state. Bush has commented that "we've got four years under our belt, and we can say that this is working, we're on the right track, and it's a far cry from what was predicted. One Florida is achieving its mission of more minority students having opportunity for higher education" (Fineout 2003, 3). However, critics point out that while the number of minority students enrolling each year has slightly increased, the overall size of the student population has grown in Florida as well.

See also Education and Affirmative Action; Harvard Model; Percentage Plans; Proposition 209; Standardized Testing; Washington Initiative 200.

FURTHER READING: Chabot, Lucy, 2000, "One Florida Worries Women Business Owners," *South Florida Business Journal* 20, no. 30 (March 10): 16; Fineout, Gary, 2000, "One Florida Initiative Having Divine Effect on State," *Black Issues in Higher Education* 17, no. 3 (March 30): 12; Fineout, Gary, 2003, "Governor Bush Touts One Florida as Success; Recent Figures Show More Minorities Attending State Universities," *Ledger*, September 3, A1.

CHRISTOPHER R. CAPSAMBELIS

One-Drop Rule

Until the 2000 census, the United States was the only country not to classify racially mixed people as mixed. Instead, the United States has relied upon the one-drop rule to maintain distinct racial categories and has utilized this rule for well over 100 years. The one-drop rule, as a method of racial classification, relates to which individuals might be entitled to receive benefits under affirmative action programs.

It is estimated that between 75 and 90 percent of African Americans have some white ancestry. Miscegenation between blacks and whites began at the same time as slavery and the forced importation of Africans to the colonies. From this time, defining who was white and who was not became a concern. Social and legal definitions were often at odds. Both custom and law varied from one region to another. During slavery, the sexual coercion of black women by slave masters was common. Racial identity was tied to the mother to define the progeny as slaves. In this way, slave masters could reproduce their workers without fear that the children would have any claim to their property.

In 1850, the U.S. census specified racially mixed nonwhites for the first time, corresponding to the growing consciousness of the danger to white supremacy posed by such mixtures. By 1890, the categories of "mulatto" (⅜ to ⅝ black), "quadroon" (¼ black) and "octoroon" (⅛ or less black) appeared. As early as the early 1700s, however, the one-drop rule was accepted in parts of the southern United States. This rule defined anyone with even one drop of black blood as black. This rule of hypodescent reflects a hierarchical definition of races. While it takes only one drop of black blood to make someone black, 99 percent white blood is not enough to make someone white. The purpose of such a rule was to guarantee white supremacy. The one-drop rule only refers to individuals with black ancestors, and there are no rules regarding the definition of other racial/ethnic groups. The concern has only been with defining who is white and preventing an individual (especially blacks) from passing as white.

By the mid-1800s, as slavery neared its end, support for the one-drop rule increased, and following the American Civil War, support was solidified throughout the southern states. Numerous state legislatures and courts embraced legal definitions of blacks as anyone with some specified fraction of black ancestry. With the advent of Jim Crow segregation and laws prohibiting miscegenation, defining race increased in importance to whites. In the now-infamous Supreme Court case *Plessy v. Ferguson*, 163 U.S. 537 (1896), Homer Plessy was less than one-eighth black. By 1915, the one-drop rule was entrenched across the United States. Whites feared mulattoes, like Homer Plessy, "passing" as whites and interacting in a non-segregated fashion and relied upon the one-drop rule to restrict legal and economic privileges to whites and to enforce segregation.

The one-drop rule also allowed white men to continue to rape or gain access to black women without concerns of legal paternity, since any children would remain with the mother and be defined as black. On the other hand, the protection of white womanhood from the supposed threat of black men was intensified, and fears of the mythological black male rapist were promulgated, justifying violence and lynching. For white Americans, this rule was essential to maintain segregation and white supremacy; clear definitions of who was and was not black were necessary. For black Americans, on the other hand, this rule contributed to greater unity and sense of identity in dealing with increasing racism and inequality.

While the civil rights movement fought for an end to legal segregation, and in 1967 laws against interracial marriage and miscegenation were struck down by the

Supreme Court, the one-drop rule remained entrenched. In some respects, support for the one-drop rule among blacks increased at this time, as a strong sense of black identity and emphases upon racial unity and strength in numbers grew.

Census classifications have always attempted to make the categories mutually exclusive: individuals could only be placed into one category, reflecting the concern with mixing. In 1910, an "Other" category was created to deal with those who could not be classified into existing categories. Throughout the 1980s and 1990s, a growing grassroots movement fought for the recognition of mixed-race identities, arguing for the creation of multiracial categories or the option to check multiple categories on the census and other governmental forms. These organizations have argued that it is offensive and inaccurate for multiracial people to have to select one racial or ethnic identity, and they have begun to dislodge the one-drop rule. Between 1980 and 1990, the number of people choosing to mark "Other" increased dramatically, and as a result of the growing multiracial movement, individuals were allowed to mark more than one category in the 2000 census. Several states have also put the issue up to the public in recent years, as is illustrated by California's recent Racial Privacy Initiative, which was defeated by referendum vote on October 7, 2003. The history of the one-drop rule highlights the problem inherent in all attempts to racially classify people: where should the boundaries be drawn? The great majority of people in the United States are the product of intermixture. Racial purity is a myth.

See also Census Classifications, Ethnic and Racial; Civil Rights Movement; De Facto and De Jure Segregation; Jim Crow Laws; *Plessy v. Ferguson*; Racial Privacy Initiative; Segregation; White Supremacy.

FURTHER READING: Davis, F. James, 1991, *Who Is Black? One Nation's Definition*, University Park: Pennsylvania State University Press; Davis, F. James, 1995, "The Hawaiian Alternative to the One-Drop Rule," in *American Mixed Race: The Culture of Microdiversity*, edited by Naomi Zack, Lanham, MD: Rowman and Littlefield; Ferrante, Joan, and Prince Browne Jr., 2001, *The Social Construction of Race and Ethnicity in the United States*, (2d ed.), Upper Saddle River, NJ: Prentice Hall.

ABBY L. FERBER

Original Intent Jurisprudence

Original intent jurisprudence (original intent) is a term typically used or understood to mean what the delegates to the Constitutional Convention of 1787 understood or believed about the Constitution. As it relates to constitutional amendments, the term is used to connote what the drafters of the amendment believed about that particular amendment regarding scope and coverage. The term first became related to affirmative action when the parties involved in *Brown v. Board of Education*, 347 U.S. 483 (1954), were asked to submit briefs and oral arguments pertaining to the "original intent" and provisions of the Fourteenth Amendment to the U.S. Constitution. The Supreme Court presented the parties with the legal issue of whether the framers of the U.S. Constitution had in mind the legal segregation of African Americans in public schools when they drafted and ratified the Equal Protection Clause of the Fourteenth Amendment. Since *Brown*, jurists will occasionally analyze whether affirmative action plans or programs are consistent with the original intent and meaning of the Fourteenth Amendment's Equal Protection Clause and the Fifth Amendment's Due Process Clause.

The term "original intent jurisprudence" is suggestive of the concept that the Court should interpret the Constitution predicated on the original understanding of the framers of the text. The utilization of original intent was designed to enhance the respectability of the Court's opinions and to deflect claims that judges were merely legislating from the bench. The concept of original intent forced those using the Constitution to analyze the Constitution under the mind-set of the framers (and the framers' intentions) when originally drafting the Constitution. Original intent jurisprudence was designed to serve as a judicial guideline when interpreting constitutional issues. Generally speaking, the Court, when referring to a constitutional issue where the resolution of the issue is unclear, may attempt to employ original intent jurisprudence. Original intent causes one to analyze and determine precisely what the framers meant when they were drafting the Constitution. Original intent affords a means whereby the Court can interpret the Constitution consistent with the original meaning of a particular constitutional provision. It becomes a key factor in determining real legal issues and requires that the framers of the Constitution essentially speak from their graves regarding constitutional interpretation. Original intent allows the Court to reason backwards in decision making with a focus on "whose" intent.

However, there are many problems associated with the original intent approach to constitutional issues. First, to have a clear understanding of original intent would require access to a myriad of original documents and notes from the Constitutional Convention of 1787 or from the legislative history of the various amendments. The record is often incomplete. Second, original intent also requires an understanding of history as well as the framers' intent, and there are often divergent views of any particular historical event. Third, it assumes the existence of a monolithic intent on a particular issue as to the meaning of the constitutional phrase in question. In reality, each delegate or legislator may have had different justifications or intentions in voting for the constitutional provision at issue. Finally, the issue of original intent is very difficult in view of the uncertainties regarding language definitions, drafting procedures, the complex legislative process, and inefficient understanding of attitudes and behaviors, as well as the composition of the Constitutional Convention.

The utilization of original intent jurisprudence allows judges not to have to review the merits of the case predicated upon public policy. Rather, under the original intent philosophy of jurisprudence, judges review the case based on the restricted perspectives of what the original intent of the Constitution was regarding that particular issue, based on the framers' intent. Thus in the area of affirmative action and racial equality, the concern before the court is not the present-day parameter of the Equal Protection Clause of the Fourteenth Amendment or modern-day notions of race relations and equality. Rather, one utilizing original intent might ask what the framers had in mind when adopting the concept of equal protection in the Fourteenth Amendment.

In *Brown v. Board of Education* (1954), original intent jurisprudence became a pivotal legal issue in the case. The Court requested both legal parties to prepare briefs and present oral arguments on the following judicial issue: "What evidence is there that Congress which submitted and the State legislatures and conventions which ratified the Fourteenth Amendment contemplated or did not contemplate, understood or did not understand, that it would abolish segregation in public schools?" The request by the Court required both parties to determine original framer intentions, as well as what the state legislatures had in mind when ratifying the Constitution. The Court in actuality required both parties in *Brown* to become involved in "law office history." After hearing and reviewing arguments presented by both legal parties, the Court failed to make a decision on the original meaning of the Fourteenth Amendment based on original intent jurisprudence. In *Brown*, the Supreme Court illustrated the problems associated with original intent jurisprudence.

Despite the Court's failure to ascertain the precise original meaning of the Fourteenth Amendment, in reaching the historic decision in *Brown* that separate but equal violated the Equal Protection Clause of the Fourteenth Amendment, the Court suggested that it was not giving "new meaning" to the Constitution. Rather, the Court was restoring the original principle of the Constitution to constitutional law. The Court noted it was correcting the damage done fifty years earlier in *Plessy v. Ferguson*, 163 U.S. 537 (1896). The Court in *Brown* held that the earlier Supreme Court had disregarded the clear intent of the framers of the Civil War Amendments to eliminate the legal degradation of blacks and thus had created a judicial philosophy to support the "separate but equal" doctrine, in contravention of the Fourteenth Amendment.

See also Brown v. Board of Education; Civil War (Reconstruction) Amendments and Civil Rights Acts; Due Process Clause; Equal Protection Clause; Fifth Amendment; Fourteenth Amendment; *Plessy v. Ferguson*; Supreme Court and Affirmative Action.

FURTHER READING: Levy, Leonard W., 2000, *Original Intent and the Framers' Constitution*, Chicago: Ivan R. Dee; Ravoke, Jack, N., 1990, *Interpreting the Constitution: The Debate over Original Intent*, Boston: Northeastern University Press.

RONNIE B. TUCKER SR.

Overt Racism

Overt racism involves blatant, transparent, unabashed outward manifestations of hatred for any other racial group than one's own racial group. Overt racism contributes to the phenomenon of de facto segregation in society. Survey studies of racial attitudes suggest that overt racism has been declining across countries. American surveys report that over time, white Americans have become more positive about integration of schools, housing, and jobs. Stereotypes about minority groups have also become more positive, and fewer people endorse negative characteristics about these groups. While overt forms of racism (overt hostility, derogatory beliefs, social distance) appear to be on the decline, the opposition to specific governmental policies that would promote racial equality (e.g., affirmative action) has remained stable.

Theorists have argued that overt racism has been replaced by other more subtle and indirect forms of racism. There are several theories about these more covert expressions of racism. These theories are similar in the idea that most people have ambivalent attitudes toward certain minority groups. Most people reject traditionally racist beliefs and embrace abstract principles of justice. However, many of these same people have negative feelings toward other racial groups. As a result, their prejudices can be only expressed in subtle ways. The more subtle forms of racism have been referred to as modern racism, symbolic racism, and aversive racism.

Modern and symbolic racists are thought to cope with their ambivalence by rationalizing their visceral negative feelings in terms of abstract political and social issues (e.g., opposition to policies such as affirmative action that are designed to promote racial equality). Symbolic racists are believed to have negative feelings toward other racial groups because those groups allegedly violate cherished values of the racist and make demands for changing the racial status quo. The theory of symbolic racism has been widely criticized on the grounds that there are many legitimate race-neutral considerations that may lead one, in good faith, to oppose affirmative action plans.

Aversive racists, in a similar way, are thought to reject overt forms of racism, but to possess unacknowledged negative feelings and beliefs toward certain other racial groups. Aversive racists alternate between positive and negative behaviors toward other racial groups depending on the normative structure within a situation and the possibility of generating a nonracial justification for a prejudiced response. When normative prescriptions are weak or ambiguous, or when a justification is readily available, aversive racists' negative tendencies will be manifested. Finally, racial ambivalence theory describes the conflict within an individual between beliefs in egalitarianism that induce sympathy for other underprivileged racial groups and beliefs pertaining to a Protestant/puritanical work ethic (individualist, devotion to work, and so on), that induce anti–affirmative action sentiments because such programs appear to be antithetical to beliefs in support of the puritanical American work ethic.

See also De Facto and De Jure Segregation; Meritocracy; Stereotyping and Minority Classes.

FURTHER READING: Gaertner, Samuel L., and John F. Dovidio, 1986, "The Aversive Form of Racism," in *Prejudice, Discrimination, and Racism*, edited by John F. Dovidio and Samuel L. Gaertner, Orlando, FL: Academic Press; Katz, Irwin, 1981, *Stigma: A Social Psychological Analysis*, Hillsdale, NJ: Erlbaum; Kinder, David R., and David O. Sears, 1981, "Symbolic Racism versus Threats to 'The Good Life,' " *Journal of Personality and Social Psychology* 40: 414–431; McConahay, John B., 1986, "Modern Racism, Ambivalence, and the Modern Racism Scale," in *Prejudice, Discrimination, and Racism*, edited by John F. Dovidio and Samuel L. Gaertner, Orlando, FL: Academic Press.

MARIA JOSE SOTELO

P

Pan-African Congresses

Frustration with the status of blacks on the African continent and in the Diaspora (locations in which people of African descent live outside of the African continent) gave rise to a series of meetings called Pan-African Congresses. The Pan-African Congresses were part of the Pan-Africanism intellectual movement, which stressed black unity, eliminating colonialism and European influence on the African continent, eradicating white supremacy, and promoting African culture. The Pan-African Congresses were held in the first half of the twentieth century as a break-off branch of the civil rights movement. The participants wanted primarily to foster unity of African Americans. The Pan-African Congresses relate to the history of affirmative action (and African American history) because Black Nationalism constitutes a subbranch of the Pan-African movement. Proponents of Black Nationalism seek black cultural, social, and political autonomy and often reject assimilation of blacks into white society, which some adherents of Black Nationalism see as a result of affirmative action programs. Interestingly, proponents of affirmative action (especially in the education context) argue that one of the main points of affirmative action is to ensure that black culture is injected into the majority white culture, and while assimilation does occur, diversity of culture is preserved (as opposed to separatism).

Henry Sylvester Williams has been referred to as the grandfather of Pan-Africanism, along with W.E.B. Du Bois. Born in Trinidad, Williams was a law student in London. Williams and W.E.B. Du Bois organized the first Pan-African Conference there in 1900. This Pan-African Conference drew delegates from the Caribbean, America, Canada, and Europe. Africans from the continent were conspicuously absent. There was discussion about starting a movement for African people's rights. The delegates petitioned Queen Victoria, denouncing Britain's treatment of people in its African colonies. This initial conference laid the foundation for others to follow. The driving force behind the Pan-African Congress movement was W.E.B. Du Bois, the African American scholar, journalist, and activist. He attended the first meeting and was the main organizer of subsequent ones, which were held in 1919, 1921, 1923, 1927, and 1945.

In 1919, the first of five Pan-African Congresses met in several sessions in London, Paris, and Brussels. Shapuiji Sakalaatvala, an Indian revolutionary, was introduced, and Gold Coast journalist W.F. Hutchinson delivered a stirring speech. This congress issued the radical London Manifesto, also known as the Declaration to the World. One delegate did not support the tone of the proceedings or the Manifesto. He was Blaise Diagne from Senegal, who sat in the French Chamber of Deputies. He broke from the group and the concept of Pan-Africanism. In 1923, the third Pan-African Congress was held in London and Lisbon. Again, demands were made for self-rule in colonial territories and the suppression of lynching and mob law in the United States. New York was the site of the 1927 Pan-African Congress. Resolutions emerged that continued to call for actions similar to those from prior conferences. The fifth Pan-African Congress in 1945 marked the end of one era and the beginning of another for many delegates. It was convened in Manchester, England, with ninety delegates present. Twenty-six of these came from Africa, thirty-three came from the West Indies, and thirty-five represented a number of organizations. Many of them were destined to return to their countries as political leaders. Some were Hastings Banda (Nyasaland, now Malawi), Kwame Nkrumah (Gold Coast, now Ghana), Olafemi Awolowo (Nigeria), Jomo Kenyatta (Kenya), Peter Abrahams (South Africa), Wallace Johnson (Sierra Leone), Ralph Armattoe (Togo), and Amy Ashwood Garvey (Jamaica). Also in attendance were George Padmore (Trinidad) and the grand old man of the movement, septuagenarian W.E.B. Du Bois from the United States.

Many resolutions were released from this 1945 conference. The proposals were bolder than ever. One unprecedented demand was to make racial discrimination a criminal offense. There was a strong denunciation of imperialism and capitalism. At the Manchester Congress, Kwame Nkrumah founded the West African National Secretariat to promote a United States of Africa. He assumed leadership in the attempt to forge unity among African nations as they gained independence.

See also Afrocentrism; Civil Rights Movement; Du Bois, William Edward Burghardt.

FURTHER READING: Abdul-Raheem, Tajudeen, 1996, *Pan-Africanism*, New York: New York University Press; Hatch, John, 1965, *A History of Postwar Africa*, New York: Praeger; Thompson, V.P., 1984, *Africa and Unity: The Evaluation of Pan-Africanism*, London: Longmans.

BETTY NYANGONI

Paternalistic Race Relations Theory

The paternalistic race relations theory is a sociological theory that postulates that the dominant group in society exercises almost entire or absolute control and power over subordinate and minority groups. Additionally, under the paternalism system, a system once governing group relationships in South Africa and in the Old South in the Reconstruction and antebellum periods, the dominant group can utilize virtually any means of coercion and violence to maintain social order. Paternalistic systems can be contrasted with competitive systems, whereby a degree of reciprocity exists between majority and minority groups, so that majority groups are accountable to minority groups. Most scholars classify the United States as a competitive system today and point to such programs as affirmative action as proof of this, as affirmative action programs presumably are implemented in part based upon some pressure and lobbying from minority groups. Also, many assert that split labor markets, based upon a paternalistic system, can only be overcome by workers when another actor (usually a government actor) intervenes in such a way as to break up the power monopoly of the dominant class and challenge the preexisting stratification. Affirmative action programs would be an example of this approach. Also, labor laws, like the Wagner Act (the National Labor Relations Act of 1935), are an example of legislation intended to break up the power monopoly.

In the political science realm, the theory of paternalism takes on a slightly different form. The theory of paternalism in political science is meant to connote a derogatory reference to an organization or entity's paternal, or fatherly, efforts to improve the welfare of its members. For example, organizations that institute voluntary affirmative action programs may be accused of engaging in paternalism, or a "father-knows-best" approach to race relations. In the government context, an overconcern or overregulation by the government in an effort to promote the welfare of its populace through means such as affirmative action might also be criticized as paternalistic. For those who believe in little or no governmental regulation and the power of the individual in society (power or right of self-reliance), a government's paternalistic interference in their lives is viewed in a very negative fashion.

Paternalism in the United States first appeared in the relationship between master and slave, whereby the master acted as caretaker and the slave as a child to be cared for and controlled. This relationship derived largely from the need of white slave owners to keep their slaves alive and well cared for once the transatlantic slave trade had been abolished in 1808. Based on this economic need, a philosophy of paternalism developed: the white race was superior (exemplified by Western legal and governmental systems) and had an obligation to teach and care for the black race. Slavery had Christianized blacks and halted their barbarism, yet they remained backward, requiring protection from the misdeeds of bad whites as well as from those who advocated social equality. A master's family often saw their slaves as their black family, in need of guidance and protection. In return, the black race was obligated to show obedience, devotion, and deference to their white caretakers. Although many slaves did not accept their subordinate position, many sought status within the slave system. This behavior was marked by submissiveness with the expectation of preferential, if not affectionate, treatment by a master.

The principles and practices of paternalism endured through Reconstruction. Wealthy whites remained powerful, while former slaves were now subject to the additional threat of poor whites. Whereas during slavery, the competition between slaves and poor whites was kept to a minimum, abolition meant that blacks were "free" to enter all sectors of labor. This freedom, however, did not mean that blacks were paid wages equal to those of their white competitors. Indeed, free blacks had a lower standard of living than whites, which made them more appealing to white employers because they could pay them less and require more work. This open competition with poor whites increased the animosity between these two groups and therefore increased the likelihood of violence. This was particularly dangerous because blacks no longer had the legal protection of white plantation owners. In addition, the majority of blacks (particularly in the South) had been slaves and brought with them many problems associated with slavery such as poverty and lack of organizations to mobilize for their needs. To avoid assault and to advance themselves financially, many blacks found it necessary to maintain paternalistic relationships. Wealthy whites were encouraged to provide their black workers with protection and facilitate small loans to reduce labor turnover and maintain loyalty and diligence from this less costly workforce.

Eventually, economic and social changes in the South and the advent of industrialism in the North effected a significant change in relations between blacks and whites and decreased the opportunity and need for paternalism. Not only was there a mass exodus by blacks to the North in search of better opportunities, but the resulting urbanization fostered the growth of racially segregated communities as well as increasingly segregated social institutions such as transportation, public facilities, and education. This segregation diminished the interaction between blacks and wealthy whites and thus lessened the paternalistic relationships made possible by close interactions.

See also Gender Stratification; Racial and Ethnic Stratification; Racism; Segregation; Slavery; South Africa and Affirmative Action; Split-Labor-Market Theory; Uncle Tom.

FURTHER READING: Alston, Lee J., 1999, *Southern Paternalism and the American Welfare State: Economics, Politics, and Institutions in the South, 1865–1965*, New York: Cambridge University Press; Brueggeman, John, 2000, "The Power and Collapse of Paternalism: The Ford Motor Company and Black Workers, 1937–1941," *Social Problems* 47, no. 2 (May): 220–231; Dusinberre, William, 1996, *Them Dark Days: Slavery in the American Rice Swamps*, New York: Oxford University Press; Parrillo, Vincent N., 2003, *Strangers to These Shores: Race and Ethnic Relations in the United States*, Boston: Allyn and Bacon; Shafritz, Jay M., 1988, *The Dorsey Dictionary of American Government and Politics*, Chicago: Dorsey Press.

MAYA ALEXANDRA BEASLEY

Patterson v. McLean Credit Union, 491 U.S. 164 (1989)

In *Patterson v. McLean Credit Union*, the Supreme Court held that adverse employment actions, such as racial harassment, were not covered under section 1981 of the Civil Rights Act of 1866 because there was no breach of contract. Justice Anthony Kennedy, who delivered the opinion of the Court, stated that racial harassment was not actionable under section 1981 "because that provision does not apply to conduct which occurs after the formation of a contract and which does not interfere with the right to enforce established contract obligations."

Congress passed the Civil Rights Act of 1866 that forbade discrimination on account of race. The act was amended in 1871 because it did not cover such activities as "the right to sell, purchase, lease, or inherit real and personal property where the state has jurisdiction" (Sovereign 1994, 27). Brenda Patterson, an African American woman, was an employee of the McLean Credit Union for ten years. After she was laid off in July 1982, she filed suit in the U.S. District Court for the Middle District of North Carolina, alleging that the credit union was in violation of 14 Stat. 27, 42 U.S.C. § 1981. Patterson claimed that her employer "had harassed her, failed to promote her to an intermediate accounting clerk position, and then discharged her, all because of her race." She further claimed that this action caused her emotional distress, which was a cause for action under North Carolina tort law.

The federal district court determined that racial harassment was not actionable under section 1981 and did not submit that portion of the suit to the jury. The court did, however, submit Patterson's section 1981 claim of alleged discrimination in her discharge and failure to be promoted to the jury, which found in her favor on both claims. The court, however, said that Patterson failed to prove her claim for "intentional infliction of emotional distress under applicable standards of North Carolina law." On appeal, Patterson raised two issues. One issue was the failure of the district court to submit her section 1981 claim of racial harassment to the jury. The other claim was that the district court erred when it instructed the jury that the claim of discriminatory failure to promote would prevail only if Patterson could show that she was better qualified than the white woman who had been promoted. The Supreme Court affirmed the lower court's ruling. On the racial harassment issue, the Court stated that it might fall under the purview of Title VII of the 1964 Civil Rights Act, but not under section 1981. The Supreme Court also declined to overturn the decision in *Runyon v. McCrary*, 427 U.S. 160 (1976). In *Runyon*, the Court held that section 1981 of the 1866 Civil Rights Act prohibited private schools from excluding qualified children for admission solely based on their race.

After the *Patterson* case, part of the ruling was overturned by federal statute. The Civil Rights Act of 1991 amended Title VII of the 1964 Civil Rights Act, the 1866 statute, and other antidiscrimination acts, as well as voiding several state statutes. Section 101 of the 1991 Civil Rights Act amended section 1981 to provide for the enjoyment of more benefits, privileges, terms, and conditions of contractual relationships (Sovereign 1994, 29). The act also allows an individual to sue for actual compensatory and punitive damages.

See also Civil Rights Act of 1866; Civil Rights Act of 1991; Title VII of the Civil Rights Act of 1964.

FURTHER READING: Sovereign, Kenneth L., 1994, *Personnel Law*, 3d ed., Englewood Cliffs, NJ: Prentice Hall.

NAOMI ROBERTSON

Percentage Plans

Put forth as color-blind alternatives to affirmative action in higher education, percentage plans are admissions policies and programs that guarantee the admission of a specified percentage or number of college admittants based on specific race-neutral academic criteria. Admission is guaranteed to all students meeting the set criteria in a defined geographic area, normally the entire state in state university systems. These plans have predominantly been instituted in states that have abandoned their race-based affirmative action admissions programs, either voluntarily, by statute, or as a result of lawsuits. However, few states have confirmed that these programs were developed as a replacement or supplement of former affirmative action programs. Notable examples in recent years of state university systems that have abandoned their race-based affirmative action programs and have instituted percentage plans are Texas (10 Percent Plan), Florida (20 Percent Plan) and California (top 4 percent for schools within the University of California system).

The first state to experiment with percentage plans was Texas in 1996. The Texas 10 Percent Plan guaranteed to any high-school student in the top 10 percent of his or her class automatic admission to the state university system, including its flagship institution. When first adopted by Texas, the percentage plan was viewed as a way to maintain diversity by automatically admitting the top 10 percent of high-school graduates from every high school in the state as a way to maintain diversity in the wake of the Fifth Circuit Court of Appeals' ban on the use of affirmative action in higher education in *Hopwood v. Texas*, 78 F.3d 932 (5th Cir. 1996). Early proponents of the Texas plan viewed it as a way to circumvent the affirmative action prohibition put forth in *Hopwood* and still ensure diversity at the state universities.

Florida and California soon followed Texas's example in passing their own variations of the Texas 10 Percent Plan. After the University of Florida system eliminated its affirmative action programs pursuant to the One Florida Initiative, Governor Jeb Bush instituted his "Talented 20" plan in July 2000, guaranteeing admission to one of the universities in the state system for any high-school senior in the top 20 percent of his or her public high-school class and who had completed the required nineteen college-preparation credits. The plan does not require an SAT or ACT score for admissions consideration, tests that have been criticized as racially biased. Governor Bush's plan included steps to boost the achievement of the state's poorer students by spending $1.6 million to help high-school sophomores better prepare for college entrance tests, adding $20 million to the state's financial aid budget, guaranteeing admission to a state university to the top 20 percent of all high-school seniors, and providing training to teachers and faculty in low-performing schools. The program does not guarantee admission to a particular state-run university, however, but only to one of the state universities operating within the state.

In July 2001, the University of California system approved a new admissions policy that guarantees admission to California students who graduate in the top 4 percent of their class. According to the *Chronicle of Higher Education*, "The 4 percent policy plays a limited role in admitting students to the most-selective campuses, Berkeley and Los Angeles," and California "relies more heavily on other programs, including public school outreach and financial aid, to encourage diversity." Another variation of the percentage-plan approach can be seen in Georgia. Since 1993, Georgia has used the proceeds from that state's lottery to fund the HOPE (Helping Outstanding Pupils Educationally) Scholarship Program, which provides college scholarships to all high-school students graduating with at least a B average to any of the state's public colleges, universities, or technical colleges. The HOPE scholarship includes funds for student tuition, covers college mandatory fees, and provides a book allowance. Since 1993, fourteen other states have offered broad-based merit scholarships modeled after the Georgia HOPE scholarship. In June 2003, Tennessee became the fourteenth state to implement a scholarship program mirrored after the Georgia HOPE scholarship.

Many proponents of race-based affirmative action oppose percentage plans as being inadequate and unable to guarantee that minorities are equally represented in admitted student populations. Since the plans are race neutral, there are no assurances that minority students will represent the diversity of each state's population. Plan proponents argue that diversity will be promoted rather than eliminated because all students with superior academic abilities, particularly those from the low economic backgrounds from which minority students originate, will be given the same access to educational opportunities and financial support.

See also Hopwood v. Texas; One Florida Initiative.

FURTHER READING: Berry, Mary Frances, 2000, "How Percentage Plans Keep Minority Students out of College," *Chronicle of Higher Education*, August 4, A48; Blum, Edward, and Roger Clegg, 2003, "Percent Plans: Admissions of Failure," *Chronicle of Higher Education*, March 21, B10; Hebel, Sara, 2003, " 'Percent Plans' Don't Add Up," *Chronicle of Higher Education*, March 21, A22; Selingo, Jeffrey, 2001, "Small Number of High Schools Produces Half of Students at U. of Texas at Austin," *Chronicle of Higher Education*, April 13, A37; U.S. Commission on Civil Rights, 2000, "Toward an Understanding of Percentage Plans in Higher Education: Are They Effective Substitutes for Affirmative Action?" http://www.usccr.gov/pubs/percent/stmnt.htm.

GLENN L. STARKS

Performance-Based Selections

Performance-based selection is the process of selecting applicants based on their actual abilities, knowledge, and skills rather than by using subjective measures of their qualifications gained through such methods as paper-and-pencil tests. While aptitude and skills tests indirectly measure an applicant's ability to perform future work tasks or succeed in college, performance tests directly assess an applicant's skills and abilities by testing physical skills, determining existing knowledge of job duties, or requiring applicants to provide evidence of past performance such as completed reports or other portfolio-based work samples. Standardized tests are used as predictive measures of future performance based on a "one-shot" approach (i.e., applicants have one chance to perform well on a test). Performance-based selection methods evaluate past performance to assess the applicant's competency to perform well in a position when provided adequate training and mentoring.

Opponents of affirmative action and proponents of testing view standardized tests as a "meritocratic" selection (a process that assures merit) that is both fair and democratic (treats all candidates as equal) and functional (can be used to select the best candidates). Proponents of affirmative action view testing as favoring privileged groups. Members of privileged groups have such benefits as being able to attend better schools and pay for expensive preparation courses. Thus proponents of affirmative action often argue that standardized testing fails to accurately measure applicants' true abilities. Susan Sturm and Lani Guinier have been among the most vocal supporters of performance-based selection and opponents of solely using standardized tests for selecting applicants. They analogize using standardized testing to measure a student's future performance to using a ruler to make a standard physical measurement. They argue that when testing is used to make selections, "institutions are assumed to know what they are looking for (to continue the yardstick analogy, length), how to measure it (yards, meters), how to replicate the measurement process (using the ruler), and how to rank people accordingly (by height)" (Sturm and Guinier, 965). They further state that testocracy (the use of standardized tests to select qualified candidates) does not "reliably identify those applicants who will succeed in college or later in life, nor consistently predict those who are most likely to perform well in the jobs they occupy. Used alone or in combination with informal networking and subjective assessment, timed paper-and-pencil tests screen out applicants who could nevertheless do the job" (Sturm and Guinier, 976).

The use of testocracy's one-size-fits-all method of selection is also viewed as favoring those from higher socioeconomic backgrounds and ignoring such innate characteristics as drive and motivation. Performance-based selection uses on-the-job training and performance assessment, allowing an applicant's merit to be based on functional abilities. Applicants are also judged on their creativity and ability to collaborate in a teaming environment. According to Sturm and Guinier, "A performance-based framework of selection is the equivalent, in employment and education, to the elimination of poll taxes and restrictive registration laws in the arena of voting" (Sturm and Guinier 2000–2001).

Opponents of affirmative action who favor standardized tests believe that their reliance on and use of such tests is fair in selecting applicants for jobs and enrollment slots because selections are made based upon merit accorded to the success of individual applicants. Conversely, proponents of affirmative action often believe that standardized tests restrict opportunities for applicants who are poor and part of the working class, and these tests base performance on inadequate predictors. Many universities are questioning the viability of the continued use of standardized tests as a selection criterion for new student entrants. On February 18, 2001, at a meeting of the American Council of Education in Washington, D.C., University of California president Richard C. Atkinson called for the elimination of the SAT as a requirement for admission to all eight of the University of California's undergraduate campuses. Many public and private employers have long abandoned using standardized tests to select new employees, but rely on such performance-based measures as work history.

Many of those who advocate the repeal of affirmative action view tests as both a reliable predictor of merit and democratic. All applicants are given equal chances of succeeding, and applicants are not identified by race and gender. While testing services and academic administrators admit that standardized tests alone should not be the sole measure of academic ability and predictor of success, they view these tests as the only universal mode of candidate assessment. Many standardized tests (such as the SAT) were developed to identify those students who deserved the opportunity for a college education despite weak backgrounds or poor past performance. Further, test scores are seen as one of the best available predictors of academic performance, and there is a clear correlation between scores and grades earned in college.

See also Guinier, Lani; Merit Selections; Meritocracy; Standardized Testing.

FURTHER READING: Case, Mary Anne C., 1995, "Disaggregating Gender from Sex and Sexual Orientation: The Effeminate Man in the Law and Feminist Jurisprudence," *Yale Law Journal* 105:1–105; Crouse, James, and Dale Trusheim, 1988, *The Case against the SAT*, Chicago: University of Chicago Press; Shipler, David K., 1995, "My Equal Opportunity, Your Free Lunch," *New York Times*, March 5, 1; Sturm, Susan, and Lani Guinier, 1996, "Race Based Remedies: The Future of Affirmative Action: Reclaiming the Innovation Ideal," *California Law Review* 84:953–1036; Sturm, Susan, and Lani Guinier, 2000–2001, "The Future of Affirmative Action: Promoting Diversity in Education and Employment Requires Us to Rethink Testing and 'Meritocracy,' " *Boston Review*, December–January, http://www.bostonreview.net.

GLENN L. STARKS

Persons with Disabilities and Affirmative Action

To a greater degree than is true for race and gender, discrimination against persons with disabilities is institutionalized, which means that full participation in society is often physically difficult or in some cases impossible even without explicitly discriminatory behavior on the part of the nondisabled. Congress has to some limited degree recognized this fact and has incorporated this reality into disability policy. While in general, civil rights policies are designed to achieve parity between disadvantaged groups and the dominant majority by outlawing discrimination and instituting programs to hire, recruit, and promote women and people of color based on the same criteria that are used for white Americans and men, disability policy recognizes that disability affects major life functions and that civil rights policies for the disabled must incorporate the idea of reasonable accommodation (e.g., Braille signage in public spaces and additional time on exams for dyslexic individuals) to break down the existing forms of institutionalized discrimination.

A wide range of programs is referred to under the umbrella of affirmative action. In reality, the government uses the phrase to refer only to programs to increase representation of disadvantaged groups in federally administered programs and as a remedy for established past discrimination in private firms. Here the term "affirmative action" will be used in a broader sense that reflects popular use of the phrase. There are many laws that aim to outlaw discrimination against the disabled in a spectrum of arenas from employment to education, transportation, and access to public facilities, and few programs that meet the narrower definition of affirmative action.

One law that does fit the more tailored definition of affirmative action is the Rehabilitation Act of 1973. The Rehabilitation Act established Congress's intent to provide equal employment opportunity and affirmative action procedures to individuals with disabilities. Section 501 of the Rehabilitation Act enumerates the congressional directives for affirmative action in relation to persons with disabilities. Subsection (b) requires that federal agencies develop procedures to ensure the employment and fair promotion of persons with disabilities within the federal government. Subsection (c) gives the Equal Employment Opportunity Commission (EEOC) the responsibility of developing affirmative action programs for the disabled. Subsection (d) directs the EEOC to submit yearly reports to Congress summarizing the current procedures for and advancements in employment of persons with disabilities within the federal government. In total, section 501 of the Rehabilitation Act of 1973 establishes that the federal government is to serve as an example of how other organizations might successfully employ persons with disabilities.

Section 503 of the Rehabilitation Act requires federal contractors and subcontractors with contracts exceeding $10,000 to act affirmatively to hire and promote qualified individuals with disabilities. Unlike the laws that apply to race and gender, governmental and public employers can consider disability status in determining an individual's qualification for a position. For instance, fire departments can refuse to hire wheelchair users as firefighters on the grounds that wheelchair riders cannot fulfill fundamental requirements of the job.

Despite the radical increase in rights and protections afforded by the Rehabilitation Act of 1973, it was criticized for failing to fully protect individuals with disabilities from employment discrimination. While the act made it clear that the federal government was to extend employment opportunities to persons with disabilities, it did not explicitly prohibit the federal government from discriminating against applicants or employees with disabilities. In contrast, section 504, which applies to federally sponsored programs and activities conducted by any executive agency, expressly states that discrimination based solely on the fact that an individual has a disability is illegal. In adjudicating legal cases where plaintiffs claimed to be discriminated against in federal employment, many courts found that section 504 did not apply because section 501 explicitly addressed the issue of federal employment and did not establish antidiscrimination law in this area. This position was further supported by the fact that the act did not discuss remedies for federal employment discrimination against individuals with disabilities.

In 1978, Congress amended the Rehabilitation Act to address these criticisms. In particular, Congress ordered federal agencies to establish regulations to ensure nondiscrimination. Section 505(a) was created and extended the protections, rights, and remedies outlined in Title VII of the Civil Rights Act of 1964 to federal employees and job applicants with disabilities. The Rehabilitation Act was further amended in 1992 to make it consistent with the Americans with Disabilities Act of 1990 (ADA).

The ADA extended antidiscrimination protections for people with disabilities into a wider category of employers and employment-related services than the Rehabilitation Act. The ADA prohibits discrimination against people with disabilities by private employers with more than fifteen employees (both full-time and part-time employees are protected), all state and local government agencies, employment agencies, and labor organizations. In addition, Title I of the ADA outlaws discrimination against people associated with people with disabilities. For example, it is illegal to refuse to employ the parent of a child with a disability or someone who shares a household with a person with HIV. Though Congress assigned oversight responsibility to the EEOC, the burden of proving discrimination falls on the individual claiming that discrimination has occurred.

Employment is a multifaceted process, and the EEOC regulations outline and prohibit discrimination in all aspects of employment. For example, employers may not recruit or advertise jobs in ways that discriminate against people with disabilities. It is also illegal to discriminate against disabled people in terms of hiring, promotion, demotion, layoff, firing, or rehiring. Persons with disabilities are entitled to the same rates of pay, job assignments, fringe benefits, and opportunities for training as all other employees. In addition, federal laws prohibit practices that have a disparate impact on persons with disabilities even if the employer is not engaging in these practices with the explicit intent to adversely affect individuals

Kate Gainer, left, receives the ADA torch from Mary Norman, right, with the aid of Marc Koretzky, center, as the Spirit of ADA Torch Relay celebrates the tenth anniversary of the Americans with Disabilities Act. © AP/Wide World Photos.

with disabilities unless these practices are necessary for business function, there are no accommodations that can be made to allow persons with disabilities to function, or instituting such accommodations would not be reasonable because it would impose undue hardship on the employer. Not surprisingly, the terms "undue hardship" and "reasonable accommodation" have been the foundation of a great deal of tension and litigation.

Employment discrimination against the disabled can only occur under conditions in which there are otherwise qualified applicants with disabilities. Central to creating qualified job applicants are appropriate primary and secondary education facilities and programs to educate children with disabilities. The Individuals with Disabilities Education Act (IDEA), which has also been titled the Education of the Handicapped Act and the Education for All Handicapped Children Act, was signed into law in 1975 to provide for the needs of students with education-related disabilities. Disabilities that fall into this category include mental retardation, hearing, speech, and language impairments, visual impairments, emotional issues, autism, and "specific learning disabilities." However, children with attention deficit disorder are not necessarily covered under the IDEA.

The IDEA is a federal law designed to correct perceived deficiencies in state education systems. Before the passage of the IDEA, educational experts estimated that 8 million American children with disabilities were not receiving adequate and appropriate educational services, about 1 million children were completely excluded from public schools, and many more children were likely receiving ineffective instruction because they had undetected disabilities.

The IDEA is enforced by the Department of Education's Office of Special Education Programs and does three things to provide education for children with disabilities. First, the IDEA guarantees all children a right to a "free appropriate public education." Second, it creates safeguards to ensure that the interests of children with disabilities will not be overlooked. The cornerstone of IDEA protection is the "individualized education program" (IEP). In theory, the IEP is revised annually through collaboration between parents, school personnel, and other relevant experts to determine the needs, abilities, and appropriate placement for children with disabilities. The IEP determines what kind of services educators should provide for children with disabilities and incorporates the belief that public school providers must respect the opinions of parents of children with disabilities. The IDEA outlines procedures that allow parents to contest IEP assessments that they feel are inaccurate or violate the rights of their child. The process of educating children with disabilities as mandated by the IDEA is often expensive, so Congress established a grant program though which states apply for additional funding support for special education programs.

The IDEA provisions apply only to children who require special education services. However, many disabilities have no adverse impact on a student's ability to learn the material taught in mainstream classrooms, especially when schools make reasonable accommodations. Some examples of disabled students who do not require special education are paraplegic wheelchair users, children with substance addictions, or children who have tested positive for HIV/AIDS. Nevertheless, historically, many children with disabilities were denied educational services because school systems were unable to provide reasonable transportation, lacked classrooms that could accommodate wheelchairs or medical equipment, or did not have accessible toilet facilities, or simply because teachers or parents of other children were unwilling to have disabled children in their classrooms. Section 504 of the Rehabilitation Act prohibits these forms of discrimination.

Disability policies affect other major life areas of people with disabilities. First, one way that people with disabilities have been barred from full participation in society is that many buildings are not accessible to people with physical disabilities. Second, due to inadequate and inaccessible transportation, many people with disabilities have been unable to live full independent lives. Third, the ability to live independently requires that accessible housing be available in reasonable quantity and at affordable prices. Finally, full participation in society by persons with disabilities must include the ability to access all public services.

The Architectural Barriers Act (ABA) of 1968 was the first federal law implemented to reduce physical barriers to access by individuals with disabilities in public facilities. Because the ABA lacked enforcement provisions, compliance with it was not particularly stringent. Section 502 of the Rehabilitation Act created the Architectural and Transportation Barriers Compliance Board (Access Board), a twenty-five-member board that establishes minimum guidelines for compliance with the ABA, researches ways to eliminate architectural barriers, and makes access-related recommendations to the president and Congress. Finally, the Access Board is responsible for identifying barriers in transportation and housing that might affect individuals with disabilities. Section 504 provides even broader regulations for the creation of a barrier-free environment for people with disabilities. It requires that all new and recently renovated facilities that are wholly or partially used by federally assisted programs be constructed to minimize or completely eliminate access barriers for persons with disabilities. Title III of the ABA establishes that private entities that operate facilities for the public must be accessible by persons with disabilities. Examples of facilities governed by Title III are movie theaters, hotels, stores and shops, museums, amusement parks, and bus stations. While not exhaustive, the list shows an assortment of places where barriers previously circumscribed access to civic spaces for people with disabilities.

The Fair Housing Amendments Act of 1988 extends the protections of the Fair Housing Act of 1968 to prohibit discrimination against persons with disabilities in public and private real-estate transactions, including the rental and sale of housing. In addition, section 504 has been used to require landlords who receive federal funds to make reasonable accommodations for persons with disabilities. An example is the requirement that landlords with no-pet clauses make exceptions for guide dogs. This vast web of policies might be rightly classified as affirmative action because they not only prohibit discrimination against persons with disabilities, but also outline procedures for affirmative actions to increase participation in public spaces by people with disabilities.

See also Civil Rights Act of 1964; Civil Rights Act of 1968; Contracting and Affirmative Action; Department of Education; Equal Employment Opportunity Commission; Fair Housing Amendments Act of 1988; Housing; Housing and Urban Development Act of 1968; Rehabilitation Act of 1973; Title VII of the Civil Rights Act of 1964.

FURTHER READING: Berkowitz, Edward D., 1987, *Disabled Policy: America's Programs for the Handicapped,* New York: Cambridge University Press; Scotch, Richard K., 1984, *From Good Will to Civil Rights,* Philadelphia: Temple University Press; Tucker, Bonnie P., and Bruce A. Goldstein, 1990, *Legal Rights of Persons with Disabilities: An Analysis of Federal Law,* Horsham, PA: LRP Publications.

KYRA R. GREENE

Philadelphia Plan

See Nixon, Richard Milhous.

Plantation System

The plantation system was in many respects a microcosm of the wider society. To a large extent, it determined the role, status, and opportunities of the various groups constituting the plantation unit. A plantation system may be described as the totality of institutions involved in the production, distribution, and export of a particular crop or set of crops. It became the dominant mode of economic organization in most of the colonies of the former imperial powers and was based largely on unfree labor. As a total form of organization, it became a well-organized bureaucratic, authoritarian, and hierarchical system, which exploited individuals and the land. The land was generally worked by black slaves, who were viewed as fungible items, and bought, sold, and traded for the betterment of the plantation.

The life of a slave on a plantation was generally that of extreme regimentation and surveillance. This was a mode of organization that until recently characterized the southern United States, the Caribbean and South America, and parts of Asia and the Pacific.

Companies, families, tenants, or the state owned these plantations. Tenant plantations have been important in the Cotton Belt of the United States and in some areas of Brazil and the Philippines. Much of the investment on plantations went toward land, labor, plant, and equipment, although the actual proportions varied with the nature of the plantation itself. The largest cost, however, was that of labor. Ownership of a plantation was either foreign or local. If it was large, it was usually foreign owned and administered by a resident attorney; if it was small, it was generally family owned, with the family resident on the plantation. The decisive feature of the plantation system was that it brought various groups together under a total system and with a variable status within the social order. On many plantations, the size and origins of the groups would vary. Generally, however, the proportion of whites was small, giving rise to fears of revolt or attack, especially where the labor was unfree. In the case of large plantations, absentee planters delegated their powers to their local agents either on commission or on a salaried basis. It was generally agreed that control of labor in these structures was much harsher than on family plantations. In the case of plantation slavery, and especially on family plantations, the plantation became in many respects a social system with its peculiar social structure and other systems. As the dominant group, the whites became the reference group for other groups on the social ladder, yet there was important ranking between and among them, the chief ranking being the "principal" and "secondary" whites. The "principal" whites were made up of plantation owners or senior officials; other whites were classified as "secondary," with lesser status. It was common for whites to have colored or black concubines, a practice that soon developed into a status symbol. The whites, however, exercised a virtual monopoly of control over major official institutions. Since rights went with status, there was a constant preoccupation with status among groups in plantation society. Next in rank was the colored population comprising free persons as well as slaves. Free colored persons, though not slaves, were debarred from a number of rights.

For this group, acculturation into white norms of behavior was a major goal. Colored slaves were employed either as craftsmen or domestics to distinguish them from the field gangs that ranked lowest in the social order. This was the class that enjoyed greater social and economic mobility that allowed some to purchase their freedom at an early stage. When, however, a slave purchased his freedom, he lost all the allowances and benefits to which he was entitled from his master. The slaves themselves were differentiated by occupation, tribal origin, or color, while among domestics the principle of differentiation was based on the particular activity. Marriage and missionary work among the slaves on the plantation were discouraged, although slaves did possess certain recognized rights. Where tensions existed, they had to do with positions in the ranking system or with mating. Given the fact that whites were the reference group, all other groups tended to strive after the values and lifestyle of the dominant group.

Thus there was a tendency for slaves to move upwards in the color strata and to reject their own institutions and color. Slaves also held evening parties with music, dancing, and feasting. At night they would seemingly play at being scholars, royalty, or the upper class; however, they also plotted against the owners and management of the plantations, so the plantation system possessed an inherent instability as reflected in the recurring revolts, runaway slaves, and underground railroads. The plantation system was indeed the larger society writ small, which explains why it became a model for Latin America and the Caribbean economists inquiring into questions of development.

See also Assimilation Theory; Integration; Slavery; Split-Labor-Market Theory.

FURTHER READING: Allen, J.S., 1936, *The Negro Question in the United States*, New York: International Publishers; Braithwaite, Lloyd, 1953, "Social Stratification in Trinidad," *Social and Economic Studies*, October, 1–175; Furnivall, J.S., 1948, *Colonial Policy and Practice*, London: Cambridge University Press; Harris, Marvin, 1964, *Patterns of Race in the Americas*, New York: Walker; Pan American Union, 1959, *Plantation Systems of the New World*, Washington, DC: Pan American Union; Patterson, H.O., 1967, *The Sociology of Slavery*, Madison, NJ: Farleigh Dickinson University Press; Reuter, E.B., 1918, *The Mulatto in the United States*, Boston: Badger; Thompson, E.T., ed., 1939, *Race Relations and the Race Problem*, Durham, NC: Duke University Press.

ANN MARIE BISSESSAR

Plessy v. Ferguson, 163 U.S. 537 (1896)

Plessy v. Ferguson was the Supreme Court case decided in 1896 that asserted that a state law requiring blacks to sit in designated railroad cars set the legal basis for many state laws requiring blacks to attend separate schools, use separate washrooms, sit at the back of public buses, and use a myriad of other segregated facilities and services. This decision established the legal pattern for racial segregation in the South and elsewhere in the United States. Years of antidiscrimination laws and efforts through such programs as affirmative action have sought to reverse this pattern.

An 1890 Louisiana law required railroad companies to provide "equal but separate" accommodations for white and "colored" passengers. Blacks in New Orleans organized to challenge the new law and asked Homer Plessy, who claimed to be one-eighth black and seven-eighths Caucasian, to purchase a ticket. Plessy refused to sit in the coaches reserved for blacks and was arrested. On appeal, the Louisiana Supreme Court held that there was no conflict between the Louisiana law and the Thirteenth and Fourteenth Amendments added to the U.S. Constitution soon after the Civil War. Plessy's legal counsel had argued that Louisiana's segregation law violated the Thirteenth Amendment in that the Thirteenth Amendment prohibited slavery, and the segregation law had the effect of placing upon black citizens a badge of inferiority and de facto slavery. The counsel for Plessy argued that the Fourteenth Amendment was also violated by the Louisiana law in that the law unfairly distinguished between white and black citizens, an arguable violation of the Equal Protection Clause of the Fourteenth Amendment. When Plessy was unsuccessful at the Louisiana Supreme Court, Plessy's legal counsel appealed this decision to the U.S. Supreme Court, which again upheld the Louisiana law and rejected Plessy's claim that this law violated his constitutional rights.

In the majority opinion, authored by Justice Henry B. Brown, the Court delineated the following major points: first, in the Court's view, the Louisiana law was reasonable, especially since Congress then required separate schools for black children in the District of Columbia; second, the Louisiana law did not stamp the colored race with "a badge of inferiority"; third, legislation seeking to "eradicate racial instincts or abolish distinctions" will "accentuate difficulties"; and fourth, the law was powerless to effectuate social changes in society: "if one race be inferior . . . , the Constitution cannot put them on the same plane."

Only one precedent was cited in the *Plessy* majority opinion, *Roberts v. City of Boston*, 59 Mass. 198 (1849), holding that black children could be assigned to separate schools. Then and now, American courts usually rely on earlier decisions to justify their decision in the case before the court. However, the *Roberts* decision was a weak precedent because (1) it was rendered before the Civil War, Reconstruction, and the addition of the Thirteenth and Fourteenth Amendments to the Constitution, (2) it was an interpretation by a state court, not a federal court, and pertained only to the Massachusetts Constitution, and (3) by 1855, the Massachusetts legislature banned racial segregation in public schools in the state.

Justice John Marshall Harlan in his now-famous sole dissenting opinion in the *Plessy* case rightly stated that the intent of the Louisiana law was to exclude colored people from coaches occupied by whites, and it had no other legitimate governmental purpose. He wrote the now-often-quoted phrase "our Constitution is color-blind, and neither knows nor tolerates classes among citizens," and that in regard to civil rights, "all citizens are equal before the law." From his dissent, the notion or doctrine of a color-blind constitution emerged. With remarkable foresight, he wrote, "The [majority] judgment . . . will prove to be as pernicious as . . . the *Dred Scott* case." Ignoring Justice Harlan's eloquent dissent, state legislatures embraced the *Plessy* decision as the constitutional basis for laws segregating the races in transportation, schools, parks, hospitals, cemeteries, hotels, and restaurants. The dual society flowing from the *Plessy* decision was especially evident in those parts of the nation with a substantial black population, including all former Confederate states. The move away from the *Plessy* "separate-but-equal" decision began in 1938 when the Supreme Court held that denial of admission of blacks, on the basis of race, to the University of Missouri Law School denied those applicants Fourteenth Amendment "equal protection of the law." Even then, more than twenty years would pass before "affirmative action" would be widely recognized as a remedy for racial segregation.

See also Civil War (Reconstruction) Amendments and Civil Rights Acts; Color-Blind Constitution; *Dred Scott v. Sandford*; Equal Protection Clause; Fourteenth Amendment; *Roberts v. City of Boston*; Segregation; Thirteenth Amendment.

FURTHER READING: Epstein, Lee, and Thomas G. Walker, 1995, *Constitutional Law for a Changing America*, 2d ed., Washington, DC: Congressional Quarterly; Mason, Alpheus Thomas, and Donald Grier, Jr., Stephenson, *American Constitutional Law*, 13th ed., Upper Saddle River, NJ: Prentice Hall, 2002.

GAYLE AVANT

Pluralism

Pluralism is an analytic framework theorizing that political power and influence are widely and unequally distributed among multiple entities according to specialization of interest, degree of concern, and availability of slack power resources. This theory suggests that parties directly affected by affirmative action, including the U.S. Equal Employment Opportunity Commission, contractors, unions, minorities, and women's groups, dominate decision making concerning affirmative action policy even though they may not have similar influence over other types of policy.

Pluralist theorists support this framework and test a polity's degree of policy pluralism by analyzing the number and makeup of observable entities that influence public decisions. A polity is considered very pluralistic if many entities, which include individuals, governmental bodies, and volunteer associations, exert influence over its policy decisions and if the entities exerting the most effective influence vary according to the policy in question. An entity's ability to exert effective influence on a policy is directly related to its relevant specialization of interest and degree of concern on the issue and to the amount of slack power resources that it can mobilize. An entity has specialization of interest in a policy as a beneficiary, administrator, advocate, or opponent of that policy. Its degree of concern refers to the degree of effect that a policy has or may have on its interests. Slack power resources include voluntary associations, the media, private pressure, and public pressure and protest. Political theorists critical of the pluralist approach suggest that review only of observable influence denies the influence of behind-the-scenes pressures that may control seemingly independent political actors or that keep policy proposals off agendas so that they can never be observed.

See also Affirmative Action Plan/Program; Contracting and Affirmative Action; Equal Employment Opportunity Commission.

FURTHER READING: Hamilton, Richard F., 2001, *Mass Society, Pluralism, and Bureaucracy*, Westport, CT: Praeger; Ross, Bernard H., and Myron A. Levine, 1996, *Urban Politics: Power in Metropolitan America*, 5th ed., Itasca, IL: F.E. Peacock.

MARK J. SENEDIAK

Plus Factor

See Harvard Model; *Regents of the University of California v. Bakke.*

Podberesky v. Kirwan, 38 F.3d 147 (4th Cir. 1994)

In *Podberesky v. Kirwan*, Daniel J. Podberesky claimed that the University of Maryland violated his rights by denying him a scholarship offered only to African Americans. Podberesky, a Hispanic American, graduated from high school with a 3.56 grade point average and scored 1340 on the SAT. The Banneker Scholarship, which he claimed he was denied, was a "full-ride" scholarship program funded by the state. In 1994, the U.S. Court of Appeals for the Fourth Circuit reversed the district court's grant of summary judgment to the university and ruled that the scholarship program failed to meet the strict scrutiny test, although the university asserted that the program's goal was to remedy the present effects of past discrimination.

The University of Maryland established the Banneker Scholarship as a result of a 1969 order by the Office for Civil Rights of the Department of Health, Education, and Welfare (now in the Department of Education), which notified the state of Maryland that its segregated higher-education system was in violation of Title VI of the Civil Rights Act of 1964. The state was ordered to submit a desegregation plan. Part of the final plan, which was not approved until 1985, included race-targeted scholarships, which included the Banneker program as part of the university's Black Undergraduate Recruitment Program.

The *Podberesky* case highlighted the practice of some universities to employ a narrow definition of what ethnicities were classified under the umbrella of minorities for purposes of affirmative action plans or programs. Although Podberesky was a Hispanic American (Costa Rican), he was not eligible for the African American–targeted scholarship program because he was not black. The university specifically pointed to its unfavorable reputation within the African American community, the racial tension on campus, the underrepresentation of African American students, the low retention and graduation rates of African Americans at the university, and the racially hostile atmosphere on the campus as justification for the minority scholarship.

The district court relied on the ruling in *City of Richmond v. J.A. Croson Co.*, 488 U.S. 469 (1989), in deciding that the effects of past discrimination justified the University of Maryland's scholarship. Phrased another way, the district court held that attempting to remedy the effects of past discrimination was a compelling governmental interest needed to pass the strict scrutiny test that is utilized to test the permissibility of affirmative action that discriminates on account of race. Additionally, according to the district court, the university narrowly tailored the program with the goal of recruiting and retaining black students by offering a race-based scholarship to black applicants while still offering race-neutral and other sources of aid to all other applicants. The decision was reversed on appeal. The Fourth Circuit Court of Appeals disagreed with the district court that there was evidence to show the continuing effects of past discrimination. Furthermore, knowledge of past discrimination alone was insufficient to justify a race-conscious program, and there must be some present or continuing effects of the previous discrimination. The Fourth Circuit held that "mere knowledge of historical fact is not the kind of present effect that can justify a race-exclusive remedy." Finally, the court held that the program also was not a narrowly tailored program, as is required under the strict scrutiny test, because it was not limited in duration.

The Fourth Circuit also stressed the need to apply the strict scrutiny analysis in cases such as this. The court articulated its denial of the university's defenses of the scholarship by stating:

> Racial and ethnic distinctions of any sort are inherently suspect and thus call for the most exacting judicial examination. The rationale for this stringent standard of review is plain. Of all the criteria by which men and women can be judged, the most pernicious is that of race. The injustice of judging human beings by the color of their skin is so apparent that racial classifications cannot be rationalized by the casual invocation of benign remedial aims. While the inequities and indignities visited by past discrimination are undeniable, the use of race as a reparational device risks perpetuating the very race-consciousness such a remedy purports to overcome. . . . It thus remains our constitutional premise that race is an impermissible arbiter of human fortunes.

The university was ordered to reexamine Podberesky's qualifications and determine his eligibility for the scholarship without regard to race. The Supreme Court refused to grant review of the case.

See also *City of Richmond v. J.A. Croson Co.*; Civil Rights Act of 1964; Compelling Governmental Interest; Department of Education; Education and Affirmative Action; Hispanic Americans; Narrowly Tailored Affirmative Action Plans; Strict Scrutiny; Title VI of the Civil Rights Act of 1964.

FURTHER READING: Spann, Girardeau A., 2000, *The Law of Affirmative Action: Twenty-five Years of Supreme Court Decisions on Race and Remedies*, New York: New York University Press.

GLENN L. STARKS

Powell, Adam Clayton, Jr. (1908–1972)

Adam Clayton Powell Jr. was called "Mr. Civil Rights" before the civil rights movement gained momentum in the United States. He was a powerful leader in the U.S. House of Representatives and had a controversial presence. In 1999, the *Journal of Blacks in Higher Education* conducted a survey listing the most important African Americans of the twentieth century. In this study, Powell was ranked second of all African American elected officials who made the greatest contributions to American society in the twentieth century (Barbara Jordan was ranked first), which is an indication of the political power and influence he held during his service in Congress. Powell used his considerable influence to promote civil rights legislation. When he was elected in 1944, from Harlem, New York, he was one of two African Americans in the U.S. House of Representatives.

During his service in the House, Powell introduced more than fifty pieces of major legislation aimed at ending segregation and promoting civil rights. One of his most successful strategies in accomplishing this unprecedented feat was the frequent use of the "Powell Amendment," a rider he would attach to proposals for federal funds. If a bill had the Powell Amendment successfully attached to it, federal funds would not be granted to local governments or agencies that would use those funds in a discriminatory or racially segregated manner. The utilization of the Powell Amendment sought to change discriminatory or segregationist practices through the power of the purse.

Through his seniority in the House, Powell assumed chairmanship of the powerful House Committee on Education and Labor in 1961, a position he maintained throughout the 1960s. During the 1960s, Powell was at the pinnacle of his power in the House and also served as a strategist for President Lyndon Johnson's Great Society agenda, being responsible for steering through the House a myriad of grand social legislation, including federal aid to higher education, training for the unemployed and the handicapped, and the monumental Civil Rights Act of 1964 that eliminated many aspects of previously permissible discrimination against blacks. Ramsey Clark, former attorney general of the United States, summarized Powell's influence and power in the House when he stated that "his personal force, the power that he accumulated in the Congress, probably isn't equaled by a single member in the [Black] Caucus, even now, and that's amazing" (Garland, 62).

Adam Clayton Powell Jr. was born into a solid middle-class family on November 29, 1908, in New Haven, Connecticut. At the time, his father was a pastor and a student at Yale University. Adam Clayton Powell Sr. was a founder of the National Urban League and an early leader of the National Association for the Advancement of Colored People. He was actively involved in fighting racism. The Powell family moved to New York City when young Adam was six months old. The father assumed the ministry of the most prestigious African American church in the country, Abyssinian Baptist Church. Later, the son was to take over this thriving ministry. Adam Clayton Powell Jr. attended public schools in New York City and graduated from Colgate University in upstate Hamilton, New York, in 1930. He earned a master's degree in religious education from Columbia University in 1932. He also studied at Shaw University in Raleigh, North Carolina. In between, his parents presented their only son with a trip to Europe, the Holy Land, and Egypt.

During the depression years, African Americans, like other Americans, were experiencing great economic difficulties. Adam Jr., through his father's church, administered a popular community outreach program that provided food, clothing, and jobs for thousands of unemployed Harlemites. This community activism surprised some because he had a reputation of being a playboy. He organized the people in the community and expanded his work to presiding over mass meetings, rent strikes, and picket lines to demand that restaurants, stores, utility companies, bus companies, Harlem Hospital, and the 1939 World's Fair hire or promote black employees. His successes in these efforts commanded the respect and loyalty of the people of Harlem. With each new victory, the black press broadcast it far and wide. Every time a segregation barrier toppled, this gave hope and inspiration to African Americans throughout many parts of the country. Gone were the days when Adam Clayton Powell Jr. was known only as a handsome, partying playboy. He had earned a stellar reputation as a bona fide religious leader and civil rights champion.

Powell assumed leadership of his father's Abyssinian Baptist Church in 1937. In addition to leading a church with a membership of nearly 14,000, he simultaneously launched a career of public service that eventually landed him in the U.S. Congress. His constituency was already in place. In 1941, running as an independent, he won a seat on the New York City Council. He was the first African American to serve in this capacity. He edited and published the *People's Voice*, a weekly newspaper, from 1941 to 1945. In 1945, he began a two-year service in the New York State Office of Price Administration. During much of that same time, he was a member of the Manhattan Civilian Defense.

In 1944, he was selected to serve in the U.S. Congress and was sworn in as a member of the Seventy-ninth Congress on January 3, 1945. Upon his arrival in Washington, Powell's first order of business was to take issue with the practice that did not allow black representatives to use Capitol facilities, reserved for members only. He ushered in his black constituents to dine with him in the "whites-only" House restaurant. He told his staff to eat there regardless of whether they were hungry or not. He was proud, brash, and eloquent, all traits that did not endear him to some of the staid or more reserved members of this august body. The staunch segregationists who still held a stronghold in Congress at that time were definitely unimpressed with their new colleague.

Powell introduced legislation to outlaw lynching and the use of poll taxes and to end discrimination in the armed forces, housing, employment, and transportation. After serving multiple successful terms in the House, he gained enough seniority to become chairman of the House Education and Labor Committee in 1961. Some of Powell's most important and long-lasting contributions were accomplished in this position. He facilitated the successful passage of the social legislation of President John F. Kennedy's New Frontier and President Lyndon Johnson's Great Society. Bills Powell introduced targeted the reduction or elimination of poverty and an increased minimum wage and included the Defense Education Act. Powell also attended the historic Bandung Conference of African and Asian nations in 1955. He admonished the U.S. government for not being more involved in their struggle for self-determination and independence. Having been elected as a Democrat, Powell chose to campaign for President Eisenhower, a Republican in 1956. Powell said that he made the decision to support the Republican candidate because the Republican Party had a stronger platform on civil rights.

In spite of all the contributions made by Powell while serving in the U.S. Congress, he managed to make many enemies. His lifestyle was often reported in the press as being flamboyant and irreverent. In the 1960s, at the pinnacle of his power in the House, he began a downward spiral that included a contempt of court citation for a libel suit, a House vote to deprive him of his congressional seat, and accusations of missing House funds, tax evasion, and conduct unbecoming a House member. He was accused of taking numerous trips abroad using public funds, chronic absenteeism, and not visiting his home district to avoid possible arrest relating to the libel case. He spent an increasing amount of time sailing his boat in the Bahamas.

On January 9, 1967, the House Democratic Caucus removed Powell from the chairmanship of the Committee on Education and Labor. Following this, the committee voted to censure and fine him and take away his seniority. Later the full House rejected these measures and voted to exclude him altogether from the Ninetieth Congress. Powell challenged this action all the way to the U.S. Supreme Court and won, for the Court ruled that the committee's action against Powell was unconstitutional. His constituents in New York then reelected Powell in a special election on April 11, 1967; however, Powell refused his seat. Again he was elected in the regular election to fill the congressional seat from which he was excluded. Once more Powell did not take his seat in the Ninety-first Congress. His final bid for election failed after he lost the Democratic primary in 1970 to Charles Rangel, a supporter of affirmative action and civil rights who has held the seat since 1971.

One year later, in 1971, Powell resigned from the ministry at Abyssinian Baptist Church and retired to the island of Bimini in the Bahamas. Throughout all of his trials, he cited what became his mantra at the time "Keep the faith, baby." Powell died of prostate cancer in 1972 at the age of sixty-three. A state office building and a street bearing his name are in Harlem as a tribute to Adam Clayton Powell Jr.

See also Civil Rights Act of 1964; Johnson, Lyndon Baines; Kennedy, John Fitzgerald; Rangel, Charles.

FURTHER READING: Garland, Phyl, 1990, "I Remember Adam," *Ebony* 45, no. 5 (March): 56–60; Hamilton, Charles V., 1991, *Adam Clayton Powell, Jr.: The Political Biography of an American Dilemma*, New York: Atheneum; Haygood, Wil, 1993, *King of the Cats: The Life and*

Times of Adam Clayton Powell, Jr., Boston: Houghton Mifflin; Powell, Adam Clayton, 1971, *Adam by Adam*, New York: Dial Press.

BETTY NYANGONI

Powell, Colin (1937–)

Appointed in the George W. Bush administration in 2001 as the first African American secretary of state, Powell was a career soldier who served as chairman of the Joint Chiefs of Staff (JCS) from 1989 to 1993 during the administrations of George Bush Sr. and then Bill Clinton. The son of poor Jamaican immigrants, Powell is depicted by some as a model for American youth: a modern-day Horatio Alger hero figure who rose from modest roots primarily due to the content of his character. Powell himself attributes his success primarily to hard work. There is no doubt that Colin Powell is a man of considerable intelligence, and he projects a commanding presence, both physically and ethically. To some, however, Powell is the quintessential "token" black who was promoted to the chairmanship of the JCS primarily because he is dark skinned and to deflect and undermine any and all claims that racial barriers still deny blacks and other racial minorities equal opportunity, either in the U.S. military or in America generally. This view is illustrated by the derogatory comments made in 2002 by entertainer Harry Belafonte, who referred to Powell as an "Uncle Tom" and a "house slave."

Powell's shifting views on affirmative action, as an influential minority leader in the United States, have been closely monitored. In his autobiography in 1995, Powell stated that "preferences, no matter how well intended, ultimately breed resentment among the non-preferred." Powell further stated that "preferential treatment demeans the achievements that minority Americans win by their own efforts . . . if [affirmative action] leads to preferential treatment or helps those who no longer need help, I am opposed" (Millard, S4). Yet soon thereafter, Powell qualified his position in a 1996 speech at Bowie State University in Maryland, where he stated that "some people will say that affirmative action stigmatizes the recipients. Nonsense . . . affirmative action provides access for the qualified" (Powell, S9312). Hence Powell appeared to be supportive of affirmative action if it was implemented properly.

Although Powell rejected overtures from some members of the Republican Party to campaign for a presidential nomination in 1996, he did deliver the keynote address at the Republican National Convention that year. In this address, Powell urged his party to remain the party of Abraham Lincoln. More specifically, he urged his party to maintain its historical commitment to equal opportunity. He also stated his support for affirmative action, at least with respect to programs that attempt to counter the effects of past discrimination, even though support for any kind of affirmative action that addresses past acts of discrimination is not a popular position within the Republican Party today. In 2003, Powell gave a nationally aired talk in which he not only stated that he supports affirmative action, but also specified that he supported affirmative action plans utilized by universities, like the plans at issue in *Gratz v. Bollinger*, 123 S. Ct. 2411, 2003 U.S. LEXIS 4801 (2003), and *Grutter v. Bollinger*, 123 S. Ct. 2325, 2003 U.S. LEXIS 4800 (2003).

Powell was born on April 5, 1937, in New York City, and was raised by his immigrant parents in the South Bronx. Powell did not distinguish himself academically in high school or at the City College of New York (CCNY), where he earned a degree in geology. He did distinguish himself, however, in his ROTC program at CCNY. In his senior year, he was voted outstanding cadet. Shortly after graduation, Powell was commissioned as a second lieutenant in the U.S. Army, and he rose steadily through the ranks. In 1989, Powell became chairman of the JCS, the youngest man (as well as the first black man) ever appointed to this prestigious position. Powell did not attend the U.S. Military Academy at West Point, the traditional path to high-level command in the U.S. Army, and he was the least senior of the fifteen four-star generals eligible for the JCS chairmanship in 1989. Powell himself acknowledged that there were several senior candidates with more impressive military credentials. These facts have led some to argue that Powell's appointment as chairman of the JCS was a political decision determined more by the color of his skin than by his credentials or character.

As chairman of the JCS, Powell received considerable public exposure during the Gulf War, and he became an even more prominent public figure after his retirement from the army in 1993. As chairman of the JCS in the Clinton administration, Powell opposed President Clinton's desire to allow homosexuals to serve in the military. In particular, Powell objected to Clinton's idea of issuing an executive order to achieve this goal. Powell came under considerable fire from some members of the national press, who noted that Powell himself was commanding white troops because President Harry S. Truman had issued Executive Order 9981, which desegregated the U.S. military despite the objection of many members of the U.S. Congress as well as most high-ranking members of the military. Powell drew a distinction, however, between discrimination based on race and discrimination in all cases. For Powell, there was no good reason to discriminate on the basis of racial factors. Given the "intimate" nature of barracks life and some combat environments, however, the differences in sexual orientation could undermine the efficiency as well as the morale of military units in the same way, Powell argued, that the integration of women into some (but not all) combat situations could undermine the military mission. Powell did not oppose the "right" of women to participate in some combat roles provided these roles did not entail integrating women and men domestically.

See also Bush, George Herbert Walker; Bush, George W.; Clinton, William Jefferson; *Gratz v. Bollinger/Grutter v. Bollinger*; Military and Affirmative Action; Truman, Harry; Uncle Tom.

FURTHER READING: Benenson, Lawrence, 1996, *Colin Powell Story*, New York: Random House; Blue, Rose, and Corinne Naden, 1997, *Colin Powell: Straight to the Top*, Brookfield, CT: Millbrook Press; Cummings, Judith, 1995, *Colin Powell and the American Dream*, New York: Penguin; Dalton, Harlon, 1995, "Horatio Alger," in *Rereading America*, 5th ed., edited by Gary Colombo, Robert Cullen, and Bonnie Lisle, New York: St. Martin's, 2001; Hughes, Libby, 1996, *A Man of Quality*, Parsippany, NJ: Dillon Press; Killian, Lewis M., 1999, "Generals, the Talented Tenth, and Affirmative Action," *Society* 36, no. 6 (September): 33–46; Lanning, Michael, 1997, *The African-American Soldier: From Crispus Attucks to Colin Powell*, Secaucus, NJ: Birch Lane Press; McAllister, J.F., 1995, "The Candidate of Dreams," *Time*, December 13, 88–90; Millard, Max, 1996, "Colin Powell's 'Vision,'" *Sun Reporter* 52, no. 8 (February 22): S4; Powell, Colin, 1995, *My American Journey*, New York: Random House; Powell, Colin, 1996, Commencement Address: Bowie State University, reprinted in 142

Cong. Rec. S9311–S9312; Roth, David, 1993, *Sacred Honor: A Biography of Colin Powell*, San Francisco: HarperSan Francisco.

MICHAEL D. QUIGLEY

Powell, Lewis Franklin, Jr. (1907–1998)

Of all his life accomplishments, Lewis Franklin Powell Jr., associate justice of the U.S. Supreme Court from 1972 to 1987, is perhaps best known and remembered for his position and opinion in the seminal affirmative action case *Regents of the University of California v. Bakke*, 438 U.S. 265 (1978). In the *Bakke* case, Justice Powell was the crucial swing vote, joining both the conservative and liberal blocs on different holdings in the case. Thus Powell joined with the conservative bloc in *Bakke* in striking down fixed racial quotas as being a violation of Title VI of the Civil Rights Act of 1964 and the Equal Protection Clause of the Fourteenth Amendment and, at the same time, joined the liberal bloc in upholding the possibility of using race-conscious affirmative action in certain circumstances. Justice Powell's position in the *Bakke* case is representative of his overall view of affirmative action while on the Court, neither entirely for or against affirmative action in all circumstances. Rather, a study of Powell's record on affirmative action while he was on the Court reveals that he favored affirmative action, but only when the government had a compelling governmental interest in putting forth a race-conscious affirmative action plan and the plan was based upon clear findings and justifications.

Lewis F. Powell was born on November 19, 1907, in Suffolk, Virginia. Powell's family was considered one of the oldest Virginia families, and his direct ancestors could be found in Virginia as early as the Jamestown Colony in 1607. With the exception of Powell's time as a student at Harvard and three years as an officer in World War II, he spent almost all of his life in Virginia. He attended college at Washington and Lee College in Lexington, Virginia, where he was elected to Phi Beta Kappa, was elected student body president, and graduated first in his class in 1929. He also earned an LL.B. from Washington and Lee College in 1931 and an LL.M. from Harvard University in 1932. During his studies at Harvard, Powell took classes under both Felix Frankfurter and Roscoe Pound, two of the great legal minds of America during this time period.

After graduating from law school, Powell returned to Virginia, where he spent the majority of his legal career in private practice. Powell became one of the most respected members of the Virginia bar, serving as chairman of several prestigious bodies, including the American Bar Association, the American College of Trial Lawyers, the Virginia State Board of Education, and the Virginia Constitutional Revision Commission. From private practice, he was nominated by President Richard Nixon to serve on the Supreme Court, was confirmed in the Senate by a vote of 89–1, and took his seat on January 7, 1972.

As evidence of his views on race, it is notable that while he was on the Virginia State Board of Education, he supported desegregation and opposed those who encouraged a "massive resistance policy" to desegregation in the state of Virginia. Upon his nomination to the Supreme Court, Powell received the backing of, among other organizations, Virginia's Chapter of the National Association for the Advancement of Colored People. Once he was on the Court, Powell "quickly became the Court's most revered and popular member. Cautious and basically conservative, yet moderate and utterly non-doctrinaire . . . he was on the winning side . . . more than any other member of the Court" (Abraham 1992, 661).

In the realm of affirmative action, Powell was best known for his deciding vote and position in the *Bakke* case, and "even though he is no longer on the Court, Justice Powell's *Bakke* opinion is still treated with a certain deference" (Spann 2000, 16). In the *Bakke* decision, Powell ultimately voted for striking down fixed racial quotas while upholding the constitutionality of race-conscious affirmative action plans when needed to advance a compelling governmental interest. For Powell, in the *Bakke* decision, a compelling governmental interest could be the elimination of past discrimination by that institution, so long as the institution clearly documented prior discrimination at the institution when it formulated the affirmative action plan. Second, for Powell, diversity in higher education might constitute a compelling governmental interest if the affirmative action plan was narrowly tailored. According to Powell, in the academic environment, race might be used one factor (among many) that might be considered by admissions departments. Powell wrote in his opinion in *Bakke* that "it is not an interest in simple ethnic diversity, in which a specified percentage of the student body is in effect guaranteed to be members of selected ethnic groups, with the remaining percentage an undifferentiated aggregation of students." Rather, commented Powell, "the diversity that furthers a compelling state interest encompasses a far broader array of qualifications and characteristics of which racial or ethnic origin is but a single though important element." This position of Powell's has become known today as the "diversity rationale" and has been the subject of several lower court cases (e.g., *Hopwood v. State of Texas*, 78 F.3d 932 [5th Cir. 1996], *Smith v. University of Washington Law School*, 233 F.3d 1188 [9th Cir. 2000], and *Johnson v. Board of Regents of the University of Georgia*, 263 F.3d 1234 [11th Cir. [2001]), as well as the milestone 2003 Supreme Court cases *Gratz v. Bollinger*, 123 S. Ct. 2411, 2003 U.S. LEXIS 4801 (2003), and *Grutter v. Bollinger*, 123 S. Ct. 2325, 2003 U.S. LEXIS 4800 (2003). In the *Grutter* case, the Supreme Court specifically affirmed Powell's diversity rationale, that race may be utilized as one of many factors, as the opinion of the Supreme Court in 2003.

In dealing with employment and affirmative action, Powell took a similar approach to his position in the *Bakke* case. He was supportive of affirmative action, but only if the state was advancing a compelling governmental interest and the plan was being implemented after clear findings and documentation of prior discrimination by the institution. Powell has been described as the "Court's strongest proponent of formal findings" (Spann 2000, 171). In dissecting the major affirmative action cases over which Powell presided, outside of the *Bakke* decision, Powell appeared to support affirmative action only in response to specific prior discrimination by the institution. Thus in *Fullilove v. Klutznick*, 448 U.S. 448 (1980), he joined the majority in allowing congressionally imposed set-asides for minority contractors; however, in a concurring opinion he stressed the need for clear findings made by a competent body concerning past discrimination before implementing affirmative action. In *Wygant v. Jackson Board of Education*, 476 U.S. 267 (1986), Powell "rejected both the role-model and general societal discrimination justifications for affirmative action; insisted on a very tight fit between the state interest and the nature of the remedy; and disfavored layoffs of innocent whites" (Spann 2000, 30).

See also Affirmative Action Plan/Program; Civil Rights Act of 1964; Compelling Governmental Interest; Education and Affirmative Action; Equal Protection Clause; Fourteenth Amendment; *Fullilove v. Klutznick; Gratz v. Bollinger/Grutter v. Bollinger; Hopwood v. Texas; Johnson v. Board of Regents of the University of Georgia;* Narrowly Tailored Affirmative Action Plans; *Regents of the University of California v. Bakke;* Role Model Theory; *Smith v. University of Washington Law School;* Title VI of the Civil Rights Act of 1964; *Wygant v. Jackson Board of Education.*

FURTHER READING: Abraham, Henry J., 1992, "Powell, Lewis Franklin, Jr.," in *The Oxford Companion to the Supreme Court of the United States,* edited by Kermit L. Hall, New York: Oxford University Press; Schmidt, Peter, 2003, "Affirmative Action Survives, and So Does the Debate: The Supreme Court Upholds Race-Conscious Admissions in Principle, but Not Always as Practiced," *Chronicle of Higher Education,* July 4, S1; Spann, Girardeau A., 2000, *The Law of Affirmative Action: Twenty-five Years of Supreme Court Decisions on Race and Remedies,* New York: New York University Press.

JAMES A. BECKMAN

Preferences

At its most basic level, the concept of "preferences" refers to a social attitude or behavior that is exhibited by human beings when favoring or giving prior rights to some thing, idea, or action before another in the scale or hierarchy of multiple alternatives while, at the same time, resources, capabilities, and materials to make decisions are limited. Situations of multiple needs and wants matched against limited available resources lead to ranking of preferences on a scale that assigns and allocates higher scores and priorities to the most favored choice of item, idea, activity, or decision. Preferences are also all about how individuals, groups, governments, families, and institutions rank or compare desirability of any two or more combinations or allotments of goods, ideas, and actions, assuming that these allotments are available to the individual at no cost. In the affirmative action area, preferences are often given to, or resources allotted to, members of a historically underrepresented class in the employment or educational context. Supporters of affirmative action are quick to point out that giving resources to a particular group based upon a preference is not just a program specific to helping minorities; rather, a variety of groups gained resources historically through preferences and preferential treatment, such as veterans through the GI program, sons or daughters of alumni through legacy admissions programs, and so on.

Preferences are universal human characteristics as well. They are born out of the human insatiable nature for wanting more than resources can accommodate. Preferences operate mostly in activities that involve our day-to-day life, like the making of purchasing decisions, or expressions through surveys, election of political officers, domestic decisions among family members, public policy enactments, and so on. Preferences are influenced by the tastes of individuals, ethnic background, gender, education, social status, occupation, income, race, social group, and other factors. For example, a European will likely prefer the temperate to the tropical climate; a more educated person will likely prefer better aesthetics; those

with higher socioeconomic status are more likely to prefer more expensive orna-
ments to make the difference between the haves and the have-nots. Uneducated
women are likely to prefer the continuation of female circumcision in practicing
communities in Africa. The consideration of "value" and "importance" has a great
influence on individual preferences. Thus preferences are ranked in line with the
estimation of their worth at that point in time. They are about choices that are
deemed more desirable or given higher priority. Preferences act as factors that
motivate human actions and decisions. Subject areas include, but are not limited
to, communication, conflict, violence, and wars; consumer behavior; culture and
cultural perception; education; history; ideologies; language; political, economic,
and social behavior; social structures; religion; and socioeconomic status.

Preferences permeate all institutions and endeavors of human existence. Even
social, economic, and political policies in heterogeneous and homogeneous societies are ranked on a preference scale because of the multiplicity of ideas and
alternatives. Elections are conducted to ensure that the most preferred candidates
get elected to limited positions. On the domestic front, families are confronted
with preferences in common decisions of what could be prepared for meals at
home. Contextually, preferences are universal denominators of human-motivated
actions and behaviors in the choice game.

See also Affirmative Action Plan/Program; Education and Affirmative Action;
Employment (Private) and Affirmative Action; Employment (Public) and Affirmative Action; GI Bill; Legacy Admissions Policy; Quotas.

FURTHER READING: Fried, Charles, 1999, "Uneasy Preferences," *American Prospect*, Sep-
tember, 50–57; "Preferences," 1985, *American Heritage Dictionary*, 2d ed., Boston: Houghton
Mifflin; Zuckerman, Mortimer B., 1999, "Piling on the Preferences," *U.S. News & World
Report* 126, no. 25 (June 28): 88.

KINGSLEY UFUOMA OMOYIBO

Prejudice

Prejudice is defined as any preconceived unreasonable or unfavorable opinion.
Sociologists have suggested that prejudice predicts discrimination better than do
stereotypes. It seems that measures of emotions related to prejudice are stronger
predictors of evaluations of and behavior toward prejudiced members. One purpose of affirmative action programs is to expose members of different groups to
each other in the work and school environment, thereby arguably limiting the
amount of prejudice (and therefore discrimination) in society.

According to Susan Fiske and Janet Ruscher, prejudice has its origin in an
intergroup context related to the perception of threat to one group, or the perception that outsider/prejudiced members interfere with the perceiver's (in-
group's) goals. People consider that outsiders interfere with in-group goals, and
this produces strong emotions directed against the members of the outsider group
as a whole. Direct contact with outsider members also can produce prejudice
because in the interaction outsider-minority group members can block perceived
in-group goals or because people can believe that outsider-minority group members present different characteristics from the familiar in-group majority characteristics. Thus while one of the purposes of affirmative action programs is to create

diversity in the workplace and reduce prejudice, one should recognize that direct contact may actually increase prejudices rather than reduce them. For example, in the affirmative action context, majority-group members may resent the presence of minority members that the majority group perceives as only being in the position by virtue of affirmative action, and not by virtue of the individual's merit or accomplishments (even though the minority individual may not even have been a beneficiary of affirmative action and may be in the position based upon traditional qualifications or merit). Thus even though there is direct interaction, this interaction may increase the amount of prejudice rather than decrease it.

John Dovidio, in an article published in the *Journal of Social Issues* in 2001, identified three "waves" in the social-psychological study of prejudice. In the first, which characterized research from the 1920s through the 1950s, prejudice was seen as "an aberration from normal thinking," that is, as a psychopathological process (a mental disease or ailment). In the second wave, prejudice was seen as a normal process associated with socialization and social norms that support prejudice. In the 1970s appeared two approaches within this second wave, the social identity theory, which demonstrated that social identity as well as individual identity underlies prejudice, and the social categorization theory, which considers prejudice a normal cognitive process. The third wave, which began in the mid-1990s, emphasizes the multidimensional aspect of prejudice and has used new technologies to study processes that were early hypothesized but not directly measurable.

See also Discrimination; Stereotypes, Gender; Stereotyping and Minority Classes.

FURTHER READING: Dovidio, John, 2001, "On the Nature of Contemporary Prejudice: The Third Wave," *Journal of Social Issues* 57, no. 4:829–850; Esses, Victoria, Geoffrey Haddock, and Mark P. Zanna, 1993, "Values, Stereotypes, and Emotions as Determinants of Inter-group Attitudes," in *Affect, Cognition, and Stereotyping: Interactive Processes in Group Perception*, edited by Diane Mackie and David Hamilton, San Diego: Academic Press; Fiske, Susan T., and Janet B. Ruscher, 1993, "Negative Interdependence and Prejudice: Whence the Effect?" in *Affect, Cognition, and Stereotyping: Interactive Processes in Group Perception*, edited by Diane M. Mackie and David L. Hamilton, San Diego: Academic Press; Tajfel, Henry, and John C. Turner, 1979, "An Integrative Theory of Intergroup Conflict," in *The Social Psychology of Intergroup Relations*, edited by William G. Austin and Stephen Worchel, Monterey, CA: Brooks/Cole.

MARIA JOSE SOTELO

President's Committee on Equal Employment Opportunity

John F. Kennedy established the President's Committee on Equal Employment Opportunity in Executive Order 10925 on March 6, 1961. The committee's purpose was to promote and ensure equal opportunity without regard to race, creed, color, or national origin for those seeking employment by the federal government and its contractors. Executive Order 10925 combined the President's Committee on Government Contracts and the President's Committee on Government Employment Policy and was the first government document to utilize the phrase "affirmative action." According to the executive order, the committee was established "to scrutinize and study employment practices of the Government of the

United States, and to consider and recommend additional affirmative steps which should be taken by executive departments and agencies to realize more fully the national policy on nondiscrimination within the executive branch of the Government." More specifically, the committee was charged with overseeing studies of current government employment practices, reviewing statistics on employment patterns, reviewing employment procedures, and making recommendations to end discrimination.

The committee was composed of senior-ranking federal government officials, including the vice president of the United States acting as chairman, the secretary of labor acting as vice chairman, the chairman of the Atomic Energy Commission, the secretary of commerce, the attorney general, the secretary of defense, the secretaries of the army, navy, and air force, the administrator of the General Services Administration, the chairman of the Civil Service Commission, and the administrator of the National Aeronautics and Space Administration. The committee was empowered to investigate claims of discrimination by the government and its contractors, hold public and private hearings, terminate or refuse contracts, and recommend possible legal proceedings to the U.S. Department of Justice. The committee was different from previous antidiscriminatory committees in that it also had the power to withhold federal funding and could issue public reports on contractors who violated its policies.

Despite these powers, however, critics believed that without the direct power to prosecute violators, the committee would be ineffective. They also criticized its ability to oversee only the federal government and its contractors and wanted the committee to have more responsibility. The committee's best-known endeavor, Plans for Progress, worked with construction contractors. The committee trained forty individuals from various federal agencies to educate contractors about affirmative action policies. As early as June 1962, nearly eighty-five contractors were participating in the plan, and nearly 90 percent of the AFL-CIO's affiliated unions were also in accordance with the committee's policies. The committee reported that by 1965, the number of blacks who worked in the federal government had increased by at least 15 percent.

The committee's policies marked a shift from government policies designed to prohibit discrimination to policies designed to actively promote compliance with equal employment opportunity initiatives. By the time President Lyndon B. Johnson abolished the committee on September 4, 1965, the more powerful and sweeping reforms of the 1964 Civil Rights Act were in place. The committee's responsibilities were distributed to the Equal Employment Opportunity Commission (EEOC), which processed complaints of discrimination in private businesses not holding federal contracts; the Civil Service Commission, which oversaw discrimination within the federal government; and the secretary of labor, who reviewed discrimination complaints by companies with federal contracts.

See also Civil Rights Act of 1964; Civil Service Commission; Department of Justice; Department of Labor; Equal Employment Opportunity Commission; Executive Order 10925; Johnson, Lyndon Baines; Kennedy, John Fitzgerald.

FURTHER READING: Kennedy, John F., 1961, "Executive Order 10925," http://www.lib. umich.edu/govdocs/jfkeo/eo/10925.htm; Saunders, Doris, ed., 1964, *The Kennedy Years and the Negro: A Photographic Record*, Chicago: Johnson Publishing Co.; Sobel, Lester A., ed., 1967, *Civil Rights, 1960–1966*, New York: Facts on File.

JAYSON J. FUNKE

Price Waterhouse v. Hopkins, 490 U.S. 228 (1989)

Price Waterhouse v. Hopkins was a landmark case that identified sexual stereotyping as a form of gender discrimination in violation of statutory and constitutional protections. *Price Waterhouse* is equally relevant to the affirmative action discussion because it illustrates how women can benefit from progressive employment practices while still being subject to antiquated traditions and beliefs about women's roles.

Ann Hopkins was a senior manager in the Price Waterhouse accounting firm in 1982 when she was nominated for partnership in that firm. Hopkins had worked for Price Waterhouse for five years when the partners proposed her as a candidate for partner. Eighty-eight other persons were suggested for partnership in that same year, but Hopkins was the only female. Forty-seven were selected for partnership, twenty-one were rejected, and twenty, including Hopkins, were put on hold for reconsideration in the next year.

The comments about Hopkins's candidacy were a mixed bag that in part would become the substance of the constitutional appeal to the U.S. Supreme Court. Some of the partners at Price Waterhouse lauded Hopkins's character and accomplishments and highlighted the successful $25-million contract she had negotiated with the State Department. Other partners, however, reported that she was "aggressive" and "macho" and that she often "overcompensated for being a woman." It was argued that Hopkins's aggressiveness often became abrasiveness and that staff members were frequently the recipients of her "brusque" behavior. It was this difficulty with interpersonal skills that frustrated even her supporters in the firm. Other opponents of her candidacy criticized her use of profanity, and one even suggested that Hopkins "walk more femininely, talk more femininely, dress more femininely, wear make-up, have her hairstyled, and wear jewelry." When Hopkins's partnership proposal was finally put on hold by the firm and no action was taken, Hopkins brought suit against Price Waterhouse for a violation of Title VII of the Civil Rights Act of 1964. Title VII prohibited any discrimination in the conditions of employment on the basis of race, color, religion, sex, or national origin. Hopkins claimed that she had been discriminated against on the basis of sex regarding the partnership issue.

The District Court for the District of Columbia ruled in her favor when it held that Price Waterhouse unlawfully discriminated against Hopkins by relying on a sex-stereotyping rationale to deny her partnership. The Court of Appeals for the District of Columbia Circuit affirmed the decision. Both lower courts determined that the remarks about Hopkins were sufficiently detrimental and that her gender played a negative role in the failure to reach a decision about her candidacy. The two lower courts also ruled that when an employer has permitted a discriminatory motive to affect an employment decision, the employer must show by "clear and convincing evidence" that it would have made the same decision in the absence of that discrimination. Price Waterhouse, the lower courts held, had not "carried this burden." The accounting firm subsequently appealed the decision to the U.S.

Supreme Court, and the constitutional issues in Price Waterhouse proved to be significant for future employment discrimination claims.

The primary question for the Supreme Court's attention was the conflict regarding the respective burdens of proof for a plaintiff and defendant in a Title VII discrimination suit when the decision resulted from a combination of legitimate and illegitimate motives. The failure to promote Ann Hopkins appeared to include both sets of motives—her failure with interpersonal skills (legitimate) and the correspondingly stereotypical comments about her dress and demeanor (illegitimate). The Supreme Court majority concluded that when a plaintiff (Hopkins) in a Title VII case shows that sex or gender contributed to an employment decision, the defendant (Price Waterhouse) does not have to use the clear and convincing evidentiary standard for a finding of liability, as the lower courts had insisted. Instead, the Court determined that the appropriate standard of proof for a defendant to avoid a finding of liability was the rule of a preponderance of the evidence. This new standard required that when evidence of sexual stereotyping is shown to be a factor in an employment decision, the burden falls to the employer to "prove by the preponderance of the evidence that it would have taken the same action regardless of the improper stereotyping." Simply stated, this new standard afforded the defendant (Price Waterhouse) a weaker burden of proof in showing that it had not discriminated against Hopkins. The new standard would also allow the employer to argue that the nondiscriminatory reason was the key factor in the inevitable employment decision.

What happened then to Ann Hopkins? Although Price Waterhouse was successful in securing a lower standard of proof from the U.S. Supreme Court, the case was remanded back to Judge Gerhard Gesell of the District Court for the District of Columbia. There, Judge Gesell was unpersuaded that the nondiscriminatory factors really justified the denial of Hopkins's candidacy, and he ordered the accounting firm to admit her to partnership effective July 1, 1990.

In 1991, Congress modified somewhat the negative impact of the overall *Price Waterhouse* decision by articulating new standards for victims of mixed-motive employment decisions. According to a provision of the Civil Rights Act of 1991, a plaintiff in a mixed-motive case could recover declaratory and injunctive relief for the impermissible motivating factor. The act, however, did not require reinstatement, back pay, or punitive damages for the injured plaintiff—once again permitting legitimate and illegitimate motives to remain a constant in the employment decision-making process. Overall, then, the *Price Waterhouse* decision itself remained a mixed bag in defining and clarifying the rights of workers and management in the complex and contentious world of employment practices.

See also Civil Rights Act of 1964; Civil Rights Act of 1991; Gender Norms; Stereotypes, Gender; Title VII of the Civil Rights Act of 1964.

FURTHER READING: Kay, Herma Hill, and Martha S. West, 2002, *Text, Cases, and Materials on Sex-Based Discrimination*, 5th ed., St. Paul, MN: West Group.

JANIS JUDSON

Privileges and Immunities Clause

See Fourteenth Amendment.

Proposition 209

Proposition 209, also known as the California Civil Rights Initiative (CCRI), was approved by a majority (54 percent) of California voters in the November 5, 1996, election. Supporters of Proposition 209 argued that special interests had forced government to impose quotas, preferences, and set-asides for women and minorities. According to supporters, the passage of Proposition 209 would remove discriminatory and preferential programs from state government that operate under the guise of affirmative action. Opponents of Proposition 209 argued that its passage would remove affirmative action programs in state government that had promoted gender, racial, and ethnic equity in public employment, education, and contracting. Opponents of the proposition further argued that the real purpose of the proposition was not to create a level playing field, but to curtail equal opportunity for women and minorities. One of Proposition 209's architects, Ward Connerly, used the proposition's passage as a vehicle for promoting similar ballot initiatives in other state efforts, notably in the states of Washington, Florida, Texas, and Michigan.

Proposition 209 bans discrimination or preferential treatment based on race, sex, color, ethnicity, or national origin in public employment, education, and contracting. Specifically, Proposition 209 amended Article I, Section 31, of the California Constitution to prohibit the state from discriminating against or granting preferential treatment to any individual or group on the basis of race, sex, color, ethnicity, or national origin in the operation of public employment, public education, or public contracting. To avoid actual or potential conflicts with federal law or the U.S. Constitution, the language of Article I, Section 31, was amended to avoid prohibiting the use of bona fide qualifications based on sex that are reasonably necessary to the normal operation of public employment, public education, or public contracting. The amended language also invalidated actions, such as ignoring court orders or consent degrees regarding affirmative action, that would result in a loss of federal funds to the state. Article I, Section 31, was amended to include a self-executing section stating that if any of its parts were found to be in conflict with federal law or the U.S. Constitution, they would be invalidated and severed from the remaining parts.

Upon its passage, a broad coalition of persons and groups challenged the constitutionality of Proposition 209 in federal court in *Coalition for Economic Equity v. Wilson*, 946 F. Supp. 1480 (N.D. Cal. 1996). The coalition argued that Proposition 209 violated the U.S. Constitution because it was vague regarding the definition of "discrimination" and "preferential treatment" and because it did not address the disparity in the state's oversight between public and private agencies' use of race, sex, ethnicity, color, or national origin in their deliberations and/or affairs. The court sided with the coalition and prevented the state from enforcing Proposition 209. However, a federal appeals court reversed the ruling, finding that Proposition 209 did not violate the Constitution in *Coalition for Economic Equity v. Wilson*, 110 F.3d 1431 (9th Cir. 1997), *cert. denied*, 118 S. Ct. 397 (1997). The Supreme Court ultimately refused to review the federal appeals court decision.

See also Coalition for Economic Equity v. Wilson; Connerly, Ward; Discrimination; One Florida Initiative; Preferences; Quotas; Racial Privacy Initiative; Washington Initiative 200.

FURTHER READING: Gee, Harvey, 2001, "Why Did Asian Americans Vote against the 1996 California Civil Rights Initiative?" *Loyola Journal of Public Interest Law* 2 (spring): 1–52; Gotanda, Neil, Jamila Bayati, Susan Berkman, Cherisse Lanier, Heather McMillan-Delaney, Sharon Tate, and Janeen Yoshida, 1996, "Legal Implications of Proposition 209—The California Civil Rights Initiative," *Western State University Law Review* 24:1–55; Larson, Ann, 2000, "The California Civil Rights Initiative: Why It's Here, Its Far Reaching Effects, and the Unique Situation in Hawaii," *Hawaii Law Review* 22 (spring): 279–321; Spann, Girardeau, 1997, "Proposition 209," *Duke Law Journal* 47:187–325; Volokh, Eugene, 1997, "The California Civil Rights Initiative: An Interpretive Guide," *UCLA Law Review* 44:1335–1402.

ADALBERTO AGUIRRE JR.

Public Works Employment Act of 1977

The Public Works Employment Act of 1977 authorized $4 billion in grants for local public works projects and required that 10 percent of the dollar volume of each grant be expended on materials and supplies from minority business enterprises (MBEs). MBEs were defined to be companies at least 51 percent owned by minority-group members, with minorities including "Negroes, Spanish-speaking, Orientals, Indians, Eskimos and Aleuts." Often referred to as a "set-aside," the 10 percent requirement was designed to redress past discrimination. Prior to the act, MBEs had received only about 1 percent of federal grants despite the fact that minorities, as defined, represented 17 percent of the U.S. population. As implemented, the program was seen as successful in increasing minority participation and building some competitive minority businesses. The program received criticism for increasing project costs, leading many states with small minority populations to rely on out-of-state contractors, and encouraging corrupt practices such as the formation of companies solely to qualify for the set-aside or the use of minority firms as fronts for existing contractors who were actually doing the work. The program was also challenged as an example of reverse discrimination in violation of the Fourteenth Amendment. In 1980, the Supreme Court upheld the program's constitutionality in the landmark case *Fullilove v. Klutznick*, 448 U.S. 448 (1980). Based on the Court's decision, the public works set-aside language became an often-used model both for federal legislation that authorized spending in such areas as transportation and defense and for state and local public works legislation.

Beginning in the 1960s, several executive orders and laws sought to encourage the development of MBEs and to increase their share of government contracts. Still, in open bidding, MBEs were receiving only a small fraction of the contracts because they could not match the bids of larger, more established companies. In 1976, President Jimmy Carter encouraged Congress to authorize $2 billion for local public works projects as part of his economic stimulus package. The program proved extremely popular, so in 1977 a bill authorizing an additional $4 billion was submitted. During floor debate, Representative Parren J. Mitchell, a Democrat from Maryland, argued that since the public works bill already targeted money to areas with high unemployment, an amendment should be added to target a "fair share" of money to MBEs. The only major objection to the amendment raised in floor debate was that it might force areas with small minority populations to use out-of-state minority firms to reach the set-aside target. Therefore, through an amendment to the amendment, it was agreed that the secretary of labor would be given the power to waive the 10 percent set-aside if no minority firms were available. The Mitchell amendment was then agreed to without a roll-call vote. Weeks later, a similar amendment was added to the Senate version of the bill, also without a roll call. The underlying bill had wide support and passed 71–14 in the Senate and 335–77 in the House. It is noteworthy that the Mitchell language, which would prove to have significant long-term impact, was not discussed in any committee hearings or reports and was adopted with little debate over questions such as why the requirement was set at 10 percent or which minority groups should be included.

The public works money was designed to help jump-start the economy, so all of the 1977 money was quickly allocated to a total of 8,554 local projects such as building schools and municipal office buildings, sewer projects, and water systems. Six thousand, two hundred MBEs were involved as either contractors or subcontractors, with grant values ranging from less than $1,000 to more than $1 million. The Commerce Department's Economic Development Administration (EDA), which oversaw the program, estimated that MBEs actually received around $560 million, or almost 14 percent of the total. This was a sharp increase compared to previous federal contracts and to the 1976 public works projects that were not governed by the set-aside language. A 1979 General Accounting Office (GAO) report on the program also concluded that it stimulated the development of new MBEs, increased the experience of existing companies, and helped develop business ties that would aid MBEs in years to come.

The GAO and others also identified problems with the program. The set-asides increased the overall cost of the program in three ways. First, the average bids submitted by MBEs were 9 percent higher than comparable bids from other firms. Second, the MBEs were less experienced both in technical skills and administration, resulting in 44 percent of prime contractors reporting that they had to assume extra burdens of administrative work, purchase supplies, or provide bonding when dealing with MBEs. Most often, the prime contractors passed these extra costs on by submitting higher initial bids. Third, the added paperwork and extra monitoring required by the program increased oversight costs. Some of that burden was passed on to the contractors, who were required to compile reports before starting a project and again when the project was 40 percent complete showing that they were in compliance; however, the EDA still used close to 25 percent of its overall program budget overseeing the set-asides and had to ask for a second authorization of administrative funds.

Another problem that emerged was one anticipated during the congressional debate. Areas such as Wyoming and New Hampshire had small minority populations and therefore few qualified MBEs. It was possible to ask for a waiver in such circumstances, but less than three dozen waivers were granted for more than 8,000 projects. For some states, more than 50 percent of the grants were made to out-of-state companies. In these areas, resentment of the program grew among non-minority local firms and among those who felt that the law's purpose of targeting money to economically depressed areas was being countered by relying on out-of-state firms.

In the initial phase of making grants, the EDA was under intense time pressure and therefore tended to rely on businesses to accurately report their minority status. Over time, concerns about fraud began to mount, so the EDA investigated

1,386 firms. Of that sample, 32 percent of the firms were found not to meet eligibility criteria. Some companies listed minority owners who had no significant management or other role in the company. In other cases, grants were made to MBEs with no equipment that then subcontracted the work to other firms. Extrapolating from the surveyed sample, perhaps as much as $50 million went to questionable firms.

Ultimately, the greatest criticism of the program came from those who felt that it unfairly punished non-minority-owned firms. One group of construction workers who felt that they had suffered economic injury and had been denied equal protection under the law pressed their case through to the Supreme Court. In a 6–3 decision in *Fullilove v. Klutznick*, the Court upheld the law and therefore the general concept of using set-asides as a way of addressing the impacts of past discrimination. There was, however, sharp disagreement among the justices, even within the majority, on issues such as whether the government had to establish a compelling reason for affirmative action programs or just a broad governmental goal and whether it was necessary to show that a particular group, like the Aleuts, had suffered discrimination or just that minorities in general had been hurt. In several subsequent cases, crucially *City of Richmond v. J.A. Croson Co.*, 488 U.S. 469 (1989), and *Adarand Constructors, Inc. v. Peña*, 515 U.S. 200 (1995), these issues were revisited and the impact of the *Fullilove* case was somewhat lessened. Still, the public works set-aside had an impact far beyond the more than $500 million directly affected by the law because billions of dollars of both federal and local money were expended under programs mirroring almost word for word the original provision.

See also Adarand Constructors, Inc. v. Peña; Carter, James "Jimmy" Earl, Jr.; *City of Richmond v. J.A. Croson Co.*; Disadvantaged Business Enterprises; Economic Development Administration; *Fullilove v. Klutznick*; Quotas.

FURTHER READING: Days, Drew, 1987, "Fullilove," *Yale Law Journal* 96, no. 3:453–485; General Accounting Office, 1979, *Minority Firms on Local Public Works Projects: Mixed Results*, Washington, DC: U.S. Government Printing Office; Kilgore, Peter, 1981, "Racial Preferences in the Federal Grant Programs: Is There a Basis for Challenge after *Fullilove v. Klutznick?*" *Labor Law Journal* 32, no. 5:306–314; U.S. Department of Commerce, 1978, *Audit Instructions for Local Public Works Grants under Title 1 of the Public Works and Employments Acts of 1976 and 1977*, Washington, DC: U.S. Government Printing Office.

JOHN W. DIETRICH

Q

Quotas

The term "quota" is frequently used in discussing the issue of affirmative action. It is often a word that is said with disdain and more often than not is said as a way of criticizing affirmative action programs. While the definition of the word "quota" is fairly straightforward, the word also connotes the specter of discrimination as well. According to the 1999 edition of *The Oxford American Dictionary of Current English*, a quota is "the share that an individual person, group, or company is bound to contribute to or entitled to receive from a total." Thus, for some, the word "quota" simply means compensatory actions in the form of an allotment or preference or "set-aside" for those who have been historically left out of jobs because of gender, racial, or ethnic affiliation. However, for many critics of affirmative action, a quota is usually thought of as a system that gives unqualified individuals jobs that they do not deserve or that they are not qualified to receive. As a result, these critics claim that the operation of a quota-based system also reversely discriminates against others because arguably more qualified individuals are being denied benefits on account of race or gender. According to Barbara Bergmann, these opponents have "demonized" the word and "have been working hard for decades to make quota into a word that signifies something bad, wrong, indefensible" (Bergmann 1996, 11). Furthermore, the U.S. Supreme Court has held in *Regents of the University of California v. Bakke*, 438 U.S. 265 (1978), that at least in the Title VI context, fixed racial quotas as part of an affirmative action plan are not permissible.

However, today, in all the major areas impacted by affirmative action (education, employment, and contracting), quotas are not meant to be a rigid, automatic, inflexible preference. Indeed, Bergmann argues that "numerical goals of affirmative action programs are not quotas because these goals are provisional, not hard and fast. The goals can be reduced or abandoned if no suitable African American or white female candidates can be found" (Bergmann 1996, 12–13). Thus among supporters of affirmative action, quotas are thought more appropriately to entail goals and timetables in the parlance of today's affirmative action practice. According to Tom Beauchamp, "Quotas are simply target employment percentages." Beauchamp further specifies that "in some cases a less qualified person may be hired or promoted, but it has never been a part of affirmative action to hire below the threshold of 'basically qualified,' and often significant questions exist in the employment situation about the exact qualifications needed for positions" (Beauchamp 1997, 216). Furthermore, today, as a result of a series of Supreme Court decisions, institutions do not employ rigid quotas (except as a remedial measure usually ordered by a court to rectify historical underrepresentation and discrimination), but rather consider race as a factor in attempting to achieve flexible integration goals.

Many Americans state that they are against quotas for several reasons. First, these individuals feel strongly that the use of quotas entails taking jobs away from individuals who are more qualified. Second, there is a belief that the government benefit (jobs, admission slots, and so on) is being given to individuals who do not deserve the benefit. Third, many argue that the whole notion of quotas or set-asides is "un-American" because it does not focus exclusively on merit. Further, some argue that a strong resentment many individuals have toward the notion of quotas is channeled unfairly toward minorities, creating an atmosphere of distrust when peers and colleagues feel that the minority member received his or her position because of affirmative action and quotas and not because they can do the job or were qualified for the job. Indeed, this is a major criticism of affirmative action programs, that it increases the amount of racial friction and causes more individuals to doubt the talent and merit of minorities already in a job or educational program. Clarence Thomas has expressed this as one of his objections to affirmative action.

Those who believe in affirmative action programs that utilize flexible quotas, "set-asides," preferences, or other types of allotment have a different view. These individuals and groups truly believe that because discrimination persists against many women and minorities (based on numerous empirical studies), it is necessary to have a form of affirmative action that uses some form of the "quota system." These individuals believe that racism, discrimination, and sexism are so deeply entrenched within this society that there is no way to promote minorities and women except by setting aside certain jobs or benefits. An even more tactical reason to accept affirmative action with programs that use a form of the quota system is to have a fair number of individuals that "look like" the diverse American culture, with the goal of making workplaces, institutions, and colleges and universities resemble the society in which we live. Some believe that if organizations make a concerted effort to recruit and retain qualified minorities and women, it will be better for all of society.

See also African Americans; Contracting and Affirmative Action; Discrimination; Education and Affirmative Action; Employment (Private) and Affirmative Action; Employment (Public) and Affirmative Action; Preferences; *Regents of the University of California v. Bakke;* Reverse Discrimination; Title VI of the Civil Rights Act of 1964.

FURTHER READING: Beauchamp, Tom, 1997, "Goals and Quotas in Hiring and Promotion," in *Affirmative Action: Social Justice or Reverse Discrimination?*, edited by Francis J. Beckwith and Todd E. Jones, Amherst, NY: Prometheus Books; Bergmann, Barbara R.A., 1996, *In Defense of Affirmative Action*, New York: Basic Books; Skrentny, John David, 1996, *The Ironies of Affirmative Action*, Chicago: University of Chicago Press.

NICOLE M. STEPHENS

R

Race in Colonial America

The early treatment of Africans in America is often cited by some as a reason for affirmative action or for programs even more aggressive than affirmative action, such as reparations. Those who make these arguments often posit that African Americans today should be compensated for the wrongs suffered during the colonial and antebellum periods in U.S. history. Thus a basic understanding of race in the colonial period is necessary to appreciate the arguments (pro or con) for reparations and aggressive affirmative action programs (based upon the justification of compensating members of groups that have been historically subject to institutional discrimination).

First, it should be noted that there were many different jurisdictions in the colonies, their wealth varied, and each had divergent groups of immigrants who differed in their willingness to work in the colonies in the respective climates. Each developed the institution of slavery at different junctures. Generally, however, slavery, a major component in the creation of colonial society, was a product of religious and economic factors. Since the Anglican Church was the established church of the majority of the southern colonies, its precepts molded the atmosphere under which colonial leaders such as George Washington attended church and received certain "religious" tenets dealing with the permissibility of slavery.

Given this attitude, the Church of England, for example, through its African Slave Company, the trading arm of the African slave trade, could adhere to numerous injunctions that flourish throughout the Bible rationalizing the subhuman state of forced labor for the economic betterment of the colonies. It should also be noted that the lack of large numbers of slaves in New England was not necessarily evidence of a higher moral attitude, but proof of the lack of a need for forced labor. King Tobacco, indigo, and soon cotton became the arbiters of slave relationships throughout the Chesapeake, Virginia, the Carolinas, and Maryland.

Virginia was the first colony to be infected by problems of slavery in 1619 when the Dutch sold the first Africans in the Jamestown Colony. Some historians allege that the first Africans came to Virginia as indentured servants, and their status gradually changed because of the need for cheap labor. The change was dramatic; in 1639 Virginia passed a law that excluded blacks from bearing arms and ammunition, and for violations they would be fined at the desires of the colonial governor and council. This legislation was important, since the increase in the number of slaves meant that the white settlers had to develop methods of controlling the social and political environment. By 1640, only one year after the passage of laws prohibiting slaves from bearing arms or ammunition, blacks were only accepted in the colonies as slaves, not indentured servants, a status reserved for the white immigrants. The colonists realized that slaves were inexpensive labor, had no legal protection, were an inexhaustible source of supply, and did not blend in with the white population. Many white colonists also believed that Africans were not civilized. Based upon this belief that Africans lacked acceptable "civilization," their skin color and whites' religious beliefs confined them to a zone of mercy beyond the pale of humanity

To create an environment that justified the segregation of races, laws against miscegenation were put into effect. While it may be alleged that this policy was instituted to keep the races apart, and one in subjugation, church theology reinforced the notion that the races should remain separate, as blacks were originally viewed as not accepting the Christian faith, and therefore they should not be permitted to marry into white families accepting the Christian faith. Therefore, those with dark skin were acceptable as slaves, but intermingling of the races was against the religious beliefs of the white colonists. The fact that such a philosophy coincided with the economic needs of the colonists was all to the better. Furthermore, the various states quickly realized that they could not support slavery if slaves converted to Christianity. Virginia, among other slave states, passed a law in 1667 prohibiting conversion of a slave as grounds for emancipation. This law applied to both blacks and Indians.

Maryland and Virginia were concerned about the retention of cheap labor; both passed ordinances in 1650 relating to blacks and white indentured servants. Depending upon the literature one peruses, Maryland and Virginia lay claim to being the first colony to have enacted such regulations. Maryland, a colony established for persecuted Catholic colonists, followed Virginia's miscegenation law in 1664. Maryland's law imposed harsh restrictions upon the free female who married a slave; she had to serve as a slave for the life of her husband, and any of their children born to them would be the slave property of the master.

Further restrictions were on the horizon for those lacking the virtues of Christianity. In 1682, Virginia led the other states in broadening the restrictions against nonwhite non-Christians. Individuals imported into the colonies whose parentage and native countries were not Christian at the time of their being first purchased by Christians were considered slaves according to the laws extant at the time, regardless of any law or customs. Virginia again expanded its restrictive laws in 1691 to include any marriage between a white man and a Negro, Indian, or mulatto. The punishment for violating this law was banishment from the colony forever. The Maryland law reminded white women that they were free, that to marry a black was a debasement of their station in society, and that to engage in intercourse with a heathen would endanger their immortal souls. As the number of slaves in the colonies increased, and the colonial economy more and more depended upon a slave population, more restrictive laws were passed. Virginia passed laws defining the racial distinction between servants and slaves. This distinction was included in the federal Constitution when that document prohibited indentured servitude.

Recognizing the conflict between their religious professions and reality, some colonies passed laws denying the right of assembly or burial in consecrated ground. As slaves learned more about their environments, they increasingly attempted to escape. Their owners then prohibited slaves from riding horses, carrying weapons, or leaving an owner's lands. Other ominous restrictions included the prohibition on learning to read or obtaining an education.

It is not fair to pillory the southern colonies by comparison with the North. The northern colonies were not hotbeds of abolitionism as much as some revisionists might allege. The New England colonies also made their contributions to slavery's growth. While their slaves were denied freedom and many were not initially manumitted, slavery did not gain the same economic hold as in the South. This was largely not out of any sense of purity, but rather because the economic need was not present. Skilled labor was in short supply, and wages for skilled labor tended to be higher in the colonies than in Europe. Southern slave owners did not need urban help; the sizes of the family plots kept getting smaller because of the rules of primogeniture, whereby the oldest son inherited the entire estate, which governed inheritance. Thomas Jefferson was responsible for removing this odious provision from the Virginia Constitution. As a result, the slaves in larger estates in Virginia tended to be housekeepers and artisans. Eventually, when family fortunes changed, the skilled artisans were contracted out and the artisan's earnings supplemented the family income. There were even instances where a slave could buy his freedom.

Finally, any discussion of race in the colonial period would not be complete without drawing attention to the class of blacks called free men/women of color. These free men or women of color lived throughout the colonies and obtained their freedom through diverse means. Most were manumitted by means of a contract, and others as a gift or reward for services. In New Orleans, for example, the class of freed black men was extremely large. These people were merchants whose expertise helped the New Orleans economy prosper in the pre–Civil War period. The mayor of New Orleans on one occasion admonished the city police chief, who was allegedly too harsh on the blacks, and reminded the chief of their contributions. This element in the discussion of race in colonial America has not been given its needed attention.

See also African Americans; American Civil War; Articles of Confederation; Bill of Rights; Constitution, Civil Rights, and Equality; Declaration of Independence and Equality; Reparations; Segregation; Slavery; Slavery and the Founding Fathers.

FURTHER READING: Miller, Loren, 1966, *The Petitioners: The Story of the Supreme Court of the United States and the Negro*, New York: Pantheon Books; Rubio, Philip F., 2001, *A History of Affirmative Action, 1619–2000*, Jackson: University Press of Mississippi.

ARTHUR K. STEINBERG

Race-Based Affirmative Action

Race-based affirmative action is a term used to refer to a set of procedures aimed at increasing the proportion of underrepresented minority groups in organizations, often by the use of racial preferences. Since the late 1960s, affirmative action has remained one of America's most controversial public policies. Prior to that time, there was very little historic precedent for government-mandated affirmative action programs in business, contracting, employment, and higher education. The foundation for government intervention is deeply rooted in the Constitution of the United States. The First Amendment to the Constitution essentially prohibits discrimination on the basis of religion, while the Fifth, Thirteenth, Fourteenth, and Fifteenth Amendments prohibit discrimination on the basis of race. Additionally, a number of pieces of federal legislation have been enacted to further regulate both the public and private sectors regarding discriminatory practices involving treatment of minority groups. One of the most important such statutes is the 1964 Civil Rights Act, which forbids discrimination "because of an individual's race, color, religion, sex, or national origin" in employment, housing, public accommodations, and education.

As a result of both the legislation that has been passed and the variation among interpretations of our constitutional guarantees, it is not surprising that the primary battleground for proponents and opponents of affirmative action policies has been the courts and, in particular, the Supreme Court of the United States. The Supreme Court has historically reflected American society's attitude toward the issue of race and equality. After the Civil War, the separation of the races emerged as a reaction to the passage of the Thirteenth, Fourteenth, and Fifteenth Amendments. This separation was furthered by the Supreme Court's majority decision in the case *Plessy v. Ferguson*, 163 U.S. 537 (1896), which involved the constitutionality of a statute in the state of Louisiana that required separate rail cars for African American and white passengers. The Court ruled nearly unanimously that a state or local jurisdiction could separate the races so long as the separated facilities were equal. The lone dissenter was Justice John Marshall Harlan, who argued, "our Constitution is color-blind, and neither knows nor tolerates classes among its citizens. In respect of civil rights, all citizens are equal before the law."

The *Plessy* decision established the now-infamous separate-but-equal doctrine that led to the continuation of practices of separation, particularly in the southern states. It was not until 1954, in the landmark case *Brown v. Board of Education*, 347 U.S. 483 (1954), that the Supreme Court unanimously decided that the separate-but-equal doctrine in place for more than fifty years had no place in public education. In essence, the Court was saying that separate educational facilities discriminated against African Americans, and as a result, unequal educational opportunities existed as well.

Following passage of the Civil Rights Act of 1964, the Supreme Court continued to be the battleground for proponents and opponents of affirmative action policies. In particular, cases regarding entrance requirements into institutions of higher education, employment issues related to both hiring and promotion procedures, and the granting of contracts involving minority-owned businesses became issues that the Court decided to address.

Affirmative action policies have provoked both a philosophical and political debate. Proponents of affirmative action defend its use on grounds that it is justified to remedy the past decades of discrimination against racial minority groups in the United States while promoting the idea of inclusiveness that would benefit persons of all races and ethnicities in their pursuit of educational and economic opportunities. In contrast, critics of affirmative action policies argue that its use actually does away with the principle of color blindness in America and believe that it is individuals, not members of racial or ethnic groups, who must be protected regardless of their race or ethnicity. Opponents view granting preferences to some people because of their race as denying these same benefits to others because of their race. In response to proponents' view that past discrimination justifies current affirmative action policies, opponents see such group preferences as seriously disadvantaging white Americans who had nothing to do with past racial or ethnic discriminatory practices and as leading to "reverse racial discrimination." These opponents believe that the bitterness that whites may feel when racial preference is used actually leads to the very racial tensions that affirmative action was designed to eliminate.

With regard to the use of affirmative action policies in higher education, proponents cite diversity as inherently beneficial to the university community by enabling college students to interact with other students who are different from them. They believe that color-blind admissions procedures do not provide an accurate estimate of the quality of the minority candidate. Opponents of the use of affirmative action in higher-education admissions argue that admissions decisions should be based on criteria such as individuals' standardized test scores, high-school grade point average, and extracurricular activities, and not on factors related to one's particular racial or ethnic background. They believe that denying a white person admission to a university due to race, with all other criteria for admission being equal, discriminates against the applicant in violation of his or her constitutional rights.

In *Regents of the University of California v. Bakke*, 438 U.S. 265 (1978), the first challenge to the constitutionality of an affirmative action program used for university admissions was made. Some observers called this case the most important civil rights case since segregation was outlawed in the 1950s. In the lawsuit, Allan Bakke, a white applicant for admission to the University of California at Davis School of Medicine, charged that he was rejected for admission so the institution could fill a minority quota. The Court's controversial 5–4 decision sent a contradictory and confusing message. The Court ruled that although Title VII of the 1964 Civil Rights Act prohibited the university from establishing fixed quotas for minorities, the Constitution did not bar college admissions officials from introducing race as a factor in their selection process. As a result, Bakke was ordered admitted to the medical school, and universities were permitted to continue considering race in their admissions policies. In his majority opinion, Justice Lewis Powell Jr. wrote that "the atmosphere of speculation, experiment, and creation—so essential in the quality of higher education—is widely believed to be promoted by a diverse student body."

Nearly twenty years later, another case involving preferential higher-education admissions policies was heard in federal court. *Hopwood v. Texas*, 78 F.3d 932 (5th Cir. 1996), was a case that challenged the preferential admissions policy at the University of Texas School of Law. Cheryl Hopwood, along with three other white applicants, challenged the policy that evaluated minority candidates under a separate standard from those standards used to evaluate white applicants. A federal district court judge upheld the law school's numerical goals in the admissions plan but did not agree with the use of separate screening procedures. Hopwood appealed to the U.S. Fifth Circuit Court of Appeals when the judge did not also award punitive damages to Hopwood or the other plaintiffs nor order their admission to the law school. The appeals court reversed the district court's order and invalidated the law school's entire preferential admissions policy. In making their ruling, the judges specifically rejected the diversity argument made by Justice Powell in the *Bakke* case. Proponents of affirmative action policies saw this decision as the appeals court overstepping its bounds, agreeing with the lone dissenting judge, who stated, "If *Bakke* is to be declared dead, the U.S. Supreme Court, not a three-judge panel of a circuit court, should make that pronouncement."

Arguments similar to those made by proponents and opponents of the use of affirmative action policies in higher-education admissions have also been brought forth with regard to hiring practices. Proponents see the need for diversity in the workplace as a reason for race-based affirmative action. These proponents believe that the inequalities in the racial imbalance that has existed for decades must be corrected by the establishment of numerical hiring goals for employers to accomplish. Critics see this as opening the door for an illegal racial quota system. They believe that employment decisions should be based on the individual applicant's ability to perform the job and that equality of opportunity for individuals is what is to be achieved.

The Supreme Court has ruled on several important cases involving affirmative action programs used for employment purposes. One of the most important early Title VII cases was *Griggs v. Duke Power Co.*, 401 U.S. 424 (1971). The Court ruled that job qualification standards must be based on job relatedness and that the burden of proof that practices that cause a disparate impact upon racial minorities are legitimate belongs with the employer. Additionally, the Court, in its unanimous decision, ruled that Title VII is specifically designed to address "discriminatory preference for any group, minority or majority."

Later, in *Wygant v. Jackson Board of Education*, 476 U.S. 267 (1986), a group of white teachers who had been laid off due to budgeting constraints argued that the school district's collective-bargaining agreement that gave preferential protection to minority teachers violated their rights under the Fourteenth Amendment's Equal Protection Clause. In a 5–4 decision, the Supreme Court struck down the school board's policy for laying off teachers in a manner that gave preference to minority faculty over white faculty members with more seniority on the job.

The Supreme Court has also been asked to rule on the constitutionality of the implementation of affirmative action programs geared to ensure that minority-owned businesses receive preference when work contracts are awarded. In *City of Richmond v. J.A. Croson Co.*, 488 U.S. 469 (1989), the Court in a 6–3 vote struck down a Richmond, Virginia, ordinance that required that 30 percent of the city's municipal construction contracts be awarded to minority business enterprises. In six separate opinions—which in itself was indicative of continued disagreement among the justices regarding affirmative action—the Court held that the ordinance violated the constitutional rights of white contractors to equal protection of the law under the Fourteenth Amendment. The Court rejected the city's claim that the ordinance was a good-faith attempt to remedy past and present racial discrimination in awarding construction contracts. The Court viewed the city's effort to remedy past discrimination as rigid and overinclusive and stated that past history, "standing alone, cannot justify a rigid numerical quota in the awarding of public contracts in Richmond, Virginia."

In a more recent decision, the Supreme Court again responded to the issuance of contracts to minority-owned businesses. By a 5–4 vote in the case *Adarand Constructors, Inc. v. Peña*, 515 U.S. 200 (1995), the Court dealt a further blow to government-sponsored race-based affirmative action. In the case, Adarand, a white-owned construction company that unsuccessfully bid on a subcontract for highway guardrails, challenged the constitutionality of the subcontracting compensation clause imposed by the federal Department of Transportation. The clause called for incentives to be given to prime contractors who awarded subcontracts to small disadvantaged businesses under race-based provisions. The Court ruled that "strict scrutiny" was the standard that should be employed to determine whether equal protection was violated by the challenge of this federal agency's affirmative action program. In other words, along with any state or local plans, a federal affirmative action plan that uses racial classifications will survive a legal challenge only if the court determines that the classifications are narrowly tailored to achieve a compelling governmental interest.

If the past has been any indicator, the future of race-based affirmative action will be dependent on the cases that will be heard in the federal courts. However, as history has also clearly shown, the decisions made by these courts are going to reflect the views of future presidents who will be in a position to nominate those individuals who will sit on these federal courts. Others believe that the survival of affirmative action programs may actually depend more on the attitudes of the American public. Until the recent past, many individuals and corporations have welcomed affirmative action as a way to attract more minority applicants into institutions of higher education and places of employment. Still, opponents see affirmative action as a form of reverse discrimination against whites who must somehow pay a penalty for the discrimination against racial minorities in the past. The key will be to find an acceptable alternative to affirmative action policies that both proponents and opponents can embrace and that will continue to advance the position of racial minorities.

See also Adarand Constructors, Inc. v. Peña; Affirmative Action, Arguments for; Affirmative Action, Criticisms of; Affirmative Action Plan/Program; *Brown v. Board of Education*; *City of Richmond v. J.A. Croson Co.*; Civil Rights Act of 1964; Color-Blind Constitution; Constitution, Civil Rights, and Equality; Fifteenth Amendment; First Amendment; Fourteenth Amendment; *Griggs v. Duke Power Co.*; *Hopwood v. Texas*; *Plessy v. Ferguson*; Powell, Lewis Franklin, Jr.; Quotas; *Regents of the University of California v. Bakke*; Reverse Discrimination; Strict Scrutiny; Supreme Court and Affirmative Action; Thirteenth Amendment; Title VII of the Civil Rights Act of 1964; *Wygant v. Jackson Board of Education*.

FURTHER READING: Kahlenberg, Richard, 1996, *The Remedy: Class, Race, and Affirmative Action*, New York: Basic Books; Rubio, Philip F., 2001, *A History of Affirmative Action, 1619–2000*, Jackson: University Press of Mississippi; Skrentny, John David, 1996, *The Ironies of Affirmative Action*, Chicago: University of Chicago Press; Spann, Girardeau A., 2000, *The Law of Affirmative Action: Twenty-five Years of Supreme Court Decisions on Race and Remedies*, New

York: New York University Press; Yates, Steven, 1994, *Civil Wrongs: What Went Wrong with Affirmative Action*, San Francisco: Institute for Contemporary Studies.

CHRISTOPHER R. CAPSAMBELIS

Race-Neutral Criteria

Race-neutral criteria, as the term implies, involve using standards in a given selection process in which race is not a deciding factor toward the outcome. As the term has been commonly interpreted, it has been used to describe such criteria as income or grade point average or other nonracially descriptive quantifying tools on which to base selection. The idea of race-neutral criteria has its historical foundations in the Civil Rights Act of 1964, which mandates no distinction is to be made in the right to vote, in the provisions of public service, the right to public employment, the right to public education, on the grounds of race, color, religion, or national origin. The administration of this policy has led to the inclusion of statistics and studies on race, sex, and national origin in all aspects of employment for the purpose of ensuring compliance with Title VI and Title VII of the Civil Rights Act, which outlawed discrimination in federally funded programs and prohibited discrimination by both private and public employers.

Race-neutral criteria have become a politically charged concept that has served to polarize much of the United States. Opponents of affirmative action cite the concept as a means to prevent discrimination without specific regard to race, while proponents of affirmative action claim that race-neutral criteria are a thinly veiled effort to undo programs. The desire of elected officials to appease constituents on both sides of this issue has forced much of the debate from the political arena to the jurisdiction of the courts. Advocates of the use of race-neutral criteria cite a number of justifications in favor of the use of this concept, probably the most prominent of which is the idea of reverse discrimination. In an effort to ensure compliance with the current interpretation of the Civil Rights Act of 1964, certain underrepresented classes of society have been given advantages not afforded to the majority of applicants. This has led to the selection of individuals who otherwise would possibly not have been competitive in the selection process. In a zero-sum game in which there are only a finite number of positions to fill, this has inevitably led to cases in which someone with lower qualifications at the time was selected over individuals with higher qualifications because of race. Charges of reverse discrimination have provided opponents of affirmative action with a powerful tool to sway public opinion against specific programs.

Proponents of race-neutral criteria assert that they can be used to ensure that diversity in the selection process is maintained without alienating segments of the population. One example of this would be weighing economic factors. In U.S. society, minorities have a tendency to fall at the lower end of the economic spectrum. By giving advantages to this economic class of society, it is reasonable to expect a rise in minority selection. Other factors of a nonracial nature that have been mentioned include such characteristics as geographical area and class standing (e.g., percentage-plan programs).

Opponents of the use of race-neutral criteria argue that distinctions such as economic criteria are superficial at best. The root of the problem lies within the fact that the system is set up in such a fashion that a "suspect class" of minorities will not get a fair share of the resources available. It is the responsibility of government to legislate and enforce the equal representation of all classes of society in the sharing of these common resources. Court decisions such as *Regents of the University of California v. Bakke*, 438 U.S. 265 (1978), allow for the use of a racially motivated criterion as one of several criteria in the selection process in the interests of achieving a diverse student body. Another argument against race-neutral criteria relies on the idea that it is acceptable to give certain categories of society advantages in reparation for past wrongs. Because certain suspect classes of society have been systematically discriminated against in the past, it is incumbent upon society to make up for these past wrongs.

Current trends within advocacy of race-neutral criteria rely on the conflicting language presented in *Bakke*. The split decision advanced the idea that it is not acceptable to adopt a racial quota system because this violates the Equal Protection Clause of the Fourteenth Amendment; however, it is allowable to use race as one of several factors in admissions. This less-than-precise language has left it up to individual courts to decide what exactly represents a legal use of race in selection criteria.

One contemporary trend has been the increasing use of race-blind admissions systems for higher education. One example of this trend is the passage of Proposition 209 ("The Prohibition against Discrimination or Preferential Treatment by State and Other Public Entities") in California in 1996. This ballot initiative eliminated affirmative action programs in that state. Also in 1996, the U.S. Fifth Circuit Court ruled in *Hopwood v. Texas*, 78 F.3d 932 (5th Cir. 1996), that different admission standards for minorities that were enacted to improve minority selection chances in Texas, Mississippi, and Louisiana were illegal except where it could be proven that vestiges of discrimination still existed.

The *Hopwood* ruling and the ratification of Proposition 209 have led to a resurgence of anti–affirmative action activism. Recent polls of the American public have shown negative feelings toward the way affirmative action has been used in the past. Two states have passed legislation similar to Proposition 209, Initiative 200 in the state of Washington and the One Florida Initiative in Florida. In 2003, the Supreme Court decided to weigh in on this issue of race-neutral criteria following the U.S. Court of Appeals for the Sixth Circuit's ruling in *Grutter v. Bollinger*, which apparently contradicted the findings in the Fifth Circuit Court of Appeals and the Eleventh Circuit in *Hopwood* and *Johnson v. Board of Regents of the University of Georgia*, 263 F.3d 1234 (11th Cir. 2001), respectively. The "Michigan cases" (*Gratz v. Bollinger*, 123 S. Ct. 2411, 2003 U.S. LEXIS 4801 [2003], and *Grutter v. Bollinger*, 123 S. Ct. 2325, 2003 U.S. LEXIS 4800 [2003]) were expected to lay the foundation for both affirmative action and race-neutral decisions for years to come, and the decisions lived up to their expectations in this regard.

In these two landmark cases, the Court reaffirmed that considerations of race are permissible as a type of criteria to utilize in making selection decisions, as long as race (as a factor) is weighted no more heavily or significantly than other race-neutral criteria. In reaffirming diversity in higher education as a compelling governmental interest, the Supreme Court upheld the University of Michigan Law School's affirmative action plan (*Grutter* case) and endorsed affirmative action plans that utilize race as one factor or ingredient (among many) in the overall evaluation of candidates.

See also Civil Rights Act of 1964; Discrete and Insular Minority; Economically Disadvantaged; Equal Protection Clause; Fourteenth Amendment; *Gratz v. Bollinger/Grutter v. Bollinger*; *Hopwood v. Texas*; One Florida Initiative; Proposition 209; *Regents of the University of California v. Bakke*; Reparations; Reverse Discrimination; Title VI of the Civil Rights Act of 1964; Title VII of the Civil Rights Act of 1964; Washington Initiative 200.

FURTHER READING: Broadnax, Walter D., 2000, *Diversity and Affirmative Action in Public Service*, Boulder, CO: Westview; Darity, William A., and Samuel L. Myers Jr., 1998, *Persistent Disparity: Race and Economic Inequality in the United States since 1945*, Northampton, MA: Edward Elgar Publishers; Forde-Mazrui, Kim, 2000, "The Constitutional Implications of Race-Neutral Affirmative Action," *Georgetown Law Journal* 88 (August): 2331–2398; Glazer, Nathan, 1975, *Affirmative Discrimination: Ethnic Inequality and Public Policy*, New York: Basic Books; Goldman, Alan, 1979, *Justice and Reverse Discrimination*, Princeton, NJ: Princeton University Press; Hall, Francine, and Maryann Albrecht, 1979, *The Management of Affirmative Action*, Santa Monica, CA: Goodyear Publishing; Wyzan, Michael, ed., 1990, *The Political Economy of Ethnic Discrimination and Affirmative Action: A Comparative Perspective*, New York: Praeger.

TOM LANSFORD and JACK A. COVARRUBIAS

Racial and Ethnic Stratification

Racial and ethnic stratification is merely one mode of societal organization. Although the dream of the egalitarian and classless societies has persisted over the years, the stubborn fact is that stratification continues unabated in almost every region and location. Stratification in society exists where there is a rank ordering of positions based on criteria such as gender, income, wealth, prestige, age, or some other characteristic. Members who form these strata that make up the stratification system and its various gradations tend to have similar life chances and lifestyles and often display a sense of common identity. It has been argued by many writers that stratification systems meet certain functional needs of the society as a whole. They assert that in all societies, some positions are deemed more important than others, and that it is accordingly necessary to motivate individuals to develop their skills by suitable rewards. It is also contended that especially in advanced economies, achievement criteria ensure rationality when occupations are arranged on a hierarchical basis relative to their importance for the economy and the society as a whole.

Critics counter that functional justifications for stratification systems betray circular reasoning since they assert that high-income jobs are functional since they are high paying. They also claim that the conflict and power dimensions of stratification have been ignored. Others contend that stratification merely ignores the advantages of inherited wealth and property that come with class position. For these and other reasons, class analysis became fashionable during the 1960s and 1970s in the United States. With the rise of doctrines of race and ethnicity and of feminist movements, however, other dimensions of stratification became more prominent. Certain writers have contended that gender struggles nowhere even remotely approached the class struggle and in any case were devoid of the usual legal, religious, and other boundaries associated with class.

In the case of racial and ethnic stratification, however, there is a stronger case for ethnicity/race as a distinct criterion of stratification, especially in what are regarded as "plural" societies. As defined by M.G. Smith (1965), who derived his model from J.S. Furnivall, a plural society is one that is characterized by cultural pluralism and a corresponding cultural incompatibility. For Smith, Furnivall, and Leo Kuper, what distinguishes different forms of stratification is the mode of incorporation of citizens into the state. In societies where there is both de jure and de facto equality in their public domain, stratification is usually based on class. In those like the Deep South of the United States, in which until recently society was based on inequality of access to the public domain as a result of legal segregation, there is a system of ethnic/racial stratification.

Ethnic/racial stratification accordingly exists where ethnic/racial groups rather than classes constitute the hierarchy that makes up the social order. In "plural societies," the ruling ethnic/racial group usually differs in culture from the subjugated groups. According to Smith, the leading exponent of this plural society thesis, the state in the plural society is the executive committee of the ruling cultural section for the control of the subjugated groups who are "simultaneously denied political rights, citizenship, and opportunities for their own organization by prescriptions of the state" (Smith, 10).

As a description of ethnic/racial relations at certain periods in countries such as the United States, South Africa, and other ex-colonies, this was no doubt an accurate account of the relations between the dominant group and the dominated. It should be noted also that under ethnic/racial stratification systems, the status quo is discontinuous. Thus each ethnic group within the society has its own rank order. This is the fundamental difference between social and ethnic/racial stratification.

Ethnic/racial stratification is thus much like caste stratification. However, rapid political and economic changes have been taking place in countries such as the United States, the United Kingdom, and South Africa and elsewhere. As sociologist Max Weber pointed out, the development of capitalism necessarily leads to the erosion of status and its replacement by class criteria of stratification. The emergence of new elites as a result of political and economic change will certainly erode the principles on which ethnic/racial stratification rests. Blacks fled to the North because of its expanding capitalism and the greater freedom that it provided. Legal reform has also been an important agent of change and has been the goal of ethnic/racial reformers almost everywhere. In South Africa and the United States, civil and political rights movements have substantially eroded ethnic/racial stratification systems. The size of the respective groups is also a critical factor in the persistence of ethnic/racial stratification. In South Africa, the whites were a small minority; in the United States, the blacks were a mere 12 percent of the population. It is accordingly easier to break down the system of stratification in South Africa than it is in the United States. Equal opportunity and other kinds of legislation certainly remove some barriers.

Ethnic/racial stratification affects the outlook of the individual and provides him or her with his or her worldview. Affirmative action can only be a temporary palliative since the object of such action is to render such actions unnecessary in the future. There are signs that ethnicity is losing its power in areas such as the film industry, the military, the intelligentsia, advertising, and the professions. There are individuals, however, who have a vested interest in selling ideas of ethnic/racial domination. No doubt there will be some persistence of ethnic/racial stratification, given the historical origins of the society in question. The high visibility of some groups will also ensure the tenacity of some stereotypes from the past; yet the experience of countries such as France, Trinidad, Jamaica, Barbados, and Guyana clearly demonstrates that societies can be restratified to ensure that elites are drawn from different ethnic groups.

See also Assimilation Theory; Caste System; Gender Stratification; Great Britain and Affirmative Action; Integration; Pluralism; Segregation; South Africa and Affirmative Action; Weber, Max.

FURTHER READING: Davis, Kingsley, and Wilbert Moore, 1945, "Some Principles of Stratification," *American Sociological Review* 10:242–249; Furnivall, J.S., 1948, *Colonial Policy and Practice*, London: Cambridge University Press; Kuper, Leo, and M.G. Smith, eds., 1965, *Pluralism in Africa*, Berkeley and Los Angeles: University of California Press; Lipset, S.M., and R. Bendrix, 1953, *Class, Status and Power: A Reader in Social Stratification*, Glencoe, IL: Free Press; Smith, M.G., 1965, *The Plural Society in the British West Indies*, Kingston, Jamaica: Sangster Books; Weber, Max, 1947, *The Theory of Social and Economic Organizations*, translated by A.R. Henderson and Talcott Parsons, London and Paris: William Hodge and Sons.

ANN MARIE BISSESSAR

Racial Discrimination

Discrimination has been defined as behavior that "comes about only when we deny to individuals or groups of people equality of treatment which they may wish" (Allport 1954, 51). It has also been described as "inappropriate treatment of individuals due to their group membership" (Dovidio et al. 1996, 279). Discrimination is the behavioral component of prejudice. The primary process that underlies racial discrimination is the self-fulfilling prophecy, the perceiver stereotypes and prejudices, through which the perceiver acts behaviorally to confirm those stereotypes and prejudices. Other studies following the social identity theory and self-categorization suggest that mere group membership elicits intergroup discrimination in the distribution of rewards.

Susan Fiske suggests that there are two kinds of discrimination, hot and cold discrimination. "Hot discrimination" is based on disgust, resentment, hostility, and anger. People high in right-wing authoritarianism might follow this kind of discrimination. "Cold discrimination" is based on stereotypes of a minority group's interests, knowledge, and motivations. Stereotypes predict discrimination less than prejudices do. Like stereotypes and prejudice, both hot and cold discrimination may be automatic.

One social psychology study (Mummendey and Otten 2001) has established three types of discrimination differing in the intention of the minority-group rejection: first, mindless majority-group favoritism and positive evaluation without explicit social comparison between majority and minority groups; second, ambivalent discrimination, where many people endorse principles of egalitarianism and want to avoid discrimination, but will discriminate in favor of their group when the situation is ambiguous (these individuals are described as "aversive racists" in the literature); and third, intentional discrimination, where actors perceive minority members as different and specifically deserving negative treatment.

The social justification for discrimination toward minority members could be traditional beliefs, because majority-group members want a stable society and feel that minority members threaten their group status, their economic situation, or their values. There are individual differences in respect to minority-group hostility. Dogmatic people conceive value differences as incompatible. Those who adhere to right-wing authoritarianism submit to authorities and direct aggression at those groups targeted or sanctioned by authorities. Also, there are those who adhere to social dominance/superiority, who perceive their group as superior to the values and norms of a minority group.

See also Afrocentrism; Discrimination; Eurocentrism; Prejudice; Scapegoating/Displaced-Aggression Theories; Stereotyping and Minority Classes; White Supremacy.

FURTHER READING: Allport, Gordon W., 1954, *The Nature of Prejudice*, Cambridge, MA: Addison-Wesley; Dovidio, John F., J. Brigham, B.T. Johnson, and Samuel L. Gaertner, 1996, "Stereotyping, Prejudice, and Discrimination," in *Foundations of Stereotypes and Stereotyping*, edited by Neil Macrae, Charles Stangor, and Miles Hewstone, Hillsdale, NJ: AUM; Fiske, Susan T., 1998, "Stereotyping, Prejudice, and Discrimination," in *The Handbook of Social Psychology*, 4th ed., edited by Daniel T. Gilbert, Susan T. Fiske, and Gardner Lindzey, New York: McGraw-Hill; Mummendey, Amelie, and Sabine Otten, 2001, "Aversive Discrimination," in *Blackwell Handbook of Social Psychology: Intergroup Processes*, edited by Rupert Brown and Samuel Gaertner, Oxford: Blackwell; Snyder, Mark, 1984, "When Beliefs Create Reality," in *Advances in Experimental Social Psychology*, vol. 18, edited by Leonard Berkowitz, New York: Academic Press.

MARIA JOSE SOTELO

Racial Group

See Census Classifications, Ethnic and Racial.

Racial Privacy Initiative

The Racial Privacy Initiative (RPI) was a California ballot initiative (Proposition 54) designed to eliminate racial checkoff boxes on most California government forms. Specifically, the initiative would have prohibited state and local governments from using race, ethnicity, color, or national origin to classify any individual in the operation of public education, public contracting, or public employment. This initiative would not have prohibited classification by sex. Kevin Nguyen, executive director of the American Civil Rights Coalition, submitted the Racial Privacy Initiative to California's attorney general, Bill Lockyer, on September 28, 2001. The Racial Privacy Initiative was on the October 7, 2003, special election ballot and was rejected by almost 60 percent of the voters. If passed, the RPI would have added Article 1, Section 32, to the California Constitution, and its provisions would have taken effect on January 1, 2005. University of California regent Ward Connerly spearheaded the campaign in support of the initiative.

Proponents of the initiative argued that classifying people into boxes is divisive and encourages the mind-set that we are different. Conservative affirmative action critics such as Ward Connerly, George Will, and Nathan Glazer rallied behind this initiative. George Will, commenting in a March 2002 article in *Newsweek* magazine, stated that passing the RPI would be a color-blind step forward for civil rights, and that the RPI should be equated to abolishing the racist one-drop rule in California. Will argued that the only people who opposed the RPI were those "who make their living by Balkanizing America into elbow throwing grievance groups clamoring for government preferment. Such people include blacks in the civil-rights industry who administer today's racial spoils system of college admissions and contract set-asides and white liberals" (Will, 64). Nathan Glazer, Harvard sociologist and long-time affirmative action critic, similarly wrote in a fall 2002 *Public Interest* article that the federal government should eliminate racial information on the federal census as well. The argument of proponents was that the United States cannot be a truly color-blind society when there are government classifications (and preferences based upon these classifications) at every turn. However, opponents of the initiative argued that it would damage California's ability to address racial and ethnic disparities in a variety of areas, including health and illness, educational resources and achievement, hate crime, and discrimination. Also, without access to vital statistics and information about racial and ethnic minorities, affirmative action would be impossible to practice. The National Association for the Advancement of Color People labeled the RPI "racist."

See also Census Classifications, Ethnic and Racial; Color-Blind Constitution; Connerly, Ward; Glazer, Nathan; National Association for the Advancement of Colored People; One-Drop Rule.

FURTHER READING: Glazer, Nathan, 2002, "Do We Need the Census Race Question?" *Public Interest*, fall, 21–33; Racial Privacy Initiative, web site: http://www.racialprivacy.org; Will, George, 2002, "Dropping the 'One Drop' Rule: A Good Idea in California May Help America Discard One of the Worst Ideas It Ever Had," *Newsweek*, March 25, 64.

PAULINA X. RUF

Racial Profiling

Racial profiling, as a concept, means the use of race or national origin as a vehicle for law enforcement to stop, question, search, and sometimes arrest an individual. Racial profiling, like affirmative action, involves the use of racial characteristics as a key factor in supporting certain governmental determinations and actions. Ironically, conservative and liberal scholars often change positions on the permissibility of utilizing race as a factor in governmental action depending on whether one is referring to the practice of racial profiling or race-based affirmative action. Additionally, since the courts and many commentators have come to accept race as a relevant and permissible factor in creating a criminal profile for law-enforcement purposes, affirmative action and diversity in the law-enforcement community impact how fairly the practice of racial profiling is applied to the populace. As discussed later, since courts have generally legitimized the use of racial profiling by law enforcement, it is necessary for law enforcement to be ever vigilant to ensure that all Americans are provided with the same protections that the laws afford. Some proponents of affirmative action may argue that affirmative action programs help ensure a racially diverse police force, which in turn may help in how fairly or justly racial profiling tactics are utilized by law enforcement.

The controversial practices of racial profiling and affirmative action often result in the same person holding different beliefs as to the permissibility of utilizing race as a factor in governmental decisions, depending on which program is being debated. The proponents of affirmative action often argue that race is relevant based upon past incidents of discrimination, and racial preferences are needed to "level the playing field." Yet many of these same individuals dismiss the use of race in the racial profiling context as irrelevant, unworkable, or a violation of the Equal Protection Clause of the Fourteenth Amendment. Conversely, critics of affirmative action often argue that race is irrelevant to decisions on employment or education because only individual merit should matter, and the preferences have the effect of reverse discrimination upon qualified white applicants (i.e., racial preferences are unfair and do not work). Yet many of these same individuals promote the use of race as a relevant and effective way to prevent, investigate, and prosecute crimes (i.e., racial preferences are fair and do work).

Today, racial profiling is a relatively common technique used in the United States by all types of law enforcement and has direct implications for affirmative action. While racial profiling is often viewed as a practice with origins in the late twentieth century, the same tactics of profiling individuals were used as early as the 1600s against North American colonists by the British. Thus, throughout the history of the United States, governmental representatives, such as law enforcement, immigration officials, and legislators, have authorized the use of racial profiling in one form or another.

Early American colonists were fully aware of governmental intrusion into their homes by the British. Officially seeking violators of the Stamp Act, these soldiers would frequently destroy property and terrorize the colonists. This practice, ultimately resulted in strong support for the inclusion of the Fourth Amendment guarantees against unreasonable searches and seizures in the Bill of Rights. At no time since has our support, as a nation, for protection against unreasonable searches and seizures been so strong. The reason is clear: the intrusions by British soldiers into the homes of colonists were widespread and well known. Thus colonists had a common reason for the fear produced by actions of a governmental power when that power went unchecked.

Perhaps less well known, at least to white America, was the impact of the Jim Crow laws upon black citizens. These laws, along with formal racial segregation, were seen as necessary by white Americans to keep black Americans in their place. These same laws when viewed by blacks in America were seen as just one more example of how they were not treated as true and equal citizens and participants in the American experience. The U.S. history of slavery assisted in the pervasive belief that black Americans and white Americans were qualitatively different in terms that went far beyond skin color.

The widespread belief that it is permissible to treat people differently because of some outward feature allowed the U.S. government to lead more than 100,000 Japanese Americans into internment camps in 1942. This experiment with Japanese Americans during World War II resulted in their loss of property, possessions, and liberty because of their ancestry. Again, like the institutionalized segregation in the twentieth century, most white Americans were either unaware of or unmoved by their plight. So, unlike during the colonial period, when nearly all colonists had been the target of British intrusion or knew someone who had been, white America did not see the connection between Jim Crow laws, racial segregation, and the internment of Japanese Americans as potential violations of the Fourth Amendment or the Equal Protection Clause of the Fourteenth Amendment.

Much of the literature on racial profiling focuses upon law-enforcement officers stopping people of color as a pretext for a more extensive search of their person or vehicle. This practice originated and received approval in part because of the war on drugs. The war on drugs has been a part of American life since the passage of the Harrison Act in 1914. However, the 1980s saw an increased law-enforcement focus upon identifying, arresting, prosecuting, and incarcerating those individuals in the drug trade, from the casual user to the top-level drug trafficker. Federal assistance to local law enforcement through programs such as Operation Pipeline taught officers how to identify drug offenders in their own jurisdictions. Inevitably, the assistance included a profile of who the culprits might be, people of color. Certainly skin color was not the only criterion, but it underscored the belief that some people in U.S. society are more dangerous and allegedly have a stronger propensity to criminal behavior, and these people can be identified by skin color. Proponents of racial profiling often describe this process as "rational racism"—the allegedly high statistical correlation between race and crimes makes race relevant.

As a result, law-enforcement agencies across America were implementing policies that resulted in the singling out of individuals for closer examination based upon skin color. Some studies have attempted to assess the frequency of vehicle stops based on race in states such as Maryland, New Jersey, and Pennsylvania. On Interstate 95 outside Baltimore, it was discovered that of all those traveling, 17 percent were black, yet when stops were examined, it was discovered that 73 percent of the drivers stopped were black, a very disproportionate figure. Vehicle stops are not the only area of law enforcement subject to racial profiling. In the case of customs checkpoints, one study found that most individuals (more than 66 percent) subjected to intrusive body searches were people of color, and 96 percent of those searches resulted in nothing illegal being found.

Likewise, in what are known as *Terry* stops (after the Supreme Court case *Terry v. Ohio*, 392 U.S. 1 [1968])—the ability of law enforcement, without a warrant and without probable cause, to stop a person and frisk him or her for weapons—racial profiling is also prevalent. While race alone is never a constitutionally permissible reason to stop an individual pursuant to *Terry*, an individual's presence in a high-crime location and an evasive attitude constitute sufficient reasonable suspicion to allow a stop under *Terry*. As some minorities work or live in high-crime areas, this makes these individuals especially subject to *Terry* stops. *Terry* stops, like customs searches and traffic stops, are difficult to measure since most departments keep little or no statistical data on the race and outcome of the initial encounter. In one study done in New York City in the late 1990s, it was found that of the 45,000 *Terry* stops recorded, 9,500 people were arrested and that two-thirds of those stopped were people of color. Of the 9,500 people arrested, at least half had charges dropped because of lack of evidence.

While most of the preceding deals with blacks or Hispanics as the victims of racial profiling (or Japanese Americans in the case of World War II), people of

Arab descent and followers of Islam have also been the targets of racial profiling in the wake of the terrorist actions on U.S. soil on September 11, 2001. Due in part to the 1996 Antiterrorism and Effective Death Penalty Act passed in the wake of the Oklahoma City bombing of the Murrah Federal Building on April 19, 1995, and the Patriot Act passed in the aftermath of the terrorist actions on September 11, 2001, the government has greater powers than ever before to hold a person, question a person without counsel, and deport aliens suspected of terrorist actions. The law also provides that these individuals can be held, questioned, and deported based upon secret evidence not available to the subject or his/her attorney.

Thus the concept of racial profiling, which started early in U.S. history, is still a viable government practice and has been legitimized by Congress with the passage of laws designed to allow for greater law-enforcement discretion. The judiciary, of course, has the final word on the legality of practices by the government and its agents. Cases dealing with racial profiling have worked their way through the system to the U.S. Supreme Court. The most significant case yet decided by the Court dealing with racial profiling is *Whren v. United States*, 517 U.S. 806 (1996).

In *Whren*, a truck driven by a person named Brown was stopped after making an allegedly illegal turn at a stop sign. Following the stop, officers found crack cocaine in plastic bags in the driver's hand. The defendants claimed that the traffic stop was actually a pretext for a drug search. The state argued that the traffic violation gave probable cause for the stop. The U.S. Supreme Court held that when a traffic violation occurs and the police initiate a stop, the temporary detention of the driver and occupants does not violate the Fourth Amendment's protection against unreasonable searches and seizures regardless of whether the "reasonable officer" would have initiated such a stop. That is, the *Terry* stop is unconstitutional only if the stop is unexplainable on any other basis (giving a reasonable suspicion) than race. The net result of the *Whren* decision is to legitimize racial profiling and pretextual stops so long as law enforcement can articulate nonracial reasons creating reasonable suspicion. Justice Antonin Scalia, writing the majority opinion for a unanimous Court, held in part that the constitutional basis for objecting to intentionally discriminatory laws is not the Fourth Amendment's unreasonable search provision, but rather the Equal Protection Clause of the Fourteenth Amendment. Thus far, practices of racial profiling have not been overturned by the Court as unconstitutional under the Fourteenth Amendment's Equal Protection Clause. In fact, in *Korematsu v. United States*, 323 U.S. 214 (1944), the Court specifically approved of racial profiling–type actions during World War II.

See also Criminal Justice System and Affirmative Action; Equal Protection Clause; Fourteenth Amendment; Japanese Internment and World War II; Jim Crow Laws; *Korematsu v. United States*; Level Playing Field; Scalia, Antonin; Segregation; Slavery.

FURTHER READING: Glasser, Ira, 2000, "American Drug Laws: The New Jim Crow Laws," *Albany Law Review* 63:703–724; Jernigan, Adero S., 2000, "Driving While Black: Racial Profiling in America," *Law and Psychology Review* 24:127–138; Romero, Victor C., 2000, "Racial Profiling: Driving While Mexican and Affirmative Action," *Michigan Journal of Race and Law* 6 (fall): 195–207; Walter, Lisa, 2000, "Eradicating Racial Stereotyping from *Terry* Stops: The Case for an Equal Protection Exclusionary Rule," *University of Colorado Law Review* 71:255–

294; Weeder, Darnell L., 1999, "It Is Not Right under the Constitution to Stop and Frisk Minority People Because They Don't Look Right," *University of Arkansas at Little Rock Law Review* 21:829–840.

SUSAN F. BRINKLEY

Racial Stereotyping

Racial stereotypes comprise the beliefs, perceptions, attitudes, prejudices, and worldview that one group of people has of another. Such attitudes, perceptions, and beliefs normally center on ideas relating to the capacity of the groups for intellectual and other kinds of achievement. In other cases, they have to do with the capacity of such groups for attaining certain levels of civilization, while in yet others, certain qualities are assumed to be inherent in the genetic makeup of the discriminated group relating to their tendency toward violence, sexual prowess, work habits, and sometimes even hygiene. Racial stereotyping was, until very recently, a universal phenomenon encapsulated in terms of national characteristics. Even in classical Athens, there was a distinction between Greeks and barbarians.

To understand the concept of racial stereotyping, it is necessary first to distinguish carefully between race and ethnicity. Banton (1967) has argued that race refers to the physical categorization of people, while ethnicity has to do with their cultural styles and identification. Racism, therefore, obviously builds on the assumption that a race or a racial group shares distinct features such as hair texture or other physical attributes that are mainly hereditary in nature. These features differ systematically between "races," and this, of necessity, gives the term "racism" sociological importance.

A number of writers (Poliakov 1974; Williams 1944) have argued that race was viewed historically not in national (or ethnic) terms but rather in class or caste terms. The domination of one superior group over another subordinate group was often justified in terms of genetic or cultural attributes. Balibar (1999) noted that this conclusion could be drawn from the power relationship that the aristocrat or the hereditary nobles maintained over their serfs or in the slave owners' representation of those populations subject to the slave trade as inferior races. Thus these racial groups, according to the groups in power, were predestined for servitude and were believed to be incapable of producing an autonomous civilization.

To maintain this kind of enforced superior/subordinate order, a number of mechanisms were employed, including laws, institutions, practices, the use of "self-referential racism" that elevated the group controlling the discourse, or the accumulation of capital. Another common form was racial stereotyping.

In social anthropology, the concept of stereotyping refers to the creation and consistent application of standardized notions of the cultural distinctiveness of a group. Stereotypes are held by dominated groups as well as those who dominate and according to Ericksen (1993) are widespread in societies with significant power differences. He observed that to a large extent, stereotypes are often mentioned in connection with racism and discrimination. For example, white Americans may justify discrimination against blacks by referring to the latter as "lazy." Some common stereotypes he observed that are held of certain races include the following: Creoles are lazy, merry, and careless; Hindus are stingy, dishonest, and hardworking; Muslims are religious fanatics and nonminglers; coloreds are clever, conceited, and too ambitious (Ericksen 1993, 23).

It has been suggested, though, that while stereotyping by its very labeling creates an order that places groups into superordinate and subordinate positions, according to Ericksen (1993), there are a number of advantages that could be derived from the use of stereotyping. In the case of Mauritius, for example, he argued that stereotypes assisted in creating "order" by providing a simple classificatory system that placed every "race" in its place. In addition, he observed that racial stereotyping could justify privileges and differences in access to a society's resources. Third, he observed that stereotypes were crucial in defining the boundaries of one's own group.

It is important, therefore, to recognize the mechanisms that generate and sustain racial stereotypes. What might have started as a stereotyping of the lower classes is soon generalized for the group as a whole since individuals from the dominant group tend to perceive things in "group" rather than "class" terms. The dominant institutions of society—the schools, the organizations, the family, and the various academic disciplines—also help to socialize individuals in the society as a whole into the adoption of racial stereotypes. Indeed, in some cases, the individuals against whom these stereotypes are directed embrace them themselves.

It is also important to recognize that generally, stereotyping has a number of negative consequences. Indeed, to a large extent, the mass murder of Jews in Germany during World War II was in part sustained by the widespread use of negative racial stereotyping. In the case of the United States, it has been suggested that stereotyping against "blacks" is a common phenomenon and one that was largely nurtured by whites. Dollard (1937) pointed out that the black/white relationships and the stereotyping that emerged during the 1930s and 1940s were promoted by active social and physical pressures that were exerted on blacks. He observed that during the period of slavery, blacks were granted sexual freedom among their own people, greater freedom of aggression, and the psychological luxury of a dependent relationship on whites. Whites, on the other hand, had the satisfaction that went with mastery, superiority, control, maturity and duty well fulfilled. They also had the pleasure of despising blacks. Negroes were permitted slack work habits, irresponsibility, and, within limits, more personal freedom than was possible in a competitive, economically progressive society. This "freedom" and "laxity" set the pace for the stereotypes that later developed and perhaps, he argued, helped to explain why blacks did not bother to change the system.

It is obvious, then, that racial stereotyping is a tool that helps to maintain the status quo and existing order. However, perceptions and stereotyping can be changed by continuing education and exposure.

See also African Americans; Asian Americans; Model Minorities (Stereotyping Asian Americans); Prejudice; Stereotypes, Gender; Stereotyping and Minority Classes.

FURTHER READING: Balibar, Etienne, 1999, "Class Racism," in *The Ethnicity Reader: Nationalism, Multiculturalism, and Migration,* edited by Montserrat Guibernau and John Rex, Cambridge: Polity Press; Banton, Michael, 1967, *Race Relations,* New York: Basic Books; Dollard, John, 1937, *Caste and Class in a Southern Town,* New Haven, CT: Yale University Press; Ericksen, Thomas Hylland, 1993, *Ethnicity and Nationalism: Anthropological Perspectives,*

London: Pluto Press; Poliakov, Leon, 1974, *The Aryan Myth: A History of Racist and Nationalist Ideas in Europe*, New York: New American Library; Williams, Eric, 1944, *Capitalism and Slavery*, Chapel Hill: University of North Carolina Press.

ANN MARIE BISSESSAR

Racism

Racism is central to the affirmative action debate. Proponents commonly argue that affirmative action benefiting racial minority groups is fair and necessary to make up for racism and the resulting discrimination against minority groups. Some also argue that all opposition to race-based affirmative action expressed by whites is racist.

Defining the term "racism" can be both difficult and controversial. This is illustrated by the activities of the United Nations' 2001 World Conference Against Racism, Racial Discrimination, Xenophobia, and Related Intolerance (WCAR). Despite the fact that some of the conference participants desired that the group clearly define racism, a clear definition of racism does not appear in the report of the conference. Perhaps this should have been foreseen as the Report of the Consultation on the World Conference against Racism, Racial Discrimination, Xenophobia and Related Forms of Intolerance held at The Rockefeller Foundation's Study and Conference Center in Bellagio, Italy, in 2000, states: "It is . . . abundantly clear that there is no one form, type or definition of 'racism' " (www. un.org).

It is generally agreed that the essence of racism is the belief that one group of people is inherently superior to another because of the difference in the lines of descent and the perceived biological characteristics of the two groups. Controversy exists, however, as to whether this definition should be either expanded or qualified.

It is now obvious to most that all people belong to one race. However, according to Etienne Balibar, professor of moral philosophy and politics at the University of Paris, X Nanterre, the term "racism" was "coined in Germany to describe the racism of the Nazi state" based on the principle that Aryans were inherently superior to other groups considered to be subhuman (Balibar, 14). Although German scientists, among others in history, have attempted to demonstrate a relevant genetic difference between groups that might support a claim that the groups are of different races, it is now generally accepted that the concept of race as used in the term "racism" is not scientifically based but is a social invention used to elevate one group of people by subjugating another. Indeed, some argue that the definition of racism includes the concept of power. In other words, only members of groups that have power in a society can be racist. Ian F. Haney Lopez, Assistant Professor of Law, University of California, Berkeley, expresses a similar theory. He states: "Racism is racial status-enforcement undertaken in reliance on racial institutions" (Haney López, 1809). He defines racial institutions as "any understanding of race that has come to be so widely shared within a community that it operates as an unexamined cognitive resource for understanding one's self, others, and the-way-the-world-is" and racial status-enforcement as "action that has the effect of enforcing a racial status hierarchy" (Haney López, 1809–1810). Professor Lopez asserts that action that does not actually enforce a racial status hierarchy, even if based on racial institutions, is not racist.

Others vehemently disagree with the claim that power is a necessary element of racism. This camp can be further subdivided. One group argues that a person can be racist or hold racist views regardless of his or her position of power in society. The other group argues that although the wielder of racism must have power, whether such power exists must be assessed on an individual basis. For example, assume that two persons are hanging on to and about to fall off of a cliff. One is African American and the other is Caucasian. Another African American person is in the position of being able to save one and only one of them. The good Samaritan has the ultimate power over the two cliff hangers—the power of life and death. If the good Samaritan chooses to save the African American cliff hanger because she believes African Americans are inherently superior than Caucasians, she is practicing racism.

Theorists have distinguished between individual racism and institutional racism. Individual racism requires relative power in interactions between individuals and institutional racism requires power within the society's social or economic institutions. Institutional Racism has been defined as follows:

> those established laws, customs, and practices which systematically reflect and produce racial inequalities in society. If racist consequences accrue to institutional laws, customs, or practices, the institution is racist whether or not the individuals maintaining those practices have racial intentions. (British Council)

Affirmative action seeks to remedy both institutional racism and the cumulative effects of individual racism by members of the majority racial groups as manifested in racial discrimination.

Few seriously deny that racial discrimination against minority groups has been rampant in most, if not all, social and economic institutions in the United States, and in many other countries. Majority racial groups in control of these institutions have used their power to exclude minority racial groups from the benefits of participation in these institutions and have justified their actions with the precept that their racial group is inherently superior to the others. Other institutions exclude minority groups perhaps unintentionally by, for example, operating according to the norms of the majority group culture. Nevertheless, the effect is the same—minority groups have not been well represented in the social and economic institutions that govern daily life. Affirmative action debates are often over whether the effects of racism expressed in past racial discrimination are present and sufficiently identifiable to justify affirmative action and whether racism continues in society's institutions.

Some affirmative action supporters argue that evidence of contemporary racism is the strong opposition to affirmative action among whites and believe all such opposition is racist. There are some majority group members who oppose all affirmative action (whether involving racial preferences or not) because they believe minority groups are inferior. These views are obviously racist. However, some whites argue their opposition to preference-type affirmative action on the principled grounds that it is contrary to the emphasis in American culture upon self-made success. This view is also considered to be racist by some affirmative action supporters. John David Skrentny describes this argument in his book *Color Lines: Affirmative Action, Immigration, and Civil Rights Options for America* (2001):

> This racism is more subtle than the coarse racism of the Jim Crow era that bluntly advocated racial segregation, discrimination, and the inherent inferiority of blacks to whites. It involves a blend of early learned antiblack feelings and beliefs with traditional American values of hard work and self-reliance. It is expressed in resentment and hostility toward blacks' demands for special treatment and toward government recognition of blacks' demands, and in unreasoned denial of the modern potency of racial discrimination or bias. It has no meaningful dependence on material contingencies in the private lives of individual whites." (Skrentny, 194)

The central role racism plays in affirmative action debates helps to explain why affirmative action is among the most heated and emotional issues on the contemporary social agenda.

See also Convention on the Elimination of All Forms of Racial Discrimination; Discrimination; Gendered Racism; Ideological Racism; Overt Racism, Racial and Ethnic Stratification; Racial Discrimination; Racial Stereotyping; Scientific Racism; White Supremacy.

FURTHER READING: Balibar, Etienne, 1996, "Racism and Anti-Racism," *UNESCO Courier*, March, 14–17; British Council, "Race and Ethnicity," http://britishcouncil.org/diversity/race_reports2.htm; Carter, Stephen L., 1991, *Reflections of an Affirmative Action Baby*, New York: Basic Books; Eberhardt, Jennifer L., and Susan T. Fiske, eds., 1998, *Confronting Racism: The Problem and the Response*, Thousand Oaks, CA: Sage Publications; Haney López, Ian F., 2000, "Institutional Racism: Judicial Conduct and a New Theory of Racial Discrimination," *Yale Law Journal* 109, no. 8:1717–1884; Jacquard, Albert, 1996, "An Unscientific Notion," *UNESCO Courier*, March, 22–28; Jones, J.M., 1997, *Prejudice and Racism*, 2d ed., New York: McGraw Hill; Perea, Juan F., Richard Delgado, Angela P. Harris, and Stephanie M. Wildman, 2000, *Race and Races: Cases and Resources for a Diverse America*, St. Paul, MN: West Group; Sears, David O., "Is It Really Racism? The Origins of White Americans' Opposition to Race-Targeted Policies," *Public Opinion Quarterly* 61:16–53; Skrentny, John David, 2001, *Color Lines: Affirmative Action, Immigration, and Civil Rights Options for America*, Chicago: University of Chicago Press; Sniderman, Paul M., 1993, *The Scar of Race*, Cambridge, MA: Harvard University Press; West, Cornel, 1993, *Race Matters*, Boston: Beacon Press.

MARIA D. BECKMAN

Racist Ideology

See Ideological Racism/Racist Ideology.

Radical Republicans

See Abolitionists.

Radicalism

Developing essentially out of the concept of liberalism, radicalism is more than just an extreme form of liberal thought. Historically, it has advocated the essential rejection of the status quo rather than a modification of it. In America, the American Revolution was arguably a radical act in that the colonists rejected the basic system of British rule as well as its agency. The history of radicalism in America, however, is dominated by rejections of the American federalist model as well as this country's commitment to capitalism and to big business in particular. While some erroneously label affirmative action as a form of radicalism, the goal of affirmative action is ultimately integration and ensuring fairness and equality under the Constitution. As such, affirmative action (or the civil rights movement) should not be considered a type of radicalism. Rather, those arguing for separatism or segregation today would more properly be labeled as engaged in radicalism.

As far back as Daniel Shays's Rebellion (August 1786–February 1787) the Haymarket Square Riot of 1886 as well as with the rise of labor unions under the leadership of men such as Eugene Debs, the history of radicalism in the United States has been dominated by populist and Marxist sentiments, albeit within the context of a commitment to the ideals of an American democracy, especially from the New Left, such as the Students for a Democratic Society (SDS), a radical group that developed initially through resistance to the war in Vietnam. Essentially, however, the SDS was resisting what President Dwight Eisenhower had called the military-industrial complex. The radical view of the New Left was that a real democratic society could not emerge from the American Constitution as long as the political process was dominated by big business generally and the business of war in particular.

Thus it is not completely accurate to describe the civil rights movement of the 1950s and 1960s as a radical movement, at least compared to the more extreme responses to racism in America. The message of Martin Luther King was radical only within the context of the institution of slavery, both literal (antebellum slavery) and de facto (Jim Crow and economic and/or social enslavement as a fact). Essentially, however, Martin Luther King was committed to a relatively traditional view of the American dream. The goal of his movement was one of assimilation and integration rather than transformation. This goal is perhaps better understood by contrast with the goals of separatist movements such as those of Marcus Garvey, Malcolm X, and the Nation of Islam.

Similarly, within the women's movement, the primary goal of most American feminist movements has been to achieve complete integration, both politically and economically, within the existing system. Arguably, women simply want the same opportunity as men to make a killing in the market. They want to play on the same level field. They want to start at the same place in the race. All these metaphors accept the ideology of human interaction as competitive more than cooperative. The more radical fringes of feminism seek to redefine human relationships in communal as well as egalitarian terms. In this context, radical feminists are not necessarily Marxist, but they do recognize the role that American capitalism plays in the enslavement of most individuals, both male and female.

A more recent development in American radicalism turns to the extreme right in the form of groups such as the Posse Comitatus, which adheres quite literally to Henry David Thoreau's idea that the best form of government is no government at all. Situated primarily in the mountain states, these groups essentially espouse the principles of anarchism and survivalism. Referred to as the New Right, these survivalist groups are typically well armed and are committed to the idea of personal defense against any and all enemies, including and perhaps especially the federal government. Originating in the myth of the frontier hero, the New Right is neither committed to nor opposed to capitalism. Its rejection of American government is framed both rhetorically and ideologically in terms of political rights, not economics.

See also Assimilation Theory; Civil Rights Movement; Garvey, Marcus; Integration; King, Martin Luther, Jr.; Level Playing Field; Malcolm X; Marxist Theory and Affirmative Action; Segregation.

FURTHER READING: Coates, James, 1987, *Armed and Dangerous: The Rise of the Survivalist Right*, New York: Hill and Wang; Cone, James, 1994, "Martin Luther King, Jr.," in *The American Radical*, edited by Mari Jo Buhle, Paul Buhle, Harvey J. Kaye, and Eric Foner, New York: Routledge; Darsey, James, 1999, *Prophetic Tradition and Radical Rhetoric in America*, New York: New York University Press; Dyson, Michael, 1994, "Malcolm X," in *The American Radical*, edited by Mari Jo Buhle, Paul Buhle, Harvey J. Kaye, and Eric Foner, New York: Routledge; Howe, Irving, 1970, *Beyond the New Left*, New York: McCall Publishing; Jacobs, Paul, and Saul Landau, 1966, *The New Radicals*, New York: Random House; Lummings, C. Douglas, 1996, *Radical Democracy*, Ithaca, NY: Cornell University Press; Malloy, Scott, 1994, "Eugene Debs," in *The American Radical*, edited by Mari Jo Buhle, Paul Buhle, Harvey J. Kaye, and Eric Foner, New York: Routledge; Marks, Kathy, 1996, *Faces of Right Wing Extremism*, Wellesley, MA: Branden Books; Morgan, Iwan, 1994, *Beyond the Liberal Consensus*, New York: St. Martin's Press; Robinson, Cedric, 2000, *Black Marxism: The Making of the Black Radical Tradition*, Chapel Hill: University of North Carolina Press; Shrank, Robert, 1999, *Wasn't That a Time? Growing Up Radical and Red in America*, Cambridge, MA: MIT Press.

MICHAEL D. QUIGLEY

Rainbow PUSH Coalition

The Rainbow PUSH Coalition (RPC) is an organization founded by the Reverend Jesse L. Jackson Sr. that, as an organization, strongly supports affirmative action initiatives. Prior to 1985, two separate organizations existed: Operation PUSH and the Rainbow Coalition. However, in 1985, Jackson merged Operation PUSH and the National Rainbow Coalition to help in focusing the goals of the two organizations. The purpose of this organization, according to its founder and members, is to bring together people of diverse backgrounds to fight for equal opportunity and equal access through such means as affirmative action. The Rainbow Coalition also has threatened protests and boycotts of businesses and institutions that do not hire and promote blacks. In April 2003, the Rainbow PUSH Coalition organized protests at the U.S. Supreme Court on the eve of oral arguments in the landmark affirmative action cases *Gratz v. Bollinger*, 123 S. Ct. 2411, 2003 U.S. LEXIS 4801 (2003), and *Grutter v. Bollinger*, 123 S. Ct. 2325, 2003 U.S. LEXIS 4800 (2003).

The main interest of RPC is to focus on areas such as elections, mediation, lobbying for more minorities in coaching and upper administrative positions in college and university sports, and pushing the entertainment industry to have more positive minority representation in television media. The organization also negotiates deals with corporations so that minorities and women can open, own, and run businesses and small franchises. The most important issues that RPC concentrates on are issues involving economic empowerment and access in varied educational arenas, fair housing for the poor, increases in wages, voting and voter registration, affirmative action, and civil rights.

Another area of importance that Jackson and the Rainbow PUSH Coalition has focused on, particularly within the last ten years, is education and prevention of the spread of HIV/AIDS in communities of color. Jackson also formed the organization called "1,000 Black Churches," a conglomeration of churches coming together to assist in alleviating the economic plight of the African American community. The organization also wishes to emphasize the need for spiritual guidance in dilemmas that continue to persist in many African American communities in regard to those areas or groups and persons that may cause problems within the community.

The Rainbow PUSH organization through its Economic Literacy core seeks to educate African Americans and to make them aware of economic injustices that continue to plague U.S. society. RPC files litigation against companies and other financial organizations that are overcharging or have overcharged blacks for services because of their ethnic and racial affiliation. RPC is also active in researching and presenting data and evidence to both minority consumers and large companies concerning fair and equitable employment practices. Some of the data that RPC presents to consumers and companies demonstrate the large disparities between minority consumerism and the number of upper-level positions. Fair minority representation in sports and the media is also a main area and focus within the Economic Literacy core of RPC.

Some of the tactics that the organization uses to achieve its goals are boycotts and small and massive demonstrations. The organization has also filed litigation in civil rights and housing rights areas. The Rainbow PUSH Coalition has several offices within the United States, for example, in Washington D.C., Los Angeles, and Atlanta. The main headquarters is in Chicago, Illinois.

See also Gratz v. Bollinger/Grutter v. Bollinger; Jackson, Jesse; Media and Affirmative Action.

FURTHER READING: Clarke, Liz, 1994, "Rainbow Coalition to Urge Boycotts of Schools That Don't Hire, Promote Blacks," Knight Ridder/Tribune News Service, November 16; Hamill, Sean D., 2003, "Rev. Jesse Jackson Organizes March for Affirmative Action on April 1," *Knight Ridder/Tribune Business News*, March 20; Rainbow PUSH Coalition, web site: http://www.rainbowpush.org/.

NICOLE M. STEPHENS

Randolph, Asa Philip (1889–1979)

An influential civil rights activist and labor leader, A. Philip Randolph is best known in the affirmative action context as being a significant force behind President Franklin D. Roosevelt's issuance of Executive Order 8802 (prohibiting discriminatory hiring practices in defense-related industries that had federal contracts) and President Harry S Truman's issuance of Executive Order 9981 (integrating the U.S. armed forces). Randolph also believed that the civil rights movement was "wholly inadequate" to rectify racial problems in America, and more governmental action was needed. A lifelong activist and labor leader, he fought discrimination in the labor context by organizing a labor union called the

Asa Philip Randolph seated with President Lyndon Johnson. Courtesy of Library of Congress.

Brotherhood of Sleeping Car Porters and, in 1955, served as a vice president in the AFL-CIO. In a 1935 speech, Randolph declared that class and economic hardships were a more appropriate factor for government action and aid to focus on than utilizing race as a factor.

A. Philip Randolph's childhood was spent in Jacksonville, Florida. He was the class valedictorian of the 1907 class of historically black Cookman Institute, which would later become known as Bethune-Cookman College. Randolph moved to New York City in 1911, where he worked as an elevator operator. While living in the community of Harlem, New York, he took classes at the City College of New York and New York University and later was employed by an employment agency. Randolph took an interest in socialism and politics, which fueled his sometimes-scathing editorials in the *Messenger*, a newspaper he founded with Chandler Owen. The newspaper was not profitable; however, it was successful in becoming an instrument for the strong radical voice of the antiaccommodationists in the African American community. The *Messenger* became a staple in the reading of many of the porters who worked for the white-owned Pullman Railroad Company, the single largest employer of African American men, many of whom were college graduates. Although many of the porters were well respected and held in high regard in the African American community, they were subject to discriminatory practices within the Pullman Company.

In 1925, Randolph began organizing a labor union called the Brotherhood of Sleeping Car Porters. For ten years, Randolph was the catalyst in keeping the union organized and energized. After years of tough negotiations with Congress and the president, the company recognized the union in 1935. It was hailed as a victory by African Americans and Caucasians alike. In a May 1935 speech, Randolph called for an alliance of blacks, labor, and poor individuals to combat discrimination and employment problems in America. He also believed that economic class was more important than race in getting at problems of disparities in education and the workforce.

In 1941, before the United States entered World War II, Randolph threatened to lead an African American march on Washington to protest racial discrimination in the defense industries. Randolph's activism in large part prompted President Franklin D. Roosevelt to issue Executive Order 8802, which prohibited racial discrimination in the hiring practices of defense-related industries that had federal contracts. Randolph likened Roosevelt's Executive Order 8802 to the "second Emancipation Proclamation." In 1948, Randolph again pressured the White House to integrate the armed forces. Randolph threatened to lead a nationwide black draft resistance, which in part prompted President Truman to issue Executive Order 9981, integrating the armed forces.

In the 1950s, Randolph joined with Martin Luther King Jr. in conducting peaceful protests throughout the South. Among other events, Randolph sponsored a Prayer Pilgrimage in 1957 and Youth Marches for Integrated Schools in 1958 and 1959. Perhaps most memorable, Randolph first proposed, and then helped organize, King's March on Washington in 1963. However, by 1964, Randolph was the subject of criticism by black militants, who claimed that Randolph's notion of nonviolent peaceful protest. Many black militants were particular enraged when Randolph signed the Moratorium on Demonstrations, which vowed to eschew demonstrations until President Johnson was reelected.

Randolph never lost an interest in labor affairs. In 1955, Randolph again immersed himself in labor negotiations, when he assisted in the merger between the AFL and CIO. Partly in recognition for his roll in the merger, Randolph became a vice president in the combined ALF-CIO. Randolph also founded the black Negro American Labor Council (NALC) to combat the racism within labor. In 1968, with his health failing, Randolph resigned his prominent labor positions. Until his death in 1979, he held disdain for black militants and firmly believed that economics held the key to integration and ultimate racial equality in society.

See also Brotherhood of Sleeping Car Porters; Civil Rights Movement; Economically Disadvantaged; Executive Order 8802; Military and Affirmative Action; Roosevelt, Franklin Delano; Truman, Harry.

FURTHER READING: Anderson, Jervis, 1972, *A. Philip Randolph*, Berkeley: University of California Press; Rubio, Phillip F., 2001, *A History of Affirmative Action, 1619–2000*, Jackson: University Press of Mississippi; Skrentny, John David, 1996, *The Ironies of Affirmative Action*, Chicago: University of Chicago Press.

F. ERIK BROOKS

Rangel, Charles (1930–)

A staunch supporter of affirmative action in the U.S. Congress, Charles B. Rangel is serving his sixteenth term as the representative from the Fifteenth Congressional District, comprising East and Central Harlem, the Upper West Side, and Washington Heights of New York City. Rangel also serves as a senior member of the Congressional Black Caucus, which also supports affirmative action initiatives in Congress. Rangel is a ranking member of the U.S. House Committee on Ways and Means, deputy Democratic whip of the House of Representatives, a cochair of the Democratic Congressional Committee, and the dean of the New York State congressional delegation owing to his years of serving his constituency in the U.S. House of Representatives.

As a founding member and former chairman of the Congressional Black Caucus and also as a chairman of the New York State Black Elected Democrats, Rangel has played a pioneering role in shaping the agenda for empowerment of African Americans who have been historically marginalized and discriminated against. He is vehemently opposed to racial profiling and has called for an end to this practice. Rangel is in favor of greater transparency on matters of sentencing for drug offenses and the death penalty and has striven to make sure no racial disparities occur. In concert with other members of the Congressional Black Caucus, Rangel has been proactive in working to end racial discrimination against African Americans in American society by means such as affirmative action.

Rangel is also the principal author of the Federal Empowerment Zone project for revitalizing urban neighborhoods in the United States. In particular, Rangel is extremely sensitive to the needs of his constituency in the Harlem district of New York and has taken steps to turn urban decadence around by authoring the low-income housing tax credit so that persons belonging to minority and economically disadvantaged groups can afford to have housing. Rangel also has authored the work opportunity tax credit, through which thousands of people belonging to minority cultures and veterans' groups are able to get jobs. During his long service as a congressman, he has authored much legislation to benefit minorities and veterans within the Department of Veterans Affairs.

Rangel is a vocal supporter of voters' rights. During the 2000 U.S. presidential election, he voiced his strong opposition to and disapproval of cases of voter disenfranchisement in parts of Florida, which ultimately was won by Republican candidate George W. Bush through a lengthy process of judicial intervention. As an active member of the Democratic Party, Rangel brought to the attention of the U.S. attorney general instances of voting irregularities and worked to ensure that they would not be repeated in future elections.

Rangel was born in Harlem on June 11, 1930, and was raised during his early childhood by his mother and grandmother after his parents' separation. He served in the U.S. Army from 1948 to 1952, including in the Korean War, and for heroic acts was awarded the Purple Heart and the Bronze Star. He earned a B.S degree from New York University in 1957. Later, Rangel earned a juris doctorate (law degree) from St. John's University in 1960. Before starting his public career as a congressman, he was assistant U.S. attorney for the Southern District of New York and later was legal counsel for the New York City Housing and Redevelopment Board. In 1970, Rangel defeated Adam Clayton Powell Jr. in a closely contested election and took his seat in 1971. He has been reelected to the House sixteen times since his original term. Rangel and his wife Alma Rangel have two children and they divide their time between Harlem and Washington, D.C.

See also Congressional Black Caucus; Democratic Party and Affirmative Action; Powell, Adam Clayton, Jr.; Racial Profiling.

FURTHER READING: Hayood, Wil, 1993, *King of the Cats: The Life and Times of Adam Clayton Powell, Jr.*, Boston: Houghton Mifflin; Marable, Manning, 1995, *Beyond Black and White: Trans-*

forming African-American Politics, New York: Verso; Ragsdale, Joel D. Tresse, 1996, *Black Americans in Congress, 1870–1989*, New York: Diane Publishing Company.

MOHAMMED B. ALAM

Rational Basis Scrutiny

The rational basis scrutiny test is a judicial standard that is utilized in deciding cases where the government has utilized some sort of classification in its actions. When the Supreme Court reviews equal protection cases using the rational basis standard, the Court asks whether a particular classification has a "rational relationship to any legitimate government interest." The rational basis test is the least exacting/strenuous test, and almost every governmental classification survives this rational basis review. The rational basis standard is used for general discrimination claims, classifications that are not based upon a "suspect class" (or "semisuspect class") or do not impair a "fundamental right." The rational basis standard has been described as "minimal scrutiny in theory and virtually none in fact." This standard of review grants a large amount of deference to the legislature and governmental action. The law will only be struck down if the classification is "purely arbitrary." In the area of affirmative action, which usually involves classifications based on race or gender, either strict scrutiny or intermediate scrutiny is applied. However, if affirmative action programs are based upon economics or social class, a court reviewing such a program should apply rational basis scrutiny.

Initially, the Supreme Court reviewed all equal protection cases under the rational basis standard. The standard has been traced back to 1897. The rational basis standard provides a requirement that all classifications must satisfy if they are to pass the test of constitutional validity. The development of a higher level of scrutiny began in a footnote in *United States v. Carolene Products Co.*, 304 U.S. 144 (1938), where Justice Harlan Fiske Stone indicated that a higher level of scrutiny should be applied to statutes directed at "discrete and insular minorities."

Most legislation does not involve race, gender, or other traits that might trigger strict scrutiny. Instead, the vast majority of legislation involves social or economic welfare. Any social or economic legislation must pass the rational basis test. Under this standard, the legislation is given a strong presumption of constitutionality. The burden is on the individual to show that the statute does not have any rational relationship to any legitimate government interest. When the Court applies this level of scrutiny, it is very unusual for a statute to be declared unconstitutional.

A court applying rational basis scrutiny might ask: "Given the information that was actually before the legislature, or information that might have been available to the legislature, or information which the legislature reasonably might have thought existed, or information of which the court can take judicial notice, could the legislature conceivably have believed (not did it actually believe) that this statute would or might, even if only in the most remote or tenuous way, further or promote a legitimate actual or hypothetical goal?" If the answer is yes, the statute is constitutional. The answer is almost always yes, prompting one scholar to remark that "judicial scrutiny under rational basis review is typically so deferential as to amount to a virtual rubber stamp" (Fallon, 79).

However, there have been cases in which statutes have been struck down using the rational basis standard. For example, in *City of Cleburne v. Cleburne Living Center, Inc.*, 473 U.S. 432 (1985), the Court considered a challenge to the refusal of the city of Cleburne, Texas, to permit the owners of land to use it for the purpose of operating a group home for the mentally retarded. The landowners claimed that the refusal to permit this use violated their right to equal protection and also argued that the mentally retarded should be considered a "quasi-suspect" class and, therefore, should receive intermediate scrutiny. The Supreme Court disagreed and applied the rational basis standard. However, the Court concluded that the city's exclusion of the group home (while permitting other similar facilities) was not supported by a rational basis. The Court found that to the extent that the city's action was based upon naked prejudice, fear, or ill will toward the mentally retarded, it did not further a legitimate governmental interest. Thus the Court has added some bite to the rational basis standard, making the constitutionality of a statute subject to such scrutiny less certain.

See also Discrete and Insular Minority; Equal Protection Clause; Intermediate Scrutiny; Stone, Harlan Fiske; Strict Scrutiny; Suspect Classification.

FURTHER READING: *City of Cleburne v. Cleburne Living Center, Inc.*, 473 U.S. 432 (1985); Fallon, Richard H., 1997, "The Supreme Court, 1996 Term: Foreword: Implementing the Constitution," *Harvard Law Review* 111:54–152; Saphire, Richard B., 2000, "Equal Protection, Rational Basis Review, and the Impact of *Cleburne Living Center, Inc.*," *Kentucky Law Journal* 88:591–639.

PAMELA C. CORLEY

Reagan, Ronald (1911–)

Elected in 1980, President Ronald Reagan did more to impede affirmative action programs than any other U.S. president. His hostility to racial preferences and affirmative action and his belief in a color-blind constitution and society are best illustrated through a comment he made on February 11, 1986, when he said that "[w]e must have a colorblind society. Things must be done for people [regardless] of any differences between us in race, ethnic origin, or religion" (*New York Times* 1986, A13). Reagan made it clear that he had two goals regarding affirmative action. The first was to put an end to the practice of giving preference to individuals based solely on their race or gender. The second was to limit the enforcement of federal antidiscrimination and civil rights laws that, he felt, needlessly cost businesses a substantial amount of money. From the very onset of his presidency, Reagan set about achieving his goals. In 1981, the Justice Department, under orders from President Reagan, announced that it would no longer demand that employers maintain affirmative action programs. In 1982, the Reagan administration fought against extension of the Voting Rights Act of 1965 and announced that it would grant tax-exempt status to schools that practiced racial discrimination. Reagan's biggest push against affirmative action came when he tried to eliminate Executive Order 11246, the order signed by President Lyndon Baines Johnson that established the federal affirmative action program. The Reagan administration also opposed the Civil Rights Restoration Act, which protected women from discrimination at educational institutions that receive federal funds. Finally, President Reagan's influence over the affirmative action continues to be substantial today through his appointments of people openly hostile to affirmative action to key positions.

Born on February 6, 1911, in Tampico, Illinois, Ronald Reagan went to high school in nearby Dixon and then worked to put himself through Eureka College, where he studied economics and sociology. After graduation in 1932, he worked for a brief period as a radio announcer (1932–1937) before signing an acting contract with Warner Brothers in 1937. During the next two decades, he appeared in fifty-three films and served as president of the Screen Actors Guild. In 1966, Reagan was elected governor of California, defeating his opponent by more than 1 million votes. As governor of California, Reagan established the Career Opportunities Development Program, the first formal affirmative action effort in the state. Reelected in 1970, Reagan stated that laws against discrimination were not enough. He said that it was necessary for each and every citizen to be committed to affirmative action.

By the time he was campaigning for the presidency, however, Reagan's position had changed. When asked about affirmative action, Reagan said, "I'd like an opportunity to put an end to this federal distortion of the principle of equal rights." Although he said that he would vigorously support federal action against intentional discrimination, he viewed affirmative action programs and President Johnson's Executive Order 11246 as "a quota system . . . a kind of reverse discrimination."

As president, Reagan appointed fewer minorities to cabinet-level and policy-making positions than his predecessors. Once he was in office, not all of those within the Reagan administration dealt with affirmative action the same way. In fact, there appeared to be three distinct approaches to the issue. The Department of Justice's (DOJ) approach was the most visible and the most confrontational. The DOJ called for immediate judicial and legislative reform. Most other civil rights agencies within the administration left the laws and regulations in place, but limited their enforcement. For example, the number of discrimination cases filed by the Equal Employment Opportunity Commission (EEOC), under the direction of Clarence Thomas, fell by 25 percent, and the number of cases settled fell from 32 percent to just under 15 percent. In contrast, the Departments of Transportation and Commerce continued to favor and implement the affirmative action programs that had been passed during the Nixon and Carter administrations. They never altered their approach to or enforcement of these regulations. In fact, they favored them.

The Department of Justice led the charge against affirmative action. Its assault against the programs took many forms. It began in 1981, at the very start of the Reagan presidency, when the DOJ announced that it would no longer require employers to maintain affirmative action programs. With these words, the civil rights community sprang into action, ready for a fight. Reagan had campaigned on an anti–affirmative action platform, so the announcement was not a surprise. Those who favored affirmative action programs were prepared to fight for them throughout the president's term.

There was very little worry within the Reagan administration about possible ramifications of reforming affirmative action, such as losing the African American vote in the next election. Nine out of ten African Americans voted against Ronald Reagan in the presidential election of 1980. He had nothing to lose. There was also no strategy like Richard Nixon's southern strategy employed during Reagan's first term of office to win over the African American vote.

In 1982, the administration made the momentous decision to extend tax-exempt status to private schools that discriminated based on race, specifically Bob Jones University and the Goldsboro Christian Schools, even though the federal courts had ruled against such exemptions in the past and their decisions had been affirmed without comment by the U.S. Supreme Court. The decision to allow the exemptions prompted NAACP leaders to say that the Reagan administration was "mighty close to racism." Although the president proposed a bill allowing the exemptions, the Democratic-controlled Congress quickly and easily voted against the idea. Shortly thereafter, the U.S. Supreme Court, in an 8–1 decision, stated that such exemptions were clearly unconstitutional.

During that same year, the Voting Rights Act of 1965 was up for renewal. The Voting Rights Act of 1965 had assured federal protection for African Americans in registering and voting in the years following 1965. The Reagan administration declared that it opposed renewing the law. It argued that the standard of proof in the statute was inappropriate. The law required individuals to prove that discrimination was an effect of the government's action, even if the government did not intend to discriminate through its actions. The Reagan administration argued that this standard was too easy to prove. The administration wanted the standard changed so that individuals had to prove that the discrimination was the intent of the government's action. There was very little support in Congress for Reagan's position, and the law was easily renewed. Ultimately, the "effects test" remained in the statute, but the statute was rewritten to state that the totality of the circumstances must be considered before a decision regarding discrimination could be made. This was the only compromise the congressional Democrats granted to their opponents to persuade them to vote for renewal. However, even when the law passed, the DOJ then refused to investigate many alleged violations of the law, a tactic it adopted from the EEOC.

The Department of Justice made several attempts to discredit race and gender preferences in the courts as well. Almost all of its attempts to do so failed. In fact, the Supreme Court, during the course of Reagan's presidency, validated several different hiring and promotion schemes that benefited nonvictims. Some of these cases include *Local 28 of the Sheet Metal Workers' International Association v. EEOC*, 478 U.S. 421 (1986); *Wygant v. Jackson Board of Education*, 476 U.S. 267 (1986); and *Johnson v. Transportation Agency, Santa Clara County*, 480 U.S. 616 (1987). That is not to say that the DOJ made no progress toward its goal. The Supreme Court did find state-sponsored nonremedial set-asides and layoffs of senior nonminority employees unconstitutional.

Central to President Reagan's agenda was the reformation, or elimination, of Executive Order 11246, signed by Lyndon Johnson in 1965. This order established the federal affirmative action program. It required every federal department to have a "positive program of equal employment opportunity" regardless of race or color. It also required federal contractors to take affirmative action to ensure that they were not discriminating in their recruiting, hiring, or promotion processes. Reagan agreed with the executive order insofar as it provided for outreach programs to female and minority candidates. However, he opposed, the provisions of the order that called for preferential treatment in the hiring and promotion processes. He felt that these provisions were in effect reverse discrimination against white men. In their place, he advocated color-blind laws, whereby an applicant was judged solely on his or her ability and merit, without regard to his or her race or gender. On many occasions he claimed that he was simply continuing the work of Martin Luther King Jr., promoting the idea that individuals be judged "not on the color of their skin, but by the content of their character."

No sooner did Reagan announce his intention to reform Executive Order 11246 than the civil rights community mounted a campaign to oppose his actions. The Leadership Conference on Civil Rights, which is composed of more than 180 organizations representing racial minorities, women, labor, the elderly, the disabled, and civil libertarians, began lobbying for the order to remain intact. Ralph Neas, executive director of the Leadership Conference on Civil Rights, sent a letter to the White House promising that his organization and all of its allies on Capitol Hill would fight any amendments to the order.

Ultimately, the civil rights community was too powerful. The efforts of the Reagan administration gave way under the pressure. In the spring of 1986, Reagan dropped his plans to reform the order. In 1987, Reagan again fought against the Democrats in Congress and many civil rights organizations in his attempt to have Robert Bork appointed to the U.S. Supreme Court. Robert Bork, well known for his adherence to the strict "original intent" constitutional jurisprudence of interpretation, was ultimately defeated during his Senate confirmation process. Many opponents of Robert Bork feared that he would roll back programs like affirmative action, which arguably are not consistent with the "original meaning" or "intent" of the framers of the Constitution.

In 1987, the Reagan administration faced its final civil rights battle. This involved the Civil Rights Restoration Act, which prohibited institutions that received funding from the federal government from discriminating according to gender. Reagan opposed this law. He stated that the law was too overreaching and argued that the law would allow the federal government to regulate virtually every aspect of private and public institutions. This, he said, was against not only the will of the people, but the spirit of the Constitution.

The passage of the Civil Rights Restoration Act was hard won. The Reagan administration lobbied Congress with all its might and promised to veto the law if it did pass. The promise was one that Reagan had to see through. The act passed both houses of Congress easily, under Democratic control. The presidential veto came quickly. Congress, however, was able to override Reagan's veto and make the act law with 292 votes, a very slim margin.

President Reagan and his administration fought hard to reform affirmative action, but with the efforts of the civil rights community and its allies on Capitol Hill, at the end of Reagan's presidency federal civil rights laws remained essentially unchanged. That does not mean, however, that Reagan failed to change the face of affirmative action. Reagan's influence over the program continues to be substantial today through his appointments of people openly hostile to affirmative action to key positions, most notably Clarence Thomas to the EEOC and Antonin Scalia and Anthony Kennedy to the U.S. Supreme Court, and the elevation of William Rehnquist from associate justice to chief justice of the Supreme Court.

After leaving the presidency in 1988, Ronald Reagan retired with his second wife, Nancy Reagan, to their ranch in California. Reagan was diagnosed with Alzheimer's disease several years later. For approximately the last decade, Reagan has been kept out of the public eye, as his Alzheimer's disease has unfortunately gained in strength.

See also Carter, James "Jimmy" Earl, Jr.; Civil Rights Restoration Act of 1988; Color-Blind Constitution; Democratic Party and Affirmative Action; Department of Justice; Equal Employment Opportunity Commission; Executive Order 11246; Johnson, Lyndon Baines; *Johnson v. Transportation Agency, Santa Clara County*; Kennedy, Anthony McLeod; King, Martin Luther, Jr.; Leadership Conference on Civil Rights; *Local 28 of the Sheet Metal Workers' International Association v. EEOC*; National Association for the Advancement of Colored People; Nixon, Richard Milhous; Original Intent Jurisprudence; Preferences; Quotas; Rehnquist, William Hobbs; Republican Party and Affirmative Action; Reverse Discrimination; Scalia, Antonin; Thomas, Clarence; Voting Rights Act of 1965; *Wygant v. Jackson Board of Education.*

FURTHER READING: Annaker, Norman C., 1988, *Civil Rights and the Reagan Administration*, Washington, DC: Urban Institute Press; Devins, Neal, 1989, "Affirmative Action after Reagan," *Texas Law Review* 68 (December): 353–379; Dugger, Ronnie, 1983, *On Reagan: The Man and His Presidency*, New York: McGraw-Hill; Laham, Nicholas, 1998, *The Reagan Presidency and the Politics of Race: In Pursuit of Colorblind Justice and Limited Government*, Westport, CT: Praeger; "Reagan Tells of Weighing Plans to Revise Minority Hiring Rules," 1986, *New York Times*, February 12, A13; Schaller, Michael, 1992, *Reckoning with Reagan: America and Its President in the 1980s*, New York: Oxford University Press.

AIMÉE HOBBY RHODES

Red Lion Broadcasting Co. v. FCC, 395 U.S. 367 (1969)

In *Red Lion Broadcasting Co. v. FCC*, the Supreme Court held for the first time that the Federal Communications Commission (FCC) had broad control over the utilization of airwaves because the airwaves are a limited resource that may be regulated to allow "others whose views should be expressed to use the medium." The U.S Supreme Court later relied on this holding in *Metro Broadcasting, Inc. v. FCC*, 497 U.S. 547 (1990), to uphold the power of the FCC to grant preferences in distributing broadcasting licenses to minorities to promote a diversity of viewpoints. That is, the allocation of broadcast licenses by the FCC to promote diversity in broadcasting was constitutionally permissible. The Court also affirmed the FCC's substantial governmental interest in ensuring that news and public issues are depicted fairly and accurately.

The underlying case involved a radio station owned by Red Lion Broadcasting Company that aired a program allegedly slandering a writer for being sympathetic to communism. At the time, the FCC employed a rule called the "Fairness Doctrine," which required that radio stations provide free airtime for rebuttals from individuals claiming to have been the subject of slanderous materials during a broadcast. The individual then requested a rebuttal pursuant to the Fairness Doctrine. When the company refused to allow him to respond over its broadcast, the FCC became involved and ordered that the broadcaster air the rebuttal pursuant to the Fairness Doctrine. The broadcaster then sued, arguing that this was a violation of its First Amendment rights, as the government was attempting to force it to carry speech that it did not wish to carry.

The Court began by noting that while broadcasters were entitled to First

Amendment protections, there was no First Amendment violation, as differences in the different types of media (and speakers) justified differences in the First Amendment standards and rules to be applied. The Court ultimately upheld the Fairness Doctrine (the rule would later be revoked), noting that the goal of the First Amendment was to ensure the "marketplace of ideas," and, as such, the Fairness Doctrine "enhance[d] rather than abridge[d] the freedoms of speech and press protected by the First Amendment." According to the Court, "It is the right of the viewers and listeners [to receive balanced and fair information], not the right of the broadcasters, which is paramount" under the First Amendment.

Most relevant to the affirmative action debate, in upholding the FCC's broad authority to regulate the airwaves, the Court held that "because of the scarcity of electromagnetic frequencies, the Government is permitted to put restraints on licensees in favor of others whose views should be expressed on this unique medium." This broad FCC authority allows the FCC to require that as a condition of receiving a federal broadcast license, broadcasters agree not to engage in discrimination against designated minorities and are required to maintain affirmative action plans. The broad FCC authority recognized in *Red Lion* was also used by the U.S. Supreme Court in *Metro Broadcasting, Inc. v. FCC* to uphold the FCC's authority to utilize preferences in ensuring that federal broadcast licenses are issued to minority-owned enterprises. However, the constitutionality of these preferences is arguably in doubt after the 1995 U.S. Supreme Court case *Adarand Constructors, Inc. v. Peña*, which applied a more strict standard to all explicit racial preferences employed by the federal government than was applied in *Metro Broadcasting*.

See also Adarand Constructors, Inc. v. Peña; Affirmative Action Plan/Program; First Amendment; Federal Communications Commission; Licensing and Affirmative Action; *Metro Broadcasting, Inc. v. FCC*; Preferences.

FURTHER READING: Darlin, Damon, 1994, "Quota Queen: Esther Renteria May Have Figured a Way to Reap Profit from Affirmative Action Guidelines," *Forbes* 153, no. 13 (June 20): 42; Ferris, Charles D., and James A. Kirkland, 1985, "Fairness: The Broadcaster's Hippocratic Oath," *Catholic University Law Review* 34:605–622; Fields, "Licensing Preferences to Women, Minorities: What Do They Achieve?" *Television/Radio Age* 34 (May 11): 89–90; Rumble, Wilfrid C., 1994, "Comment: The FCC's Reliance on Market Incentives to Provide Diverse Viewpoints on Issues of Public Importance Violates the First Amendment Right to Receive Critical Information," *University of San Francisco Law Review* 28:793–857.

JAMES A. BECKMAN

Redlining

See Lending Practices and Affirmative Action.

Regents of the University of California v. Bakke, 438 U.S. 265 (1978)

More than a quarter of a century after the decision was handed down, the landmark case *Regents of the University of California v. Bakke* remains one of the most discussed and debated cases in the affirmative action context. The *Bakke* case may be appropriately labeled the first major case involving a modern affirmative action program or plan to reach the Supreme Court and where the constitutionality of affirmative action was the central issue before the Court. The case has been referred to as "one of the Court's most famous affirmative action decisions" (Spann 2000, 15). The seminal *Bakke* decision, dealing with the permissibility of race-conscious affirmative action in higher education, has been widely studied by scholars, practitioners, educational institutions, and lower courts in the past quarter century. While the majority holding in the case was fairly clear, that "fixed [racial] quotas" could not be utilized as part of a university's admissions process and violated the Fourteenth Amendment's Equal Protection Clause (as well as Title VI of the Civil Rights Act of 1964), that simple holding disguised a very sharp and profound disagreement among the justices as to the permissible constitutional parameters of race-conscious affirmative action plans under the Fourteenth Amendment.

Put plainly, the nine justices could not agree as to when (if at all) race could be utilized as a selection factor in the admissions process. As a result, underneath the simple holding that fixed racial quotas could not be utilized, a variety of disagreements emerged as to when, outside the racial quota context, race could still be utilized as part of an affirmative action plan. This disagreement resulted in a severely fractured Court, with six separate opinions in the case, forcing each of the justices to "concur in part" and "dissent in part" to the plurality decision of the Court. The swing vote in the case, Justice Lewis Powell, was truly a "swing vote," joining four other justices (Justices John Paul Stevens, Warren Burger, Potter Stewart, and William Rehnquist) in forming the majority opinion that racial quotas were unlawful under the Fourteenth Amendment, and also joining the other four justices (Justices William Brennan, Byron White, Thurgood Marshall, and Harry Blackmun) in holding that in some circumstances race-conscious affirmative action plans might be permissible.

The disagreement among the Supreme Court justices is not surprising if one considers that the Supreme Court is often a microcosm of society, in a rough way representing the same passions and disagreements that exist in society as a whole. Yet individuals, institutions, and the lower courts turn to the Supreme Court for guidance, and the *Bakke* decision raised more questions than it answered. Clearly, as a result of the *Bakke* decision, institutions of higher learning knew that the utilization of fixed racial quotas as part of an affirmative action plan was impermissible. However, what remained unclear to the lower courts, and the country as a whole, was to what extent race might be utilized as a factor in plans. Furthermore, what justification or reason was suitable for instituting an affirmative action plan that might hurt innocent nonminorities? Could an institution promulgate an affirmative action plan in order to ensure diversity in the classroom or to enhance the educational experience? Could an institution promulgate a plan in order to increase minorities in the various professions (law, medicine, accounting, and so on)?

Furthermore, from 1978 (the date of the *Bakke* decision) until 2003 (the date of the *Gratz v. Bollinger*, 123 S. Ct. 2411, 2003 U.S. LEXIS 4801 [2003], and *Grutter v. Bollinger*, 123 S. Ct. 2325, 2003 U.S. LEXIS 4800 [2003], decisions), the U.S. Supreme Court remained silent on the issue of affirmative action and higher education and left it to the lower courts to apply the conflicting guidance contained in the *Bakke* decision, and specifically the rationale of six different opinions in the case. During this time period, the most significant lower court post-*Bakke* challenges to affirmative action in higher education came almost a decade and a half after the *Bakke* decision in *Hopwood v. Texas*, 78 F.3d 932 (5th Cir. 1996), *Smith v. University of Washington Law School* 233 F.3d 1188 (9th Cir. 2000), *Johnson v. Board of Regents of the University of Georgia*, 263 F.3d 1234 (11th Cir. 2001), and *Grutter v. Bollinger*, 288 F.3d 732 (6th Cir. 2002). However, in each of these cases, the lower courts made varying interpretations of the *Bakke* decision and what was permissible or not permissible under the Fourteenth Amendment. The Supreme Court arguably granted certiorari (legal review) in the *Gratz* and *Grutter* cases in order to clarify the ambiguities caused by the *Bakke* decision and to harmonize the disagreements among the federal circuits as to affirmative action in higher education that had become pronounced in the late 1990s and early 2000s.

Thus today, the *Bakke* decision is generally regarded as the focus point for discussion of diversity and affirmative action in higher education, not because of what the decision specifically prohibited (i.e., racial quotas), as will be described later, but rather for what was left unsaid in the decision. Opponents of diversity and affirmative action measures in higher education have used *Bakke* to challenge the use of race, ethnicity, sex, or national origin in student admissions, financial aid, and staff and faculty employment. These opponents point to the fact that the Supreme Court rejected the affirmative action plan at issue in *Bakke* as being inconsistent with the Fourteenth Amendment and to the bloc of conservative justices in the case (Justices Stevens, Rehnquist, Burger, and Stewart) who, along with Justice Powell, held that fixed quotas were impermissible and that the University of California affirmative action plan violated Title VI of the Civil Rights Act of 1964. However, proponents of affirmative action justify affirmative action plans as being ultimately consistent with the *Bakke* decision, which also did suggest the possibility of utilizing race or gender as a factor to be considered in the admissions process. These proponents focus on the opinion and position of the liberal bloc of justices (Justices Brennan, White, Marshall, and Blackmun) who, along with Justice Powell, held that race might be a permissible consideration to utilize in admissions decisions in some contexts. Thus an understanding and working knowledge of the *Bakke* case and decision are indispensable even today for students and scholars of the affirmative action debate.

The genesis of the *Bakke* case can be traced back to 1968, a full decade before the actual Supreme Court decision, when the University of California at Davis opened its medical school. When the medical school was opened in 1968, it had an original entering class of 50 students, but the entering class number was soon increased to 100 new students each year. From the onset, administrators at the medical school were concerned with low minority enrollment. Thus in the second year of operation, admissions officials at the medical school decided to set aside 16 of the 100 seats for applicants from nontraditional backgrounds. In 1973, the application materials indicated that nontraditional backgrounds would include applicants who were "economically and/or educationally disadvantaged." The following year, in 1974, the application materials stated that those considered as having nontraditional backgrounds and eligible for the 16 special set-aside seats included members of a minority group, which included "Blacks," "Chicanos," "Asians," and "Native Americans."

Out of this concern for recruiting and selecting "nontraditional" students, a dual admissions system evolved, depending on the background of the applicant. Under the regular admissions process for the medical school (i.e., for those competing for the unreserved 84 seats out of the original 100), the application process operated as follows: First, the admissions department of the medical school automatically disqualified any applicant with a grade point average below 2.5. Second, of the remaining applicants, each applicant was interviewed and was given a rating on a scale from 1 to 100. The applicant's ultimate rating was determined by the interviewer and four other members of the admissions committee and was based upon the applicant's performance in the interview, as well as other information in the applicant's file (e.g., grade point average, standardized test scores, and letters of recommendation). Once a composite score/rating was obtained for each applicant, the rating for each applicant was added together, which yielded an aggregate rating number for the entire applicant pool. This aggregate number was divided by the number of applicants to yield the average applicant score in the process (which was used as a benchmark), and the applicants were ranked. Offers of admission were then made depending on the applicant's position on the overall ranking and his or her individual composite score.

However, the applicants from "nontraditional" backgrounds were handled differently. First, on the application materials, students were asked (in 1973) if they wished to be considered "economically and/or educationally disadvantaged." In 1974, applicants were asked if they wished to be listed as a member of a minority group. If so, that individual's application was routed to a special admissions committee charged with reviewing these applications and deciding which applicants should receive one of the 16 set-aside seats in the entering class (based upon the same 1–100 applicant score/index approach). While in theory, the "nontraditional" minority applicant could gain one of the 84 unreserved regular seats by scoring sufficiently high on the applicant index, relatively speaking, few were qualified to gain admittance by this means. From 1971 to 1974, only one African American, six Mexican Americans, and thirty-seven Asian Americans were admitted via the normal admissions process. This process meant that minority applicants were competing for 100 available possible seats (with 16 seats specially reserved for minorities), while white applicants were competing for only 84 available possible seats. While several whites attempted to apply for admittance under the special admissions program allowance for "economically and/or educationally disadvantaged" applicants, none were accepted. The final advantage given to a minority applicant was that the minimum 2.5 grade point average was waived for minority students, and all were given an interview, ranked, and permitted to compete for the special set-aside seats.

Under this special admissions procedure, from 1971 through 1974, a total of sixty-three minority applicants were admitted: twenty-one African American students, thirty Mexican American students, and twelve Asian American students. During the years ultimately at issue during the *Bakke* case, the admissions process was very competitive. At the medical school in 1973, there were 2,464 applications for admission, and in 1974, there were 3,737 applicants for admission. Also, in 1974, only 38 percent of the applicants even secured an interview.

Allan Bakke, the plaintiff in the *Bakke* case, applied for admission to the medical school in 1973–1974. Bakke, a white individual of Jewish ethnicity, has been described as an overly qualified applicant, having a standardized test score (Medical

College Admission Test, MCAT) that put him in the top percentile of all test takers, as well as an above-average 3.44 grade point average. He also earned an interview, which in 1974, was granted to only 38 percent of the applicants. Yet he was denied admission. Some have speculated that his denial may have been based on the fact that he was an older applicant and that his application came late in the admission year. Because he applied late in the year, many of the available eighty-four seats were already filled under the rolling admissions policy, which arguably detracted from the competitiveness of his application. However, in litigation, Allan Bakke later learned that there were four empty seats from the reserved sixteen minority seats that could not even be filled for that year.

Upon his rejection from the medical school, Allan Bakke wrote to the dean of the admissions department, George H. Lowrey, and questioned the admissions decision and the use of race and ethnicity as a factor, which Bakke deemed to be unfair and damaging to his application. Bakke then applied again for admission the following year, in 1974, and was again denied admission. Coincidentally, in the second year, Allan Bakke's main interviewer was the dean of admissions (George Lowrey) to whom he had written a year earlier. At the conclusion of the interview, Lowrey recorded that his opinion was that Allan Bakke was "rather limited in his approach to medical problems" and that he had "very definite opinions which were based more on his personal viewpoints than upon the total problem."

After being rejected for the second time, Bakke filed suit in the California state court system, where he sought "mandatory, injunctive, and declaratory relief" that would compel his admission to the medical school. Bakke based his lawsuit upon the claim that the medical school's affirmative action program, which reserved seats only for minority applicants, was in essence a racial quota. Furthermore, Bakke's attorneys argued, quotas that distinguished or discriminated on account of race were a violation of Title VI of the Civil Rights Act of 1964 (prohibiting racial discrimination in public educational institutions or in institutions receiving federal funds) and the Equal Protection Clause of the Fourteenth Amendment (prohibiting states from denying their citizens the "equal protection of the laws"). The University of California's response to Bakke's arguments was that while nondiscrimination was the general norm, "the meritocratic promise of nondiscrimination was offset by the state's equally compelling concern for the victims of past and continuing racial injustice" (O'Neill 1992, 714). The university additionally argued that its affirmative action program was needed in order to ensure that minority professionals were being educated (and would after graduation return to minority communities and provide needed medical services), that minorities could establish themselves in the medical profession and thereby become role models to disadvantaged youths, and that increasing the diversity of the student body during medical school would improve the overall educational experience.

In interpreting the Equal Protection Clause of the Fourteenth Amendment, both the California state trial court and the California Supreme Court ruled in favor of the plaintiff and held that racial quotas or exclusionary racial preferences (like the one at issue in the medical school plan), absent a specific finding and justification by the institution that it had in the past engaged in discrimination, violated the Fourteenth Amendment. Phrased another way, the California Supreme Court in *Bakke* held that in the educational context, quotas or racial preferences in an affirmative action plan could not be utilized unless the plan was implemented by the institution to remedy its own prior discrimination and mistreatment of minority students. Thus the stage was set for Supreme Court review.

The Supreme Court heard the *Bakke* case during the 1977–1978 term. The plaintiff had the assistance of Reynold Colvin (his original counsel) during oral arguments, while the Regents of the University of California were represented by Archibald Cox, an eminent constitutional law scholar (now a professor of law at Harvard Law School) and the solicitor general of the United States under the Kennedy administration. At the strong behest of President Jimmy Carter, Wade McCree, the solicitor general during the Carter administration, made an appearance on behalf of the United States of America in the case and argued strongly in favor of race-conscious affirmative action programs as a means to correct past wrongs traditionally suffered by minorities. Thus the *Bakke* case had two solicitors general-making oral arguments, both of whom served under presidents deemed to be favorable to affirmative action. Exactly a quarter century later, President George W. Bush's solicitor general, Theodore Olson, would make an appearance in the *Gratz/Grutter* case, just as Solicitor General McCree had done twenty-five years earlier on behalf of Carter. However, Olson's (and therefore Bush's) position was the exact opposite from McCree's (and therefore Carter's) position in *Bakke*, with Olson in essence arguing that race-conscious affirmative action plans should not be utilized under the Fourteenth Amendment, except as a remedy of very last resort.

On June 28, 1978, the Supreme Court released its eagerly awaited decision just before its traditional summer break. The central holding of the Court was decided by a narrow 5–4 vote (Justices Stevens, Burger, Stewart, Rehnquist, and Powell in the majority; Justices Brennan, Blackmun, Marshall, and White in dissent), ruling that the use of "fixed" racial quotas was impermissible under the Fourteenth Amendment. However, another different five-justice majority (Justices Brennan, Blackmun, Marshall, White, and Powell) coalesced to also hold that the use of racial criteria as part of a university's affirmative action program might be permissible in some contexts. Thus the "simple" holdings of the case belied the Court's true views on affirmative action. Indeed, the Court was so divided on the permissibility of race-conscious affirmative action under both the Fourteenth Amendment and Title VI of the Civil Rights Act of 1964 that six separate opinions were issued in the case.

In essence, the Court was divided into two major blocs, one bloc being composed of justices opposed to the affirmative action plan at issue in the *Bakke* case, the other bloc being composed of justices favorable to the affirmative action plan at issue, with Justice Powell serving as the crucial swing vote and joining both groups in different conclusions in the case. The first group or bloc of justices (Justices Stevens, Burger, Stewart, and Rehnquist) believed that the affirmative action plan was illegal under Title VI of the Civil Rights Act of 1964. Title VI of the Civil Rights Act of 1964, a codification of the *Brown v. Board of Education*, 347 U.S. 483 (1954), decision a decade earlier, specified in relevant part that "no person in the United States shall, on the ground of race, color, or national origin, be excluded from participation in, be denied the benefits of, or be subjected to discrimination under any program or activity receiving federal financial assistance." This group of justices thought that the "broad prohibition against the exclusion of any individual" on account of race under Title VI was sufficient to order Allan Bakke admitted to the medical school and the affirmative action plan thrown out.

The second group or bloc of justices (Brennan, Blackmun, Marshall, and White), known as the "antidiscrimination four" as a result of this case, thought that the requirements of Title VI were no different than the requirements under the Equal Protection Clause of the Fourteenth Amendment. Furthermore, according to this group (in a concurring opinion authored by Justice Brennan), as the affirmative action program did not engage in invidious discrimination and promote the "presumption that one race is inferior to another," it should not be tested under the Fourteenth Amendment under a strict scrutiny analysis. Rather, as the affirmative action program at issue was benignly discriminating to help "those least well represented in the political process," this second group thought that affirmative action programs like the one at issue in the case should be upheld so long as the government could show an important purpose for the plan. As all the reasons put forth by the University of California in support of its plan arguably were "important" state interests, this second group of justices would have upheld the plan.

Justice Thurgood Marshall wrote a separate opinion that is also worthy of mention, especially for the reader to understand the relevancy of the history leading up to modern affirmative action plans. Marshall's separate opinion put forth his conclusion that the first affirmative action programs in the United States came immediately following the American Civil War. Reconstruction civil rights legislation like the Civil Rights Act of 1866 and the creation of the Freedmen's Bureau were earlier examples of affirmative action. As far as Marshall was concerned, affirmative action was consistent with the purpose and requirements of the Fourteenth Amendment, as "[a]fter the Civil War our Government started several affirmative action programs," and these programs were created by many of the very same people responsible for drafting and ratifying the Fourteenth Amendment.

However, the most remembered opinion in the case was that of Justice Lewis Powell. In casting the deciding vote and joining both of the competing blocs in different points, Powell's position in the case became symbolic of the overall import of the *Bakke* case. Powell joined the first bloc's conclusions that racial quotas were illegal (unless they were implemented to remedy the institution's own discrimination in the past), but joined the second bloc as to the permissibility of utilizing race in some circumstances during the admissions process. For Powell, racial quotas were too inflexible and "totally foreclosed" nonminorities from the process; however, for Powell, less exclusionary racial practices might be permissible.

In his plurality opinion in the case, Powell argued for what has been called a "diversity rationale" in higher education. Powell wrote in his opinion that ethnic and racial diversity could be considered as one factor in a range of factors for attaining heterogeneity in higher education, and that affirmative action plans were permissible to obtain a "diverse student body." Justice Powell specifically cited a program at Harvard (the Harvard Plan) with approval. However, Justice Powell warned against the use of ethnic diversity to establish quotas that would harm the interests of "genuine" diversity. Powell wrote as follows regarding diversity:

It is not an interest in simple ethnic diversity, in which a specified percentage of the student body is in effect guaranteed to be members of selected ethnic groups, with the remaining percentage an undifferentiated aggregation of students. The diversity that furthers a compelling state interest encompasses a far broader array of qualifications and characteristics of which racial or ethnic origin is but a single though important element.

Hence the fractured Court's position in the *Bakke* case has posed a dilemma for institutions of higher education in the quarter century since that decision. All that was clear from the holding was that fixed racial quotas were not permissible unless they were implemented to remedy a clear discriminatory practice by that institution in the past. However, beyond that, it was unclear as to whether race might be utilized in a less exclusionary fashion. In the years after the *Bakke* decision, institutions of higher learning began to develop admissions policies that took race into consideration, but did not formulate quotas based on race. These institutions of higher education interpreted *Bakke* as identifying a diversity rationale that allowed them to use race as a selective factor in admissions as long as racial quotas were not promoted. According to one article, "Rather than providing a definitive answer on affirmative action, *Bakke* nibbled at the question, settling only the narrower issue of racial quotas in admissions to state-supported schools and leaving later cases to test the propriety of affirmative action in other realms" (O'Neill 1992, 714).

Interestingly, the diversity rationale adopted by institutions of higher education after *Bakke* (and as originally delineated by Justice Powell in his plurality opinion) became a central issue in the challenge to affirmative action in higher education in the late 1990s and early 2000s. In 2003, coming full circle exactly twenty-five years after Powell first penned his diversity rationale for an extremely divided Supreme Court, the Supreme Court announced its decision in the *Gratz* and *Grutter* cases, which have been described as the most monumental affirmative action cases since the *Bakke* decision. However, in the twenty-five years since the *Bakke* decision, all of the Supreme Court justices who ruled in the *Bakke* had passed away except Chief Justice Rehnquist and Justice John Paul Stevens, and Rehnquist and Stevens had the rare opportunity to go back and redecide in *Gratz* and *Grutter* whether affirmative action should exist in higher education.

In these two landmark cases, the Court reaffirmed the diversity rationale that Justice Powell had enunciated twenty-five years earlier in the *Bakke* case. In reaffirming diversity in higher education as a compelling governmental interest, the Supreme Court upheld the University of Michigan Law School's affirmative action plan (*Grutter* case) and endorsed affirmative action plans that utilize race as one factor or ingredient (among many) in the overall evaluation of candidates. Thus race could be considered as a "plus" factor, just as other factors such as one's athletic ability or musical talent or letters of recommendation might be considered. However, the Court also warned in the *Gratz* decision that fixed racial quotas and mechanized formulas (which have the effect of operating as a quota) would not be tolerated. In the *Gratz* decision, the Court struck down the University of Michigan undergraduate admissions affirmative action plan that gave extra points for race alone. The plan struck down by the Court had awarded African American, Hispanic, and Native American applicants an automatic 20 points on a 150-point undergraduate admissions scale. This, the Court held, was akin to racial quotas, which violate the Fourteenth Amendment.

See also Affirmative Action Plan/Program; African Americans; Asian Americans; Blackmun, Harry Andrew; Brennan, William Joseph; *Brown v. Board of Education*; Burger Court and Affirmative Action; Bush, George W.; Carter, James "Jimmy" Earl, Jr.; Civil Rights Act of 1964; Economically Disadvantaged; Education and Affirmative Action; Equal Protection Clause; Fourteenth Amendment; *Gratz v. Bollinger/Grutter v. Bollinger*; Harvard Model; Hispanic Americans; *Hopwood v. Texas*; *Johnson v. Board of Regents of the University of Georgia*; Kennedy, John Fitzgerald; Marshall, Thurgood; Meritocracy; Minority Professionals and Affirmative Action; Powell, Lewis Franklin, Jr.; Quotas; Rehnquist, William Hobbs; Role Model Theory; *Smith v. University of Washington Law School*; Standardized Testing; Stevens, John Paul; Strict Scrutiny; Suspect Classification; Title VI of the Civil Rights Act of 1964; White, Byron Raymond.

FURTHER READING: Ball, Howard, 2000, *The Bakke Case: Race, Education, and Affirmative Action*, Lawrence: University Press of Kansas; Edley, Christopher, Jr., 1996, *Not All Black and White: Affirmative Action, Race, and American Values*, New York: Hill and Wang; Friendly, Fred W., and Martha J.H. Elliot, 1984, *The Constitution, That Delicate Balance: Landmark Cases That Shaped the Constitution*, New York: Random House; O'Neill, Timothy J., 1992, "*Regents of the University of California v. Bakke*," in *The Oxford Companion to the Supreme Court of the United States*, edited by Kermit L. Hall, New York: Oxford University Press; Purdy, Lawrence R., 2003, "Prelude: *Bakke* Revisited," *Texas Review Law and Politics*, spring, 313–384; Rubio, Philip F., 2001, *A History of Affirmative Action, 1619–2000*, Jackson: University Press of Mississippi; Spann, Girardeau A., 2000, *The Law of Affirmative Action: Twenty-five Years of Supreme Court Decisions on Race and Remedies*, New York: New York University Press; Wilkinson, J. Harvie, III, 1979, *From Brown to Bakke: The Supreme Court and School Integration, 1954–1978*, New York: Oxford University Press.

JAMES A. BECKMAN

Rehabilitation Act of 1973

The Rehabilitation Act of 1973 was the first major statutory enactment to extend civil rights protections and affirmative action programs to disabled Americans. Although the act's primary purpose was to authorize funds for federal and state programs designed to enable the disabled to receive job training and lead independent lives, Title V of the act has had the most significant long-term impact. Sections 501 and 503, respectively, require that all executive branch agencies and major federal contractors take affirmative action in hiring and promoting disabled workers. In contrast to European laws on the disabled and some U.S. affirmative action legislation for other groups, these sections do not require set goals, quotas, or timetables. Section 504, which prohibits discrimination against otherwise qualified disabled individuals in any executive branch agency or program receiving federal aid, such as programs for housing, education, or health care, has had the greatest overall impact. Importantly, the act's requirements do not apply to private-sector employers. Protections for the disabled were not extended to all public and private activities until the Americans with Disabilities Act of 1990 (ADA). ADA borrowed many important passages from the 1973 act and supplements rather than replaces it. The 1973 act was an important first step in pushing businesses and educational institutions to make accommodations for disabled citizens and in increasing awareness of the rights and concerns of disabled citizens.

The 1964 Civil Rights Act outlawed employment discrimination on the basis of race, color, religion, sex, or national origin, but it said nothing about the rights of disabled workers. Advocates for the disabled recognized the importance of including them on the list of groups that were guaranteed rights, as opposed to those simply granted privileges in certain cases. On the more practical level, they were concerned by very high unemployment rates among the disabled, which were often attributed to business wariness of the costs involved in accommodating workers with special needs and to widely held views that disabled workers could perform few important tasks. The federal government had been providing assistance for rehabilitation programs since the 1920s, but the programs needed periodic reauthorization and restructuring. In 1972, legislation requiring major revision of federal programs for the disabled passed easily through Congress. It was, however, vetoed by President Nixon, who cited cost concerns. In 1973, similar legislation was again passed and vetoed, but a third version, with some concessions to the administration's budget concerns, was passed unanimously by both houses and signed by Nixon on September 26, 1973 as the Rehabilitation Act of 1973 (P.L. 93-112). Interestingly, the far-reaching Title V sections, which were quietly added by Senate staff members, received little attention or debate.

Because the Rehabilitation Act is an authorization bill, it must be reviewed and reauthorized at set intervals. This has encouraged revisions to Title V over time. In 1974, a crucial change was made in the definition of handicap. Prior to 1974, a narrow definition existed since it was tied to eligibility for federal vocational training. The definition was broadened when the term became tied to the rights of a class of individuals. The broader definition, though, has created contention over whether such wide-ranging conditions as attention deficit disorder, HIV infection, and drug addiction constitute disabilities. Section 505, which details the remedies and procedures for complaints, was added in 1978. In 1992, the word "handicapped" was replaced by the then-preferred word "disabled." Section 508, which deals with equal access to information technology, was added in 1998. There also have been a series of court cases that have helped clarify key terms such as "reasonable accommodation" and "otherwise qualified."

Advocates for the disabled were naturally pleased by the act's passage, but they have been less satisfied with how it has been implemented. In 1977, regulations outlining compliance with the law still had not been issued by executive agencies, prompting protests and sit-ins at federal buildings. In subsequent years, the Reagan administration, which favored a reduced role for government in business, was not aggressive in pursuing complaints. Critics also pointed out that with the majority of disabled citizens out of the workforce and the section 503 and 504 protections not extending to the majority of private businesses, the act only affected a small subsection of the disabled. From the other side, businessmen and others worried about the costs of compliance. Early estimates were that reasonable accommodations would cost businesses $50 million and modifications of buildings for full compliance perhaps as much as $500 million. Others, though, later argued that these early numbers were simply guesses, given the uncertainty about how many people qualified under the act's definition, and that the estimates were high-end projections reflecting business confusion on necessary accommodations. Surveys in fact found that most businesses were able to comply relatively cheaply. A final criticism of the act stemmed from the unique problems of the disabled. In attacking racial or gender discrimination, the goal was to achieve equal opportunity. In contrast, increasing the number of disabled workers necessitated going beyond equality to accommodation of special needs. This requirement set up complex disputes on what accommodations were necessary and whether affirmative action was really the same thing as requiring accommodations.

Despite these problems and criticisms, most observers have judged the Rehabilitation Act to be an overall success. Directly measuring how many people have received jobs or educational opportunities nationwide as a result of the act is difficult; however, the number of disabled workers in federal employ increased by 170,000 between 1970 and 1982, and the proportion of government workers with disabilities rose from 9.9 percent to 10.2 percent in that same period. It is also difficult to know whether the relatively small number of complaints pursued under sections 503 and 504 reflect good compliance with the law or simply an unwillingness of potential complainants to wade through the long, complex complaint process. A 1986 Louis Harris poll did show, though, that two-thirds of the disabled polled felt that laws passed since the 1960s had helped somewhat or a great deal. Additionally, the act was important because it helped stimulate political activism among the disabled, clarified definitions that would be employed in future legislation, and increased awareness of both the problems faced by the disabled and the important contributions they could make to businesses and society.

See also Civil Rights Act of 1964; Nixon, Richard Milhous; Persons with Disabilities and Affirmative Action; Reagan, Ronald.

FURTHER READING: Deane, Richard H., 1975, "Affirmative Action: A New Impact," *Journal of Rehabilitation* 41:23–25; O'Brien, Ruth, 2001, *Crippled Justice: The History of Modern Disability in the Workplace*, Chicago: University of Chicago Press; O'Neill, D.M., 1977, *Discrimination against Handicapped Persons: The Costs, Benefits, and Economic Impact of Implementing Section 504 of the Rehabilitation Act of 1973*, Washington, DC: U.S. Government Printing Office; Scotch, Richard K., 2001, *From Good Will to Civil Rights: Transforming Federal Disability Policy*, 2d ed., Philadelphia: Temple University Press; West, Jane, ed., 1991, *The Americans with Disabilities Act: From Policy to Practice*, New York: Milbank Memorial Fund.

JOHN W. DIETRICH

Rehnquist Court and Affirmative Action

See Rehnquist, William Hobbs.

Rehnquist, William Hobbs (1924–   )

During his more than a quarter of a century on the Supreme Court, both as an associate justice and chief justice of the U.S. Supreme Court, the Arizona transplant from Wisconsin William Hobbs Rehnquist has left a stylistic conservative imprint on the Court, just as the 1960s served as a mirror image to a legally liberal Court shaped by the Warren era. Rehnquist was a clerk to Supreme Court justice Robert H. Jackson, led the Office of Legal Counsel in the Justice Department from 1969 to 1971, was appointed to the U.S. Supreme Court at the age of forty-seven by President Richard M. Nixon (to the seat vacated by Justice John Marshall Harlan) in 1972, and was elevated to chief justice in 1986 by President Ronald Reagan and confirmed by a Democratic-controlled Senate. Once known as the "Lone Ranger," Rehnquist was at one time early in his tenure on the Court standing alone against the majority of his colleagues in attempting to curb the direction that expansive social programs such as affirmative action were taking.

Rehnquist was born in Milwaukee, Wisconsin, on October 1, 1924, and attended law school at Stanford University after having obtained two master's degrees from Stanford and Harvard. Rehnquist graduated at the top of his law school class, along with future Supreme Court justice Sandra Day O'Connor, who graduated third in the class. After clerking for Justice Robert H. Jackson, he spent the next sixteen years in private practice in Arizona. During this phase of his career, Rehnquist has been described as being very conservative, especially on race issues. During his clerkship with Jackson, the Court was deciding the famous desegregation case *Brown v. Board of Education*, 347 U.S. 483 (1954). Rehnquist authored a memo to Justice Jackson arguing that the separate-but-equal doctrine of *Plessy v. Ferguson*, 163 U.S. 537 (1896), should be upheld. Furthermore, while he was in Phoenix, he was accused of harassing black voters. During his confirmation hearings, Rehnquist denied that he had ever harassed voters and claimed that he was playing the "devil's advocate" in the memo to Jackson. After serving in the Office of Legal Counsel, he was nominated and appointed to the Supreme Court in 1972. He has served as chief justice since 1986.

Like a pendulum in motion, the Court led by Chief Justice Rehnquist for nearly two decades has pulled back on the reins of affirmative action and has insisted that race not be a "deciding factor" in affirmative action plans. Until 2003, the decisions in the Rehnquist era had rejected every affirmative action plan in whole or in part in programs that included law school admissions, scholarships, voting districts, and public contracts. The Rehnquist Court has repeatedly taken the stance that the same level of scrutiny applied in cases of invidious discrimination against racial minorities should be used in assessing affirmative action efforts.

Rehnquist is said to abide by a strict constructionist viewpoint and the doctrine of "original intent" (or "legal positivism") as it relates to his jurisprudence. Thus Rehnquist believes in interpreting the Constitution (if possible) as it was intended by the framers. As he wrote in his book *The Supreme Court: How It Was, How It Is*, "To go beyond the language of the Constitution, and the meaning that may be fairly ascribed to the language, and into the consciences of individual judges, is to embark on a journey that is treacherous indeed" (Rehnquist, 317). Therefore, in the area of the Fourteenth Amendment, Rehnquist has strictly construed the language and what is permissible under the Equal Protection Clause. As the Fourteenth Amendment requires "state action," Rehnquist has held the view that the amendment does not apply when the case does not deal with state-initiated or sponsored discrimination.

Additionally, in the specific areas of affirmative action and civil rights, Rehnquist adheres to the belief that the amendment is color blind and does not permit preferences or preferential treatment to minority classes. His views on this subject are apparent in a number of key affirmative action and Title VII cases, such as *United Steelworkers of America v. Weber*, 443 U.S. 193 (1979), *City of Richmond v. J.A.*

Croson Co., 488 U.S. 469 (1989), *Wards Cove Packing Co. v. Atonio*, 490 U.S. 642 (1989), and *Adarand Constructors, Inc. v. Peña*, 515 U.S. 200 (1995). He also believes that since the Fourteenth Amendment was enacted to deal with racial inequalities, the Equal Protection Clause of the Fourteenth Amendment should not be grounds for prohibiting disparate treatment based upon gender. Rehnquist illustrated these views in such cases as *Craig v. Boren*, 429 U.S. 190 (1976), and *Michael M. v. Superior Court of Sonoma County*, 450 U.S. 464 (1981).

An interesting observation that has been noted in the Rehnquist era is that the Court has not recognized any new suspect classifications that would effectuate intermediate or strict scrutiny review. This is especially so when efforts in affirmative action are involved. The Rehnquist-led Court has created no extensions of protections beyond those previously established by the Burger and Warren Courts. Thus, as alluded to earlier, the Rehnquist Court has also not been as aggressive as the Warren or Burger Courts in viewing affirmative action as a vehicle for remedying past discrimination. The Rehnquist Court's decisions on affirmative action have evolved through a series of decisions to the point that the same level of scrutiny (strict scrutiny) is applied to affirmative action plans as is applied under suspect classification to cases involving invidious discrimination against minorities. In the 1990 case *Metro Broadcasting, Inc. v. FCC*, 497 U.S. 547 (1990), the Rehnquist Court applied only the intermediate standard of scrutiny to congressionally imposed affirmative action plans (a federally imposed licensing scheme was at issue in *Metro Broadcasting*). In *Metro Broadcasting*, the Court stated that Congress had the power to remedy past discrimination. Rehnquist dissented in this case, along with Justices Sandra Day O'Connor (who wrote the dissenting opinion), Antonin Scalia, and Anthony Kennedy. However, *Metro Broadcasting* was overruled five years later in *Adarand*, and the majority said that the strict scrutiny analysis should apply to the constitutionality of all affirmative action efforts that employ race-conscious measures. Arguably the difference between the 1990 *Metro Broadcasting* case and the 1995 *Adarand* case was that four justices in the majority in the former case left the Court from 1990 to 1995, with the four dissenters remaining, thereby becoming the majority with one additional member by 1995 (Justice Clarence Thomas).

Indeed, prior to the 2003 cases *Gratz v. Bollinger*, 123 S. Ct. 2411, 2003 U.S. LEXIS 4801 (2003), and *Grutter v. Bollinger*, 123 S. Ct. 2325, 2003 U.S. LEXIS 4800 (2003), affirmative action cases in the education context had not been successful in even being heard during the seventeen years that Rehnquist had presided as chief justice. Review was denied twice in the Fifth Circuit Court of Appeal's invalidation of the admissions programs at the University of Texas Law School in *Hopwood v. Texas*, 78 F.3d 932 (5th Cir. 1996), as well as affirmative action admissions programs arising from the Ninth Circuit and the Eleventh Circuit Court of Appeal cases *Smith v. University of Washington Law School*, 233 F.3d 1188 (9th Cir. 2000), and *Johnson v. Board of Regents of the University of Georgia*, 263 F.3d 1234 (11th Cir. 2001), respectively.

In the two landmark affirmative action cases *Grutter* and *Gratz*, the Court moved away from the historical trend against affirmative action during much of the Rehnquist era and issued an opinion allowing the use of affirmative action in higher education (to promote diversity) at least for the next couple of decades (the majority opinion specified that it was unlikely that affirmative action in higher education would be needed by 2028). The majority opinion in *Grutter*, to which

Rehnquist dissented, held that diversity in higher education was a compelling governmental interest that could be addressed through narrowly tailored affirmative action programs. The majority opinion in *Grutter* reaffirmed the diversity rationale that Justice Lewis Powell had enunciated twenty-five years earlier in *Regents of the University of California v. Bakke*, 438 U.S. 265 (1978), a position to which Rehnquist had also dissented in 1978. Rehnquist, in his dissent, disagreed with the majority opinion that the Court's strict scrutiny analysis had been satisfied in the case and called the majority's deference to the University of Michigan's affirmative action program "unprecedented."

However, Rehnquist wrote the majority opinion in *Gratz*, the companion case to *Grutter*. In *Gratz*, the Court warned that fixed racial quotas and mechanized formulas (which have the effect of operating as a quota) would not be tolerated. In the *Gratz* decision, the Court struck down the University of Michigan undergraduate admissions affirmative plan that gave extra points for race alone. The plan struck down by the Court had awarded African American, Hispanic, and Native American applicants an automatic 20 points on a 150-point undergraduate admissions scale. This, the Court held, was akin to racial quotas, which violate the Fourteenth Amendment.

As the new century begins, the Rehnquist era is winding down. In the evening glow of an era in which the torch of chief justice will soon be passed, the U.S. Supreme Court as a body has found itself on the defensive in an affirmative action attack on the Court's own minority hiring practices. Of the 428 law clerks hired by the current Court, only seven (1.6 percent) have been African American, eighteen (4.2 percent) Asian, and five (1.2 percent) Hispanic, and none have been Native American Indian. Chief Justice Rehnquist worried about the power of the Supreme Court law clerk as far back as 1957, believing that most clerks were "to the 'left' of either the nation or the Court" and had a bias of "extreme solicitude for the claims of Communists and other criminal defendants, expansion of federal power at the expense of State power, great sympathy toward any government regulation of business" (Perry, 72).

Just as the Warren Court worked to define and give new direction to the protections of what were viewed as the fundamental rights of the individual, the Rehnquist Court has done so as well in a different direction with decisions that have shaped this country. While the Rehnquist era has been marked by what some legal scholars have labeled conservative activists, Chief Justice William H. Rehnquist has guided, articulated, and defined its tone, direction, and philosophical views away from what some consider individual rights and toward a narrower view of the Constitution in its "plain meaning." The Rehnquist Court and its influence on affirmative action may or may not survive, but its decisions today affect what happens tomorrow.

See also Adarand Constructors, Inc. v. Peña; *Brown v. Board of Education*; Burger Court and Affirmative Action; *City of Richmond v. J.A. Croson Co.*; Department of Justice; Equal Protection Clause; Fourteenth Amendment; *Gratz v. Bollinger/Grutter v. Bollinger*; *Hopwood v. Texas*; *Johnson v. Board of Regents of the University of Georgia*; *Metro Broadcasting, Inc. v. FCC*; Nixon, Richard Milhous; O'Connor, Sandra Day; Original Intent Jurisprudence; *Plessy v. Ferguson*; Reagan, Ronald; *Smith v. University of Washington Law School*; State Action Doctrine; Thomas, Clarence; Title VII of the Civil Rights Act of 1964; *United Steelworkers of America v. Weber; Wards Cove Packing Co. v. Atonio;* Warren Court and Affirmative Action.

FURTHER READING: Ashe, Bernard F., 2001, "Government Efforts to Erase Employment Discrimination," *Experience—American Bar Association* 11 (winter): 14; Chermerinsky, Erwin, 1999, "Access to Justice: The Rehnquist Court and Justice: An Oxymoron?" *Washington University Journal of Law and Policy* 1:37–53; Dean, John W., 2001, *The Rehnquist Choice: The Untold Story of the Nixon Appointment That Redefined the Supreme Court,* New York: Free Press; Friedelbaum, Stanley H., 1994, *The Rehnquist Court: In Pursuit of Judicial Conservatism,* Westport, CT: Greenwood Press; Giordano, Timothy K., 2000, "Different Treatment for Non-Minority Plaintiffs under Title VII: A Call for Modification of the Background Circumstances Test to Ensure That Separate Is Equal," *Emory Law Journal* 49 (summer): 993–1031; Lazarus, Edward, 1998, *Closed Chambers: The Rise, Fall, and Future of the Modern Supreme Court,* New York: Penguin Press; Maxwell, Susan M., 1998, "Racial Classifications under Strict Scrutiny: Policy Considerations and the Remedial-Plus Approach," *Texas Law Review* 77:259–296; Perry, Barbara A., 1999, *The Priestly Tribe: The Supreme Court's Image in the American Mind,* Westport, CT: Praeger; "Race Law and Justice: The Rehnquist Court and the American Dilemma" (conference), 1996, *American University Law Review* 45, no. 3 (February): 567–635; Rehnquist, William H., 1987, *The Supreme Court: How It Was, How It Is,* New York: William Morrow; Starr, Kenneth W., 2002, *First among Equals,* New York: Warner Books; Woodward, Bob, and Scott Armstrong, 1979, *The Brethren: Inside the Supreme Court,* New York: Simon and Schuster.

ROBERT DON GIFFORD II

Relative Deprivation Theory

Relative deprivation theory represents an attempt to explain behavior based upon social inequalities within a society. This theory basically postulates that levels of delinquency in society are the result of societal frustrations, inequities, negative events in life, and a sense of injustice based upon the perceived economic advantages of others in society. These social inequalities often are the result of race and poverty and thus are connected with affirmative action. One of the purposes of affirmative action programs is to alleviate the economic hardships suffered by minority groups because of previous incidents of racial discrimination. The basis for this relative deprivation theory is that any society where there are vast differences in wealth and power will result in some citizens feeling left out of opportunities to succeed. This is especially true in a society such as that existing in the United States.

In the United States, the media through television, magazines, advertising, and movies offer a portrait of success for the average citizen. This portrait often focuses upon those individuals who are able to influence their future by means of their wealth. These individuals are the ones who are holders of power, corporate executives, and others who can use money to better their station in life. While this may be a portrait of the "American dream," that dream has not been and arguably is still not available to all within our society. Some minority groups are disproportionately represented in statistics covering the poor in America. Thus traditionally these groups have less access to education and the opportunity for good jobs. Once in a job, minority members of these groups are less likely to advance, again because of lack of education. Some minority groups live disproportionately in poverty-ridden public housing and find themselves with little chance of leaving these conditions. With these conditions facing many in America, it is no wonder that when the media illustrate what advantages many whites enjoy, some minority groups feel deprived in a relative way.

Among other things, relative deprivation theory attempts to explain why some citizens are more likely to commit crimes than others. Those living in poverty see the criminal justice system as unfair based upon lack of access to money. The poor feel that they are subjected to law-enforcement surveillance more than the wealthy, are less likely to be afforded bail once they are arrested because of their lack of money, are less likely to be successful at trial because of court-appointed counsel, and finally, once they are found guilty of an offense, are more likely to go to prison because of their financial position. When the poor weigh their position against that of a wealthier individual, they feel deprived of the standard of justice that all Americans should enjoy. The poor want the same things that the wealthy want. Because of these factors, the poor, comprised disproportionately of certain minority groups, are considered more likely to commit crimes according to relative deprivation theory. As long as there is institutionalized disparity in wealth and income, the poor will be thrust into a situation where they feel that the only way to succeed is through illegal means.

See also Criminal Justice System and Affirmative Action; Kerner Commission; Riots, Economically and Racially Motivated.

FURTHER READING: Blau, Judith, and Peter Blau, 1982, "The Cost of Inequality: Metropolitan Structure and Violent Crime," *American Sociological Review* 147:114–29; Harrison, Jeffrey, 1997, "Piercing Pareto Superiority: Real People and the Obligation of Legal Theory," *Arizona Law Review* 39 (spring): 1–14; Martin, Joanne, 1981, "Relative Deprivation: A Theory of Distributive Injustice for an Era of Shrinking Resources," *Research in Organizational Behavior* 3:53.

SUSAN F. BRINKLEY

Reparations

The practice of reparations is an aggressive means of compensating an individual or a group for a wrong or injury. In legal parlance, the reparations are a remedial measure meant to return an injured party to its original condition before the injury. The debate over whether African Americans in the United States should be paid monetary reparations for the U.S. history of slavery and racial oppression is related to the debate over affirmative action. Although affirmative action programs that benefit African Americans are sometimes viewed as a type of reparations, the commonly understood concept of reparations is a more direct means of compensation. Many reparations proposals would require direct payment of money from the federal government to all African Americans. Other reparations proposals are narrower, requiring monetary payments from entities (such as corporations or state governments) that participated in or benefited from slavery to all African Americans or to descendants of slaves. Just as affirmative action is a more aggressive and controversial means than antidiscrimination measures in attempting to "level the playing field," the theoretical practice of reparations for African Americans is an even more aggressive and controversial means than affirmative action in the attempt to level the playing field. Proponents of reparations argue that affirmative action in education, employment, and other segments of society is insufficient compensation for injuries resulting from slavery and racial oppression, while opponents of reparations argue that affirmative action programs have more than compensated for slavery and its aftermath.

Advocates of reparations argue that all African Americans in the United States should be compensated for atrocities committed against blacks in the South who were enslaved from the 1600s through the abolition of slavery in 1865. As historian Roger Wilkin once famously stated, "Blacks have a 375-year history on this continent: 245 involving slavery, 100 involving legalized discrimination, and only 30 involving anything else" (Plous, 28). In the words of another author, "African skills and accomplishments were overlooked, ignored, or denied outright, a situation that has yet to be rectified. Slavery's human toll can never be calculated, but it clearly ranks among the worst crimes of humankind" (Altman 1997, 232). The estimates of economists on the actual damage of slavery to the African American community in terms of lost labor and production, and excluding the incalculable amounts of emotional damage and loss of liberty, run in the range of $600 billion (conservative figure) to trillions of dollars. Several economists have estimated that this figure is as high as $777 trillion dollars. Reparations, some argue, are therefore justified and required in order to compensate for this lost capital and also for the tremendous "pain and suffering" caused by slavery.

Proponents of reparations point out that the concept of providing reparations for individuals or a group that has been subject to systematic discrimination and mistreated by society has several historical precedents. The Freedmen's Bureau's famed 1865 promise of "forty acres and a mule" for all freed slaves certainly could be construed as a promise of reparations (although recent scholarship has argued that the federal government never made this promise). The Black Panther Party justified its claim for reparations by this promise, arguing in its ten-point manifesto that "this racist government has robbed us and now we are demanding the overdue debt of forty acres and two mules. Forty acres and two mules were promised 100 years ago as restitution for slave labor and mass murder of Black people. We will accept the payment in

African Americans working in the fields of Georgia in the 1890s. © Bettmann/Corbis.

currency which will be distributed to our many communities." In 1988, the United States paid $20,000 to every Japanese American survivor, or his or her immediate family, for being wrongfully removed from their homes and, in essence, imprisoned in Japanese internment camps during World War II. In 1999, Germany, the United States, and several other countries of Eastern Europe agreed to pay $5 billion in reparations to the victims, as well as the immediate direct descendants of the victims, who were forced into a condition of involuntary servitude and forced to labor on behalf of Germany and Austria in World War II. Madeleine Albright, serving as U.S. secretary of state at the time, called the decision "the first serious attempt to compensate those whose labor was stolen or coerced during a time of outrage and shame. It is critical to completing the unfinished business of the old century before entering the new" (Ince, 49–50). Another example of reparations in U.S. history is the partial payment to certain Native American tribes for federal government land seizures and treaty violations (or outright treaty abrogation). On the state level, in 1994, reparations were paid by the state of Florida to the survivors of the Rosewood massacre in 1923, in which an all-white mob descended on the black town and committed countless acts of cold-blooded murder. Reparations for slavery have also been contemplated on the international level, most recently in the United Nations Conference on Racism that was held in South Africa in 2001, in which reparations for the descendants of black slaves were proposed.

These historical precedents set the framework for those arguing that providing reparations for slavery is feasible. Proponents of reparations argue that "mild" social programs such as affirmative action are not sufficient compensation and represent "traditional tokenism" by society (Rubio 2001, 191). Proponents argue that an aggressive compensation scheme is required to compensate for both the psychic and the economic damage the African American community has suffered because of slavery and its aftermath.

Opponents of reparations raise a host of problems ranging from fairness and legal objections to the practical infeasibility of massive societal compensation for slavery. First, opponents argue that all of the historical precedents cited by proponents of reparations are distinguishable in that the previous compensation schemes were paid to the actual victims (or their immediate family members) for the wrong suffered, and not to an entire group of people three or four generations and more then 150 years removed from the institution of slavery. Furthermore, critics argue, not all blacks in America during the eighteenth and nineteenth centuries were enslaved, and therefore it is overbroad to compensate descendants of those not actually in bondage.

Second, the currently proposed reparation schemes exclude other ethnic and minority groups who were oppressed or even enslaved in the past. In this vein, Thomas Sowell, an African American critic of reparations and affirmative action, has argued that "slavery itself was not unique to Africans. The very word 'slave' derives from the name of a European people—the *Slavs*, who were enslaved for centuries before the first African was brought to the Western Hemisphere. The tragic fact is that slavery existed all over the world, for thousands of years" (Sowell 2000). Likewise, there are countless other groups who suffered institutional discrimination and oppression, both within the United States and abroad, who arguably are also entitled to reparations. Native Americans, for example, had much of the current landmass of the United States seized from them by European colonists. Critics postulate that the arguments for these reparations make more sense (and are less amorphous) than reparations for slavery.

A third argument against reparations is that the "sin of slavery" was not just a white sin, but was indeed multiracial. Critics point out that during the eighteenth and nineteenth centuries, African tribal warlords greatly profited from the African slave trade and persecuted their own peoples. Critics argue that if one accepts the argument of reparations, liability should also be assessed on the present-day African countries that supported the slave trade, or on the approximately 3,000 black slave owners who lived in the antebellum South in the course of several centuries. In the words of one author, "Obviously the West African comes out of this unsavory business no better than anybody else—but no worse either. Horrors like slavery are seldom the fault of specific individuals or groups. They just happen at great cost to human decency and self respect" (Furnas 1959, 75). Similarly, while a small percentage of society actually owned slaves in the antebellum South (calculated by historians as about 10 percent of whites in the South), 350,000 white Union soldiers died in ridding the country of slavery. As conservative writer George Will has argued, if society awards compensation to an entire race for the evils of slavery, should not the white descendants of individuals (including non-English-speaking immigrants of German and Irish descent) who died on such battlefields as Gettysburg and Antietam also be entitled to compensation? David Horowitz, a nationally known critic of reparations, has asked: "What about the descendants of the 350,000 Union soldiers who died to free the slaves? They gave their lives. What possible moral principle would ask them to pay (through their descendants) again?" (Horowitz 2001). Furthermore, given the fact that a great majority of Americans came in immigrant waves after the American Civil War (and were therefore not connected with the institution of slavery), critics argue that it is not fair that these individuals be held responsible. In this vein, newspaper columnist Mona Charen has asked, "What about immigrants like Koreans or Vietnamese, who only just arrived? They did not participate in discrimination against blacks, nor did their ancestors" (Charen, 7B).

Fourth, critics argue that it is simply not feasible or politically realistic for the government to provide meaningful compensation as argued for by the proponents of reparations. As author Richard America has commented, "It really is the stuff of fantasy to imagine white America turning more than $1 trillion over to black America" (America 1990, 11). Critics argue that the modest payment of $20,000 per family for the actual survivors of World War II internment camps, which was an incredibly large compensation funded through general taxation, would only be a drop in the bucket compared with the mammoth amount of government revenue needed to distribute trillions of dollars.

Furthermore, as Rubio points out, there are some who view "affirmative action as a form of reparations" (Rubio 2001, 188). Horowitz has argued that various social programs such as welfare programs, race-conscious job preferences, race-conscious admissions preferences, and special set-aside provisions for minority contractors have been specially compensating the black community. Specifically, in Horowitz's controversial "Ten Arguments against Reparations," he argues that "since the passage of the Civil Rights Acts and the advent of the Great Society in 1965, trillions of dollars in transfer payments have been made to African Americans . . . all under the rationale of redressing historical racial grievances." Furthermore, Horowitz muses, "If trillion dollar restitutions and a wholesale rewriting of American law (in order to accommodate racial preferences) for African Americans is not enough to achieve a 'healing,' what will?" (Horowitz 2001).

Proponents of reparations dismiss these arguments. For example, Derrick Bell, a law professor and author, has argued that each of these antireparations arguments can be addressed and refuted. According to Bell, all of the civil rights legislation since the Civil War was passed, not because of white America's concern for blacks, but rather because it served a white interest. As Bell commented in 2001, "Every civil rights measure all the way back to the Emancipation Proclamation that has been implemented has had as a major characteristic that it was a great help to whites" (Taylor, W3). For Bell, the issue of reparations can be boiled down to the issue of compensation and justice. In responding to reparations objections, Bell commented in 2001 that "it's interesting that the argument is only made with regard to doing stuff for black people. When the Mississippi overflows its banks when people are told not to build [houses there], nobody makes [those] argument[s]. The government does all manner of things through our tax money to correct things" (Taylor, W3).

One strategy used to refute the overbreadth argument that providing reparations for all African Americans is overbroad in terms of both the persons benefited and burdened (many of whom were not affected by slavery) is to focus on specific postslavery wrongs for which compensation is justified. One commentator, Charles J. Ogletree Jr., cites several violent events that took place during the Jim Crow era in the South, including the Tulsa race riot of 1921 in which hundreds of people (mostly African Americans) were killed in an attempt by whites to enforce racial segregation, as examples of postslavery tragedies for which reparations should be paid. The overbreadth argument may also arguably be refuted by noting that in the United States, the intense racial bias that has permeated society since the time of slavery and is the direct result of attitudes formed during slavery has significantly benefited every non–African American and has significantly burdened every African American whether or not a person's ancestors were directly involved with slavery.

The argument that the welfare system is fair compensation for African American slavery is infuriating to some proponents of reparations who do not see the welfare system as providing any assistance toward self-reliance justly due to African Americans. The welfare system, it is argued, is a method to placate recipients so that they remain dependent on the government rather than taking desperate action to improve their situation. Reparations, on the other hand, involve a recognition that African Americans were grievously injured and deserve compensation. This argument is also infuriating to some because of its implication that only African Americans are on welfare rolls. This implication, it is argued, demonstrates that persons advancing this argument are laboring under racially biased stereotypes.

The reparations debate has been raging for years. During the 1960s, several black organizations called for reparations. In 1994, the National Coalition of Blacks for Reparations in America held a summit, attended by Jesse Jackson and Rosa Parks, among others, calling for reparations for all descendants of slavery. Additionally, every year since 1989, Congressman John Conyers has introduced a bill calling for the study of the feasibility of African American reparations. More specifically, according to Conyers, this bill has four functions:

(1) It acknowledges the fundamental injustice and inhumanity of slavery; (2) It establishes a commission to study slavery, its subsequent racial and economic discrimination against freed slaves; (3) It studies the impact of those forces on today's living African Americans; and (4) The commission would then make recommendations to Congress on appropriate remedies to redress the harm inflicted on living African Americans. (Conyers 1989)

In 2001, David Horowitz caused a firestorm on college campuses across the country when he ran an antireparations advertisement in college newspapers. Many colleges refused to print the advertisement, censored it, or were excoriated by students if the school's paper decided to publish it. Yet despite these efforts by proponents and opponents to resolve the issue, as the United States begins its journey in the new millennium, perhaps only one thing is clear: There is no quick or easy solution to the reparations debate that will satisfy all of the parties involved. This debate promises to rage well into the twenty-first century.

See also African Americans; American Civil War; Bell, Derrick A., Jr.; Civil War (Reconstruction) Amendments and Civil Rights Acts; Declaration of Independence and Equality; Freedmen's Bureau; Jackson, Jesse; Japanese Internment and World War II; Level Playing Field; Race in Colonial America; Slavery; Slavery and the Founding Fathers.

FURTHER READING: Altman, Susan, 1997, *The Encyclopedia of African-American Heritage*, New York: Facts on File; America, Richard F., ed., *The Wealth of Races: The Present Value of Benefits from Past Injustices*, Westport, CT: Greenwood Press; Bittker, Boris I., 1973, *The Case for Black Reparations*, New York: Vintage Books; Conyers, John, Jr., "Major Issues—Reparations," http://www.house.gov/conyers/new_reparations.htm; "Do African-Americans Deserve Reparations?" (panel discussion), 1997, *Essence* 28, no. 6 (October): 64–67; Furnas, J.C., 1959, *The Road to Harpers Ferry*, New York: William Sloane Associates; Horowitz, David, 1999, *Hating Whitey*, Dallas: Spence Publishing; Horowitz, David, 2001, "Anti-Reparations Ad," http://www.adversity.net; Horowitz, David, 2002, *Uncivil Wars: The Controversy over Reparations for Slavery*, San Francisco: Encounter Books; Irons, Peter, 1999, *A People's History of the Supreme Court*, New York: Viking Press; Ogletree, Charles J., 2003, "The Current Reparations Debate," *University of California at Davis Law Review* 36 (June): 1051–1072; Parker, Jay, 2000, "An Apology and Reparations for Slavery?" *World and I Magazine*, February, http://www.worldandi.com; Plous, S., 2003, "Ten Myths About Affirmative Action," *Journal of Social Issues* 52:25–31; Robinson, Randall, 1999, *The Debt: What America Owes Blacks*, New York: Dutton Plume; Rubio, Philip F., 2001, *A History of Affirmative Action, 1619–2000*, Jackson: University Press of Mississippi; Smith, John David, 2003, "The Enduring Myth of 'Forty Acres and a Mule,' " *Chronicle of Higher Education*, February 21, B11; Sowell, Thomas, 2000, "Reparations for Slavery," *Jewish World Review*, July 17, http://www.jewishworldreview.com; Taylor, Lynda Guydon, 2001, "Professor Says Civil Rights Changes Always in Favor of Whites," *Pittsburgh Post-Gazette*, May 20, W3; West, Cornel, 1994, *Race Matters*, Boston: Beacon Press.

MARIA D. BECKMAN

Republican Party and Affirmative Action

Since the 1960s, the American political party system has become increasingly polarized along racial lines. The Republicans, once the party of Lincoln and emancipated blacks, have become a largely white political party that is perceived as being hostile to affirmative action. In contrast, the Democrats have lost substantial support among white southerners and white ethnics in the North and have been perceived as the "black party," defenders of affirmative action. However, this political divide is not always that clear.

The racial polarization of the party system emerged in 1964 when the Republicans nominated Senator Barry Goldwater of Arizona for President. Goldwater, who voted against the 1964 Civil Rights Act, attracted the votes of southern segregationists and carried five southern states. Goldwater offered a political rationale for his position in a 1961 Atlanta speech when he said, "We're not going to get the Negro vote as a block in 1964 and 1968, so we ought to go hunting where the ducks are." During the next four decades, the issue of race in American politics evolved from fundamental civil rights to affirmative action.

Modern usage of the term "affirmative action" often connotes laws, court decisions, and executive orders that emerged during the Democratic Kennedy and Johnson administrations in order to aid minorities and women. While originally intended to counter job discrimination against African Americans, affirmative action now covers a number of areas, including education and employment, housing and economic development, and veterans' rights.

Richard Nixon, who would win the presidency in 1968, developed what he called his "southern strategy," which was intended to win southern whites away from the Democratic Party by opposing busing and other forms of racial integration opposed by southerners. Yet Nixon also approved the first federal initiative, the Philadelphia Plan, requiring federal contractors to institute goals and timetables for minority hiring as a precondition for securing government contracts and strengthened the enforcement powers of the U.S. Equal Employment Opportunity Commission (EEOC).

Perhaps the Republican administration perceived as the most hostile to affirmative action (and to African Americans in general) was the Reagan administration (1981–1989). This administration favored tax exemptions for segregated schools. It advocated a voucher system that would allow whites to send their children to private schools while ending their financial support for predominantly black public systems. The administration convinced the Supreme Court to narrow the application of civil rights statutes in *Grove City College v. Bell*, 465 U.S. 555 (1984). Four years later, Reagan vetoed the Civil Rights Restoration Act of 1988 that was intended to reverse the Supreme Court's decision in *Grove City College v. Bell*, only to have his veto overridden by a two-thirds majority in Congress.

Following their 1994 takeover of Congress, conservative Republicans were willing to roll back preferences. As Puddington (1995, 22) wrote, "In what looked like a harbinger of things to come, Republicans had succeeded in eliminating a set-aside program for the communications industry, and another set-aside was dropped by the Federal Communications Commission because of the threat of litigation by white-owned businesses." President Bill Clinton, in response to his party's loss of Congress, proposed a "mend it, don't end it" policy toward affirmative action in 1995.

In the 2000 presidential campaign, George W. Bush attempted to distance himself from the perception that African Americans held of his party. Speaking to the annual meeting of the National Association for the Advancement of Colored People (NAACP), the presidential candidate stated that his party "had failed to conduct itself as the party of Lincoln." However, in the second presidential debate against Vice President Al Gore in October 2000, Bush indicated that he was opposed to affirmative action if it involved quotas. Shortly after taking office, the Bush administration filed a brief defending affirmative action in a Supreme Court case involving a Latino-owned business, *Adarand v. Mineta.* Yet despite these public statements, Bush has repeatedly denounced the use of quotas as being unfair and has stated that he does not believe in affirmative action, but rather "affirmative access," a term he created to connote equal access to facilities and services. In January 2003, the Bush administration argued against affirmative action in the cases *Gratz v. Bollinger*, 123 S. Ct. 2411, 2003 U.S. LEXIS 4801 (2003), and *Grutter v. Bollinger*, 123 S. Ct. 2325, 2003 U.S. LEXIS 4800 (2003). In a January 2003 press conference, Bush declared affirmative action usage in higher education to be "divisive, unfair and impossible to square with the Constitution" and "fundamentally flawed" (Schmidt, A20). In oral arguments in the case in April 2003, Bush's solicitor general, Theodore Olson, argued strongly against the use of race-conscious affirmative action programs in higher education.

See also Affirmative Access; African Americans; Bush, George W.; Civil Rights Act of 1964; Civil Rights Restoration Act of 1988; Clinton, William Jefferson; Democratic Party and Affirmative Action; Equal Employment Opportunity Commission; Federal Communications Commission; *Gratz v. Bollinger/Grutter v. Bollinger*; *Grove City College v. Bell*; Johnson, Lyndon Baines; Kennedy, John Fitzgerald; National Association for the Advancement of Colored People; Nixon, Richard Milhous; Reagan, Ronald.

FURTHER READING: Balz, Daniel J., 1996, *Storming the Gates: Protest Politics and the Republican Revival*, Boston: Little, Brown; Black, Earl, and Merle Black, 2002, *The Rise of Southern Republicans*, Cambridge, MA: Harvard University Press; Branch, Taylor, 1998, "The Year the GOP Went South," *Washington Monthly* 30, no. 3 (March): 34; Connerly, Ward, 2001, "Losing the Soul of the GOP: Republicans Make a Rotten Peace with Racial Preferences," *National Review* 53, no. 19 (October 1): 42–45; Edwards, Lee, 1999, *The Conservative Revolution: The Movement That Remade America*, New York: Free Press; Greenberg, Stanley B., 1995, *Middle Class Dreams: The Politics and Power of the New American Majority*, New York: Times Books; Greenhaw, Wayne, 1982, *Elephants in the Cottonfields: Ronald Reagan and the New Republican South*, New York: Macmillan; Judis, John B., 1988, "Black Donkey, White Elephant: Race and American Politics," *New Republic* 98 (April 18): 25–29; 25; Laham, Nicholas, 1998, *The Reagan Presidency and the Politics of Race: In Pursuit of Colorblind Justice and Limited Government*, Westport, CT: Praeger; Lind, Michael, "The Southern Coup: The South, the GOP, and America," *New Republic* 212 (June 19): 20–26; Puddington, Arch, "Will Affirmative Action Survive?" *Commentary* 100, no. 4 (October): 22; Schmidt, Peter, 2003, "Bush Asks Supreme Court to Strike Down University of Michigan's Affirmative Action Policy," *Chronicle of Higher Education*, January 24, A20; Shull, Steven A. 1993, *A Kinder, Gentler Racism? The Reagan-Bush Civil Rights Legacy*, Armonk, NY: M.E. Sharpe; Wolters, Raymond, 1996, *Right Turn: William Bradford Reynolds, the Reagan Administration, and Black Civil Rights*, New Brunswick, NJ: Transaction Publishers.

JEFFREY KRAUS

Reservation System

See Quotas.

Reverse Discrimination

With the possible exception of quotas, no term or concept in the debates over affirmative action has been as volatile, divisive, and misunderstood as "reverse discrimination." *The American Heritage Dictionary of the English Language* (4th edition) has defined the concept of "reverse discrimination" as "discrimination against members of a dominant or majority group, especially when resulting from policies established to correct discrimination against members of a minority or disadvantaged group." Even with such a concise and relatively straightforward definition as this, the concept has, on the one hand, been dismissed as nonexistent and, on the other hand, has been considered identical with affirmative action.

Yet this confusion and angst over "reverse discrimination" did not enter the public scene with the advent of affirmative action, but rather developed for many over the nearly four-decade history of affirmative action and its metamorphosis from a positive, temporary action that would simply eliminate discrimination in hiring, promotions, and college admissions into an ongoing social condition that has not only given opportunities for jobs, promotions, and admissions to minority (or female) applicants, but has also engineered the giving of the actual jobs, promotions, and admissions, arguably negatively impacting those who, while otherwise qualified, except for race or sex, are rejected or not considered for the same position or benefit.

The much-cited metaphor of the chained runner of Lyndon Johnson's 1965 speech at Howard University vividly and poetically portrays the unfairness of a color-blind, competitive "level playing field" for those who had been deprived of the education, training, and opportunities to enable them to compete without some assistance or preference. The image works fine as poetry, but modern critics point out that the metaphor fails to lay out a case for exactly what would be done, how it would be done, for how long, in what circumstances, at whose expense, and why. Indeed, in regard to the metaphor, critics of affirmative action also point out that the chained runner has been unchained and as the playing field has been leveled, and thus the originally temporary affirmative action programs or preferences should now be terminated.

Although first John F. Kennedy's and then Lyndon Johnson's executive orders gave the impression of "color blindness" in their insistence that applicants and employees be treated "without regard to their race, creed, color, or national origin," it soon became clear that the government's vision for the future of the formerly chained runners went far beyond seeking out and recruiting qualified applicants from the disadvantaged group, or establishing training programs to make applicants qualified and competitive and then allowing them to compete on an equal footing, but rather included preferences for them. Such preferential treatment may take two major forms: "weak preferences," selecting members of the disadvantaged group when they are just as qualified as their competitors, or "strong preferences," selecting them when they are not as qualified as their competitors. In both cases, but especially the latter, the competitors who lack the advantage of being in the "disadvantaged" group may claim that they are being discriminated against on the basis of race. In fact, many of those who most strongly oppose affirmative action as leading to reverse discrimination actually find the term "reverse discrimination" distasteful. Having a special label for this kind of discrimination does prompt a different reaction than one would have for "discrimination." It suggests that it is an unusual circumstance; it also, by implication, in an environment in which "affirmative action" is the law, seems to strip the act of discrimination of its "wrongness" and minimize the legitimacy of the complaints of the victims.

One mistaken view of many whites is that reverse discrimination is involved whenever a minority person gets a job or promotion or college admission that might have gone to a white. A mistaken view of many minorities is that reverse discrimination does not exist. Both positions are incorrect, and examining the real intertwining of affirmative action and reverse discrimination—both in theory and in actual practice—reveals questions of equality and fairness that are troubling and convoluted, offering few simple solutions except to those ideologically committed to or against affirmative action regardless of the consequences.

To what extent, if at all, affirmative action becomes equivalent to reverse discrimination, both in theory and in practice, is intricately tied to different concepts of justice that may be invoked, and how these theoretical concepts are actually applied in practice. Theories of justice that focus on rectifying wrongs or injuries done in the past may be characterized as "backward looking" and are generally labeled either "compensatory justice" or "corrective justice," while theories of justice that focus on the distribution of society's goods, services, benefits, and opportunities may be characterized as "forward looking" and are called "distributive justice."

To those who point out that the country's past history of explicitly denying opportunities to some persons because of their skin color (e.g., black) and granting opportunities to others because of skin color (e.g., white) illustrates the impermissibility of making such determinations based on racial classifications, proponents of affirmative action respond that this description of the affirmative action and reverse-discrimination situation misses the mark. To them, under affirmative action, opportunities are to be granted not merely because persons are members of a certain minority class, but rather because they are in a category of injured persons deserving compensation.

Application of this principle may not always be simple in a tort, in which one party sues for restitution or compensation for injury done by another party, but when this principle is used as the basis for affirmative action, complexities abound. These complexities may start in the problem of identifying, on the large scale, the injuries done to different minority classes. To say that affirmative action is a solution to discrimination is to gloss over the complex history of discrimination itself. Lack of equal opportunity in education and employment in contemporary society is only the tail end of a much longer history that began in centuries of slavery, brutality, and dehumanization and, following emancipation, was transformed into a divided society of institutionalized and legally and culturally sanctioned segregation and discrimination.

Therefore, as opposed to a tort in which an individual or corporation or other limited and identifiable party is named as having caused some specific injury to another limited and identifiable party, the application of "compensatory justice" as the justification for affirmative action does not investigate claims of specific acts done by one party to another, nor does it weigh how much compensation is due in any particular case, or how that compensation is to be awarded. It is instead taken as a given that the whole structure of American society is implicated in past discrimination.

A related contemporary argument growing out of this view is the question of American reparations for slavery. This is a discussion separate from but related to questions of the "compensatory justice" claims for affirmative action, and comparisons to the American internment of Japanese Americans during World War II and the atrocities of the Jewish Holocaust may be inevitable, but they are not necessarily legitimate. In the case of slavery, reparations are being demanded not for those who were enslaved, or even for their immediate descendants, but for descendants generations later who were untouched by slavery. "Compensatory justice" claims for slavery reparations may then be linked to claims that though no living African Americans lived under slavery, they are heirs to those who did and are justly entitled to "inherit" the compensation that would have been due their enslaved ancestors. Other claims may rest on the assertion that though slavery did not exist during the lifetimes of today's African Americans, the inequalities, the segregation, and the discrimination in modern American society are the remnants of the slavery system, and African Americans are justly entitled to compensation on that basis.

However, even though just "compensations" or just "correctives" for some "disadvantaged" group may be considered to be assessed against society at large, the actual cost in many situations turns out to be paid by those who have done nothing warranting having any penalty assessed against them and who consequently perceive "just compensation" for others to be discrimination against them—which has come to be called "reverse discrimination." The "compensatory" justice claims for affirmative action arguably are further weakened when the scope of affirmative action extends, on the basis of "diversity," beyond African Americans to encompass women and other minorities who have no history of slavery and segregation in this country.

Although the argument about affirmative action and reverse discrimination based on claims of "compensatory" justice or "corrective" justice seems mired in these complexities, an argument about affirmative action and reverse discrimination based on claims of "distributive" justice is not necessarily simpler. Where limited resources exist (society's goods, services, benefits, and opportunities), justly meting these out falls under theories of distributive justice. However, just distribution does not demand mathematically equal distribution among all persons, if such a thing were even possible, but rather proportionally equal distribution, based upon what one deserves. But desert may be calculated in different ways, and a "just distribution" under one calculation may turn out to be an "unjust distribution" under another.

Behind the much-maligned practice of "quotas" or even the softer term "goals" lies the notion, often ill defined or unarticulated, that a just distribution will lead to proportional, or near-proportional, representation of minorities through all levels of American society. From this perspective, affirmative action is a form of social engineering that brings about a more just society through the just (proportional) distribution of benefits. However, since such an approach may take race into account, it may be seen as a form of discrimination, only one called "reverse discrimination." Those opposing affirmative action see the program as social engineering trampling upon an individual's rights to fair treatment.

A further complication injected into discussions of justice relating to affirmative action and reverse discrimination is the much-used but seldom-defined term "merit." Opponents of affirmative action who believe that it is equivalent to, or at least leads into, reverse discrimination often argue that justice requires a color-blind system in which race plays no part, and one in which people are judged only upon objective qualifications or merit.

For college admission, a high grade point average (GPA) in high school and a high score on the Scholastic Assessment Test (SAT) are often assumed to be the criteria that determine "qualifications" or "merit." For graduate and professional school admissions, the same may be said for college grade point average and performance on such exams as the Graduate Record Exam (GRE), the Law School Admission Test (LSAT), and the Medical College Admission Test (MCAT). These assumptions are further grounded on the often-unspoken assumption that the highest "score" demonstrates the highest "qualification" or "merit" because grade point averages and test scores are taken to be predictors of success. Thus likelihood of success, which is a prediction about a future outcome, is taken to be a "qualification" for the opportunity, and that in turn comes to be conceived of as "merit." Of course, there is much debate about whether or not standardized tests are a correct barometer of "merit."

Even though these may be the assumptions in the minds of the general public, admissions officers and employers may conceive of qualifications and/or merit in a variety of different ways, some of which may involve race, gender, or ethnicity. When these issues are factored in in any way, it is only a small step to claims about "unqualified," "less qualified," or "underqualified" applicants, and then to claims of reverse discrimination.

Proponents of affirmative action are quick to point out that evaluating qualifications is more an art than a science and that to rely solely on grades or scores is to focus too narrowly on one aspect of a very complex picture. Additionally, various preferences or benefits are given to athletes, veterans, or legacies (sons and daughters of alumni) and may be cited as examples of the multiform possibilities that may be given consideration along with the more easily measured "qualifications." Moreover, the issue of "diversity," which may be brought in under the argument from proportional distribution, can easily shift over to "qualifications" as an aspect that given individuals bring to an institution that enriches the institution. For example, it may be argued not that a black candidate who scores lower on a test than many whites deserves an opportunity because she is black, but rather that a better education is given to all students by the institution's creation of a diverse student body. In essence, the good of the many (the diverse student body) outweighs the good of the few (the excluded students). Again, opponents who see reverse discrimination focus on the individuals who are excluded and thereby pay the price for "diversity."

The argument about the benefits that "diversity" brings to an institution may have a more legitimate ring to it in higher education than in the workplace, especially in the more selective colleges and universities, whose students, were it not for affirmative action, would receive an education lacking much of the diversity of American society. But similar arguments may be made in business and industry, especially in arenas dealing with public interaction, and most especially where the issue of "role models" may be brought in, as it was in *Porcelli v. Titus,* 431 F.2d 1254 (3rd Cir. 1970), cert. denied, 402 U.S. 944 (1971), one of the first reverse-discrimination cases and one that set the stage for the history of complex and competing issues that would create a quagmire for affirmative action.

In this case, Newark, New Jersey, had experienced some of the worst race riots of 1967, and the school board, following the recommendation of Franklyn Titus, the superintendent of schools, suspended the established procedures for promoting teachers to administrative positions within the school system. Titus had argued for the changes in the procedures based on the changes within the city, changes in educational philosophy, and the need for racially "sensitive" administrators. In addition to the rioting, which had already created an atmosphere of racial tension surrounding the case, testimony from educational experts, elaborating on the "educational crisis" in Newark's schools, argued for the right of blacks to have black school leaders and the need of black students to have positive role models. It would also be better, the argument went, for blacks to discipline black students, and black parents would respond better to black teachers and administrators and be more likely to become involved in their children's education. In this case, the charge of discrimination, or reverse discrimination, was countered by making race a "legitimate" qualification for job performance. According to John Skrentny, "Racial hiring was thus successfully equated with merit hiring in a case that almost certainly would never have happened had Newark not been rocked by rioting in the summer before Titus began to reevaluate the promotion procedure" (Skrentny 1996, 103).

More typical questions of "merit" and reverse discrimination in the educational context were raised several years later in the case *DeFunis v. Odegaard,* 416 U.S. 312 (1974). In 1971, Marco DeFunis, a white male Jewish applicant, had applied for admission to the University of Washington Law School. The law school had received 1,600 applications for 150 places in the first-year class, and DeFunis was denied admission. Thirty-seven applicants were admitted under the minority admissions program, based on a question about ethnic origin on the admission form, and DeFunis filed suit, claiming that the admissions policy had resulted in the unconstitutional denial of his application. The trial court found in his favor and ordered his admission. DeFunis was in his second year in law school when the Washington Supreme Court reversed the decision and found that the school's policy did not violate the Constitution. By the time the case reached the U.S. Supreme Court, DeFunis was in his third and final year in law school and was going to be allowed to finish regardless of the Court's decision. Therefore, the Court found the case moot and did not address the issues.

However, when the Court did finally agree to hear a case involving reverse discrimination, that case proved to have complex and long-standing ramifications for affirmative action. "Bakke" became a household name, and the case *Regents of the University of California v. Bakke,* 438 U.S. 265 (1978), attained the status of an icon in the reverse-discrimination argument, even among those unfamiliar with the details of the case. In 1972, Allan Bakke, a white student, applied for admission to the University of California at Davis Medical School. Sixteen of the 100 spaces had been reserved for minority students, and when Bakke was rejected, he filed suit alleging that he was better qualified than those admitted under the special program, who had been admitted with combined GPAs 0.63 points lower than his and MCAT scores 20 to 30 points lower, and that he had been a victim of discrimination based on his race.

The philosophical contradictions that lay behind the affirmative action and reverse-discrimination quagmire are vividly represented in the Supreme Court's opinion in *Bakke*. First, the Court ordered the medical school to admit Bakke and in fact denounced the school's "special admissions program" for using an "explicit racial classification" that completely excluded other applicants from a number of seats set aside for minority applicants. The program, the Court said, was fatally flawed in its "disregard of individual rights as guaranteed by the Fourteenth Amendment." But instead of giving the death knell for anything but the weakest of affirmative action programs, the Court endorsed the possibility, in theory, of programs that took race into consideration and suggested the kind of justification that would be required in such cases. While "diversity" in university admissions was indeed of compelling state interest, reserving a set number of seats based on race or ethnicity had not been shown to be the only way to achieve diversity, and in any case, racial or ethnic diversity was only one kind of diversity, and the medical school's program would therefore hinder rather than promote "genuine diversity." Thus while the *Bakke* case may have been a victory for Allan Bakke himself, it was not such a victory for the opponents of affirmative action, or for those who saw the danger of "reverse discrimination" inherent in affirmative action.

A chance for greater clarity in distinguishing affirmative action from reverse discrimination was missed in the case of *Taxman v. Piscataway Township Board of Education*, 91 F.3d 1547 (3rd Cir. 1996), *cert. granted*, 117 S. Ct. 2506 (1997), *cert. dismissed*, 118 S. Ct. 595 (1997). This case originated in the decision of the Piscataway Township Board of Education to eliminate one job in the high-school business department. Two teachers were considered for the elimination, and since both had been hired on the same day, the state of New Jersey's seniority system could not be applied to make the decision. One teacher, Debra Williams, was black, and one, Sharon Taxman, was white. Despite differences in degrees, backgrounds, and professional certifications, the board considered the two equal, with equal seniority, and invoked the district's affirmative action policy to make the determination. The school had no history of discrimination, but wanted to ensure that the business department, in which both Taxman and Williams taught, remained "diverse" and reflected the student population. Based upon these concerns, Williams was retained, and Taxman was fired. Two weeks later, Taxman filed a complaint with the Equal Employment Opportunity Commission, which found that there was "probable cause" to believe that the school district had discriminated against Taxman, and in 1991, the federal government filed suit against the board on behalf of Taxman. In September 1993, a U.S. district court in Newark found in Taxman's favor and awarded her $144,000 in back pay. On appeal, the U.S. Court of Appeals for the Third Circuit upheld the lower court's ruling that an employer may consider race in voluntary affirmative action only if it is used to remedy past discrimination or to correct distinct underrepresentation of minorities in traditionally segregated jobs. The Piscataway school board, the federal appeals court found, did not meet either standard, and even if the board had identified a problem, employee termination would have been an extreme way to deal with it.

As the case headed to the Supreme Court with the expectation that the Court would use the case to clarify the permissible application of affirmative action, the Black Leadership Forum, an alliance of various civil rights organizations, including the National Association for the Advancement of Colored People (NAACP), the Urban League, and the Southern Christian Leadership Conference, entered the case to help settle the matter before the Supreme Court could make a ruling detrimental to affirmative action. Of the final $433,500 settlement—for back pay, interest, and lawyer's fees—the Black Leadership Forum paid $308,500, and the school board, $125,000.

In *Taxman*, the abundant ironies of the case underscore the complexities and conflicted feelings involving the idea of reverse discrimination and its interaction with affirmative action. First, it is conceivable that the school board could have taken the action it did without citing the district's affirmative action plan, but rather basing the decision on the teachers' qualifications, since Williams had a master's degree and Taxman only a bachelor's degree. In addition, during the course of the case's journey through the EEOC and the court system, Taxman did not permanently lose her job. Rather, in 1991, she returned to her old job temporarily when another teacher in the department went on maternity leave, and she was permanently rehired in 1993. Since, of the total settlement, the school board paid a sum equal to her lost wages, the board, in the long run, did not even save the money that was the motivation for eliminating one teacher from the business department. Finally, mixing political agendas in with irony, the federal government actually changed sides in the case. Initially, the suit had been filed by the government under the Bush administration, which had seized on it as a case that could help eliminate race-based preferences. However, the Clinton administration, supporting affirmative action, decided to side with the school board on appeal. The final irony is that for all of the attention that the case has gained, and for all of its symbolic power in arguably representing the excesses of affirmative action, the settlement in the case, partially funded by the Black Leadership Forum, prevented the case from being heard by the Supreme Court and prevented the Court from delivering an opinion that could have provided clearer understanding of the proper application of affirmative action.

The anguish aroused by the conflicting notions of justice, fairness, and equity surrounding the issue of reverse discrimination suggests that the issue will not go away. The claims that the "benign" reverse discrimination of affirmative action is only the inevitable price to be paid for curing the malignancy of the original discrimination winds up being totally unsatisfying to those whose own opportunities become part of that price. Additionally, where past cases have failed to reach a satisfactory end—either through inconclusiveness, as in *Bakke*, or through settlement, as in *Taxman*—new cases arise to challenge perceived discrimination.

The case *Hopwood v. Texas*, 78 F.3d 932 (5th Cir. 1996), for example, arising nearly twenty years after *Bakke*, could easily be considered *Bakke II*. In this case, in 1992, Cheryl Hopwood applied for admission to the University of Texas Law School. Despite excellent academic qualifications—in fact, superior to those of most of the blacks and Mexican Americans admitted—Hopwood was rejected and sued, arguing, against Justice Lewis Powell's opinion in *Bakke*, that considering race or ethnicity in admissions to achieve a diverse student body is not a compelling state interest under the Fourteenth Amendment. Hopwood's 1996 victory in this case led Texas and Louisiana to abolish race as a consideration in college admissions. The Supreme Court refused to hear Texas's appeal in the case.

A similar case was that of Jennifer Gratz and Patrick Hamacher, who had applied to the University of Michigan at Ann Arbor in 1995 and 1997, respectively. Their applications, they alleged, were rejected because they were white. In support of this claim, they pointed to a "grid" system that had explicitly different qualifications for white applicants than for minority applicants. This process was found to be unconstitutional and to exclude a certain class from equal consideration solely on account of their race. In 1998, the University of Michigan changed the application system from the "grid" to a point system, awarding points to such factors as SAT scores, application essays—and race. The university claimed that this process produces results nearly identical to those of the "grid" system, yet the court found the revised system to be constitutional.

A similar case in the same university's law school involved its rejection of applicant Barbara Grutter, who with an LSAT score of 161 and a 3.8 GPA faced an 8.6 percent chance of admission, while black applicants with the same credentials faced a 100 percent admission rate. Illustrative of the war over what is permissible and what is impermissible in considering race as an admissions factor, after the federal court found one version of the undergraduate college's program unconstitutional (the "grid" plan) and another constitutional (the "points" plan), when it came to the law school's program, the federal court found that the law school's admissions policies were unconstitutional, and the Sixth Circuit Court of Appeals reversed that decision.

Both cases (*Gratz v. Bollinger*, 123 S. Ct. 2411, 2003 U.S. LEXIS 4801 [2003], and *Grutter v. Bollinger*, 123 S. Ct. 2325, 2003 U.S. LEXIS 4800 [2003]) then headed for the Supreme Court, and the anti–affirmative action Center for Individual Rights, which represented plaintiffs in both cases, predicted a verdict that would be the "Alamo for Affirmative Action." This prediction was unfulfilled, and the usage of affirmative action remains in doubt, since the Court in *Grutter v. Bollinger* held that diversity in higher education is a compelling governmental interest that may be permissibly addressed through narrowly tailored affirmative action programs that consider race as one of many factors to be considered—at least for the next quarter century. The Court in *Gratz v. Bollinger* also yet again warned against the use of fixed racial quotas or mechanized formulas that would violate the Fourteenth Amendment's Equal Protection Clause.

Thus after the *Gratz* and *Grutter* decisions, acrimonious battles will continue to be waged in defining the concept and practice of affirmative action. As Justice Antonin Scalia stated in dissent in the *Gratz* case, "[T]oday's *Grutter-Gratz* split double header seems perversely designed to prolong the controversy and the litigation." History has shown that when placed under pressure for having "unconstitutional" plans, proponents of affirmative action will revise these plans to achieve the desired results, and when one justification, such as "corrective justice," does not work, another, such as "diversity," will be called on to defend the practice. What is also clear is that while denominating this kind of discrimination as "reverse" (a characterization that might be contested by proponents of affirmative action) and characterizing it as "benign" may soften its image and minimize the legitimacy of the complaints, individuals who bear the brunt of it will continue to oppose it and expose it as discrimination.

A report by the Department of Labor in March 1995 illustrates some of the ambiguities in which the issue of reverse discrimination is mired. The report, prepared by Alfred Blumrosen, an architect of affirmative action, was dismissive of the significance of "reverse discrimination" in cases of discrimination, finding that such cases comprised between 1 and 3 percent of all discrimination cases, with "a high proportion" of these claims being "without merit." "This research," he claims, "suggests that the problem of 'reverse discrimination' is not widespread" ("Reverse Discrimination 1995). Although Blumrosen's statistics may be correct, others find fault with his conclusion. Specifically, since the law permits a variety of strategies favoring minorities under the rubric "affirmative action," it may be impossible to gauge the extent of the problem of "reverse discrimination" based on claims filed. "Precisely because the law is tilted against a successful lawsuit," Terry Eastland writes,

> the paucity of cases from 1990–1994 doesn't say anything about the extent of the problem of "reverse discrimination." We don't know how much discrimination results from affirmative action in the workplace, just as we don't know the extent to which employers engage in preferential treatment. What we do know is the state of the law. And if the diversity rationale wins acceptance in the federal courts and spreads beyond the "narrow" context endorsed by the Clinton administration, we can be confident that there will be fewer "reverse discrimination" cases for the next Blumrosen to report—assuming anyone is still interested. (Eastland 1996, 116)

Despite "official" claims critical of the prevalence of reverse discrimination, others see it and see that it is a by-product of affirmative action. Like the Center for Individual Rights, which represented Cheryl Hopwood and the plaintiffs in the University of Michigan cases, among others, Adversity.net is a high-profile opponent of affirmative action that considers the preferential treatment derived from such plans to be just another form of discrimination.

Adversity.net was founded, it says, "to promote fair and equal treatment under the law without regard to race, gender or ethnicity." Although it claims to be a civil rights organization ("A Civil Rights Organization for Color Blind Justice"), its self-proclaimed mission distinguishes it from most civil rights organizations and stridently equates affirmative action with reverse discrimination. Its goals are as follows: (1) to broaden and inform the public debate on the issue of racial preferences, targets, and goals that are, by definition, racially discriminatory; (2) to distribute facts about the adverse impact of racial preferences on those who are not members of any government-defined preferred class; and (3) to provide a resource and support system for victims of reverse discrimination. Like many other groups and individuals who oppose affirmative action and, rightly or wrongly, equate it with reverse discrimination, the board of Adversity.net is critical of the very term. "We use the term *reverse discrimination* reluctantly," it says, "and only because it is so widely understood. In our opinion there really is only one kind of discrimination."

The concept of "reverse discrimination" naturally arises, first, in cases involving discrimination against whites, in situations in which blacks or other minorities receive preference, or second, in cases involving discrimination against males, in situations in which women receive preference. However, the notion that discrimination can manifest itself "in reverse" in any case in which protected categories are favored in an unusual way creates implications for possible reverse discrimination in categories rarely considered—age and national origin, for example. Whereas discrimination based on age or national origin would usually be conceived of as violations against older persons and those of foreign origin, it is possible to conceive of preference being given to exactly these same people, with possible "reverse-discrimination" claims being made by younger persons or those who are American born.

A case that may have serious future implications is *Cline v. General Dynamics Land Systems Inc.*, 296 F.3d 466 (6th Cir. 2002). A group of 196 defense-contractor employees between the ages of forty and forty-nine filed suit when the terms of the employer's retirement health benefits plan were changed so as to apply to those aged fifty when a new collective-bargaining agreement went into effect. After an Ohio federal district court ruled against them on the basis that the situation amounted to "reverse age discrimination," which is not covered by the federal Age Discrimination in Employment Act, the federal appeals court disagreed, finding the situation discrimination "plain and simple," without the dubious modifier "reverse," and the court even noted that "the expression 'reverse discrimination' has no ascertainable meaning under the law."

See also Affirmative Action, Arguments for; Affirmative Action, Criticisms of; African Americans; Benign Discrimination; Center for Individual Rights; Color-Blind Constitution; Compelling Governmental Interest; *DeFunis v. Odegaard*; Department of Labor; Discrimination; Diversity; Education and Affirmative Action; Employment (Private) and Affirmative Action; Employment (Public) and Affirmative Action; Equal Employment Opportunity Commission; Executive Order 10925; Executive Order 11246; Fourteenth Amendment; *Gratz v. Bollinger/Grutter v. Bollinger*; *Hopwood v. Texas*; Japanese Internment and World War II; Johnson, Lyndon Baines; Kennedy, John Fitzgerald; Level Playing Field; Meritocracy; National Association for the Advancement of Colored People; Powell, Lewis Franklin, Jr.; Preferences; Quotas; *Regents of the University of California v. Bakke*; Reparations; Role Model Theory; Segregation; Slavery; Social Engineering; Southern Christian Leadership Conference; Standardized Testing; *Taxman v. Piscataway Township Board of Education*; Urban League.

FURTHER READING: Beckwith, Francis J., and Todd E. Jones, eds., 1997, *Affirmative Action: Social Justice or Reverse Discrimination?* Amherst, NY: Prometheus Books; Eastland, Terry, 1996, *Ending Affirmative Action: The Case for Colorblind Justice*, New York: Basic Books; Gray, W. Robert, 2001, *The Four Faces of Affirmative Action: Fundamental Answers and Actions*, Westport, CT: Greenwood Press; Lynch, Frederick R., 1991, *Invisible Victims: White Males and the Crisis of Affirmative Action*, New York: Praeger; "Reverse Discrimination," 1995, http://www.mdcbowen.org//p2/rm/reports/reverse.html; Skrentny, John David, 1996, *The Ironies of Affirmative Action: Politics, Culture, and Justice in America*, Chicago: University of Chicago Press.

ROBERT A. RUSS

Review of Federal Affirmative Action Programs: Report to the President

See Clinton, William Jefferson.

Rice v. Cayetano, 528 U.S. 495 (2000)

In *Rice v. Cayetano*, the U.S. Supreme Court declared Hawaii's electoral scheme for the Office of Hawaiian Affairs (OHA) in violation of the Fifteenth Amendment. Because the OHA controls certain lands for the benefit of Native Hawaiians, state law allowed only descendants of the indigenous peoples of Hawaii to vote for the trustees of the OHA. In 2000, the Supreme Court ruled that this voting scheme constituted an infringement of the right to vote on account of race in violation of the Fifteenth Amendment to the U.S. Constitution, declining to apply the Supreme Court's earlier approval of preferential programs for Native Americans in *Morton v. Mancari*, 417 U.S. 535 (1974). This decision cast doubt on the availability of racial classifications for Native Hawaiians.

Petitioner Harold F. Rice was a citizen of the state of Hawaii who was not of Native Hawaiian descent, although his ancestors had lived in Hawaii since before the islands were annexed by the United States. When Rice was not allowed to vote in the election for OHA trustees, he brought suit against the governor of Hawaii. He argued that this voting scheme violated his Fourteenth Amendment right to equal protection and his Fifteenth Amendment right to vote. He argued that the voting qualifications, which were based on ancestry, were in fact a proxy for race and should be invalidated as such.

Respondent Benjamin Cayetano was the governor of Hawaii. He argued that the voting scheme was allowed as a reasonable means of providing for a measure of Native Hawaiian sovereignty over lands designated for their benefit, first by the U.S. Congress and later by the state of Hawaii. Cayetano reasoned that the state of Hawaii was administering a trust for the Native Hawaiians similar to the trust relationship between the federal government and many Indian tribes in the continental United States. Cayetano further argued that this voting scheme should be upheld either as a preferential arrangement designed to protect Native Hawaiian sovereignty (similar to the employment preferences upheld in *Morton v. Mancari* or to the restrictions on voting for certain tribes upheld in numerous prior cases) or as an arrangement providing for trustees to be elected by the beneficiaries of the trust.

The Supreme Court ruled for the petitioner, resting its decision primarily on the Fifteenth Amendment right to vote. The majority argued that because the Office of Hawaiian Affairs was an office of the state government, elections for its officers must be open to all citizens of the state regardless of race. The law required that an individual be a "descendent of the aboriginal peoples inhabiting the Hawaiian Islands which exercised sovereignty and subsisted in the Hawaiian Islands in 1778" to vote for OHA officers. Although this classification was not strictly racial, the majority held that this ancestry requirement was a sufficient proxy for race to run afoul of the strict language of the Fifteenth Amendment.

The majority also rejected the state's argument that its should apply *Mancari*. It distinguished *Mancari* in two ways. First, *Mancari* had approved a classification that, although explicitly racial, was primarily aimed at members of federally recognized tribes. Native Hawaiians have never been formally recognized by the U.S. Congress as an Indian tribe. Without federal recognition, Native Hawaiians do not enjoy the special relationship with the federal government that justified the preferences in question in the earlier case. Second, the law in question in *Rice* governed an election for a statewide office and thereby implicated the protections of the Fifteenth Amendment, which are more strict than the equal protection provisions of the Fourteenth Amendment. The Fifteenth Amendment prohibits the abridgment of voting rights on the basis of race without recourse to arguments about self-governance.

In concurrence, Justice Stephen Breyer, joined by Justice David Souter, argued that there was no trust at issue in the case, and that the OHA electorate did not sufficiently resemble a tribe. He found that there was no trust because the provisions of the Statehood Act governing the lands controlled by the OHA made clear that they were intended to benefit all Hawaiians in a variety of ways, as well as Native Hawaiians in particular. Further, not only Native Hawaiians were not recognized by the federal government as a tribe, but their definition here did not resemble a tribe. Nearly all tribes require that an individual have at least one-quarter to one-sixteenth blood quantum and be recognized by other tribal members as a member of the tribe, or as the child of a recognized member. Native Hawaiians have no mechanism for recognizing individuals as part of their community, and the law allows persons with as little as 1/500 blood quantum to qualify to vote as a "Hawaiian." This, he concluded, was unreasonable.

Justices John Paul Stevens and Ruth Bader Ginsburg, writing in dissent, argued that the OHA did in fact operate as a trust and had been delegated autonomy by Congress to promote the special relationship that the United States has with the Native Hawaiians. As evidence of this argument, they pointed out the numerous laws governing Native Americans that include Native Hawaiians under their jurisdiction. They suggested that these laws, considered together with the treaties between the U.S. government and the government of the Kingdom of Hawaii prior to annexation of the islands, were the functional equivalent of recognition of Native Hawaiians as a separate people. They argued further that even if the resources in question were not an "Indian trust," they were a trust for the Native Hawaiians, and that this voting restriction merely allowed the beneficiaries of the trust to control its trustees.

Because this case was decided so recently, it is not possible at this time to assess its long-term effect. While it did not actually overturn *Morton v. Mancari*, the majority declined to extend its logic. Because of that, the *Rice* decision has produced substantial concern among Native American activists, particularly those interested in protecting or extending Native American sovereignty. On a practical level, the *Rice* decision also sparked an initiative by Senator Daniel Inouye, Democrat of Hawaii, to extend federal recognition to Native Hawaiians; that bill had not left committee as of June 2003.

See also Breyer, Stephen Gerald; Equal Protection Clause; Fifteenth Amendment; Fourteenth Amendment; Ginsburg, Ruth Bader; *Morton v. Mancari*; Native Americans; Native Hawaiians; One-Drop Rule; Souter, David Hackett; Stevens, John Paul.

FURTHER READING: Corcoran, Tina L., 2000, "Recent Decision: The Fifteenth Amendment's Prohibition against State Suffrage Restrictions Based upon Race Encompasses Ancestral Restrictions That Are Used as Substitutes for Race: *Rice v. Cayetano*," *Duquesne Law*

Review 39 (fall): 217–241; Kanehe, Le'a Malia, 2001, "Recent Development: The Akaka Bill: The Native Hawaiians' Race for Federal Recognition," *Hawaii Law Review* 23 (summer): 857–906.

RACHEL BOWEN

Rigid Competitive Race Relations Theory

The goal of affirmative action programs is to increase the representation of minorities in organizations and communities from which they have historically been excluded (predominantly by systematic discrimination) by fostering a "level playing field." According to rigid competitive race relations theory, the likelihood of racial conflict and discord increases as the number of minorities increases in these organizations and communities. Therefore, only increasing structural diversity (increasing the number of minorities) is not sufficient for a full realization of diversity benefits. Rather, there must be active commitment and engagement by organizational leaders in fostering an institutional transformation embracing diversity with such programs as diversity management.

Rigid competitive race relations theory was originated by Robert Park of the University of Chicago, who believed that modern American race relations were based upon and grew out of conflict and competition among groups. Park developed the "race relations cycle" to describe the stages of race conflict: contact, competition, conflict, and accommodation. He did not assume that conflict disappears once accommodation is reached. According to Park, "Competition determines the position of the individual in the community; conflict fixes his place in society. Location, position, ecological interdependence—these are the characteristics of the community. Status, subordination, and superordination, control—these are the distinctive marks of a society" (Coser, 359–360).

According to this theory, rigid competition exists when the dominant and non-dominant groups compete for available resources (admission slots, housing, jobs), and the nondominant group already holds fewer resources or the opportunity to increase its share of resources than the dominant group. Rigid competition is most often characterized by groups divided along racial lines. While members of both groups may have similar jobs, for instance, members of the nondominant group are paid less for the same work. There is a tendency for the dominant group to separate the two groups under the philosophy of "separate but equal." Mass action by the nondominant group is prone to occur. Park believed that the process of social change involved a three-stage sequence, or "natural history," beginning first with one group's dissatisfaction with current social conditions and leading to disturbances and social unrest, followed second by mass movements, and finally ending in accommodations within a new institutional order. Social unrest "represents at once a breaking up of the established routine and a preparation for new collective action" (Coser, 360). This theory does not apply only to race. It also applies to groups that are economically or socially disadvantaged and are vying for equality or representation (Native Americans, poor whites, and others). The two groups generally come into contact due to members of one or both populations migrating. The three conditions that exist under this theory are ethnocentrism (judging one's own group to be superior to others and/or judging other groups to be inferior), competition and the opportunity for exploiting another group, and unequal power.

In speaking of race relations in the United States, Park stated, "There is probably less racial prejudice in America than elsewhere, but there is more racial conflict and more racial antagonism. There is more conflict because there is more change, more progress. The Negro is rising in America and the measure of the antagonism he encounters is, in some very real sense, the measure of his progress" (Coser, 362).

See also Diversity Management; Ethnocentrism; Level Playing Field; Relative Deprivation Theory; Riots, Economically and Racially Motivated; Segregation; Socialization Theory of Equality.

FURTHER READING: Coser, Lewis, 1977, *Masters of Sociological Thought: Ideas in Historical and Social Context*, 2d ed., New York: Harcourt, Brace and Jovanovich; Gurin, Patricia, 1999, "Expert Report of Patricia Gurin," in *The Compelling Need for Diversity in Higher Education: Gratz et al. v. Bollinger et al. No. 97-75231 (E.D. Mich.) and Grutter et al. v. Bollinger et al. No. 97-75928 (E.D. Mich.)*, 99–234, Ann Arbor: University of Michigan; Palmer, P., 1990, "Good Teaching: A Matter of Living the Mystery," *Change* 22, no. 1 (January/February): 10–17; Park, Robert, 1950, *Race and Culture*, Glencoe, IL: Free Press; Park, Robert, and Ernest Burgess, 1921, *Introduction to the Science of Sociology*, Chicago: University of Chicago Press.

GLENN L. STARKS

Riots, Economically and Racially Motivated

Many factors and forces (nature, economics, physical threats, psychological fears, and so on) have motivated humans for many centuries to move to other locations. The African American community (and, to a lesser extent, other ethnic cultures) of the twentieth century is no exception. African Americans' quest for economic independence, improved living conditions, and social freedom led them to move from the conservative, overtly segregated South to the more liberal, more subtly segregated climate of the North. As the century progressed, migration continued to other parts of the United States, including the West and, ironically, an economically revived South. As a result of the influx of new residents competing for jobs and housing with existing, predominantly white people, economically and racially motivated riots occurred. Affirmative action programs have therefore been described as a means of crisis management to reduce and/or avoid the phenomena of these riots. In the context of the riots, affirmative action additionally has been described as a "safety valve."

One of the first major economically and racially motivated riots was the East St. Louis, Illinois, riot of 1917. White workers who had attempted to organize a union at the Aluminum Ore Company were replaced by African Americans. Because East St. Louis had been a segregated city prior to the event (schools, housing, and other areas), despite the existence of state and federal laws prohibiting riotous activities, city leaders and others were determined to maintain the status quo with retaliation against the African American Community. Based on a news report that a white man had been wounded by an African American suspect during a liquor store holdup, the white Aluminum Ore strikers burned black-owned homes and stores. The African American community retaliated, Illinois National

Guard troops were called in, and forty-one people (thirty-nine African Americans and two whites) were killed, with an additional 750 injured.

Continuing a nationwide trend of economically and racially motivated riots that took place during and after World War I from 1917 to 1923, the Tulsa Race War of 1921 resulted in the burning of thirty city blocks in the segregated area of Tulsa, Oklahoma, known as Greenwood. The riot developed in response to an African American–led protest of an impending lynching of a black man for assaulting a white woman. Because the protesters were armed, white residents, fearing for their safety, retaliated. Once again, National Guard (Oklahoma) troops were called in to quell the violence.

Another major riot in this period of unrest took place not in the African Americans' migratory destination of the North but in the South, where Jim Crow laws and blatant discrimination were common. In Rosewood, Florida, a series of lynching deaths and other acts of white retaliation against blacks came to a climax during January 1923 when the entire town was destroyed by angry white protesters. More than 500 whites descended on Rosewood over a two-day period to cause the calamity.

Analysis of what could be classified as the early economically and racially motivated riots reveals the conditions that contributed to their generation (as well as the incubation and generation of later economic/racial riots). After World War I, the massive influx of veterans who reentered the workforce caused the competition for jobs to increase in an economic environment no longer supported by the war effort. Since more African Americans (and other ethnic groups) were entering the traditionally white-dominated workforce, the job pool became crowded. Furthermore, no laws restricting employment based on race or other factors existed, and such employments reinforces the socially based racial inequality that existed at the same time.

The Great Depression was a period of relative calm, as whites and ethnic groups generally suffered economic distress together. However, World War II changed the economic and social climate once again and led to another onslaught of riots. The Zoot Suit Riots of 1943 (also called the Sailor Riots) involved another minority group, Latin Americans. White fears of Latinos from a social and economic standpoint—further enhanced by goods rationing (e.g., food, clothing, and petroleum) and threats to American patriotism as a result of World War II—incited more than 200 navy sailors on shore leave to attack Mexican American *pachucos* ("gang" members noted for wearing "zoot suits," a tailored suit popular at that time) in East Los Angeles. More than 600 Latin Americans were arrested while no military personnel were punished.

Another major riot occurred during this same period in Detroit, Michigan. The result of racially motivated events that took place at a popular amusement park, Belle Isle, the Detroit riots of 1943 lasted for several days and required the positioning of 6,000 Michigan National Guard troops throughout the city, the closing of schools and offices, and the elimination of all unnecessary activity by order of Michigan governor Harry Frances Kelly. As in prior riots, white fears of a social and economic nature—including a strong presence of the Ku Klux Klan in Detroit factories and neighborhoods—led to racial strife and property destruction.

Immediately following World War II, the country experienced an unprecedented postwar economic boom. There were no major race riots during this period. The next round of major riots did not occur until the mid-1960s. At this time, the rioting reached its peak, with a series of major riots occurring within a two-year period. Scholars say that these riots resulted from the changing social structure and economic landscape brought to the forefront of American consciousness by the ongoing Vietnamese conflict.

Passage of California Proposition 14, legislation aimed at blocking the fair-housing portion of the 1964 Civil Rights Act, resulted in a six-day riot. The Watts riots of 1965 left thirty-four people dead, 1,000 injured, 4,000 arrested, and millions of dollars in property damage. Similarly, the existence of overcrowding, overpriced housing, poverty, and joblessness in the Hough neighborhood of Cleveland's East Side led to the Hough and Glennville riots of 1966. Four days of intense unrest resulted in four African American deaths and destruction of millions of dollars in property throughout the Cleveland area. In 1967, another Detroit riot ensued. This time, 43 people were killed, 700 were injured, and 7,231 people were detained by government order due to the destruction of $50 million in property from 1,685 fires.

While major riots occurred during the latter third of the twentieth century, including riots in Baltimore, Maryland (1974), Miami–Liberty City, Florida (1989), Los Angeles, California (1992), and St. Petersburg, Florida (1996), significant changes in workers' rights laws and affirmative action lessened the impact of potential riots and their widespread catastrophic effects on human life and property. It is for this reason that some have described affirmative action as a crisis management tool needed in the 1960s and 1970s to avoid riots and other acts of violence.

See also Civil Rights Act of 1964; Civil Rights Movement; Jim Crow Laws; Kerner Commission; Relative Deprivation Theory; Segregation.

FURTHER READING: Brophy, Alfred C., 2002, *Reconstructing the Dreamland: The Tulsa Riot of 1921*, New York: Oxford University Press; Bullock, Paul, ed., 1969, *Watts: The Aftermath: An Inside View of the Ghetto*, New York: Grove Press; Conot, Robert, 1968, *Rivers of Blood, Years of Darkness: The Unforgettable Classic Account of the Watts Riot*, New York: William Morrow; D'Orso, Michael, 1996, *Like Judgment Day: The Ruin and Redemption of a Town Called Rosewood*, New York: G.P. Putnam's Sons; Dye, R. Thomas, 1996, "Rosewood, Florida: The Destruction of an African American Community," *Historian: A Journal of History* 58, no. 3 (spring): 605–622; Hendrickson, Wilma Wood, ed., 1991, *Detroit Perspectives: Crossroads and Turning Points*, Detroit: Wayne State University Press; Hirsch, James S., 2002, *Riot and Remembrance: The Tulsa Race War and Its Legacy*, Boston: Houghton Mifflin; Mazon, Mauricio, 1984, *The Zoot Suit Riots*, Austin: University of Texas Press; Norris, Harold, 1991, "Oral History," in *Untold Tales, Unsung Heroes: An Oral History of Detroit's African American Community, 1918–1967*, edited by Elaine Latzman Moon, Detroit: Wayne State University Press; Shogan, Robert, and Tom Craig, 1963, *The Detroit Race Riot: A Study in Violence*, Philadelphia: Chilton Books; Taylor, John, 1994, "The Rosewood Massacre," *Esquire* 122, no. 1 (July): 46–53.

THOMAS A. ADAMICH

Roberts v. City of Boston, 59 Mass. 198 (1849)

Roberts v. City of Boston was the first case in which a court articulated the separate-but-equal doctrine. The case, mounted by black citizens of Boston, Massachusetts, was a challenge to the segregated school system of which they were forced to be a part. The Supreme Court of Massachusetts held that "colored persons are entitled by law, in this commonwealth, to equal rights, constitutional and political, civil and social"; however, providing separate schools for black children did not violate these rights. The lawsuit was based upon equal protection provisions in the Massachusetts Constitution. The lawsuit did not rely on federal law and preceded the advent of the Fourteenth Amendment's Equal Protection Clause by nearly two decades.

The Boston School Committee was charged with overseeing all public schools within the city limits. The committee established and administered 160 primary schools for the children of its jurisdiction. Two of these schools were designated to be used exclusively to educate the black children of the city. The remaining 158 were reserved for whites only. The plaintiff in this case was a black child named Sarah Roberts. Sarah's father had attempted to enroll her in the primary school nearest her home. Sarah was denied enrollment because this school was reserved for white students only. Instead, she was forced to travel past five white schools on her way to the exclusively black school that she was ordered to attend. On her behalf, her father challenged this order and the school committee's establishment of separate schools for black children as unfair and a violation of the equality of rights among different citizens in the Commonwealth of Massachusetts.

The attorney for the plaintiff was Charles Sumner, the famed abolitionist, a future U.S. senator from Massachusetts, and one of the chief architects of the Civil War (Reconstruction) Amendments. Sumner argued that separating children into different schools purely because of their race was tantamount to establishing a caste system. This was a violation of the equality guaranteed to all citizens by the courts and the legislature of the Commonwealth of Massachusetts. In his argument, he stated that "a school exclusively devoted to one class must differ essentially, in its spirit and character, from that public school known to the law, where all classes meet together in equality. . . . [Black children] have an equal right with the white children to the general public schools." This argument is almost identical to that adopted 105 years later by the U.S. Supreme Court in its *Brown v. Board of Education*, 347 U.S. 483 (1954), opinion.

The decision of the Massachusetts Supreme Court was written by Chief Justice Lemuel Shaw. He found that Sumner's principles of equality were correct. All citizens were entitled to equal protection under the law of the commonwealth. However, he stated that the law could, and should, treat people differently in accordance with their station in life. The prejudice to which Sumner was referring, he stated, was not created by the law and, in turn, could not be changed by the law. He concluded that the establishment of exclusively black schools was not a violation of equality. Therefore, the decision of the school committee to require Sarah Roberts to attend the all-black school was upheld.

Forty-seven years later, the United States faced the question of equality in separate facilities for black and white persons in *Plessy v. Ferguson*, 163 U.S. 537 (1896). Despite the difference in public facilities at issue in the two cases (separate railroad car in *Plessy*; separate school in *Roberts*), the Court's opinion in the *Plessy* case was remarkably similar to that of Chief Justice Shaw's opinion in the *Roberts* case. The Court found that although blacks and whites were each segregated to different public facilities based upon race, the treatment each group received was equal to that received by their counterparts, at least according to the Court. It would not be until more than half a century after *Plessy* in the famous *Brown v. Board of Education* case that the Supreme Court would reverse the separate-but-equal doctrine in the education context.

See also Brown v. Board of Education; Caste System; Civil War (Reconstruction) Amendments and Civil Rights Acts; Equal Protection Clause; Fourteenth Amendment; *Plessy v. Ferguson.*

FURTHER READING: Kull, Andrew, 1992, *The Color-Blind Constitution*, Cambridge, MA: Harvard University Press.

AIMÉE HOBBY RHODES

Role Model Theory

The role model theory has been put forth by proponents of affirmative action in the last several decades in an attempt to justify affirmative action plans. The role model theory claims that traditionally underrepresented minority students (minority racial and/or female students) require teachers and leaders of their own race and/or gender who will serve as role models to the students, thereby enabling the students to reach their highest academic and professional potential. The theory argues that by being exposed to other members of the same race or gender who have achieved academic and/or professional success and accomplishments, the students are then inspired to achieve the same or a greater level of success.

Proponents of this theory also allege that the most prominent colleges and universities have a duty to extend special admissions privileges to minorities or women. These individuals will then graduate as lawyers, teachers, and doctors from the best college programs available, return to their minority communities, and inspire young people from their respective races to also aspire to attend prominent schools and increase the ranks of minorities in professional fields. Promoters of the theory argue that if minority students are only exposed to white male teachers and doctors, they will never fully believe that they too can progress in these fields.

The role model theory has been utilized in support of the use of racial preferences or affirmative action plans. In *Regents of the University of California v. Bakke*, 438 U.S. 265 (1978), for example, the University of California attempted to justify its affirmative action program, in part, because some of the minority students would later serve as role models for other students. Likewise, in two other Supreme Court cases (*Taxman v. Piscataway Township Board of Education*, 118 S. Ct. 595 [1997], and *Wygant v. Jackson Board of Education*, 476 U.S. 267 [1986]), the role model theory was utilized by the defendants in the hopes that the theory would lend justification to their actions based upon racial considerations. In *Taxman*, the defense sought to justify the school board's continued employment of the only black teacher in the business department over the firing of a white teacher with equal seniority by contending that there was a need for a black role model for students and the promotion of racial diversity. In *Wygant v. Jackson Board of Education*, the defense justified its race-conscious layoff of a white teacher as necessary to maintain minority faculty role models and to remedy past discrimination.

Despite these attempts to utilize the role model theory as a legal justification for racial preferences or discrimination, the U.S. Supreme Court has rejected the notion that the role model theory serves as a compelling state interest and has held that it cannot justify discrimination. In the *Wygant* decision, Justice Lewis Powell expressly rejected the role model theory under the Fourteenth Amendment and held that such a theory had "no logical stopping point," which would permit "the Board to engage in discriminatory hiring and layoff practices long past the point required by any legitimate remedial purpose." Further, Justice Powell likened the race role model theory to the rationale utilized to support separatist theory in *Plessy v. Ferguson*, a rationale ultimately rejected in *Brown v. Board of Education.*

The Supreme Court has subsequently reaffirmed its rejection of reliance on the role model theory to support efforts at diversification. In *City of Richmond v. J.A. Croson Co.*, 488 U.S. 469 (1989), for example, the Court was deciding whether Richmond's set-aside program for minority contractors was valid under the Fourteenth Amendment. In rejecting Richmond's attempts at promoting minority contractors, the Court stated: "Like the 'role-model' theory employed in *Wygant*, a generalized assertion that there has been past discrimination in an entire industry provides no guidance for a legislative body to determine the precise scope of the injury it seeks to remedy. It 'has no logical stopping point.' "

Notwithstanding the constitutional problems, opponents of the role model theory have also put forth other criticisms. First and foremost is that the potential achievement of some students based on racial factors cannot be supported at the expense of the rest of society. Second, the role model theory promotes the interests of a particular race while denying the civil rights of individuals. For example, while the interests of many minority students may be promoted by the retention of a minority teacher, this is done by sacrificing and ignoring the civil rights of nonminority teachers. Third, the concept of a role model diverts attention away from real problems and impediments of infrastructure and power.

See also Brown v. Board of Education; City of Richmond v. J.A. Croson Co.; Drug Abuse Education Act of 1970; *Plessy v. Ferguson*; Powell, Lewis Franklin, Jr.; *Regents of the University of California v. Bakke*; Talented Tenth; *Taxman v. Piscataway Township Board of Education; Wygant v. Jackson Board of Education.*

FURTHER READING: Addis, Adeno, 1996, "Role Models and the Politics of Recognition," *University of Pennsylvania Law Review* 144 (April): 1377–1468; Chin, Gabriel J., ed., 1998, *Affirmative Action and the Constitution*, vol. 3, *Judicial Reaction to Affirmative Action, 1989–1997: Things Fall Apart*, New York and London: Garland Publishing; Thomas, June Manning, and Marsha Ritzdorf, eds., 1997, *Urban Planning and the African American Community: In the Shadows*, Thousand Oaks, CA: Sage Publications.

GLENN L. STARKS

Roosevelt, Eleanor (1884–1962)

Eleanor Roosevelt (ER) will long be remembered as one of the most influential women of the twentieth century. While living through some of the most dramatic and challenging events in modern history, she was steadfastly committed to American democracy, humanitarian ideals, and the inherent worth of every human being. ER repeatedly challenged America to recognize that racial injustice was the biggest threat to American democracy. She was also instrumental in the passage of the now-famous Universal Declaration of Human Rights, which today forms the international law foundation regarding notions of individual equality and affirmative action programs. Her commitment to racial justice was so public and common that she became synonymous with early demands for civil rights. Upon her death, Martin Luther King wrote of her that "the courage she displayed taking sides on matters considered controversial, gave strength to those who risked only pedestrian loyalty and commitment to the great issues of our times" (Black 1996).

Eleanor Roosevelt was born in New York City on October 11, 1884, to a prominent family, her uncle being Theodore Roosevelt. Her parents died at an early age, and she was raised by her maternal grandmother. At the age of fifteen, she was sent to a boarding school in England and returned to the United States in 1902. In 1905, she married a distant cousin, Franklin Delano Roosevelt, and her uncle, the current president, gave away the bride. They had six children, one of whom died in infancy. From marriage to the day of Franklin's death, Eleanor dedicated her life to his purposes. She diligently aided Franklin's political career, starting from his early days in the New York State Senate to the successful presidential election of 1932. ER dramatically changed the role of the first lady into that of a critical assistant to the president. In general, she was more liberal than the president and worked hard to promote racial equality.

As soon as she became first lady in 1933, ER let the country know that she believed that racism was wrong and that she would try to improve the life of African Americans. A few days after moving into the White House, she announced that she would only hire black servants. This may seem peculiar today, but the blacks on the White House staff from the previous president anticipated being removed due to their race. During her tenure as the nation's longest-serving first lady, she consistently lobbied to help the disadvantaged and sought a gradual removal of segregation, often traveling to black communities and institutions and representing civil rights in New Deal days when the term was not even known. On one notable occasion in 1939, when the Daughters of the American Revolution had refused to let the great black contralto Marian Anderson sing in Constitution Hall in segregated Washington, D.C., the First Lady resigned her membership in the group and sponsored a free open-air concert at the Lincoln Memorial. Seventy-five thousand people attended, and the incident became a symbolic landmark in the struggle to end discrimination. Subsequently, ER invited Anderson to the White House to perform before Britain's king and queen. ER had many significant black political colleagues, including Mary McLeod Bethune, A. Philip Randolph, W.E.B. Du Bois, Pauli Murray, and Walter White.

During World War II (1939–1945), ER visited American soldiers around the world and championed desegregation of the armed forces. After Franklin passed away in 1945, she was nominated to the national board of the NAACP and expected a much quieter life at her New York farm, Val Kill. However, President Harry Truman had other ideas. With the formation of the United Nations (UN) after World War II, shrewd, effective communicators were necessary to serve as delegates, and Truman appointed her as a member of the U.S. delegation in 1945. One of the critical tasks of the UN was to create and have ratified an international treaty that deftly articulated the fundamental and inalienable rights of all members of the human family. The delegates on the subcommittee responsible for drafting this document elected Eleanor as their chairperson. After several years of work, the Universal Declaration of Human Rights (UDHR) was ratified on December 10, 1958. It represented the first comprehensive agreement among nations as to the specific rights and freedoms of all human beings. The UDHR has become a cornerstone of customary international law, binding all governments to its principles.

Though ER participated little in the actual drafting of the UDHR, it is hard to imagine how it could have been brought to completion without her. Mary Ann Weldon wrote that ER's efforts in drafting the UDHR were historically "analogous to George Washington's chairmanship of the Constitutional Convention. While the Constitution was framed by others, Washington's presence is commonly held to have been decisive for its acceptance, owing to the great respect in which he was held" (Weldon, 206). ER felt that the UDHR was her greatest lifetime accomplishment, and Martin Luther King warmly embraced it.

ER did not take an active part in the 1948 and 1952 presidential campaigns because of her responsibilities to the UN. However, after resigning from her appointment, she vocalized her increasing disenchantment with Dwight Eisenhower's leadership and became a strong proponent of Democratic Party leader Adlai Stevenson. In the 1960 election, she redirected her support to the more civil rights–oriented Democratic candidate, John F. Kennedy. Eleanor Roosevelt died in 1962 and was buried in the rose garden at Hyde Park next to her husband. Her Democratic protégé Adlai Stevenson best summed up her lifelong philosophy: "She would rather light a candle than curse the darkness" (New York Times 1962, 34).

See also African Americans; Bethune, Mary Jane McLeod; Du Bois, William Edward Burghardt; Eisenhower, Dwight David; Kennedy, John Fitzgerald; King, Martin Luther, Jr.; Randolph, Asa Philip; Roosevelt, Franklin Delano; Truman, Harry.

FURTHER READING: Black, Allida M., 1996, *Casting Her Own Shadow: Eleanor Roosevelt and the Shaping of Postwar Liberalism*, New York: Columbia University Press; Black, Allida M., 1996, "Championing Civil Rights, http://www.thirdworldtraveler.com/Roosevelt_Eleanor/ Championing_ER_CHOS.html; Lash, Joseph P., 1984, *A World of Love*, Garden City, NY: Doubleday; New York Times, 1962, "Tribute to Eleanor Roosevelt," November 7, 34; Weldon, Mary A., 2001, *A World Made New: Eleanor Roosevelt and the Universal Declaration of Human Rights*, New York: Random House.

PETER L. PLATTEBORZE

Roosevelt, Franklin Delano (1882–1945)

As the thirty-second president of the United States, Franklin Delano Roosevelt served from 1933 to 1945 and was considered supportive of early civil rights efforts, in large part due to the efforts of his wife, Eleanor Roosevelt. In the area of racial equality, Roosevelt issued Executive Order 8802, which forbade employment discrimination in the government and in defense industries. This executive order served as a model for later executive orders issued by Presidents Harry Truman, and John F. Kennedy, and Lyndon Johnson to achieve a semblance of racial equality in the public employment and federal contracting contexts, notably Kennedy's famous Executive Order 10925, which mandated "affirmative action" in federal contracting.

Roosevelt was elected to serve four terms as president and is the only U.S. president to have this distinction. He won presidential elections over Herbert Hoover in 1932, Alfred Landon in 1936, Wendell Willkie in 1940, and Thomas Dewey in 1944. The country suffered a number of unprecedented challenges during the time he was president. Under his leadership, the nation emerged from the devastation of the Great Depression. He was in the forefront of the Allies' struggle to win World War II. Along with Winston Churchill, Great Britain's prime minister, Roosevelt made strategic and military decisions that ultimately resulted in victory for the Allies over the Axis powers in World War II. He also forged a new and different role for government on the domestic front.

Roosevelt's presidency left an indelible mark on the country. He and his reform-minded advisors introduced and implemented a model interventionist state. Government's role was greatly expanded through the establishment of numerous agencies, programs, and initiatives that stimulated a wave of social and economic change. While many Americans benefited from these governmental changes, by far the major enthusiasts of the new governmental policy known as the New Deal were minorities (primarily African Americans), urban dwellers, and the working class.

Franklin Delano Roosevelt was born on January 30, 1882, in Hyde Park, New York, to James and Sara Delano Roosevelt. His family was wealthy. Governesses and private tutors were responsible for his early education. He traveled to Europe and generally enjoyed a life of privilege. By 1896, he had entered prestigious Groton School in Massachusetts. It is widely believed that it was at Groton that the passion for public service was awakened in this future president. His formal education continued at Harvard University, where he completed his studies in three years, and at Columbia University Law School. While Roosevelt left Columbia before receiving his law degree, he was able to pass the bar examination prior to leaving law school. Thus he was able to practice law, which he did for several years.

On March 17, 1905, Franklin Delano Roosevelt and Anna Eleanor Roosevelt (distant cousins) were married. Another distant relative, President Theodore (Teddy) Roosevelt, gave the bride away. Eleanor's father, Elliott, was the brother of President Theodore Roosevelt. From that union, six children were born, Anna, James, Elliott, Franklin, John, and one child who died in infancy.

Despite the fact that young Franklin cast his first presidential vote in 1904 for his Republican relative, Theodore Roosevelt, and that he had been an active member of a Young Republican group at Harvard, he himself was an unabashed liberal and a Democrat throughout his adult life. He rose from New York state senator to assistant secretary of the navy, candidate for vice president, and governor of New York.

In the midst of what appeared to be a charmed political career, Roosevelt suffered a debilitating blow. In 1921, he contracted poliomyelitis, which left him confined to a wheelchair for the rest of his life. Sometimes he would use heavy, awkward leg braces to assist him in standing and limited walking. His indomitable spirit and support from family and friends triumphed. After getting polio, he went on to become governor of New York and later president of the United States.

Upon assuming the presidency, Roosevelt began the massive government reform agenda that is known as the New Deal. Relief, recovery, and reform were the goals of this bold new plan. The following are some of the results: the Federal

President Franklin D. Roosevelt waves a hearty greeting to neighbors who ended a torchlight parade on election night at his home in Hyde Park, New York, on November 7, 1944. Roosevelt was reelected, becoming the only president of the United States to serve four consecutive terms in office. Standing directly behind him is his daughter, Anna Eleanor, and at his right is First Lady Eleanor Roosevelt. © AP/Wide World Photos.

Banking Act/Federal Deposit Insurance Corporation (FDIC); the Federal Emergency Relief Administration (FERA); the Civil Works Administration (CWA); the National Industrial Recovery Act (NIRA); the Indian Reorganization Act of 1934; the Public Works Association (PWA); the Securities and Exchange Commission (SEC); the Home Owners Loan Corporation (HOLC); the Agricultural Adjustment Administration (AAA); the Tennessee Valley Authority (TVA); the Works Progress Administration (WPA); the Farm Security Administration (FSA); the National Labor Relations Board (NLRB); the Fair Labor Standards Act; the Social Security Act (SSA); and the National Youth Administration (NYA).

All of these initiatives served to change the way that the government operated and the perception that many citizens had of their government prior to the New Deal. Often the government, programs, projects, and agencies were known by letters of the alphabet. Collectively they were labeled as "alphabet soups." It has been observed that even the president was frequently referred to as FDR instead of by his full name.

Millions of ordinary Americans from all walks of life were helped by the New Deal, including many blacks and other minorities. For the first time, many who had not believed in the government in the past began to have faith in the power of inclusion by their government. Although affirmative action had not yet become a familiar phrase, the policies and practices of the New Deal opened doors for some that previously had been closed.

During the New Deal, not only did the president rely on his trusted advisors, referred to as the "brain trust," but he frequently consulted with another group known variously as the "black cabinet" or the "kitchen cabinet." The role of this group was to advise the president on all matters relative to African Americans. The leader of this group was Mary McLeod Bethune, the respected educator and social activist. Some other well-known members of the group were William H. Hasties, lawyer and judge, and Robert Weaver, future cabinet member and college president. Bethune became the first African American woman to be appointed to a position at this level in the federal government, as the director of the Division of Negro Affairs in the National Youth Administration (NYA).

These were encouraging signs of change for African Americans, but all was not perfect. First, while the New Deal was notably supported by some voters, there were others who strongly opposed it. Some who spoke out against the new government policies and programs accused the administration of moving the country toward socialism. Second, even among Roosevelt's staunchest supporters, there was discontent. Responding to rising frustrations by African Americans, specifically about their exclusion from employment in the thriving defense industry, A. Philip Randolph, a leader of the Brotherhood of Sleeping Car Porters, and others proposed a huge protest march on Washington, D.C. President Roosevelt responded to this by issuing Executive Order 8802 forbidding employment discrimination in government and the defense industry. Also, the Fair Employment Practices Commission was created to handle discrimination complaints. The march was called off. In addition to including minorities in the New Deal, Roosevelt was the first president in the history of the United States to appoint a woman to a cabinet position. She was Frances Perkins, secretary of labor.

While Roosevelt was conducting the formal business of government in the executive branch, his wife, Eleanor Roosevelt, was working vigorously and tirelessly on social and racial issues as the first lady. She was friendly with several African Americans of the era and advocated for equality on their behalf. Some of her high-profile friends among the leadership ranks in the African American community were Mary McLeod Bethune, Walter White, and Ralph Bunche. From the time of the marriage, Eleanor Roosevelt was a partner to her husband. Often she is described as being among the most, if not the most, active, hardworking, and effective first ladies in U.S. history. As her husband's health declined, Eleanor Roosevelt became even more involved. Many African Americans viewed her as a direct pipeline to the president. She demonstrated in many ways her support for social and political equality for all Americans. In the eyes of many, she solidified this perception when in 1939, Marian Anderson, the famous African American contralto, was refused the right to perform in Constitution Hall by the Daughters of American Revolution. In protest, Eleanor Roosevelt resigned her membership in the organization.

The president, the New Deal reformers, his wife, and those who believed in the New Deal laid the foundation for a new vision of liberalism and a kind of responsiveness by government that had not been seen before. It resonated decades later in new affirmative action and equal opportunity policies by the government.

After the experience of World War II, President Roosevelt supported the founding of the United Nations. His vision was to ensure peace in the world. His wife, Eleanor, was instrumental in securing passage of the United Nations General Assembly's Universal Declaration of Human Rights. While Franklin Roosevelt did not live to see the United Nations, Eleanor Roosevelt was able to exercise a prominent role in the founding meeting and in the eventual promulgation.

President Franklin D. Roosevelt died of a cerebral hemorrhage on April 12, 1945, in Warm Springs, Georgia, just a few months after winning his fourth and last election. His death occurred less than a month before Germany surrendered in World War II. He was buried far from Washington in his mother's rose garden in Hyde Park, New York.

See also African Americans; Bethune, Mary Jane McLeod; Brotherhood of Sleeping Car Porters; Executive Order 8802; Johnson, Lyndon Baines; Kennedy, John Fitzgerald; Randolph, Asa Philip; Roosevelt, Eleanor; Truman, Harry.

FURTHER READING: Burns, James M., 1990, *Roosevelt: The Soldier of Freedom, 1940–1945*, Harcourt; New York: Goodwin, Doris Kearns, 1995, *No Ordinary Time: Franklin and Eleanor Roosevelt: The Home Front in World War II*, New York: Simon and Schuster; Patterson, James T., 1967, *Congressional Conservatism and the New Deal: The Growth of the Conservative Coalition in Congress, 1933–1939*, Lexington: University of Kentucky Press; Schlesinger, Arthur M., Jr., 1940, *The New Deal in Action, 1933–1938*, New York: Macmillan; Tugwell, Rexford, 1977, *Roosevelt's Revolution*, New York: Macmillan.

BETTY NYANGONI

S

Sacrificial Lamb

See Scapegoating/Displaced-Aggression Theories.

San Antonio School District v. Rodriguez, 411 U.S. 1 (1973)

The Supreme Court case *San Antonio School District v. Rodriguez* addressed the question of equity in public school funding. The suit charged that the method the state of Texas employed to generate school revenues violated the Equal Protection Clause of the Fourteenth Amendment of the U.S. Constitution in that the method employed resulted in the affluent school districts receiving roughly twice the funding that the poorer school systems received. In a close 5–4 ruling, the Supreme Court ruled that Texas's method was not unconstitutional in that the difference in funding between school districts was based not upon an impermissible classification (race), but rather upon indigence. The Court in essence held that socioeconomic discrimination is not a classification that violates the Fourteenth Amendment. Socioeconomic status is often put forward as a race-neutral alternative to race-based or race-conscious affirmative action plans.

The suit in *San Antonio School District* was brought on behalf of schoolchildren who resided in one of the poorer school districts in San Antonio, Texas. The children in more affluent school districts received almost twice as much funding for their education as those in poorer districts. Public schools in Texas were funded primarily from local property taxes rather than general state revenues. State law forbade any local municipality from taxing the property in one school district at a higher rate than in any other district: that is, a school district with property values lower than other school districts could not make up the difference by taxing property at a significantly higher rate. There was no disagreement within the Court that the method of generating school revenues in Texas resulted in uneven levels of support throughout the state as well as in the city of San Antonio. Nor was there any substantial disagreement that these uneven levels of support might well contribute to uneven levels of educational opportunity. Nonetheless, the majority held that this inequity was a political matter, not a constitutional one.

The majority opinion focused first on the question of substantive rights. There was no right to an education, either stated or implied, in the U.S. Constitution, the majority held. Each state was free to develop a method of public education or not to develop one. If a state chose to initiate a public education system, then it must do so for all children within the state. The state of Texas was doing just this, the majority concluded. Although the method Texas employed did lead to inequities among school districts, no child was denied the opportunity to receive some kind of public education. The Court took judicial notice of earlier rulings with respect to substantive rights more clearly guaranteed or at least implied in the federal Constitution, such as the right to counsel in a criminal proceeding even if the accused cannot afford counsel. The majority noted that such a right did not entitle the indigent to the best counsel money could buy, but only to some kind of counsel.

The majority further rejected the argument that there was any discriminatory behavior on the part of the state. There was no claim that the method Texas employed was designed to segregate students on the basis of race or any other specific characteristic. The majority noted that all the states but one employed the same method of generating public school revenue. The fact that there was a greater proportion of blacks and other racial minorities living in poorer school districts did not on its face suggest that the purpose of the state's method of funding schools was to establish or maintain racial barriers. The majority rejected as well the argument that "the poor" were themselves a "suspect class" of people and were therefore entitled to a stricter method of judicial scrutiny. Essentially, the majority rejected the idea that wealth is a basis for establishing a case of discrimination.

In short, the majority held that there were no violations of the Fourteenth Amendment based upon the treatment of individuals from different socioeconomic characteristics. Further, if the "right" in question were a fundamental one, such as the freedom of speech, especially political speech, then a state attempting to restrict this right must show a legitimate state interest compelling enough to overcome a presumption that strongly favored the freedom of speech. However, in this case, there was no federal, constitutional right to an education at all, much less a fundamental right. Second, the method of public school funding in Texas did provide each and every student in Texas with a public education. The fact that some school districts, as a result of higher property tax revenues, could afford to spend more money on education than other, poorer school districts did not result in denying any child a public education. Whether the state of Texas should provide equal funding to all students was a political question as well as one of policy better left to the Texas legislature, the majority concluded. It was not a federal, constitutional question.

In a concurring opinion, Justice Potter Stewart wrote, "The method of financing public schools in Texas, as in almost every other State, has resulted in a system of public education that can fairly be described as chaotic and unjust." Nonetheless, Stewart voted with the majority that this system did not violate any part of the U.S. Constitution. In a dissenting opinion, Justice Thurgood Marshall argued that the method of school funding in Texas did lead to racial segregation in effect. Most blacks and other racial minorities could not afford to live within wealthier school districts with a tax base high enough to provide for a quality education. The disenfranchised could not compete "on a level playing field" for jobs or opportunities in higher education, especially at the more prestigious universities. As a result, Marshall argued, they earned less and could not, in turn, afford to live within a school district that provided their children with a quality education. The system in Texas was self-perpetuating and discriminatory in its effect, Marshall concluded.

See also Economically Disadvantaged; Equal Protection Clause; Fourteenth Amendment; Level Playing Field; Marshall, Thurgood; Rational Basis Scrutiny; Segregation; Suspect Classification.

FURTHER READING: Bell, Derrick, 2000, *Race, Racism, and American Law,* 4th ed., New York: Panel Publishers; Clune, William, 1992, "New Answers to Hard Questions Posed by *Rodriguez:* Ending the Separation of School Finance and Educational Policy by Bridging the Gap between Wrong and Remedy," *Connecticut Law Review* 24:721–755; Howe, Kenneth, 1997, *Understanding Equal Educational Opportunity: Social Justice, Democracy, and Schooling,* New York: Teachers College Press; Kahlenberg, Richard, 2001, *All Together Now: The Case for Economic Integration in the Public Schools,* Washington, DC: Brookings Institution Press; Powell, John, 2001, "The Tensions between Integration and School Reform," *Hastings Constitutional Law Quarterly* 28:655–697; Sayfie, Justin, 1994, "Education Emancipation for Inner City Students: A New Legal Paradigm for Achieving Equality of Educational Opportunity," *University of Miami Law Review* 48:913–947; True-Frost, Cora, 2001, "Beyond Levittown towards a Quality Education for All Children: Litigating High Minimum Standards for Public Education," *Syracuse Law Review* 51:1015–1041; Washburn, Andrew, 2001, "Campaign for Fiscal Equity v. State: A Template for Education Transformation in New York," *Buffalo Law Review* 49:489–512; Wise, Arthur, 1969, *Rich Schools, Poor Schools: The Promise of Equal Opportunity Education,* Chicago: University of Chicago Press.

MICHAEL D. QUIGLEY

Scalia, Antonin (1936–   )

Associate Justice Antonin Scalia was appointed to the U.S. Supreme Court by President Ronald Reagan in 1986. One scholar noted that "[c]ertainly, on one issue, affirmative action, Scalia came to the bench and the High Court as close to a 'sure thing' as any President could desire on any administration's social agenda." Scalia is known for his conservative ideology and for his outspoken views regarding constitutional interpretation. Scalia believes that the Constitution should be interpreted according to its original meaning. He looks for "a sort of 'objectified' intent—the intent that a reasonable person would gather from the text of the law." (Scalia 1997, 17). On the Supreme Court, Scalia has consistently voted against affirmative action plans, arguing that affirmative action perpetuates racial hatred by dividing the country into races. According to Scalia in his concurring opinion in *Adarand Constructors, Inc. v. Pena* (1995), the U.S. Constitution is color blind. "In the eyes of government, we are just one race here. It is American." Scalia believes that the way to end discrimination is through race-neutral laws.

Scalia was born in Trenton, New Jersey, on March 11, 1936. His father, an Italian immigrant, was a college professor, and his mother was an elementary-school teacher. Scalia was an intelligent student, graduating first in his high-school class. He also graduated first in his class from Georgetown University. He then attended Harvard Law School, where he was a member of the law review. After graduation, he married and worked for six years as an associate with Jones, Day, Cockley, and Reavis in Cleveland. He then accepted a position on the faculty of the University of Virginia Law School. He developed a specialty in administrative law and became general counsel to the White House Office of Telecommunications. In 1974, Scalia moved to the Department of Justice as assistant attorney general in charge of the Office of Legal Counsel, the office that provides legal advice to the president. Scalia remained at the Justice Department until January 1977 and then spent six months at the American Enterprise Institute, a conservative research organization. He then accepted a position as a professor at the University of Chicago School of Law.

While Scalia was a professor at Chicago, he wrote a law review article titled "The Disease as Cure," in which he criticized the Supreme Court's affirmative action jurisprudence, stating that it was an "embarrassment to teach." Scalia objected to affirmative action both on principle and because he did not believe that it could effectively overcome discrimination. According to Scalia, "I owe no man anything, nor he me, because of the blood that flows in our veins." He argued that affirmative action is racist, and "from racist principles flow racist results." However, Scalia did state that he was in favor of giving preferences to the poor and disadvantaged. "But I am not willing to prefer to the son of a prosperous and well-educated black doctor or lawyer—solely because of his race." Scalia also objected to gender affirmative action for essentially the same reasons (Scalia, 151–153).

In 1982, Scalia was appointed to the U.S. Court of Appeals for the District of Columbia Circuit, where he served until he was appointed to the Supreme Court in the summer of 1986. During his confirmation hearings, Scalia was questioned regarding his views on affirmative action and specifically about the law review article he had written when he was a professor at the University of Chicago. Scalia stated that the opinions in the article were "policy views" that he held at the time and that the article did not address the constitutionality of affirmative action programs. The Senate voted 98–0 to confirm Scalia's nomination, and he became the first Italian American to sit on the Supreme Court.

In Scalia's first term on the Supreme Court, the Court considered, in *Johnson v. Transportation Agency, Santa Clara County*, 480 U.S. 616 (1987), whether a voluntary affirmative action plan that directed sex or race to be considered for the purpose of remedying underrepresentation of women and minorities in traditionally segregated job categories violated Title VII of the Civil Rights Act of 1964. The Supreme Court held that the county agency did not violate Title VII. Scalia dissented from this opinion, arguing that "[t]he Court today completes the process of converting [Title VII] from a guarantee that race or sex will not be the basis for employment determinations, to a guarantee that it often will." According to Scalia, the Court had replaced the goal of a discrimination-free society with a new goal of proportionate representation by sex and by race in the workplace. Scalia especially disagreed with the fact that the majority permitted affirmative action not to overcome the employer's own discrimination, but to remedy general societal discrimination. "[I]t is the alteration of social attitudes, rather than the elimination of discrimination, which today's decision approves as justification for state-enforced discrimination."

Next, in *Johnson*, Scalia criticized the Court's extension of *United Steelworkers of*

America v. Weber, 443 U.S. 193 (1979), a private-employer case, to this case, which involved a public employer. In *Weber*, the Supreme Court held that Title VII permitted a private employer to adopt a voluntary, race-conscious affirmative action plan. In any event, Scalia did not agree with the underlying rationale of *Weber* and concluded that *Weber* should be overruled. Scalia closed by remarking that "[a] statute designed to establish a color-blind and gender-blind workplace has thus been converted into a powerful engine of racism and sexism, not merely permitting intentional race- and sex-based discrimination, but often making it, through the operation of the legal system, practically compelled."

Two years later, the Court, in *City of Richmond v. J.A. Croson Co.*, 488 U.S. 469 (1989), considered a challenge to the city's plan requiring prime contractors awarded city construction contracts to subcontract at least 30 percent of the dollar amount of each contract to one or more "minority business enterprises." Although the plan was remedial in nature, the Court applied strict scrutiny and struck down the plan as unconstitutional. In his concurrence, Scalia agreed that strict scrutiny must be applied to all governmental racial classifications, whether the purpose of the classifications is remedial or benign. However, he did not agree with the Court that discrimination was allowed in order "to ameliorate the effects of past discrimination." Consistent with the views he expressed in "The Disease as Cure," Scalia argued that affirmative action could not overcome the effects of past discrimination. "The difficulty of overcoming the effects of past discrimination is as nothing compared with the difficulty of eradicating from our society the source of those effects, which is the tendency—fatal to a Nation such as ours—to classify and judge men and women on the basis of their country of origin or the color of their skin. A solution to the first problem that aggravates the second is no solution at all."

Although Scalia noted that the Court had permitted racial classifications by the federal government to remedy the effects of past discrimination, he argued that there was a valid distinction between federal and state or local action. In Scalia's view, "[T]here is only one circumstance in which the States may act by race to 'undo the effects of past discrimination': where that is necessary to eliminate their own maintenance of a system of unlawful racial classification." Scalia gave as an example school desegregation.

Scalia further argued that "[r]acial preferences appear to 'even the score' . . . only if one embraces the proposition that our society is appropriately viewed as divided into races, making it right that an injustice rendered in the past to a black man should be compensated for by discriminating against a white. Nothing is worth that embrace." Scalia posited that the only program that is constitutional is a race-neutral program aimed at the disadvantaged.

In *Adarand Constructors, Inc. v. Peña*, 515 U.S. 200 (1995), the Court remanded to a lower court a case involving a federal remedial program designed to provide highway contracts to disadvantaged black enterprises. The Court held that all racial classifications, even those imposed by the federal government, must be reviewed using strict scrutiny analysis. Scalia's concurrence pointed out that the government can never have a "compelling interest" in discriminating on the basis of race in order to "make up" for past discrimination. "Individuals who have been wronged by unlawful racial discrimination should be made whole; but under our Constitution there can be no such thing as either a creditor or debtor race. That concept is alien to the Constitution's focus upon the individual." Scalia further argued that affirmative action reinforces the way of thinking that produced race hatred in the first place. "In the eyes of government, we are just one race here. It is American."

Most recently, in *Gratz v. Bollinger,* 123 S. Ct. 2411, 2003 U.S. LEXIS 4801 (2003), and *Grutter v. Bollinger,* 123 S. Ct. 2325, 2003 U.S. LEXIS 4800 (2003), Scalia again positioned himself firmly against the use of race-conscious affirmative action plans in higher education. He joined the majority opinion authored by Chief Justice William Rehnquist in the *Gratz* decision, striking down the University of Michigan's undergraduate admissions policy as unconstitutional under the Equal Protection Clause of the Fourteenth Amendment and a violation of Title VI of the Civil Rights Act of 1964. The Court held that Michigan's program put too much focus on race and was too akin to racial quotas. In the companion case of *Grutter,* Scalia dissented from the majority opinion upholding the race-conscious program utilized by the University of Michigan Law School. Scalia argued that the Court was putting forth no intelligible standard for institutions to follow, and the allowance of affirmative action in the *Grutter* decision seemed "perversely designed to prolong the controversy and the litigation." In closing his dissent, Scalia again made clear his long-standing opposition to race-conscious affirmative action, commenting that "the Constitution proscribes government discrimination on the basis of race, and state-provided education is no exception."

See also Adarand Constructors, Inc. v. Peña; City of Richmond v. J.A. Croson Co.; Civil Rights Act of 1964; Color-Blind Constitution; Economically Disadvantaged; Gender-Based Affirmative Action; *Gratz v. Bollinger/Grutter v. Bollinger;* Johnson v. Transportation Agency, Santa Clara County; Original Intent Jurisprudence; Race-Based Affirmative Action; Reagan, Ronald; Strict Scrutiny; Suspect Classification; Title VII of the Civil Rights Act of 1964; *United Steelworkers of America v. Weber.*

FURTHER READING: Boling, David, 1991, "The Jurisprudential Approach of Justice Antonin Scalia: Methodology over Result?" *Arkansas Law Review* 44:1143–1205; Brisban, Richard A., Jr., 1997, *Justice Antonin Scalia and the Conservative Revival,* Baltimore: Johns Hopkins University Press; Mcalister, James L., 1994, "A Pigment of the Imagination: Looking at Affirmative Action through Justice Scalia's Color-Blind Rule," *Marquette Law Review* 77 (winter): 327–359; Scalia, Antonin, 1979, "The Disease as Cure," *Washington University Law Quarterly* 1979:147–157; Scalia, Antonin, 1997, *A Matter of Interpretation: Federal Courts and the Law,* Princeton, NJ: Princeton University Press.

PAMELA C. CORLEY

Scapegoating/Displaced-Aggression Theories

The term "scapegoating" comes from a biblical practice of the ancient Hebrews in which a high priest would pray over the head of a goat on the Day of Atonement for the sins of the Jewish people before letting the goat run off into the wilderness (Leviticus 16:7–26). Scapegoating, or scapegoating theory, is related to the process of blaming some person, group, or thing for an incident, crime, mistake, or issue over which the person, group, or thing had no control or influence. This theory suggests that it is actually prejudiced people who feel that they are the victims in society. Scapegoating has to do with pointing the finger at some person, group, or thing because it simplifies blame and often takes a complicated matter and reduces it to elementary terms. In many cases, the person, group, or thing who becomes the scapegoat may be indirectly related to the issue in question. In a related sociological theory, the person, group, or thing who becomes the scapegoat may also be referred to as a "sacrificial lamb" to be sacrificed in order to pay for the sins of another.

Scapegoating is a form of displaced aggression because the real cause for an incident or issue is not addressed. Scapegoating and displaced aggression allow others to direct and rationalize their anger, fear, or other irrational emotions and justify verbal chastisements and behavioral acts toward the innocent party. This has often led to taunts, teasing, vilification, and in many instances violence against a person or group that had nothing to do with the outcome. Scapegoating often takes the form of the written word as well and may be couched in scholarly concepts or theories, such as black inferiority. Scapegoating and displaced aggression, then, may have serious consequences for the target of that aggression. Blacks as a group have served as scapegoats for a criminal element that makes up only a fraction of the total American population. As a race of people, particularly in, but not limited to, the South, individual black men often were the scapegoats when a white woman claimed that she had been raped or when she incurred violence at the hands of other whites. Scapegoating had particularly deadly consequences for blacks in the state of Mississippi, where there were more than 550 recorded lynchings from 1880 to 1960. Often, the victim of violence and lynch mobs was innocent of any crime.

One of the best, yet most tragic, examples of scapegoating and misplaced aggression in the twentieth century was that of Adolf Hitler, who blamed Jews for all of the ills of a social and economic nature in Germany in the 1930s. As a result, many anti-Jewish laws that were repressive in nature were passed prior to World War II in Germany. The societal hysteria against Jews, in turn, led to the concentration camps and mass extermination campaigns of Jews at these camps. Similarly, the black codes were instituted in southern states after the American Civil War as a means of "putting blacks back in their place." Blacks were blamed for the Civil War and the suffering of whites who fought to defend the practice of slavery. Blacks were not responsible for the war, slavery, or the status of southern whites.

During the era of affirmative action from the 1960s into the new millennium, blacks and affirmative action not only have become synonymous, but have become the scapegoat for other societal ills that brought affirmative action to the forefront of the political agenda. Charges of "reverse racism" and "reverse discrimination" often are made because a male did not get a job or promotion over a female who got it, or because a black was awarded a job over a white. In many instances, it is felt that the female or black was not really qualified for the position, and they serve as scapegoats for lesser qualifications held by males or whites. Conversely, white males often feel that they have been made scapegoats over systemic and historical racial discriminatory policies in jobs that they had nothing to do with or over which they had no control. Affirmative action is perceived as an unjust remedy in which white males are made to suffer the consequences for something for which they were not responsible.

See also American Civil War; Prejudice; Reverse Discrimination; Slavery.

FURTHER READING: Burke, Peter J. 1969, "Scapegoating: An Alternative to Role Differentiation," *Sociometry* 32, no. 2:159–168; *The Holy Bible: Old and New Testament*, (King James version), 2001, Nashville: World Bible Publishers; Peterson, Christopher, and Martin E.P. Seligman, 1983, "Learned Helplessness and Victimization," *Journal of Social Issues* 39, no. 2: 103–116; Schaefer, Richard T., 2001, *Race and Ethnicity in the United States*, 2d ed., Upper Saddle River, NJ: Prentice Hall.

MFANYA D. TRYMAN

Scientific Racism

For more than two centuries, there have been scientists who have been intent on proving that minorities, foreigners, the poor, and women are inherently inferior to the upper-class white males of northern European ancestry. Some scientists have curried the favor of bigots by generating seemingly useful data for them. For example, in America in the 1840s, the challenge to end slavery had been started in earnest by the abolitionists, but so had the strong defense of the peculiar institution. Defenders used the 1840 census as a major political weapon because its flawed data suggested that Northern blacks suffered from higher rates of lunacy than Southern slaves. Hence Southerners concluded that the Negro suffered unduly from "mental activity and where there is the greatest mental torpor, we find the least insanity." Slavery, it would seem to those who analyzed these data, was the appropriate social state for blacks.

The development of scientific racism began with Francis Galton, a cousin of renowned scientist Charles Darwin. Galton was not interested in the details of his cousin's evolution theories as much as he was fixated on the idea of controlling human evolutionary development via proper breeding. Just as dog fanciers could control the development of canine breeds, he felt that scientists could develop techniques that would promote the proper human being through scientifically paired mating. This became the pseudoscience called eugenics, which is based on two premises. The first is that there are many separate human races, with distinct physical and moral characteristics. According to this theory, some "races" are morally superior, mentally superior, physically superior, harder working, less criminal, and so on, and conversely, other lower races are sexually depraved, given to criminality and sloth, and filled with people of low intelligence. Second, these racial characteristics are fixed and immutable, and offspring inherit them from their parents.

Eugenics was readily embraced by the governing class in Victorian England, at the time Europe's most advanced, progressive, and evolved nation. To the bulk of scientists and anthropologists, these eugenic premises seemed paradoxical. First, humans cannot be divided into distinct races the way the eugenicists perceived. The recent completion of the human genome sequence has clearly shown that the majority of the estimated 30,000 genes in our repertoire are amazingly similar. The genes responsible for our phenotypic, or external, differences of skin color and hair texture represent only 0.01 percent of each person's total genetic makeup. Second, it has been illustrated that the characteristics defined by the eugenicists as "fixed and unchangeable" are indeed quite malleable (e.g., head size, eye color, and so on).

Eugenics was brought to the United States by politically and socially elite groups who sought to protect the burgeoning country against the incursions of "undesirables." Prior to 1880, American immigrants arrived mostly from northern and western Europe, which eugenicists theorized contained the better races, so the American race had good ancestors. From 1880 to 1924, immigration came increasingly from southern and eastern Europe, proposed to be a home of lower races. It was felt that these immigrants would primarily bring crime and poverty to America. Eugenicists sought data to prove the inferiority of these recent immigrants, which led to an early version of the intelligence quotient (IQ) test. In World War I, almost 2 million draftees completed an IQ test, and largely from these data, eugenicists testified to Congress that approximately 75 percent of immigrants from southern and eastern Europe were mentally defective. Harry Laughlin, the superintendent of the Eugenics Records Office, wrote in 1913 that about "10 percent of our population, primarily through inherent defect and weakness, are an economic and moral burden on the 90 percent and a constant source of danger to the national and racial life." He recommended an aggressive policy of involuntary sterilization of the 10 percent.

In 1921, the House Committee on Immigration and Naturalization took up the issue of postwar controls on American immigration. Its chairman requested just one scientific expert, Harry Laughlin, to conduct a statistical survey of the national effect of recent immigration. Not surprisingly, Laughlin reported that "the recent immigrants (largely from Southern and Eastern Europe) as a whole present a higher percentage of inborn socially inadequate qualities than do older stocks" (Lindzen, 12). Shortly thereafter, Congress took the historic step of imposing a quota system on immigration that was based on national origin.

The eugenicists became a more pervasive public force after the 1927 Supreme Court case *Buck v. Bell*, 274 U.S. 200, which involved involuntary sterilization. Justice Oliver Wendell Holmes asserted that "instead of waiting to execute degenerate offspring for crime, or to let them starve for their imbecility, society can prevent those who are manifestly unfit from continuing their kind. The principle that sustains compulsory vaccination is broad enough to cover cutting the Fallopian tubes." Holmes further infamously commented that society should not have to put up with inferior offspring, stating, "[T]hree generations of imbeciles are enough." This judicial endorsement of compulsory sterilization proved a landmark victory for eugenicists, and several states revised sterilization laws or passed new ones. By 1932, twenty-eight states had such legislation in place. By the time compulsory sterilization had ended in the 1970s, more than 60,000 Americans had been subjected to the procedure.

The effects of scientific racism have also been felt in biomedical research involving human subjects. A notably onerous violation began in 1932 when the Public Health Service (PHS) recruited 600 black men in Macon County, Alabama, to participate in "A Study of Untreated Syphilis in the Negro Male." Approximately one-third served as a control group, while the remainder had the sexually transmitted disease syphilis. None were informed of their health status, and all were told that they were receiving treatment for "bad blood." Sadly, the researchers withheld penicillin, an effective treatment for syphilis in the 1940s, from the infected men and requested that other health professionals do likewise. This clinical study continued for forty years and ceased only after public protest. A 1973 report by the Department of Health, Education, and Welfare found the study "ethically unjustified" because subjects had not given their informed consent, participants should have been provided penicillin, and the sponsor used subjects' blood to develop profitable new syphilis tests that are still used today. These and other unethical, outlier clinical studies resulted in the establishment of the National Commission for the Protection of Human Subjects of Biomedical and Behavioral Research. Its work provided the basis for subsequent federal regulations titled "Protection of Human Subjects" in Title 45, Code of Federal Regulations. It is currently unethical to conduct experiments on people without their free and informed consent, to use harmful procedures that offer little or no therapeutic benefit, or to exploit people's body tissues or fluids for profit without their agreement.

In the name of eugenics, select scientists have eschewed morality and political judgment, preferring that their pseudoscience prove the worthiness of citizens. Fortunately, the purity of true science and societal common sense have exposed the mental gymnastics of these individuals who abused the system in the name of ideology. Though humans will undoubtedly continue to be divided by culture and environment, true science has clearly shown that when all is said and done, we really are one big family. Thomas Jefferson, when regarding the distinction between science and morality for blacks or the poor, elegantly said, "Whatever be their degree of talents, it is no measure of their rights."

See also Abolitionists; American Civil War; Darwinism; Eugenics; Immigration Act of 1965.

FURTHER READING: Gallin, John I., 2002, *Principles and Practices of Clinical Research*, San Diego: Academic Press; Gould, Stephen J., 1981, *The Mismeasure of Man*, New York: W.W. Norton; Grant, Madison, 1970, *The Passing of the Great Race*, Manchester, NH: Ayer Co. Pub.; Graves, Joseph, Jr., 2001, *The Emperor's New Clothes: Biological Theories of Race at the Millennium*, Rutgers University Press; Lindzen, Richard S., 1996, "Science and Politics: Global Warming and Eugenics," in *Risks, Costs, and Lives Saved*, edited by Robert W. Hahn, New York: Oxford University Press; Quinn, Peter, 2003, "Race Cleansing in America," *American Heritage* 54, no. 1:34–43; Tucker, William H., 1994, *The Science and Politics of Racial Research*, Urbana: University of Illinois Press.

PETER L. PLATTEBORZE

Scottsboro Boys

The infamous case of the "Scottsboro Boys" in Alabama in 1931 brings back awful memories of inequalities in America and the often-racist operation of the criminal justice and jury system on the state level (particularly in the southern states). The case stands as one of the milestone events of race relations in the twentieth century in the United States. First, several scholars date the modern civil rights movement, with whites and blacks working together to achieve equality, from the Scottsboro Boys case. Second, the Scottsboro Boys incident resulted in two important U.S. Supreme Court rulings (*Powell v. Alabama* and *Norris v. Alabama*) related to race relations and the operation of the criminal justice and jury systems at the state level. Third, as a result of these two important Supreme Court rulings, many scholars have argued that the Scottsboro Boys incident is the beginning of the period in which the Supreme Court became concerned with more aggressively protecting the rights of minorities by policing state criminal proceedings via the Due Process Clause of the Fourteenth Amendment. Also implicit in the Supreme Court decisions stemming from the Scottsboro Boys case was the notion that minorities in the South needed extra protection from the state and additional scrutiny by the courts of state action aimed at minorities. Fourth, the Scottsboro Boys incident, even today, is cited as an example of why racial equality and fairness are essential within the criminal justice and jury system. Indeed, many authors advocating affirmative action in the criminal justice and/or jury system begin by discussing the Scottsboro Boys case. The Scottsboro Boys case often comes up in the literature on the use of affirmative action in jury selection or in the criminal justice system generally.

The term "Scottsboro Boys case" actually connotes the collective experience of nine black youths who were accused of raping two white females on a train. The year was 1931, the depression was raging, and for many people, riding the rails was a common pastime and means of getting from one place to another. In March 1931, several dozen people, mostly males, were riding a train from Chattanooga to Memphis. Among this group were four black teenagers from Chattanooga riding to Memphis in hopes of finding a job. Also on board were five other black teens from different parts of Georgia. Four white individuals were also riding that day, two males and two females. A fight ensued after one of the white males stepped on the hand of one of the black young men. The two white males were forced off the train, leaving the nine black teens with the two white females. The males who were thrown off the train contacted the stationmaster in the next town to declare that they had been assaulted by a gang of blacks, and the stationmaster wired ahead to have the train stopped. After the train was stopped by dozens of men with guns drawn, the nine young black men were taken into custody. The tensions were running so high, with the fear of a lynching, that Alabama governor Benjamin Meeks Miller ordered the National Guard to Scottsboro to protect the defendants.

One of the females on the train, Victoria Price, accused six of the nine boys of raping her on the train. The assumption was that Ruby Bates, the other female on the train, was raped by the other three blacks. The climate surrounding this event was hostile, to say the least. The judge asked "all members of the bar" to represent the defendants, and two lawyers actually appeared with them at trial, but offered minimal to no actual legal representation. Stephen Roddy, a Chattanooga real-estate attorney who was drunk the first day of the trial, was unpaid. Milo Moody, the other attorney, was a seventy-year-old who had not tried a case in decades. In retrospect, both attorneys were clearly incompetent. They did not argue for separate trials, even though one of the defendants was only twelve years old, they failed to cross-examine important government witnesses, they offered no defense witnesses other than the defendants themselves, and finally, they offered no closing statements at all. The trial also took place a mere six days after the defendants' arrests, offering little time for case preparation. The result of the first round of trials was that eight of the nine were convicted and sentenced to death, while one trial, of the twelve-year-old Roy Wright, ended in a mistrial.

In January 1932, the Alabama Supreme Court affirmed all but one of the eight convictions and sentences. From there the cases were appealed to the U.S. Supreme Court, resulting in the case *Powell v. Alabama*, 287 U.S. 45 (1932), the first of several "Scottsboro cases" to be decided by the U.S. Supreme Court. The case specifically dealt with one of the defendants, Ozzie Powell, who had been arraigned with his eight friends on March 31, 1931, for the crime of rape, had pled not guilty, and had been found guilty after the short trial mentioned earlier. At issue in the case was the lack of adequate counsel afforded to the nine black youths during the trial. The judge hearing the case appointed "all members of the bar" for the purposes of arraigning the defendants with the anticipation that "all members of the bar" would continue to assist with the case at trial. Compounding the issue of inadequate legal representation was the fact that all nine defendants were from out of state and were not allowed to contact family and friends not living in Alabama. None of the nine received any assistance by counsel in the most important time of a case, from arraignment until trial. Thus no investigations were made, and no gathering of witnesses and no evaluation of the evidence were conducted on their behalf. The defendants were broken up into three different groups and tried in groups of three, all but one of whom were convicted and sentenced to death.

The question before the Court was whether this lack of representation violated the Due Process Clause of the Fourteenth Amendment to the Constitution of the United States. The Supreme Court concluded that it did, reversed the convictions, and remanded the case back to Alabama for further action. Justice George Sutherland, who delivered the opinion of the Court, stated that

> the ordinary layman, even the intelligent and educated layman, is not skilled in the science of law, and needs the advice and direction of competent counsel. It is apparent from the settled facts that the Negroes were in effect denied the right to counsel. In the light of the facts outlined in the forepart of this opinion—the ignorance and illiteracy of the defendants, their youth, the circumstances of public hostility, the imprisonment, and the close surveillance of the defendants by the military forces, the fact that their friends and families were all in other states and communications with them necessarily difficult, and above all that they stood in deadly peril of their lives—we think the failure of the trial courts to give them reasonable time and opportunity to secure counsel was a clear denial of due process.

Thus for the first time, the Supreme Court held that in some circumstances, a state must afford legal counsel in criminal cases at the state level. Prior to this decision, the Sixth Amendment "right to counsel" provision had been applicable only to the federal government. A result of the Court's ruling in *Powell v. Alabama* was to incorporate the Sixth Amendment "right to counsel" provisions as being applicable to the states for capital offenses through the Due Process Clause of the Fourteenth Amendment (through the legal doctrine that is today referred to as selective incorporation).

Alabama decided to try all of the defendants again, starting with Haywood Patterson. The new trial began in March 1933. One of the most famous criminal lawyers in America at the time, Samuel Liebowitz, was appointed to represent Haywood Patterson in his second trial and offered a much different explanation of the events surrounding the alleged crime. Liebowitz was aggressive in his cross-examining, especially of one of the main witnesses for the government, Victoria Price. She was identified as being a liar, an adulterer, a prostitute, and fearful of being arrested for violating the federal Mann Act (a federal statute criminalizing the act of prostitution that involves movement across state lines) when she originally met with the government agents stopping the train. The other alleged victim, Ruby Bates, finally made a dramatic appearance at trial (after disappearing for a time) and stated that the rape had never happened. Despite the differences in this trial, Patterson was found guilty and sentenced to death. The same fate soon followed for the other defendants. The prosecutors made many anti-Semitic (Liebowitz was Jewish) and racist remarks to the all-white jury during the trial and during closing arguments (e.g., one prosecutor argued in closing arguments, "Show them, show them that Alabama justice cannot be bought and sold with Jew money from New York").

Once again the case was appealed to the U.S. Supreme Court, this time because of the lack of black representation on the jury roll, resulting in the Supreme Court case *Norris v. Alabama*, 294 U.S. 587 (1935). Once again, the issue before the Court was whether or not the state proceedings violated the Due Process Clause of the Fourteenth Amendment. Specifically, the due process issue addressed in this case primarily revolved around the lack of blacks on the jury. The case specifically related to the trial of Clarence Norris, who was another of the nine black young men charged with the crime of rape in Jackson County, Alabama.

The trials had taken place in Morgan County, Alabama, after a change of venue from Jackson County. The population of Morgan County was larger than that of Jackson County, as was the proportion of blacks. The total population of Morgan County in 1930 was 46,176, and of this number, 8,311 were black. However, under questioning, a clerk of the circuit court indicated that in the thirty years he had lived in the county, not one person of color had ever been called for jury duty. Under Alabama law at the time, the qualifications to serve on a jury included

> all male citizens of the county who are generally reputed to be honest and intelligent men, and are esteemed in the community for their integrity, good character and sound judgment, but no person must be selected who is under twenty-one or over sixty-five years of age, or who is an habitual drunkard, or who, being afflicted with a permanent disease or physical weakness, is unfit to discharge the duties of a juror, or who cannot read English, or who has ever been convicted of any offense involving moral turpitude.

Nowhere in the statute did it declare that blacks were legally precluded from serving as potential jurors, even though that was the practice. When questioned about the lack of blacks on the jury roll, the jury commission presented a list of names from the county that included the names of six blacks. What is of interest is that all six names of the black citizens were the last on the list, which was otherwise in alphabetical order. It was clear that these names had been fraudulently added at a later date to give the appearance of the inclusion of black citizens.

The U.S. Supreme Court again overturned the convictions and remanded the case back to Alabama. The Court overturned the convictions on the grounds that the defendants had been denied due process of law since there was no presence of black individuals on the jury, even though there were many qualified blacks living in the jurisdiction. According to the Court, this lack of representation on juries by blacks in the two counties in question presented a prima facie case that there was a clear violation of the Due Process Clause of the Fourteenth Amendment. The Court had held as early as 1879 in *Strauder v. West Virginia*, 100 U.S. 303 (1879), that excluding blacks from juries was a violation of the Fourteenth Amendment's Equal Protection Clause. The Court, in *Strauder*, had held that excluding blacks from jury service violated the litigant's rights to equal protection of the laws. The Court further noted that blacks were treated so poorly by whites that blacks needed the affirmative protection of the Court. Just as in *Powell v. Alabama*, the Court incorporated a provision of the Sixth Amendment (right to trial by impartial jury) that previously had been applicable only to the federal government and made it applicable to state governments via the Due Process Clause of the Fourteenth Amendment and the practice of selective incorporation.

After two more trials, five of the original nine defendants were convicted of rape and were sentenced to death, ninety-nine years, or seventy-five years. President Franklin D. Roosevelt and Eleanor Roosevelt petitioned the Alabama governor for pardons, but with no success. The four remaining defendants had all their charges dropped. Through either parole or escape, all five of the convicted black defendants finally left Alabama over the next several decades. The last of the Scottsboro Boys was released from Alabama prison in 1950 after serving approximately nineteen years in prison for a crime he did not commit. All of the defendants went on to live largely troubled lives. However, in the 1970s, the last surviving member of the nine Scottsboro Boys (Clarence Norris) traveled to Alabama to officially receive a pardon from the state of Alabama and Governor George Wallace. At this presentation, the state of Alabama apologized for its racist treatment of the nine defendants and officially exonerated the nine of all wrongdoing. Unfortunately, Norris was the only remaining living member able to actually hear this acknowledgment and apology from the State of Alabama.

See also Bill of Rights; Criminal Justice System and Affirmative Action; Fourteenth Amendment; Jury Selection and Affirmative Action; *Strauder v. West Virginia*.

FURTHER READING: Boser, Ulrich, 2002, "The Black Man's Burden," *U.S. News and World Report*, August 26, 50; Carter, Dan T., 1979, *Scottsboro: A Tragedy of the American South*, Baton Rouge: Louisiana State University Press; Goodman, James E., 1995, *Stories of Scottsboro*, New York: Vintage Books; Thernstrom, Abigail, 1996, "From Scottsboro to Simpson," *Public Interest*, no. 122 (winter): 17–28.

SUSAN F. BRINKLEY

Section 1981

See Civil Rights Act of 1866.

Segregation

Segregation is a social or natural process of separation, polarization, stratification, and "putting apart" from others. It is best conceptualized from the nature-nurture context. Segregation emphasizes the dissimilarity characteristics in man influenced by natural or artificial creation. The segregation occurs as a result of differences in biological makeup of people and through a process of socialization that influences the behavior, attitude, and thought processes of individuals or groups against one another. Legally mandated segregation, or de jure segregation,

White students in class at the University of Oklahoma and G.W. McLaurin, an African American, seated in a separate anteroom. McLaurin would successfully challenge this segregationist practice as being unconstitutional in the U.S. Supreme Court in *McLaurin v. Oklahoma.* Courtesy of Library of Congress.

has been primarily eliminated in American society through the use of antidiscrimination laws. However, vestiges of segregation in fact throughout society, or de facto segregation, still exist, although the degree of existence is subject to debate. One of the purposes of affirmative action plans or programs is to proactively improve diversity and integration and tear down the remaining walls of de facto segregation.

The features that are crucial in understanding segregation vary with the complex conceptualization of the alternate definitions of the term. Recent social research shows that segregation is still manifest in residential patterns by ethnicity, gendered patterns of occupation, polarized income patterns in family economics, the social composition of school education, racial patterns of superiority, religious patterns of differences in denominations and sects, sexual preferences and partner selection, and other areas. Segregation has been used largely as a strategy to maintain the "purity of elites," and a central part of this strategy has been that of domination to keep minorities or "inferior races" from mixing with majority, superior, and dominant races or groups. This was a dominant trend in the United States during the period of slavery, during Reconstruction, and generally prior to the modern civil rights movement in America. Segregation was used in all of these periods to enforce separation of races and ethnic groups.

One key factor of segregation is the restriction it places or creates between contact groups, such as dominant and minority groups or superordinate and subordinate groups, manifested even in the same neighborhoods, schools, and clubs and in the use of public facilities. Until the 1950s in the United States, and between 1948 and 1991 in South Africa, segregation enjoyed institutional support from the state governments. The emergence of the modern civil right movement in the United States in the early 1950s saw massive protests against the legal enforcement of discrimination and segregation—protests against de jure segregation. But the institutional crackdown by the law on segregation did not end racial inequality and separation called de facto segregation (the innate feeling and acting of segregation as part of social existence, and not necessarily mandated by law). Thus segregation was tacitly enforced by the doctrine of separate but equal until 1954, when the U.S. Supreme Court in its landmark decision in *Brown v. Board of Education*, 347 U.S. 483 (1954), declared segregated schools inherently unequal and, by implication, any form of segregation unconstitutional under the Equal Protection Clause of the Fourteenth Amendment. De facto segregation has also given way to self-segregation, which developed from all sides of the racial divide for self- or alike-group identification based upon notions of ethnocentrism or racism.

Some stimulating factors that propel segregation are relative deprivation in the existing social structure, perceived differences in abilities, differential status symbols, racial divisions, and perceived ethnic and religious differences. However, there are situations where segregation is still enforced by state policies in the public interest. This form of segregation is evident in the separation of criminals from law-abiding citizens through the creation of prisons for the temporary isolation of criminals for deterrent, reformatory, and rehabilitative purposes, as well as the universal enforcement of separation between males and females in the use of certain social facilities like restrooms or bathrooms. Contextually, antidiscrimination laws and programs like affirmative action are used to break some biologically or naturally occurring segregation and to ensure the integration of society and the maintenance of social order.

See also Brown v. Board of Education; Civil Rights Movement; De Facto and De Jure Segregation; Equal Protection Clause; Ethnocentrism; Eugenics; Fourteenth Amendment; Gender Stratification; Integration; Racial and Ethnic Stratification; Relative Deprivation Theory; Slavery.

FURTHER READING: Blackburn, R., and J. Jarman, 1997, "Occupational Gender Segregation," *Social Research Update* 53, no. 4 (spring): 513–523; Calhoun, Craig, Donald Light, and Suzanne Keller, 1994, *Sociology*, 6th ed., New York: McGraw-Hill; Marshall, Gordon, ed., 1998, *A Dictionary of Sociology*, New York: Oxford University Press; Taylor, Chris, Stephen Gorard, and John Fitz, 2000, "A Re-examination of Segregation Indices in Terms of Compositional Invariance," *Education Research* 30:1–9.

KINGSLEY UFUOMA OMOYIBO

Seneca Falls Convention

The first major meeting established to discuss the rights of women took place at the Wesleyan Methodist Church in Seneca Falls, New York, on July 19–20, 1848. It is considered to be the initial event that launched the women's movement in the United States. Two hundred and forty women attended the conference, with the first day designated for women only and the second day open to the general public. Organizers Elizabeth Cady Stanton, Lucretia Mott, her sister Martha Wright, Jane Hunt, and Mary Ann McClintock wrote the premier document to come out of the conference, titled "The Declaration of Sentiments and Resolutions." It was signed by sixty-eight women and thirty-two men. Based on the Declaration of Independence, it stated that all men and women are created equal. A total of eighteen societal injustices were listed and discussed at the conference, with a dozen resolutions put up for ratification.

All twelve passed unanimously except the resolution that demanded the right to vote for women. The suffrage resolution was considered too radical and extreme for passage. Elizabeth Cady Stanton demanded woman suffrage at the conference, and her demand was seconded by the renowned antislavery advocate Frederick Douglass. The suffrage resolution was not passed, however, until the Rochester, New York, conference at the Unitarian Church, which followed two years after the Seneca Falls Convention. It remained a core issue of the women's movement until the Nineteenth Amendment was ratified in 1920.

Lucretia Mott, an established advocate of abolitionism, was selected as a delegate to the World Anti-Slavery Conference in London in 1840. Because she was a woman, however, she was denied seating at the conference and could only observe the proceedings from a gallery seat. Angered at the treatment of women, Mott found herself in the company of another American woman relegated to the gallery, Elizabeth Cady Stanton. Their outrage highlighted the need for a conference specifically designed to address the issues of women's rights. Eight years later, their conversation materialized in the Seneca Falls Convention. Lucretia Mott's husband, James Mott, chaired the convention, both because it was unthinkable for a woman to hold such a position in that day and to give credibility to the cause. The Rochester conference two years later was, however, chaired by a woman, Abigail Bush.

In 1845, Margaret Fuller published a book titled *Women in the Nineteenth Century*. This early feminist text is believed to have directly influenced the formation and proceedings of the Seneca Falls Convention. The entire conference was ridiculed by the media. As news of this initial women's rights conference spread, however, subsequent women's conferences followed throughout New York, Pennsylvania, Massachusetts, Ohio, and Indiana.

See also Declaration of Sentiments; Douglass, Frederick; Mott, Lucretia Coffin; Nineteenth Amendment; Stanton, Elizabeth Cady; Suffrage Movement.

FURTHER READING: Gurko, Miriam, 1974, *The Ladies of Seneca Falls*, New York: Schocken Books; Hymowitz, Carol, and Michaele Weissman, 1978, *A History of Women in America*, New York: Bantam Books; Lunardini, Christine, 1994, *What Every American Should Know about Women's History*, Holbrook, MA: Bob Adams; O'Melveny, Mary K., 1996, "The Sesquicentennial of the 1848 Seneca Falls Women's Rights Convention: American Women's Unfinished Quest for Legal, Economic, Political, and Social Equality: Playing the Gender Card: Affirmative Action and Working Women," *Kentucky Law Journal* 84 (summer 1996): 1249–1275.

SHEILA BLUHM

Separate-but-Equal Doctrine

See Plessy v. Ferguson.

Set-Aside Programs

See Economically Disadvantaged; Quotas.

Sex and Gender

Affirmative action programs have arguably benefited white women more than any other group. Women have made tremendous inroads into all occupations during the past thirty years. Historically, women had been barred from attending most colleges and universities, as well as from the majority of occupations, based on their assumed differences from men. For many years, it was argued that women's monthly cycles prevented them from holding a job, and doctors charged that women should not be allowed to seek higher education because their brain would drain away energy from their reproductive systems, leaving them sterile. While in reality the differences between men and women are insignificant, our culture has been obsessed with finding differences to justify exclusion and inequality.

The use of the terms "sex" and "gender" has been at the center of debates over inequality between men and women. The two terms are frequently confused and are often used interchangeably. Historically, the term "sex" was commonly used in the United States to refer to one's identity as either male or female. Sex was assumed to be inborn, determined by God or biology. Because sex was seen as given and unchanging, it was used to rationalize the different treatment of men and women. Beginning in the 1960s, the term "gender" was introduced to distinguish between one's sex and the social roles and cultural expectations that shape individuals' behavior and sense of identity. Gender has been widely used since that time to refer to the cultural and social norms that we learn and perform based on our sex. The term "gender" was introduced to emphasize that the significant differences between men and women are determined by society rather than biology. While sex refers to whether one is male or female, gender refers to our masculinity and femininity, which are learned.

Sociologists and anthropologists have documented that gender behavior and identity vary tremendously from one culture to another and over time. Tasks that are considered feminine in one culture may be considered part of the male role in another. Gender is socially constructed, whereas it is still largely assumed that sex is biological.

Differences between men and women are largely the product of gender. In other words, we learn to talk, feel, and act differently, beginning at infancy. Research shows that even the most egalitarian parents still treat male and female infants differently. Children grow up playing with different toys, being dressed differently, and being encouraged to express themselves differently. While it is often assumed that males and females are very different, research disconfirms this. There is instead such tremendous variation among men and among women that any generalization about men or about women tells us nothing about any individual man or woman. For example, while overall, men have greater upper body strength (and women greater lower body strength), this cannot be used as a basis for excluding women from a specific job, since there are individual women who possess tremendous upper body strength, and many men who do not. Additionally, the few differences that have been found between men and women are very slight, with tremendous deviation. In fact, the differences among men and among women far exceed the differences between men and women. Additionally, differences are narrowing over time, demonstrating that even physical differences are shaped by the culture's expectations and gender training.

In recent years, a number of scholars, including biologists, have argued that sex is a social construct as well. For example, there are many "intersexed" people, those born with ambiguous genitalia. In numerous cultures, such persons have been classified as a third sex. Biologist Anne Fausto-Sterling argues that there are actually five sexes, while others argue that sex falls along a continuum rather than into only two discrete categories. It is common in the United States to operate on infants born with ambiguous genitalia to make them conform to our two-sex classification system. A growing field of research by biologists, psychologists, anthropologists, sociologists, and historians documents that categories of sex are social/cultural constructs imposed upon bodies.

See also Discrimination; Gender Segregation in Employment; Gender Stratification; Glass Ceilings; Stereotypes, Gender.

FURTHER READING: Fausto-Sterling, Anne, 1985, *Myths of Gender: Biological Theories about Men and Women*, New York: Basic Books; Fausto-Sterling, Anne, 2000, *Sexing the Body: Gender Politics and the Construction of Sexuality*, New York: Basic Books; Hubbard, Ruth, 1992, *The Politics of Women's Biology*, New Brunswick, NJ: Rutgers University Press; Kimmel, Michael S., 2000, *The Gendered Society*, New York: Oxford University Press; Laquer, Thomas, 1990, *Making Sex*, Cambridge, MA: Harvard University Press.

ABBY L. FERBER

Sex Discrimination

Title VII of the Civil Rights Act of 1964 originally was proposed to prohibit employment discrimination on the basis of race and national origin. "Sex" was added to the original civil rights bill by Representative Howard Smith of Virginia. Some have argued that "sex" was added as a protected category to generate sufficient opposition to defeat the bill. However, the bill was passed. Accordingly, section 703(a) of Title VII provides that it is an unlawful employment practice for an employer of fifteen or more employees "to discriminate against any individual with respect to his compensation, terms, conditions, or privileges of employment, because of such individual's race, color, religion, sex, or national origin."

Although legal prohibition against sex discrimination was not originally contemplated in the Civil Rights Act of 1964, the need became readily apparent when a third of the charges filed with the Equal Employment Opportunity Commission (EEOC) in its 1966 fiscal year alleged sex discrimination. Perhaps because discrimination "based on sex" was not originally envisioned by Congress, there is little legislative history to guide courts "in interpreting the Act's prohibition against discrimination based on 'sex' " (*Meritor Savings Bank v. Vinson*, 477 U.S. 57 [1986], 63–64). As a result, courts' interpretation of that portion of Title VII prohibiting sex discrimination and EEOC guidelines over the years have been crucial in fashioning the parameters of unlawful sex discrimination.

From its inception, the EEOC took the position that various outmoded, paternalistic, and stereotypical practices adversely affecting employment opportunities and advancement of women in the workplace were unlawful. Significant early interpretations of the law included the position that state protective laws that provided extra benefits for women (such as extra work breaks and shorter work hours), failure to hire or promote women because they were married or had children, and classifying jobs as "male" or "female" violated Title VII. In addition, section 703(e) of Title VII provides an exception to the act's prohibition against sex discrimination if gender is a bona fide occupational qualification. Since 1965, the EEOC has maintained that the BFOQ exception as to sex should be construed narrowly, and its position has been upheld by the courts. This has limited employers' use of the exception to restrict women from jobs requiring physical labor, to comply with customer preferences to work only with members of one gender, and the like. The courts' adoption of the EEOC's position on these matters has opened many doors and formerly traditionally male jobs to women.

Title VII sex discrimination proscriptions led to the invalidation of state protective laws passed in the late nineteenth and early twentieth centuries aimed at protecting women and children from exploitation. Prior to the passage of Title VII, some courts had held that such laws served the government's interest in public health and safety. However, they often also restricted women's equal employment opportunities. With the passage of the Civil Rights Act of 1964, virtually all such laws conflicted with and were superseded by Title VII.

Since 1965, the EEOC also has taken the position that maintaining separate lines of progression and seniority lists based on sex and classifying jobs as "male" or "female" are unlawful. The EEOC guidelines pertaining to seniority systems are set forth in 29 C.F.R. § 1604.3. Statutory authority for this position is set forth in section 703(h) of Title VII. Section 703(a)(1) prohibits sex discrimination in the provision of fringe benefits. According to the EEOC, fringe benefits include "medical, hospital, accident, life insurance and retirement benefits; profit-sharing and bonus plans; leave; and other terms, conditions, and privileges of employment" (29 C.F.R. § 1604.9).

Whenever sex is a factor in an employment rule or practice, it may run afoul of Title VII. Thus the EEOC has successfully taken on so-called sex-plus practices in which sex is coupled with another factor that discriminates on the basis of gender. For example, restricting employment of married women or women with children (but not married men or men with children) cannot be justified if it is not shown to be a BFOQ. However, courts have held that some appearance and grooming standards, such as restrictions on beards or men's hair length, have been deemed not to violate Title VII.

In recent years, Title VII prohibitions against sex discrimination have been extended and strengthened. For example, in 1978 Congress passed the Pregnancy Discrimination Act (PDA). Embodied in section 701(k), it amended Title VII to provide that "women affected by pregnancy, childbirth, or related medical conditions shall be treated the same for all employment-related purposes, including receipt of benefits under fringe benefit programs, as other persons not so affected but similar in their ability or inability to work." Recently, the EEOC took the position that a health plan that excludes health insurance coverage for prescription contraceptives while covering other preventive drugs discriminates on the basis of sex and pregnancy, thereby violating Title VII, as amended by the Pregnancy Discrimination Act.

A major extension of Title VII proscriptions occurred when sexual harassment was determined to constitute a form of sex discrimination (see, e.g., *Harris v. Forklift Systems, Inc.*, 510 U.S. 17 [1993]; *Meritor Savings Bank v. Vinson*, 1986). EEOC guidelines define sexual harassment as "unwelcome sexual advances, requests for sexual favors, and other verbal or physical conduct of a sexual nature" (29 C.F.R. § 1604.11[a]). Two types of sexual harassment have been recognized as actionable. The first is known as "quid pro quo" harassment. It occurs when the benefits of employment are conditioned on the employee (harassee) providing sexual favors. A sexual harassment claim can also be based on a "hostile work environment" theory. Under this theory, employer liability can be established when the employer's conduct unreasonably interferes with an employee's work performance or creates "an intimidating, hostile, or offensive working environment" (29 C.F.R. § 1604.11[a]).

The EEOC also has taken on sex discrimination in professional and executive employment. In 1995, the Glass Ceiling Commission issued its report. The commission found numerous examples of impediments that inhibit opportunities for women in corporations in the United States. The commission found that these impediments help maintain a glass ceiling that hampers the ability of women to move into senior-level executive and professional positions. Such barriers to the promotion of women in the workplace are a subset of unlawful employment practices upon which the EEOC has placed greater focus since 1995.

See also Civil Rights Act of 1964; Employment (Private) and Affirmative Action; Employment (Public) and Affirmative Action; Equal Employment Opportunity Commission; Gender Segregation in Employment; Glass Ceiling Commission; Glass Ceilings; Title VII of the Civil Rights Act of 1964.

FURTHER READING: *Harris v. Forklift Systems, Inc.*, 510 U.S. 17 (1993); Lindemann, Barbara, and Paul Grossman, 1996, *Employment Discrimination Law*, 3d ed., vols. 1 and 2, Washington, DC: Bureau of National Affairs; Lindemann, Barbara, and David D. Kadue, 1992, *Sexual Harassment in Employment Law*, Washington, DC: BNA Books; *Meritor Savings Bank v. Vinson*, 477 U.S. 57 (1986).

PAUL M. HARIDAKIS and RICHARD J. BENNETT

Sexism

Attitudes toward gender roles have been changing over time. Men and women have become more liberal in their attitudes toward women's roles. However, several studies suggest that new forms of sexist attitudes are developing that affect affirmative action. A distinction is now made between old-fashioned sexism and modern sexism. The old-fashioned notion of sexism was characterized by an adherence to traditional gender roles, a disparate treatment of women and men, and traditional gender stereotypes and beliefs about female competency. Modern sexism is characterized by a rejection of stereotypes of women's inferiority and good-faith egalitarian treatment (i.e., overt discrimination is not a perceived problem). However, modern sexism also entails negative feelings toward women who make political and economic protests and belief that governments pay excessive attention to women.

Neosexism, similar to modern sexism, is defined as a manifestation of a conflict between values of equality and residual negative feelings toward women. Researchers have suggested that a belief in neosexism predicts men's negative attitudes toward gender-based affirmative action. Another approach to the study of sexism is the ambivalent sexism theory. According to this theory, sexism has two components: hostile and benevolent. Hostile sexism is characterized by competitive relations between women and men, heterosexual hostility, and the endorsement of dominant status for men, whereas benevolent sexism emphasizes the good qualities of women while continuing to reflect beliefs in strong differences between women and men.

Research on sexism has traditionally studied people's preference for traditional gender roles, demonstrating that many women and men showed a preference for division of labor by gender in which the husband provides for the family and the wife takes care of the house and children. Recently, measures of sexism have incorporated other elements, like perceptions of how women and men are treated. In these measures, the belief that "discrimination is no longer a problem" is used as one indicator of sexist beliefs, because denial of discrimination can serve to maintain gender inequality. For example, one study found that the neosexism scale correlated with lack of support for affirmative action programs as a way to achieve gender equality.

See also Discrimination; Gender Norms; Glass Ceilings; Prejudice; Sex Discrimination; Stereotypes, Gender.

FURTHER READING: Eagly, Alice 1987, *Sex Differences in Social Behavior: A Social-Role Interpretation*, Hillsdale, NJ: Erlbaum; Glick, Peter, and Susan T. Fiske, 1996, "The Ambivalent Sexism Inventory: Differentiating Hostile and Benevolent Sexism," *Journal of Personality and Social Psychology* 70:491–512; Swim, Janet K., Kathryn J. Aikin, Wayne S. Hall, and Barbara A. Hunter, 1995, "Sexism and Racism: Old-Fashioned and Modern Prejudices," *Journal of Personality and Social Psychology* 68:199–214; Tougas, Francine, Rupert Brown, Ann M. Beaton, and Stephane Joly, 1995, "Neosexism: Plus Ça Change, Plus C'est Pareil," *Personality and Social Psychology Bulletin* 21, no. 8:842–849.

MARIA JOSE SOTELO

The Shape of the River

In 1998, two former Ivy League university presidents, William G. Bowen and Derek Bok, published a widely acclaimed work on affirmative action in higher education titled *The Shape of the River: Long-Term Consequences of Considering Race in College and University Admissions*. The book is considered a sweeping defense of the use of affirmative action in higher education. Bowen and Bok conclude in the book that affirmative action programs at elite institutions have been significantly beneficial to African American students while not unnecessarily trammeling the rights of nonminority students or being significantly harmful to nonminorities. They also assert in the book that eliminating affirmative action would result in reducing African American enrollment at elite schools by as much as 50 percent.

The book largely is an analysis of data from roughly 90,000 students at twenty-eight elite institutions of higher learning covering the specific years 1951, 1976, and 1989. The data were collected and maintained by the Andrew W. Mellon

Foundation, an organization that Bowen presided over as president. Therefore, Bowen and Bok had unfettered access to this data, a fact that has not been lost on critics of the book, such as Stephan and Abigail Thernstrom, who have objected to the use of a "restricted access data base." Using these data, Bowen and Bok strongly defend affirmative action based upon how the students did during college, as well as what students did after graduation. Among other findings, Bowen and Bok discovered that African Americans achieved notable success after graduation, earning advanced degrees at rates identical to those of their white classmates, and that African Americans were more active in civic and community organizations than their white classmates.

See also African Americans; Education and Affirmative Action; Minority Professionals and Affirmative Action; Thernstrom, Stephan, and Thernstrom, Abigail.

FURTHER READING: Bowen, William, and Derek Bok, 1998, *The Shape of the River: Long-Term Consequences of Considering Race in College and University Admissions,* Princeton, NJ: Princeton University Press; Gose, Ben, 1998, "A Sweeping New Defense of Affirmative Action," *Chronicle of Higher Education,* September 18, A46; "Review of Book Defending Affirmative Action Criticizes Availability of Data," 1999, *Chronicle of Higher Education,* June 18, A14.

JAMES A. BECKMAN

Shaw v. Reno, 509 U.S. 630 (1993)

In *Shaw v. Reno,* the U.S. Supreme Court ruled that race-conscious redistricting warranted strict scrutiny under the Equal Protection Clause of the Fourteenth Amendment even if the motivation behind the redistricting was to benefit a minority race. The Court articulated that such a redistricting plan, even if it was facially race neutral, was only constitutional if it was narrowly tailored to further a compelling governmental interest. Consistent with its affirmative action jurisprudence, the U.S. Supreme Court refused to relax the standard of scrutiny for a reapportionment plan enacted to help historically disenfranchised minority groups and adopted the same standard of scrutiny as for a reapportionment plan enacted to discriminate against such minority groups.

The federal Voting Rights Act of 1965 required states to get federal authorization, either from the U.S. attorney general or from the U.S. District Court for the District of Columbia, before changing a "standard, practice, or procedure with respect to voting" in certain areas. The act's purpose was to ensure that states did not pass laws designed to abridge individual voting rights (especially those of African Americans) based on race. For example, several states had designed what they claimed to be race-neutral devices to disenfranchise black voters, including literacy tests with "grandfather" clauses and "good-character" provisions. Another tool used by the states to achieve the same purpose was racial gerrymandering— "the deliberate and arbitrary distortion of district boundaries . . . for [racial] purposes." The U.S. Congress passed the Voting Rights Act to end such discriminatory practices.

To comply with the Voting Rights Act, the North Carolina General Assembly gave the U.S. attorney general a reapportionment plan that included one black-majority congressional district. The attorney general objected, claiming that a second black-majority district could have been created to further enhance minority voting strength. The General Assembly acquiesced and created another black-majority district, though in a different part of North Carolina than where the attorney general had recommended. According to the Court, the new district contained boundaries "of dramatically irregular shape"; it wound "in snakelike fashion through tobacco country, financial centers, and manufacturing areas" until the district, as expressed by the lower court, "gobble[d up] enough enclaves of black neighborhoods."

Five white North Carolina residents filed an action against state and federal officials, alleging that the second black-majority district was an instance of racial gerrymandering in which the sole motivation behind the district was race and, as such, violated the Fourteenth Amendment's Equal Protection Clause. The plaintiffs claimed that the two black-majority districts had combined black voters arbitrarily (that is, without considering compactness, contiguousness, geographical boundaries, or political subdivisions) to create congressional districts along racial lines and to ensure the election of black representatives. They alleged that the deliberate segregation of voters into separate districts on the basis of race violated their constitutional rights to participate in a color-blind electoral process. Their arguments echoed previous challenges to affirmative action in employment and education in which predominantly white plaintiffs argued that the law should be color blind.

The U.S. District Court for the Eastern District of North Carolina dismissed the claims against the federal officials for lack of subject-matter jurisdiction because the U.S. District Court for the District of Columbia had exclusive jurisdiction over these claims. The North Carolina district court dismissed the complaint as to the state officials because it found that the North Carolina redistricting plan did not violate the Equal Protection Clause. According to its ruling, race-based redistricting favoring minority voters was not discriminatory in the "constitutional sense," especially because North Carolina's plan did not leave white voters underrepresented or dilute white voting strength.

The Supreme Court disagreed. In its 5–4 majority opinion written by Justice Sandra Day O'Connor, the Court first noted that North Carolina's scheme appeared to be so irrational that it could be understood only as an effort to segregate voters on the basis of race. Unlike the district court, the Court found that the redistricting plan had to pass strict scrutiny to be constitutional under the Equal Protection Clause, echoing the level of scrutiny the Court had applied to other affirmative action programs based on race. The Court, therefore, remanded the case to the district court to consider whether the plan had been narrowly tailored to serve a "compelling governmental interest." If not, the Supreme Court indicated, the lower court should find the plan in violation of the Equal Protection Clause.

The Supreme Court acknowledged the difficulty in determining from the face of a redistricting plan whether it purposefully distinguished voters on the basis of race, particularly since reapportionment plans do not classify people but, rather, tracts of land and addresses. The Court noted that such difficulty was compounded because districting rules were unique in that they reflected a state legislature's awareness of race, age, economic status, religion, political persuasion, and a variety of other demographic factors, so that racial consciousness was not always equated with racial discrimination. Based on prior case law, the Court noted that when members of the same racial group lived together in a single community, a reapportionment plan that placed them in the same district could be completely legitimate. On the other hand, the Court suggested that any plan that put into the same district individuals of one race who had only their skin color in common and who were otherwise separated by physical or political boundaries or other demographic factors "bears an uncomfortable resemblance to political apartheid." On this basis, the Court ruled, the North Carolina reapportionment plan did invoke the Equal Protection Clause.

The Supreme Court asserted that classifications of citizens based solely on race are suspect "because they threaten to stigmatize persons by reason of their membership in a racial group and to incite racial hostility." Accordingly, any state law that makes racial distinctions, either explicit or neutral but unexplainable on grounds other than race, must be analyzed under "strict scrutiny," which presumes that a racial classification is invalid unless it is "narrowly tailored to further a compelling governmental interest." The Court adopted the same standard that it had adopted to scrutinize affirmative action programs in employment and education.

The state had argued that its "compelling interest" was compliance with the Voting Rights Act, but the Court found that a reapportionment plan that satisfied the act could still be unconstitutional under the Equal Protection Clause if it went beyond what the act required. In response to North Carolina's claim that the General Assembly's revised plan was necessary to avoid diluting black voting strength, the Court said that such an issue could serve a "compelling interest" and that the district court should consider whether such dilution was supported by the particular facts of the case.

North Carolina also argued that the General Assembly's plan advanced a compelling governmental interest by seeking to erase the effects of past racial discrimination. Justice O'Connor was skeptical of that argument, ruling that for such an effort to be considered a "compelling interest," the state had to provide strong evidence showing that such remedial action was necessary. Justice O'Connor suggested that the district court could consider the issue but expressed doubt that the state could present sufficient evidence.

There were three dissenting opinions. Justice John Paul Stevens found that the North Carolina redistricting plan was constitutional because, although race conscious, it was otherwise permissible and had been enacted "to benefit an underrepresented minority group." Justice Stevens's dissent reflected his affirmative action jurisprudence of giving less scrutiny to race-conscious laws designed to benefit rather than to discriminate against minority groups that had suffered past discrimination.

Justice David Souter also thought that the North Carolina redistricting plan did not warrant strict scrutiny; however, he sought the same level of scrutiny for the North Carolina plan as the Court had given to other state voting initiatives. Justice Souter believed that to prevail, the North Carolina plaintiffs had to allege and prove that they would be specifically harmed by the redistricting plan, or else the plan was constitutional as long as there was a legitimate state interest for redistricting. Justice Souter would have affirmed the decision of the district court because the plaintiffs alleged no harm from the redistricting, and the plan was otherwise constitutional.

Last, Justice Byron White noted that the Court had found only two types of state voting practices that could implicate a constitutional right—practices that outright denied individuals in a certain racial or political group the right to vote and practices that diminished a racial or political group's influence on the political process. Because neither of these types of practices was at issue in this case, Justice White believed that the plaintiffs failed to raise a constitutional claim and that the Court should have affirmed the decision of the district court.

See also Apartheid; *Baker v. Carr*; Color-Blind Constitution; Compelling Governmental Interest; Equal Protection Clause; Fifteenth Amendment; Fourteenth Amendment; Narrowly Tailored Affirmative Action Plans; O'Connor, Sandra Day; Souter, David Hackett; Stevens, John Paul; Strict Scrutiny; Suspect Classification; Voting Rights Act of 1965; White, Byron Raymond.

FURTHER READING: Kousser, J. Morgan, 1999, *Colorblind Injustice: Minority Voting Rights and the Undoing of the Second Reconstruction*, Chapel Hill: University of North Carolina Press; Parker, Frank R., 1995, "The Constitutionality of Racial Redistricting: A Critique of *Shaw v. Reno*," *District of Columbia Law Review* 3:1–59; Peacock, Anthony, ed., 1997, *Affirmative Action and Representation: Shaw vs. Reno and the Future of Voting Rights*, Durham, NC: Carolina Academic Press; Yarbrough, Tinsley E., 2002, *Race and Redistricting: The Shaw-Cromartie Cases*, Lawrence: University Press of Kansas.

GREGORY M. DUHL

Sipuel v. Regents of the University of Oklahoma, 332 U.S. 631 (1948)

Sipuel v. Regents of the University of Oklahoma was one of the important U.S. Supreme Court cases in the effort to integrate institutions of higher education. The *Sipuel* case was also one of the important cases leading up to *Brown v. Board of Education*, 347 U.S. 483 (1954). In *Sipuel*, Ada Lois Sipuel and attorneys for the National Association for the Advancement of Colored People (NAACP) took aim at state segregation statutes in the higher-education context. Despite the Equal Protection Clause of the Fourteenth Amendment indicating that no state shall deny its citizens the "equal protection of the laws," the state of Oklahoma had a deep and long history of segregation and opposition to integration. An Oklahoma state statute prohibited schools from operating with a student body composed of blacks and whites; moreover, it imposed a fine of from $100 to $500 per day for schools teaching blacks and whites together. Under the statute, any student attending such a school could be fined up to $25 a day.

Ada Sipuel was a twenty-one-year-old daughter of a clergyman. She had graduated from Langston State College for Negroes with excellent accolades and credentials. Sipuel was turned down for admission to the School of Law of the University of Oklahoma. The state advised her that it had plans to build a separate and equal facility for black residents at some point in the future. She was also informed that Oklahoma provided an out-of-state scholarship for black students for professional and graduate courses that were not offered at Langston State College. Put plainly, Oklahoma would rather ship its black residents outside the state and pay for the out-of-state tuition than allow black students to study alongside white students in Oklahoma.

Sipuel sought a writ of mandamus to gain admission to the state's sanctioned law school available, which was at the University of Oklahoma. Sipuel argued that not allowing her to attend a state institution deprived her of the equal protection of the laws. In response, the state district court ruled that the university did not have to open a separate law school to comply with the Fourteenth Amendment's Equal Protection Clause until there were an acceptable number of black students showing interest in attending law school within the state.

The case was appealed to the Oklahoma Supreme Court, but that court upheld the district court's ruling. The case was then appealed to the U.S. Supreme Court. Thurgood Marshall, attorney for the NAACP Legal Defense Fund and future Supreme Court justice, argued the case before the U.S. Supreme Court. He argued that the precedent of providing out-of-state tuition for black residents had been previously disapproved by the Supreme Court in *Missouri ex rel. Gaines v. Canada*, 305 U.S. 337 (1938). Furthermore, Marshall argued that even if Oklahoma created a separate law school, such a school would not be equal to the existing white law school.

The U.S. Supreme Court ruled in favor of Sipuel and sent the case back to the Oklahoma Supreme Court, which ordered the state to admit Sipuel immediately or open a black law school. Furthermore, the court ordered the Oklahoma Board of Regents to cease operation of the white law school until a black law school could be established. The Oklahoma Board of Regents responded to the court's ruling by establishing a makeshift law school for black students at the state capitol in Oklahoma City by roping off a small section of the basement and providing a few part-time law instructors. Sipuel refused to attend the mock/facade law school, and Oklahoma later established a law school at Langston College.

In March 1948, Sipuel returned to court arguing that Oklahoma had not fulfilled its obligation of an equal facility and opportunities. Sipuel's suit also requested that she immediately be admitted to the University of Oklahoma, and the district court judge denied her petition. In 1949, the state legislature passed a law that allowed black students to attend white graduate and professional schools if those programs were not available at black institutions; however, black students would be segregated from white students within the university. Sipuel was admitted to the University of Oklahoma, graduated in 1951, and was later admitted to the state bar.

See also Brown v. Board of Education; Equal Protection Clause; Fourteenth Amendment; Integration; Marshall, Thurgood; National Association for the Advancement of Colored People; Segregation; *Sweatt v. Painter.*

FURTHER READING: Hall, Kermit L., William M. Wiecek, and Paul Finkelman, 1991, *American Legal History: Cases and Materials*, New York: Oxford University Press; Irons, Peter, 1999, *A People's History of the Supreme Court*, New York: Viking Press; Miller, Loren, 1972, *The United States Supreme Court and the Negro*, New York: Pantheon Books; Wasby, Stephen L., Anthony A. D'Amato, and Rosemary Metrailer, 1977, *Desegregation from Brown to Alexander*, Carbondale: Southern Illinois University Press.

F. ERIK BROOKS

Skocpol, Theda (1947–)

Theda Skocpol serves as the Victor S. Thomas Professor of Government and Sociology at Harvard University, and her work and writings on the allocation of government resources occasionally are cited in the literature on affirmative action. She has written profusely on governmental programs geared toward veterans, such as the GI Bill. She is a sociologist and political scientist who studies societies and social policies, social revolution, civic engagement, and modern welfare states in both Europe and North America. She has written that throughout U.S. history, some groups have been viewed as morally worthy of governmental assistance (e.g., veterans, mothers), while others have not been viewed as worthy (e.g., certain racial groups). She has argued that "institutional and cultural opposition between the morally 'deserving' and the less deserving run like fault lines through the entire history of American social provisions" (Skocpol 1992, 149).

A Michigan native, Skocpol earned her bachelor of arts degree at Michigan State University and her master's and doctoral degrees from Harvard University. She worked at the University of Chicago from 1981 to 1986, but returned to Harvard in 1986 as a professor of sociology and most recently as the director of the Center for American Political Studies at Harvard. She has served as president of the American Political Science Association since August 2002, and previously served as the president of the Social Science History Association in 1996. She has been recognized in *A New Handbook of Political Science* (1996) as one of ten "Powerhouses" (those most frequently cited in the discipline and subdisciplines) among seventy-six "Leading Figures in Political Science." She is also the recipient of multiple academic and professional sociological and political science awards. She serves on many editorial boards for prestigious academic journals. She is the recipient of many major research grants, including the Ford Foundation grant (2000–2001) for research on "African American Popular Associations: Religion, Gender, and Democratic Possibilities"; the Russell Sage Foundation grant (2000–2001) for a study of civic and political consequences of increasing economic inequality in the United States since the 1970s; and the Ford Foundation grant (1998–2000) for research on "The Religious Bases of Women's Leadership in American Civil Society."

Her publications include a winner of two major scholarly awards that was translated into six additional languages, *States and Social Revolutions: A Comparative Analysis of France, Russia, and China* (1979); a winner of five major scholarly awards, *Protecting Soldiers and Mothers: The Political Origins of Social Policy in the United States* (1992); *Social Revolutions in the Modern World* (1997); *Social Policy in the United States: Future Possibilities in Historical Perspective* (1995); *State and Party in America's New Deal* (1995); *Boomerang: Clinton's Health Security Effort and the Turn against Government in U.S. Politics* (1996); *The Missing Middle: Working Families and the Future of American Social Policy* (2000); and *Civic America Transformed: From Membership to Advocacy— and Beyond* (2001). She has also published many edited books, a monograph titled *Lessons from History: Building a Movement for America's Children* (1997), and many scholarly articles and chapters. She acts as cochair of the Working Group on States and Social Structures at the Russell Sage Foundation.

See also GI Bill; Race-Based Affirmative Action; Veterans' Preferences.

FURTHER READING: Skocpol, Theda, 1992, *Protecting Soldiers and Mothers: The Political Origins of Social Policy in the United States*, Cambridge, MA: Harvard University Press.

SHEILA BLUHM

Slavery

Slavery in the United States of America was a phenomenon whereby individuals were owned either partially or completely by others on the basis of one's racial characteristics. The institution of slavery predated the birth of the nation and initially involved indentured servitude for both blacks and whites. However, over time, the practice of indentured servitude decreased, and outright slavery based upon skin color increased. The practice of slavery went hand in hand with the establishment of the colonies and, eventually, the new republic. The institution of slavery and the history of slavery relate strongly to social programs such as affirmative action and more aggressive compensation schemes such as reparations, as they serve as reasons for the special treatment or compensation. In the words of one author, "African skills and accomplishments were overlooked, ignored, or denied outright, a situation that has yet to be rectified. Slavery's human toll can never be calculated, but it clearly ranks among the worst crimes of humankind" (Altman 1997, 232). As historian Roger Wilkin once famously stated, "Blacks have a 375-year history on this continent: 245 involving slavery, 100 involving legalized discrimination, and only 30 involving anything else" (Plous, 26).

There is evidence to show that slave labor was in use in South Carolina in the sixteenth century while it was under Spanish control—a documented African slave revolt in the Pedee River area in 1526. The building of the city of St. Augustine in Florida, in 1565, is also an indicator of the existence of the institution of slavery in another non-English American colony. A year before the Mayflower crossing of 1620, a Dutch man-of-war sold twenty Africans at Jamestown, Virginia, for food and provisions, thus marking the beginning of slavery in what would become the United States of America within the English American environment. While there is some dispute as to whether the Africans became indentured servants or actual slaves, it is clear that the arrival of these twenty individuals represents a landmark date in the institution of slavery.

At this early stage of slavery, the ugly dynamics of the evil institution had not yet assumed their proper positions. There was no clear-cut distinction between black and white indentured servants. It is remarkable that by the middle of the seventeenth century, some of the twenty African indentured servants had not only gained their freedom, but had also become prosperous. With the passage of time, however, the status of subsequent indentured servants faced a decline, and slavery also assumed a racial character.

The stage was thus set for Massachusetts to become the first colony to legally recognize slavery in 1641. After the middle of the seventeenth century, all blacks (and no whites) entering the colonies came under the slave laws. By the late 1600s and early 1700s, the institution of slavery was spreading like wildfire among the colonies. By 1661, Virginia had recognized slavery in its laws and in 1662 declared that children could be born into slavery if their mother was a slave. The Constitution of Carolina conferred on every white in 1669 "absolute power and authority over his negro slaves." Georgia formally adopted a resolution to the effect that African slave labor should be used as the principal means in the development of agriculture in the area.

A demographic analysis by Okon Edet Uya (Uya 1987, 247–249) shows that the black population spread displayed marked variations. In New England, where African slaves were introduced as early as 1638 in Massachusetts, black slaves never featured prominently in the population. Black slaves numbered about 550 in 1708, constituting 2.2 percent of the population. In the Middle Atlantic states of New Jersey, New York, and Pennsylvania, there was a considerably larger black representation. East and West Jersey had 8 percent, New York, 12.5 percent, and Pennsylvania, 2.5 percent. Further south, in the Virginia colony, the black population accounted for 41 percent in 1780. In South Carolina, evidence shows that by 1750, there were 39,000 blacks and only 25,000 whites. By 1780, there were 97,000 blacks and 83,000 whites. The black population was concentrated in the sea island area, especially around Charleston, where, on the eve of the American Civil War, they made up 83 percent of Beaufort County, South Carolina. It has been posited that on the whole, supplemented by imports from the Caribbean and natural birth, the black slaves from Africa to the United States eventually yielded a population of 4.5 million enslaved individuals in America on the eve of the American Civil War.

After the successful conclusion of the American Revolution, the Articles of Confederation were instituted as the first constitution of the new republic. While the Articles of Confederation did not explicitly mention the institution of slavery, they did contain several provisions that set up separate treatment for both black and white inhabitants of the nascent republic. The Articles notably spoke of "free persons" and also included a provision for a return of "fugitives."

But at the Continental Convention of 1787, there was a great compromise that negated the very principle upon which the new nation was founded. The new Constitution, which replaced the Articles of Confederation in 1789, contained new provisions indirectly dealing with the "peculiar institution." While some northern framers of the Constitution were opposed in principle to legalizing the institution of slavery in the new Constitution, the northern framers basically compromised with the southern delegates on the issue of slavery to bring the southern states into the new union, earning the Constitutional Convention the appellation of the "Great Compromise of 1789." While the words "slave" or "slavery" never appeared in the Constitution (and would not appear until ratification of the Thirteenth Amendment in 1865), the Constitution did contain several clauses euphemistically dealing with the institution of slavery. These included the infamous "Three-Fifths Compromise" and the compromise over the abolishment of the international slave trade, in which it was agreed that the importation of slaves from Africa would not be prohibited before 1808. Since blacks were considered property without any rights, the new Constitution also specified that runaway slaves had to be returned to their owner through the process of extradition. Hence the document left untouched the practice of slavery in the various states.

Some constitutional historians and scholars like Joseph Ellis have argued that but for this "Great Compromise," the new United States of America would not have been possible. Others argue that nonetheless, by not dealing directly with the slavery issue, the framers gave slavery the imprimatur of law and legal backing. As slavery became a "total institution," and the slave was now considered a legal nonperson, the property of the owner, an outsider, and a "socially dead person," the conditions of living of the slaves declined further. Hence, whether in the large plantations or small farms, the master's household or dockyards, railroads, mining

Fugitive slaves forging the Rappahannock River during Pope's retreat. © Photography Collection, Miriam and Ira D. Wallach Division of Art, Prints, and Photographs, New York Public Library, Astor, Lennox, and Tilden Foundations.

companies, or the cotton mills, slavery meant hard work. As the slave cabins were crudely built, cramped, and poorly ventilated and the slaves themselves were poorly clothed and fed, morbidity and mortality rates were very high. As the degradation of the slaves increased, the institution of slavery assumed a critical position in the life of the nation, especially in the industry of the southern states.

Under the institution of slavery, slaves also had very few legally enforceable rights. While the laws of each state were different, slaves generally could not be witnesses in a court of law (except in cases involving other slaves), did not have the capacity to enter into contracts, were prohibited from owning firearms, could not assemble without the presence of a white individual, were prohibited from reading, and were prohibited from traveling without permission. Additionally, families were often broken up by the sale of one of the family members, and corporal punishment of slaves unfortunately occurred throughout the South.

While the institution of slavery itself was inexcusable and the amount of human degradation was very hard on the enslaved, it is pertinent to note that there were white slave owners who acted humanely despite their absolute power over their slaves. That is, in spite of the legal provisions in respect to the status of their slaves, some slave masters treated their slaves with a certain degree of humanity because local conditions and interpersonal relationships between the slave masters and their slaves, as well as financial considerations, moderated the institution to some degree.

Following the outbreak of the American Civil War in 1861, the institution of slavery in the United States was in its last days. First, President Abraham Lincoln issued his presidential Emancipation Proclamation of January 1, 1863, declaring that slaves in the Deep South states "then in rebellion" were forever free. The Emancipation Proclamation was expanded beyond the Confederacy and made permanent by the ratification of the Thirteenth Amendment in 1865, forever abolishing the institution of slavery throughout the United States.

See also American Civil War; Articles of Confederation; Civil War (Reconstruction) Amendments and Civil Rights Acts; Constitution, Civil Rights, and Equality; Race in Colonial America; Reparations; Slavery and the Founding Fathers; Thirteenth Amendment; Three-Fifths Compromise.

FURTHER READING: Altman, Susan, 1997, *The Encyclopedia of African-American Heritage*, New York: Facts on File; Berlin, Ira, Marc Favreau, and Steven Miller, eds., 1998, *Remembering Slavery: African Americans Talk about Their Personal Experiences of Slavery*, New York: New Press; Campbell, Edward D., and Kym S. Rice, 1991, *Before Freedom Came: African American Life in the Antebellum South*, Richmond, VA: Museum of the Confederacy and University Press of Virginia; Countryman, Edward, 1999, *How Did American Slavery Begin?* New York: Bedford/ St. Martin's Press; Ellis, Joseph, 2000, *Founding Brothers: The Revolutionary Generation*, New York: Knopf; Johnson, Charles, and Patricia Smith, 1998, *Africans in America: America's Journey through Slavery*, New York: Harcourt Brace and Company; Plous, S., 2003, "Ten Myths About Affirmative Action," *Journal of Social Issues* 52:25–31.

PAUL OBIYO MBANASO NJEMANZE

Slavery and the Founding Fathers

The relationship of the issue of slavery and the responses of the Founding Fathers has been the subject of some controversy in recent years. A modern quasi-intellectual movement has sprung up, criticizing Founders like George Washington and Thomas Jefferson for their arguable support of the institution of slavery. The debate goes to the heart of the issue of whether the United States was founded on the Jeffersonian declaration that all men are created equal and endowed by their creator with certain unalienable rights. This topic has had ripple effects in other areas concerned with equality, such as affirmative action today.

Any conclusions about the Founding Fathers and the issue of slavery must consider an assessment or explanation of the atmosphere extant in 1776. Further, the Founders' condemnation (or lack thereof) must be viewed within a holistic approach: they created a document that allowed for the legal emancipation of involuntary labor within the four corners of the Constitution of the United States. But for the efforts to negotiate, compromise, and devise documents, the Civil War Amendments, for example, would not have become law. While all will agree that slavery was central to James Madison's drafting of the Constitution and the Bill of Rights, those of his colleagues who allowed ambiguity to pervade much of the Constitution had no choice if the United States was not to be stillborn.

The fifty-five members of the Committee of the Whole, had the task of finding commonalities allowing for the supplanting of the moribund Articles of Confederation with a new and more effective document. The Articles of Confederation, the first American constitution, failed because of their internal organizational defects that prevented effective national governance. The states were the center of authority, and the proposed central government was devoid of real power and authority to conduct national or foreign affairs. The recognition of this problem led to the meeting in Annapolis where many of the Founding Fathers recognized the weaknesses of the Articles; the subsequent sessions in Philadelphia convened not to alter them, but to draft a document that would become the Constitution of the United States.

There was general agreement that the Philadelphia sessions would be held in secret until the completion of the work by those assembled. While many issues required compromise, the most intransigent problem stemmed from slavery's continued existence in the southern United States with the complicity of some northern commercial interests. While the southern states are condemned for their retention and support of slavery, it was an industry that involved many northerners. For example, many Boston Brahmins owned the slave ships that plied the trade routes from Africa's west coast to the United States in collaboration with various African leaders. Many New England Puritans, and others, historically preferred cheap labor in the form of indentured servitude to legal slavery.

Faced with the possibility of another defeat, the Founders resolved among themselves to compromise on many issues, especially slavery, should the need arise. The realization that a protracted debate would increase animus compelled the Founders to emphasize the immediate common goals. The acceptance of the South's "peculiar institution" was not a moral surrender, but a recognition of the realism of the moment. The purpose was to draft the requisite documentation for the functioning of a viable nation. Their collective concern for the creation of a government was based on prudence and expediency, not morality. Criticism and/or nonaction by many of slavery's opponents did not offer the opportunity to ruminate about morality and the long-term fibers of America. One need only image the consequences of an independent South devoid of a restraint to the fostering of slavery and possibly its spread beyond the Mississippi River.

The majority of the Founders were not maximists, but they recognized the problems of dealing with encrusted views that could not, and would not, be changed without force. Economic and religious self-interest would rule until America evolved into a more democratic republic as envisioned by the optimistic Founders. Allegations that all the Founders did not believe that all men were created equal are false. Political correctness has also decried many whose conduct was not pure or instantaneous in the defense of their fellow human beings. The legacy of Thomas Jefferson reflects this fact. In 1779, Thomas Jefferson, reviled over a then-unproven relationship with Sally Hemming, proposed a law in Virginia for the gradual emancipation of slaves; in 1784, he challenged the federal Congress when he sought legislation that would prohibit slavery in the entire western territories and lost by one vote. Jefferson's *Notes on the State of Virginia*, while containing derogatory descriptions of blacks, also contained an attack on slavery that was not accepted by his fellow Virginians. Finally, in 1807, he supported the legislation for the abolition of slavery, an extremely unpopular action among his fellow Virginia planters. Jefferson did question the biological equality of blacks, but he was not opposed to their natural rights. He made the connection between the slaves' environment and ability to function; he recognized that the educational deprivation inflicted upon the enslaved Africans was a cause of their social and legal situation in America.

Southerners such as the Rutledges and John Clay of South Carolina and the Lees of Virginia and a multitude of others accepted slavery as a vehicle to the best of all possible worlds. While they influenced their compatriots in Philadelphia, they were concerned with economic states' rights. Southern Founders did have a great effect upon their brethren enduring the heat and discomfort of Philadelphia. Fortunately for the evolution of democratic America, their ultimate influence was not great nor long lasting.

See also African Americans; American Civil War; Articles of Confederation; Bill of Rights; Constitution, Civil Rights, and Equality; Declaration of Independence and Equality; Race in Colonial America; Reparations; Segregation; Slavery.

FURTHER READING: Bowen, Catherine Drinker, 1966, *Miracle at Philadelphia: The Story of the Constitutional Convention, May to September 1787*, Boston: Little, Brown and Company; Irons, Peter, 1999, *A People's History of the Supreme Court*, New York: Viking Press; Miller, Loren, 1966, *The Petitioners: The Story of the Supreme Court of the United States and the Negro*, New York: Pantheon Books; Rubio, Philip F., 2001, *A History of Affirmative Action, 1619–2000*, Jackson: University Press of Mississippi.

ARTHUR K. STEINBERG

Small Business Administration

See Disadvantaged Business Enterprises.

Smith v. Allwright

See White Primary.

Smith v. University of Washington Law School, 233 F.3d 1188 (9th Cir. 2000)

The U.S. Court of Appeals for the Ninth Circuit decided in the case of *Smith v. University of Washington Law School* that consideration of race as a factor in state universities in order to reap the educational benefits of a diverse student body may be both constitutional and permissible under Title VI of the Civil Rights Act of 1964 if "properly designed and operated." The case is particularly important because it approved the use of a racial classification for a purpose other than to remedy demonstrated past discrimination. This conclusion, that diversity in higher education is a compelling governmental interest, was subsequently adopted by the U.S. Supreme Court in *Gratz v. Bollinger*, 123 S. Ct. 2411, 2003 U.S. LEXIS 4801 (2003), and *Grutter v. Bollinger*, 123 S. Ct. 2325, 2003 U.S. LEXIS 4800 (2003).

In *Smith v. University of Washington Law School*, Caucasian applicants sued the University of Washington Law School because it maintained an admissions affirmative action program that used racial minority status as a positive criterion and they were not admitted. That the school used race as a factor was undisputed in the case. The school justified the practice not as a remedial measure necessary to overcome the effects of past discrimination against minorities in its admissions practices, but in order to obtain the educational benefits of a diverse student body.

The court recognized that the race-conscious admissions program was subject to strict scrutiny constitutional review and thus could be upheld only if it was narrowly tailored to achieve a compelling governmental interest. The crucial question before the court was whether any interest other than a remedial one could qualify as "compelling" under this standard. Following the opinion of U.S. Supreme Court justice Lewis Powell in the famous case *Regents of the University of California v. Bakke*, 438 U.S. 265 (1978), case the court held that a university could have a compelling governmental interest in achieving a diverse student body because of the educational value that was likely to accrue benefiting the entire student body as long as race or ethnicity was only one of a range of factors considered to contribute to diversity and that consideration of race did not completely isolate applicants from competition because of their race. The court recognized that Justice Powell's opinion had been criticized as not binding because it was not a majority opinion. The court noted that the U.S. Court of Appeals for the Fifth Circuit had determined not to follow Powell's opinion and had declared that a diverse student body could not be a compelling governmental interest to justify consideration of race in university admissions even as only one of a number of factors (in *Hopwood v. Texas*, 78 F.3d 932 [5th Cir. 1996]). The court explained the legal doctrine that when the Supreme Court issues a split decision, the binding aspect of the several decisions is the narrowest position shared by a majority of the justices. The court then explained that Justice Powell's opinion was the narrowest and was, therefore, the law. The court then concluded that Powell's opinion required a "determination that a properly designed and operated race-conscious admissions program at the Law School of the University of Washington would not be in violation of Title VI or the Fourteenth Amendment." The court noted, however, that after the case was filed, Initiative 200, which outlawed preferential treatment on the basis of race or ethnicity in public education, became law in the state of Washington and forbade the affirmative action program challenged in the case. The Supreme Court declined in May 2001 to hear an appeal in the case.

See also Civil Rights Act of 1964; Compelling Governmental Interest; Fourteenth Amendment; *Gratz v. Bollinger/Grutter v. Bollinger*; *Hopwood v. Texas*; Narrowly Tailored Affirmative Action Plans; Powell, Lewis Franklin, Jr.; *Regents of the University of California v. Bakke*; Title VI of the Civil Rights Act of 1964; Washington Initiative 200.

FURTHER READING: Einat, Philip, 2002, "Diversity in the Halls of Academia: Bye-bye *Bakke*," *Journal of Law and Education* 31:149–166; Schmidt, Peter, and Jeffrey Selingo, 2002, "A Supreme Court Showdown: The Justices Take Up 2 Michigan Cases—and the Debate over Affirmative Action in Admissions," *Chronicle of Higher Education*, December 13, A20.

MARIA D. BECKMAN

Social Contract

Under the classic social contract theory, sovereignty-supported governments must take affirmative action to ensure that the benefits of collective action are conferred on all of their citizens. In general, social contract theory states that individuals move from a natural state of total freedom into a restricted society by entering into a contract in which they agree to give up or "sell" some of their personal freedoms and the personal freedoms of future generations to sovereignty to utilize societal collective action for the good of all to survive. In exchange for being a party to this contract, each individual receives influence over and benefits generated by sovereignty and societal collective action. In cases where benefits are not conferred, sovereignty must take affirmative action to remedy the situation to maintain and validate the contract.

Social contract theory, which traces its roots back to the Sophists of ancient Greece, has evolved as circumstances have changed, often justifying both sides of opposing points of view regarding the government allocation of goods and resources in society. Since the seventeenth century, the theory has progressed through two phases. Initially, it was described as a contract between the people and their government. The people agreed to "sell" their individual freedoms to a sovereign crown bearer in exchange for order, prosperity, and safety provided by the crown bearer. The sovereign crown bearer was held liable and could be punished or overthrown for not providing order, prosperity, and safety to his or her people, which was in sharp contrast to traditional authoritarian beliefs suggesting that the crown bearer was sovereign by the will of God and was accountable and answered only to God.

As power shifted to popularly elected assemblies, the people-government social contract evolved into a contract between individuals to create a government to provide peace, prosperity, and order for all of the people. The second phase was split into two divergent points of view. Thomas Hobbes, who wrote to oppose revolutions against the crown bearer, suggested that individuals of their own will created a governmental sovereign in the form of the crown bearer and sold to that individual/government all of their individual rights bound in posterity in exchange for order, prosperity, and safety. He placed the crown bearer/government/sovereign outside any obligation to the contract while binding individuals to passive obedience for all time. John Locke and Jean-Jacques Rousseau, who wrote to justify revolutions, theorized that the "general will" of the people was sovereign because individuals "sold" their freedoms to each other through the "general will." The government proper was an agent providing and maintaining distribution of societal benefits and enforcement of individual rights granted by the sovereign "general will" of the people. If the government no longer acted as an agent of the "general will" for the benefit of all, it no longer retained the support of popular sovereignty and should be altered.

See also Discrimination; National Labor Relations Act of 1935 (Wagner Act); National Labor Relations Board; Split-Labor-Market Theory.

FURTHER READING: Hobbes, Thomas, 1996, *Leviathan*, Cambridge: Cambridge University Press; Rousseau, Jean-Jacques, 1950, *The Social Contract and Discourses*, New York: E.P. Dutton; Sidorsky, David, 1970, *The Liberal Tradition in European Thought*, New York: G.P. Putnam's Sons.

MARK J. SENEDIAK

Social Darwinism

See Darwinism.

Social Engineering

Social engineering refers to intentional, proactive attempts to influence human interaction and ultimately serves as the social agent that propels change and development in society. The relevance of social engineering to affirmative action is important, as affirmative action plans are in essence a type of social engineering. The government is imposing a preferential plan, or group of benefits, for a historically discriminated-against class as a means for compensating members of these groups and promoting diversity. As such, the government is engaged in intentional, proactive actions to orchestrate a planned social change or development in society and, in the case of affirmative action, a breakdown of de facto segregation, discrimination, and racism in society.

Social engineering has a long history and significance in the social, scientific, artistic, and humanistic realms. In the late eighteenth century, it was a strong tool of positivistic science—an attempt to understand social life by applying scientific methodology. Social engineering was also used to understand social change in the context of development and progress of society called "social dynamics." Social engineering is a human interactive magic or elixir for reforming the social, economic, cultural, religious, and political institutions of society such that the existing needs are satisfied by alternative structures, unless it involves a change that eliminates these needs altogether.

Conflict theorists like Karl Marx and John Stuart Mill perceive social engineering as a continual social process in society because of the different ideological positions of active social agents in society. Social engineering is fundamental to these thinkers as an important ingredient of social change and progress or devolution of society. The continuous state of flux, tension, disagreement, and hostility that society undergoes is evaluated on the basis of the divergent ideological thoughts and ideas involved in social engineering. Radical and revolutionary ideological minds are believed to be those engaged in objective social engineering, while reactionary and conservative ideological social agents are believed to engage in dysfunctional and undesirable social engineering. Hostility over goals and values is a contentious area in social engineering.

See also Darwinism; De Facto and De Jure Segregation; Discrimination; Marxist Theory and Affirmative Action; Scientific Racism.

FURTHER READING: Kahlenberg, Richard D., 1996, *The Remedy: Class, Race and Affirmative Action*, New York: Basic Books; Merton, Robert K., 1957, "Manifest and Latent Functions," in *Social Theory and Social Structure*, 60–69, Glencoe, IL: Free Press; Mills, Wright C., 1959, *The Sociological Imagination*, New York: Oxford University Press.

KINGSLEY UFUOMA OMOYIBO

Socialization Theory of Equality

The socialization theory of equality, sometimes referred to as the social contact theory, is a process by which individuals are inculcated with learning based on norms, values, orientation, and ideology of equity and fairness through interaction with others in the performance of social roles and obligations as members of society. That is, by ensuring diversity in the workplace or in the school, members of different groups and walks of life begin to view each other equally and treat each other with fairness when they have enjoyed extensive social contact with each other. Thus affirmative action plans or programs, which place a premium on promoting diversity, are thought to improve equity and fairness among different ethnic and/or racial groups based upon their socialization and social contact with each other. The socialization theory of equality also seeks to dissipate problems stemming from xenophobia, or fears of things foreign and unknown.

The idea of the theory is to combat the potential threat to national or societal solidarity inherent in the value of inequality embedded in the different worldviews of individuals, groups, societies, or cultures who remain separated from other groups. The gender perspective conceptualizes it as an exhibition of hope against the unbridled masculinization of patriarchy and seeks a new being in a balanced personality in men and women. Pragmatically, it is more a theory of gender and an opposite of the social dominance theory. The socialization theory of equality seeks equality enhancement and a more balanced society and links equality to the focal value of the legitimate aspiration of all individuals to maximal self-realization.

Both functionalist and conflict theoretical perspectives hold that the theory is related to the process of progressive social change in society. The main area of polemics is in the belief by functionalists that it helps in the integration of all interests in society, while the conflict theoretical perspective asserts that the socialization theory is important as a method of correction of inequality and injustices in relationships among the existing social class differences ingrained in society. Thus the theory is applied to redress social inequality and relative deprivation in relationships among existing social forces in society. Put differently, the conflict theoretical perspective advocates the employment of socialization between groups in order to improve the lot of those groups that have previously suffered inequality and discrimination without regard to the impact on the majority group. This can be contrasted again by the functional approach, which adheres to the belief that socialization and social contact are beneficial for all groups. Under either approach to the socialization theory, the idea is to put values in place and make relevant the outcome of order and justice in the learning process acquired by individuals. The socialization of different groups thus ensures adequate integration of all segments and interests for the positive development of society and amalgamates all the divergent interests resulting from differences in ethnicity, race, class, religion, and so on into a uniform value orientation for progress to be attained, and it recognizes and helps to mobilize all interests to perform their social roles and obligations without recourse to discrimination and inequity.

The contemporary reemergence of active civil rights movements, feminist and human rights activism, and the struggle for women's empowerment in many developing and developed societies formed the basis for this theory. Over time, the family institution has played a less important role in the socialization theory of equality in the individual; instead, churches, schools, educational institutions, associations, clubs, and the mass media have been more effective at ingraining attitudes in individuals that emphasize more extensive social contacts based on equity, social justice, and recognition of the rights and dignity of other individuals in the social system. Application of the socialization theory reinforces the degree and sensitivity of feelings of individuals involved in interactions and the frequency of such interactions based on the democratic principles of justice, equality, and respect.

The socialization theory of equality, which is geared toward the overall positive development of society and its members, is influenced by the physical, social, and ideological environment, as well as attitudes and values of people who should be seen as active participants in the interactive process. The theory includes the realization of the self in a context that does not necessarily imply the development of highly personalized and idiosyncratic values of superiority, but rather egalitarian traits.

See also Civil Rights Movement; Diversity Management; Integration; Relative Deprivation Theory; Segregation; Xenophobia.

FURTHER READING: Cover, J. Daniel, 1995, "The Effects of Social Contact on Prejudice," *Journal of Social Psychology* 135, no. 3 (June): 403–406; Delgado, Richard, 1987, "The Ethereal Scholar: Does Critical Legal Studies Have What Minorities Want?" *Harvard Critical Legal Studies Law Review* 22:301–320; Helve, Helena, 1993, "Socialization of Attitudes and Values among Young People in Finland," *Young-Nordic Journal of Adults* 1, no. 3:27–39; Marshall, Gordon, ed., 1998, *A Dictionary of Sociology*, New York: Oxford University Press.

KINGSLEY UFUOMA OMOYIBO

Socially Disadvantaged and Affirmative Action

See Class-Based Affirmative Action; Economically Disadvantaged.

Socioeconomic Preferences

See Class-Based Affirmative Action; Economically Disadvantaged; Preferences.

Souter, David Hackett (1939–   )

David Hackett Souter, who has served as an associate justice of the U.S. Supreme Court since 1990, was nominated by President George H.W. Bush to fill the vacancy caused by the retirement of liberal justice William Brennan. While generally a moderate on the Court, Souter is considered to be strongly supportive of affirmative action. According to Georgetown University law professor Girardeau Spann, "In addition to Justice Stevens, the other three justices who make up the present Court's liberal bloc on affirmative action—Justices Souter, Ginsburg, and Breyer—have voted to uphold each affirmative action program that they considered in a constitutional case" (Spann 2000, 161). In 2003, he again aligned himself as being firmly in favor of affirmative action in the landmark cases *Gratz v. Bollinger*, 123 S. Ct. 2411, 2003 U.S. LEXIS 4801 (2003), and *Grutter v. Bollinger*, 123 S. Ct. 2325, 2003 U.S. LEXIS 4800 (2003), joining the majority in the *Grutter* decision and dissenting in the *Gratz* decision.

David Souter was born on September 17, 1939, in Melrose, Massachusetts, and spent his early childhood in the greater Boston area. In 1950, his family moved to Weare, New Hampshire, where his relatives still reside and he returns each summer to visit during the Supreme Court's summer breaks. Souter went on to attend Harvard College, where he was selected as a Phi Beta Kappa and as a Rhodes scholar, earning an A.B. degree in 1961. After attending Oxford University on his Rhodes scholarship and earning both an A.B. degree in jurisprudence and a master's degree, Souter returned to the United States and attended Harvard Law School, earning an LL.B. degree in 1966.

Upon graduation from Harvard, Souter returned to New Hampshire, where he worked as an associate for a law firm in Concord, New Hampshire, from 1966 to 1968. From 1968 to 1978, he served in the New Hampshire attorney general's office, first as an assistant attorney general (1968–1971), second as a deputy attorney general (1971–1976), and finally as the attorney general of New Hampshire

(1976–1978). In 1978, Souter transitioned to the state court system and served as a judge on the New Hampshire Superior Court (1978–1983) and the New Hampshire Supreme Court (1983–1990). During his time in the state court system (and in the attorney general's office), Souter had the reputation of being a frequent supporter and defender of Republican administrations in New Hampshire. He was also viewed as "tough on crime" and rarely supported the reversal of criminal convictions. In May 1990, during President George H.W. Bush's administration, Souter was confirmed as a judge on the U.S. Court of Appeals for the First Circuit. However, approximately two months later, before Souter could even settle into his new federal judgeship on the First Circuit, President Bush nominated Souter to the U.S. Supreme Court.

Since 1990, Souter has served on the Supreme Court, often joining Justice Sandra Day O'Connor as part of the Court's center, consistently joining neither the conservative bloc (Justices William Rehnquist, Clarence Thomas, Antonin Scalia, and Anthony Kennedy) nor the liberal bloc (Justices John Paul Stevens, Ruth Bader Ginsburg, and Stephen Breyer). Before ascending to the high court, Souter was expected to be a conservative jurist who would align himself with Justices Scalia and Rehnquist on most issues. After Souter's nomination, the White House even assured conservatives that Souter was a "home run." Yet on the Court, Souter has defied being labeled as a consistent member of either the conservative or the liberal bloc of the Court. Souter is best considered a moderate who is unafraid to oscillate between the conservative and liberal blocs. Although he was nominated by a conservative president, Souter is one of the supporters of affirmative action on the high court. He has voted consistently and uniformly in favor of affirmative action. In perhaps the biggest three affirmative action cases that he has reviewed on the high court, *Adarand Constructors, Inc. v. Peña*, 515 U.S. 200 (1995), and the *Gratz v. Bollinger* and *Grutter v. Bollinger* (2003) decisions, Souter has come out as a firm supporter of affirmative action, as illustrated by his position in these cases.

See also Adarand Constructors, Inc. v. Peña; Blackmun, Harry Andrew; Brennan, William Joseph; Breyer, Stephen Gerald; Bush, George Herbert Walker; Ginsburg, Ruth Bader; *Gratz v. Bollinger/Grutter v. Bollinger*; Kennedy, Anthony McLeod; O'Connor, Sandra Day; Rehnquist, William Hobbs; Scalia, Antonin; Stevens, John Paul; Thomas, Clarence.

FURTHER READING: Spann, Girardeau A., 2000, *The Law of Affirmative Action: Twenty-five Years of Supreme Court Decisions on Race and Remedies*, New York: New York University Press.

JAMES A. BECKMAN

South Africa and Affirmative Action

From 1948 until 1991, a formalized system of racial segregation prevailed in South Africa much like that which existed in the United States. Known by the Afrikaans term "apartheid," which literally means "separateness," the system segregated South Africans of European descent from those who were not, categorizing people of non-European and indigenous lineage into "coloured" or mixed, Bantu, Indian, and various other racial/ethnic denominations. The term "apartheid" has since evolved into a more general label for social, educational, political, economic, and other objectionable forms of racial/ethnic differentiation and separation. South Africa's past experiences are similar to those of the United States in two chief ways: first, both the U.S. system of segregation and South Africa's apartheid system show how the legal system operated as a tool to oppress minorities; and second, both countries are now attempting to overcome this history of legal discrimination by investigating the feasibility of, and implementing, various measures needed to ensure equality under the law. One such type of program recently being investigated and debated in South Africa is that of affirmative action programs for minorities. The comparisons between the United States and South Africa are especially important in the race relations and affirmative action context. An indication of the importance of the comparison is that in the April 2003 oral arguments in the cases *Gratz v. Bollinger*, 123 S. Ct. 2411, 2003 U.S. LEXIS 4801 (2003), and *Grutter v. Bollinger*, 123 S. Ct. 2325, 2003 U.S. LEXIS 4800 (2003), U.S. Supreme Court Justice Ruth Bader Ginsburg asked counsel to explain why the United States should not employ affirmative action plans when such programs have been used successfully in South Africa, India, and Canada in recent times.

The official rationale for apartheid offered by the white minority rulers who governed South Africa from the mid-1900s until 1991 was that complete separation by race/ethnicity was in the best interests of each racial/ethnic group and offered the best means to establish a harmonious multiracial/multiethnic nation. An institutionalized system of racial classification in which housing, employment, and all other areas of social life were structured around racial/ethnic identification would allegedly ensure a separate yet nevertheless equal social system. However, this white supremacist ideology not only classified people according to race/ethnicity, but used such classifications to "justify" assigning such groupings to specific geographical areas within South African cities, towns, and rural districts, with minority whites controlling the most desirable land and people of color legally restricted (e.g., via a "passbook" system) to more desolate and harsh interior regions of the country. This geographical separation was used to enforce (and was reinforced by) racial/ethnic exclusion from important social, educational, economic, and political opportunities. This formal system of inequality was brought to an official close in 1991 when the South African people freely elected a democratic government and along with it endorsed the formal legal equality of all people, which was to be guaranteed by a democratically constructed constitution. The Constitution of the Republic of South Africa, highly contested and slowly crafted over the better part of six years, was finally signed into law by President Nelson Mandela in December 1996 and implemented in February 1997. Today, though real egalitarianism still remains more an ideal than a reality, efforts are ongoing to dismantle the white supremacist structures of privilege and power that long dominated South Africa.

There are no comprehensive formal policies of "affirmative action" currently in place in South Africa. However, the implementation of new affirmative action–type programs, such as those that have been utilized in the United States, has been supported by the African National Congress (ANC) and was encouraged by President Nelson Mandela during his last days in office. For example, shortly before leaving office in 1998, President Mandela stated, "We shall not be discouraged by the concerns of the self-interested. Affirmative action is corrective action. There is no other way to move away from racial discrimination to true equality."

In the same spirit, the ANC passed the Employment Equity Act of 1999, which includes substantial affirmative action hiring requirements in order to reduce the inequity in the labor market among the races. Several South African laws refer to the permissibility of "positive discrimination," which is analogous to notions of benign discrimination under American affirmative action plans. Ironically, South Africa has also been experimenting with positive discrimination laws that benefit whites, who represent the current minority in South Africa.

Additionally, a number of constitutional principles and provisions, government-appointed commissions, and various nongovernmental organizations (NGOs) provide de facto mechanisms for achieving the ends for which formal affirmative action programs and policies have elsewhere (e.g., in the United States) been crafted. Specifically, the Constitution of the Republic of South Africa adopted in 1996 consists of thirty-four constitutional principles, many of which articulate the value of racial and gender equality as well as the need to develop the legal means of ensuring meaningful equality. For instance, the first principle of the Constitution asserts South Africa's commitment to "achieving equality between men and women and people of all races" via a democratic governmental system. The third expresses a constitutional prohibition on racial, gender, "and all other forms of discrimination" and a concomitant pledge to "promote" unity and equality among the people of South Africa. The fifth principle explicitly links these ideals of equality to the legal system, making clear that all South Africans are equal in the eyes of the law. This principle, moreover, insists that it is appropriate and expected that the law be used to ameliorate "the conditions of the disadvantaged, including those disadvantaged on the grounds of race, colour, or gender." Thus the law is envisioned both as a proactive and as a reactive instrument in simultaneously generating the conditions of meaningful equality while addressing the legacy effects of past racial/ethnic discrimination. The eleventh principle of the Constitution articulates support for diversity by explicitly announcing the recognition and promotion of diverse languages and cultures within South Africa. In these and related ways, the South African Constitution expresses its agreement with the moral ideals and principles animating affirmative action policies and practices in the United States and elsewhere around the world.

As noted, these ideals and principles of equality and nondiscrimination are also made practical via such organizations as the Office of the Public Protector, an office independent of the state and required to investigate impropriety or prejudice in any sphere of government. The Human Rights Commission, which aims to promote a culture of human rights while monitoring their observance by all individuals and institutions in South Africa, acts as an additional watchdog organization committed to real equality. Other groups, such as the Commission on Gender Equality (CGE) and the Truth and Reconciliation Commission (TRC), have also been of central importance in establishing substantive equality in South Africa.

One especially important arena of reform in the South African struggle for equality is the justice system itself. The Department of Justice and Constitutional Development, responsible for the administration of the courts and for developing the constitution, has been restructured to make justice more accessible and affordable for all citizens of South Africa. The system has defined and implemented guidelines on sexual offenses, crafted a "gender policy statement," and created a unit on "sexual offenses and community affairs" to assist in identifying and responding to gender discrimination and violence against women. The justice system also established a "human rights investigative unit" to assist the TRC in identifying and responding to gross human rights violations during the apartheid era. Although the TRC was dissolved in May 2001, a final report about its investigation into human rights violations and amnesty for perpetrators of such wrongs is forthcoming. Other reforms of the justice system include the establishment of so-called community courts in recognition of the fact that less formal decentralized tribunals composed of local community members may help ease the burden placed on the formal legal system while rendering more meaningful resolutions to petty crimes and social disputes. In the aftermath of the work of the TRC, the question of the need for and legitimacy of a final policy of reparations for victims of apartheid-era atrocities has taken center stage.

The final lines of Alan Paton's *Cry, the Beloved Country* are a forlorn worry: "But when that dawn will come, of our emancipation, from the fear of bondage and the bondage of fear, why, that is a secret" (Paton 1987, 236). Thus real human emancipation, and with it true equality, remains a mystery to contemporary South Africa as it continues to enact its break with apartheid and its transition to a postapartheid democratic government committed to racial/ethnic equality. The transition has to date been relatively free of violence; however, progress remains slow. Indeed, what counts as progress remains much debated. Discussions continue about the nature of political forms of apology, truth, and reconciliation and their ability to create the conditions for future justice and equality. In a nation that has for so long been bitterly divided along racial and ethnic lines, concerns about the nature of historical "memory" and its implications for South Africa's identity have begun to surface. These concerns focus on the role of collective memory in adequately responding to a morally tragic past in a way that preserves the past without distorting it, yet in a way that enables the nation to move forward. These and other complex political and moral issues make South Africa's struggle to achieve racial/ethnic equality very much a work in progress.

See also Apartheid; Benign Discrimination; Canada and Affirmative Action; Ginsburg, Ruth Bader; Global Implementation of Affirmative Action Programs; *Gratz v. Bollinger/Grutter v. Bollinger*; India and Affirmative Action; Segregation.

FURTHER READING: Berger, D., ed., 2001/2002, *South Africa Yearbook, 2001/02*, http://www.gcis.gov.za/docs/publications/yearbook02/chap2.pdf; "Confrontation, Communication, Reconciliation" (collected papers on political reconciliation and amnesty from the Congress 2001 Conference on "Communication: From Confrontation to Reconciliation"), 2001, *Media Development* 48, no. 4; Higginbotham, Michael F., 1999, "Affirmative Action in the United States and South Africa: Lessons from the Other Side," *Temple International and Comparative Law Journal* 13 (fall): 187–230; Hughes, Paul, 2001, "Moral Atrocity and Political Reconciliation: A Preliminary Inquiry," *International Journal of Applied Philosophy* 15, no. 1: 123–135; Jeffery, Anthea, 1999, *The Truth about the Truth Commission*, Johannesburg: South African Institute of Race Relations; Langston, Lundy R., 1997, "Affirmative Action: A Look at South Africa and the United States: A Question of Pigmentation or Leveling the Playing Field," *American University International Law Review* 13:333–377; Malan, Rian, 1990, *My Traitor's Heart*, New York: Grove Press; Palakow-Suransky, Sasha, 2002, "Reviving South African History," *Chronicle of Higher Education*, June 14, A36–A38; Paton, Alan, [1948] 1987; *Cry, the*

Beloved Country, reprint, New York: Charles Scribner's Sons; South African Government Justice, web page: www.gov.za/structure/justice.htm; Tutu, Desmond, 1999, *No Future without Forgiveness*, New York: Doubleday; Villa-Vicencio, Charles, ed., 2000, *Transcending a Century of Injustice*, Rondebosch, South Africa: Institute for Justice and Reconciliation.

PAUL M. HUGHES

Southern Christian Leadership Conference

The Southern Christian Leadership Conference (SCLC) is a civil rights organization founded by, among others, Martin Luther King Jr. and Ralph Abernathy. The SCLC had its genesis in the civil rights movement and was instrumental in lobbying for civil rights laws and conducting boycotts and protests throughout the South. Today, the SCLC has an on-line web site and a magazine dedicated to civil rights issues, as well as chapters and affiliates throughout the country that continue to engage in the civil rights dialogue. In the 1990s, the SCLC became an advocate of affirmative action. In 1995, then Vice President Al Gore delivered a keynote address at the thirty-eighth annual SCLC conference, calling for the continuation of affirmative action. Gore stated that "there are those who would say the time for affirmative action has come and gone . . . but anybody who denies that racism still exists is less than honest about the true state of America today. Affirmative action can and must continue to play a role in our society" (Jet, 10). The SCLC's 2003 Program Goals state that the "SCLC has had a leadership role for at least the past decade in the area of affirmative action. We will continue our role as advocates in this area" (SCLC, "Program Goals," http://www.selenational.org).

In 1997, Martin Luther King III, the son of Martin Luther King Jr., was elected as the fourth president of SCLC and took office on January 15, 1998, his father's birthday. King succeeded the Reverend Joseph Lowery, who had led the organization for twenty years prior and was occasionally criticized for lacking vision in leading the SCLC into the twenty-first century. Since the SCLC's involvement in the civil rights movement, some have suggested that the SCLC lost the focus that it had during the 1960s. When King III took office in January 1998, he called for focusing the SCLC's attention on external problems facing the black community, like recent assaults on affirmative action. Prior to his ascendancy to SCLC's presidency, King founded a group called Americans United for Affirmative Action.

The history of the SCLC goes back more than four decades. In January 1957, a conference concerning integration and other African American issues was held in Atlanta, Georgia. Several community and civil rights activists were present. Among those who attended the meeting were Stanley Levison, Ella Baker, Bayard Rustin, Fred Shuttlesworth, C.K. Steele, Ralph D. Abernathy, Joseph Lowery, William H. Borders, and Martin Luther King Jr. After an initial meeting, the nucleus of what would become the SCLC was formed. Shortly after the organization was formed, Martin Luther King Jr. was elected president. The mission of the organization was to transform America through nonviolent strategies adopted from the teachings of Mahatma Gandhi. The organization used the powerful influence of the African American church as the main avenue of reaching the larger African American community. The SCLC also advocated compensatory justice solutions to the race problem throughout the 1960s.

The SCLC's first efforts were very modest and mild. The organization's first major campaign against segregation took place in November 1961 in Albany, Georgia, when the SCLC entered an existing integration campaign. After being unsuccessful in its effort to receive national support, the SCLC ended its efforts in the protests in Albany. In 1963, the SCLC began a campaign in the segregationist stronghold of Birmingham, Alabama. The new project was called "Project C" and aimed to end segregation in Alabama. Project C drew criticism from segregationists as well as white liberal leadership that suggested that Birmingham's African American citizens wait until a new city administration enacted reforms promised by city leaders while campaigning for city public offices. Protesters who demonstrated and defied segregative laws were jailed. In May 1963, African American children marched in Birmingham and were arrested and placed in jail. The next day, more children marched. However, on this occasion, the police used powerful water hoses on them. This brutal attack was captured by the media and soon garnered national and international attention. As a result of the aforementioned developments, the city of Birmingham went into negotiations with civil rights leaders.

After the success in Birmingham, the SCLC organized protest campaigns in several other cities in the Deep South. In 1965, the SCLC began a new campaign tackling the poll tests, which were being used as a requirement for African American voters in the Deep South. In some states, African Americans were blatantly denied voting privileges. The SCLC organized a fifty-mile march from Selma to Alabama's state capital in Montgomery. As the marchers began their trek to Montgomery, the Alabama State Police used batons and tear gas to disperse the marchers. After the images of protesters being trampled and beaten reached the national media spotlight, the march attempt was called "Bloody Sunday." About a week later, a second march from Selma to Montgomery was organized and successfully carried out. After assisting in securing voting rights for African Americans, the organization shifted its attention to economic inequality in America. However, after the death of Martin Luther King Jr. and subsequent infighting over the changing mission and leadership, the group was not able to fully regain its stature as one of the quintessential leading organizations in the civil rights movement.

See also African Americans; Americans United for Affirmative Action; Civil Rights Movement; King, Martin Luther, Jr.

FURTHER READING: Peake, Thomas R., 1987, *Keeping the Dream Alive: A History of the Southern Christian Leadership Conference from King to the Nineteen-eighties*, New York: P. Lang; Sack, Kevin, 1997, "Rights Group Gives Martin Luther King 3d His Father's Old Post," *New York Times*, November 2, 1:29; Southern Christian Leadership Conference, web site: http://www.sclcnational.org; "Vice President Al Gore Gives Keynote Address at SCLC Convention," 1995 *Jet* 88, no. 19 (September 18): 10.

F. ERIK BROOKS

Sowell, Thomas (1930–)

Thomas Sowell is an economist, a columnist, and a leading black conservative voice in the United States. He is also a senior fellow at the conservative Hoover Institution in Stanford, California. Sowell has prolifically argued that affirmative action programs are antithetical to the goal that Americans be treated equally;

therefore, he has opposed affirmative action programs that target individuals based on race, gender, or age. Sowell rejects the idea that differences in statistical representation between groups should serve as evidence of discrimination and expresses doubt about affirmative action's ability to correct past injustices. He believes that these policies encourage hostility, separation, and dependence by the targeted groups and that affirmative action policies contribute to continuing racial polarization.

According to Sowell, without discrimination, all groups would not necessarily be represented in a proportion equal to their representation in the population. Rather, he argues that because individuals differ in their abilities and preferences, perfect statistical representation cannot be reasonably expected. Thus, for Sowell, the idea that affirmative action policies should be used to correct statistical discrimination is not rational. Additionally, he believes that affirmative action policies are at their base discriminatory. He argues, on the one hand, that the broadening umbrella of policies has created a situation whereby two-thirds of Americans are given preferences over the one-third of Americans who are young, male members of nonprotected ethnic/racial groups. On the other hand, Sowell writes that affirmative action policies are fundamentally based on the idea that protected groups cannot be held to the same standards as others.

A recurring theme in his work is the idea that America has consistently discriminated against new groups of immigrants and that these groups have nevertheless been able to succeed. He argues that African Americans have shown a great deal of improvement in material conditions in the recent past and that without affirmative action programs, we might reasonably expect this progress to continue. However, he worries that affirmative action tends to coddle African American youngsters and give them the impression that they need not work to their full potential, since they will be favored in affirmative action programs. Further, he rejects the idea that white racism continues to be the main barrier to African American success. Finally, Sowell has argued that not all black students ought to be considered for Ivy League institutions. Like other races and ethnicities, there are students of different talents, and (according to Sowell) one must be cognizant of realistic limitations. In this vein, Sowell has commented that "youngsters who could have succeeded at San Jose State University may be failing at Berkeley, while youngsters who could have succeeded at a community college are failing at San Jose State."

Sowell is a prolific writer. Though he is certainly an opponent of affirmative action, most of Sowell's writing does not focus specifically on this issue. Rather, his work speaks to issues of culture, economics, education, and social change as well as social policies designed to compensate for past discrimination. He advocates limited government involvement in social issues, such as housing and employment. He has written more than twenty books and has published seven collections of his columns, in addition to the scores of essays and articles that can be found under his name. His writing has been directed to a broad audience. He has written both academic works and columns for publications as diverse as the *New York Times*, *Forbes*, the *Washington Star*, and the *Los Angeles Herald Examiner*, among others.

Sowell is the Rose and Milton Friedman Senior Fellow at the Hoover Institution, which is housed at Stanford University. Sowell has been a Hoover fellow since

1977. Sowell trained as an economist at a series of prestigious institutions: Harvard, Columbia, and the University of Chicago, where he earned his bachelor's degree, a master's degree in economics, and a doctorate in economics, respectively. He has held positions in the public and private sectors, serving as a labor economist as well as an economic analyst. In addition, he has held a variety of academic positions over the course of his nearly forty-year career.

See also Affirmative Action, Criticisms of; Color-Blind Constitution; Disparate Treatment and Disparate Impact, Reverse Discrimination; Statistical Proof of Discrimination.

FURTHER READING: Megalli, Mark, 1995, "The High Priests of the Black Academic Right," *Journal of Blacks in Higher Education*, autumn, 71–77; Sowell, Thomas, 1981, *Ethnic America: A History*, New York: Basic Books; Sowell, Thomas, 1981, *Pink and Brown People: and Other Controversial Essays*, Stanford, CA: Hoover Institution Press; Sowell, Thomas, 1999, *Barbarians inside the Gates: and Other Controversial Essays*, Stanford, CA: Hoover Institution Press; Sowell, Thomas, 2000, *A Personal Odyssey*, New York: Free Press; Sowell, Thomas, 2002, *Controversial Essays*, Stanford, CA: Hoover Institution Press.

KYRA R. GREENE

Split-Labor-Market Theory

The split-labor-market theory explains racial conflict as the result of competition between labor-price-differentiated racial groups in the labor market. In this theory, groups collectively differentiate the price of their labor, separating labor markets into high- and low-priced segments. These segments become antagonistic to each other when low-priced labor undercuts the value of high-priced labor, and high-priced labor utilizes power to restrict the access of low-priced labor to the market through exclusion or caste systems.

The price of a group member's labor includes the sum of all costs that an employer must bear to utilize that labor for production: wages, recruitment, transportation, housing, education, health care, labor unrest, and social unrest. A group's relative costs in each category are determined by the resources and motives that it wields in the labor marketplace. Price-deflating resources include low wage requirements to induce mobility, sparse comparable labor-market wage information and weak political resources in wage negotiations, and price-deflating motivations such as pursuing only temporary or fortune-seeking employment.

Labor markets split when two or more ascribed, mutually exclusive groups with different prices of labor compete for the same jobs. Business interests fill available jobs with low-priced labor first, forcing high-priced labor to either leave the labor market or reduce its price. Low-priced labor groups weaken high-priced labor groups by utilizing this cost advantage to get a foothold in and eventually monopolize labor markets. In anticipation of or response to these actions, high-priced labor groups utilize their economic, political, and social power to prevent a split in the labor market by resisting the entry of low-priced labor into competitive labor markets through exclusion laws or by removing existing low-priced labor through the establishment and enforcement of a social caste system that increases the labor and social unrest costs of formerly low-priced labor.

Ascribed racial and ethnic groups that have lived separately from each other or that have different employment goals often have different prices of labor. When two or more of these different groups are forced to compete for the same jobs, the labor market splits, and racial or ethnic antagonism occurs. For example, after the Civil War, former slaves who competed with whites for employment became the victims of ethnic persecution by groups such as the Ku Klux Klan.

See also American Civil War; Caste System; Good-Old-Boy Factor; Ku Klux Klan; National Labor Relations Act.

FURTHER READING: Bonacich, Edna, 1972, "A Theory of Ethnic Antagonism: The Split Labor Market," *American Sociological Review* 37, no. 5 (October): 547–559, reprinted in *From Different Shores: Perspectives on Race and Ethnicity in America*, edited by Ronald Takaki, New York: Oxford University Press, 1987; Segura, Denise, 1984, "Labor Market Stratification: The Chicana Experience," *Journal of Sociology* 29:57–80, reprinted in *From Different Shores: Perspectives on Race and Ethnicity in America*, edited by Ronald Takaki, New York: Oxford University Press, 1987.

MARK J. SENEDIAK

Standardized Testing

Large-scale educational and psychological assessments have been used for many years as tools to attempt to provide more equitable access to education and employment. These forms of assessment, sometimes referred to as standardized tests, have been the target of extensive criticism and debate. Many critics see these forms of tests as playing too large a role in the selection of individuals for employment and admission to institutions of higher learning, and they maintain that the tests are biased and exclusionary. Conversely, many critics of affirmative action argue that selection and promotion should not be based upon race or gender, but rather on merit, which is often defined by how well one performs on standardized tests.

The standardized-testing movement to test aptitude and achievement began in the early twentieth century. The work of Alfred Binet, a French physiological psychologist, led to the creation of the first successful intelligence scale. Subsequent revisions of Binet's scale by Lewis Terman of Stanford University resulted in the development of the Stanford-Binet intelligence test. After the success of the intelligence test administrable to individuals, American psychologists began to explore the possibility of developing intelligence tests that could be administered simultaneously to groups of examinees. The impetus for the widespread use of group intelligence tests in the United States began with its entry into World War I. The Army Alpha Intelligence Test was developed as a rapid means of sorting and classifying recruits for the army to effectively staff its military operations. The Army Alpha was used to test almost 2 million men in the largest mass testing of the century. The success of the army testing program was unprecedented, leading to the explosive growth of the testing movement.

In the post–World War II era, a renewed focus on standardized testing resulted from the need to evaluate the millions of GIs returning to civilian life and preparing to attend America's colleges on the GI Bill. The Scholastic Aptitude Test (SAT), now referred to as the Scholastic Assessment Test, originally introduced in 1926, was the testing instrument selected to evaluate the GIs' scholastic aptitude. Subsequently, other forms of standardized tests were developed for making admissions and employment decisions.

The author of a standardized test must be able to ensure that the instrument is both valid and reliable. Validity is the most important consideration in test evaluation. The validity of a test is the degree to which the inferences from the test are accurate and meaningful. In more general terms, the concept of validity relates to the extent to which a test measures what it purports to measure. The methods to ensure evidence of validity of a test are typically grouped into three major categories that include content-related, construct-related, and criterion-related evidence of validity. Content-related evidence of validity demonstrates the degree to which a sample of items, tasks, or questions on a test is representative of a defined domain. On a test for employment selection, for instance, a systematic observation of the tasks one performs on a specific job combined with expert judgment from those individuals familiar with the job can be used for the purpose of determining the domain of critical tasks that the test should measure. Construct-related evidence of validity relates to a test score that is intended to be a measure of some defined characteristic of interest. Examples of the characteristics that may be found on a college admissions test are reasoning ability and reading comprehension. Finally, the third category of validity is criterion-related evidence of validity. Criterion-related evidence shows that the test scores are related to one or more outcome criteria. Criterion-related evidence of validity is therefore based on the extent to which an examinee's score on a test permits the inference of the examinee's performance on a criterion variable. With regard to college admission, an example of criterion-related validity evidence would be the use of a verbal aptitude test administered to a student in high school for the purpose of predicting that student's academic performance in college. This evidence is more specifically referred to as predictive criterion-related evidence of validity. In employment selection testing, this category of validity is targeted at predicting successful job performance.

The issue of reliability is the second important consideration of the test developer. The reliability of a test instrument relates to the degree to which the resulting test scores are free from measurement errors. Two important considerations in assessing the reliability of an instrument are consistency and stability. A test is considered to be reliable if an examinee's performance is "consistent" and stable after multiple administrations. This is sometimes called test-retest reliability. To verify stability, a test is repeated on the same test group at a future time, and the results are compared to give the test a measure of stability.

Critics of tests used for both college admissions and employment selection often believe that bias exists within commercially created standardized tests. Bias in relationship to standardized testing refers to the extent to which test items offend or unfairly penalize any group of examinees on the basis of personal characteristics such as gender, race, or ethnicity. A test item that may be considered offensive to a particular group might portray a female in the stereotypical role of housewife sending her businessman husband off to work. A test item that depicts a white police officer interviewing a group of minority youth representing gang members may offend minority examinees. Test items that unfairly penalize a particular group of examinees would be items on which those examinees perform less well than other groups of examinees with similar levels of achievement or aptitude. Inner-city youths, for instance, may perform less well when drawing conclusions from a reading selection about growing up on a farm, not because they are less able to draw conclusions, but because they may have less prerequisite knowledge about farm life.

Test bias can come in many forms, including gender bias, religious bias, geographic bias, or linguistic bias. The form of bias that has been considered most insidious by the critics of standardized testing is ethnic bias. Critics claim that testing practices that are ethnically biased have contributed to continued unfair treatment of individuals who have already been victims of social injustices and inequities. Lani Guinier, a high-profile advocate of affirmative action, has coined the term "testocracy" to describe the arguably undue reliance on unfair tests. Guinier argues that if the United States is truly to adhere to the notion of meritocracy, it must do away with its propensity for "testocracy."

Standardized testing is commonly associated with admissions to undergraduate colleges and universities as well as graduate and professional schools. Results on the Scholastic Assessment Test (SAT) or the American College Test (ACT) are required by most colleges and universities as part of the undergraduate admissions process. The Graduate Record Examination (GRE), the Law School Admission Test (LSAT), and the Medical College Admission Test (MCAT) are typically used for entrance into graduate schools, law schools, and medical schools, respectively.

A standardized test is not the sole criterion used in the admissions process. Many institutions use a variety of criteria, including grade point average, rank in class, letters of recommendation, extracurricular activities, and writing samples. Additionally, background data such as gender, age, and racial- or ethnic-group designation are often requested. This information is sometimes used for affirmative action considerations. Making admissions decisions by taking an applicant's gender, age, or racial and ethnic designation into consideration has been a source of controversy. Proponents of the use of affirmative action in admissions decisions most often point to the used of standardized testing for selection as most detrimental to minority applicants.

Criticism of standardized tests has taken a very consistent tone over the years. Opponents see the tests as racist, classist, and not accurately reflective of students' potential achievement. Some opponents argue that the tests are not a measure of one's intellectual aptitude, but are instead influenced by such things as the quality of a student's secondary education or even a student's affluent background. Students who are members of affluent families have the ability to pay for tutors or commercially offered test-preparation courses. Some students simply test well while others do not, further raising questions about the tests' credibility. When affirmative action programs are recommended to neutralize the negative effects that opponents of standardized testing cite, there is opposition from testing proponents. Critics of testing counter by claiming that entrance into America's most prestigious schools is often left to those students of wealth and familial connections, which, in and of itself, is a form of affirmative action. They see the emergence of affirmative action programs as a way to correct the negative effects of testing on minority access to opportunities previously made available only to the elite.

Both sides of the debate on the effects of admissions tests on group differences believe that the academic research supports their view on the use of such tests. Much of the research indicates that there are substantial differences among groups in mean scores on standardized tests. Standardized differences used to compare white test takers to other ethnic and racial groups indicate that group differences appear fully consistent across standardized admissions tests. The largest gaps have been found between white and African American test takers, followed by Hispanic test takers.

Proponents of the use of standardized tests for admissions decisions claim that the tests are a good indicator of potential achievement and success in the first year of college. They argue that the tests are not unfair to minority groups. They point out that researchers studying the fairness of the SAT, for instance, do not ordinarily focus on the average scores achieved by each racial or ethnic group. Instead, they consider how well the SAT predicts college grades for each group. Their research indicates that using the SAT to predict first-year college grade point average results in a more positive prediction for African American and Hispanic test takers than is warranted. The indication is that the test tends to provide an overprediction of future success in college for these groups. In other words, African Americans and Hispanics tend to have lower freshman-year grades than white students who score the same on the SAT. According to the proponents of testing, these results show that standardized admissions tests are benefiting minority groups seeking college admissions.

Recent court decisions and actions by state legislatures have also influenced the use of standardized testing in admissions decisions. In *Hopwood v. Texas*, 78 F.3d 932 (5th Cir. 1996), four white students claimed that they deserved admittance to the University of Texas at Austin Law School more than the Hispanic students who had been admitted. The plaintiffs based their claim on the fact that their Texas Index scores, which included a combination of college grade point average and scores on the LSAT, were higher than the scores of the Hispanic students. The U.S. Fifth Circuit Court of Appeals agreed and dismantled the university's affirmative action program on that basis.

Several states have also made changes to develop "race-neutral" standards in admissions. These changes may both eliminate the use of affirmative action programs and lessen the emphasis on a standardized test such as the SAT. In Texas, the federal appellate court's decision in *Hopwood* banning affirmative action prompted the legislature to adopt a policy of admitting all students in the top 10 percent of their high-school graduating class to the state's universities. Florida followed suit by replacing race preferences with a policy of admitting the top 20 percent of the high-school graduating class to its state public universities. California and Washington have also passed legislation prohibiting considerations of race and ethnicity in admissions decisions in public colleges and universities. Opponents of plans such as those implemented in Texas and Florida argue that because some high schools are segregated, these plans raise academic disparity questions similar to those in more straightforward affirmative action plans.

Employment selection decisions are typically made by the use of application completion, background checks, previous work history inquiries, letters of recommendation, and/or interviews. Tests are also a common method used to make a variety of personnel and employment decisions. Tests that have been used to make employment decisions typically have been measures of cognitive skills, called aptitude or ability tests. Aptitude tests that have been professionally developed have been considered to be valid predictors of job performance. The selection of individuals for entry-level positions or the promotions of individuals from within an organization to higher-level positions are employment situations in which such tests are typically used. The use of competent tests can contribute to fair treatment of individuals in employment settings and be the most valid and least discriminating personnel decision aids available.

Government intervention in issues of personnel selection decisions has a longer history and is more commonplace than that in college admissions. The federal government's initial major involvement in the personnel selection of private and public organizations began with the passage of the Civil Rights Act of 1964. Specifically, Title VII of the act made it unlawful for employers to fail to hire, to discharge, or otherwise to discriminate against any individual with regard to his or her compensation, terms, conditions, or privileges of employment because of an individual's race, color, religion, sex, or natural origin.

The Civil Rights Act was expanded in 1972 with the passage of the Equal Employment Opportunity Act. This act established the Equal Employment Opportunity Commission (EEOC), which was charged with the task of adopting a common federal position regarding testing and selection procedures for personnel decision making. This task led to the development of the Uniform Guidelines on Employment Selection Procedures in 1978. There are several essential features within the guidelines that must be considered when developing tests for employment selection. The fundamental principle underlying the Uniform Guidelines is that employer policies and practices that have an adverse impact on employment opportunities for any race, sex, or ethnic group are illegal unless they are justified by business necessity. Adverse impact refers to substantial disparities in the rate at which different groups are affected by personnel decisions involving employment opportunities. The guidelines adopted a "rule of thumb" referred to as the four-fifths or 80 percent rule as a practical means of determining adverse impact for use in employment proceedings. This rule requires that the selection rate or, in the case of an employment test, the passing rate for minority candidates must be at least 80 percent of the rate for majority candidates. Personnel selection tests that meet the criteria of this rule will help the employing agencies avoid possible discrimination suits. The guidelines also specify the establishment of test validity using criterion-related, content-related, and construct-related evidence. Technical standards and documentation requirements for the application of each of the three approaches are contained in the guidelines.

There have also been several significant court cases that serve as a foundation for governmental intervention in the employment testing procedures of organizations. A first application of Title VII came as a result of *Griggs v. Duke Power Co.*, 401 U.S. 424 (1971). The Supreme Court held in the *Griggs* case that employment selection devices not clearly related to the job to be performed are unlawful. Additionally, job applicants should be selected on qualifications having a demonstrable relationship to successful job performance. This decision emphasizes the necessity for developing an employment selection test that is based on a job-task analysis to ensure job relatedness. In *Albemarle Paper Co. v. Moody*, 422 U.S. 405 (1975), the Supreme Court expanded the effects of *Griggs*. The Court required employers not only to show that tests were job related, but also to demonstrate that other less discriminating means of selection were unavailable.

The Supreme Court showed some discontent with the rigid application of its own prior decisions in the case *Washington v. Davis*, 426 U.S. 229 (1976). In *Washington*, the Court upheld the use of tests in spite of evidence of adverse impact. Black applicants who had failed a verbal skills test administered by the District of Columbia Police Department charged that the test disproportionately screened out black applicants. The failure rate for black applicants was found to be four times that of white applicants. The city claimed that the test was job related, since the scores were highly correlated with police academy performance. The Court ruled that if the test appears to be "on the face" related to job performance, it is not violating any constitutional right. Additionally, the Court noted that there is no single method of validating employment tests for their relationship to job performance. This ruling indicated that content-, construct-, or criterion-related evidence of validity is considered professionally acceptable.

Thus the efficacy of testing for the purpose of university admissions and for employment selection decisions has been an issue of debate. The creation of a diverse workforce or college classroom by attempting to attract minority participation is both a noble pursuit and oftentimes a legal necessity. The methods used to achieve this participation are the point of contention. Many universities seeking to maintain a fair representation of minority students while responding to the criticism of suspected bias inherent in standardized testing have deemphasized test scores in favor of the more traditional methods, including class rank, grade point average, and recommendations. Complete elimination of the use of standardized tests, while occurring at some institutions, is not expected any time in the near future. With regard to employment testing, from a legal perspective, a court judgment against an organization in an employment discrimination lawsuit can be quite costly, making compliance with guidelines for personnel selection such as the four-fifths rule paramount. One method for increasing diversity in the workforce is the implementation of an affirmative action program. Affirmative action is rooted in Title VII, which is designed to afford equal employment opportunities. The use of the four-fifths rule is intended to ensure that any test developed and used for employment selection or promotion provides equal employment opportunities for protected groups. The challenge is to strike the proper balance that will afford employment access to qualified minority candidates while also ensuring fair treatment of majority candidates.

See also African Americans; *Albemarle Paper Co. v. Moody*; Civil Rights Act of 1964; Education and Affirmative Action; Employment (Private) and Affirmative Action; Employment (Public) and Affirmative Action; Equal Employment Opportunity Act of 1972; Equal Employment Opportunity Commission; GI Bill; *Griggs v. Duke Power Co.*; Guinier, Lani; Hispanic Americans; *Hopwood v. Texas*; Meritocracy; One Florida Initiative; Percentage Plans; Proposition 209; Race-Neutral Criteria; Title VII of the Civil Rights Act of 1964; Washington Initiative 200.

FURTHER READING: "Affirmative Action and Standardized Testing" (colloquy), 1998, *Texas Hispanic Journal of Law and Policy* 4:85–97; American Psychological Association, 1999, *The Standards for Educational and Psychological Testing*, Washington, DC: American Psychological Association; Camara, W.J., and A.E. Schmidt, 1999, *Group Differences in Standardized Testing and Social Stratification*, College Board Report No. 99-5, New York: College Entrance Examination Board; Delgado, Richard, 2001, "Official Elitism or Institutional Self Interest? 10 Reasons Why UC–Davis Should Abandon the LSAT (and Why Other Good Law Schools

Should Follow Suit)," *University of California at Davis Law Review* 34 (spring): 593–614; Kidder, William C., 2001, "Does the LSAT Mirror or Magnify Racial and Ethnic Differences in Educational Attainment? A Study of Equally Achieving Elite College Students," *California Law Review* 89 (July): 1055–1124; Lemann, Nicholas, 1999, *The Big Test: The Secret History of the American Meritocracy*, New York: Farrar, Straus and Giroux; Williams, Wendy, 2000, "Perspectives on Intelligence Testing, Affirmative Action, and Educational Policy," *Psychology, Public Policy, and Law* 6 (March): 15–19.

CHRISTOPHER R. CAPSAMBELIS

Stanton, Elizabeth Cady (1815–1902)

As a writer, orator, and political activist, Elizabeth Cady Stanton is often considered the founder of the women's rights movement in the United States. She has been variously described as a freethinker, radical revisionist, original feminist, and champion of the rights of women. While her life predates modern affirmative action programs, her ideas and struggle impact the affirmative action debate today. Stanton was convinced that "prejudice against sex" was worse than racial prejudices. She also believed that notions of patriarchy and religious doctrines worked to subjugate women in society and keep them from achieving economic and political equality. Organized religion, thought Stanton, did much to further gender stereotypes in America. Therefore, Stanton penned the controversial book *The Women's Bible*, a revision of the Bible that removed or revised all provisions that were perceived as being negative to women. Stanton also coined the phrase "Men, their rights and nothing more; women, their rights and nothing less." She also helped pen the Declaration of Sentiments, which mirrored the Declaration of Independence, but was directed at gender equality. The document radically declared that "all men and women are created equal . . . and are endowed by their Creator with certain unalienable rights."

Elizabeth Cady was born in Johnstown, New York, on November 15, 1815. Cady's parents, Margaret Livingston and Daniel Cady, were strict Scotch Presbyterians. While all six of the Cady children were exposed to the strict discipline and conservatism of their parents, they were also exposed to more radical ideas and people through Daniel Cady's law office. Although her parents were strict, the bright and active Elizabeth was allowed to pursue educational goals. Recognizing her intelligence, Elizabeth's father allowed her to come to his law office and observe. The time in her father's office exposed Elizabeth to numerous legal issues affecting women. Laws that denied married women property especially disturbed Elizabeth. Aside from her father's influence, her intellectual development was greatly affected by her relationship with Presbyterian minister Simon Hosack. Despite her frustration with the Scotch Presbyterian religion, she and the reverend developed a close friendship that lasted into adulthood. She also studied at the Johnstown Academy, where she excelled in Greek, Latin, and math, and then enrolled at the Troy Female Seminary. When her brother died, Elizabeth was even more determined to do well in the hope that her success would ease her father's pain. Despite Elizabeth's efforts, her father often stated that he wished she were a boy.

Elizabeth's interest in reform movements blossomed during her yearly visits to the Peterboro, New York, estate of her cousin, Gerrit Smith. Smith, one of the wealthiest men in New York, was an active participant in the abolitionist movement before the Civil War, was a secret supporter of John Brown's 1859 raid on the federal arsenal in Harpers Ferry, Virginia, and often held abolitionist meetings in his home. During one meeting, Elizabeth was introduced to abolitionist and reformer Henry Brewster Stanton. Despite objections from her father, Elizabeth married Stanton on May 10, 1840. Through Henry, Elizabeth met a number of influential abolitionists, including the Grimké sisters and Lucretia Mott.

By the time the Stantons moved to Seneca Falls, New York, in 1847, Elizabeth was an ardent reformer. Just a year later, she called for a women's rights convention to demand equality for women. During the July 19–20, 1848, convention, the attendees wrote the Declaration of Sentiments outlining women's grievances. A recognized reform leader through her writings and speeches, once she met Susan B. Anthony in 1851, her reform activities mushroomed. While Stanton remained at home to care for her seven children, Anthony used her mobility as a single woman to advance the women's rights movement. The suffragists' movement split in 1869, with Anthony and Stanton forming the National Woman Suffrage Association, but by 1890 the groups merged again into the National American Woman Suffrage Association. Stanton started to slow down when she reached sixty-five but continued to travel and lecture. She also published five books, including the two-volume *History of Woman Suffrage* (1881–1882). Stanton died in her sleep on October 26, 1902.

See also Abolitionists; American Civil War; Anthony, Susan Brownell; Declaration of Independence and Equality; Declaration of Sentiments; Stereotypes, Gender; Suffrage Movement.

FURTHER READING: Chorlian, Meg, 2000, "It's a Family Affair," *Cobblestone* 21, no. 3 (March): 30; Greene, Meg, 2000, "Progress Is the Law," *Cobblestone* 21, no. 3 (March): 2; Griffith, Elisabeth, 1985 (reprint), *In Her Own Right: The Life of Elizabeth Cady Stanton*, New York: Oxford University Press; Leuchtag, Alice, 1996, "Elizabeth Cady Stanton: Freethinker and Radical Revisionist," *Humanist* 56, no. 5 (September–October): 29–33; Rynder, Constance, "All Men and Women Are Created Equal," *American History* 33, no. 3 (August): 22–28.

LISA A. ENNIS

State Action Doctrine

Historically, the state action doctrine is closely associated with both the principle of federalism and the Equal Protection Clause of the Fourteenth Amendment to the U.S. Constitution, which states that no "state" (any governmental agency or any officer acting "under the color of law") shall act in any way "to deny any person within its jurisdiction the equal protection of the laws." Initially, this doctrine was limited to affirmative acts committed by the state or its officers, and it was limited further to individual rights deemed fundamental constitutionally, such as the right to due process in criminal matters. Later, however, the scope of individual rights was expanded, as was the definition of state action, which eventually entailed an affirmative obligation of state officials to attempt to prevent some acts of discrimination committed by private citizens, such as lynching. Eventually, the doctrine reached acts of discrimination and other civil rights violations by private citizens provided there was at least some connection, or nexus, between the actions of the individual and the actions, either directly or indirectly, of the state.

As one of the Civil War Amendments, the primary purpose of the Fourteenth Amendment was to protect the rights of blacks as equal citizens under the law. Presumably, this amendment enabled the U.S. Congress to prevent individual states or local governments from enacting and enforcing discriminatory laws with respect to rights guaranteed to each and every American citizen under the U.S. Constitution. The amendment was intended as well to prevent states or local governments from granting any right or privilege to whites without granting the same right or privilege to blacks. Initially, however, the Supreme Court limited the power of Congress to enforce the Civil Rights Act of 1875, which prohibited private acts of discrimination in public places such as hotels, restaurants, and theaters. In the *Civil Rights Cases*, 109 U.S. 3 (1883), the Court established the state action doctrine with respect to acts of discrimination. Initially, the Court interpreted this doctrine narrowly, confining it quite literally to affirmative acts, such as discriminatory laws, enacted or enforced by individual states or local governments, as well as their officers. Thus the Court invalidated the Civil Rights Act of 1875 because it attempted to regulate the acts of private citizens.

With the decision in *Plessy v. Ferguson*, 163 U.S. 537 (1896), and the Court's sanction of the separate-but-equal doctrine, the states were free to enforce segregation or Jim Crow laws. Eventually, *Plessy* and the doctrine of separate but equal were repudiated by the Warren Court in *Brown v. Board of Education*, 347 U.S. 483 (1954), and the prohibition against state action was reaffirmed. Moreover, the Court began to expand the scope and definition of state action. It had already ruled in *Screws v. United States*, 325 U.S. 91 (1945), that the doctrine applied to a sheriff who had beaten a black prisoner to death. The Court rejected the argument that since the sheriff's conduct was in clear violation of state law, he was not acting under the "color" of law and thus not subject to the Civil Rights Act. That the sheriff had acted within an "official place" (the jail) was the controlling fact for the Court.

This trend continued in *Lynch v. United States*, 343 U.S. 934 (1951), in which the Court upheld a federal civil rights conviction of a Georgia sheriff for not attempting to prevent a Ku Klux Klan mob from kidnapping and beating black prisoners in his custody. In *Terry v. Adams*, 345 U.S. 461 (1953), the Court invalidated a "private" primary election in Texas because it excluded blacks. The Court held that any election affecting the public is essentially an activity of the state and thus within the reach of the state action doctrine. In *Pennsylvania v. Board of Directors of City Trusts*, 353 U.S. 230 (1957), the Court held that the discriminatory policies of the Girard College of Education, which was administered by city board members, violated the state action doctrine. In *Evans v. Newton*, 382 U.S. 296 (1966), the Court ruled that a public park in Macon, Georgia, that excluded blacks was in clear violation of the state action doctrine. That city officials had appointed a "private" board of trustees to oversee the park did not remove the taint of state action.

In *Shelley v. Kraemer*, 334 U.S. 1 (1948), the Court struck down a restrictive covenant that forbade the sale of property to blacks. The Court did not rule that two or more people could not agree privately, as private citizens, not to sell their property to blacks. The Court did rule, however, that such an agreement was unenforceable as a matter of law because the enforcement of the covenant legally entails state action by the utilizing of the state court system. With respect to public accommodations, in *Peterson v. Greenville*, 373 U.S. 244 (1963), the Court invalidated a city ordinance that required the separation of races in restaurants. In *Lombard v. Louisiana*, 373 U.S. 267 (1963), the Court went even further, holding that even though there was no city ordinance mandating the segregation of races in restaurants, there was clear evidence that city officials had coerced the owner of the restaurant into discriminating against blacks. Therefore, this was state action.

In *Heart of Atlanta Motel v. United States*, 379 U.S. 241 (1964), the Court upheld a federal statute forbidding racial discrimination in any public place, including privately owned places of accommodation open to the public, such as hotels and restaurants. It is important to note, however, that the statute was upheld under the constitutional jurisdiction of the Commerce Clause, not the Fourteenth Amendment. Neither the Commerce Clause nor the state action doctrine can reach the discriminatory acts of private citizens, at least with respect to private clubs, for example, that are not open to the public. A private club is free to exclude members on the basis of race as long as it is in fact an exclusive organization, not open to the public and not supported in any way by the state (which would implicate the state action doctrine). Nor can the state have any close contact with such an organization. In *Burton v. Wilmington Parking Authority*, 365 U.S. 715 (1961), for example, the Court ruled that a privately owned restaurant operating in a parking complex owned by the state of Delaware could not bar blacks because the state leased the property, thus establishing a nexus between the actions of the individual and those of the state. In *Moose Lodge v. Irvis*, 407 U.S. 163 (1972), however, the Court held that a private club could keep its liquor license, issued by the state, even though its membership policy discriminated against blacks. The Court ruled that merely issuing a license to sell liquor did not constitute a sufficient nexus between private and state action.

Strictly considered, the state action doctrine was not established to promote integration or even to enable the federal government to enforce the Fourteenth Amendment. Rather, it was established to restrict the reach of the federal government to intercede in cases of discrimination that were not clearly within the province of governmental activity and not clearly within the realm of constitutionally protected rights, such as the right to vote. The Rehnquist Court has been far more reluctant than earlier, more liberal courts to find a nexus between state action and private acts of discrimination that will enable the federal government to intercede. This trend is just one of many that reflect the states-rights movement of the Court today. Ironically, the state action doctrine has figured more prominently in the "reverse-discrimination" cases such as *Regents of the University of California v. Bakke*, 438 U.S. 265 (1978), and its progeny.

See also Brown v. Board of Education; Civil Rights Act of 1875; *Civil Rights Cases*; Civil War (Reconstruction) Amendments and Civil Rights Acts; Discrimination; Equal Protection Clause; Fourteenth Amendment; Integration; Jim Crow Laws; *Plessy v. Ferguson*; *Regents of the University of California v. Bakke*; Segregation.

FURTHER READING: Cortner, Richard, 2002, *The Supreme Court and the Second Bill of Rights: The Fourteenth Amendment and the Nationalization of Civil Liberties*, Ann Arbor: Books on Demand; Davis, Sue, 1983, "The Supreme Court: Finding State Action . . . Sometimes," *Howard Law Journal* 26:1395–1423; Fisher, Louis, 1999, *American Constitutional Law*, 3d ed., Durham: Carolina Academic Press; Lieberman, Jethro, 1992, *The Evolving Constitution*, New York: Random House; Nelson, William, 1995, *The Fourteenth Amendment: From Political Principle to Judicial Doctrine*, Cambridge, MA: Harvard University Press; Perry, Michael, 1999, *We the People: The Fourteenth Amendment and the Supreme Court*, New York: Oxford University Press.

MICHAEL D. QUIGLEY

Statistical Proof of Discrimination

In *Griggs v. Duke Power Co.*, 401 U.S. 424 (1971), when first upholding the disparate impact theory of Title VII of the Civil Rights Act of 1964 in a case where employment criteria disqualified black applicants "at a substantially higher rate than white applicants," the Supreme Court took for granted that statistical proof was an essential element of such a case. Six years later, in *International Brotherhood of Teamsters v. United States*, 431 U.S. 324 (1977), the Court also firmly established the validity of statistical evidence to prove intentional discrimination in employment. The Court found that "longstanding and gross disparity between the composition of a work force and that of the general population" could be significant evidence of purposeful discrimination, even though "Title VII imposes no requirement that a work force mirror the general population." The Court cautioned, however, that "statistics are not irrefutable; they come in infinite variety and, like any other kind of evidence, they may be rebutted. In short, their usefulness depends on all the surrounding facts and circumstances."

That same term, in *Hazelwood School Dist. v. United States*, 433 U.S. 299 (1977), the Court introduced the concept of statistical significance into the analysis of statistical evidence in employment discrimination cases. Referencing a formula for calculating the standard deviation from the expected number of selections of the subject group given the group's representation in the candidate pool that the Court had set out in *Castaneda v. Partida*, 430 U.S. 482 (1977), a jury selection case, the Court concluded that " 'if the difference between the expected value and the observed number [of black teacher hires] is greater than two or three standard deviations,' then the hypothesis that teachers were hired without regard to race would be suspect."

The Court next offered guidance on the use of statistics in employment discrimination nine years later in *Bazemore v. Friday*, 478 U.S. 385 (1986). There the Court overturned an appeals court ruling that regression analyses of salary differences between whites and blacks were "unacceptable evidence of discrimination" because they had failed to include "all measurable variables" thought to affect salary. The Court concluded that where regression analysis had accounted for the "major factors" affecting salary, the failure to include additional factors would go only to the probative value of the studies, not to their admissibility.

Three years later, the court again considered statistical issues in the case of *Wards Cove Packing Co. v. Atonio*, 490 U.S. 642 (1989). Rejecting claims that a prima facie case of disparate impact could be established on the basis that minority cannery workers comprised far higher proportions of unskilled jobs than of skilled workers, the Court held that a case of disparate impact could generally be established only by comparing minority representation in the jobs at issue with minority representation in the labor force with the skills for such jobs.

In general, however, these cases have given very limited guidance on the use of statistical evidence. Though the lower courts have issued many rulings on the subject, they have done little to develop a sophisticated jurisprudence in this area. With respect to disparate impact, there is no consensus and limited guidance in lower court decisions on how substantial a disparity must be to require that an employer satisfy the burden of showing the job relatedness and business necessity of the practice causing the impact. At times, courts have looked either to differences in rates of meeting some standard or criterion or to differences in rates of failing to meet the standard, and they have done so without recognition, for example, that the less stringent a standard, the greater will be the disparity in failing to meet the standard and the smaller will be the disparity in meeting the standard. In other words, if a cutoff is lowered on a test on which minorities have lower average scores than whites, racial disparities in failure rates will increase while racial disparities in pass rates will decrease.

With respect to determining whether a particular disparity is caused by intentional discrimination, courts have tended to focus on statistical significance without consideration that the statistical significance of a disparity, being a function of both the size of a disparity and the number of observations, is a poor indicator of whether a disparity is sufficiently large to compel an inference of discrimination. Even when courts have attempted to evaluate the size of a disparity, they have done so without recognition that fair selection in the face of some difference in qualifications will yield disparities of varying sizes depending on the selectivity of the employment process at issue.

The *Wards Cove* case, which concerned the demographic disparity between cannery and noncannery workers, involved a fundamentally flawed claim founded not on a showing that minorities comprised a smaller proportion of hires into the better (noncannery) jobs than they comprised of persons seeking such jobs, but on a showing merely that minorities comprised a much higher proportion of cannery hires than noncannery hires. More commonplace counterparts to such claims may be found in claims in the retail and grocery industries, for example, that women are disproportionately assigned to cashier or salesclerk jobs compared with more remunerative jobs like commission sales. Yet a variety of social and labor-market-wide forces lead to the high female representation among persons seeking certain traditionally female jobs, and whether the particular employer excludes women from its better jobs will have little bearing on the matter. Hence comparison of female representation in an employer's poorer jobs with the female representation in its better jobs is not probative that the employer is excluding women from the better jobs.

The Supreme Court rejected the flawed claim in *Wards Cove*, even terming it "nonsensical," but the Court failed to establish the illegitimacy of so-called assignment claims in sufficiently definitive terms. Hence in the years that followed the *Wards Cove* decision, large-scale cases in the grocery and retail industries were pursued on the same theory underlying the claims in the *Wards Cove* case, with several resulting in settlements in excess of $100 million. Thus much remains to be done in the development of jurisprudence in this area.

See also Disparate Treatment and Disparate Impact; *Griggs v. Duke Power Co.*;

Title VII of the Civil Rights Act of 1964; *Wards Cove Packing Co. v. Atonio*; *Yick Wo v. Hopkins.*

FURTHER READING: Baldus, David C., and James W.L. Cole, 1980, *Statistical Proof of Discrimination*, Colorado Springs: Shepards-McGraw Hill; Scanlan, James P., 1988, "Illusions of Job Segregation," *Public Interest*, fall, 54–70; Scanlan, James P., 1991, "The Perils of Provocative Statistics," *Public Interest*, winter, 3–15; Scanlan, James P., 1993, "Getting It Straight When Statistics Can Lie," *Legal Times*, June 28, 40–43; Scanlan, James P., 1995, "Multimillion-Dollar Settlements May Cause Employers to Avoid Hiring Women and Minorities for Less Desirable Jobs to Improve the Statistical Picture," *National Law Journal*, March 27, B5.

JAMES P. SCANLAN

Steele, Shelby (1946–   )

Shelby Steele, a research fellow at the Hoover Institution who specializes in race relations and affirmative action, is a leading critic of affirmative action programs. He has authored numerous articles in periodicals, journals, and newspapers on the efficacy of affirmative action. Steele contends that affirmative action programs do more harm than good for those whom such programs are attempting to help. In 1990, Steele authored the book *The Content of Our Character: A New Vision of Race in America*, a controversial work about race, the dilemma of black/white power divisions, and affirmative action. The book is considered an influential work on affirmative action and contains a collection of essays on race. In this book, which won the National Book Critics Circle Award in 1991, Steele acknowledges both the subjugation of blacks in American history and the injustices of white oppression, but reserves the apex of his essay for a criticism of the claim of black entitlement that arose from these conditions. Steele argues that in the late 1960s and early 1970s, affirmative action initiatives grew out of the concurrent rise of black power and white guilt. Affirmative action plans resulted in racial quotas, set-asides, and preferential treatment, thus offering whites redemption from past sins and blacks a guarantee of new economic power. Steele's most recent book, *A Dream Deferred: The Second Betrayal of Black Freedom in America* (1998), picks up the theme of white guilt being the primary reason for affirmative action programs today. According to Steele, affirmative action programs are put forward in an effort to placate white guilt rather than being based upon a sole motivation to improve the plight of the intended beneficiaries of such programs.

For Steele, affirmative action in America came with a high cost. Preferential treatment that used race as a criterion for opportunity was simply, as Steele describes in his book *The Content of Our Character*, an "old sin . . . in a new guise." It was a wrongful plan that "re-burdened society" with the very problem it was trying to eliminate, that of racial injustice. According to Steele, decades after the implementation of affirmative action as a form of social engineering, blacks were worse off and had even more to lose. They could not, he insisted in *The Content of Our Character*, be "repaid for the injustice done to the race, but could be corrupted by society's gestures of repayment" (Steele 1990, 119).

Steele believes that preferential treatment promotes the view of the black self as a perpetual victim. It encourages a false belief in entitlement. More problematic is the fact that racial preference for blacks creates a profound sense of demoralization that results in self-doubt and "implied inferiority." Although no objective basis might exist for his claim, it was white perception of black inferiority that perpetuated the image of black ability or inability. This "debilitating" doubt about black worth was evidenced, Steele argues, in the fact that blacks were five times more inclined to drop out of college than whites. As social policy, affirmative action also failed to offer blacks the skills, education, or motivation necessary to succeed in a competitive marketplace. In *The Content of Our Character*, Steele points to the fact that the number of blacks earning Ph.D.'s has declined in recent years as support for this argument.

Steele is in concert with those Supreme Court decisions that eroded racial preferences in affirmative action. His provocative thesis in *The Content of Our Character* and the subsequent legal retraction of some affirmative action policies brought much criticism from both blacks and whites. For Steele, affirmative action is morally problematic and politically disruptive, and it is necessary to abolish it. Does Steele then offer an alternative to affirmative action? He acknowledges the need for some kind of social and public policy that will help historically disenfranchised people. His suggestions are more philosophical and abstract than concrete. His point that commonality and not difference should be highlighted does not adequately address the economic inequalities that continue to permeate contemporary society. In spite of the criticisms, however, Steele's arguments remain provocative, controversial, and very much part of the ongoing contentious debate about affirmative action.

Steele has served as a research fellow at the Hoover Institution since 1994. He was a professor of English literature at San Jose State University from 1974 to 1991. He holds a Ph.D. in English from the University of Utah, a master's degree in sociology from Southern Illinois University, and a bachelor's degree from Coe College in Cedar Rapids, Iowa. Among his numerous awards, he earned an Emmy Award in 1990 for "Seven Days in Bensonhurst," a PBS documentary examining a racially motivated killing in New York City.

See also Affirmative Action, Criticisms of; King, Martin Luther, Jr.; Stereotyping and Minority Classes.

FURTHER READING: Edwards, Wayne, 1991, "Going It Alone: Author Shelby Steele Says Affirmative Action May Do More Harm than Good," *People Weekly* 36, no. 8 (September 2): 79; Roach, Ronald, 1998, "Seeing No Evil," *Black Issues in Higher Education* 14, no. 23 (January 8): 18; Steele, Shelby, 1990, *The Content of Our Character: A New Vision of Race in America*, New York: St. Martin's Press; Steele, Shelby, 1993, "Rise of the 'New Segregation:' The 'Politics of Differences' Threatens to Produce a Divided Society," *USA Today* (Magazine) 121, no. 2574 (March): 53; Steele, Shelby, 1996, "The Race Not Run: Fear and the Roots of Affirmative Action," *New Republic* 215, no. 15 (October 7): 23.

JANIS JUDSON

Stereotypes, Gender

Stereotypes are generalizations or widely held beliefs about a person or group of people based on their race, sex, age, or other social characteristics. Unfortunately, these generalizations do not have to be and often are not based in any truth whatsoever. Despite evidence against them, stereotypes do not dissipate.

They are embraced and often passed down to new generations. Although the stereotype is most often not true, its consequences are very real. The vast majority of stereotypical attributes assigned to various groups of people are negative, demeaning, and insulting. At times, however, "positive" stereotypes are applied to certain groups of people. These are positive attributes believed to be true about a group of people. These, too, are most often not based in any truth. Positive stereotypes are, however, just as generalized as negative stereotypes and certainly just as damaging as negative stereotypes.

Many stereotypes exist about women, based on their sex, gender, and sexuality. Following are some examples: Women are kind, loving, caring, and nurturing. They are emotional (rather than rational) and will change their minds often (they are not decisive). These are general female stereotypes that are often applied to all women. Female stereotypes, however, also exist for different groups of women. Stereotypes of subdivisions of women abound throughout society and may be specifically based on gender plus socioeconomic status, gender plus marital status, gender plus race, gender plus age, gender plus sexual orientation, or any other combination of sociological variables.

Women who hold high positions in their careers and who have made it to the upper echelons of the corporate world are stereotypically bossy, demanding, brash, loud, ruthless, and obnoxious. Their work and achievement imply that they are so selfishly wrapped up in their own advancement that they are both bad in relationships and terrible mothers. Because "career women" often postpone marriage and childbearing, they are seen as denying a "natural" function of womanhood: being wife and mother, first and foremost. This makes them "unnatural" and "freaks" of nature and the natural evolutionary process. Historically, single women have also been viewed as deviant, since they have not entered the norm of marriage. Their stereotypical "unnatural" nature was viewed not only as aberrant behavior, but also as a mental illness. The *Diagnostic and Statistical Manual (DSM)* of psychiatric disorders maintained that singlehood was a mental disorder until the diagnosis was removed in the mid-1950s.

Women of color also carry their own subset of stereotypes, which may further be divided by specific race or ethnicity. For example, African American women could be seen as the historical stereotype of strong maid, mammy, and authoritative mother or the more modern stereotype of outspoken, overly defensive on race issues, single head of household or drug-addicted woman. Latina American women may be stereotypically viewed as undereducated, submissive to male authority figures, highly religious, and constantly pregnant. Asian American women carry the stereotype of being silent, submissive, and passive while at the same time holding the positive stereotype of being intelligent, clean, small bodied, and diligent.

Women of age are heavily stereotyped within American society, often without the consciousness that such stereotypes are even harmful. A vast array of birthday cards in any store embodies many of the currently held stereotypes of old women. They are portrayed as forgetful, without any type of physical strength, asexual, full of gossip and meaningless talk, invasive, pushy, cranky, overly perfumed, "blue haired," and slow drivers. The positive stereotype for women of age is that all old women are sweet and loving grandmas whose main joy in life is to "baby-sit" grandchildren and bake apple pies. A stereotype that is rather unique to this group is that they are invisible in society. The lack of women in the media, for example, perpetrates a stereotype, not by the act of commission, but by the consistency of portrayal omission. Further subdivisions within this category include stereotypes of the spinster, bag lady, rich widow, old maid, crone, and eccentric old hag.

The sexuality and sexual orientation of women also have their own set of stereotypical characteristics. Stereotypically, all lesbians are malelike, men haters, and sexually obsessive women who have been shunned or somehow hurt by a man in the past. Their sexuality is often considered a passing experimentation that they will eventually abandon for the more "normal" heterosexual relationship. Although these and other negative stereotypes abound for lesbians, the demeaning impacts of the stereotypes lessen if they are sexually uniting for the pleasure of a man. The popular male fantasy of "two women" does not carry the same negative connotations about the women that their sexual involvement does without the presence of a man.

Female stereotypes are perpetuated in society through four main avenues of gender socialization. Parents, peers, the educational system, and the media begin socializing a child early and continue generating stereotypes throughout the life course. Gender socialization begins as early as parents dressing female infants in pink and male infants in blue. Girls are given toys that are deemed appropriate for their stereotypical roles in society. Since girls are stereotypically kind, loving, nurturing, and natural mothers, they are given baby dolls with which to play. Since girls are more emotional than logical, they are encouraged to take classes in school that fit their stereotypical portrait. Girls should study literature, music, art, and creative writing, while boys should study mathematics, natural science, nuclear physics, and engineering.

What is being described here is known as the "vicious cycle." A constant and lifelong cycle exists between female stereotypes and gendered roles. The two empower each other, creating a cycle that is "vicious" in that it is nearly impossible to break. The female stereotype is that women are caring, mothering, nurturing, and loving. The roles then available to women in society include jobs that embody these characteristics: nurse, elementary-school teacher, secretary, nanny, and day-care worker. When women are predominantly seen in these roles, the stereotypes are reinforced. She is nurturing, therefore she is a nurse. She is a nurse, therefore she is a nurturing person. The cycle reinforces itself, as the stereotypes and roles not only interact, but also strengthen each other. If the stereotypical belief exists that women are emotional and not rational, the result is that women should not be given rational privileges (such as the right to vote) and not hold positions or roles of power that require rational, not emotional, responses. Hence the lack of women in executive positions and the lack of high-end salaries among women are said to be a result of these characteristics. When women are not seen in these positions, the stereotype of nonrational beings is reinforced against women, and they remain unselected for these positions.

This has a particularly important significance for women, known as the "feminization of poverty." Throughout the life course, women are stereotypically socialized into gendered roles and jobs. Unfortunately, these jobs are not CEOs of corporations, physicians, top administrators, or other high-level positions. Instead, they are low-paying jobs with limited or no employment benefits. Throughout a woman's working adult life, she may be able to make ends meet and survive on an adequate income, but because of the lower-paying positions and the inequity of male/female wages, she is unable to save the money throughout her life course that her male counterpart is able to put away for late life. It is in her old age, then, that a woman most emphatically experiences the consequences of societal stereotypes and the vicious cycle. The feminization of poverty takes place over the entire life course, from pink bows in the infant girl's hair to encouragement to take gender-appropriate school courses, holding a female-acceptable job, accepting lower wages and lower societal positions, and financial problems, often dire, in late life.

The Thomas theorem, developed by Robert Merton, holds that what is perceived to be real is in fact real in its consequences. All stereotypes confirm this theorem. The most erroneous stereotypes, based on complete untruths, still guarantee very real consequences. Stereotypes of women in general, and stereotypes of specific subgroups of women in particular, no matter how faulty or untrue, have very real consequences. Until society can offer up a majority of female executives, female physicians, female professors, female attorneys, female scientists, and female mathematicians, it remains obvious that female stereotypes are effective, societally pervasive, and extremely detrimental to women.

See also Gender Norms; Gender Segregation in Employment; Gendered Racism; Glass Ceilings; Sex Discrimination; Stereotyping and Minority Classes.

FURTHER READING: Burke, Phyllis, 1996, *Gender Shock: Exploding the Myths of Male and Female*, New York: Anchor Books; Crittenden, Ann, 2001, *The Price of Motherhood: Why the Most Important Job in the World Is Still the Least Valued*, New York: Metropolitan Books; Hubbard, Ruth, 1990, *The Politics of Women's Biology*, New Brunswick, NJ: Rutgers University Press; Kimmel, Michael S., 2000, *The Gendered Society*, New York: Oxford University Press.

SHEILA BLUHM

Stereotypes, Racial

See Racial Stereotyping.

Stereotyping and Asian Americans

See Model Minorities (Stereotyping Asian Americans).

Stereotyping and Minority Classes

Stereotyping is the action of observing a trait of an individual who belongs to a larger group and generalizing that trait to the larger population. In one sense, stereotyping may be seen as the action of one who has a lazy mind and refuses to probe or investigate further to find out if one observation or several observations can really be generalized to the larger population. Stereotypes tend to perpetuate myths and misconceptions regarding members of a particular group. Stereotypes are utilized extensively in affirmative action debates, normally to argue that a particular group is not worthy of benefits (or not qualified to receive benefits except through preferential treatment). There are an abundance of stereotypes regarding women, blacks, Hispanics, Jews, and other socioeconomic, ethnic, racial, and religious groups in America. White ethnic groups that immigrated to the United States in the nineteenth and twentieth centuries were often the butt of stereotypical jokes, which only perpetuated misconceptions regarding these groups.

Racial stereotyping does not recognize the complexity of socioeconomic classes and income levels within a race. Hence blacks are often stereotyped as being lazy, conniving, wanting a handout or wanting to live on welfare, oversexed, intellectually inferior, and criminally prone. The mass media may help to perpetuate such racial stereotypes, since a disproportionate amount of blue-collar crime in the inner city is committed by blacks, and the media report such crimes on a daily basis.

Conversely, some racial minorities (hereafter referred to as persons of color) tend to stereotype each other as well as whites. For instance, many blacks think that all whites are prejudiced, if not racist, based upon their experiences and contact with a limited number of whites. Many blacks feel that all whites are insensitive to the needs and aspirations of blacks and do not understand "the black way of life." Stereotypes can be dangerous if they are held by persons who make public policy, because such policies may become the law of the land and affect millions of people at a time.

Racial stereotypes in particular have implications for higher education, one of the areas where there has been much controversy over affirmative action and admissions policies. It has been argued that lax admissions policies that admit black students who are not qualified to do college-level work set them up for failure in college and weaken academic standards to the point that college is no longer an experience for the gifted and better-qualified student. Rather, college has now become a haven for mediocre students as well as the better qualified, and the former are a drag on the latter's full potential.

The stereotype-vulnerability theory suggests that racial stereotypes confront very intelligent black students in college who begin to have some degree of trepidation that regardless of their past performance and excellence, they will not do well, and that this fear consequently undermines their performance. In stressful situations, this vulnerability manifests itself and as a result affects performance in a negative way. This tends to be reinforced on tests in which these gifted blacks are reminded of their racial or group affiliation. While this is just a theory, it may explain why some highly intelligent blacks do not do well on tests in biracial settings. At the same time, when black students were told that exams that they were taking would not be used to evaluate their ability, the performance of whites was no better than that of blacks.

Racial and gender stereotypes also exist in the public sector, particularly government, and the private sector in the field of business as the result of affirmative action programs and policies in which white males feel that people of color and women are given preferential treatment in jobs or promotions simply because of their race and gender. As a result of such stereotypes, white prejudice and racism and sexism may be reinforced. But such prejudice and racism may be reinforced even in the absence of preferential treatment when subliminal racism or sexism surfaces when evaluating candidates of color or women in the context of equal opportunity rules. The racism and sexism, in turn, reinforce stereotypes.

Racial and gender stereotypes based upon preferential treatment have, in many cases, led to court suits in which white males have alleged "reverse discrimination" and "reverse racism." The plaintiff in the seminal Supreme Court case *Regents of the University of California v. Bakke,* 438 U.S. 265 (1978), made just that very argument. Allan Bakke, a white male who sued the Regents of the University of California, alleged that the admissions system at the University of California at Davis Medical School had a quota system that guaranteed people of color slots in the medical program that amounted to preferential treatment, and according to Bakke, these students were not qualified for these admissions slots.

See also Education and Affirmative Action; Media and Affirmative Action; Model Minorities (Stereotyping Asian Americans); Preferences; Prejudice; Racial Stereotyping; *Regents of the University of California v. Bakke;* Reverse Discrimination; Sexism; Standardized Testing; Stereotypes, Gender.

FURTHER READING: Bowen, William G., and Derek Bok, 1998, *The Shape of the River: Long-Term Consequences of Considering Race in College and University Admissions,* Princeton, NJ: Princeton University Press; Carter, Richard F., 1962, "Stereotyping as a Process," *Public Opinion Quarterly* 26, no. 1:77–91; Steele, Shelby, 1990, *The Content of Our Character,* New York: St. Martin's Press.

MFANYA D. TRYMAN

Stereotyping and Persons with Disabilities

People with physical, developmental, and psychological disabilities have long been discriminated against in American society. In the words of a U.S. court of appeals case, this discrimination "often occurs under the guise of extending a helping hand or a mistaken, restrictive belief as to the limitations of [disabled] persons" (*Pushkin v. Regents of the University of Colorado,* 658 F.2d 1372, 1385 [10th Cir. 1982]). The underpinning of discrimination is stereotypes—generalized beliefs about a category of people that are used to make determinations and decisions about individuals.

Perhaps the most damaging of all stereotypes of the disabled is the idea that disabled people should be pitied. One of the most visible examples of this stereotype is the set of images associated with telethons. Both the posters that advertise these telethons and the televised segments featuring individuals with disabilities emphasize the perceived helplessness of the disabled. These images are designed to encourage the audience to give to the charity because of their sympathy for the disabled. Pity for the persons with disabilities discourages the nondisabled population from interacting with persons with disabilities as equal and similar to nondisabled people. This distance is what makes the continued survival of all the other stereotypes of disabled people possible.

A closely related stereotype is the perception of disabled people as a burden on their families and on society. One way that this stereotype is expressed is the perception of disabled children as not fulfilling the parental wish for a "healthy child." The reality is that disabilities are not necessarily illnesses. For example, a blind or deaf person may have no illnesses whatsoever. Yet these individuals are often perceived as in need of special care from their families, friends, and even strangers. Because disabled children are viewed as a greater burden than other children, it is perceived as more appropriate to wish not to have a disabled child, to place a disabled child for adoption, and to avoid adopting disabled children in lieu of a "healthy" child.

The polar opposite of the preceding two stereotypes, yet equally damaging, is the image of the disabled person as a being superhumanly heroic. Many media features about disabled people are designed to give a view of the courageous disabled individual overcoming great obstacles to live a "normal" life. In reality, the lives being portrayed are generally extraordinary in comparison to the lives of the average disabled and nondisabled person (e.g., crutch users finishing a marathon). However, the only category of reference suggested by these features is other disabled individuals, and such features imply that if obstacles stop disabled individuals from fully participating in society, it is because these people lack the inner rectitude to overcome their disabilities.

A fourth stereotype is the idea of the disabled, especially the psychologically impaired, as evil and criminal. Villains, in literature and movies, often incorporate a wide range of characteristics that are associated with disability (e.g., hearing voices and wearing a hook). Thus these portrayals encourage fear of and aversion to people with disabilities. The result is increased isolation of people with disabilities, which may degrade their self-esteem. Second, this makes it even more difficult to dismantle stereotypes, since it is unlikely that people who hold these sorts of beliefs will engage in meaningful and potentially transformative interactions with disabled individuals.

Another stereotype is the belief that disabled people need to be fixed or might be better off dead. Discussions of the rising cost of health care, the cost/benefit analysis of extraordinary medical procedures, and the widespread support for cochlear implants for the deaf by medical professionals, politicians, and the general public are all predicated on this sort of belief. Underlying all of these debates is the idea that the cost of "coping" with the disabled might not be worth it to the rest of society. In addition, these conversations seldom include the voices of disabled people, who would be in the best position to inform society about the benefits of a life after a disabling accident or the realities of cochlear implants.

A sixth stereotype of the disabled is the idea that if they would only adopt a positive outlook, their lives would be much better. This stereotype is based on a condescending view of the disabled, one in which individuals who have not experienced disability are in the best position to provide advice about how disabled people should perceive their situation. It also denies disabled people the right to the full range of emotions that mark human existence. Everyone gets frustrated, angry, and sad; however, these same emotions when expressed by the disabled are likely to be treated as self-pity and self-defeating.

Taken together, these stereotypes suggest that disabled individuals are incapable of living complete, successful lives filled the same joys and defeats as the nondisabled. Disability rights activist Justin Dart summarizes society's perception of the disabled thus: "Our society still is infected by an insidious, now almost subconscious, assumption that people with disability are less than fully human and therefore not entitled to the respect, the opportunities, and the services and support systems that are available to other people as a matter of right" (Dart 1993, 12). Disability rights activists have countered these stereotypes through mobilization and the creation of alternative visions of the disabled. The independent living movement, which focuses on the fact that many people with disabilities desire to and are fully capable of living fully independent lives, shows how we might organize our society in ways that allow for the full participation of people with disabilities. In many cases, only small changes in the organization of public spaces can make the world easier for people with disabilities to negotiate, and despite claims about the cost of accommodating the disabled, seldom do these advantages benefit only people with disabilities. Two clear examples are the implementation of audible crossing signals and incorporation of curb cuts into public walkways. Audible crossing signals not only benefit the blind, but also help children to know when it is possible to safely cross the street. Curb cuts allow wheelchair riders to access public sidewalks, but they also help parents with strollers.

Still, the only hope of breaking down stereotypes about people with disabilities is to have disabled people more incorporated into our society. Especially important is the need for highly visible disabled people in the media, in political positions, in the lives of children, and in the public places that we all frequent. For this to occur, it is imperative that greater accommodation for the wide range of physical bodies be incorporated into the design and implementation of homes, public buildings, and civic spaces.

See also Discrimination; Persons with Disabilities and Affirmative Action; Stereotyping and Minority Classes.

FURTHER READING: Bilken, Douglas, and Robert Bogdan, 1977, "Media Portrayals of Disabled People: A Study in Stereotypes," *Interracial Books for Children*, Bulletin 8, no. 6:4–9; Dart, Justin W., Jr., 1993, "Introduction: The ADA: A Promise to Be Kept," in *Implementing the Americans with Disabilities Act: Rights and Responsibilities of All Americans*, edited by Lawrence O. Gostin and Henry A. Beyer, Baltimore: Paul Brookes; Switzer, Jacqueline Vaughn, 2003, *Disabled Rights: American Disability Policy and the Fight for Equality*, Washington, DC: Georgetown University Press; Tucker, Bonnie Poitras, 1998, *Federal Disability Law in a Nutshell*, 2d ed., St. Paul, MN: West Group.

KYRA R. GREENE

Stevens, John Paul (1920–   )

Appointed to the Supreme Court by President Gerald Ford in 1975, Associate Justice John Paul Stevens for a time seemed destined to be one of the Supreme Court's most vigorous opponents of affirmative action. Ultimately, however, as a result of an expressed deference to *stare decisis* (case law precedent) and evolving views concerning the value of race- and gender-conscious measures, Stevens became one of the Court's strongest defenders of such measures. According to Georgetown University law professor Girardeau Spann, "In addition to Justice Stevens, the other three justices who make up the present Court's liberal bloc on affirmative action—Justices Souter, Ginsburg, and Breyer—have voted to uphold each affirmative action program that they considered in a constitutional case" (Spann 2000, 161).

Born to an upper-class family in Chicago, on April 20, 1920, Stevens attended Northwestern University Law School. After law school, Stevens, a World War II veteran, was selected for a prestigious Supreme Court clerkship with Justice Wiley Rutledge. After his clerkship, he returned to Illinois and engaged in private practice, specializing in antitrust law. In 1970, he was appointed to the U.S. Court of

Appeals for the Seventh Circuit by President Richard Nixon, where he earned a reputation for writing concise and well-worded judicial opinions. With five years' experience on the Seventh Circuit Court of Appeals, he was elevated to the Supreme Court by President Gerald Ford.

A year after Stevens's appointment, in *McDonald v. Santa Fe Trail Transportation Co.*, 427 U.S. 273 (1976), the Court considered whether Title VII of the Civil Rights Act of 1964 and section 1 of the Civil Rights Act of 1866 (42 U.S.C. § 1981) prohibited private employers from discriminating against white persons. Justice Stevens joined in Thurgood Marshall's opinion for the Court, which, after reviewing the legislative histories of the two statutes, concluded that both protected whites from discrimination in employment.

Two years later, Stevens partially concurred in the judgment that struck down the race-conscious admissions policy in *Regents of the University of California v. Bakke*, 438 U.S. 265 (1978). Stevens, however, declined to reach the constitutional issue addressed in varied opinions by the remainder of the Court, for he found it "crystal clear" that Title VI of the Civil Rights Act of 1964 prohibited all race-conscious affirmative action at institutions receiving federal funds. In reaching that conclusion, Stevens relied on the *McDonald* decision, but he also explored at length the legislative history of the 1964 Civil Rights Act, emphasizing that individual fairness was the focus of both Title VI and Title VII and indicating that he would consider it equally clear that Title VII prohibited all race-conscious affirmative action in employment. More generally, the opinion reflected strong disapproval of practices that disadvantage individuals because of race, regardless of the race of the person disadvantaged.

The following year, in *United Steelworkers of America v. Weber*, 443 U.S. 193 (1979), the Court considered whether Title VII prohibits all race-conscious affirmative action in employment. Justice William Brennan's majority opinion explored Title VII's legislative history, concluding that the statute had been intended to encourage voluntary measures to abolish traditional patterns of racial segregation and hierarchy. The Court therefore found that notwithstanding *McDonald*'s holding that Title VII prohibits discrimination against white persons, the statute does not prohibit all private, race-conscious affirmative action plans aimed at eliminating conspicuous racial imbalances in traditionally segregated job categories.

Stevens did not participate in the consideration of *Weber*, though, as discussed later, he later revealed that consistent with his opinion in *Bakke*, he believed that *Weber* was wrongly decided. Moreover, the following year, dissenting from the Court's decision in *Fullilove v. Klutznick*, 448 U.S. 448, 523–524 (1980), which upheld congressionally mandated minority set-asides for federally funded construction projects, Stevens revealed that he continued to disapprove strongly of any distinctions based on race. Reflecting on the potential harm of racial classifications to the body politic, he noted that "the very attempt to define with precision a beneficiary's qualifying racial characteristics is repugnant to our constitutional ideals" and suggested that a serious effort to define racial classes by objective criteria would require study of the racial classification laws of Germany's Third Reich. After observing that "racial classifications are simply too pernicious to permit any but the most exacting connection between justification and classification," he went on to serially discuss and reject each of the proffered justifications for the set-aside program at issue. Thus, as of 1980, no member of the Court seemed more opposed to race-conscious measures than Stevens.

The Court did not again consider an affirmative action case until 1984. That year, in *Firefighters Local Union No. 1784 v. Stotts*, 467 U.S. 561 (1984), the Court overturned a district court's modification of a race-conscious consent decree in a Title VII action to restrain a city from implementing a layoff in a manner that would reduce the minority representation among firefighters. The Court merely found that the district court had exceeded its authority in modifying the decree. At the time, however, the Court had not yet addressed the issue of whether a court could order race-conscious relief for a Title VII violation. In particular, it had not considered whether the last sentence of section 706(g) of Title VII, 42 U.S.C. § 2000e-5(g), precluded a court from ordering race-conscious relief to persons who were not themselves victims of discrimination (though the courts of appeals that had considered the matter had been unanimously of the view that it did it not). While not specifically reaching that issue, Justice Byron White's opinion for the Court nevertheless based its decision in part on an interpretation of the sentence that precluded such relief, thus calling into question a standard remedy for findings of broad violations of Title VII.

Although Stevens concurred in the judgment, he wrote a separate opinion noting that in his view, "the Court's discussion of Title VII is wholly advisory." He appeared to share the majority's view that section 706(g) would preclude a court from awarding the type of race-conscious relief at issue in the case, but he maintained that the same limitation would not apply to what parties could voluntarily do in a consent decree. As of that date, the view that parties could agree to race-conscious action as a Title VII remedy was the position most accepting of affirmative action that Stevens had yet expressed.

But he went rather farther two years later. In *Wygant v. Jackson Board of Education*, 476 U.S. 267 (1986), the Court considered the constitutionality of a collective-bargaining agreement of a public school system that prevented the school system from laying off minority teachers in numbers that would decrease the minority representation among teachers. The Court found that unless the provision were directed at correcting discrimination by the governmental unit involved, the racial classification was not sufficiently narrowly tailored to survive constitutional scrutiny.

Stevens dissented in the case. Observing that "in our present society, race is not always irrelevant to sound government decisionmaking," he maintained that rather than focusing on whether the affected minority teachers were entitled to positions because of past discrimination, the inquiry should first address whether the policy advanced the public interest in educating children for the future. Reasoning that "it is quite obvious that a school board may reasonably conclude that an integrated faculty will be able to provide benefits to the student body that could not be provided by all white, or nearly all white, faculty," Stevens stated that he would uphold the program.

In addition to being the first instance in which Stevens indicated that he would uphold a racial classification, his *Wygant* dissent was also his first articulation of the type of forward-looking justification for racial classifications that would underlie much of his reasoning in affirmative action cases in the ensuing years. Even before the *Wygant* decision was issued in May 1986, however, there had been at least one indication (apart from the *Stotts* concurrence) that Stevens's view of affirmative action was changing. In February 1986, the court heard arguments in *Local 28 of the Sheet Metal Workers' International Association v. EEOC*, 478 U.S. 421 (1986), a case that, in the context of court-ordered race-conscious hiring goals for a Title VII violation, squarely raised the issue of whether section 706(g) of Title VII prohibited a court from ordering race-conscious relief benefiting persons who were not actual victims of discrimination. The Reagan administration took the position that the section did prohibit such relief, maintaining that the issue had been resolved in *Stotts*. While Stevens had appeared to accept that interpretation of section 706(g) in his *Stotts* concurrence (though not agreeing that the Court had properly reached the issue), during oral argument in *Sheet Metal Workers*, Stevens pressed the government's counsel for an acknowledgment that the language of section 706(g) did not on its face require that interpretation. Five months later (six weeks after *Wygant*), when the Court issued its opinion upholding the hiring goals in *Sheet Metal Workers* and specifically finding that section 706(g) did not preclude such relief, Stevens joined in every part of Brennan's opinion for the Court. That same day, in *Local Number 93, International Association of Firefighters v. City of Cleveland*, 478 U.S. 501 (1986), Stevens joined in Brennan's opinion upholding affirmative action provisions of a consent decree and finding that regardless of any limitations section 706(g) might impose on the powers of a court to order race-conscious relief, the provision did not apply to consent decrees.

The following year, in *United States v. Paradise*, 480 U.S. 149 (1987), the Court upheld a court-ordered requirement that blacks receive 50 percent of promotions to Alabama state trooper corporal positions, finding that the measure was permissible under the Equal Protection Clause because it served a compelling governmental interest in the elimination of past discrimination and was narrowly tailored to serve that purpose. Stevens concurred in the judgment, but he wrote a separate opinion, maintaining that in contrast to measures imposed by a governmental entity where a strong presumption exists against the measure, there exists no such presumption against a race-conscious measure imposed by a district court to remedy a proven constitutional violation. Relying on school desegregation jurisprudence, he maintained that district courts had broad discretion to fashion remedies for such violations without having to satisfy the requirement that the measure be narrowly tailored to achieve a compelling governmental interest. Thus on this occasion, Stevens for the first time showed himself to be even more accepting of race-conscious measures than those other members of the Court who generally approved of race-conscious measures, at least in situations where the measure was intended to correct a constitutional violation, situations he termed to be "dramatically different" from the "response to a past societal wrong" that he believed was at issue in *Fullilove*.

The same year, in *Johnson v. Transportation Agency, Santa Clara County*, 480 U.S. 616 (1987), the Court reaffirmed its holding in *Weber* that Title VII did not prohibit race- or gender-conscious measures to eliminate conspicuous imbalances in the labor force. Stevens concurred in the result, but he did so solely on the basis that the case was controlled by *Weber* and because of his respect for *stare decisis*, making clear that he believed that *Weber* had been wrongly decided and had itself been contrary both to the legislative intent of Title VII and to the prior construction of the statute in *McDonald*. Yet while concurring solely on the basis of the

Weber decision that he maintained had been erroneous, Stevens went on to argue for an expansive interpretation of that precedent. Arguing that there was no reason why an employer should have to determine whether its past practices might constitute an arguable violation of Title VII, he went on to suggest that there might be a wide range of forward-looking rationales to justify such measures. Quoting from a law review article, he suggested that improving the quality of education, as well as "improving [an employer's] services to minority communities, averting racial tension over the allocation of jobs in a community, or increasing the diversity of the workforce, to name but a few examples," might justify such measures in appropriate circumstances.

Two years later, in *City of Richmond v. J.A. Croson Co.*, 488 U.S. 469 (1989), the Court struck down Richmond, Virginia,'s minority set-aside in a decision that suggested that governmental entities would have great difficulty justifying a race-conscious measure of any sort that did not directly address past discrimination by the governmental entity. Stevens concurred in the result, but took issue with the premise that racial classifications are never permissible except as a remedy for a past constitutional violation. He maintained that sound governmental decision making should also take into account a racial classification's impact on the future, as with, for example, consideration of the benefits of an integrated faculty. He joined in the judgment, however, because he did not regard set-asides to serve forward-looking ends as lawful, and, citing the dangers of stereotypical thinking and the potential stigma to beneficiaries of racial preferences, he concluded by quoting at length from portions of his dissent in *Fullilove* that had been strongly critical of such measures.

The next affirmative action case considered by the Court was *Metro Broadcasting, Inc. v. FCC*, 497 U.S. 547 (1990), in which the Court upheld the congressionally mandated race-conscious preferences in the distribution of broadcast licenses. Stevens joined in Brennan's opinion for the majority that found that congressionally sanctioned "benign" racial classifications were subject only to intermediate scrutiny, but he also filed a concurrence to emphasize that the Court's ruling "squarely rejects the proposition that a governmental decision that rests on a racial classification is never permissible except as a remedy for a past wrong," and to endorse "this focus on the future benefit" of such measures. While observing that race might be legitimately taken into account by a governmental entity only in extremely rare circumstances, he indicated that in addition to promoting diversity in broadcasting, integrating police forces and promoting diversity in public school faculties and student bodies of professional schools were among those rare circumstances.

By the time the Court considered the next affirmative action case, Stevens was the only member of the *Metro Broadcasting* majority still on the Court. In *Adarand Constructors, Inc. v. Peña*, 515 U.S. 200 (1995), a much-changed court struck down a congressionally mandated program giving general contractors incentives to hire "socially and economically disadvantaged individuals" as subcontractors where a race-based presumption was used in identifying such individuals. In reaching that result, the Court rejected the *Metro Broadcasting* precedent and for the first time applied the strict scrutiny standard to congressionally mandated race-conscious measures. Stevens filed a vigorous dissent. The dissent partly relied on the *stare decisis* effect of *Fullilove* and *Metro Broadcasting*, but it also argued at length concerning the differences between racial classifications intended to benefit a minority group and those that were intended to disadvantage or stigmatize a minority group. The dissent presents a striking contrast to the *Fullilove* dissent in which Stevens first articulated his views as to the wisdom and morality of racial classifications intended to benefit minority groups.

In 2003, in possibly Stevens's last affirmative action cases, he also aligned herself as being firmly in favor of affirmative action in the landmark cases *Gratz v. Bollinger*, 123 S. Ct. 2411, 2003 U.S. LEXIS 4801 (2003), and *Grutter v. Bollinger*, 123 S. Ct. 2325, 2003 U.S. LEXIS 4800 (2003). His strong support of affirmative action in these cases (as part of the majority in *Grutter* and dissenting in *Gratz*) illustrates his evolution on the issue of affirmative action and his strong support of affirmative action today.

See also Adarand Constructors, Inc. v. Peña; Brennan, William Joseph; *City of Richmond v. J.A. Croson Co.*; Civil Rights Act of 1866; Civil Rights Act of 1964; *Firefighters Local Union No. 1784 v. Stotts*; Ford, Gerald Rudolph; *Fullilove v. Klutznick*; *Gratz v. Bollinger/Grutter v. Bollinger*; *Johnson v. Transportation Agency, Santa Clara County*; *Local 28 of the Sheet Metal Workers' International Association v. EEOC*; *Local No. 93, International Association of Firefighters v. City of Cleveland*; Marshall, Thurgood; *Metro Broadcasting, Inc. v. FCC*; Reagan, Ronald; *Regents of the University of California v. Bakke*; Title VI of the Civil Rights Act of 1964; Title VII of the Civil Rights Act of 1964; *United States v. Paradise*; *United Steelworkers of America v. Weber*; White, Byron Raymond; *Wygant v. Jackson Board of Education*.

FURTHER READING: Funston, Richard Y., 1992, "Stevens, John Paul," in *The Oxford Companion to the Supreme Court of the United States*, edited by Kermit Hall, New York: Oxford University Press; Popkin, William, 1989, "A Common Lawyer on the Supreme Court: The Opinions of Justice Stevens," *Duke Law Journal* 1989 (November): 1087–1139; Sickels, Robert Judd, 1988, *John Paul Stevens and the Constitution: Search for Balance*, University Park: Pennsylvania State University Press; Schauer, Frederick, 1996, "Symposium: Perspectives on Justice John Paul Stevens," *Rutgers Law Journal* 27 (spring): 543–561.

JAMES P. SCANLAN

Stone, Harlan Fiske (1872–1946)

Harlan Fiske Stone was a U.S. Supreme Court justice from 1925 to 1941 and chief justice from 1941 to 1946. His famous footnote 4 in *United States v. Carolene Products Co.*, 304 U.S. 144 (1938), suggested that in certain instances the Court may closely review legislation that impinges on certain civil rights and liberties. Stone defined such instances as those in which the government threatened the constitutional provisions protected by the Bill of Rights and the Fourteenth Amendment, when it threatened to restrict political processes (such as political assembly), and when it threatened the rights of particular religious, national, or racial minorities. The footnote became the basis for subsequent judgments that aimed to protect the rights of "suspect" classifications like race, gender, and religion. The footnote is often viewed as the critical point when the Supreme Court began emphasizing the protection of civil liberties and rights.

Harlan Fiske Stone was born on October 11, 1872 in Chesterfield, New Hampshire. He graduated from Amherst College in 1894 and from Columbia University

Law School in 1898. He taught and practiced law from 1898 to 1924 and then served for a year as attorney general before Calvin Coolidge appointed him to the Supreme Court on February 2, 1925. Throughout his early years on the bench, Stone and his fellow justices debated primarily whether the Court should review the constitutionality of economic legislation. The Court was split between the older and more conservative judges, who defended traditional notions of economic rights that heavily favored property owners, and the younger judges like Stone, who favored individual rights and liberties. In 1937, in an event often referred to as the Constitutional Crisis of 1937, President Franklin D. Roosevelt sought to appoint to the Court additional liberal judges who would be more favorable to his New Deal ideas. His attempt failed. As a result, some of his New Deal legislation was struck down, but a series of retirements over the next few years allowed him to slowly appoint sympathetic justices, and his legislation was eventually upheld. Stone supported Roosevelt's New Deal legislation, but did not like Roosevelt's attempt to pack the Court. Shortly after the crisis, Stone laid out in his footnote the special circumstances in which the judicial review of legislation, the point so hotly contested during the crisis of 1937, might occur. He was appointed chief justice by President Roosevelt in 1941 and went on to oversee the Supreme Court's subtle transformation from concern for property rights to concern for individual rights and liberties.

United States v. Carolene Products Co. dealt with a federal law prohibiting interstate transportation of "filled milk"—skimmed milk containing mixtures of animal fat—and was primarily concerned with existing governmental boundaries and economic rights. Footnote 4, however, delineates three circumstances when there should be a more critical judicial review of noneconomic legislation. According to Stone, in all other circumstances but for the three noted exceptions, the courts should not interfere with legislation. The third paragraph is specifically directed at addressing the circumstances involving racial and other minority rights (one of the three exceptions) and reads as follows: "Nor need we enquire whether similar considerations enter into the review of statutes directed at particular religious . . . or national . . . or racial minorities . . . whether prejudice against discrete and insular minorities may be a special condition, which tends seriously to curtail the operation of those particular processes ordinarily to be relied upon to protect minorities, and which may call for a correspondingly more searching judicial inquiry." As discussed earlier, this footnote became the basis for subsequent judgments that aimed to protect the rights of "suspect" classifications like race, gender, and religion and is often viewed as the critical point when the Supreme Court began emphasizing the protection of civil liberties and rights.

See also Bill of Rights; Discrete and Insular Minority; Fourteenth Amendment; Roosevelt, Franklin Delano; Suspect Classification.

FURTHER READING: Mason, Alpheus Thomas, 1956, *Harlan Fiske Stone: Pillar of the Law*, New York: Viking Press; Rosenberg, Gerald N., 2000, "Footnote Fetishism: Carolene Products Footnote 4 and the Changing Meanings of Supreme Court Decisions," http://www.artsci.wustl.edu/~polisci/epstein/conference/archive00/Rosenberg.pdf; Urofsky, Melvin I., 1997, *Division and Discord: The Supreme Court under Stone and Vinson, 1941–1953*, Columbia: University of South Carolina Press.

JAYSON J. FUNKE

Stone, Lucy (1818–1893)

Lucy Stone, Elizabeth Cady Stanton, and Susan B. Anthony led the women's rights movement for more than half of the nineteenth century, converting many people to the causes of antislavery and women's rights. Known as a great lecturer and editor and one of America's great suffragists, Stone was the founder of the American Woman Suffrage Association (AWSA), formed in November 1869 in Cleveland, Ohio. In May of that same year, Susan B. Anthony and Elizabeth Cady Stanton had organized the National Woman Suffrage Association (NWSA).

Stone helped organize one of the first national women's rights convention, held in Worcester, Massachusetts, in 1850. Her speech at this convention drew Anthony into the suffrage movement. The two disagreed on principles and policy and split the suffrage movement into these two main factions (AWSA and NWSA) after the Civil War. Stone's organization (AWSA) is considered to have been the more conservative of the two. The first president of the AWSA was a man, Henry Ward Beecher. While the AWSA supported a national suffrage amendment, it conducted a lecture tour focused on changing individual state constitutions.

Lucy Stone, a strong advocate of equality in marriage, is remembered for being the first woman in the United States to keep her own name after marriage. Women since her who keep their maiden name have been called "Lucy Stoners." Stone was also the first woman in Massachusetts to earn a college degree and was one of the few early feminists who did not have their father's financial and emotional support for their education. Although her brothers were sent to college, Lucy Stone had to earn her own way. At age twenty-five, she attended Oberlin College (founded in 1833) in Ohio, the first college in America to admit both women and African Americans. After working her way through college as a housekeeper and a teacher, she graduated in 1847 in the company of such early graduates as Antoinette Brown Blackwell, Emeline Horton Cleveland, and Anna Julia Cooper. She returned home to Massachusetts, where she gave her first speech on women's rights, much to the embarrassment of her family.

The American Anti-Slavery Society hired her as a lecturer in the spring of 1848 to travel and give speeches on abolition. William Lloyd Garrison said, "She [Stone] is a very superior young woman, and has a soul as free as the air, and is preparing to go forth as a lecturer, particularly in the vindication of the rights of women" (Lewis 2000). When her suffragist speeches became a cause of concern for the Anti-Slavery Society, she arranged to speak on abolition on weekends and women's rights on weekdays, charging for the latter. Such large crowds gathered to hear her speak that in three years, her women's rights speeches brought in $7,000. They also brought violence, heckling, and hatred, with reports of many disturbances during her lectures. She was also ridiculed as she joined other feminists of the day in donning the controversial "bloomers" costume, which caused a public outcry. For twenty years (1869–1889), Stone served as editor of the *Woman's Journal*, a feminist magazine that she founded and published weekly. With her knowledge of Greek and Hebrew, she challenged the biblical translations that were demeaning to women and argued against unfair church practices that excluded women. She was expelled by the Congregational Church and became a member of the Unitarian Church.

Lucy Stone was born the eighth of nine children to Francis and Hannah Stone on August 13, 1818, on a poor 145-acre farm in West Brookfield, Massachusetts. On May 1, 1855, she married Henry B. Blackwell, a man seven years her junior. He was not only active in the antislavery movement, but also firmly believed in women's rights and the concept of total and absolute equality in marriage. Both of his sisters, Elizabeth and Emily, were physicians, with Elizabeth Blackwell being the first woman physician in the United States. Stone and Blackwell had two children, a son who died at birth and a daughter, Alice Stone Blackwell, who was born in 1857. Lucy Stone retired to raise her daughter, and the family moved from Cincinnati to New Jersey. There she refused to pay property taxes on a house that was in her name alone. She challenged the authorities, claiming "taxation without representation" since she could not vote. Her furniture was publicly auctioned to pay the debt, but the incident brought much attention to the voting status of women in society. In 1883, Lucy Stone gave a eulogy at the funeral of Sojourner Truth, where more than 1,000 people gathered for the service. Stone and Truth had shared the fight for the rights of both African Americans and women.

Lucy Stone's daughter, Alice Stone Blackwell, attended Boston University and became very active in the suffrage movement. In 1890, she organized and accomplished a union of the NWSA and the AWSA, forming the unified National American Woman Suffrage Association. Elizabeth Cady Stanton was named president, Susan B. Anthony was vice president, and Lucy Stone was chairman of the executive committee. Lucy Stone's last words to her daughter were "make the world better." She died before the passage of the Nineteenth Amendment, on October 18, 1893, in Worcester, Massachusetts. Completing her string of "firsts," Lucy Stone was also the first person in New England to be cremated.

See also Abolitionists; Anthony, Susan Brownell; Mott, Lucretia Coffin; Nineteenth Amendment; Stanton, Elizabeth Cady; Suffrage Movement.

FURTHER READING: Gurko, Miriam, 1974, *The Ladies of Seneca Falls: The Birth of the Woman's Rights Movement*, New York: Schocken Books; Hymowitz, Carol, and Michaele Weissman, 1978, *A History of Women in America*, New York: Bantam Books; Lewis, Jone Johnson, 2000, "A Soul as Free as the Air: Profile of Lucy Stone," http://womenshistory.about.com/libraryweekly/aa062899.htm; Lunardini, Christine, 1994, *What Every American Should Know about Women's History*, Holbrook, MA: Bob Adams.

SHEILA BLUHM

Strauder v. West Virginia, 100 U.S. 303 (1879)

The Supreme Court case *Strauder v. West Virginia* was significant in the area of racial discrimination in the selection of juries under the Fourteenth Amendment for several reasons. First, it was one of the few major decisions under the Fourteenth Amendment favorable to African Americans during this period in U.S. history. Second, the Court noted that under the Fourteenth Amendment, it was permissible to protect minority classes with affirmative measures. The Court specifically noted that "they [newly freed African Americans] needed the protection which a wise government extends to those who are unable to protect themselves. They especially needed protection against unfriendly action in the States where they were residents." Interestingly, a short four years later, the Court stated that blacks should no longer be treated as "the special favorites of the law" under preferential legislation in the *Civil Rights Cases*, 109 U.S. 3 (1883).

The underlying facts of the *Strauder* case date back to the early 1870s. West Virginia law in the 1870s prohibited blacks from serving on juries, thus ensuring that black defendants were always judged by white citizens, and that white citizens were always judged by white individuals. The specific genesis of this case revolved around the indictment and subsequent conviction of a black man in Ohio County, West Virginia. The West Virginia law at the time (1873) stated that "[a]ll white male persons who are twenty-one years of age and who are citizens of this State shall be liable to serve as jurors, except as herein provided." Thus no West Virginia man of color was eligible to be a member of the grand jury or to serve on a petit jury in the state. The defendant, being black and a former slave, had reason to believe that he could not receive a full and equal hearing of his case before an all-white jury. On the heels of emancipation, blacks at the time were still regarded as ignorant, "mere children" (in the words of the Supreme Court in *Strauder*), and in need of protection that could be afforded by whites. What this belief left out was the fact that black slaves were not taught to read, were made to be dependent upon their white owners, and were just beginning to find their way in a free America when this case came to the forefront. It was because of this belief on the part of white America that the Fourteenth Amendment was framed and adopted. It was designed to ensure that persons of color, primarily African Americans, would enjoy the same civil rights as whites and be protected from state laws that were designed on their face to deny equal access to these protections.

The U.S. Supreme Court ruled that the law in West Virginia "amounts to a denial of the equal protection of the law to a colored man when he is put upon trial for an alleged offense against the State." As a result, the case was reversed and remitted with specific instructions back to the state of West Virginia, the Circuit Court of Ohio County. This case became the footing upon which all further cases dealing with issues of racial exclusion from the jury process would rest. It was one of the first clear indications that when state laws discriminate against persons of one race, the courts will step in and affirmatively uphold the rights of the race being disadvantaged. Additionally, as noted earlier, the Court set forth the notion that minorities needed affirmative protection in the United States through proactive, preferential legislation and laws.

See also *Civil Rights Cases*; Civil War (Reconstruction) Amendments and Civil Rights Acts; Fourteenth Amendment; Jim Crow Laws; Jury Selection and Affirmative Action; Paternalistic Race Relations Theory.

FURTHER READING: Miller, Loren, 1966, *The Petitioners: The Story of the Supreme Court of the United States and the Negro*, New York: Pantheon Books.

SUSAN F. BRINKLEY

Strict Scrutiny

Strict scrutiny is a standard of review used by the Supreme Court to test the constitutional validity of a challenged law (including affirmative action cases). A standard of review refers to the manner and focus the Court gives to a particular law to determine its consistency with provisions of the Constitution. For example, what is the standard of review for the evaluation of equal protection challenges under the Fourteenth Amendment? The Court has set in place three recognizable standards of review for equal protection challenges: strict scrutiny, intermediate review, and the rational basis test. The Court has determined that when a state law classifies a person according to an "immutable characteristic determined solely by the accident of birth," or when the state impinges upon a "fundamental right" of an individual, then a suspect classification has occurred. If a suspect classification is acknowledged, then the standard of review for that particular law requires strict scrutiny.

Strict scrutiny is the highest level of evaluation, and the strict scrutiny test, as it has come to be known, requires the state to show a compelling governmental interest to sustain the constitutionality or integrity of that law. Historically, the Supreme Court has been divided on the matter of identifying a suspect classification that requires such close judicial scrutiny. All the justices have agreed that race constitutes a suspect class. Constitutional jurisprudence has shown that blacks constitute a suspect class, but there is some confusion about whether whites can constitute a suspect class if a statutory arrangement discriminates against this group. In the 1995 Supreme Court case *Adarand Constructors, Inc. v. Peña*, 515 U.S. 200 (1995), the Supreme Court held that all affirmative action programs that classify by race (even if benignly) are subject to strict scrutiny by the courts. The Court in *Adarand* specified that "all racial classifications, whether overtly invidious or purportedly benign, were subject to strict scrutiny." One of the few cases to have held that the governmental discriminatory action at issue survived the strict scrutiny analysis was *Korematsu v. United States*, 323 U.S. 214 (1944), which dealt with the internment of Japanese Americans in World War II. The fact that the strict scrutiny analysis is so rigorous prompted Justice Thurgood Marshall once to remark that "strict scrutiny is strict in theory, but fatal in fact."

As for age, gender, sexual orientation, or indigence classifications, the Court has also been badly divided. Gender, by a narrow margin of 5–4 in *Frontiero v. Richardson*, 411 U.S. 677 (1973), has been relegated to an intermediate level of review that calls for a less stringent standard of judicial scrutiny. Gender-based classifications will be upheld if the government meets the burden of showing a "legitimate" and "exceedingly persuasive justification" and can prove a "substantial relationship" between the government objective and the means it uses to achieve that objective. The lowest level of review, the rational basis test, permits classifications in which the state can reasonably be assured that a law does not offend the Equal Protection Clause. Hence a strict scrutiny analysis should always be used by the Court for classifications based on race and ethnicity. As for the disparate treatment given to additional classifications such as gender, sexual orientation, or age, the question is still unresolved on how the Supreme Court will address these statutory categorizations in the future.

See also Adarand Constructors, Inc. v. Peña; Compelling Governmental Interest; Discrete and Insular Minority; Equal Protection Clause; Fourteenth Amendment; *Frontiero v. Richardson*; Intermediate Scrutiny; Japanese Internment and World War II; *Korematsu v. United States*; O'Connor, Sandra Day; Rational Basis Scrutiny; Suspect Classification.

FURTHER READING: Anderson, Elizabeth, 2002, "Integration, Affirmative Action, and Strict Scrutiny," *New York University Law Review* 77, no. 5:1195–1271; Chang, Mitchell J., Daria Witt Chang, James Jones, and K. Hakuta, eds., 2003, *Compelling Interest: Examining the Evidence on Racial Dynamics in Colleges and Universities*, Stanford, CA: Stanford University Press.

JANIS JUDSON

Suffrage Movement

The suffrage movement was the movement in the United States to gain the right to vote for women. The suffrage movement represented a concerted effort by many in society to ensure gender equality in the political realm. At the first women's rights convention, the issue of women's right to vote was proposed as one of twelve resolutions. Considered to be too controversial, the right to vote was not added to the constitutional demands of the Seneca Falls Convention of 1848, despite the support of antislavery advocate Frederick Douglass. Two years later, however, at the Rochester women's right conference, the suffrage resolution was passed. The fight for women's right to vote continued from that date until the Nineteenth Amendment was passed by the U.S. Senate in 1919 and ratified by the states in 1920.

After the Civil War, women's rights advocates expected that women would gain the right to vote. Instead, when the Fourteenth Amendment to the Constitution was ratified in 1868, its one voting provision (Section 2, dealing with the abridgment of the right to vote in elections for the federal offices of president, vice president, and Congress) specifically applied only to men. Its language spoke of "male citizens" and "male inhabitants," using the word "male" for the first time in the Constitution. It thus clearly excluded women from its coverage. While the Fourteenth Amendment spoke of the right of males to vote, it not only prohibited women's vote, but, for the first time, made necessary an additional constitutional amendment to grant women's voting privileges. More than half a century passed before this occurred and women were given the same right to vote that was extended to black men in the Fifteenth Amendment.

First-wave feminists such as Susan B. Anthony, Lucy Stone, and Elizabeth Cady Stanton protested against the Fourteenth Amendment for its exclusion of women. On the heels of the Fourteenth Amendment, the Fifteenth Amendment was also added to the Constitution in 1870. The Fifteenth Amendment provided that the right to vote could not be denied on the basis of race, color, or previous condition of servitude. Women demanded that the word "sex" also be added to this list, but to no avail. In fact, many abolitionists struck out against the women's movement and its suffrage efforts, claiming that Reconstruction was a time for the rights of black men to be established and not diminished by the additional issue of women's rights. It was believed that society could and would handle only one voting reform at a time, and the issue of women's right to vote clouded, complicated, and potentially harmed the issue of the black man's right to vote.

Feminist alignment with the abolitionist movement became the source of division within the women's movement. New York–based feminists, such as Stanton and Anthony, believed that women's rights (specifically women's right to vote) must be the first and foremost concern of any feminist movement. Finding themselves excluded from the right to vote after having supported the abolitionist movement, they set out to gain their own rights and privileges. In 1869, Stanton and Anthony withdrew from the Equal Rights Association and formed the National Woman Suffrage Association (NWSA). Boston-based feminists, such as Lucy Stone and Julia Ward Howe, also wanted women to have the right to vote, but believed that their cause should wait until the vote was secured for black men. This caused a great division in the women's movement. After learning of the formation of the NWSA and their subsequent exclusion from the group, Stone and Howe moved to form their own group, which they called the American Woman Suffrage Association (AWSA).

It took until 1890 for the two factions of the women's movement to unite once again. The NWSA and the AWSA joined to become the National American Woman Suffrage Association NAWSA. Elizabeth Cady Stanton served as president of the association for its first two years of operation. After the suffrage convention of 1894, the focus of the fight for the right to vote shifted. Instead of seeking a federal constitutional amendment, the association's strategy was to make changes on the state level. The visionary and ideological leader, Elizabeth Cady Stanton, was out of leadership. Although women's right to vote was of high importance to Stanton, she saw it as one of many central issues of female equality that had to be addressed. The two succeeding presidents of the association, Anna Howard Shaw (1847–1919) and Carrie Chapman Catt (1859–1947), had more practical goals in mind. They saw the right to vote as the essential move that would bring about any other needed changes. Therefore, they sought the support of middle-class women in America and fought exclusively for women's right to vote.

England's suffrage movement began later than the American efforts, but used different tactics, including violence. Many of these tactics were adopted by women of the American effort, particularly younger women of the second generation of suffragettes. Protests, picketing at the White House, imprisonment, parades, and rallies were all used to raise social awareness and encourage support for the vote. Radical feminist Alice Paul led a women's suffrage movement that formed the National Woman's Party (NWP) and adopted many of the British tactics. On March 3, 1914, Paul led a parade of protest at Woodrow Wilson's inauguration. Some 8,000 people participated in the parade, with an estimated 500,000 spectators on Pennsylvania Avenue. Participants included representatives from every local, state, and national suffrage organization, as well as people from every occupation that employed women. The parade resulted in a delegation meeting with the new president, and vast public sympathy and financial support.

The NAWSA suspended its suffrage efforts during World War I to help the nation present a solidified and patriotic image to the world. The National Woman's Party, however, refused to be silenced, even for the war. Instead, its members picketed the White House and would not allow Wilson's claims to democracy for the world without a vote for women. The NWP members brought worldwide attention to their suffrage cause through multiple arrests and imprisonments. Wilson responded by addressing Congress in a plea to consider suffrage an emergency war measure, claiming that it was essential to his ability to bring about world peace.

Jeannette Rankin of Montana, the first woman representative in Congress, introduced the suffrage amendment to the House of Representatives on January 10, 1918. The amendment passed with only one more vote than the two-thirds needed, 274 votes in its favor and 136 votes against it. It took another year and a half for the Senate to pass it, and then the states had to ratify it. After seventy-two years, the vote for women was finally gained on August 26, 1920. Charlotte Woodward was the only woman who survived from the time of the initial Seneca Falls Convention (when she was nineteen years old) to actually cast a vote in 1920 at the age of ninety-three. The NAWSA later became the League of Women Voters.

In 1922, a six-volume *History of Woman Suffrage* was published, recording the long struggle for women's right to vote. Begun in 1876 by Elizabeth Cady Stanton, Susan B. Anthony, and Matilda Joslyn Gage, it remains a rich collection of letters, convention notes, memoirs, and recorded history of the American women's suffrage movement.

Three women attaching a "Votes for Women" poster to a telephone pole in New Jersey during the suffrage campaign days. Courtesy of Library of Congress.

See also Abolitionists; Anthony, Susan Brownell; Douglass, Frederick; Fifteenth Amendment; Fourteenth Amendment; Mott, Lucretia Coffin; Nineteenth Amendment; Seneca Falls Convention; Stanton, Elizabeth Cady; Stone, Lucy.

FURTHER READING: Gurko, Miriam, 1974, *The Ladies of Seneca Falls*, New York: Schocken Books; Hymowitz, Carol, and Michaele Weissman, 1978, *A History of Women in America*, New York: Bantam Books; Lunardini, Christine, 1994, *What Every American Should Know about Women's History*, Holbrook, MA: Bob Adams; O'Melveny, Mary K., 1996, "The Sesquicentennial of the 1848 Seneca Falls Women's Rights Convention: American Women's Unfinished Quest for Legal, Economic, Political, and Social Equality: Playing the Gender Card: Affirmative Action and Working Women," *Kentucky Law Journal* 84 (summer): 863–901.

SHEILA BLUHM

Supreme Court and Affirmative Action

African Americans and other minorities in pursuit of equal representation, equal employment, and equal opportunity frequently have had to rely on the federal court system as a mechanism for relief. It has often been suggested that the Supreme Court was the protector of the rights of African Americans during much of the twentieth century. Starting with the "Scottsboro Boys" cases of the early 1930s and continuing through the 1970s, the Court was viewed as the one institution that would protect minorities in America. However, with the appointments of conservative Supreme Court justices Sandra Day O'Connor, William Rehnquist, Anthony Kennedy, Antonin Scalia, and Clarence Thomas, the Supreme Court is now considered hostile to affirmative action and unsympathetic toward the rights and concerns of African Americans and other minorities. Supreme Court affirmative action cases decided since 1978 reveal that a slow evolution in legal and political philosophy has resulted in decisions that have restricted affirmative action programs as the years have progressed toward the present.

During the years from 1971 to 1988, the Supreme Court, it could be argued, was generally protective of the rights of the employee as well. The composition of the Court was important in how decisions were reached. A clear liberal bloc existed in the early years of this period. Justices William Brennan, Byron White, Thurgood Marshall, and Harry Blackmun constituted the liberal votes in each case pertaining to affirmative action. The judicial philosophy of these four justices became known for championing the rights of protected groups in affirmative action cases. The slow dissolution of the influence of this liberal bloc resulted in many of the affirmative action cases during the latter part of this period going against the liberal bloc on the Court, in large part because of the changing composition of the Court in the 1980s. In the late 1980s, William Brennan, along with Thurgood Marshall and Harry Blackmun, comprised a three-justice bloc that always voted to uphold affirmative action plans when the constitutionality of such plans was called into question. However, Justice White, a strong supporter of affirmative action during the 1970s, began to grow increasingly critical of affirmative action by the 1980s. By the mid-1980s, White was more consistently aligned with conservative Justices opposed to affirmative action than with the liberal bloc.

Initially, Supreme Court decisions were viewed as friendly to affirmative action and as providing judicial protection for those promoting affirmative hiring and promotional practices. In many of the early affirmative action cases, the Court avoided the large issue of the constitutionality per se (or lack thereof) of affirmative action plans. In *Griggs v. Duke Power Co.*, 401 U.S. 424 (1971), the Supreme Court for the first time approved an affirmative action–type remedy in response to the disparate impact of discriminatory employment practices. In 1974, in *DeFunis v. Odegaard*, 416 U.S. 312 (1974), the Court was able to avoid the larger issue of the constitutionality of affirmative action and the arguments that a white male applicant was reversely discriminated against under the Fourteenth Amendment by virtue of an affirmative action program at a law school because it declared that the case was moot, as the plaintiff was entering the third and final year of law school.

However, the issue of whether affirmative action constitutes reverse discrimination and therefore violates the Equal Protection Clause of the Fourteenth

Amendment, and whether affirmative action violates the Civil Rights Act of 1964, particularly Title VI, confronted the Court four years later in *Regents of the University of California v. Bakke*, 438 U.S. 265 (1978). In *Bakke*, the Court dealt with the permissibility of rigid racial quotas under affirmative action plans and held such quotas to be a violation of the Equal Protection Clause of the Fourteenth Amendment. However, *Bakke* resulted in several different plurality/concurring opinions of the Court, each taking a different opinion on the general constitutionality of affirmative action plans. In Justice Lewis Powell's famous plurality opinion, race could still be utilized as a factor in making admissions decisions. Thus the *Bakke* decision left intact the bulk of affirmative action programs that gave special consideration for constitutionally protected groups, so long as rigid racial quotas were not utilized. The Court also held that the use of race in any program benefiting from statutory-provided federal financial assistance was impermissible under Title VI of the Civil Rights Act of 1964.

In 1979, in *United Steelworkers of America v. Weber*, 443 U.S. 193 (1979), the Supreme Court was confronted with the legal issue of a voluntary affirmative action plan in the employment context and dealt with whether such a plan (and the use of quotas as part of the plan) was a violation of Title VII of the Civil Rights Act of 1964. In this case, the Court ruled that Title VII of the 1964 Civil Rights Act did allow for preferential treatment and that Title VII allowed employers and unions in the private sector to use quotas and to institute race-conscious programs to eliminate racial imbalances in traditionally segregated job categories in order to eradicate historical racial discrimination in employment.

Next, in *Fullilove v. Klutznick*, 448 U.S. 448 (1980), the Court addressed the issue of whether setting aside contracts for minority business enterprises (MBEs) was constitutional. The case ultimately established the permissibility of set-aside contracts in the area of affirmative action, so long as the set-aside programs were "narrowly tailored and did not unnecessarily trammel the interests of others." It was the view of the Court at this time that set-asides were constitutional if they were designed to eradicate the effects of past racial discrimination in the area of employment. This view would change with the passage of time and with changes to the composition of the Court.

In 1984, in *Firefighters Local Union No. 1784 v. Stotts*, 467 U.S. 561 (1984), the Supreme Court reviewed the legality of bona fide seniority systems in conjunction with affirmative action programs during periods of employee layoffs. One of the key issues in the case dealt with whether minorities hired under affirmative action plans should be laid off before white employees with more seniority on the job. This case was important in the area of affirmative action because the Court held that because the individual minority employees could not prove that they were themselves the victims of past discrimination, the seniority system in place was legitimate and took precedence over affirmative action plans. Under this decision, the Court held that white employees with more seniority on the job could not be laid off in lieu of newer minority employees on the job, regardless of the existence of affirmative action plans. That is, a bona fide seniority system was a legitimate and protected practice under Title VII of the 1964 Civil Rights Act.

Two years later, in *Wygant v. Jackson Board of Education*, 476 U.S. 267 (1986), the Supreme Court again confronted an employment case involving layoffs, affirmative action, and charges of reverse discrimination by white workers. In *Wygant*, the Court declared unconstitutional, as a violation of the Equal Protection Clause of the Fourteenth Amendment, a local school board's plan for laying off teachers that gave preference to people of color. The Court also used the strict scrutiny legal principle in analyzing the affirmative action plan at issue and held that employers must present convincing evidence that the remedial action was essential in order for the plan to pass constitutional muster.

After the *Wygant* decision, the Supreme Court decided three subsequent cases dealing with the constitutionality of affirmative action plans imposed by courts as remedies in response to defendant employers who engaged in egregious and aggravated forms of racial discrimination. In the first case, *Local 28 of the Sheet Metal Workers' International Association v. EEOC*, 478 U.S. 421 (1986), local minorities were found to have been excluded from the union and discriminated against in a blatant fashion in violation of Title VII of the Civil Rights Act of 1964. For more than a decade after the case was initiated in 1975, a federal district court, through remedial measures, attempted to improve the local union's recruitment and hiring of minority workers up to the level at which these minorities were represented in the work force at large. However, these remedial efforts failed, and the lower court fined the union $150,000 and placed this money in a special relief fund to be used for the recruitment and training of minority workers. The lower court also ordered the fund to be replenished by the union at several junctures. These court-imposed "affirmative action" remedial efforts were approved by the federal court of appeals, and the case was appealed to the Supreme Court. In a narrow 5–4 decision that would become the norm in many subsequent affirmative action cases, the Court affirmed the lower court's use of judicially imposed affirmative action plans as a permissible remedial plan in response to defendant employees who engaged in egregious discrimination and willful contempt of Title VII. The Court further held that the ordered relief fund was constitutional because it was a temporary measure. The Court also indicated that "the language of Title VII does not preclude the implementation of a race-conscious relief as a remedy for past historical discrimination." Similarly, in *Local 93 of the International Association of Firefighters v. City of Cleveland*, 478 U.S. 501 (1986), the Court again upheld the court-ordered race conscious hiring and promotion plans after the lower court had documented prior past discrimination by the parties involved.

During the 1987 term of the Supreme Court, the Court addressed the post-*Wygant* decision dealing with the legality of a court-ordered affirmative action plan in *United States v. Paradise*, 480 U.S. 149 (1987). This case stemmed from the hiring practices of the Alabama State Troopers. In 1972, a federal district court had found that Alabama had discriminated against minorities so blatantly that not one black trooper had ever been hired by Alabama in the entire history of the Alabama State Troopers (leading up to the case). In response, as in the *Sheet Metal Workers* case, a federal district court attempted for more than a decade through remedial efforts to ensure that Alabama hired and promoted black state troopers. After eleven years, the federal district court had ordered in 1983 and 1984 the implementation of a one-for-one promotion scheme. The purpose of the promotion requirement was to promote one African American state trooper for each white trooper who was promoted. This affirmative action court-imposed remedial plan called for the continuation of this one-for-one promotion scheme until black troopers comprised 25 percent of the force (the proportion of blacks in the labor force in Alabama) or until the Alabama State Troopers adopted a permanent promotion plan that would not adversely impact blacks. Ultimately, the federal court of appeals affirmed this lower court remedial plan, as did the U.S. Supreme Court in another close 5–4 decision. This case was arguably different from *Sheet Metal Workers* in that the focus was now on promotional practices rather than hiring practices, but both cases dealt with the permissibility of court-imposed mandatory affirmative action plans as a remedy to cure previous incidents of discrimination. The Court in *Paradise* established the guideline that "strict racial quotas in promotions meet constitutional muster in the public sector" as a remedy for previous racial discrimination.

Four weeks after *Paradise*, in *Johnson v. Transportation Agency, Santa Clara County*, 480 U.S. 616 (1987), the Court decided arguably the most significant affirmative action/reverse-discrimination decision since the *Bakke* case in 1978. The issue in *Johnson* involved the constitutionality of an affirmative action plan that was adopted unilaterally and voluntarily, and not as a mandatory remedial measure imposed by a court. Also, the affirmative action plan at issue involved not only minorities, but also women and persons with disabilities. The specific portion of the plan at issue in *Johnson* was the part that gave women preferences in promotion in order to cure the problem of occupational segregation and the traditional underrepresentation of women in certain areas of the workforce. Ultimately, in yet another 6–3 decision, the Court held that the plan established in *Johnson* met the judicial criteria of *Weber* and was permissible. The Court further ruled that it was permissible to take gender and race into consideration as a factor in employment decisions and that women and African Americans can receive preferential treatment. Thus *Johnson* marked the first time that the Court ruled on an affirmative action plan that provided preferences to women based upon concerns of occupational segregation in the workforce.

Yet in 1989, the Supreme Court began to view affirmative action differently and less favorably than it from 1971 to 1988. In 1989, the composition of the U.S. Supreme Court changed significantly as it related to affirmative action adjudication. Anthony Kennedy, an appointee of President Ronald Reagan, replaced Lewis Powell, a Richard Nixon appointee. This change produced a significant shift in how the Court voted in cases involving affirmative action and reverse discrimination. Powell had become a generous supporter of affirmative action during his years on the Court and is well remembered for his famous plurality opinion in the *Bakke* case. Kennedy's appointment had an immediate impact on decisions reached by the Court. His views were revealed in the six cases decided by the Supreme Court in 1989. In each of these cases, Kennedy voted on the side favorable to a reduction and reversal of affirmative action programs. His addition to the Court allowed a move from mainly having plurality decisions (which was the case in most of the affirmative action cases listed earlier) to formulating majority decisions that generally restricted or reversed affirmative action plans.

Thus 1989 is considered a swing year or transition year for the Court in the realm of affirmative action. The Court handed down several decisions of tremendous impact pertaining to the longevity of affirmative action in 1989. The bulk of the Court's agenda during this term focused on two issues: first, whether reverse discrimination violated the Equal Protection Clause of the Fourteenth Amendment; and second, whether affirmative action plans violated the Civil Rights Act of 1964, particularly Title VII. The Court's decisions during this time had a direct impact on personnel and the composition of the workforce in the public and private sectors. The Court was requested to address the principles related to set-asides, to establish guidelines for strict scrutiny, to consider disparate impact, and to rule on consent decrees. Six cases related to affirmative action were ruled on during the 1989 term of the Supreme Court. Indeed, the Civil Rights Act of 1991 was an effort to reverse some of the effects of the sweeping decisions made by the Court during 1989.

During this term, the Supreme Court addressed the issue of set-asides, the permissibility of which had been viewed as leading to the establishment of quotas. In *City of Richmond v. J.A. Croson Co.*, 488 U.S. 469 (1989), the Supreme Court narrowed the earlier decision in *Fullilove* (1980) and, at the same time, issued its first majority opinion disapproving of the affirmative action plan at issue. *Fullilove* had led to the establishment of court-approved set-asides designed to improve the economic plight of minority contractors. Thus the focal point of *Croson* was the constitutionality of set-asides. The Supreme Court, in resolving this legal issue, employed its "strict scrutiny" analysis. A key area of concern for the Court was the lack of evidence demonstrating prior discrimination. The Court held that the set-aside plan lacked sufficient proof of discrimination in the construction industry and, therefore, failed to meet the very high standard of strict scrutiny.

The decision in *Croson* simplified the process for whites who were challenging set-aside provisions under reverse-discrimination arguments. According to the Court, cases now required that state and local governments must demonstrate a compelling state interest in order to establish a prima facie case for set-asides. Furthermore, the Court also required that race-neutral alternatives must be narrowly tailored so as to rectify the effects of past discrimination.

Justice Marshall, in his dissent, wrote that the Court's decision in *Croson* was a giant step backward in the realm of affirmative action. Marshall strongly suggested that the Court had refused to accept documented proof of historical discrimination. He also asserted that the Court exhibited judicial inconsistency in reaching this decision. Marshall argued that the decision of *Croson* was a reversal of *Johnson v. Transportation Agency*, as well as inconsistent with *Fullilove*.

The decision that followed next in 1989 was considered to be another severe blow to affirmative action. In *Wards Cove Packing Co. v. Atonio*, 490 U.S. 642 (1989), the Court in essence held that race-based statistical comparisons were not enough to prove disparate impact. The Court also held that a statistical imbalance between jobs and employee groups was insufficient for employee groups supporting a prima facie case of illegal discrimination. Rather, the appropriate statistical comparison was between the racial composition of the at-issue jobs and the racial composition of the qualified population in the relevant labor market. The ruling of the Court in *Wards Cove* made it difficult for protected classes of individuals and groups to use statistics as support for claims of illegal discrimination under a disparate impact/treatment argument. The Court was concerned with what it considered the proper assessment of the burden of proof. Thus in *Wards Cove*, the Court placed the burden of proof on the plaintiff to win a case involving a disparate impact.

One week later, in *Martin v. Wilks*, 490 U.S. 755 (1989), the Supreme Court ruled on the issue of consent decrees relating to affirmative action plans. The

Supreme Court held that white workers could challenge race-conscious promotion decisions alleged to be required by a consent decree even though the workers were not parties to the underlying decree. Thus the Court settled the issue of when one could become a party to an affirmative action lawsuit. In *Martin v. Wilks*, it became apparent that the Supreme Court had changed its judicial view on the mechanism utilized in the implementation of affirmative action goals. The Court in *Martin* reasoned that a consent decree settled matters among the immediate parties; it did not, however, exclude the rights of those that were strangers to the proceedings. Thus the decision in *Martin* in effect opened the potential for large numbers of lawsuits challenging consent decrees that had been implemented over the past two years in affirmative action cases. In essence, the Court held that under Title VII, white employees could challenge, without time limitations, affirmative action consent decrees settling employment disputes, even if the current litigants were not original parties to the lawsuit. The decision in *Martin* reduced the impact of consent decrees designed to eradicate historical racial discrimination in employment and promotional practices.

In June 1989, the Supreme Court issued yet another decision narrowing the impact of affirmative action plans. In *Price Waterhouse v. Hopkins*, 490 U.S. 228 (1989), the Court required that an employee in a Title VII discrimination action demonstrate the burden of proof by objective evidence. Phrased another way, the Court held that liability under Title VII could be avoided if the employer showed that the employer would have taken the same action for legitimate business reasons. According to one opinion in the case, the decision made it clear that employers must exercise legal and moral propriety in the establishment of employee appraisal systems. Thus the decision shifted the burden of proof to the plaintiff and the employer merely had to prove by a preponderance of evidence that the major factor in the decision was made absent gender discrimination. The Court's decision had the practical effect of making it difficult to bring a successful case based on gender discrimination. The Court relied on the principle of intentional discrimination and suggested that gender discrimination could still play a role as long as it was a secondary rather than a primary role.

The issue of the legality of seniority systems and the application of the statute of limitations in affirmative action plans was the focus in *Lorance v. AT&T Technologies, Inc.*, 490 U.S. 900 (1989). The key issue was whether a discriminatory employment practice disguised as a facially neutral practice met constitutional muster under Title VII. The Court held that in cases of alleged discrimination under seniority systems, a plaintiff must show that the system was intentionally discriminatory and held that the statute of limitations began to run at the time the seniority system is adopted, rather than when the practice was applied to the harmed plaintiffs. Justice Marshall, again in a dissenting opinion, stated that the decision of *Lorance* diminished the congressional intent of seniority systems under Title VII. Marshall suggested that the Court in *Lorance* required an employee to anticipate discrimination or forever hold their peace. Marshall concluded with the rationale that the Court in *Lorance* had created a situation that rewarded employers ingenious enough to cloak their acts of discrimination in a facially neutral guise identical to a facially discriminatory seniority plan.

The next 1989 case decided by the Court dealing with the issue of affirmative action was *Patterson v. McLean Credit Union*, 491 U.S. 164 (1989). The foundation of the *Patterson* case went all the way back to the Civil Rights Act of 1866 (section 1981). The legal issue in the *Patterson* case centered on discrimination in a private contract involving an African American woman. The Court in *Patterson* had to resolve the legal issue of whether or not the discriminatory practice was prohibited during the formation of the contract or the conditions that arose from the contract.

The Court held that under Section 1981, the prohibition against racial discrimination in making and enforcing private contracts applied only to discrimination in the formation of the contract. Thus the Court reasoned that Section 1981 did not extend protection against discriminatory conduct after the contractual relationship was initially established. This, according to the Court, was inclusive of a breach of contract or discriminatory work conditions after the establishment of the contract. Regarding the issue of racial harassment, the Court held that the conditions were not covered under section 1981 of the Civil Rights Act of 1866 because the provision did not apply to conduct occurring after the formation of the contract. In essence, the Court held that section 1981 barred racial discrimination in hiring and (at times) promotion, but not in posthiring employer actions (e.g., harassment).

In 1990, the Supreme Court, in *Metro Broadcasting, Inc. v. FCC*, 497 U.S. 547 (1990), finally ruled in favor of an affirmative action plan, but not in the area of employment. Rather, the *Metro Broadcasting* case dealt with minority licensing and preferences in the field of broadcast media. Specifically, the Court held that the Federal Communications Commission's minority preference policies did not violate the Equal Protection Clause because they provided appropriate remedies for the victims of discrimination and were consistent with legitimate congressional objectives of program diversity. Thus for the first time since 1988, the Court viewed an affirmative action plan favorably.

In 1993, the Supreme Court was again confronted with the issue of the legality of set-aside contracts. In *Northeastern Florida Chapter of the Associated General Contractors of America v. City of Jacksonville, Florida*, 508 U.S. 656 (1993), the issue was set-aside contracts for MBEs. The legal question was whether the practice violated the Equal Protection Clause of the Fourteenth Amendment. The facts in *Northeastern* differed from those in *Croson* in that prior to adjudication by the Supreme Court; the city of Jacksonville repealed the MBE ordinance and replaced it with an ordinance that set aside contracts for certified African American and female-owned businesses. The city argued that the case was now moot. However, the Court's response was that it was a settled legal principle that the voluntary cessation of a challenged practice did not deprive a federal court of the power to determine the legality of the practice simply because a defendant was not precluded from reinstating the said practice. The Court noted that the city's new ordinance allowed preferential treatment in the awarding of contracts, thus violating the Equal Protection Clause of the Fourteenth Amendment. The Supreme Court in 1993 affirmed the view that race-conscious preferential treatment was unconstitutional.

In 1995, the Supreme Court again took a very unfavorable view of affirmative action. In the seminal case *Adarand Constructors, Inc. v. Peña*, 515 U.S. 200 (1995), the Court held that race-based classifications were subject to strict scrutiny regardless of whether enacted by Congress or other governmental decision makers. The

Court held that all racial classifications, whether overtly invidious or purportedly benign, were subject to strict scrutiny. Therefore, in the *Adarand* decision, the Court continued to reduce the viability of affirmative action programs, a trend that it had first begun developing in 1989. The cases presented during the years from 1989 to 1996 demonstrated a continuous reduction in decisions favorable to proponents of affirmative action.

Finally, after years of declining cases involving affirmative action in higher education, and after several years during which a significant rift developed in the federal circuit courts regarding the constitutionality of affirmative action plans in higher education, the Supreme Court announced in December 2002 that it had agreed to hear two cases involving the University of Michigan and its affirmative action programs, *Gratz v. Bollinger*, 123 S. Ct. 2411, 2003 U.S. LEXIS 4801 (2003), and *Grutter v. Bollinger*, 123 S. Ct. 2325, 2003 U.S. LEXIS 4800 (2003), which were combined as a single case for purposes of Supreme Court review. This set the stage for the Supreme Court's decision of the "Michigan cases" in June 2003. The Supreme Court's resolution of the Michigan cases (and harmonizing of the prior conflicting decisions of lower courts on the permissibility of utilizing race in making admissions decisions in higher education) has earned the Michigan cases the title of the most significant Supreme Court decision on affirmative action and education since the *Bakke* decision. The decision, while certainly not the final word on affirmative action by the Court, is significant in that it represents yet another effort by the Court to resolve the thorny issue of race relations in the context of affirmative action and the Fourteenth Amendment.

In Grutter, the Supreme Court upheld the University of Michigan Law School's affirmative action plan and endorsed affirmative action plans that utilize race as one factor or ingredient (among many) in the overall evaluation of candidates. However, the affirmative action plan at issue at the University of Michigan's undergraduate campus was held to be a violation of the Fourteenth Amendment, as the plan did not allow for an individual assessment of an applicant's application, leading to too great an emphasis on race in granting or denying admissions. The Court also warned in the *Gratz* decision that fixed racial quotas and mechanized formulas (which have the effect of operating as a quota) would not be tolerated. In the *Gratz* decision, the Court struck down the University of Michigan undergraduate admissions affirmative plan that gave extra points for race alone. The plan struck down by the Court had awarded African American, Hispanic, and Native American applicants an automatic 20 points on a 150-point undergraduate admissions scale. This, the Court held, was akin to racial quotas, which violate the Fourteenth Amendment.

See also Adarand Constructors, Inc. v. Peña; Blackmun, Harry Andrew; *City of Richmond v. J.A. Croson Co.;* Civil Rights Act of 1866; Civil Rights Act of 1964; Civil Rights Act of 1991; Compelling Governmental Interest; *DeFunis v. Odegaard;* Disadvantaged Business Enterprises; Disparate Treatment and Disparate Impact; Equal Protection Clause; Federal Communications Commission; *Firefighters Local Union No. 1784 v. Stotts;* Fourteenth Amendment; *Fullilove v. Klutznick; Gratz v. Bollinger/Grutter v. Bollinger; Griggs v. Duke Power Co.; Johnson v. Transportation Agency, Santa Clara County;* Kennedy, Anthony McLeod; *Local 28 of the Sheet Metal Workers' International Association v. EEOC; Lorance v. AT&T Technologies, Inc.;* Manifest Imbalance Standard; Marshall, Thurgood; *Metro Broadcasting, Inc. v. FCC;* Narrowly Tailored Affirmative Action Plans; O'Connor, Sandra Day; *Patterson v. McLean Credit Union*; Powell, Lewis Franklin, Jr.; *Price Waterhouse v. Hopkins*; *Regents of the University of California v. Bakke*; Rehnquist, William Hobbs; Scalia, Antonin; Scottsboro Boys; Strict Scrutiny; Thomas, Clarence; Title VI of the Civil Rights Act of 1964; Title VII of the Civil Rights Act of 1964; *United States v. Paradise*; *United Steelworkers of America v. Weber*; *Wards Cove Packing Co. v. Atonio*; White, Byron Raymond; *Wygant v. Jackson Board of Education*.

FURTHER READING: Bell, Derrick, 1992, *Race, Racism, and American Law*, Boston: Little, Brown and Company; Farber, Daniel A., William N. Eskridge Jr., and Philip P. Frickey, 1993, *Constitutional Law: Themes for the Constitution's Third Century*, St. Paul, MN: West Publishing Company; Jones, Elaine R. 1996, "Race and the Supreme Court's 1994–95 Term," in *The Affirmative Action Debate*, edited by George E. Curry, Reading, MA: Perseus Books; Spann, Girardeau A., 2000, *The Law of Affirmative Action: Twenty-five Years of Supreme Court Decisions on Race and Remedies*, New York: New York University Press; Tucker, Ronnie B., 2000, *Affirmative Action, the Supreme Court, and Political Power in the Old Confederacy*, Lanham, MD: University Press of America.

RONNIE B. TUCKER SR.

Suspect Classification

The Fourteenth Amendment of the U.S. Constitution mandates that no state shall deny to any person the equal protection of the laws. The Supreme Court has interpreted the Equal Protection Clause to mean that states cannot classify people according to their race or their ethnicity and consequently make that law applicable to them on the basis of that classification. A suspect class results when a state relies on "immutable characteristics of birth"—on those qualities we cannot alter, such as race or ethnicity, to classify people and deprive them of a fundamental right. When and if a state does violate the principle and spirit of the Equal Protection Clause by drafting a law that impermissibly classifies, the state creates a suspect classification. When there exists the possibility of a suspect classification, the Fourteenth Amendment requires that courts provide a standard of heightened judicial scrutiny to that classification. The following two cases illustrate how the Supreme Court has had the occasion to address the issue of suspect classifications.

One important example of the Court's initiative to review a state classification based on race was the decision in *Brown v. Board of Education*, 347 U.S. 483 (1954). Following the separate-but-equal doctrine of the *Plessy v. Ferguson*, 163 U.S. 537 (1896), precedent, Kansas and many other states had required the segregation of public schools on the basis of race, whereby black students were not permitted to attend white institutions. This mandate of separate schools prevented black children from receiving an equal education and illustrated the detrimental impact of a suspect classification. Segregated schools, sanctioned by state law, were unequivocally a system that burdened a class of people based on a factor they were fundamentally unable to change—in this instance, race. In the landmark decision in *Brown v. Board of Education*, the Supreme Court ruled that racial classifications were not only suspect, but also "inherently unequal." The *Brown* decision was historic in its promotion of the idea that great harm could be done by the creation of a suspect classification.

In contrast to the Court's decision in *Brown* was the challenge of a suspect class in the case of *Korematsu v. United States*, 323 U.S. 214 (1943). The *Korematsu* case addressed President Franklin D. Roosevelt's Executive Order 9066, requiring Japanese American citizens to be evacuated and then interned in detention camps after the bombings at Pearl Harbor. The executive order clearly created a suspect classification—this one based solely on ethnicity, as only Japanese Americans were arrested and detained. On appeal to the Supreme Court on grounds that the exclusion and detention order violated the Fourteenth Amendment's Equal Protection Clause, the Court majority upheld the detention order. In doing so, the Court failed to acknowledge its own mandate of preventing suspect categorizations. Even in the absence of any evidence that indicated disloyalty on the part of the 112,000 imprisoned Japanese Americans, the Court persisted in validating the suspect classification. In its reasoning, the Court insisted that national security interests outweighed the harm to fundamental rights. In his dissent to the Court's majority opinion, Justice Frank Murphy eloquently wrote, "[T]he exclusion of all persons of Japanese ancestry, both alien and non-alien, from the Pacific Coast area . . . goes over the very brink of constitutional power and falls into the ugly abyss of racism." Murphy's comment resonates today as a reminder that the Court has an institutional obligation to prevent not only the evocation of a suspect class, but the ultimate revocation of fundamental rights.

Although race and ethnicity have been acknowledged as suspect classifications, the Court has been reluctant to make sex a suspect category in its gender-based decisions. By a narrow majority vote of 5–4, the Court ruled in *Frontiero v. Richardson*, 411 U.S. 677 (1973), that women are not considered a "suspect class," thus suggesting that classification by sex is not always suspect as discrimination. The Court then created an intermediate or middle level of scrutiny in spite of the "immutable characteristic" argument that governed race and ethnic discrimination. This substantially lower standard of review by the Court on issues of sex and gender has resulted in much criticism from those who believe that sex and gender deserve the same protections as other suspect classifications. Suspect classifications on the basis of race or national origin should always be held to a heightened standard of scrutiny by courts. As for the disparate treatment given to other classifications such as gender, sexual orientation, and disability, there is still contentious debate in the legal community on how to address and mediate these particular classifications.

See also Brown v. Board of Education; Discrete and Insular Minority; Equal Protection Clause; Fourteenth Amendment; *Frontiero v. Richardson*; Japanese Internment and World War II; *Korematsu v. United States*; *Plessy v. Ferguson*; Roosevelt, Franklin Delano; Segregation.

FURTHER READING: Mason, Alpheus Thomas, and Stephenson, Donald Grier, Jr., 2002, *American Constitutional Law: Introductory Essays and Selected Cases*, 13th ed., Upper Saddle River, NJ: Prentice Hall; Rossum, Ralph, and Alan Tarr, 1999, *American Constitutional Law*, New York: St. Martin's Press; Spann, Girardeau A., 2000, *The Law of Affirmative Action: Twenty-five Years of Supreme Court Decisions on Race and Remedies*, New York: New York University Press.

JANIS JUDSON

Sweatt v. Painter, 339 U.S. 629 (1950)

The case *Sweatt v. Painter*, 339 U.S. 629 (1950), gave the U.S. Supreme Court the opportunity to review the exact meaning of the legal principle of "separate but equal" in the public education context. More than fifty years earlier, the Supreme Court had announced the separate-but-equal doctrine in *Plessy v. Ferguson*, 163 U.S. 537 (1896), as it applied to public accommodations. During the ensuing half century, many states applied the separate-but-equal doctrine to a wide array of circumstances, including (but certainly not limited to) public education. The separate-but-equal doctrine formed the basis of countless interactions between African Americans and whites as well as the delivery (or the failure of the delivery) of governmental services to African Americans. This Texas law school case provided the opportunity for the Supreme Court to explain the exact meaning of the separate-but-equal formula, and how the formula must be applied in the public education context to not run afoul of the Equal Protection Clause of the Fourteenth Amendment.

Herman Sweatt, an African American postal clerk, applied for admission to the University of Texas Law School in 1945. Sweatt was denied admission because of his race. At the time of his rejection, there was no law school in Texas for African Americans. Thus Sweatt filed suit in state court seeking admission to the University of Texas Law School. The state district court did not order Sweatt's admission immediately, but warned that the state must either open a black law school at the Texas State University for Negroes, or admit Sweatt to the white school at Austin. The state court did understand that the state's action denied Sweatt equal protection of the laws as guaranteed by the Fourteenth Amendment. That is, under the Fourteenth Amendment and the separate-but-equal doctrine, if the state segregated, it must provide substantially equal separate facilities to those excluded from the white facilities. As a result of this state court decision, the state hired two African American lawyers to teach law courses in some rented rooms in a Houston motel and called it a law school. The state court was then satisfied that the newly established law school was equal to the white law school. Sweatt appealed the decision to the U.S. Supreme Court.

Thurgood Marshall was the chief legal counsel in this case for both Sweatt and the National Association for the Advancement of Colored People (NAACP). Marshall used the legal strategy of not directly attacking the separate-but-equal principle as set forth in *Plessy*. Rather, Marshall argued that the law school established by Texas was unequal to the University of Texas Law School. Marshall's strategy was to force the state to provide substantially equal facilities and thereby make the operation of a segregated system too costly. Interestingly, the U.S. Department of Justice for the first time in a public education case filed a brief arguing that *Plessy* had been incorrectly decided.

Chief Justice Fred M. Vinson wrote the majority opinion for the Court. The Supreme Court ordered the University of Texas to admit Sweatt. For the first time, the Court gave a specific remedy for violation of the *Plessy* separate-but-equal doctrine. The majority opinion focused on the constitutional issue pertaining to the Equal Protection Clause of the Fourteenth Amendment. The Court gave the legal rationale that Sweatt was denied his full constitutional rights in not being admitted to the law school or being provided with substantially equal separate facilities. The legal education equivalent to that offered by the state to students of other races was not available to Sweatt in a separate law school offered by the state.

The Court in reaching its decision in *Sweatt* recognized the significance of intangible differences between the two schools. The Court made the comparison that the faculty of the Texas Law School consisted of sixteen full-time professors and three part-time professors, of whom some had national recognition. The library contained more than 65,000 volumes along with other qualities that were incapable of objective measurement but that made for greatness in a law school. The law school established for African Americans had no independent faculty or library. The faculty was composed of four professors who were required to teach at both institutions. The library for the African American law school contained only 10,000 volumes. At the time of the case, few of those books had arrived, and the school was not accredited. It was clear that the African American law school was not equal in facilities. The Court reasoned that the law school was in essence the proving grounds for legal learning and practice, and this objective could not be attained in a system of isolation from individuals and institutions with which the law interacted. The Court also pointed out that the law school to which Texas was willing to admit Sweatt excluded from its student body members of the racial groups that numbered 85 percent of the population of the state and included most of the lawyers, witnesses, jurors, and other officials with whom Sweatt would eventually have to interact upon becoming a member of the Texas bar. In *Sweatt*, the Supreme Court did not overturn the separate-but-equal doctrine as established in *Plessy*, but instead narrowed its scope. While the Court did refuse to reexamine the purpose of the Fourteenth Amendment, effects of racial segregation, or the constitutionality of the separate-but-equal doctrine, the *Sweatt* decision was a significant step toward the Court's ultimate reversal of separate but equal and segregation in *Brown v. Board of Education*, 347 U.S. 483 (1954).

See also Brown v. Board of Education; Equal Protection Clause; Fourteenth Amendment; Marshall, Thurgood; National Association for the Advancement of Colored People; *Plessy v. Ferguson*; *Sipuel v. Regents of the University of Oklahoma*.

FURTHER READING: Barker, Lucius J., 1994, *Americans and the American Political System*, Englewood Cliffs, NJ: Prentice Hall; Bell, Derrick, 1992, *Race, Racism, and American Law*, Boston: Little, Brown and Company; Farber, Daniel A., William N. Eskridge Jr., and Philip P. Frickey, 1993, *Constitutional Law: Themes for the Constitution's Third Century*, St. Paul, MN: West Publishing Co.; Perry, Huey L., and Wayne Parent, eds., 1995, *Blacks and the American Political System*, Gainesville: University Press of Florida; Tucker, Ronnie B., 2000, *Affirmative Action, the Supreme Court, and Political Power in the Old Confederacy*, Lanham, MD: University Press of America.

RONNIE B. TUCKER SR.

T

Talented Tenth

The Talented Tenth was a concept put forth in 1903 by African American author and educator W.E.B. Du Bois that emphasized the need for higher education to develop the potential of the most able 10 percent of African Americans. That is, to achieve social and political equality and cast off the mantle of second-class citizenship, Du Bois believed that the black race would be uplifted by the Talented Tenth, a few black intellectual leaders within the race. These leaders would not only possess exceptional intellect (education), but also broad sympathy, knowledge of the world (experience), and an understanding of the relation of man to the world (social experience). These leaders would then in turn motivate and empower the more marginalized of the race and serve as role models for others in the community. Some proponents of affirmative action programs today argue that Du Bois's Talented Tenth theory sought the same goals as modern affirmative action programs, namely, the promotion of social and political equality through educational opportunities for minorities, and the promotion of minority leadership in historically underrepresented professional areas to serve as role models for others in the community.

The phrase "Talented Tenth" appeared in an article by Du Bois titled "The Negro Problem" published in 1903. Du Bois believed that African Americans should be given the opportunity to take full advantage of education, but had been continually hindered by slavery and race prejudice. With the end of slavery, only the Talented Tenth could rise and pull "all that are worth the saving up to their vantage ground" (Du Bois, 35–36). Since not all African Americans could attend college, Du Bois believed that the best and most capable youth should attend college. Unlike Booker T. Washington, Du Bois believed that African Americans should be exposed to more than just learning industrial trades such as carpentry. Du Bois wrote in his essay on the Talented Tenth that "Work alone will not do unless inspired by the right ideals and guided by intelligence. Education must not simply teach work—it must teach life. The Talented Tenth of the Negro race must be made leaders of thought and missionaries of culture among their people. No others can do this work and Negro colleges must train men for it. The Negro race, like all other races, is going to be saved by its exceptional men." Teaching African Americans a trade only taught them how to make money, not how to become responsible men who could be role models for others (Du Bois, 33).

Du Bois was seen by some as being elitist for his views of an educated group leading the rest of the black race and as being out of touch with the needs, beliefs, and daily realities of black workers. He was also criticized for his belief that integration would not be achieved through racial compromise, but through the artistic and intellectual advancement of this selective group of blacks. His views were also radically different from those of Washington, who believed that African Americans would advance through industrial education and thus be more respected and accepted by whites. Du Bois argued that industrial education would keep African Americans in a lower class and in occupations of service to the more fortunate.

See also Du Bois, William Edward Burghardt; Role Model Theory; Washington, Booker T.

FURTHER READING: Aptheker, Herbert, ed., 1982, *Writings by W.E.B. Du Bois in Non-Periodical Literature Edited by Others*, Millwood, NY: Kraus-Thomson; Du Bois, W.E.B., 1903, "The Talented Tenth" in *The Negro Problem: A Series of Articles by Representative American Negroes of Today*, 33–75, New York: J. Pott & Company; James, Joy, 1997, *Transcending the Talented Tenth*, New York: Routledge; Killian, Lewis M., 1999, "Generals, the Talented Tenth, and Affirmative Action," *Society* 36, no. 6 (September): 33–46.

GLENN L. STARKS

Taxman v. Piscataway Township Board of Education, 91 F.3d 1547 (3rd Cir. 1996), *cert. granted*, 117 S. Ct. 2506 (1997), *cert. dismissed*, 118 S. Ct. 595 (1997)

The case titled *Taxman v. Piscataway Township Board of Education* was predicted in 1997 to be a landmark and milestone case in the affirmative action debate. At issue in the case was whether any affirmative action program, whether instituted by a public or a private employer, could ever be permissible under Title VII of the Civil Rights Act of 1964. As the underlying lawsuit was instituted under Title VII and not the Equal Protection Clause of the Fourteenth Amendment, the Supreme Court's ruling in the case could have impacted the permissibility of all voluntary affirmative action programs, whether instituted by a public employer (also subject to Fourteenth Amendment restrictions) or a private employer (under Title VII). The lower federal court had ruled that the affirmative action program implemented by the local school board that gave a layoff preference or protection to a black teacher over an equally qualified white teacher to promote diversity was a violation of Title VII. However, after the Supreme Court announced its decision to grant review in the case, but prior to Supreme Court action in the case, the case was settled by the parties, and the school board agreed to pay all of the dismissed white teacher's damages in the case. This settlement was backed by a variety of prominent civil rights organizations (who had previously supported the school board's affirmative action policy), who feared a very negative decision by the Supreme Court on the permissibility of voluntary affirmative action plans under Title VII. Thus as a result of settlement, the nation was deprived of what was predicted to be a landmark decision on affirmative action.

In 1975, the local school board of Piscataway, New Jersey, adopted an affirmative action program that was designed to promote diversity among faculty and students, and not as a remedy for previous past discrimination by the school board in question. The affirmative action program called for qualified teachers to be promoted, but allowed for considerations of race and ethnicity when the candidates were equally qualified as a means to determine advancement or termination. In May 1989, the school board discharged a white female under its affirmative action plan when the board learned that it had to decrease its faculty in the local high school. The specific problem dealt with the reduction of one in a department of ten. The two individuals who were considered for elimination were both tenured faculty personnel who had been hired on the same day nine years earlier; Sharon Taxman was white and Debra Williams was black. According to the school board's representatives, the two female employees had performed to the same standards and were equally qualified by "seniority, work performance, certifications, evaluations, teaching ability, and volunteerism" (Spann, 74). While Taxman's range of topics taught, and extracurricular work favored her, Ms. Williams held a masters degree while Taxman did not.

While no direct evidence was offered that the board acted with malicious intent to discharge Taxman, other than race, the evidence describing Williams's and Taxman's respective qualifications deserves further examination. The rationale for Taxman's discharge was the board's erroneous (according to the federal courts' review of this case) application of the 1975 affirmative action policy. The board had asserted that Williams was retained, and Taxman terminated, because the business department had only one black faculty member (Williams), and that should Williams be discharged or moved, then the department would be all white. Thus the school board relied on its affirmative action plan to terminate a qualified teacher primarily on the grounds that she was white.

After termination, Taxman filed a complaint with the Equal Employment Opportunity Commission. The United States then filed a lawsuit in the U.S. District Court for the District of New Jersey against the school board alleging that the termination and the affirmative action policy violated antidiscrimination provisions of Title VII. Taxman then intervened as a plaintiff in the case as well. At the district court level, the court ruled in favor of Taxman and the United States and ordered the school board to pay Taxman's damages for back pay and benefits in the amount of $134,014.62. She had previously been rehired, so the court did not need to order reinstatement.

The school board then appealed the district court's ruling to the U.S. Court of Appeals for the Third Circuit. The United States attempted to change sides in the litigation (which the court refused), and ultimately the United States withdrew from the litigation. The United States had taken several conflicting positions during the course of the litigation. In 1991, during President George H.W. Bush's administration, the United States sided with Taxman at the district court level. In 1994, during President Clinton's administration, the United States attempted to change sides after the district court's ruling, and when that was denied, withdrew from the litigation. Later, after the Third Circuit Court of Appeals ruled in the case, the United States again appeared to change sides when it recommended against the Supreme Court reviewing the school board's appeal. Additionally, once the case ultimately reached the Supreme Court, the United States filed an amicus brief recommending that the Court rule in Taxman's favor.

In August 1996, the Third Circuit, in a rare en banc decision, affirmed the lower court ruling that Taxman's termination under the voluntary affirmative action plan was a violation of Title VII. The court's majority decision was quite clear in its interpretation of the applicable statutory law. Title VII states that one's position cannot be terminated because of his/her race and continues by commenting that "the burden of racial preferences, whatever their social utility may be, cannot be visited entirely on innocent non-minority (or minority) group individuals." In Taxman's case, race was the determinate factor causing her to be discharged.

Interestingly, while the language of Title VII (as the court concluded) clearly prohibits racial classifications in employment, the Supreme Court had previously ruled in *United Steelworkers of America v. Weber*, 443 U.S. 193 (1979), that voluntary affirmative action plans in the private employment context were permissible so long as the plans mirrored the purposes of Title VII and did not unnecessarily trammel the interest of other nonminority employees. Furthermore, the Court had ruled in 1987 in *Johnson v. Transportation Agency, Santa Clara County*, 480 U.S. 616 (1987), that in the public employment context, affirmative action programs could be utilized to select minorities or women to remedy a manifest imbalance or an underrepresentation of these groups in traditionally segregated work categories, so long as (consistent with *Weber*) the affirmative action program did not result in the termination of other (nonminority and/or male) employees.

In the Third Circuit's decision in *Taxman*, the court concluded that the local school board's affirmative action program violated Title VII and did not adhere to what the Supreme Court had specified in the *Weber* and *Johnson* decisions. Specifically, the Third Circuit held that Congress had dual goals in enacting Title VII: first, to end employment discrimination in the workplace; and second, to provide a remedy for segregation and underrepresentation caused by specific past discrimination. The *Weber* and *Johnson* decisions both dealt with affirmative action plans instituted to provide a specific remedy based upon specific past discrimination. Phrased another way, an affirmative action program could not be said to mirror or comply with Title VII if the plan was not implemented to remedy or cure prior past discrimination.

According to the Third Circuit, the problem with the affirmative action plan at issue in the *Taxman* case, however, was that it was not instituted as a remedial plan to remedy previous discrimination (as had been the case in both the *Weber* and *Johnson* decisions), but was instituted only in the interests of promoting diversity. The transcript in the case indicates that there had not been any previous administrative decisions or concern on the departmental level dealing with federal compliance with affirmative action racial policies. The purpose of selecting Taxman for discharge was that the board wanted a racially diverse staff in the department. Taxman offered evidence that the business department did not learn and study in a vacuum; students had to attend classes in other disciplines, and not all were white students. In essence, the board justified its actions by alleging that cultural diversity was the goal; compliance with the federal standards was mandated. Several board representatives admitted in their depositions that the reason for their choice and conduct was race. The board asserted that it had the authority to achieve departmental diversity for "education's sake," an argument that the Court rejected. Since no evidence was introduced that a special need existed for the retention of a black, and that the problems could be rectified by Williams's retention, there was no legal basis for retention on racial lines. If the board had provided evidence of a special need for a black employee, Title VII had provisions for such an exception.

The admission was contrary to the law, which required racial neutrality, unless such a program mirrored the purposes of Title VII, which, according to the Supreme Court in *Weber* and *Johnson*, meant that the plan had to be narrowly tailored as a remedy for previous instances of past discrimination. Otherwise, Title VII protects white employees when black employees are favored without just cause. The Court specifically rejected the argument that recognition of diversity in implementing an affirmative action plan was sufficient to satisfy the requirements of Title VII. Ironically, statistics for 1985 indicated that the percentage of blacks employed by the board as teachers exceeded the percentage of blacks in the entire work force.

The court noted that the board also failed to properly apply the "narrowly tailored" approach mandated by Title VII. According to the court, the Piscataway affirmative action plan also failed to meet the requirements the Supreme Court imposed in *Weber*, specifically that the affirmative action plan not unnecessarily trammel the rights of nonminority workers (like Taxman). According to the court, Taxman's termination was too high a price and therefore constituted an unnecessary trammeling of Taxman's rights. The court also held that the Piscataway affirmative action plan utterly lacked structure and definition, was unlimited in duration, and had no real benchmarks or standards. The plans that were upheld in *Weber* and *Johnson* were both implemented to achieve remedial purposes, were limited in duration, did not unnecessarily trammel the rights of nonminorities, and had defined standards, all of which the court found lacking in the Piscataway plan.

The proportional representation and diversity arguments offered by the board were viewed by the Third Circuit as a shibboleth. The court's interpretation of the applicable statutes was that they "prohibited all racial discrimination in employment without exception." This broad stroke was intended to protect all Americans from any form of vested interests advocating a particular goal. According to the Supreme Court in the *Weber* and *Johnson* decisions, special consideration in developing affirmative action plans could be given to instances where historic imbalances existed, but there were no assertions in *Taxman* that this was at issue.

The anticipated Supreme Court review of the case raised the specter of a decision that might be unfavorable to voluntary affirmative action plans under Title VII. The Black Leadership Forum (BLF), an umbrella organization of twenty-one different civil rights groups, was especially concerned. Aware of the potential negative results for its interpretation of affirmative action, the BLF chose to raise funds to resolve the case rather than have the Supreme Court examine the legality of voluntary affirmative action plans under Title VII. The BLF raised and contributed $308,500 toward the $433,500 in back pay, interest, and legal fees that were ultimately paid to Taxman. The BLF's intentions in helping to fund the settlement were to prevent the issue from being adjudicated by the high court, which would have defined the limits of racial preference and voluntary affirmative action plans in the private employment context. The BLF alleged in its web site that this case was a poor "vehicle for testing the legitimacy of affirmative action." If Taxman, after having been rehired, had permitted the case to be heard by the high court, both American jurisprudence and American society might have been better served.

See also Bush, George Herbert Walker; Civil Rights Act of 1964; Clinton, William Jefferson; Discrimination; Diversity; Employment (Private) and Affirmative Action; Employment (Public) and Affirmative Action; Equal Employment Opportunity Commission; Equal Protection Clause; Fourteenth Amendment; *Johnson v. Transportation Agency, Santa Clara County*; Narrowly Tailored Affirmative Action Plans; Segregation; Title VII of the Civil Rights Act of 1964; *United Steelworkers of America v. Weber.*

FURTHER READING: Patterson, Katrina, 1999, "What May Have Become a New Title VII Precedent on Affirmative Action in the Workplace: *Piscataway Township Board of Education v. Taxman*—Permissible or Impermissible?" *New York Law School Journal of Human Rights* 15 (winter): 355–383; Spann, Girardeau A., 2000, *The Law of Affirmative Action: Twenty-five Years of Supreme Court Decisions on Race and Remedies*, New York: New York University Press.

ARTHUR K. STEINBERG

Testocracy

See Performance-Based Selections; Standardized Testing.

Texas Top 10 Percent Plan

See Percentage Plans.

Thernstrom, Stephan (1934–), and Thernstrom, Abigail (1936–)

Stephan and Abigail Thernstrom are best known nationally as vociferous critics of affirmative action and have written several highly publicized works on this topic. They are perhaps most widely known as the authors of a 1997 book titled *America in Black and White: One Nation, Indivisible*, which takes a very critical look at affirmative action and race in America. The book is a survey of race relations in the United States from the 1940s to the present day and presents and discusses the achievements made by African Americans in the areas of education, employment, and housing. The book and its authors stirred significant controversy when it claimed that race relations are generally good today and that racial preferences are harmful and divisive. The book also claimed that African Americans present their plight to be much worse than it is in reality. In December 1997, Abigail Thernstrom had a public confrontation over affirmative action with President Bill Clinton in Akron, Ohio, in Clinton's first "town meeting on race." Stephan and Abigail Thernstrom have both written extensively on affirmative action, equal opportunity, and the use of racial preferences in the United States.

The first six chapters of their 1997 book *America in Black and White* outline the history of the civil rights movement and how blacks have progressed as far as they have in society. The Thernstroms then argue that legislation, such as the various civil rights acts and affirmative action policies, has done little to help the situation of African Americans. They state that most of the progress blacks have made during the last fifty years has come from self-help and self-effort, not quotas or programs of equal opportunity. The Thernstroms also argue that affirmative action programs are simply condescending and paternalistic insofar as they assume that blacks cannot compete unless they are issued a lower standard to achieve. They argue that the only way for blacks to truly achieve equality is for them to meet the same standards that are prescribed for whites. The Thernstroms also take issue with the findings in the milestone 1968 Kerner Commission Report, which held that the United States was heading into two separate societies, one black and one white. They offer a plethora of statistics to rebut the findings of the Kerner Commission in this regard. Critics of their work claim that the Therstroms magnify the gains made by African Americans while at the same time minimizing the gap that still remains. Some critics have even referred to the Thernstroms and their claims and conclusions as racist. The Thernstroms' 1997 book remains a controversial work on affirmative action and engenders debate on both sides of the political spectrum.

The Thernstroms have organized the Citizens' Initiative on Race and Ethnicity, a conservative group formed in response to President Clinton's Initiative on Race in 1995. The Thernstroms also believe that if the education of African Americans and Hispanics were better, there would be no need for affirmative action. In essence, the Thernstroms believe that equality is best achieved through self-help and hard work and that, in words taken from their book *America in Black and White*, "race-conscious policies make for more race-consciousness; they carry America backward" (Thernstrom and Thernstrom 1997, 539).

Stephan Thernstrom is the Winthrop Professor of History at Harvard University and has served as a full professor at Harvard since 1973. He earned his Ph.D. from Harvard in 1962 and has received a myriad of academic and publishing awards. Among others, he was awarded the prestigious Bancroft Prize in American History. He has authored numerous books and articles and is the editor of the *Harvard Encyclopedia of American Ethnic Groups*. In addition to his academic duties and writing, he has served as an expert witness in many affirmative action cases. His wife, Abigail Thernstrom, is a senior fellow at the Manhattan Institute in New York. She also serves on the board of the Center for Equal Opportunity, an anti–affirmative action research group, and as a member of the U.S. Commission on Civil Rights. Abigail Thernstrom is also the author of the 1987 book *Whose Vote Counts? Affirmative Action and Minority Voting Rights*, which critiques the Voting Rights Act of 1965. She also holds a Ph.D. from Harvard University.

See also African Americans; Center for Equal Opportunity; Citizens' Initiative on Race and Ethnicity; Hispanic Americans; Kerner Commission; U.S. Commission on Civil Rights; Voting Rights Act of 1965.

FURTHER READING: Shatz, Adam, 2001, "The Thernstroms in Black and White," *American Prospect* 12, no. 5 (March 12): 32–41; Thernstrom, Stephan, and Abigail Thernstrom, 1997, *Black and White in America: One Nation, Indivisible*, New York: Touchstone.

AIMÉE HOBBY RHODES

Thirteenth Amendment

The Thirteenth Amendment to the Constitution, which formally ended the institution of slavery in the United States, was ratified at the conclusion of the American Civil War. The amendment was ratified by the requisite number of state governments by December 6, 1865. The amendment provides that "neither slavery nor involuntary servitude, except as a punishment for crime whereof the party shall have been duly convicted, shall exist within the United States, or any place subject to their jurisdiction." The amendment also provided that "Congress shall have power to enforce this article by appropriate legislation." Thus the amendment legally ended the institution of slavery and gave Congress the power to pass further implementing legislation. In passing the Civil Rights Act of 1866, Congress relied on this new authority given to it by the Thirteenth Amendment.

To fully understand the Thirteenth Amendment, one must consider the history leading up to the amendment. The first ten amendments to the Constitution, known as the Bill of Rights, covered a wide range of liberties, but none of these touched on the rights of slaves. In fact, the Fifth Amendment's Due Process Clause (i.e., that no person shall be deprived of life, liberty, or property without due process of law) was construed by the Supreme Court in *Dred Scott v. Sandford*, 60 U.S. (19 How.) 393 (1857), as giving white slave owners a property interest in their black slaves. Other clauses of the Constitution, such as the Three-Fifths Compromise and the fugitive slave provision, solidified the legality of slavery in the Constitution. Thus slavery continued to occupy a central position in the life of the nation. As slavery was a serious moral and legal issue as well as an economic institution, the nation was for a long time divided on its continued existence.

Following the outbreak of the American Civil War, the legal abolition of slavery was finally addressed. In 1862, President Abraham Lincoln issued the Emancipation Proclamation, effective January 1, 1863, declaring:

Illustration from the *Illustrated London News* from the September 27, 1856, edition depicting a slave auction in Richmond, Virginia. Such auctions would become illegal after Lincoln's Emancipation Proclamation in 1863 and the ratification of the Thirteenth Amendment in 1865. Courtesy of Library of Congress.

That on the 1st day of January, in the year of our Lord 1863, all persons held as slaves within any state or designated part of a state, the people whereof shall there be in rebellion against the United States, shall be then, thenceforth and forever free; and the Executive Government of the United States, including the military and naval authorities thereof, will recognize and maintain the freedom of such persons, and will do no act nor acts to repress such persons, or any of them, in any effort they may make for their eventual freedom.

The Emancipation Proclamation freed those slaves in the Deep South, in "any state . . . the people whereof shall there be in rebellion." However, in those states that were not currently "in rebellion," the proclamation did not apply. Thus the Emancipation Proclamation did not affect the status of slaves in the border states, such as Delaware, Kentucky, Maryland, Missouri, and parts of Virginia and Louisiana that were already occupied by Union troops, as those areas were not then "in rebellion." Additionally, President Lincoln issued the proclamation as a wartime measure as commander in chief, which meant that the institution of slavery could possibly be reinstated after the war by the act of a subsequent president or Congress. Finally, while the proclamation freed individuals in the Deep South, it did not impact the Supreme Court's decision in the *Dred Scott* case, which was still on the books and had not been reversed.

These weaknesses inherent in the Emancipation Proclamation itself necessitated that the institution of slavery be abolished via a constitutional amendment. A constitutional amendment would ensure that the institution could not be revived by a subsequent president or Congress and would supersede the Supreme Court's ruling in *Dred Scott*. Finally, a constitutional amendment would expand the Emancipation Proclamation beyond the Deep South to the country as a whole. Thus the Thirteenth Amendment was ratified in 1865, legally ended slavery, and laid the foundation for the empowerment of ex-slaves. It was the first of three amendments that today comprise the Civil War (Reconstruction) Amendments (the Thirteenth, Fourteenth, and Fifteenth Amendments).

See also American Civil War; Bill of Rights; Civil Rights Act of 1866; Civil Rights Movement; Civil War (Reconstruction) Amendments and Civil Rights Acts; Constitution, Civil Rights, and Equality; *Dred Scott v. Sandford*; Fifth Amendment; Slavery; Three-Fifths Compromise.

FURTHER READING: Du Bois, W.E.B., 1970 (reprint of 1935 work), *Black Reconstruction in America, 1860–1880*, New York: Atheneum; Litwack, Leon F., 1980, *Been in the Storm So Long: The Aftermath of Slavery*, New York: Vintage Books; Miller, Loren, 1966, *The Petitioners: The Story of the Supreme Court of the United States and the Negro*, New York: Pantheon Books.

PAUL OBIYO MBANASO NJEMANZE

Thomas, Clarence (1948–)

A firm critic of affirmative action, Clarence Thomas has served as an associate justice of the U.S. Supreme Court since 1991. He is one of several justices in a conservative bloc on the Court who are overtly critical of affirmative action. According to Georgetown University law professor Giradeau Spann, "A five-justice conservative voting bloc has formed on the present Court consisting of justices who have almost never voted to uphold an affirmative action plan in a constitutional case. The members of this conservative bloc are Chief Justice Rehnquist, and Justices O'Connor, Scalia, Kennedy and Thomas" (Spann 2000, 159–160). Thomas, in his professional and personal comments, has denounced affirmative action programs as detrimental to African Americans.

Born in a dirt-floored shack in the Jim Crow marshes of Pin Point, Georgia, to a mother who plucked crabmeat and served as a maid in white-owned households, Clarence Thomas overcame great odds in life to become the 106th Supreme Court justice and only the second African American to serve on the high court. With the guidance of a stern grandfather, Thomas received his undergraduate education at the College of the Holy Cross, a Jesuit institution, after the school implemented a black recruitment program, with an honors degree in English and then entered law school at Yale under yet another minority preference program. Thomas's career in the law began with the Missouri attorney general's office under John Danforth, but he left public service after two years to become a corporate lawyer for the Monsanto Corporation when Danforth was elected to the U.S. Senate. After two years in the pesticide and agriculture division of Monsanto, Thomas joined Senator Danforth once again as his legislative aide.

After attending a conference of black conservatives in 1980, Thomas was the subject of an article in the *Washington Post* that brought him to the attention of the Reagan administration. After accepting a job as the assistant secretary for civil rights in the Department of Education, Thomas was appointed to serve as the head of the Equal Employment Opportunity Commission (EEOC) from 1982 to 1990, the government agency charged with preventing workplace discrimination on the job. At the EEOC, "he took positions at odds with those of established civil rights groups, thus marking him as a prominent black conservative and potential nominee for the Court" (Hall 1992, 870–871).

In 1990, Thomas was appointed to the federal bench for the Court of Appeals for the District of Columbia Circuit. After he had served only eighteen months and authored twenty opinions as an appellate judge, President George H.W. Bush nominated Thomas in July 1991 to the U.S. Supreme Court to replace the retiring Associate Justice Thurgood Marshall, the first African American Supreme Court justice. Thomas's confirmation hearing became a battle due to his unwillingness to express opinions about personal approaches to constitutional interpretation as well as an undecided position on the controversial abortion decision *Roe v. Wade*, 410 U.S. 113 (1973). Thomas's confirmation hearing became even more of a marathon and bitterly divisive in the wake of sexual harassment allegations by University of Oklahoma professor Anita Hill, a last-minute witness and a former EEOC colleague. To some, the nomination and confirmation of Thomas exemplified the hypocrisy of the opportunities provided by affirmative action. Thomas believed that he was being attacked by black groups because he refused to toe the standard race line as it related to affirmative action and policies of race, and referred to his confirmation process as a "high-tech lynching." However, after one of the longest confirmation hearings in history, in the end the appointment was won by the narrowest Senate voting margin in the history of Court confirmation with a vote of 52–48 on October 15, 1991.

Justice Thomas has often been considered the polar opposite in judicial philosophy of his patron justice, Thurgood Marshall, and, therefore, has met strong opposition from minority groups who oppose Thomas's views on civil rights. Thomas, with a core philosophy arising from natural law (e.g., "survival of the fittest"), broke from the traditional civil rights path with his own views of affirmative action programs. In Thomas's view, affirmative action weakens minorities by making them dependent on and complacent about what he has labeled as "handouts," rather than encouraging self-reliance and education. In a law review article by Thomas in the late 1980s, he emphasized the need to shift the focus to the specific needs of individuals to create a true "equal opportunity" rather than attempt to remedy the needs of any minority group as a whole. Under often-used goals and timetables forced upon employers, minorities are often placed in dead-end positions with no real room for valuable experience or advancement. According to Thomas, minorities would always be relegated to positions in which they would never be able to excel, rather than to areas that provide training and education for further growth and advancement. In Thomas's controversial philosophy, the government should not attempt to solve the problems of minorities with set-aside programs, but only give minorities the opportunity to solve their own ills. Additionally, Thomas has frequently argued that affirmative action increases racial friction and causes many to doubt the achievements of minorities who can succeed and survive by "merit" alone.

As an associate justice known to ask few questions at oral argument, Thomas has opposed affirmative action as a vehicle that belittles minorities. In 1995, the affirmative action pendulum swung back decisively to the conservative bloc with a vote by Thomas that changed the direction of affirmative action in the watershed case *Adarand Constructors, Inc. v. Peña*, 515 U.S. 200 (1995), which involved a federal program that authorized racial preferences in subcontracting highway projects. Thomas voted with Justices William Rehnquist, Sandra Day O'Connor, Antonin Scalia, and Anthony Kennedy to overturn the federal program as unconstitutional and hold that any racial preference, even benign discrimination, was to be viewed by the Court with suspicion and to be subject to the rigorous strict scrutiny analysis. While Thomas agreed with much of O'Connor's majority opinion, he concurred in part with the opinion and wrote that affirmative action programs not only "raise grave constitutional questions," but also "undermine the moral basis of the equal protection principle" that was "[p]urchased at the price of immeasurable human suffering." In clearly indicating his position on affirmative action, Thomas went on to say that "in my mind, government-sponsored racial discrimination based on benign prejudice is just as noxious as discrimination inspired by malicious prejudice."

Most recently, in *Gratz v. Bollinger*, 123 S. Ct. 2411, 2003 U.S. LEXIS 4801 (2003), and *Grutter v. Bollinger*, 123 S. Ct. 2325, 2003 U.S. LEXIS 4800 (2003), Thomas again positioned himself firmly against the use of race-conscious affirmative action plans in higher education. He joined the majority opinion authored by Chief Justice Rehnquist in the *Gratz* decision, striking down the University of Michigan's undergraduate admissions policy as being unconstitutional under the Equal Protection Clause of the Fourteenth Amendment and a violation of Title VI of the Civil Rights Act of 1964. The Court held that Michigan's program put too much focus on race and was too akin to racial quotas. In the companion case of *Grutter*, Thomas dissented from the majority opinion upholding the race-conscious program utilized by the University of Michigan Law School. Thomas, in dissent, argued that the use of race as part of the admissions decision was a violation of the Equal Protection Clause of the Fourteenth Amendment.

Thomas did not understand how the majority in *Grutter* could uphold the affirmative action plan at issue then, but comment that it would not be permissible in another twenty-five years. Thomas stated, "I believe that the Law School's current use of race violates the Equal Protection Clause and that the Constitution means the same thing today as it will in 300 months." In closing his dissent, Thomas again made clear his long-standing opposition to race-conscious affirmative action, commenting that the practice of affirmative action "can only weaken the principle of equality embodied in the Declaration of Independence and the Equal Protection Clause." Thomas then quoted Frederick Douglass and Justice John Marshall Harlan:

> "Our Constitution is color-blind, and neither knows nor tolerates classes among citizens." *Plessy v. Ferguson*, 163 U.S. 537, 559 (1896) (Harlan, J., dissenting). It has been nearly 140 years since Frederick Douglass asked the intellectual ancestors of the Law School to "[d]o nothing with us!" and the Nation adopted the Fourteenth Amendment. Now we must wait another 25 years to see this principle of equality vindicated.

See also Adarand Constructors, Inc. v. Peña; Affirmative Action Plan/Program; African Americans; Benign Discrimination; Bush, George Herbert Walker; Civil Rights Act of 1964; Color-Blind Constitution; Declaration of Independence; Department of Education; Douglass, Frederick; Equal Employment Opportunity Commission; Equal Protection Clause; Fourteenth Amendment; *Gratz v. Bollinger/Grutter v. Bollinger*; Kennedy, Anthony McLeod; Marshall, Thurgood; O'Connor, Sandra Day; *Plessy v. Ferguson*; Reagan, Ronald; Rehnquist, William Hobbs; Scalia, Antonin; Strict Scrutiny; Title VI of the Civil Rights Act of 1964.

FURTHER READING: Abramson, Jill, and Jane Mayer, 1994, *Strange Justice: The Selling of Clarence Thomas*, Boston: Houghton Mifflin; Friedelbaum, Stanley H., 1994, *The Rehnquist Court: In Pursuit of Judicial Conservatism*, Westport, CT: Greenwood Press; Greenya, John, 2001, *Silent Justice: The Clarence Thomas Story*, NJ: Barricade Books; Hall, Kermit, ed., 1992, *The Oxford Companion to the Supreme Court of the United States*, New York: Oxford University Press; Lazarus, Edward, 1998, *Closed Chambers: The Rise, Fall, and Future of the Modern Supreme Court*, New York: Penguin Press; Maxwell, Susan M., 1998, "Racial Classifications under Strict Scrutiny: Policy Considerations and the Remedial-Plus Approach," *Texas Law Review* 77:259; "Race Law and Justice: The Rehnquist Court and The American Dilemma" (conference), 1996, *American University Law Review* 45, no. 3 (February); Spann, Girardeau, 2000, *The Law of Affirmative Action*, New York: New York University Press; Thomas, Andrew Peyton, 2001, *Clarence Thomas: A Biography*, San Francisco: Encounter Books; Thomas, Clarence, 1987, "Affirmative Action Goals and Timetables: Too Tough? Not Tough Enough!" *Yale Law and Policy Review* 5 (spring/summer): 402–411.

ROBERT DON GIFFORD II

Three-Fifths Compromise

The Three-Fifths Compromise, contained in Article 1, Section 2, of the U.S. Constitution, was a political agreement struck during the Constitutional Convention of 1787. The compromise set the apportionment of direct taxes and congressional seats in the House of Representatives among the states, counting three-fifths of the slave population for both purposes. It was one of four clauses in the Constitution that protected the institution of slavery and attempted to ensure preferential treatment under the Constitution for whites over black slaves in perpetuity. The clause represents one of the earliest attempts by the United States to utilize race as a way to allocate taxation burdens and decide representational issues.

The origin of the Three-Fifths Compromise has been debated since the ratification of the U.S. Constitution of 1787. Traditionally, the clause was theorized to be a sectional compromise between northerners and southerners to balance congressional power and the direct tax burden between the two sectional interests. Northerners wanted slaves counted for direct taxes, but not counted for representation, and southerners wanted slaves counted for representation, but not counted for direct taxes.

During the Civil War era, abolitionists theorized that the clause was a compromise legitimizing slavery and a counterrevolution betraying the Revolution fought under the guise of the Declaration of Independence's principle that all men were created equal. Modern historians building on this theory have suggested that the clause was a purely sectional compromise between southerners attempting to secure slavery in the South via the Constitution and northerners attempting to prohibit slavery in the territories north of the Ohio River via the Northwest Ordinance of 1787.

During the early part of the twentieth century, progressive historians theorized that the establishment of the three-fifths "federal ratio" for representation purposes was only an extension of the New Jersey Plan crafted and approved by eleven states in the Congress of the Articles of Confederation, which suggested that three-fifths of the slave population would be counted to determine each state's share of direct taxation. Modern historians building on this view have suggested that the compromise was not over the numeric value of the ratio, but was a nonsectional agreement between all states to set the ratio in the Constitution instead of leaving it up to the new U.S. Congress.

See also Articles of Confederation; Bill of Rights; Constitution, Civil Rights, and Equality; Color-Blind Constitution; Declaration of Independence and Equality; Slavery; Slavery and the Founding Fathers.

FURTHER READING: Lynd, Staughton, 1967, *Class Conflict, Slavery, and the United States Constitution*, Indianapolis: Bobbs-Merrill; O'Connor, Karen, and Larry J. Sabato, 1993, *American Government: Roots and Reform*, New York: Macmillan; Ohline, Howard A., 1971, "Republicanism and Slavery: Origins of the Three-Fifths Clause in the United States Constitution," *William and Mary Quarterly* 28, no. 4:563–584.

MARK J. SENEDIAK

Title VI of the Civil Rights Act of 1964

Title VI of the landmark Civil Rights Act of 1964 prohibits discrimination on the basis of race, color, or national origin in the conduct of any federally financed program. If a funding recipient does not voluntarily comply with the statute, federal funds can be terminated. The law gave the federal government and civil rights activists powerful new leverage to force states to integrate their schools, hospitals, and other institutions and programs receiving federal funds. Also, since federal agencies were charged with implementing the law and since all related rules and regulations required specific presidential approval, the law took some of the civil rights focus away from the court system and shifted it to the executive branch. Some observers have credited Title VI with a major role in achieving integration. Others, though, have criticized the statute on various grounds. First, they cite general problems in enforcing the statute. Second, federal agencies have been inconsistent in implementation, with some being aggressive, but others preferring to protect existing funding programs. Finally, now that cases of intentional discrimination have been reduced, some feel that the law has been applied too broadly to policies that have a "discriminatory impact."

In June 1963, facing mounting racial tensions and a real fear of possible violence, President John Kennedy submitted a major legislative proposal on civil rights. Included in that proposal was a Title VI that provided that no federal program could be construed as requiring the disbursement of funds where discrimination existed. In the Senate, little immediate action was taken on the proposal, but in the House, the legislation was referred to a subcommittee of the House Judiciary Committee. This subcommittee essentially created the Title VI that would eventually become law. The subcommittee changed the wording to an outright prohibition on discrimination and thus created a right to federal benefits irrespective of race, color, or national origin. The subcommittee version also called for the termination of assistance for those failing to comply. As the legislation moved through the committee level and debate on the floor, modifications were made in three areas. First, explicit roles were created for both the president and Congress. The president has to approve all implementing regulations, and congressional committees with legislative jurisdiction have to receive a report before fund termination can occur. Second, certain types of programs, such as those with a contract of insurance or guaranty, were exempted. Third, enforcement mechanisms were clarified. Initial language that allowed civil actions in federal courts was dropped, but the idea of judicial review of agency decisions was adopted. The overall bill was heavily contested in the Senate, with long filibusters and heated debates, but the Title VI provisions proved less controversial than other parts of the bill.

Initially, Title VI affected programs totaling about $18 billion in federal assistance and overseen by almost two dozen federal agencies. In subsequent years, the amount of assistance and number of agencies involved grew substantially as the federal government created new programs. Early on, two major areas of focus were education and health care. In 1964, despite the ruling in *Brown v. Board of Education*, 347 U.S. 483 (1954), several southern states still had less than 10 percent of black students attending integrated schools. Federal aid to local schools, however, had increased threefold in the preceding decade. Advocates argued that the threat of funding termination could now achieve what court rulings had not. In its first decade, Title VI concerns were raised with more than 500 school systems, and gradually the percentage of students in integrated schools increased. In health care, discrimination was a problem both in terms of patients admitted—a 1959 study showed that only 6 percent of southern hospitals admitted African Americans without restrictions—and in staffing. Even in the North, only 20 percent of hospitals had African American physicians on staff. Here too, though, the federal government had new leverage because of the creation of Medicare, which was covered by Title VI and disbursed funds to more than 7,000 hospitals nationwide. Again, compliance was not immediate, but discrimination did greatly decrease in the health field.

Although hailed by some as a crucial step in the civil rights movement, Title VI and its implementation have also been criticized by many observers, including the U.S. Commission on Civil Rights. These critics argue that efforts to investigate compliance have been chronically underfunded and have suffered major procedural problems because compliance has been investigated by the same agencies implementing the funding programs. They also point out that full implementation requires active presidential leadership, but some administrations, such as that of Ronald Reagan, developed reputations for being relatively uninterested in pursuing discrimination cases.

Critics also point out that there have been sharp differences among federal agencies in how compliance has been pursued. Under the law, agencies can seek compliance through voluntary remedies, the termination of funds, or "other means authorized by law," which has come to mean either fund deferral or referral of the case to the Justice Department. Many agencies are wary of using fund termination because they know that it will anger constituents, possibly lead to pressure from members of congress, and limit the very programs they oversee. Disparities therefore have arisen in which of the four compliance measures agencies employ. One 1997 study found that the Department of Health, Education, and Welfare had terminated funds 200 times, deferred funds 180 times, referred 80 cases to the Justice Department, and utilized voluntary compliance 480 times. During the same time period, the Department of Labor had used voluntary compliance only 150 times and had never terminated funds, deferred funds, or referred a case to the Justice Department.

Over time, the number of cases involving a clear intent to discriminate has declined. Therefore, the focus has shifted to policies that have a discriminatory impact. For example, suits have been submitted against the state of New York that argue that disparities between achievement rates of students in various districts show an overall biased education system and a violation of students' rights. Cases have also been brought on whether the placement of toxic waste facilities in certain low-income areas shows "environmental racism." In 2001, further expansion of cases like these was set back by the Supreme Court ruling in *Alexander v. Sandoval*, 532 U.S. 275 (2001), which held that given the scope of the original law, private suits could only be brought for intentional discrimination and not for discriminatory effects.

See also Brown v. Board of Education; Civil Rights Act of 1964; Department of Education; Department of Health and Human Services; Department of Justice; Department of Labor; Education and Affirmative Action; Environmental Racism; Integration; Kennedy, John Fitzgerald; Reagan, Ronald; U.S. Commission on Civil Rights.

FURTHER READING: Halpern, Stephen C., 1995, *On the Limits of the Law: The Ironic Legacy of Title VI of the 1964 Civil Rights Act*, Baltimore: Johns Hopkins University Press; Jones, Augustus J., Jr., 1982, *Law, Bureaucracy, and Politics: The Implementation of Title VI of the Civil Rights Act of 1964*, Washington, DC: University Press of America; Reynolds, Preston P., 1997,

"The Federal Government's Use of Title VI and Medicare to Racially Integrate Hospitals in the United States, 1963 through 1967," *American Journal of Public Health* 87:1850–1858; Whalen, Charles, and Barbara Whalen, 1985, *The Longest Debate*, Cabin John, MD: Seven Locks Press.

JOHN W. DIETRICH

Title VII of the Civil Rights Act of 1964

Title VII of the Civil Rights Act of 1964 is important to the affirmative action debate not only because it was the first comprehensive statute that aimed to eliminate discrimination in the workplace, but also because it has been interpreted to permit, but impose limits upon, the voluntary affirmative action efforts of employers, to permit, but limit, the racial and gender preferences that can be imposed by a court in remedying discrimination against minorities and women, and to require federal employers to maintain affirmative programs of equal employment opportunity.

Enacted at the apex of the 1960s civil rights movement, the Civil Rights Act of 1964 was designed to eliminate discrimination in several important aspects of society such as housing and public accommodations and in all federally funded programs. Title VII of the Civil Rights Act prohibits discrimination on account of race, color, sex, religion, or national origin by most private-sector, state government, and local government employers. Before Title VII was enacted, there were other legislative attempts to prohibit employment discrimination. However, these efforts were not comprehensive and not very effective. In 1972, Title VII was amended to apply the same prohibition to federal government employers. Title VII not only prohibits discrimination by employers, but also prohibits unions and employment agencies from using discriminatory practices. Title VII also created the U.S. Equal Employment Opportunity Commission (EEOC) and assigned to it the responsibility for enforcing the statute though an administrative complaints process and the authority to bring lawsuits on behalf of victims of discrimination in federal court.

Title VII prohibits not only those employment actions, practices, and policies that are motivated by an intent to discriminate, but, as the U.S. Supreme Court held in *Griggs v. Duke Power Co.*, 401 U.S. 424 (1971), also prohibits facially neutral employment policies and practices that have an adverse impact on a group of persons because of their racial status, color, sex, religion, or national origin. For two decades, this so-called disparate impact or adverse impact theory remained a product of judicial interpretation. However, in 1991, via the Civil Rights Act of 1991, Congress codified this disparate impact theory, making it explicit in Title VII. Under this theory, an employer may be held to have violated Title VII even if there is no proof that the employer intended to discriminate.

In addition to investing the EEOC with the authority to bring discrimination claims to federal court, Title VII gave victims of discrimination the right to bring their complaints to court. An increasing number of Title VII cases are being filed by white males who believe that they have lost hiring or promotion opportunities to less qualified minority or female candidates, oftentimes pursuant to affirmative action programs. Although some courts initially held that Title VII did not protect whites from race discrimination and males from gender discrimination, it has now been recognized that Title VII does protect whites and males from racial or gender discrimination. The Supreme Court has made this holding clear in several cases, such as *McDonald v. Santa Fe Trail Transportation Co.*, 427 U.S. 273 (1976), and *Oncale v. Sundowner Offshore Services, Inc.*, 118 S. Ct. 998 (1998).

In a few circumstances, an employer may discriminate without violating Title VII. For example, an employer may use gender, religion, or national origin as a factor in making employment decisions if the protected characteristic is a "bona fide occupational qualification" (BFOQ) for the position in question (i.e., consideration of the protected characteristic is "reasonably necessary to the normal operations of the employer's business or enterprise"). For example, a church can consider the religious beliefs of applicants for church leaders. This defense is not available for employment decisions based on race or color. Another defense against reverse-discrimination cases is that the challenged action, policy, or practice was pursuant to a lawful affirmative action plan.

Title VII is crucial to the issue of affirmative action in three contexts: (1) voluntary affirmative action plans of private-sector employers and state and local governmental employers; (2) affirmative action in court orders following a finding of discrimination against women or minorities; and (3) the requirement of affirmative employment efforts for most federal government employers. Title VII allows employers to voluntarily implement affirmative action employment plans in certain circumstances, even if the plans grant race- or gender-based preferences and result in an employment benefit given to one person over another, at least in part, because of race or gender. Thus even if the defendant employer in a reverse-discrimination case admits that it would have selected the white male plaintiff but for its affirmative action plan that allowed the employer to consider race as a preferential factor in the selection process, the plaintiff would not succeed in establishing a Title VII violation as long as the affirmative action plan met Title VII's requirements and the specific decision challenged was authorized by the plan.

The first time the U.S. Supreme Court addressed the issue of whether affirmative action plans that granted racial preferences were permissible under Title VII was in its decision in *United Steelworkers of America v. Weber*, 443 U.S. 193 (1979). The affirmative action plan challenged in *Weber* was part of a collective bargaining agreement between the United Steelworkers Union and the employer, Kaiser Aluminum and Chemical Corporation. The plan included minority hiring goals for Kaiser's craft positions and established programs that would provide Kaiser's production employees with the qualifications necessary for the better-paying craft positions. Production employees were selected for the training program in seniority order, except that at least 50 percent of the production employees admitted to this training program had to be black until the percentage of blacks occupying craft positions at each plant was equal to the percentage of blacks in the local workforce. Before the affirmative action plan was implemented, nearly all of Kaiser's craft workforce was white. The plaintiffs were white male production workers who had more seniority than the black production workers selected for the training program. The plaintiffs argued that Title VII forbids all discrimination in employment because of race, and therefore, the reservation of 50 percent of the craft training opportunities for black employees was unlawful.

The Supreme Court recognized that a literal reading of Title VII would support the plaintiffs' argument. However, the Court held that the legislative history of Title VII and the historical context in which Title VII was passed counseled against an interpretation that would bar all voluntary race-conscious affirmative action programs. The Court cited comments made by senators and congressmen during the debate and passage of Title VII that indicated that the primary purpose of Title VII's prohibition against race discrimination in employment was to improve participation of black Americans in the national workforce (particularly in skilled jobs, because unskilled jobs were increasingly eliminated by automation) in order to make possible the overall goal of the Civil Rights Act: the full integration of blacks in American society. The Court noted that the unemployment rate of black Americans at the time Title VII was enacted was 124 percent of the unemployment rate for white Americans.

The Court held that Kaiser's voluntary affirmative action plan, which was designed to eliminate significant underrepresentation of blacks in traditionally segregated job categories, did not violate Title VII. The Court did not establish clear, universally applicable rules for determining when race-conscious affirmative action plans would be lawful under Title VII, but indicated why Kaiser's plan was on the permissible side of the line. The Court found that the plan (1) was voluntary, (2) mirrored the purposes of Title VII inasmuch as it aimed to correct a demonstrated gross statistical disparity between blacks in the local labor force and blacks in craft positions from which they had been traditionally excluded because of race, (3) did not unnecessarily trammel the interests of nonminorities because it did not require the discharge of white employees and was not an absolute bar to advancement for white employees, and (4) was only a temporary measure that did not aim to maintain permanent racial balance but would end when the percentage of blacks in craft positions equaled the percentage of black in the local labor force.

Eight years later, in its opinion in *Johnson v. Transportation Agency, Santa Clara County*, 480 U.S. 616 (1987), the U.S. Supreme Court further elucidated *Weber*'s requirement of a factual predicate for race- or gender-conscious affirmative action programs that are designed and intended to eliminate the effects of discrimination in traditionally segregated jobs. The affirmative action plan challenged by the male plaintiff allowed race and sex to be considered as factors in making selections among qualified candidates for hiring and promotion in those job categories where minorities and women were significantly underrepresented when compared with the available and qualified labor pool. The plaintiff complained that a less qualified female employee was promoted instead of him because of her gender and that this was sex discrimination in violation of Title VII. Like the affirmative action plan in *Weber*, the plan had been voluntarily adopted by the employer, and its purpose was to remedy the effects of past discrimination. However, the plan had no clear termination date. The plaintiff and the female employee selected for promotion had both been judged as qualified. However, the male plaintiff was rated slightly higher during the selection process than was the female selectee. The employer admitted that it took gender into account in its decision to promote the female candidate because her selection would contribute to the goals of the affirmative action plan.

The Court held that the employer's use of gender as one of many factors in selecting the female candidate for promotion to the road dispatcher position was appropriate under Title VII. The Court applied the principles set out in its *Weber* opinion and found that the Transportation Agency's plan, as applied to the challenged selection, was shown to have mirrored the purpose of Title VII to eliminate segregation in the workplace without unnecessarily trammeling the rights of the majority. The Court held that employers could demonstrate that taking sex into account in selections for certain jobs was justified to further the purposes of Title VII where there was a "manifest imbalance that reflected underrepresentation of women in traditionally segregated job categories," including the job category in question. A finding or admission of prior discrimination was not necessary to establish the required factual predicate for race- or gender-conscious action. The Court also explained the methods by which employers must determine whether women or minorities were underrepresented in traditionally segregated job categories in order to establish a sufficient factual predicate. In *Weber*, the comparison was between the racial composition of skilled craft workers at the Kaiser plants and the local general labor force. The Court explained that this comparison was appropriate when examining underrepresentation in job categories requiring no specialized skills or for training programs that would provide the special skills required for the positions in question (as in *Weber*). However, the Court explained that when an employer was determining whether there was a manifest imbalance attributable to past discrimination in job categories that did require specialized skills, the appropriate comparison was between the demographics of the persons the employer employed in the job category and the demographics of the available labor force with the qualifications for the job. The Court was impressed that the Transportation Agency's goals for the employment of women and minorities did take into account the availability of women and minorities who had the specialized qualifications desired. The Transportation Agency was able to demonstrate a manifest imbalance of women in the skilled craft worker job category at issue, where none of its 238 skilled craft worker positions were held by women. Therefore, the Court held that the Transportation Agency established a sufficient factual predicate for taking sex into account in these jobs.

The Court also found that the Transportation Agency's affirmative action plan did not unnecessarily trammel the interests of nonminorities. The Court noted that the plan did not set aside any number of positions for women or minorities, but merely authorized race or sex to be taken into account among other factors when deciding among qualified candidates. The Court also noted that the plaintiff had no entitlement to promotion, and therefore the use of sex in selecting a female "unsettled no legitimate, firmly rooted expectations on the part of" the plaintiff. The Court noted that he remained employed by the Transportation Agency and could apply for promotions in the future. Finally, the Court rejected the argument that the plan was deficient because it had no termination date. The Court explained that while an affirmative action plan with set-asides should have a specific end date to ensure that the plan would merely attain and not maintain a demographically balanced workforce and not unduly burden nonminorities, an end date was not necessary to fulfill the purposes of this plan because it had flexible, realistic goals implemented on a case-by-case basis rather than rigid set-asides. The Court concluded its opinion by stressing that because Congress emphasized the importance of voluntary efforts to eliminate discrimination and the lingering effects of discrimination in the workplace, appropriate voluntary affirmative action efforts should not be held to violate Title VII.

Guidelines for legal and appropriate affirmative action plans can be found not only in case law, but in Title VII itself and in its implementing regulations. Section 713 of Title VII provides that a defendant in a Title VII lawsuit will not be held liable for a Title VII violation if the defendant proves that the action challenged was taken "in good faith, in conformity with and in reliance on any written interpretation or opinion of the Commission." The U.S. Equal Employment Opportunity Commission issued regulations setting standards for lawful affirmative action under Title VII at 29 C.F.R. part 1608. The regulations explicitly state that an affirmative action plan that is adopted in good faith, in conformity with, and in reliance upon them will be entitled to the section 713 defense.

In its regulations, the EEOC opines not only that Title VII does not prohibit affirmative action in employment, but also that Title VII encourages voluntary affirmative action plans. The EEOC emphasizes that Congress's desire in enacting Title VII was that elimination of employment discrimination and its effects be accomplished primarily through voluntary effort. Therefore, the EEOC states, voluntary affirmative action to benefit minorities and women in the workplace "must be encouraged and protected."

The EEOC defines affirmative action in the regulations as "those actions appropriate to overcome the effects of past or present practices, policies or barriers to equal employment opportunity." The EEOC regulations both set out the circumstances under which affirmative action is appropriate and give instruction concerning how to establish an affirmative action plan. The regulations provide that affirmative action is appropriate in three circumstances. First, affirmative action is appropriate when an analysis reveals that employment policies or practices instituted or contemplated have resulted in or have the potential to result in an adverse impact on women or minorities. Second, affirmative action is appropriate to correct the effects of past discriminatory practices that may be identified by a comparison between the demographics of the workforce and the appropriate qualified labor pool. Finally, when there is evidence that the qualified labor pool itself has been artificially limited by discrimination, affirmative action may be appropriate to overcome such past discrimination by, for example, instituting training programs for women and minorities and engaging in recruiting efforts to locate qualified minority and female candidates.

When the correct circumstances exist, the EEOC's regulations provide that a lawful affirmative action plan must have the following three elements: "a reasonable self analysis; a reasonable basis for concluding action is appropriate; and reasonable action." The aim of the reasonable self-analysis must be to determine whether employment policies or practices result in the disparate treatment of or in an adverse impact upon groups because of their minority racial status or gender and/or whether the effects of such prior policies or practices are still present in the workforce. If discriminatory practices or the effects thereof are found, a reasonable basis for affirmative action exists. Finally, the action authorized by the affirmative action plan must be a reasonable response to the findings of the self-analysis. The EEOC specifically approves the use of numerical goals and other measures "which recognize the race, sex, or national origin of applicants or employees," but also states that "the race, sex or national origin conscious provisions of the plan or program should be maintained only so long as is necessary" to achieve equal employment opportunity. The regulations state that opportunities may be provided to minorities and women who are members of groups that had been subject to discrimination even if the particular persons directly benefited by such measures were not themselves subject to the discrimination. Finally, the regulations also provide that the affirmative action plan should avoid "unnecessary restrictions on the opportunities of the workforce as a whole."

Title VII is relevant not only to voluntary affirmative action efforts, but also to affirmative action–style remedies contained in court orders after a court has determined that employment policies or practices discriminated against minorities or women in violation of Title VII. Section 706(g) of Title VII provides for remedies for victims of employment discrimination. Race- or gender-conscious remedies that are necessary to "make whole" the actual victims of discrimination are permitted and uncontroversial. However, arguments have been made based on section 706(g) that courts do not have authority to impose racial or gender preferences as a remedy for discriminatory employment actions, policies, or practices that benefit persons who were not injured by the discrimination. The U.S. Supreme Court initially seemed sympathetic to this argument in *Firefighters Local Union No. 1784 v. Stotts*, 467 U.S. 561 (1984), when it held that a court could not order the suspension of a seniority system during a layoff that would have resulted in the layoff of many African Americans firefighters because the persons benefited by such an order had not been shown to have themselves been victims of discrimination. The Court appeared to change course in *Local 28 of the Sheet Metal Workers' International Association v. EEOC*, 478 U.S. 421 (1986). The Court upheld a district court order setting a minority membership goal for the union after making extensive findings that the union engaged in discriminatory membership practices. Justice William Brennan wrote for a plurality of the court that section 706(g) permits courts to order such relief, but only in limited circumstances. Brennan stated that one example of such circumstances is "where an employer or labor union has engaged in persistent or egregious discrimination, or where necessary to dissipate the lingering effects of pervasive discrimination." In *United States v. Paradise*, 480 U.S. 149 (1987), the Supreme Court again approved a trial court's decree that for every white officer promoted, one African American officer had to be promoted after finding substantial evidence of serious past discrimination. The Court provided additional guidance concerning when court-ordered race-conscious relief is permissible. The Court stated that factors that are important include but are not limited to "the necessity for the relief and the efficacy of alternative remedies; the flexibility and duration of the relief, including the applicability of waiver provisions; the relationship of the numerical goals to the relevant labor market; and the impact of the relief on the rights of third parties." Racial or gender preferences in consent decrees settling a Title VII lawsuit, however, have been viewed as more akin to voluntary affirmative action efforts than court-ordered affirmative action efforts. Therefore, the consent decrees have generally not been subject to the limitation of section 706(g).

The Civil Rights Act of 1991 amended Title VII to include a provision (section 703[l]) that prohibits adjusting scores or score standards of employment-related tests used in selection or promotion processes on the basis of race, color, religion, sex, or national origin. This provision may severely restrict race and gender preferences in affirmative action plans that involve test scores or other qualification standards.

While Title VII permits voluntary affirmative action by state and local government employers and by employers in the private sector within certain limits, it does not require these employers to take affirmative action. Section 703(j) of Title VII provides that Title VII should not be interpreted to require preferential treatment of persons because of their race, color, religion, sex, or national origin where there is an imbalance between a group's representation in a workforce and its representation in the general labor force. Although it has been argued that this section actually precludes race and gender preferences in affirmative action programs, the U.S. Supreme Court has rejected this argument. In its *Johnson* opinion, the Court stated that on the contrary, the fact that section 703(j) does not require racial or gender preferences indicates that Congress believed that such preferences, if adopted voluntarily, were permitted under Title VII.

On the other hand, section 717 of Title VII requires the federal government as an employer to maintain what the statute calls an "affirmative program of equal employment opportunity." Title VII assigns to the EEOC the responsibility of reviewing and approving the affirmative employment plans of federal agencies and requires the EEOC to make an annual report to Congress on the state of equal employment opportunity in the federal government. The EEOC has promulgated management directives to guide federal agencies in establishing affirmative employment plans. Management Directive 715 is the current version of these guidelines. Neither Title VII itself nor the EEOC's Management Directive 715 requires that affirmative employment plans utilize racial or gender preferences.

It is important to note that Title VII is not the only limitation on what affirmative action federal, state, and local governmental employers may take. The Equal Protection Clause of the Fourteenth Amendment and the equal protection guarantee that has been held to be a part of the Fifth Amendment's Due Process Clause also impose limits on governmental affirmative action that are arguably stricter than those imposed by Title VII.

See also Adarand Constructors, Inc. v. Peña; Affirmative Action Plan/Program; African Americans; Brennan, William Joseph; *City of Richmond v. J.A. Croson Co.;* Civil Rights Act of 1964; Civil Rights Act of 1991; Civil Rights Movement; Color Consciousness; Discrimination; Disparate Treatment and Disparate Impact; Employment (Private) and Affirmative Action; Employment (Public) and Affirmative Action; Equal Employment Opportunity Commission; Fifth Amendment; *Firefighters Local Union No. 1784 v. Stotts;* Fourteenth Amendment; *Griggs v. Duke Power Co.;* Integration; *Johnson v. Transportation Agency, Santa Clara County; Local 28 of the Sheet Metal Workers' International Association v. EEOC;* Manifest Imbalance Standard; *Metro Broadcasting, Inc. v. FCC;* Racial Discrimination; Reverse Discrimination; Statistical Proof of Discrimination; Supreme Court and Affirmative Action; Title VI of the Civil Rights Act of 1964; *United States v. Paradise; United Steelworkers of America v. Weber.*

FURTHER READING: Iheukwumere, Emmanuel O., and Philip C. Aka, 2001, "Title VII, Affirmative Action, and the March toward Color-Blind Jurisprudence," *Temple Political and Civil Rights Law Review* 11 (fall): 1–61; Lindemann, Barbara, and Paul Grossman, 1996,

Employment Discrimination Law, 3d ed., vol. 1–2, Washington, DC: Bureau of National Affairs; Whiteside, Janice C., 1998, "Title VII and Reverse Discrimination: The Prima Facie Case," *Indiana Law Review* 31:413–443.

MARIA D. BECKMAN

Title VIII of the Civil Rights Act of 1968

See Civil Rights Act of 1968; Housing.

Title IX of the Education Amendments of 1972

Title IX grew out of both the civil rights and feminist movements of the mid- and late twentieth century. As part of the 1972 Education Amendments of the 1964 Civil Rights Act, Title IX prohibits sex discrimination, including marital or parental status discrimination, in schools receiving federal aid. According to Title IX's preamble, "No person in the United States shall, on the basis of sex, be excluded from participation in, be denied the benefits of, or be subject to discrimination under any educational program or activity receiving federal financial assistance." Affecting kindergarten through graduate school in both private and public schools in areas such as programs, admissions, recruitment, facilities, scholarships, courses, services, and athletics, Title IX has ushered in waves of opportunities for women.

In 1968, President Lyndon Johnson amended Executive Order 11246, issued in 1965, which prohibited any federal contractor from discriminating on the basis of race, color, religion, or national origin, to include sex discrimination, making the order, now called Executive Order 11375, the impetus for Title IX. Johnson's daughter, Luci, was denied readmission to the Georgetown University School of Nursing because the school did not admit married women. The first person to realize the implications for schools was senior scholar in residence for the National Association of Women in Education Bernice R. Sandler. Arguing that because most universities and colleges held federal contracts, they could not discriminate against women, Sandler soon attracted the attention of Michigan representative Martha Griffiths. On March 9, 1970, Griffiths delivered the first congressional speech addressing sex discrimination in education. The first compliance investigation took place just three weeks later at Harvard.

By the summer of 1970, Ohio representative Edith Green initiated the first congressional hearings on sex discrimination in education and employment. Senators Birch Bayh of Indiana and George McGovern of South Dakota managed the bill. Originally, supporters planned to amend Title VII and Title VI of the Civil Rights Act of 1964, but at the request of African American leaders, who feared that Title VI would be weakened by the process, Green developed a separate and new title. After several months of working through the 250 differences between different bills in the House and Senate, the end result of the hearings was Title IX. Passed by Congress on June 8, 1972, and signed into law on June 23, 1972, by President Richard Nixon, Title IX went into effect on July 1, 1972. Once Title IX was passed into law, the Department of Health, Education, and Welfare (now the Department of Education) was charged with developing specific regulations, a three-year process. President Gerald Ford signed the regulations on May 27, 1975.

Title IX's regulations require that affected institutions have a Title IX coordinator who oversees compliance and investigates complaints, that employees and students be notified of who their Title IX coordinator is and how to contact him or her, that procedures and policies be made public, that schools complete a onetime self-evaluation, and that schools make an effort to encourage participation in areas where bias occurred.

Enforced by the Office of Civil Rights of the Department of Education, Title IX withstood a number of challenges during the 1980s. One such challenge came in 1984 when the Supreme Court ruled in *Grove City College v. Bell*, 465 U.S. 555 (1984), that Title IX was program specific. This meant that only programs receiving direct federal assistance were required to be compliant instead of schools and institutions as a whole. Thus under *Grove*, a university or college that discriminated against women could continue receiving federal funding so long as the discriminatory programs were not federally funded. The outrage among civil rights and women's groups was immediate following the *Grove* decision. In 1987, over President Ronald Reagan's veto, Congress passed the Civil Rights Restoration Act to overturn the *Grove* opinion. The Civil Rights Restoration Act of 1988 specified that Title IX applied to all programs or departments of a university or college if any part of the school received federal funding. Hence the Civil Rights Restoration Act placed compliance responsibility back on school systems and colleges as a whole, meaning that any part of a university or college's program that practices discrimination puts the entire school at risk of being held to be in noncompliance with Title IX.

In 1997, Title IX's twenty-fifth anniversary, a number of studies examined the impact and success of Title IX. The studies showed a dramatic increase in female participation in education and athletics. For instance, before Title IX, 43 percent of female high-school graduates enrolled in college. By 1994, the female enrollment percentage had increased to 63 percent. In graduate and professional degrees, the numbers were even more impressive. Before Title IX, women earned only 9 percent of medical degrees awarded each year, but in 1994, the percentage increased to 34 percent. In dentistry, the number grew from 1 percent to 38 percent; law degrees grew from 7 percent to 43 percent; and doctoral degrees rose from 25 percent to 44 percent.

However, Title IX's most visible achievements are in the area of athletics. Under Title IX, females are guaranteed equal treatment and opportunity, but schools are allowed latitude in establishing sports teams based on student interest, geography, budgetary constraints, and male-to-female ratio. A school's compliance depends on three primary areas: athletic financial assistance, accommodation of athletic interests and abilities, and everything else, which includes eleven areas. First, schools must ensure that the total amount of scholarships be proportional to the ratio of males and females enrolled in the university. The second area of accommodation of interests and abilities is more complicated. Institutions must meet one of the following three criteria to be compliant: first, schools must ensure that women have the opportunities to participate in proportion to their rate of enrollment; second, schools must show a long-term commitment to the expansion of programs for underrepresented groups; or third, schools must provide for the interests and abilities of the underrepresented gender. The third area is a grouping of other areas within athletics where institutions must provide equality,

Title IX has drastically increased female participation in a variety of educational programs and activities, including female participation in sporting activities such as soccer teams. © Fotosearch.

such as equipment and supplies, game and practice scheduling, travel and per diem monies, tutoring, coaching, publicity, support services, recruitment, practice and competition facilities, medical and training facilities, and housing and dining facilities.

As a result, the number of women participating in intercollegiate athletics has quadrupled since 1971. For instance, in 1971, women composed only 7.5 percent of high-school athletes by 1994, the percentage had jumped to 39 percent, and for college athletes the percentage grew from 15 percent to 37 percent. While Title IX has provided an increase in opportunities for women, the national *Report Card on Gender Equality* (June 1997) released by the National Coalition for Women and Girls in Education only gave the nation a C average. According to the *Report Card*, women still lag behind men in overall doctoral degrees awarded, the number of women coaches coaching women's team has fallen, and compared to the 73 percent of female teachers, only 35 percent of principals are women. The impact of Title IX, however, is profound. Women compose the majority of students in colleges and universities and earn more than half of all bachelor's and master's degrees.

In women's basketball, the changes have been dramatic. For instance, in 1972, 132,299 girls played high-school basketball. By the 1994–1995 season, the number had increased more than 200 percent to 412,576. The popularity of college basketball and the success of both the women's Olympic basketball team and the Women's National Basketball Association (WNBA) all attest to the significance of Title IX. Cheryl Miller, Olympic gold medal winner, outstanding collegiate basketball player, and WNBA coach, sums up the impact of Title IX in her life: "Without Title IX, I'd be nowhere" (U.S. Department of Education 1997).

See also African Americans; Civil Rights Act of 1964; Civil Rights Movement; Civil Rights Restoration Act of 1988; Department of Education; Executive Order 11246; Executive Order 11375; Ford, Gerald Rudolph; *Grove City College v. Bell*; Johnson, Lyndon Baines; Nixon, Richard Milhous; Persons with Disabilities and Affirmative Action; Sex Discrimination; Title VI of the Civil Rights Act of 1964; Title VII of the Civil Rights Act of 1964; Women's Education.

FURTHER READING: Gender Equity in Sports Project, 2000, "Overview of Title IX," October, http://bailiwick.lib.uiowa.edu/ge/Title_IX.html; National Collegiate Athletic Association, 1996, *Achieving Gender Equity: A Basic Guide to Title IX and Gender Equity in Athletics for Colleges and Universities*, Overland Park, KS: NCAA; Suggs, Welch, 2002, "Title IX at 30," *Chronicle of Higher Education*, July 21, A38; "Title IX: Gender Equity in College Sports: 6 Views," *Chronicle of Higher Education*, December 2, B7; U.S. Department of Education, 1997, "Title IX: 25 Years of Progress," June, http://www.ed.gov/pubs/TitleIX/; Valentin, Iram,

1997, "Title IX: A Brief History," August, http://www.edc.org/WomensEquity/pdffiles/t9digest.pdf.

LISA A. ENNIS

Truman, Harry (1884–1972)

Harry S Truman, the thirty-third president of the United States, is best known in the affirmative action context for his 1948 desegregation of the U.S. armed forces. Truman led the nation during the final months of World War II and through the early years of the Cold War, including the Korean War. Although he was known as a political pragmatist, Truman undertook a variety of steps to bolster the civil rights of African Americans even though this alienated many southern Democrats. Truman's 1948 Executive Order 9981, which ordered the integration of the military, helped pave the way for later desegregation successes in other areas. Also in 1948, Truman issued Executive Order 9980, which created the Fair Employment Board within the Civil Service Commission to ensure equal opportunity in government employment. Finally, in 1951, Truman issued Executive Order 10308, creating an eleven-person Commission on Government Contract Compliance, which was charged with studying the problems of discrimination by government contractors. This executive order was a precursor to President John Kennedy's famous Executive Order 10925, which utilized the term "affirmative action" for the first time in dealing with discrimination by government contractors.

Truman was born on May 8, 1884, in Lamar, Missouri, and grew up on a farm in Independence, Missouri. Truman served in the army during World War I and was eventually promoted to captain. Upon his return, he married Elizabeth Virginia Wallace on June 28, 1919. He became active in Democratic Party politics and was elected to an administrative post in Jackson County in 1922. In 1934, Truman was elected a U.S. senator. While serving as a senator, Truman developed a reputation for his honesty and straightforward manner. He further gained national fame for his efforts in investigating the defense industry during World War II. Truman's Senate investigatory committee is credited with saving some $15 billion by detecting waste and fraud in the defense industry. In this capacity, the future president also oversaw the efforts to end racial discrimination in government employment and in defense firms with government contracts. In 1944, President Franklin D. Roosevelt chose Truman as his vice presidential running mate. When Roosevelt died in office in April 1945, Truman became president. He served as president until 1953.

During World War II, under pressure from African American groups led by A. Philip Randolph, Roosevelt had issued executive orders against discrimination in the federal civil service and in defense firms that gained government contracts. Truman initially sought an expansion of opportunities for minority groups by proposing an enlargement of the New Deal programs (his efforts would eventually be termed the "Fair Deal"). For instance, in 1948, Truman delivered a message to Congress asking for significant civil rights legislation, including the renewal of the Fair Employment Practices Committee (which Congress had allowed to expire after World War II) to fight discrimination in employment. Truman also sought the establishment of a Civil Rights Division within the Justice Department. In his

President Harry S Truman, between the flags, speaks from a rostrum on the steps of the Lincoln Memorial at the 38th annual conference of the National Association for the Advancement of Colored People on June 29, 1947, in Washington, D.C. Courtesy of Library of Congress.

February 2, 1948, message to Congress, the president stated that "we believe that all men are entitled to equal opportunities for jobs, for homes, for good health and for education." However, the onset of the Cold War and the election of more conservative members of Congress constrained these broad efforts. Truman found much of his proposed Fair Deal legislation blocked by a coalition of Republicans and conservative southern Democrats. In addition, much of the focus of the country shifted to foreign affairs and the growing conflict with the Soviet Union. Truman was not an ardent believer in racial equality, and in fact he admittedly shared many of the misguided racial sentiments common during the period. On the other hand, he was a political pragmatist and understood the importance of African Americans to the Democratic Party, especially in light of increasing gains by the Republican Party among white southerners. The president also recognized the incongruity of continued segregation in the United States at a time when the American government sought moral leadership of the West in the conflict against a rival, totalitarian ideology based on Marxism and Leninism. Therefore, Truman took what actions he believed he could. For example, he appointed Irvin C. Mollison to the Customs Court, the highest judicial appointment of an African American to that date. He also appointed a Presidential Commission on Civil Rights in 1946 and supported the Indian Claims Commission Act of that same year. The president further issued an executive order in February 1948 that forbade segregation or discrimination in government agencies.

While many of his proposals designed to end segregation stalled in Congress, one area of domestic civil rights policy in which Truman was able to make a dramatic impact concerned the military. Because of the Cold War, Truman sought a peacetime draft to meet the growing military commitments of the United States, especially following the promulgation of the Truman Doctrine in 1947 in which the president pledged American military aid and assistance to nations fighting Communist insurgencies.

When Truman initially called upon Congress to enact the peacetime draft, he did not include provisions against continuing segregation in the military. This prompted African American groups to organize a variety of campaigns to push for desegregation in the military. The prestigious performance of segregated ethnic units during World War II undercut arguments by segregationists for the continued separation of races within the military. A. Philip Randolph founded the Committee against Jim Crow in Military Service and Training to organize protests against continued segregation, and within a year, this group was superseded by an even larger entity, the League for Non-violent Civil Disobedience against Military Segregation. One of the key tactics of the civil rights groups was to promote civil disobedience among African Americans. For instance, foreshadowing the tactics used broadly during the Vietnam War, African Americans were encouraged not to register with the Selective Service and to refuse to serve in the military if drafted.

To help preserve a domestic consensus on the need to counter the expansionist policies of the Soviet Union and to maintain the nation's military commitments, on July 26, 1948, Truman issued an executive order to desegregate the American military. Although desegregation proceeded slowly at first, the military soon became the most integrated component of American society. Truman's actions set the stage for later civil rights successes and the implementation of affirmative action programs in the government and in the civilian sectors of the American economy.

Although he could have run for office again in 1952, Truman chose to retire from politics. After leaving office, he essentially disappeared from public life. He published a two-volume autobiography in 1955 and 1956 and worked to establish his presidential library in Independence, Missouri. Truman died on December 26, 1972, in Kansas City, Missouri.

See also African Americans; Civil Service Commission; Democratic Party and Affirmative Action; Executive Order 10925; Jim Crow Laws; Kennedy, John Fitzgerald; Military and Affirmative Action; Randolph, Asa Philip; Republican Party and Affirmative Action; Roosevelt, Franklin Delano; Segregation.

FURTHER READING: Berman, William C., 1970, *The Politics of Civil Rights in the Truman Administration*, Columbus: Ohio State University Press; Egendorf, Laura K., 2002, *Presidents and Their Decisions: Harry S. Truman*, San Diego: Greenhaven; Hamby, Alonzo L., 1974, *Harry S. Truman and the Fair Deal*, Lexington, MA: D.C. Heath; McCullough, David, 1992, *Truman*, New York: Simon and Schuster.

TOM LANSFORD

U

Uncle Tom

The name Uncle Tom originated with the book *Uncle Tom's Cabin*, written in 1852 by Harriet Beecher Stowe, which depicted the cruelty and dehumanization of slavery in the American South by southern slave owners and the consequent suffering by black slaves. The book was hugely popular, selling more than 300,000 copies the first year. The book also won significant numbers of whites over to the abolitionist cause and put southerners on the defensive. The book became an ideological symbol in the fight against slavery, and the key character in the book was the noble figure Uncle Tom. However, since the Civil War, the term "Uncle Tom" has taken on negative connotations. Blacks who are critical of affirmative action today are sometimes referred to derogatorily as "Uncle Toms."

In current usage, the term "Uncle Tom" suggests a person who is overly loyal to whites, regardless of what has been done to him or her as a black person. Such persons rationalize their subservient condition and blame their status on themselves or other blacks. Whites are never to blame for anything, and an Uncle Tom will go out of his or her way to accommodate the whims of whites, at any social level, to show that he or she is different from other blacks who may be less accommodating. In most cases, self-gratification is the only thing at stake. In many cases, an Uncle Tom wants to share the limelight with no one, even though there may be others who exhibit similar behavior. There is seldom any other reward that may be forthcoming from manifesting this type of behavior. The label of Uncle Tom has occasionally been applied to black opponents of race-based affirmative action plans or programs or black individuals who refuse to challenge the current political/economic power structure in America.

Malcolm X made a distinction between the Field Negro and the House Negro, with the latter characterized as an Uncle Tom. The House Negro was a reference to servants who, during slavery, worked in the home of the slave master. They often ate the same food as the slave master, cooked the meals for the slave master and his family, kept the house clean, ran short errands, and tended to the white family's children. Black females who served in this last capacity were often referred to as "mammies." Basically, they were partly responsible for caring for if not raising many white children in the South, a practice that continued to modern times. The mammy was the female counterpart to the male Uncle Tom. Nevertheless, the most important trait of the House Negroes, whether male or female, was their loyalty to their master specifically and whites generally. Because they ate better, had better clothes, often slept in relatively decent quarters, and generally existed in an environment superior to that of other slaves, the House Negroes felt that they were better than other blacks. The House Negro would defend the slave master's property and loved the slave master more than he loved himself. The House Negro identified totally with the white slave master and served as his alter ego. Malcolm X argued that many of the civil rights leaders of the 1960s were Uncle Toms because of their passivity and docile nature and involvement in nonviolent protests.

On the other hand, Malcolm X spoke of the Field Negro as the slave who worked in the fields on the plantation in the hot sun from sunup to sundown, or from "can see" to "can't see." The Field Negro ate worse food, had ragged clothing, lived in a shack, and was often beaten or brutalized for not working hard enough or feigning illness. The Field Negro was highly resentful of the slave master and all whites associated with the system of slavery. Field Negroes were rebellious and were not beyond plotting their freedom and even killing the slave master and his family if that was necessary to win their liberation. Field Negroes fit the profile of Denmark Vesey, Nat Turner, and Toussaint L'Ouverture, slaves who plotted their own violent rebellions for freedom and, in some cases, killed whites in the process. It was the Field Negro whom every white slave master feared the most, for he was not beyond organizing other slaves for violent upheavals for their freedom. His hatred of slavery was so great that he prayed for his master's death and for strong winds if the master's house caught on fire. The Field Negro was a 180-degree or complete opposite of the House Negro. Because of his living and slave conditions, he felt that he had nothing to lose in thinking and acting the way that he did. Malcolm X identified himself as a Field Negro involved in the cause of black liberation.

Because Uncle Toms have often played a critical role in African American history in pacifying more militant and strident blacks who were more like the Field Negro identified by Malcolm X, they have often sought or been thrust into leadership positions. Consequently, they have often been labeled as "sellouts" in that they compromise the economic and political needs of the black community. In a study of New Orleans in the early 1960s, black leaders were characterized as either Uncle Toms, Race Diplomats, or Race Men, with the latter two types exhibiting a more aggressive style and boldness than the Uncle Tom, who was meek by comparison and never made demands on the power structure of the city.

A variant of the Uncle Tom is what has been referred to as the "black bourgeois." This type of Uncle Tom appears to be highly refined and sophisticated in his syntax, behavior, mannerisms, and other personal traits in an attempt to disassociate himself from the black race. The implication here is that blacks generally lack such sophistication and attributes that would put them in a more refined social and cultural context. The black bourgeois is a person who mimics whites by "talking proper," clearly and distinctly enunciating every word so that his speech and grammar are not associated with a "black dialect," but with white linguistic phonetics. The characteristic of living in an all-white neighborhood as the only black family, or other such distinctions that may set him apart from blacks generally, are associated with the black bourgeois type of Uncle Tom.

See also Abolitionists; American Civil War; Scapegoating/Displaced-Aggression Theories; Slavery.

FURTHER READING: Brandstadter, Evan, 1974, "Uncle Tom and Archy Moore: The Antislavery Novel as Ideological Symbol," *American Quarterly* 26, no. 2:160–175; Franklin, John Hope, 1967, *From Slavery to Freedom*, New York: Alfred A. Knopf; Frazier, E. Franklin, 1957, *The Black Bourgeoisie*, Glencoe, IL: Free Press; Locke, Mamie, 2002, "The Field Negro" and "The House Negro," in *The Malcolm X Encyclopedia*, edited by Robert L. Jenkins and Mfanya Donald Tryman, Westport, CT: Greenwood Press; Thompson, Daniel C., 1963, *The Negro Leadership Class*, Englewood Cliffs, NJ: Prentice-Hall.

MFANYA D. TRYMAN

United Nations Commission on the Status of Women

The United Nations Commission on the Status of Women (CSW) was established to promote women's rights in politics, economics, civil/social fields, and educational fields around the world. It was founded by the United Nations Economic and Social Council on June 21, 1946. The underlying purpose of the organization is to investigate and take concrete steps to eliminate gender discrimination worldwide. The commission consists of forty-five members, thirteen from African states, eleven from Asian states, four from Eastern Europe, nine from Latin American/Caribbean states, and eight from Western Europe and other states. Members of the commission are elected by the United Nations Economic and Social Council and serve four-year terms. The commission normally meets annually for eight working days to discuss current issues related to the furtherance of rights for women. The commission is informed by such related United Nations organs as the Committee on the Elimination of Discrimination against Women (CEDAW), which was empanelled in 1982 to monitor the implementation of the Convention on the Elimination of All Forms of Discrimination against Women. This convention, frequently described as an international "bill of rights" for women, was adopted by the United Nations General Assembly in 1979, though many nations, including the United States, have continued to balk at fully endorsing and/or implementing its provisions.

The CSW recognizes that the elimination of discrimination against women is an especially important prerequisite to human development and to the establishment of equal human rights worldwide. This fact was made clear by the United Nations Development Program report on human development in 1999, which noted that "there is no country that treats its women as well as its men, according to a complex measure that includes life expectancy, wealth, and education." The report, moreover, emphasized the connection between economic well-being and meaningful equality in its acknowledgment that "gender inequality is strongly correlated with poverty" in developing countries (Human Development Report 1999, 26).

In addition to promoting the general idea that women's rights are part of the struggle for human rights worldwide, the CSW makes specific recommendations to the United Nations Economic and Social Council on urgent problems in the field of women's rights that require immediate attention. For example, the World Conference on Women, which convened in China in 1995, adopted a twelve-point "platform for action" in service to women's rights globally. Charged by the United Nations Economic and Social Council to monitor worldwide implementation of that action platform, the CSW focused its 1998 annual meeting on the issues of human rights, the girl child, violence against women, and women and armed conflict, four of the items on the action platform's agenda. This CSW annual meeting also featured, for the first time in CSW history, a delegation of young girls from fifteen nations who presented their perspectives on how such major issues as teen pregnancy, forced prostitution, and the lack of reproductive freedom affect women and girls in their respective countries.

The Commission on the Status of Women is related to affirmative action in its commitment to establish equality for all persons, irrespective of race, creed, religion, gender, or other irrelevant personal characteristics. In countries such as the United States, in which there are formal legal provisions for mechanisms of affirmative action aimed at eliminating gender discrimination, the link between the CSW agenda and affirmative action is explicit. Insofar as affirmative action refers to policies and programs intended to increase the numbers of ethnic minorities and women in employment and education, as it does in developed nations like the United States, the CSW endorses and monitors such efforts. Today in the United States, affirmative action policies and voluntary hiring decisions have increased the presence of women at all levels of government, as well as in many other areas of employment and in higher education. Still, the evidence is compelling that some fields of employment remain male dominated, and that even within fields in which women are employed in greater numbers than ever before, "glass" walls and ceilings continue to thwart their advance to the highest echelons of private and public employment. Economic discrimination in the form of gender pay gaps and sexual harassment across personal and professional dimensions of women's lives continue to make true gender equity an unrealized goal even in so-called developed nations like the United States and Great Britain. In nations where there is either no "affirmative action" per se, or where affirmative action is practiced, but only provides steps toward eliminating non-gender-based forms of discrimination, the link between affirmative action and the global gender equity sought by the CSW would still be nonexistent. In principle, however, it seems fair to say that the CSW commitment to discover and remedy the many forms of discrimination faced by women globally shares the same broad spirit of equity that animates formal affirmative action mechanisms in place throughout the world.

See also Convention on the Elimination of All Forms of Discrimination against Women; Glass Ceilings; Global Implementation of Affirmative Action Programs; Great Britain and Affirmative Action; United Nations Conferences on Women.

FURTHER READING: Gardner, Susan, and Kathryn Lewis, 2000, "Sexual Harassment Investigations: A Portrait of Contradictions," *Advanced Management Journal* 65, no.4:29–37; "The Gender Pay Gap Must Go," 1999, *New Statesman* 128:1–2; Higginbotham, Elizabeth, and Mary Romero, 1997, *Women and Work: Exploring Race, Ethnicity, and Class*, Women and Work, vol. 6, Thousand Oaks, CA: Sage Publications; Kessler-Harris, Alice, 2001, *In Pursuit of Equity: Women, Men, and the Quest for Economic citizenship in 20th Century America*, New

York: Oxford University Press; Linder, Doris H., 2001, "Equality for Women: The Contribution of Scandinavian Women at the United Nations, 1946–66," *Scandinavian Studies* 73, no. 2:165–208; Miller, Will, and Kerr Reid, 2000, "A Study of the Advancement of Women in Municipal Government Bureaucracies: Persistence of Glass Ceilings?" *Women and Politics* 21, no. 1:35–53; Nussbaum, Martha C., 1999, *Sex and Social Justice*, New York: Oxford University Press; Nussbaum, Martha C., 2000, *Women and Human Development*, New York: Cambridge University Press; Peters, Julie, and Andrea Wolper, eds., 1995, *Women's Rights, Human Rights*, New York and London: Routledge; Tobach, Ethel, and Betty Rosoff, eds., 1994, *Challenging Racism and Sexism: Alternatives to Genetic Explanations*, Genes and Gender, vol. 7, New York: Feminist Press; United Nations Commission on the Status of Women, web page: www.undp.org/fwcw/csw.htm.

PAUL M. HUGHES

United Nations Conferences on Women

To date, there have been five United Nations Conferences on Women. Each conference is an opportunity for the participants involved to review the status of the treatment of women throughout the world and to see how women are treated economically and politically in comparison to their male counterparts, as well as an opportunity for organizations to outline ways in which all individuals can be treated equally regardless of gender or race. Conferences have been held in Mexico City, Copenhagen, Nairobi, Beijing, and New York. The preparatory committee for each conference is the United Nations Commission on the Status of Women (CSW). The CSW uses conferences of this sort to bring its issues to the forefront of the international community. The largest of these conferences was the Fourth World Conference on Women in Beijing, China. In fact, the Beijing Conference was the largest conference ever sponsored by the United Nations. Held in 1995, this meeting was a global event that attracted thousands of participants from all over the world, including representatives from governments, the private sector, and nongovernmental organizations.

The most significant outcome of this conference was *The Beijing Declaration and Platform for Action*. This document, which was adopted by representatives from 189 countries, outlines the goals of equality, development, and peace for women worldwide. Many of its goals build on the commitments made during the United Nations Decade of Women, 1976–1985.

The platform lists twelve areas of concern for the advancement of women: poverty, education and training, health, violence, armed conflict, the economy, decision making, institutional mechanisms, human rights, the media, the environment, and the girl child. In each area, the document outlines specific actions that need to be taken so that its goals can be realized. Actions are specified for each kind of participating organization. The most recent conference, in New York in 2000, was an opportunity for the organizations that adopted the platform to review their goals and objectives. An update was given on the status of women worldwide, and additional actions were outlined to accelerate the progress of obtaining equality. The CSW plans to sponsor additional conferences of this sort until all of its goals are accomplished.

See also Convention on the Elimination of All Forms of Discrimination against Women; United Nations Commission on the Status of Women.

FURTHER READING: Auth, Janice, 1998, *To Beijing and Beyond: Pittsburgh and the United Nations Fourth World Conference on Women*, Pittsburgh: University of Pittsburgh Press; Chittister, Joan D., 1996, *Beyond Beijing: The Next Step for Women: A Personal Journal*, Ashland, OH: Sheed and Ward.

AIMÉE HOBBY RHODES

U.S. Commission on Civil Rights

The U.S. Commission on Civil Rights, initially established by Congress by the enactment of the Civil Rights Act of 1957, was intended to be a temporary bipartisan agency. During the first quarter century of its existence, the commission was a leading voice for civil rights reform. During the 1970s and 1980s, the commission expanded its work to include gender-based discrimination. During the 1980s, the commission began examining issues such as the extent of income inequality between blacks and whites in various parts of the country. The commission additionally lost part of its strength during this decade due to criticisms and attacks from the Reagan administration. At the onset of the Clinton administration in 1993, however, the commission regained strength and focus and has, in recent years, studied and reported on affirmative action in higher education. Since being established in 1957, the commission has published more than 70 reports containing recommendations to Congress and the president and more than 160 additional reports on civil rights matters. Another 240 reports have been produced by the state advisory committees.

The commission was originally proposed in the Eisenhower administration by Attorney General Herbert Brownell in 1956 as part of a more comprehensive civil rights bill. The legislation eventually approved by Congress was a watered-down version intended to mute southern opposition. The commission was originally established as a six-member body, with no more than three of its appointees from any one political party. The six members would be appointed by the president with the advice and consent of the Senate. The commission was directed by Congress to investigate claims that black citizens were being deprived of their right to vote in federal elections, to study and collect information on discrimination, and to submit reports, findings, and recommendations to Congress. In President Dwight Eisenhower's words, the role of the commission was to "put the facts on the table" (Fagin 1983, 2622).

During the first twenty-five years of its existence, the commission was a leading voice for civil rights reform. The Civil Rights Act of 1964, the Fair Housing Act, and the Voting Rights Act of 1965 were among the more important pieces of legislation that the commission recommended to Congress and the president for their consideration. During the 1970s and 1980s, the commission expanded its work to include gender-based discrimination. During the 1980s, the commission began examining issues such as the extent of income inequality between blacks and whites in various parts of the country (Williams 1984, 29). Up to this point, the one controversial episode involving the commission took place when President Richard M. Nixon asked for and received the resignation of Theodore Hesburgh because of his support for the mandatory busing of schoolchildren to achieve racial balance, a position opposed by Nixon (Thompson 1985, 181–182).

The Reagan administration took a decidedly different approach to civil rights.

Breaking with the consensus that had developed during the previous two decades, the administration directed the Justice Department's Civil Rights Division to scale back its enforcement efforts, vehemently opposed affirmative action, and supported tax-exempt status for Bob Jones University, an institution that engaged in discriminatory practices. As a result, the commission became what Detlefsen called an "in-house critic of executive branch policies" (Detlefsen 1991, 140).

In 1982, President Ronald Reagan attempted to reshape the commission by firing two commissioners (Chair Arthur Flemming and Stephen Horn) who disagreed with his administration's civil rights policies. The commission persisted in opposing Reagan, demanding gender and racial data on appointments made in the executive branch. When the administration refused to provide the data, the commission issued a subpoena.

In 1983, Reagan tried again to change the commission's composition. He nominated three Democrats for the commission (one of whom, Morris Abram, had been Martin Luther King Jr.'s lawyer) who were opposed by much of the civil rights establishment because they were perceived as not being sympathetic to the movement. As part of a compromise, Reagan and congressional leaders agreed to reconstitute the commission by statute. Congress then rewrote the law creating the commission, changing its composition, method of appointment, and tenure. The commission would now be composed of eight commissioners, four appointed by the president and four by Congress. The president would designate the chair and vice chair of the commission from among its members with the concurrence of a majority of the commissioners. The commissioners, who no longer require Senate confirmation, serve six-year terms. The president may remove a member only for neglect of duty or malfeasance in office. The change gave Reagan an effective majority on the commission. It was during this time that the Citizens' Commission on Civil Rights, an independent bipartisan citizens' group headed by Flemming, was established.

During this time, Commissioner Clarence Pendleton became a lightning rod for those opposed to the administration's policies. An African American businessman, Pendleton enthusiastically confronted his opponents, at one point describing the concept of comparable worth as "the looniest idea since Looney Tunes came on the screen" (Blum, 52). Not only was Pendleton condemned by the civil rights leadership, but one of the other Reagan appointees, John Bunzel, called on Pendleton to resign. Bunzel himself resigned from the commission, calling the divided body a "little Beirut on the Potomac" (Detlefsen 1991, 148). In 1986, Democrats in Congress reduced the agency's funding as a rebuke to Pendleton. Pendleton remained as chair of the commission until his death in 1988.

During the 1990s, the commission shifted back toward what might be called the traditional view of civil rights policy that had developed during the 1960s and 1970s. Mary Frances Berry was designated by President Bill Clinton in 1993 as chair of the commission. Under her leadership, the commission has investigated police brutality, has called on colleges and professional sports teams to end the use of Native American mascots and team names, and has challenged the ending of race-based admissions policies in a number of state colleges and universities.

In 1999, Elsie Meeks became the first Native American appointed to the commission. In 2001, the commission held hearings and conducted an investigation of the disputed presidential election in Florida. The commission concluded that the election had been marred by voter disenfranchisement. In 2002, the commission sent staff to Florida to monitor the state's gubernatorial election. In 2002, the commission also attempted to block President George W. Bush's effort to replace Clinton appointee Victoria Wilson. The commission's chair, Mary Frances Berry, contended that Wilson had been appointed to a full six-year term in 2000. The Bush administration argued that Wilson had been appointed to complete the unexpired term of A. Leon Higginbotham Jr., who had died in 1998. The U.S. Court of Appeals for the District of Columbia Circuit held that Wilson's term had expired and that she could be replaced by Bush's appointee, Peter Kirsanow, a conservative black attorney who was also an opponent of affirmative action.

A full-time staff director, appointed by the president with the commissioners' approval, is responsible for the agency's day-to-day activities. The staff director serves at the pleasure of the president. The commission also maintains six regional offices (Kansas City, Kansas; Washington, D.C.; Chicago, Illinois; Denver, Colorado; Atlanta, Georgia; and Los Angeles, California). There are also fifty-one state advisory committees, one for each state and the District of Columbia. The members of these committees serve two-year terms.

The commission meets monthly and convenes several times a year to conduct hearings, conferences, consultations, and briefings. The commission lacks enforcement powers and refers complaints that it receives to federal, state, and local government agencies for action. The commission also maintains the Robert S. Rankin Civil Rights Memorial Library, named for the late member, at its headquarters in Washington, D.C.

See also Bush, George W.; Civil Rights Act of 1957; Civil Rights Act of 1964; Civil Rights Act of 1968; Clinton, William Jefferson; Department of Justice; Eisenhower, Dwight David; Fair Housing Amendments Act of 1988; Nixon, Richard Milhous; Reagan, Ronald; Voting Rights Act of 1965.

FURTHER READING: Blum, Linda M., 1991, *Between Feminism and Labor: The Significance of the Comparable Worth Movement*, Los Angeles: University of California Press; Detlefsen, Robert R., 1991, *Civil Rights under Reagan*, San Francisco: Institute for Contemporary Studies; Pear, Robert, 1985, "Civil Rights Agency Splits in Debate on Narrowing Definition of Equality," *New York Times* October 14, 13; Thompson, Robert J., 1985, "The Commission on Civil Rights," in *The Reagan Administration and Human Rights*, edited by Tinsley E. Yarbrough, New York: Praeger.

JEFFREY KRAUS

United States v. Carolene Products Co.

See Discrete and Insular Minority; Stone, Harlan Fiske.

United States v. Fordice, 505 U.S. 717 (1992)

In *United States v. Fordice*, the Supreme Court indicated that states have an affirmative duty to ensure that the public school system within the state is race neutral in its operation and is free from the results of its previous history of segregation and discrimination. This case is one of the major desegregation cases issued by the Supreme Court in recent years, is one of the longest civil rights cases in history, and is considered by some a threat to the continued viability of state-supported historically black institutions. The case also illustrates how protracted desegregation and antidiscrimination litigation can be even with judiciary action attempting to rectify the claimed problems. Finally, the case is especially important in the affirmative action debate because it arguably demonstrates that affirmative action programs are still needed in higher education to achieve and ensure racial diversity in the classroom.

The saga of desegregation in Mississippi has a long history dating back to the early 1960s when James Meredith became the first black to gain entrance into the state's flagship university, the University of Mississippi. Desegregation in the modern era began in 1975 when a group of blacks in Mississippi sued the state in federal district court claiming that the school system still had not adequately integrated. The plaintiffs claimed that Mississippi's school system was in violation of Title VI of the Civil Rights Act of 1964. Jake Ayers was designated as lead plaintiff because his name was first alphabetically among the plaintiffs, and thus the case was originally captioned *Ayers v. Fordice*, 674 F. Supp. 1523 (1987). The plaintiffs were requesting equity in the state's higher education system and wanted more funding for the state's three historically black colleges. They also asserted numerous claims of discrimination against the defendants. Among other things, they contended that at the time of *Brown v. Board of Education*, 347 U.S. 483 (1954), Mississippi had established separate systems of public higher education and that the institutions designated to serve blacks were inferior to the institutions serving whites. Plaintiffs contended that from 1954 onward the state of Mississippi had continued a racially dual system of public higher education through policies and practices governing student admissions and employment of faculty and administrative staff and through the operation of white universities or branches close to black universities. Plaintiffs also contended that black students and faculty had been denied equal opportunity by Mississippi's discrimination against the state's black institutions in respect to institutional missions, number and level of academic programs, quality of instructional staff, allocation of land-grant functions, level of quality of buildings, and distribution of financial resources. The plaintiffs sought extensive injunctive relief to remedy the alleged discrimination.

The state of Mississippi did not dispute the existence of a segregated system through 1962, but the state contended that after 1962 it had maintained nondiscriminatory admissions and operational policies and had expended substantial affirmative efforts in good faith in respect to students, faculty and staff, and resource allocation to promote desegregation of the state's public universities. The state denied that Mississippi's present university system was unlawful and denied equal opportunity to certain minority students. Mississippi operated under a unitary board, which had been created in 1910 and oversaw ten higher-education institutions in total, consisting of three comprehensive universities, four regional universities, two historically white universities, and one urban university. Five universities were classified as predominantly white institutions: the University of Mississippi (1844), Mississippi State University (1878), Mississippi University for Women (1884), the University of Southern Mississippi (1910), and Delta State University (1924). Alcorn State University (1871), Jackson State University (1940), and Mississippi Valley State University (1946) were classified as black institutions.

Many of these schools had duplicative programs, and several of these schools were only a few miles apart from each other.

In the mid-1980s, nearly all white Mississippi students attended predominantly white universities, and three-quarters of all black Mississippi students went to historically black universities. The negotiations between the two parties in the case languished for twelve years, as they were unable to reach a settlement that was satisfactory, and the case went to trial in the federal district court in 1987. After a trial in 1987, the district court concluded that no constitutional violation existed because the state's actions were racially neutral, had been developed and implemented in good faith, and did not substantially contribute to the racial identification of the schools. The court acknowledged that the state had an affirmative duty to change the policies and practices of the former segregated system, and it questioned whether the same standard of racial mixture as established in *Green v. School Board of New Kent County*, 391 U.S. 430 (1968), could be applied to higher education. The district court also considered a case that involved single-race 4-H clubs and a case that involved the construction of an extension campus for Auburn University and whether that constituted a dual system. The district court held that these cases showed that for higher education "the affirmative duty to desegregate does not contemplate either restricting choice or the achievement of any racial balance." The Fifth Circuit Court of Appeals affirmed the decision in 1990, and the decision was appealed to the U.S. Supreme Court.

On November 13, 1991, the U.S. Supreme Court heard the case. The primary issue identified by the Court was whether the state of Mississippi had met its affirmative duty to eliminate its former de jure system of segregation in its higher-education system. On June 26, 1992, Justice Byron White, in a nearly unanimous decision (with only Justice Antonin Scalia in part dissenting), wrote an opinion reversing the district court decision and held that merely implementing race-neutral policies did not constitute meeting the state's affirmative duty to eliminate de jure segregation. The Court stated that the state's affirmative duty to reform its system continued "if policies traceable to the de jure system are still in force and have discriminatory effects." Phrased another way, if policies are not educationally justified and are remnants of the past, the state has a constitutional duty under the Fourteenth Amendment and a statutory affirmative duty under Title VI of the Civil Rights Act of 1964 to dismantle its dual system. The Court also concluded that the wrong standard had been applied, since it was possible that race-neutral policies might be reinforcing policies that had been segregative in their original intent and effect. These policies, therefore, also had to be reexamined. For example, the record in the case indicated that the state continued to allow varying standardized admission scores between black and white institutions, and the Court believed that such policies continued to contribute to the existing racial identities of the state's universities and colleges. The Court agreed with the lower courts that colleges and universities were different from public schools and had specific missions, but the Court did not agree that race-neutral policies combined with a student's ability to choose a university cured the constitutional violation of a dual system.

The Court also found that a student's choice resulted from many factors, and some of these factors were traceable to the former de jure system of segregation. The Court further examined four areas of policy: admission standards, program duplication, institutional mission assignments, and the continued operation of the state's eight universities. In regard to admission standards, Mississippi's universities and colleges used the American College Testing examination for admittance, but the acceptable score and standards varied across the state. Most of the predominantly white universities used 15 as an acceptable score, while most predominantly black schools used 13 as an acceptable score. The Court specifically held:

> Although the state's current admission policy requiring higher minimum composite scores on the American College Testing Program (ACT) for the five historically white institutions than for the three historically black universities derived from policies enacted in the 1970's to redress the problem of student unpreparedness, the policy is constitutionally suspect because it was originally enacted in 1963 by three white universities to discriminate against black students who at the time had an ACT score well below the required minimum.

The U.S. Supreme Court also found this policy traceable to the segregated system. The Court attacked the validity of the mission statements when racially different schools with the same mission had different admission standards. The Court held that the mission assignments were based on the old de jure organization, and the differing missions did not justify the differing admission standards. The Court also addressed program duplication between the predominantly white and predominantly black institutions. The Court found that there was "unnecessary duplication" of programs. While the Court stopped short of saying that this issue was attributed to the former system, it ordered that this issue needed to be investigated by the lower court on remand. The Court established that Mississippi had the burden of proof to show that the duplication of programs was educationally justified and not merely the remnant of Mississippi's segregated past.

Finally, the Court questioned the need for eight separate state-operated universities in a state where four or fewer would be sufficient for its population and available funding. The Court described the excessive number of institutions (each dedicated to a different student population) as "wasteful and irrational." However, the Court did not suggest that any universities should be closed or merged. The Court stated that in remand the district court should address the issue of the need for eight public state institutions and whether the retention of all these institutions affected student choice. It also stated that the full range of the state's higher-education policy activities should be examined, including funding of the historically black universities under the proper standard to determine whether the state was taking the necessary steps to dismantle its prior system. In light of all of these holdings, the Court found that Mississippi had maintained a segregated school system and had not met its affirmative duty to dismantle its dual system. The Court denied the plaintiffs' request to upgrade only the historically black institutions of Mississippi and remanded the case for further district court action consistent with its ruling.

Two concurring opinions and one dissenting opinion were rendered in the case. Justices Sandra Day O'Connor and Clarence Thomas each issued concurring opinions stressing that it was the state of Mississippi's burden to prove that it had removed remnants of past desegregation and that there was no compulsion from the Court to eliminate the historically black universities. Justice Scalia agreed that the admissions practices by the state of Mississippi were suspect and should be changed, but he dissented from the majority of the rest of the opinion. Scalia took issue with the Court putting too great a burden on the state and with the ambiguity of terms like "educationally justifiable." He believed that the race-neutral policies and open admissions were sufficient to redress any of the remnants of Mississippi's segregated higher-education system.

On remand back to the Fifth Circuit Court, the court gave both parties time to propose remedies. The court directed counsel to report on what policies and practices were changeable and what were remnants of a dual system and to offer a proposal on how to eliminate those practices and policies. The court asked the parties to examine all areas that were agreed upon to be remnants of past segregated systems. The plaintiffs offered the following proposal: (1) the continued operation of all the public four-year institutions; (2) revision of the institutional admissions policies; (3) more minority representation on college boards and trustee boards; (4) provisions for scholarships for underrepresented populations at predominantly white universities; (5) hiring more minority faculty at predominantly white universities; (6) improvement of physical plant facilities; and (7) a redefinition of the role of the community college system as a feeder program to the four-year system.

On the contrary, the state of Mississippi proposed the following: (1) closing Mississippi Valley State University; (2) merging the Mississippi University for Women with the University of Southern Mississippi; (3) absorbing Alcorn State University, which had been designated as the state's black land-grant college administratively, and having it report to Mississippi State University, which was the white land-grant college; (4) merging Delta State University with the University of Mississippi; (5) closing the University of Mississippi School of Dentistry in Jackson; (6) closing the Mississippi State University of Veterinary Medicine in Starkville; and (7) giving control of the "Universities Center" (a facility that was centered on the Jackson State University campus, but for which black Jackson state had no control over) to the administration at Jackson State University.

As a result of these conflicting proposals, the parties did not reach an agreement in the case. Furthermore, each side accused the other of not cooperating by not providing needed information. The court threatened to place sanctions on both parties if full cooperation and progress were not made by both parties. The court issued a remedial decree that directed implementation of new admission standards at all Mississippi universities for first-time freshmen, and new academic programs and resources for Alcorn State University and Jackson State University. The decree also called for the establishment of an endowment trust for Alcorn State and Jackson State for educational enhancement and racial diversity and additional studies of ways to further desegregate Delta State University and Mississippi Valley State University as an alternative to consolidating these universities.

The original lead plaintiff died while this case crept through the courts, and in March 1996, the district court designated Congressman Bennie Thompson as the lead plaintiff. Settlement talks began again in 1997, but were unproductive, and the case returned to the district court in 1998 for instructions on how to further implement the decree. Mississippi's desegregation case became the longest civil rights case, spanning some twenty-six years. In April 2001, a tentative agreement was finally reached and now awaits the federal court's approval. The proposed settlement sends $500 million to the state's black colleges, Jackson State

University, Alcorn State University, and Mississippi Valley State University. The agreement calls for $246 million to be spent on academic programs, $75 million for capital improvements and buildings, and $70 million in public endowments, as well as $35 million in private endowments. The plaintiffs, the college board members, and the state attorney general have signed the settlement. It is unclear how many more years will elapse before this case is ultimately concluded. Some scholars estimate that further litigation may take years. As nineteen states operate historically black institutions, this case also questions the continued constitutional and statutory viability of these separate schools.

See also Brown v. Board of Education; Civil Rights Act of 1964; De Facto and De Jure Segregation; Discrimination; Fourteenth Amendment; Historically Black Colleges and Universities; O'Connor, Sandra Day; *Plessy v. Ferguson*; Scalia, Antonin; Segregation; Thomas, Clarence; Title VI of the Civil Rights Act of 1964; *United States v. Louisiana*; White, Byron Raymond.

FURTHER READING: Brown, Christopher M., 1999, *The Quest to Define Collegiate Desegregation: Black Colleges, Title VI Compliance, and Post-Adams Litigation*, Westport, CT: Greenwood Press; Dentler, Robert, Catherine Baltzell, and Daniel Sullivan, 1983, *University on Trial: The Case of the University of North Carolina*, Cambridge, MA: Abt Books; Holmes, Dwight Wendell Oliver, 1969, *The Evolution of the Negro College*, New York: Arno Press; Preer, Jean L., 1982, *Lawyers v. Educators: Black Colleges and Desegregation in Public Higher Education*, Westport, CT: Greenwood Press; Roebuck, Julian, and Komanduri Murty, 1993, *Historically Black Colleges and Universities: Their Place in American Higher Education*, New York: Praeger; Sims, Serbrenia, 1994, *Diversifying Historically Black Colleges and Universities: A New Higher Education Paradigm*, Westport, CT: Greenwood Press.

F. ERIK BROOKS

United States v. Louisiana, 9 F.3d 1159 (5th Cir. 1993)

United States v. Louisiana, along with *United States v. Fordice*, 505 U.S. 717 (1992), illustrates how protracted desegregation and antidiscrimination litigation can be even with judiciary action attempting to rectify the claimed problems. *United States v. Louisiana* and *United States v. Fordice* are also important in the affirmative action debate because they arguably demonstrate that affirmative action programs are still needed in higher education to achieve and ensure racial diversity in the classroom.

Title VI of the Civil Rights Act, which prohibits federal funding for any institution that practices discrimination, was enacted in 1964 and codified the Supreme Court's ruling in *Brown v. Board of Education*, 347 U.S. 483 (1954). Five years later, the Department of Health, Education, and Welfare (whose education part is now the Department of Education) determined that there were fifteen southern and border states, including Louisiana, that were in violation of Title VI of the 1964 Civil Rights Act. Louisiana refused to submit a desegregation plan because it believed that it had taken the necessary steps and actions to fulfill the compliance requirements of Title VI. Louisiana believed that it had an open admissions policy at all its colleges and universities and that this constituted compliance.

In 1974, the Department of Health, Education, and Welfare referred the case to the U.S. Justice Department. The Justice Department filed a lawsuit against Louisiana seeking compliance with Title VI and the Fourteenth Amendment. From 1979 until 1981, active negotiations took place. Following these two years of intense negotiations, a tentative agreement was reached. A federal district court three-judge panel approved the consent decree. Prior to the implementation of the consent decree, the U.S. Justice Department intervened and moved for additional relief in the court.

In 1988, the federal district court in Louisiana entered an order of finding of discrimination in the school systems of the state, and Louisiana was found liable. The court ordered Louisiana to submit a remedial plan; however, the litigants could not develop a plan satisfactory to all parties. In 1989, the court ordered a plan based largely on a suggested plan from a special master appointed by the court. Louisiana appealed the court's order to the federal Court of Appeals for the Fifth Circuit and then to the U.S. Supreme Court. In 1990, the U.S. Supreme Court dismissed the defendant's appeal "for want of jurisdiction." The three-judge panel was dissolved, and the case was remanded to the federal district court with instructions to revise the implementation date of the original order.

A month later, while *United States v. Louisiana* was still under consideration, the Fifth Circuit Court of Appeals met en banc (as a whole) and issued a decision in the Mississippi desegregation case *United States v. Fordice*. In October 1990, relying on the ruling in the Mississippi case, the district court vacated the earlier decision in favor of the plaintiffs and granted a summary judgment in favor of Louisiana. The U.S. Justice Department and historically black Southern University appealed the summary judgment.

In 1991, the U.S. Supreme Court decided to review the decision in *United States v. Fordice*. The Fifth Circuit Court of Appeals stayed all further proceedings in the Louisiana case pending the outcome of the Mississippi case in the U.S. Supreme Court. In 1992, the U.S. Supreme Court vacated the judgment in *United States v. Fordice* and remanded it to the Fifth Circuit Court of Appeals for further proceedings consistent with the ruling in *Fordice*. The U.S. Justice Department requested that the Fifth Circuit Court of Appeals remand the *Fordice* case back to the federal district court, and the case was so remanded.

In September 1992, the district court summoned all parties in *United States v. Louisiana* to appear and show probable cause why the court should not reissue the remedial plan rendered in 1990. The court granted a continuance in the case until November 1992 so that all parties would have an opportunity to reach a compromise. In November 1992, an agreement had not been reached. On December 23, 1992, the court issued a remedial order that closely resembled the previous order, with the exception of a merger between historically white Louisiana State University and historically black Southern University's law schools. In 1993, the U.S. Justice Department filed a motion for reconsideration and to alter or amend judgment. In January 1993, the court issued orders and reasons and denied the Justice Department's motions. Currently, Louisiana is under an out-of-court settlement that addresses governance structure and admissions as a result of this litigation and years of alleged discrimination.

See also Brown v. Board of Education; Civil Rights Act of 1964; Department of Education; Department of Justice; Equal Protection Clause; Fourteenth Amendment; Title VI of the Civil Rights Act of 1964; *United States v. Fordice*.

FURTHER READING: Preer, Jean L., 1982, *Lawyers v. Educators: Black Colleges and Desegregation in Public Higher Education*, Westport, CT: Greenwood Press.

F. ERIK BROOKS

United States v. Paradise, 480 U.S. 149 (1987)

In *United States v. Paradise*, the Supreme Court affirmed the constitutionality of a lower court order that the State Department of Public Safety in Alabama set racial quotas to hire black police officers, stipulating that one black state trooper must be hired or promoted for every white state trooper hired or promoted until at least 25 percent of the upper ranks of the department were black. A federal district court in 1972 found that there had never been a black trooper in the thirty-seven-year history of the state patrol and ordered the department to end its "pervasive, systematic, and obstinate discriminatory exclusion of Blacks." The department resisted the order and did not promote any blacks above the entry level for more than another decade, even after several more lawsuits and court rulings brought against it. The original case was brought by the National Association for the Advancement of Colored People (NAACP) in 1972 on behalf of Phillip Paradise Jr. as a challenge to "the Department's longstanding practice of excluding blacks from employment."

This case exemplified the Court's continued belief that the government had an inherent duty to provide for societal interests by supporting and providing remedies for past discriminatory public practices against blacks, particularly where discrimination was being perpetuated by public entities (*Franks v. Bowman Transportation Co.*, 424 U.S. 747 [1976]). This interest differed from requirements the Court imposed upon private firms (*United Steelworkers of America v. Weber*, 443 U.S. 193 [1979]). In its ruling, the Court stated that

> the race-conscious relief ordered by the District Court is justified by a compelling governmental interest in eradicating the Department's pervasive, systematic, and obstinate discriminatory exclusion of blacks. The contention that promotion relief is unjustified because the Department has been found to have committed only hiring discrimination is without merit, since promotion, like hiring, has been a central concern of the District Court since the action's commencement. The Department's intentional hiring discrimination had a profound effect on the force's upper ranks by precluding blacks from competing for promotions. Moreover, the record amply demonstrates that the Department's promotional procedure is itself discriminatory, resulting in an upper rank structure that totally excludes blacks. The District Court's enforcement order is also supported by the societal interest in compliance with federal court judgments. The Department has had a consistent history of resistance to the District Court's orders, and relief was imposed only after the Department failed to live up to its court-approved commitments.

The Court looked at four factors to determine whether an affirmative action program was permissible and met the strict scrutiny test: (1) the efficacy of alternative remedies; (2) the flexibility and duration of the relief; (3) the relationship of the numerical goals to the percentage of minorities in the relevant population; and (4) the impact of the relief on the rights of third parties (*Fullilove v. Klutznick*, 448 U.S. 448 [1980]).

This case also involved the use of quotas in an affirmative action program as a means to achieve racial equality. In applying this quota system, the Court defended it by testing its intent and contents against the four factors of the preceding analysis. The Court imposed a one-for-one requirement, the hiring of one black officer for every white trooper hired or promoted until at least 25 percent of the upper ranks of the department were composed of blacks, and ruled that this requirement was "necessary to eliminate the effects of the Department's long-term, open, and pervasive discrimination, including the absolute exclusion of blacks in the upper ranks; to ensure expeditious compliance with the 1979 and 1981 Decrees by inducing the implementation of a promotional procedure that would not have an adverse racial impact; and to eradicate the ill effects of the Department's delay in producing such a procedure." The one-for-one requirement met the aforementioned test because it "does not impose an unacceptable burden on innocent white promotion applicants," was "temporary and limited in nature" (it was only used once and could never be used again), "does not bar, but simply postpones, advancement by some whites," and "does not require the layoff or discharge of whites or the promotion of unqualified blacks over qualified whites."

See also Franks v. Bowman; Fullilove v. Klutznick; National Association for the Advancement of Colored People; Quotas; Supreme Court and Affirmative Action; *United Steelworkers of America v. Weber.*

FURTHER READING: Davis, Kenneth R., 2003, "Undo Hardship: An Argument for Affirmative Action as a Mandatory Remedy in Systemic Racial Discrimination Cases," *Dickinson Law Review* 107 (winter): 503–570; Donze, Patricia L., 2000, "The Supreme Court's Denial of *Certiorari* in *Dallas Fire Fighters* Leaves Unsettled the Standard for Compelling Remedial Interests," *Case Western Reserve University Law Review* 50 (spring): 759–796.

GLENN L. STARKS

United States v. Virginia

See Gender-Based Affirmative Action.

United Steelworkers of America v. Weber, 443 U.S. 193 (1979)

The 1979 U.S. Supreme Court case *United Steelworkers of America v. Weber* held that affirmative action quota plans utilized in the private sector were permissible under Title VII of the Civil Rights Act of 1964. That is, the Supreme Court interpreted Title VII as allowing employers and unions in the private sector to use quotas in instituting race-conscious programs to eliminate racial imbalances in traditionally segregated job categories, so long as they were specifically designed to eradicate past incidents of racial discrimination. Thus, in the case, the Court held that a private union and a private employer could adopt a voluntary race-conscious preference plan in order to respond to previous institutional racial discrimination.

The facts surrounding the *Weber* case had their origin with the labor practices of Kaiser Aluminum and Chemical Corp. Kaiser, as an employer, had a long history of racial segregation in certain skilled labor jobs. In order to rectify racial imbalances at certain jobs within Kaiser (and avoid Title VII lawsuits and the loss of federal contracts), Kaiser, along with the United Steelworkers union, put into place a race-based affirmative action plan. The United Steelworkers were challenged by a white employee, Weber, over its use of a quota system for training individuals. The program allegedly discriminated against more qualified whites in favor of less qualified blacks to raise the quota of blacks in the program in an effort to achieve racial balance in certain job categories. The Kaiser plan was designed to grant racial preference by reserving 50 percent of the places in its training program for blacks. During the first year of the plan's operation, seven black and six white trainees were chosen from the plant's workforce. The most senior black trainees, despite having less seniority than several white applicants who bid for admission to the program, were accepted over white applicants. Weber, who had been denied admission to the training program, filed a class-action suit in federal district court alleging that the affirmative action racial quota system had denied him his constitutional rights under the Equal Protection Clause of the Fourteenth Amendment. He declared that Kaiser, by its use of a quota, had reduced Weber's future work potential by granting preferences to less qualified junior black employees to the detriment of senior white employees.

The federal district court held that Kaiser's operative plan was racially discriminatory and a violation of Title VII since Kaiser had used race as a factor in hiring and selecting apprentices for training in the program. The court granted injunctive relief and entered judgment in favor of Weber. The federal circuit court of appeals affirmed the judgment of the lower court and further ruled that all employment preferences based on race, including those incidental to bona fide affirmative action plans, violated Title VII's mandate against racial discrimination in employment.

The case was then appealed to the U.S. Supreme Court, where it was argued on March 28, 1979, and the Court ultimately rendered its decision on June 27, 1979. Justice William Brennan, speaking for the Court, offered a rationale for permitting the affirmative action quota plan to stand in certain contexts to redress previous racial segregation and/or imbalance in the workforce. Brennan interpreted Title VII as allowing employers and unions in the private sector to use quotas in instituting race-conscious programs to eliminate racial imbalances in traditionally segregated job categories. Brennan justified the decision by alleging that the interests of white employees were not being trammeled, as no white employees were discharged or replaced by blacks. Therefore, the majority decision concluded that the Kaiser plan was not a violation of Title VII of the Civil Rights Act of 1964. The decision further asserted that the instituted quota system in this case was no bar to advancement because half of the persons involved in the program would be white. The plan was also ultimately thought to be justified by the Court given the temporary nature of the plan in question.

Finally, the majority decision relied on a previous Supreme Court decision, *Albemarle Paper Co. v. Moody*, 422 U.S. 405 (1975), wherein it stated that it was requiring "employers and unions to self-examine and self-evaluate their employment practices and to endeavor to eliminate, so far as possible, the last vestiges of an unfortunate and ignominious page in this country's history." Hence the Court held that Title VII allows the voluntary use of race-conscious preferences for temporary periods of time to eliminate the last vestiges of racial discrimination and/or segregation, even if this is to the detriment of white workers who did not individually volunteer to be subject to the plan.

See also Albemarle Paper Co. v. Moody; Brennan, William Joseph; Civil Rights Act of 1964; Equal Protection Clause; Fourteenth Amendment; Quotas; Reverse Discrimination; Supreme Court and Affirmative Action; Title VII of the Civil Rights Act of 1964.

FURTHER READING: Meyer, David D., 1989, "Finding a Manifest Imbalance: The Case for a Unified Statistical Test for Voluntary Affirmative Action under Title VII," *Michigan Law Review* 87:1986–2025; Spann, Girardeau A., 2000, *The Law of Affirmative Action: Twenty-five Years of Supreme Court Decisions on Race and Remedies,* New York: New York University Press; Yolnosky, Michael, 1998, "Whither *Weber?*" *Roger Williams University Law Review* 4 (fall): 257–292.

ARTHUR K. STEINBERG

Urban League

The National Urban League has served as one of the leading civil rights organizations for African Americans since 1910. During the early years of the organization, the Urban League was on record as opposing programs that utilized racial preferences and quotas. Yet during the same time period, the Urban League aggressively pushed for black employment opportunities, even at the ostensible detriment of white employers and employees. Over time, the Urban League has come to be a strong organizational supporter of affirmative action programs. Whitney Young Jr., former president of the Urban League, once declared that "a decade of discrimination in favor of the Negro youth" was needed (Drake, 61). In 2003, the Urban League joined with the Rainbow PUSH Coalition in jointly authoring an amicus curiae (friend-of-the-court) brief in favor of affirmative action in higher education to the U.S. Supreme Court in *Gratz v. Bollinger*, 123 S. Ct. 2411, 2003 U.S. LEXIS 4801 (2003), and *Grutter v. Bollinger*, 123 S. Ct. 2325, 2003 U.S. LEXIS 4800 (2003).

The mission of the Urban League is to "enable African Americans to secure economic self-reliance, parity and power and civil rights." To achieve these goals, the Urban League focuses on three specific areas: education and youth, economic and self-sufficiency, and racial inclusion. The Urban League is a community-based organization with approximately 115 Urban League affiliates in more than 100 cities nationwide. These affiliates serve more than 2 million people each year.

Established in 1910 and originally called the Committee on Urban Conditions among Negroes, the Urban League was founded to assist blacks who moved north during the black/African American migrations to adapt to urban life and to reduce the overwhelming discrimination they faced. The first programs offered by the Urban League included training African American social workers and attempting to bring additional employment opportunities to the African American community. The Urban League has greatly expanded its focus since the days of its founding. Today it pursues a three-pronged strategy. First, it works to ensure that African American children are well educated and equipped for economic self-reliance. Second, it organizes programs to assist African Americans in obtaining good jobs, becoming homeowners, and accumulating wealth. Finally, it works to eradicate the discriminatory barriers that preclude the first two prongs from being fulfilled. The Urban League implements these strategies at the local, state, and federal levels through direct services, advocacy, research, policy analysis, and communications. The Urban League has been instrumental in fashioning such significant efforts as including African Americans in the New Deal recovery programs, the March on Washington movement, the War on Poverty legislation, and its annual report on "The State of Black America."

See also African Americans; *Gratz v. Bollinger/Grutter v. Bollinger, Plessy v. Ferguson;* Rainbow PUSH Coalition; Randolph, Asa Philip.

FURTHER READING: Drake, W. Avon, 2003, "Affirmative Action at the Crossroads," *Western Journal of Black Studies* 27, no. 1 (spring): 57–65; Moore, Jesse Thomas, 1981, *A Search for Equality: The National Urban League, 1910–1961*, University Park: Pennsylvania State University Press; National Urban League, web site: http://www.nul.org; Parris, Guichard, 1971, *Blacks in the City: A History of the National Urban League*, Boston: Little, Brown and Company; Weiss, Nancy Joan, 1974, *The National Urban League, 1910–1940*, New York: Oxford University Press.

AIMÉE HOBBY RHODES

V

Veterans

See Veterans' Preferences.

Veterans' Preferences

Preferences for veterans of the U.S. armed forces have been a type of affirmative action that the government has employed since the earliest days of the Republic. For example, after the Revolutionary War, soldiers were given land grants of territory in Virginia and what is now Ohio. Supporters of racial preferences and affirmative action today often point to the historical usage of veterans' preferences and the GI Bill as examples of preferences being utilized to benefit other classes of individuals (e.g., white male soldiers). Since the Civil War, the federal government has given veterans preference in appointments to federal jobs. These preferences were not a way to reward individuals for serving their country, but an attempt to recognize the economic loss realized by the service members during their time of service. The current federal law granting these preferences is the Veterans Preference Act of 1944. Following the lead of the federal government, many states stepped forward and passed similar legislation awarding veterans preference for positions in state and local government. Some of these laws have been challenged in state and federal courts as discriminatory. In each case, the courts have upheld the veterans' preference laws. These laws continue to be enforced today.

The Veterans Preference Act of 1944 was specifically passed so that those returning to the civilian workforce after having served in the military during World War II would not be penalized for the time they served. The law does not guarantee veterans a job within the federal government. It states that those who served on active duty during specified military campaigns, or those who were disabled while on active duty, will receive additional points on their civil service examination when they apply to fill a job within the federal government. Those who served during a military campaign are awarded five points, while those who were disabled receive ten points. There is also a provision in the law that allows the unmarried widow or mother of a deceased veteran to receive these same benefits. Under the federal law, these additional points are awarded in only two cases: to veterans who are applying for initial employment and to determine retention standings in the event of a layoff. They are not taken into consideration for promotion, transfer, or reassignment. The law is simply Congress's attempt to recognize the sacrifices of those who serve their country during a time of need and to help them recoup some of the economic loss they suffer during their time on active duty.

In 1971, during the Vietnam War, using a rationale similar to that of the Veterans Preference Act, Richard Nixon issued Executive Order 11598 to facilitate the employment of veterans returning home from the war who might otherwise have lacked the necessary job training, qualifications, or other experience needed to be hired by federal contractors. In 1972, the Vietnam Era Veterans' Readjustment Assistance Act (VEVRAA) was passed by Congress, in essence expanding the coverage of Nixon's executive order to include educational assistance and training benefits to returning eligible veterans. In 1998, the VEVRAA was amended by the Veterans' Employment Opportunities Act to further broaden the definition of those who are entitled to veterans' preferences.

Those who are entitled to veterans' preferences depend on the preference one is dealing with. Some benefits define "veteran" broadly for purposes of eligibility to include any service member who serves continuously on active duty for more than 180 consecutive days. For example, the VA home loan (providing a low-interest home loan secured by the Veterans Administration) is available for any individual who has served on active duty for more than 180 continuous days. However, other veterans' preferences define eligibility more restrictively to include active-duty service only during times of conflict or war.

Almost every state legislature has passed its own laws granting veterans preference. The state laws, of course, differ from state to state. Like the federal statute, most states award veterans additional points on civil service examinations. Other states give a veteran preference over a nonveteran in the case of a tie score. A few states give absolute preference by ranking all veterans over all nonveterans. For example, the Commonwealth of Massachusetts has adopted an absolute lifetime preference statute. This law expands not only the group of those who are entitled to the preference, but also the extent of the preference. First, it defines a veteran as anyone who has served in the armed forces for ninety days or more and has been awarded an honorable discharge from the service. Second, it states that all of these individuals who qualify for state civil service positions must be considered for appointment ahead of any qualified nonveteran. This is the most generous kind of veterans' preference given.

The constitutionality of the Massachusetts statute was challenged in 1979. In *Personnel Administrator of Massachusetts et al. v. Feeney*, 442 U.S. 256 (1979), the U.S. Supreme Court heard arguments as to whether the absolute lifetime preference law discriminated against women. The plaintiff in this case, a female nonveteran, had taken and passed several open examinations for civil service positions. On each occasion, the position was filled by a male veteran who was given absolute preference under the state's veterans' preference law. The plaintiff claimed that the law denied women equal protection of the law, in violation of the Fourteenth Amendment of the U.S. Constitution.

In *Feeney*, the Court upheld the preference. Justice Potter Stewart, writing for the Court, stated that the law was facially neutral insofar as it was not gender based. He also held that the effect of the legislation did not reflect "invidious" gender discrimination. He concluded that the term "veteran" was defined in gender-neutral terms, and that even though there were more male service members than female, the status of a veteran was all-inclusive. The distinction made by the law was not one of man versus woman, but veteran versus nonveteran. The Court did note that absolute lifetime preference might not be a wise policy, but it went on to say that the plaintiff had failed to show that the purpose of the law was to effectuate gender discrimination. This decision set the precedent for lower courts faced with the same or similar questions. Based on the *Feeney* decision, all challenges to veterans' preference laws based on the Fourteenth Amendment have been unsuccessful.

Just as the Massachusetts statute expanded the definition of a veteran and the type of preference awarded, some states have expanded the number of cases to which the preference applies. For example, the Pennsylvania statute granted preference to veterans, not just for appointment and retention, but also in promotion for civil service positions. This difference was addressed in 1993 in a case called *Carter v. City of Philadelphia*, 989 F.2d 117 (3d Cir. 1993). There the U.S. Court of Appeals for the Third Circuit clearly stated that the Pennsylvania Veterans Preference Act granted veterans a statutory preference that was constitutionally protected. Additionally, the court held that if the preference were not granted, the plaintiff would be entitled to relief under 42 U.S.C. § 1983.

Unlike affirmative action programs based on race or gender, veterans' preference laws have undergone few constitutional challenges. In no case to date has a veterans' preference law been held unconstitutional. It has been suggested that the reason for this is threefold. Many people believe that those who serve their country deserve special treatment under the law, and that this law should not be in place simply to repair any economic loss suffered during their time on active duty, but also as a reward for their service. Others have suggested that challenging a veterans' preference law would be viewed as unpatriotic, not something an elected representative would do any time near reelection. Those who view this as a valid point have pointed to the fact that veterans tend to make up a strong voting bloc and lobbying group that could significantly impact an election. Finally, veterans' preferences do not employ race as the distinguishing factor, which clearly makes a difference under Fourteenth Amendment Supreme Court jurisprudence. In fact, as minorities make up a higher percentage of soldiers and sailors than that reflected in the general workforce population, veterans' preferences also indirectly benefit minority groups.

See also Equal Protection Clause; Fourteenth Amendment; GI Bill.

FURTHER READING: Marlowe, Keith S., 1995, "*Carter vs. City of Philadelphia*: Veterans May Have Won a Battle over Veterans' Preference in Promotions, but Have They Won the War?" *Dickinson Law Review* 99 (spring): 807–834; Murray, Melissa E., 2002, "Whatever Happened to G.I. Jane? Citizenship, Gender, and Social Policy in the Postwar Era," *Michigan Journal of*

Gender and Law 9:91–129; Skrentny, John David, 1996, *The Ironies of Affirmative Action*, Chicago: University of Chicago Press; U.S. General Accounting Office, 1995, *Federal Hiring: Reconciling Managerial Flexibility with Veterans' Preference*, GAO/GGD-95–102, June, Washington, DC: Government Printing Office.

AIMÉE HOBBY RHODES

Vietnam Era Veterans' Readjustment Assistance Act of 1974

The Vietnam Era Veterans' Readjustment Assistance Act (VEVRAA) of 1974 requires that any contractor or subcontractor receiving a contract from the federal government in the amount of $25,000 or more must take affirmative action in employing and advancing qualified special disabled veterans, veterans of the Vietnam era, and any other veterans who served on active duty during a war or in a campaign for which a campaign badge has been authorized. VEVRAA does not establish set goals or timetables for hiring. Instead, it requires that federal contractors immediately list employment opportunities with the nearest state job service office and that the job service give veterans priority in referrals to contractors. The priority referral does not obligate an employer to hire the referred veterans. To monitor compliance and success in increasing veteran's employment, contractors are required to track their hiring practices and file annual VETS-100 reports with the Department of Labor. If a veteran believes that he/she has been discriminated against, complaints are filed with the Office of Federal Contract Compliance Programs (OFCCP) or through the local veterans' representative at the state job service. In fiscal year 1999, there were 1,120,370 special disabled and Vietnam-era veterans employed by federal contractors, but national unemployment rates for veterans continue to exceed those of nonveterans.

In 1971, President Richard Nixon issued Executive Order 11598 to facilitate the employment of veterans returning from Vietnam who might otherwise have lacked the necessary job experience or other credentials to be hired by federal contractors. The next year, similar language was included in section 503 of the Vietnam Era Veterans' Readjustment Assistance Act of 1972. This bill's main purpose was to increase the rates of educational assistance and special training allowances paid to eligible veterans. In 1974, a similar bill again increased education spending and amended the earlier section 503 wording to explicitly require affirmative action for all contractors with contracts in excess of $10,000. The bill was vetoed by President Gerald Ford, who cited cost issues, but became law through a congressional override and has since remained the key affirmative action legislation for veterans.

In 1998, the Veterans' Employment Opportunities Act amended VEVRAA by increasing the contract figure that triggers the law from $10,000 to $25,000 and by expanding the eligibility criteria. Originally, the law covered special disabled veterans, defined as those who were released from active duty because of a service-connected disability or were entitled to compensation for a disability rated at 30 percent or more, and Vietnam-era veterans, defined as those serving between August 1964 and May 1975. In time, people questioned why Vietnam-era veterans should get special treatment not given to those who served before or after them, so the law was changed to cover veterans who served in other wars and also in campaigns when war was not officially declared. In 2000, the Veterans Benefits and Health Care Improvement Act of 2000 further expanded the definition of "veterans" to include "recently separated veterans." "Recently separated veterans" enjoy preferences in the federal contracting setting in the year immediately following release from active duty ("recently separated" is defined in the statute as "any veteran during the one-year period beginning on the date of such veteran's discharge or release from active duty").

The law requires contractors to take affirmative action in hiring and promoting qualified veterans. More specifically, it requires that contractors list all job openings with the state job service or by using the Internet to directly list openings in America's Job Bank. The only exceptions for this are executive or top management positions, positions filled within the organization, or those lasting three days or less. Contractors are responsible for communicating the requirements to all subcontractors with subcontracts of $25,000 or more. Department of Labor statistics for fiscal year 1999 show that 838,388 job openings were listed and 15,947 special disabled or Vietnam-era veterans entered employment through this program. Additionally, large federal contractors, those with fifty or more employees and $50,000 or more in contract funds, must go further by having written affirmative action plans and demonstrating that they have actively recruited qualified veterans.

All contractors and subcontractors with contracts in excess of $25,000 must annually file VETS-100 reports for each of their hiring locations. For example, a company with a headquarters and two affiliates in other cities would have to file three reports. Contractors report statistics for their existing employees and new hires showing how many fall into protected categories of special disabled veterans, Vietnam-era veterans, and so on. If a veteran falls into multiple categories, he/she should be listed in each; however, many contractors are not fully aware of this procedure and thus underreport certain groups. Failure to file a required report triggers action by OFCCP, which tries to negotiate an acceptable remedy with the contractor. Continued failure to report leads to the contractor being banned from receiving future federal contracts.

In fiscal year 1999, 32,222 contractors and subcontractors filed VETS-100 reports. More than 5,000 of these companies had multiple sites and thus filed multiple reports, bringing the overall total to 184,774 reports. This total was slightly decreased from the previous year because budgetary constraints meant that no delinquency notices were sent out. For fiscal year 1999, reports showed that more than 1 million disabled or Vietnam-era veterans were federal contractor employees, and that 12,968 special disabled and 100,341 Vietnam-era veterans were new hires. Most businesses comply with the reporting requirements, but some resent the burden that compiling the statistics and following other terms of VEVRAA place on their human resources staff. In the summer of 2002, Home Depot reminded the managers of its home-improvement outlets to refuse all business with the federal government, apparently so that it would not be subject to VEVRAA and other affirmative action laws for federal contractors. Weeks later, faced with pressure from activist groups and bad publicity, the company reversed its position.

In a series of cases, the courts have ruled that individuals cannot sue contractors for failing to comply with the hiring provisions of VEVRAA. The legislative intent of the law was that only the Department of Labor should supervise and enforce compliance. In fiscal year 1999, 230 individuals initiated complaints with OFCCP. Many of the complaints were rejected for untimely filing, lack of jurisdiction, or other problems, so that only eighty-two were accepted for investigation. Of the cases closed that year, some of which had been initiated the previous year, sixty-seven were closed without violations, twenty-two were closed for other reasons, and only seven were closed with violations. All seven of these cases were closed by a conciliation agreement, not by further sanctions.

See also Affirmative Action Plan/Program; Contracting and Affirmative Action; Department of Labor; Ford, Gerald Rudolph; GI Bill; Nixon, Richard Milhous; Office of Federal Contract Compliance Programs; Veterans' Preferences.

FURTHER READING: El Boghdady, Dina, 2002, "Home Depot Shies from Federal Deals; Retailer Says It Doesn't Want to Deal with Government Paperwork Requirements," *Washington Post*, June 18, E6; U.S. Department of Labor, "Frequently Asked Questions about the Federal Contractor Program," http://www.dol.gov/vets; U.S. Department of Labor, Assistant Secretary for Veterans' Employment and Training, *Annual Report to Congress 2000*, http://www.dol.gov.

JOHN W. DIETRICH

Voting Rights Act of 1965

The Voting Rights Act of 1965 was a product of the civil rights movement of the 1960s. It and the Civil Rights Act of 1964 constitute the two most influential pieces of civil rights legislation in U.S. history. The Voting Rights Act was the first modern effort by the federal government in the area of voting reforms. The Voting Rights Act was enacted on August 7, 1965, and has been amended three times, in 1970, 1975, and in 1982. The Voting Rights Act as amended was enacted to ensure that the rights of citizens to vote would not be denied or impaired because of racial or language discrimination. The original act was intended to be a temporary measure but had to be extended on more than one occasion because of intransigence on the part of those who would deny the right to vote to African Americans, women, and other protected groups. Furthermore, the Supreme Court has interpreted the Voting Rights Act quite broadly to allow a whole series of "affirmative" remedial methods for improving the right to vote by minorities. Thus the Voting Rights Act of 1965 is one of the most important civil rights statutes in American history and represents a part of the struggle for African Americans' enfranchisement over the centuries. The Voting Rights Act has been described by lawyer and presidential advisor Vernon Jordan as "probably the most significant accomplishment" of the entire civil rights movement, because "voting is power."

The original Voting Rights Act of 1965 was specifically directed at seven southern states: Alabama, Georgia, Louisiana, Mississippi, North Carolina, South Carolina, and Virginia. These seven states were targeted because of their usage of poll taxes, literacy tests, and other mechanisms designed to prevent voter registration of African Americans. Special provisions of the act also affected counties and towns in California, Colorado, Connecticut, Florida, Hawaii, Idaho, Massachusetts, Michigan, New Hampshire, New York, and Wyoming.

The Voting Rights Act of 1965 is composed of three titles. Title I is referred to as the "Voting Rights Provision," and Title II contains the "Supplemental Provisions." Title III contains regulations regarding the right of eighteen-year-olds to vote as a result of the passage of the Twenty-Sixth Amendment to the U.S. Con-

President Lyndon B. Johnson gives Dr. Martin Luther King one of the pens used in the signing of the Voting Rights Act of 1965. In the background are Florida Representative Claude Pepper, center, and Reverend Ralph Abernathy. Courtesy of Library of Congress.

stitution. The act will require congressional extension in 2007. The general provisions of the Voting Rights Act protect the voting rights of Americans in several important ways. The general provisions prohibit voting qualifications or procedures that would deny or abridge a person's right to vote predicated on race, color, or inclusion in a minority group. The provisions make it a crime for a public official to refuse to allow a qualified person to vote or for any person to use threats or intimidation to prevent an individual from voting or assisting another in voting. The general provisions also allow for increased enforcement of voting guarantees by private parties. Title I, section 3, contains provisions that permit private parties, as well as the U.S. attorney general, to file legal actions pertaining to the enforcement of voting rights guaranteed in the Fourteenth and Fifteenth Amendments to the U.S. Constitution. The general provisions provide for the appointment of federal examiners (with the power to register citizens to vote) and observers. Furthermore, under the act, certain specified jurisdictions (where voting discrimination had occurred previously) were required to obtain "preclearance" from the justice department if that jurisdiction wished to adopt new voting practices or procedures. The Voting Rights Act contains a nationwide prohibition of tests or devices as a prerequisite for voting.

The Voting Rights Act as amended in 1975 outlines the criteria for determining if a region is subject to its provisions. A jurisdiction is "covered" if it meets one of the following test or trigger mechanisms: (1) the jurisdiction maintained on November 1, 1964, any test or device as a precondition for voter registration, and less than 50 percent of the total voting age population was registered on November 1, 1964, or voted in the presidential election of 1964; (2) the jurisdiction maintained on November 1, 1968, a test or device as a precondition for voter registration, and less than 50 percent of the total voting age population was registered on November 1, 1968, or voted in the presidential election of 1968; (3) the jurisdiction maintained on November 1, 1972, any test or device as a prerequisite to voting or voting registration, and less than 50 percent of the voting population was registered on November 1, 1972, or voted in the presidential election of 1972; (4) or more than 5 percent of the citizens of voting age in the jurisdiction were members of a single-language minority group, and the illiteracy rate of such persons as a group is higher than the national illiteracy rate.

The special provisions of the Voting Rights Act as amended in 1970 were imposed on those jurisdictions that failed to comply with the 1965 act. The special provisions applied to the entire states of Alaska, Alabama, Arizona, Georgia, Louisiana, Mississippi, South Carolina, Texas, and Virginia and included counties or towns in California, Colorado, Connecticut, Florida, Hawaii, Idaho, Massachusetts, Michigan, New Hampshire, New York, North Carolina, South Dakota, and Wyoming. The special provisions of the Voting Rights Act are temporary inasmuch as there are included "bailout" features. A jurisdiction may "bail out" by proving in a suit in the U.S. District Court for the District of Columbia that its voting practices or procedures were not used in a discriminatory manner for the proper prior period (seventeen years in the case of the first two trigger mechanisms and ten years under the third trigger mechanism). Jurisdictions are unable to avail themselves of the bailout provisions if the jurisdiction is "covered" by virtue of being in the fourth trigger mechanism category. The special provisions required, as well as provided, that examiners from the Department of Justice along with observers from the Office of Personnel Management be sent into the covered jurisdictions for the purpose of guaranteeing that African American citizens would be duly registered and permitted to vote.

The Voting Rights Act provided congressional authority required to regulate voting practices as granted in the Fifteenth Amendment to the U.S. Constitution. The Fifteenth Amendment gives all citizens the right to vote regardless of race, color, or previous condition of servitude. The Voting Rights Act of 1965 was designed to bring an end to the traditional practice of allowing states to handle all matters germane to voting and elections. The passage of the Voting Rights Act of 1965 has been viewed as the most radical piece of civil rights legislation since Reconstruction.

Title I, section 5, contains a key provision of the Voting Rights Act of 1965, referred to as the "preclearance" provision. Section 5 requires covered jurisdictions to obtain preclearance before any changes in voting qualifications or prerequisites for voting or standards, practices, or procedures with respect to voting that are different from those in effect on November 1, 1964. The submissions are to be examined to determine if they have either the purpose or effect of denying or abridging the right to vote on account of race or color. Section 5 prevents the substitution of new discriminatory practices for old ones that violated the guidelines of the Voting Rights Act. Section 5 is automatic in that all covered jurisdictions must submit any changes for review by the federal government. The attorney general must act on any submission within sixty days or the submission is valid even if it contains discriminatory provisions. Those states in which elections remain covered by Section 5 today include Alabama, Arizona, Georgia, Louisiana, Mississippi, South Carolina, Texas, and Virginia. States whose elections are covered only in certain counties today include California, Florida, Michigan, New Hampshire, New York, North Carolina, and South Dakota.

The southern states, however, perceived the act as an infringement upon states' rights. The legality and constitutionality of the act were tested in the case *South Carolina v. Katzenbach*, 383 U.S. 301 (1966). In *Katzenbach*, the U.S. Supreme Court upheld the constitutionality of the Voting Rights Act, taking a very liberal judicial view of the power of Congress to pass such legislation under the Fifteenth Amendment. In Philip Rubio's *A History of Affirmative Action, 1619–2000*, it is asserted that part of the "affirmative action legacy" is the Voting Rights Act of 1965 and, more particularly, the Supreme Court adjudication of cases dealing with the Voting Rights Act. Rubio, quoting historian Steven F. Lawson in his book *Running for Freedom*, comments as follows:

> One of those legacies [of affirmative action] was the broadening of the 1965 Voting Rights Act by the Supreme Court in 1969, as noted by historian Steven F. Lawson: "Beginning in 1969, it decreed that the statute . . . was also meant to include 'all actions to make a vote effective.' In a series of decisions the judiciary empowered federal authorities to strike down electoral rules that had the purpose or effect of diluting the strength of black ballots. The conversion from single-member districts to at-large elections, the expansion of municipal boundaries through annexation of largely white areas, and reapportionment plans that produced racially gerrymandered districts were regulations of this type." (Rubio 2001, 163)

Because of the Court's liberal interpretation, relocation of polling places, changes in ballot forms, reapportionment of election districts, and revisions of rules pertaining to the qualification of candidates have been implemented.

See also African Americans; *Baker v. Carr*; Civil Rights Act of 1964; Civil Rights Movement; Department of Justice; Fifteenth Amendment; Fourteenth Amendment.

FURTHER READING: Ball, Howard, Dale Kranc, and Thomas P. Lauth, 1982, *Compromised Compliance: Implementation of the 1965 Voting Rights Act*, Westport, CT: Greenwood Press; Davidson, Chandler, and Bernard Grofman, 1994, *Quiet Revolution in the South: The Impact of the Voting Rights Act, 1965–1990*, Princeton, NJ: Princeton University Press; Rubio, Philip F., 2000, *A History of Affirmative Action, 1619–2000*, Jackson: University Press of Mississippi; Tucker, Ronnie B., 2000, *Affirmative Action, the Supreme Court, and Political Power in the Old Confederacy*, Lanham, MD: University Press of America.

RONNIE B. TUCKER SR.

W

Wagner Act

See National Labor Relations Act of 1935 (Wagner Act).

Wards Cove Packing Co. v. Atonio, 490 U.S. 642 (1989)

In *Wards Cove Packing Co. v. Atonio,* 490 U.S. 642 (1989), the U.S. Supreme Court gave guidance on what type of statistical analysis is relevant to show discrimination. This guidance has been relied upon to establish whether an affirmative action plan is justified to remedy the effects of discrimination. The opinion also made other significant holdings concerning the burden of proof in discrimination cases. The Civil Rights Act of 1991 was passed in part to overrule part of the *Wards Cove* opinion concerning burden of proof. The case involved a situation in which white employees occupied almost all of the skilled noncannery jobs at a salmon cannery in Alaska. The nonskilled jobs were filled largely by minority workers (Filipinos, Alaskan Natives, and others). The nonskilled workers claimed that the racial imbalance in the workforce was discrimination and a violation of Title VII.

Wards Cove is significant in the development of employment discrimination law in at least three respects. The first concerns the interpretation of statistical evidence. The case involved a situation where minorities comprised more than half of the employer's unskilled positions, but less than 20 percent of its skilled positions. Justice Byron White's majority opinion squarely rejected the plaintiffs' effort to establish a prima facie case of disparate impact on such a comparison, finding that plaintiffs could establish a claim of exclusion from the skilled jobs only by comparing the racial composition of employees in those jobs with the racial composition of the qualified labor market for those jobs. This principle is still followed in establishing a basis for affirmative action measures to remedy the effects of past discrimination.

The second and best-known development in *Wards Cove* involves the Court's interpretation of the burden of proof with respect to the business justification for a practice causing a disparate impact and the strength of the justification in terms of importance to the employer's business needs. For approximately two decades preceding the *Wards Cove* decision, both in the Supreme Court and lower courts, the burden of establishing the justification had been placed on the defendant. For approximately the same length of time, the justification had been phrased in terms of "business necessity," with the courts of appeals universally describing that standard as a quite stringent one, though with dicta in the Supreme Court's own opinions being somewhat interpretable.

In *Wards Cove*, the Court placed the burden of proof as to whether there was sufficient justification squarely on the plaintiffs. This seemed a clear reversal of precedent. The Court also cast the justification standard as relatively modest. It noted that "the dispositive issue is whether the practice serves in a significant way, the legitimate goals of the employer." It went on to observe that "a mere insubstantial justification in this regard will not suffice, because such a low standard would permit discrimination to be practiced through the use of spurious, seemingly neutral employment practices," but concluded that "there is no requirement that the challenged practice be 'essential' or 'indispensable.' " This ruling was arguably contrary to the Court's own earlier rulings and was certainly contrary to consistent authority among the courts of appeals. Indeed, aspects of the opinion suggested that the Court was on its way to redefining the disparate impact theory into a mere means of proving intentional discrimination.

In any event, these aspects of the decision evoked much criticism, and that criticism provided a significant part of the impetus for the Civil Rights Act of 1991. Among other things, that act placed the burden of justifying a practice causing a disparate impact again on the employer. The act also cast the justification standard in terms of a demonstration that "the challenged practice is job-related and consistent with business necessity." Legislative history was created to indicate that these terms were to be interpreted in light of pre–*Wards Cove* decisions. However, because the Court in *Wards Cove* was maintaining that it was merely interpreting existing law, the implications of the reference to pre–*Wards Cove* decisions remain unclear.

The third significant aspect of the *Wards Cove* decision involves an evolution of some casual language in an early Supreme Court opinion. Early in the development of the disparate impact theory, the courts of appeals reasoned that if a less discriminatory alternative to a challenged practice existed, the practice could not be essential to an employer's business and hence could not satisfy the business necessity standard. These courts had generally placed the burden of demonstrating the absence of such an alternative on the employer. In *Albemarle Paper Co. v. Moody*, 422 U.S. 405 (1975), however, the Supreme Court placed the burden of showing the existence of a less discriminatory alternative on the plaintiff. Having done so, the Court went on to observe that the existence of the alternative "would be evidence that the employer was using its [practices] as a 'pretext' for discrimination." Critics of this observation argue that while the existence of the alternative might well show that a practice was not justified under a stringent standard, it would do little to suggest that the practice was being employed for the purpose of discrimination. More likely, the employer did not know about the alternative, did not agree that it equally served its purposes, or simply preferred the selection procedure it had employed.

In *Wards Cove*, Justice Blackmun, relying on *Albemarle*, found that if plaintiffs "come forward with alternatives to the petitioner's hiring practices that reduce the racially-disparate impact of practices currently being used, and petitioners refuse to adopt these alternatives, such a refusal would belie a claim by petitioners that their incumbent practices are being employed for nondiscriminatory reasons." The addition of the element whereby the employer refused to adopt the alternative after its utility was shown in court might have provided a better basis for inferring that the existing practice was a pretext for discrimination than would the simple demonstration that such a practice existed, but the formula set out by White's opinion created the anomalous and perhaps unprecedented situation in which the employer's liability would turn on events occurring after trial. Nevertheless, in its effort to address the *Wards Cove* decision in the Civil Rights Act of 1991, Congress, apparently without discussing the issue, carried over the failure of the employer to adopt the remedy alternative as an element of establishing liability on the basis of the existence of a less discriminatory alternative employment practice and confirmed that it is the plaintiff's burden to demonstrate the existence of an alternative employment practice. The post–*Wards Cove* burden-of-proof rule is now codified at 42 U.S.C. § 2000e-2(j).

See also Albemarle Paper Company v. Moody; Civil Rights Act of 1991; Discrimination; Disparate Treatment and Disparate Impact; *Griggs v. Duke Power Co.*; Statistical Proof of Discrimination; Supreme Court and Affirmative Action; Title VII of the Civil Rights Act of 1964; White, Byron Raymond; *Yick Wo v. Hopkins.*

FURTHER READING: Davidson, Michael, 1992, "The Civil Rights Act of 1991," *Army Law* 1992 (March): 3–11; Player, Mark, 1989, "Is *Griggs* Dead? Reflecting (Fearfully) on *Wards Cove Packing Co. v. Atonio,*" Florida State University Law Review 17 (winter): 11–47.

JAMES P. SCANLAN

Warren Court and Affirmative Action

Earl Warren presided over the Supreme Court as Chief Justice during turbulent times in America, and the Warren Court has earned praise for how it handled the cases that percolated up to the High Court during this era, particularly cases pertaining to criminal procedure and cases pertaining to integration and the civil rights movement. Warren was born March 19, 1891, in Los Angeles, California. Warren spent much of his adult life in California, earning his bachelor of laws and juris doctorate from the University of California at Berkeley. He also served in a variety of public offices in California, including deputy city attorney (Oakland), deputy assistant district attorney, assistant district attorney, and district attorney for Alameda County, attorney general for the state of California, and governor of California. He was nominated by Eisenhower for the Chief Justice position, and began serving on the Court in 1953, a place he would have a great impact on until his resignation roughly a decade and a half later (Warren would pass away on July 8, 1974, within a few years of his resignation from the High Court).

During his tenure as chief justice, the Supreme Court entered one of its most judicially active periods. The Warren Court has been characterized as judicially active particularly in the area of civil liberties and rights and in regard to promoting equality. Critics of the Court in this period have accused the Court of aggrandizing and usurping powers from state governments and the other branches of the federal government. Warren was a proponent of racial equality, and as a result of his philosophy, the Court adopted a judicial activist decision-making approach, particularly in cases dealing with race. Warren was particularly adept at forming consensuses on the Court. Thus the Court applied the chief justice's perspective of a belief in equality before the law, equality of races, of citizens, of rich and poor. It has been said that the Warren Court's perspective regarding equality provided the mechanism and impetus for the movement of equality in America. Specifically, in regard to affirmative action, the Warren Court was instrumental in expanding the notion of "state action" and giving judicial sanction to the use of remedial action plans in relief of victims of racial discrimination. The Warren Court's willingness to protect the constitutional rights of African Americans caused African Americans to view the Supreme Court as a friend and protector of their rights. Thus the Warren Court became known as the "liberal Court."

One year after the appointment of Earl Warren as chief justice, the Warren Court laid the foundation for the application of the key principles of liberty, equality, and justice. In the case *Brown v. Board of Education*, 347 U.S. 483 (1954), the Warren Court formulated an antidiscrimination decision that was designed to undo the legacy of white supremacy and domination that had been sanctioned judicially in *Plessy v. Ferguson*, 163 U.S. 537 (1896). The decision of the Warren Court in *Brown* signaled the start of a new era in effective civil rights enforcement. In this decision, the Supreme Court moved into an area (civil rights) where Congress had refused to venture. The Court adopted Warren's viewpoint that segregation was unconstitutional. The Warren Court declared in *Brown v. Board of Education* that the principle of "separate but equal" was per se unconstitutional under the Fourteenth Amendment to the U.S. Constitution. In *Brown*, the Supreme Court concluded that separate facilities were inherently unequal. Thus the *Brown* decision gave hope that the Court was in support of removing historical barriers that had been encountered by African Americans or other minorities in public education. One year later, the Court in *Brown v. Board of Education (II)*, 349 U.S. 294 (1955), required that schools begin their desegregation plans with "all deliberate speed."

In 1958, the Warren Court again established a landmark decision in the desegregation struggle. In *Cooper v. Aaron*, 358 U.S. 1 (1958), the first school decision given by the Supreme Court after the *Brown I* and *Brown II* decisions, the Court, under the leadership of Chief Justice Warren, convened in a special session to review the judicial arguments presented by the Little Rock, Arkansas, School Board in response to the 1954 decision in *Brown*. The Little Rock School Board was seeking a stay of its 1958 desegregation plan because of public hostility. The dispatching of National Guard units by the governor designed to prevent African American students from enrolling in high school had attracted national attention. It was advocated by the school board that "normal educational" activities were impossible in view of the hostile environment. In an unprecedented move, all nine justices signed the opinion ruling that the state of Arkansas was obligated to follow the Supreme Court's decision in *Brown*. The Court noted that the hostile environment had been created by the behavior of state officials. The Court also held that the constitutional rights of African American students were not to be sacrificed or yielded to the violence and disorder that resulted from actions implemented by the governor and legislature of Arkansas. In *Cooper*, the Warren Court sharply criticized the notion of states to engage in violent resistance to *Brown*.

The composition of the Warren Court changed in 1962 with the appointments of Byron White and Arthur Goldberg by President John F. Kennedy, thereby adding to the existing liberal bloc of the Court, members who all adhered to the same general judicial philosophy as Warren. In 1965, President Lyndon B. Johnson appointed Abe Fortas. In 1967, Johnson appointed Thurgood Marshall, former attorney for the National Association for the Advancement of Colored People, a key lawyer in the *Brown* case, who successfully argued to the High Court that the "separate but equal" doctrine should be overturned as unconstitutional, and the first African American to be appointed to the Supreme Court. As by the mid-1960s, the "real" Warren Court was in place, and Warren's sway on the Court reached a pinnacle during the time period from 1962 until 1969, at which time Warren retired from the Court.

The liberal philosophy of the Warren Court in the race relations context was tested in 1962 and 1963 in the Court's deliberation of cases involving those arrested during sit-in demonstrations in the South as part of the civil rights movement. In these cases, the pivotal legal issue was the factor that the protesters had been arrested for trespassing on private property and allegedly causing a breach of the peace. The liberal Court was now required to evaluate its emphasis on fair treatment and racial equality when such rights were conflicting with normal property-related rights of others. The sit-in cases presented the issue to the Court of whether a state could use its power to help a private storeowner discriminate against African Americans. This issue was a difficult one for the Warren Court in that the Equal Protection Clause of the Fourteenth Amendment prohibited only discriminatory state action. It contained no guidelines regarding private discrimination. Indeed, the Court had historically held that if there was not "state action," there could not be a violation of the Fourteenth Amendment.

During the 1963 term, the Warren Court reviewed six sit-in cases: *Peterson v. Greenville*, 373 U.S. 244, *Avent v. North Carolina*, 373 U.S. 244, *Gober v. Birmingham*, 373 U.S. 374, *Lombard v. Louisiana*, 373 U.S. 267, *Shuttlesworth v. Birmingham*, 373 U.S. 262, and *Griffin v. Maryland*, 373 U.S. 920. The cases arose from Greenville, South Carolina, Durham, North Carolina, and Birmingham, Alabama, as a result of city ordinances that required racial segregation in restaurants. In the case of New Orleans, Louisiana, there was no segregation ordinance, but the police chief and the mayor made statements indicating that sit-in demonstrations were not allowed. In *Shuttlesworth v. Birmingham*, the legal issue was criminal trespass. The final case of *Griffin v. Maryland* involved the legal segregation of an amusement park. The key legal issue germane to these six cases was whether or not these various types of segregation were a violation of the Equal Protection Clause of the Fourteenth Amendment. For the Court to hold that these various segregation practices were a violation of the Fourteenth Amendment, the Court would have to find sufficient "state action." After a series of extensive judicial conferences and rewriting of opinions, the Warren Court ultimately determined that the convictions should be overturned in each of the cases. Thus the Warren Court loosened the requirement of "state action" and allowed for protection against private discrimination under the Equal Protection Clause of the Fourteenth Amendment, so

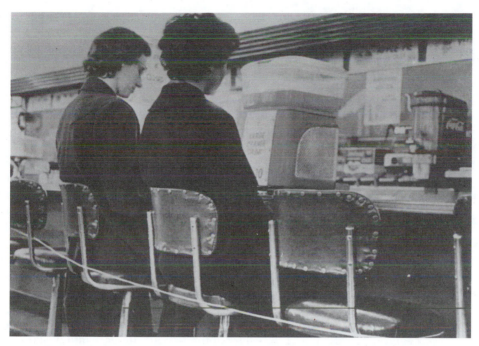

A white and a black woman protesting segregation, sitting side by side on stools at a Nashville, Tennessee, lunch counter in 1960. Several sit-in cases resulted in Supreme Court decisions on segregation in the 1960s. Courtesy of Library of Congress.

long as there was some nexus with state or local government (through its actions or through its sanctioning of the actions).

The Warren Court again reviewed sit-in cases during the 1963 term. The Court decided to review four additional sit-in cases: *Bell v. Maryland*, 378 U.S. 918, *Barr v. Columbia*, 378 U.S. 198, *Bouie v. Columbia*, 378 U.S. 347, and *Robinson v. Florida*, 378 U.S. 153. As established during the 1962 term, the Warren Court broadly interpreted the state involvement needed to satisfy the state action doctrine and again affirmed that the Equal Protection Clause of the Fourteenth Amendment provided protection against private discrimination in public places. The Warren Court's judicial perspective was adopted by Congress as part of the Civil Rights Act of 1964.

The Warren Court in *Evans v. Newton*, 382 U.S. 296 (1966), handed down an opinion that further revised the issue of state-sponsored discrimination in conjunction with the Equal Protection Clause of the Fourteenth Amendment. The case involved the segregation of a park on the basis of race. The park land was in Macon, Georgia, and had been given by state senator Augustus O. Bacon to the city. In establishing the city as trustee over the land, Bacon attached a condition to his gift to the city that the park be used solely for the enjoyment and benefit of whites. The city had provided maintenance from 1911 and enjoyed tax-exempt status. In part as a result of the *Brown* decision, the city terminated its trusteeship, and a group of private trustees was created. The Warren Court ruled that regardless of the title transfer and appointment of private trustees, as the park was a public holding, there was sufficient state action, and the action violated the Equal Protection Clause of the Fourteenth Amendment.

The Warren Court confronted the legal issue of state involvement in private racial discrimination again in *Reitman v. Mulkey*, 387 U.S. 369 (1967). The case resulted from a provision in the California Constitution prohibiting the state from interfering with the absolute discretion of an owner to sell, lease, or rent property (as well as the refusal to do so). As a result of this provision, cases were filed alleging that the denial of housing due to race was a violation of fair-housing laws, as well as a violation of the Fourteenth Amendment's Equal Protection Clause. The Court held that by including an absolute right of property ownership and right of discrimination in the California Constitution, California was specifically sanctioning and encouraging private discrimination in the state. Therefore, the Court again found sufficient state action to conclude that the California law was unconstitutional. The Court noted that "the provision in its effect, nullified previous fair housing laws, and therefore, the state had taken affirmative action to make discrimination legally possible." The decision of *Reitman* was important in that it prevented states from developing "elusive statutory schemes" that would nullify the protection of the Fourteenth Amendment.

In regard to affirmative action and racial discrimination, the Court examined the legality of "freedom-of-choice" desegregation plans in *Green v. School Board of New Kent County*, 391 U.S. 430 (1968). Freedom-of-choice desegregation plans involved the notion or concept that the local governments or institutions that historically had engaged in discrimination that resulted in de jure or de facto segregation should have freedom of choice in choosing what method to utilize in their desegregation efforts. In *Green*, a case dealing with segregated public schools, the Warren Court eliminated the freedom-of-choice argument as a viable option in desegregation. The *Green* case put forth two significant points that subsequently became relevant in affirmative action litigation in other cases: first, *Green* laid the foundation for the Court to examine the issue of remedies for the established practices of discrimination and impose mandatory remedial affirmative action measures if it deems proper; and second, *Green* served as an indicator that judicial consideration and scrutiny would be given regarding the impact of a governmental practice and that institution's attempts at remedying the past discrimination, and that both factors would be relevant in the Court forging remedial measures if necessary.

See also African Americans; All Deliberate Speed; *Brown v. Board of Education*; Civil Rights Act of 1964; Equal Protection Clause; Fourteenth Amendment; Johnson, Lyndon Baines; Kennedy, John Fitzgerald; Marshall, Thurgood; National Association for the Advancement of Colored People; *Plessy v. Ferguson*; State Action Doctrine; White, Byron Raymond.

FURTHER READING: Horwitz, Morton J., 1998, *The Warren Court and the Pursuit of Justice*, New York: Hill and Wang; Powe, Lucas A., Jr., 2000, *The Warren Court and American Politics*, Cambridge, MA: Harvard University Press; Schwartz, Bernard, 1983, *Super Chief: Earl Warren and His Supreme Court*, New York: New York University Press; Schwartz, Bernard, 1996, *The Warren Court: A Retrospective*, New York: Oxford University Press; Tushnet, Mark, ed., 1993, *The Warren Court in Historical and Political Perspective*, Charlottesville: University Press of Virginia.

RONNIE B. TUCKER SR.

Washington, Booker T. (1856–1915)

Booker T. Washington, a former slave and postbellum civil rights leader, is regarded as one of the most influential African American leaders of his time. He promoted a philosophy of self-help, racial solidarity, and accommodation. Washington urged African Americans to accept discrimination for the time being and concentrate on elevating themselves through hard work and economic prosperity. Washington's views can be contrasted with those of another great African American, W.E.B. Du Bois. Du Bois argued that the way to achieve true racial change was through agitation and challenging the status quo. Du Bois was the radical; Washington, the conservative. Du Bois argued that society must change to afford blacks equality; Washington argued that the best way to achieve equality was through hard work and self-help, not by expecting societal handouts or societal changes. Washington stressed private initiative and nonpolitical solutions to improving the plight of minorities in the South. Washington remarked that once individuals improve themselves, "friction between the races will pass away in proportion as the black man . . . can produce something that the white man wants or respects in the commercial world." Du Bois's and Washington's views on race and the different means to achieve advancement in society are relevant to the issue of affirmative action today and are often cited in affirmative action articles and debates. The current debates on affirmative action are simply a continuation of century-old debates between influential leaders (such as Du Bois and Washington) as to how best to achieve racial justice and equality in the United States.

Booker Taliaferro Washington was born a slave on the Burroughs tobacco farm in Hales Ford, Virginia. After the Civil War in 1865, Washington and his family moved to Malden, West Virginia. As a young adolescent, Washington worked in coal mines and salt furnaces. At age sixteen, he enrolled in Hampton Institute, an industrial school for African Americans located in Hampton, Virginia. After graduation, Washington became a teacher in Tinkersville, West Virginia, for three years. In 1878, he left to attend Wayland Seminary in Washington, D.C., but quit after six months. In 1879, Washington returned to Hampton Institute as a teacher. Washington's philosophy of education was based on the educational training he received at Hampton.

Washington rose to prominence primarily because of his role as the founder of Tuskegee Normal Institute. On July 4, 1881, Washington started the school in an abandoned church building. He established Tuskegee as a vocational training school for African Americans. It was a very humble beginning, but under Washington's leadership, Tuskegee and Washington grew to be well known around the world. The school made lasting and profound contributions to the South and to the United States, due in part to the work of one of its teachers, George Washington Carver. The school's name was changed to Tuskegee Institute, and today it is known as Tuskegee University. The school curriculum focused on teaching specific trade skills, including carpentry, farming, brick masonry, printing, shoemaking, and mechanics. Teacher training was also an important aspect of the Tuskegee curriculum. In his book titled *Up from Slavery*, Washington illustrated his belief in the importance of working with one's hands when he said that "the individual who can do something that the world wants done will, in the end, make his way regardless of race."

During his leadership of Tuskegee, Washington was always concerned about

Booker T. Washington at his desk in 1894. © AP/Wide World Photos.

accumulating enough funds to run the institution. The support he received from the state was neither generous nor stable enough to maintain the kind of school he was developing. Washington became an astute fundraiser. He went on speaking tours where he solicited donations. He received financial support from white northerners who were impressed with the work he was doing and his nonthreatening racial views. Northern industrialists like Andrew Carnegie and John D. Rockefeller donated money on a regular basis. As Tuskegee grew in prominence and student enrollment expanded, Washington devoted much of his time to fundraising. Due in part to his diligent leadership, Tuskegee Institute emerged as a model of industrial education. The Tuskegee Institute National Historic Site, established in 1974, includes Washington's home, student-made college buildings, and the George Washington Carver Museum.

Washington's education philosophy was grounded in the belief that African Americans needed a more practical, vocational education as opposed to a college education in the classical liberal tradition. Throughout the South and the North, during the late nineteenth century, most African Americans were living in poverty. Washington believed that to uplift the race, blacks needed to acquire vocational skills, work hard, and buy property. He thought that the acquisition of skills would lead to economic prosperity for African Americans. Washington believed that by gaining economic clout, black people would eventually be granted civil and political rights, and that economic empowerment alone would end discrimination. In his autobiography, *Up from Slavery*, Washington discussed his views on the quest of African Americans to secure their economic and political rights.

By the late 1800s, African Americans were victims of lynchings, Jim Crow laws, de facto segregation, and discrimination in the North and the South. Washington believed that African Americans should strive to simply get along with whites and refrain from demanding equal civil and political rights. At the same time, Washington encouraged whites to give African Americans better-paying jobs, Washington also promoted self-sufficiency in the black community. He urged African Americans to persevere in a segregated America, and triumph over the racist Jim Crow laws through hard work and toil. He believed in education for the development of trade, industry, and farming and the cultivation of the virtues of patience, enterprise, and thrift. This, he said, would engender the respect of whites and lead to African Americans being fully accepted as citizens and integrated into all levels of society. Because of Washington's nonthreatening racial views, he was often referred to as "the Great Accommodator." He believed that African Americans should not push to attain their civil and political rights but seek to elevate themselves to a place of respect through hard work and determination, and that African Americans were solely responsible for improving their economic, social, and political circumstances.

As Washington's influence with whites and African Americans grew, he received several honors. He became an advisor to President Theodore Roosevelt. He was the first African American ever to dine at the White House with the president. This created a huge scandal in the white community. Many whites thought that it was wrong for whites and African Americans to socialize together, and for the president to do so was unthinkable. Roosevelt defended his actions at the time and continued to seek Washington's advice, but he never invited him back to the White House. Washington became a shrewd political leader and advised not only presidents, but members of Congress and governors on political appointments for African Americans and other sympathetic whites. He actively encouraged the wealthy to contribute to various black organizations. Washington owned and financially supported many black newspapers. He was very astute at using journalists to print stories about his work and to gain support for his activities.

On September 18, 1895, Washington spoke before a largely white audience at the Cotton States and International Exposition in Atlanta, Georgia. His speech came to be known as the "Atlanta Compromise" address, a speech that many believe is one of the most important and influential speeches in American history. Although the organizers of the event worried that "public sentiment was not prepared for such an advanced step" (Harlan, 583), the organizers decided that inviting a black speaker like Washington would impress northern visitors with the evidence of racial progress in and open-mindedness of the South. Washington soothed his listeners' concerns about blacks by claiming that his race would content itself with living "by the productions of our hands" (Harlan, 584). He also made a statement that would later subject him to criticism from individuals like W.E.B. Du Bois, a statement some said sanctioned the existence of Jim Crow laws and living willfully in segregation: "In all things that are social we can be as separate as the fingers, yet one as the hand in all things essential for mutual purposes" (Harlan, 585). From this speech, Washington earned the nickname the "Great Accommodator," due to his conciliatory approach to others, even those who perpetuated a segregationist society.

In 1900, Washington established the National Negro Business League (NNBL) to support African American entrepreneurs. Washington served as president of the organization. The activities of the NNBL primarily focused on commerce and paid little attention to questions of African American civil and political rights.

Throughout much of his life, Washington attempted to pacify whites in the North and the South. When he made public speeches, he refrained from speaking about black political causes that were viewed as unpopular among southern whites. However, Washington secretly financed lawsuits opposing segregation and upholding the rights of African Americans to vote and to serve on juries. Like those who helped to fund Tuskegee Institute, Washington was highly critical of the emerging trade-union movement in the United States.

Washington was not without his public critics. A number of African Americans believed that his conservative approach undermined the quest for racial equality. The most vocal and public opposition to Washington's accommodationist strategies came from W.E.B. Du Bois, a Harvard-trained historian and sociologist. Du Bois criticized Washington's education and political philosophy and practices and advocated the education of talented African Americans who could move into leadership positions in the black community. Although Du Bois acknowledged the need for industrial and vocational training for African Americans, he believed that they should have the opportunity to pursue a college education. Du Bois thought that Washington's strategy would serve to perpetuate white oppression. Du Bois advocated political action and a civil rights agenda. As a founding member of the National Association for the Advancement of Colored People (NAACP), Du Bois argued that social change could be accomplished by developing a small group of college-educated blacks that he referred to as "the Talented Tenth."

In 1903, Du Bois spelled out his opposition to Washington's educational philosophy and practices in his book *The Souls of Black Folk*. Washington retaliated with criticism of Du Bois and his Niagara Movement. The two men also clashed over the establishment of the NAACP. Washington kept his white following by conservative policies and moderate utterances, but he faced growing black and white liberal opposition from the Niagara Movement and the NAACP, groups demanding civil rights and encouraging protest in response to white aggressions such as lynching, disenfranchisement, and segregation laws. Washington successfully fended off these critics, often by underhanded means. At the same time, however, he attempted to use his own success as a model for African American advancement by serving on the boards of Fisk and Howard Universities and directing philanthropic aid to these and other black colleges. Through his speaking engagements and private relationships, he tried to equalize public education opportunities for African Americans. The year of Washington's death in 1915 marked the beginning of the Great Migration from the rural South to the urban North. Washington's racial philosophy, pragmatically adjusted to the limiting conditions of his own era, did not survive the change.

See also African Americans; De Facto and De Jure Segregation; Du Bois, William Edward Burghardt, Integration; Jim Crow Laws; National Association for the Advancement of Colored People; Segregation; Talented Tenth.

FURTHER READING: Bontemps, Arna Wendell, *Young Booker T. Washington's Early Days*, New York: Dodd, Mead; Drinker, Frederick E., 1915, *Booker T. Washington, The Master Mind of a Child of Slavery*, Philadelphia: National Publishing Company; Harlan, Louis R., ed., 1974, *The Booker T. Washington Papers*, vols. 1–14, Urbana: University of Illinois Press; Peterson, Robert A., 1988, "Booker T. Washington: Apostle of Freedom," *Freeman* 38, no. 8 (August): 1–8; Washington, B.T., 1901, *Up from Slavery*, Tuskegee, AL: Tuskegee Institute Press.

PAULETTE PATTERSON DILWORTH

Washington Initiative 200

Washington Initiative 200 became law in 1998. It sought to terminate the ability of any government entity in the state of Washington to give preferential treatment to individuals based upon their race, sex, color, ethnicity, or national origin. In the months leading up to the November 1998 vote, Initiative 200 provoked much debate in Washington State. Many of those who discussed the initiative compared it to a similar piece of legislation arising out of California. It is argued that Washington Initiative 200 mirrors not only the language of California Proposition 209, but its purpose as well. Washington Initiative 200 has also been compared to the Houston Civil Rights Initiative. The Houston Initiative would have precluded granting preferences based upon race, gender, or national origin in the allocation of government jobs within the city of Houston, or in the awardance of government contracts. Supporters of Initiative 200 point out how its opponents attempted to employ strategies similar to those that were used to strike down the Houston initiative. Ultimately, at the close of the polls, approximately 60 percent of those who voted in the November election indicated that they supported making the initiative law in Washington.

The language used in the text of the Washington state civil rights initiative is direct and uncomplicated. Section 1, paragraph 1, reads as follows: "The state shall not discriminate against, or grant preferential treatment to, any individual or group on the basis of race, sex, color, ethnicity, or national origin in the operation of public employment, public education, or public contracting" (Washington State Civil Rights Initiative, Chapter 49.60 RCW).

Paragraph 4 of section 1 provides three exceptions to the mandate of paragraph 1. According to this paragraph, the state may classify someone based on his or her sex if it is done for medical or psychological treatment or for sexual privacy reasons. Such classification is also allowed if the classification is used for undercover law-enforcement operations or if it is done for casting purposes in films, theater, or audio or video productions. Finally, classifications are allowed if they are implemented to create separate athletic teams for males and females.

Paragraph 7 provides a rather broad definition of the term "state" as it is used in paragraph 1. The mandates of the initiative do not apply only to actions taken by state legislative, judicial, or executive bodies. Actions taken by cities, counties, or public colleges also must not violate the prohibition against discrimination or preferential treatment. The section goes on to indicate that the prohibition applies to actions taken by school districts, political subdivisions, and other governmental instrumentalities.

Much controversy surrounded the passage of Washington Initiative 200 into law. The controversy stemmed from the claim that the ultimate purpose of Initiative 200 was actually to end affirmative action. Opposition to the initiative argued that restricting the ability of the state to grant preferential treatment to minorities would effectively terminate the benefits that affirmative action programs provide to disadvantaged minorities. Supporters of the initiative argued that Initiative 200 only sought to restore the equilibrium that was intended when the 1964 Civil Rights Act was passed. Supporters have also indicated that Washington Initiative 200 was actually modeled on the 1964 Civil Rights Act and, like California Proposition 209, only intended to reaffirm the importance of protecting all citizens from the devastating impact state-sponsored race-based discrimination can have on the citizenry.

One main difference between California Proposition 209 and Washington Initiative 200 is their legal status once they were adopted in their respective elections. Proposition 209 became an amendment to the California Constitution. Washington's initiative did not become part of the state constitution. Rather, it became a generally applicable state law that finds itself on equal footing with other state laws. Initiative 200 was not provided with the added protections that are associated with constitutional amendments. After its passage, legislators were faced with the task of reconciling this new law with other laws that had potential conflicts with the new Initiative 200 mandate.

Another argument made by opponents of Initiative 200 was that the wording on the official ballot concerning the initiative was misleading. It read as follows, "Shall government be prohibited from discriminating or granting preferential treatment based on race, sex, color, ethnicity, or national origin in public employment, education, and contracting?" (Washington Secretary of State, News Release, January 21, 1998). They argued that the ballot should have been more direct and indicated that the initiative would actually end affirmative action. Supporters countered this by claiming that the initiative only sought to end quotas and preferences, not affirmative action in general. Attempting to change the ballot phraseology concerning a civil rights initiative has been referred to as the "Houston strategy." The term finds its basis in the defeat of a similar civil rights initiative in Houston, Texas. Opponents of that initiative were successful in changing the wording of the ballot, and as a result, supporters say, the initiative was defeated.

Although Washington Initiative 200 did abolish some of the tools that could be used for ensuring diversity and equal opportunity throughout Washington, it did not abolish them all. Initiative 200 prohibits discrimination or preferences based on race, sex, or ethnicity. It does not, however, prohibit giving preference to an individual based upon age or disability. Preference policies based on these factors were able to continue even after Initiative 200 became law. The initiative also allows the state to continue giving preference to veterans. Initiative 200 does not prohibit the state from employing targeted outreach programs and other preference programs not based on race, sex, or ethnicity.

See also Civil Rights Act of 1964; Preferences; Proposition 209; Veterans' Preferences.

FURTHER READING: Bond, Julian, 1998/1999, "A Call in Defense of Affirmative Action: Just Spoils of a Righteous War," *Gonzaga Law Review* 34:1–17; Brune, Tom, and Joe Heim, 1998, "New Battle Begins: Interpreting I-200," *Seattle Times*, November 4, B1; Daniel, Philip T.K., and Kyle Edward Timken, 1999, "The Rumors of My Death Have Been Exaggerated: *Hopwood*'s Error in 'Discarding' *Bakke*," *Journal of Law and Education* 28 (July): 391–418; Gee, Harvey, 2001, "Why Did Asian Americans Vote against the 1996 California Civil Rights Initiative?" *Loyola Journal of Public Interest Law* 2 (spring): 1–52; Holland, Robert, 1999, "Implementing Initiative 200: Keeping Faith with the Voters," Washington Policy Center, Policy Note 99-06, http://www.washingtonpolicy.org/ECP/PNKeepingFaithWithVoters99-06.html; Newsroom, Washington Secretary of State, 1998, "Initiative to the Legislature #200 Certified," http://www.secstate.wa.gov/office/news_releases.aspx.

SCOTT S. BRENNEMAN

WASP (White Anglo-Saxon Protestant)

WASP is an acronym that stands for white Anglo-Saxon Protestant. Among early acronyms that make reference to particular ethnic groups, WASP has been the most influential. Sociologist E. Digby Baltzell is credited with popularizing the acronym WASP with the publication in 1964 of his book *The Protestant Establishment: Aristocracy and Caste in America.* However, according to Fred Shapiro (1989), Andrew Hacker used the term first in an article published in a 1957 issue of the *American Political Science Review* in reference to the wealthy establishment.

Baltzell used the acronym to describe an elite caste of white Protestants who dominated American society. Other sociologists used it in reference to the cultural group that has dominated American history (i.e., the British). Over the years, the popular usage of WASP has evolved to refer to all white Protestants, particularly those in middle-class America. Irving Allen argues that WASP "connotes the coincidence of class privilege, suburban conformity, and the smugness of majority ethnicity" (Allen 1990, 105).

The influence of Anglo culture in the United States is undeniable. They brought with them not only their language, but also their major institutions (e.g., religion), and because of their numbers, they were able to dominate and influence the development of the United States. Today, WASP largely represents the dominant majority in the United States, that is, white European Americans. As a group, they have a history of prejudice and discrimination against those who are different. The centuries of privilege that they have enjoyed are behind the development and implementation of affirmative action programs that attempt to alter the consequences of past and present discriminatory practices and policies.

See also Assimilation Theory; Caste System; Discrimination; Ethnic Groups; Ethnocentrism; Eurocentrism; Good-Old-Boy Factor; Integration; Prejudice; White Supremacy; Xenophobia.

FURTHER READING: Allen, Irving Lewis, 1990, *Unkind Words: Ethnic Labeling from Redskin to WASP,* New York: Bergin and Garvey; Baltzell, E. Digby, 1964, *The Protestant Establishment: Aristocracy and Caste in America,* New York: Random House; Halsey, Margaret, 1977, *No Laughing Matter: The Autobiography of a WASP,* Philadelphia: J.B. Lippincott; Shapiro, Fred R., 1989, "Earlier Evidence for the Acronym WASP," *American Speech* 64 (summer): 188–189; Stalvey, Lois Mark, 1970, *The Education of a WASP,* New York: Bantam/William Morrow.

PAULINA X. RUF

Weber, Max (1864–1920)

Max Weber was a German sociologist whose work is occasionally referenced in affirmative action literature. Weber, considered the founder of sociology in Germany, wrote extensively about theory construction and understanding the role that religion and bureaucracy play in modern capitalism. Weber wrote that the traits of capitalism and bureaucracy often transcend ethnic cultures. He was also concerned about his fellow sociologists in that he felt that they let their personal values influence their theories and their research. Weber argued for a value-free type of intellectual endeavor where the researchers would put themselves in the place of those they studied and understand the world and societal impact upon the subjects. Of significance for the area of affirmative action is Weber's view of classical bureaucracy and of social hierarchy. He believed that money, power, and prestige were the driving forces in a society and that the phenomena could be understood by a society by studying the work hierarchies they produced. He also believed that the bureaucratic work hierarchy trapped the average worker into categories (referred to within the literature as the "iron cage") from which they could not escape.

According to Weber, the bureaucratic work hierarchies were necessary and involved specializations leading to a fixed division of labor. This clear-cut division of labor involves activities that are inherent in the position held and not the person holding the position. Since the hierarchical systems produce a bureaucracy that perpetuates the interests of the powerful over those of the powerless, one could argue from a feminist perspective that he was referring to gender in power roles as well. Since power, money, and prestige were often thought of as historically male attributes, Weber's discussion of bureaucracy could easily be viewed as a male-female power struggle. With the increase in bureaucracies, workers are often separated from the instruments of production, making them reliant upon the "institution" to supply the "tools" of their work. If those institutions are controlled and managed by men, the theory would suggest that women by virtue of their sex would be excluded from the workforce.

See also Marxist Theory and Affirmative Action.

FURTHER READING: "Max Weber: The Conceptualization of Bureaucracy," 2000, *Thinkers*, December, 5–8; McCaughan, Edward J., 1993, "Race, Ethnicity, Nation, and Class within Theories of Structure and Agency," *Social Justice*, spring–summer, 82–90; Stone, John, 1995, "Race, Ethnicity, and the Weberian Legacy," *American Behavioral Scientist* 38, no. 3 (January): 391–400.

SUSAN F. BRINKLEY

West, Cornel (1953–)

Cornel West has worked for racial justice since childhood and has been recognized nationally for his opinions on race and race relations. His best-selling book *Race Matters* (1993) shone the spotlight on racial issues and triggered a national debate on these issues. His most recent publications include *The Cornel West Reader* (2000) and *The African-American Century: How Black Americans Have Shaped our Country* (with Henry L. Gates Jr., 2000). While he is supportive of affirmative action, he views affirmative action as a flawed, but nonetheless necessary social program. Affirmative action redistributes wealth in a needed fashion, but does not go far enough. West has commented that "the problem is that affirmative action could never really get at the issue of corporate power in the workplace, and so you ended up with the downsizing; you ended up with the de-industrializing. You ended up with the marginalization of working people even while affirmative action was taking place." Ideally, according to West, affirmative action should be class based, not race or gender based. However, West has also commented that affirmative action is actually a "weak response" to the "legacy of white supremacy."

Cornel West was born in Tulsa, Oklahoma, on June 2, 1953. His father was a civilian air force administrator, and his mother was an elementary-school teacher and later a school principal. After moving around a great deal, the family settled in Sacramento, California. It was here that West became interested in the Baptist Church and the community-based political action advocated by the Black Panthers. Inspired by a biography of Teddy Roosevelt, at eight years of age, West decided that he would attend Harvard. Cornel West graduated in three years from Harvard magna cum laude with a degree in Near Eastern languages and literature. He then went on to Princeton University, where he received his M.A. and Ph.D. West served as professor of religion and director of the Afro-American Studies Department at Princeton until he joined the faculty at Harvard in 1994.

However, in 2001, controversy erupted. West was allegedly counseled by Harvard president Lawrence Summers for not spending sufficient time at Harvard working on another major scholarly work, spending time working on a political exploratory committee for Al Sharpton, and allegedly allowing grade inflation in his classes. West publicly countered that Summers was not fully supportive of affirmative action at Harvard. By the end of the year, West left Harvard and returned to Princeton as the Class of 1943 University Professor of Religion.

See also Class-Based Affirmative Action; Economically Disadvantaged; Gates, Henry Louis, Jr.

FURTHER READING: Fogg, Piper, and Kate Galbraith, 2002, "Gates to Remain at Harvard; Yale's Provost Will Be First Woman to Lead U. of Cambridge Full Time," *Chronicle of Higher Education*, December 13, A7; Wilson, Robin, and Scott Smallwood, 2002, "Battle of Wills at Harvard," *Chronicle of Higher Education*, January 18, A8.

PAULINA X. RUF

White, Byron Raymond (1917–2002)

Byron White, an associate justice on the U.S. Supreme Court from 1962 to 1993, has been described by Joan Biskupic (a Supreme Court reporter) as "an American hero for most of the twentieth century" (Biskupic 2002, 1). As a deputy attorney general at the U.S. Department of Justice during the first half of President John Kennedy's administration, White played a leading role in enforcing the desegregation of schools and public accommodations in the South. After being appointed to the Supreme Court by Kennedy in 1962, White joined the liberal members of the Warren Court in strictly enforcing civil rights, particularly the Civil Rights Act of 1964 and the Voting Rights Act of 1965. White also adopted an expansive interpretation of the "state action" doctrine in a series of Fourteenth Amendment Equal Protection Clause cases. In the area of affirmative action, early in his tenure on the Court, White was a strong supporter of affirmative action and aligned himself often with the liberal justices William Brennan, Thurgood Marshall, and Harry Blackmun. However, by the 1980s, White began to have problems with affirmative action and set-aside programs, and found that he was voting more and more with the conservative bloc of the Rehnquist court. In the cases he decided while on the Supreme Court, it is clear that White supported race conscious affirmative action to remedy prior discrimination. However, White opposed affirmative action plans that were not well designed and narrowly tailored, needlessly hurt innocent white individuals, or when the affirmative action plan was not designed by the federal government.

Byron White was born into a middle class family in Fort Collins, Colorado, on June 8, 1917. He spent his childhood in the nearby town of Wellington, Colorado, where his father was a lumber dealer and served as the town mayor. White graduated first in his high school class and attended the University of Colorado on a scholarship. While at the University of Colorado, White was elected student body president. However, White was best known on campus for his athletic abilities, playing on the football, baseball, and basketball teams. Because of his prowess on the gridiron (he was an All-American football player), a newspaper reporter nicknamed him "Whizzer White," a name that would stick with him (despite his displeasure with the name) throughout his entire subsequent legal career and professional life. His biographer, University of Chicago law professor Dennis Hutchinson, reported that once White (as a Supreme Court justice) was in a restaurant, approximately three decades after his football career, and a waitress walked up to him and said "Say, aren't you Whizzer White?" White replied, "I was."

After graduation from the University of Colorado in 1938, he played professional football for the Pittsburg Steelers (then named the Pittsburg Pirates) and was one of the highest paid players in the National Football League, earning $15,000. During his first season, White led the league in rushing yards. However, in 1939, White was awarded the prestigious Rhodes scholarship to study at Oxford University in England. At Oxford, White made the acquaintance of a young John F. Kennedy, who accompanied his father Joseph Kennedy on his appointment as the U.S. ambassador to the Court of St. James in England. This was the first of several times that White's path would cross with John F. Kennedy.

At the onset of World War II, White returned to the United States, where he studied law at Yale University as well as playing professional football for the Detroit Lions. However, before completing his law degree, White joined the navy in 1942. White served as an intelligence officer in the Pacific. Ironically, White's path crossed Kennedy's path again during this time. When Kennedy's PT-109 boat sank in the Pacific, it was White who was charged with writing the official navy report on the incident. By the conclusion of the war, White was the recipient of two Bronze Stars for valor and meritorious service in the Pacific theater.

After World War II, White returned to the United States and completed his studies at Yale University Law School, graduating magna cum laude with a law degree in 1946. White landed a highly competitive and sought-after Supreme Court clerkship with Chief Justice Fred Vinson. During his clerkship, he renewed his relationship with John Kennedy, who was serving in the House of Representatives from Massachusetts. Upon completion of his one-year clerkship, White returned to Colorado to practice law, which he did for the next decade and a half. In 1960, White crossed paths with Kennedy a fourth time, actively assisting in Kennedy's presidential campaign in Colorado.

As a reward for this service, when Kennedy was elected president, he named White a deputy attorney general. White earned a reputation as a strict enforcer of civil rights issues, in particular, ensuring the desegregation of schools (as mandated by *Brown v. Board of Education*, 347 U.S. 483 [1954]) and public accommodations. In one incident, White personally confronted Alabama governor John Patterson, who, in concert with the Ku Klux Klan, was not ensuring protection for the freedom riders. In 1962, a vacancy appeared on the Supreme Court (Justice Charles Whittaker resigned), giving Kennedy his first of two appointments to the

Supreme Court. Kennedy nominated White on April 3, 1962, and his confirmation was approved by a voice vote in the Senate on April 11, 1962. He was sworn in on April 16, 1962, the ninety-third justice in the history of the Supreme Court.

White's jurisprudence on the Court has been described as "nondoctrinaire pragmatism" (Israel 1992, 927) and as that of a jurist "who said he decided each case on its own merits and resisted broad judicial philosophies" (Biskupic 2002, 1). In the areas of civil rights and discrimination, especially in his first decade on the Court, White was very liberal. He sided with the liberal wing of the Warren Court on strong enforcement and support of the Civil Rights Act of 1964 and the Voting Rights Act of 1965. He also advocated broadly interpreting or construing the state action doctrine for purposes of making states responsible under the Fourteenth Amendment's Equal Protection Clause.

In the specific area of affirmative action, White was supportive of affirmative action, but only those affirmative action plans put forward by the federal government. In all of the affirmative action and Title VII cases White reviewed during his three decades on the Court, he voted to uphold only one affirmative action plan that was not sponsored by the federal government, the race-conscious admissions plan of the University of California at issue in the seminal affirmative action case *Regents of the University of California v. Bakke*, 438 U.S. 265 (1978). Therefore, it is fair to characterize White as being supportive only of federally sponsored affirmative action plans.

In *Regents of the University of California v. Bakke*, the Court was extremely fractured, issuing several different opinions in the case, none having the majority opinion status needed to make it binding precedent. While a majority of the Court in *Bakke* ultimately declared the specific affirmative action plan at issue in the case to be unconstitutional, the various members of the Court could not agree on how to view or analyze affirmative action under the Fourteenth Amendment Equal Protection Clause or under Title VI (which prohibits any institution receiving federal funds from excluding or denying benefits to any person on the grounds of race). While five justices (Lewis Powell, John Paul Stevens, Warren Burger, Potter Stewart, and William Rehnquist) ultimately agreed that the specific affirmative action plan was defective in this case, no majority opinion could be reached. Four of these five justices (excluding Powell) declined to analyze the case under the Fourteenth Amendment, as these four justices believed that the University of California violated Title VI. Powell agreed that the plan was defective, not on Title VI grounds, but rather on Equal Protection Clause grounds.

White joined the liberal bloc (known as the "antidiscrimination four" in this case) of Justices William Brennan, Thurgood Marshall, and Harry Blackmun in agreeing that race-conscious admissions plans to remedy past societal discrimination were justifiable under the Fourteenth Amendment. The "antidiscrimination four" in *Bakke*, in a plurality opinion authored by Brennen, advocated using an intermediate level of scrutiny in analyzing such race-conscious plans (as opposed to strict scrutiny). These justices, including White, believed that racial classifications could be permissibly used as part of an affirmative action program to remedy prior discrimination. The fifth vote needed to uphold the permissibility of using race-conscious factors in admissions was provided by Powell, although he issued his own opinion in the case because he did not believe that the specific plan at issue in the case satisfied constitutional requirements. Thus, as illustrated by the *Bakke* case, White's position on affirmative action early on was strongly in favor of such plans.

However, in the 1980s, Justice White has been described as drifting away from his position in *Bakke* and his general support of affirmative action. While White voted with the majority to affirm affirmative action plans at issue in three major cases spanning three decades (*United Steelworkers of America v. Weber*, 443 U.S. 193 [1979], *Fullilove v. Klutznick*, 448 U.S. 448 [1980], and *Metro Broadcasting, Inc. v. FCC*, 497 U.S. 547 [1990]), he expressed reservations or voted against affirmative action plans more often than not, either as part of the majority or in dissent (e.g., *Firefighters Local Union No. 1784 v. Stotts*, 467 U.S. 561 [1984], *Local 28 of the Sheet Metal Workers' International Association v. EEOC*, 478 U.S. 421 [1986] [in dissent], *Local No. 93, International Association of Firefighters v. City of Cleveland*, 478 U.S. 501 [1986] [in dissent], *United States v. Paradise*, 480 U.S. 149 [1987] [in dissent], and *City of Richmond v. J.A. Croson Co.*, 488 U.S. 469 [1989]).

In the *Fullilove* and *Metro Broadcasting* cases, White voted with the majority in upholding federally constructed set-aside programs as a means of remedying previous incidents of discrimination. White also approved of a private affirmative action plan adopted to comply with Title VII in *Weber*. Thus White's positions in *Fullilove*, *Metro Broadcasting*, *Weber*, and *Bakke* all supported the notion that properly drafted set-aside programs, enacted for the purpose of remedying clear prior discrimination, would survive constitutional challenges under the Fourteenth Amendment. White was a strong supporter of the rights of Congress to pass legislation to remedy racial problems or enforce civil rights legislation.

However, in cases that did not involve federally sponsored affirmative action plans or enforcement of a federal civil rights statute, White was a critic. Thus in the *Croson* case, White sided with the majority in overturning an affirmative action set-aside program adopted by the city of Richmond despite the fact that this program had been modeled after the federal program upheld in the *Fullilove* case (the only other major difference in the cases was that *Fullilove* dealt with a 10 percent set-aside for minorities, while *Croson* dealt with a 30 percent set-aside for minorities). Also, in *Croson*, White agreed with the majority, in an opinion authored by Justice Sandra Day O'Connor, that any racial classification, even benign discrimination, should be subject to strict scrutiny. Thus White had reversed his view of the appropriate level of scrutiny for racial classifications that he had taken in the *Bakke* case eleven years earlier (in *Bakke*, White had advocated using an intermediate level of scrutiny; in *Croson*, White advocated strict scrutiny).

In several affirmative action cases, White denied that federal district courts should have the power to implement broad remedial affirmative action programs as a remedy for Title VII violations. Thus in the *Paradise*, *Stotts*, and *Firefighters v. Cleveland* cases, White took the position that the federal district court in each of these cases had exceeded its powers by imposing affirmative action remedies. Finally, from his position on these cases, it is clear that White was very reluctant to approve affirmative action plans that hurt innocent majority-group members or were implemented to benefit individuals in an area that was not subject to a clear documented history of prior discrimination.

See also Affirmative Action Plan/Program; Blackmun, Harry Andrew; Brennen, William Joseph; *Brown v. Board of Education*; Burger Court and Affirmative Action; *City of Richmond v. J.A. Croson Co.*; Civil Rights Act of 1964; Department of Justice;

Education and Affirmative Action; Employment (Private) and Affirmative Action; Employment (Public) and Affirmative Action; Equal Protection Clause; *Firefighters Local Union No. 1784 v. Stotts*; Fourteenth Amendment; Freedom Riders; *Fullilove v. Klutznick*; Kennedy, John Fitzgerald; Ku Klux Klan; *Local 28 of the Sheet Metal Workers' International Association v. EEOC*; *Local No. 93, International Association of Firefighters v. City of Cleveland*; Marshall, Thurgood; *Metro Broadcasting, Inc. v. FCC*; Powell, Lewis Franklin, Jr.; *Regents of the University of California v. Bakke*; Rehnquist, William Hobbs; State Action Doctrine; Stevens, John Paul; Strict Scrutiny; Supreme Court and Affirmative Action; Title VI of the Civil Rights Act of 1964; Title VII of the Civil Rights Act of 1964; *United States v. Paradise*; *United Steelworkers of America v. Weber*; Voting Rights Act of 1965; Warren Court and Affirmative Action.

FURTHER READING: Biskupic, Joan, 2002, "Ex–Supreme Court Justice Byron White Dies," *USA Today*, April 15, 1; Hutchinson, Dennis, 1998, *The Man Who Once Was Whizzer White: A Portrait of Justice Byron R. White*, New York: Free Press; Israel, Fred L., 1992, "White, Byron Raymond," in *The Oxford Companion to the United States Supreme Court*, edited by Kermit L. Hall, New York: Oxford University Press; Spann, Girardeau A., 2000, *The Law of Affirmative Action: Twenty-five Years of Supreme Court Decisions on Race and Remedies*, New York: New York University Press.

JAMES A. BECKMAN

White Primary

The white primary was a political device and procedure used in the South for more than sixty years to control the outcome of state and local elections and ensure white supremacy in election returns. The white primary was instituted primarily as a way to circumvent the Fifteenth Amendment and keep blacks from exercising their right to vote. The utilization of white primaries is an illustration of how far southern states went in an effort to ensure that blacks were politically disenfranchised after the Civil War.

The Fifteenth Amendment, ratified in 1870, states that "the right of citizens of the United States to vote shall not be denied or abridged by the United States or by any State on account of race, color, or previous condition of servitude." On its face, the amendment appeared to guarantee the right to vote to blacks. However, on closer scrutiny, the Fifteenth amendment initially was interpreted as only prohibiting state governments from depriving citizens of the right to vote on account of race. Hence in the South (where the Republican Party of Abraham Lincoln was not a viable force after Reconstruction), the Democratic Party was the dominant political party in all elections. Due to little opposition to the Democratic Party from other parties in the general election, this meant that the Democratic candidates would automatically win the general election. Thus to ensure that the Democratic Party remained under white control, the white primary was instituted. The advocates of the white primary argued that since political parties were private, voluntary organizations, they could discriminate in elections that determined party candidates. Phrased another way, there was no "state action" that would implicate the Fifteenth Amendment and its protections. The rationale behind this move was to keep white candidates seeking nominations from appealing to black voters with promises of civil rights legislation.

The first white primary case to reach the Supreme Court was *Nixon v. Herndon*, 273 U.S. 536 (1927), brought by the National Association for the Advancement of Colored People (NAACP), which had been founded in 1909. The Court struck down a Texas law that excluded blacks from participating in the state's Democratic Party primary election. However, it only invalidated the law based on the Equal Protection Clause of the Fourteenth Amendment; it did not guarantee blacks the right to vote in the primary. In *Grovey v. Townsend*, 295 U.S. 45 (1935), the Supreme Court upheld Texas's version of the white primary because it did not involve state action, thus barring black Texans from politics.

The white primary was finally declared unconstitutional in *Smith v. Allwright*, 321 U.S. 649 (1944). The Texas Supreme Court declared the Democratic Party of Texas a "voluntary association" and allowed only whites to participate in primary elections. Lonnie Smith, a black man, brought suit against S.S. Allwright, a county election official, because he denied Smith the right to vote in the 1940 Texas Democratic primary. The lower courts dismissed the case, relying on the decision in *Grovey* that the Texas Democratic Party was a private organization and could limit its membership on the basis of race. The case was appealed to the Supreme Court in 1943 and was decided in 1944.

The question presented in *Smith v. Allwright* was, "Did denying blacks the right to vote in primary elections violate the Fifteenth Amendment?" Phrased another way, was there state action? Future Supreme Court justice Thurgood Marshall argued against the white primary. The Texas Democratic Party was certain that the Court would uphold its decision in *Grovey* and thus did not even send counsel. In an 8–1 decision, the Supreme Court overruled *Grovey* and declared the white primary unconstitutional. Speaking for the majority, Justice Stanley Reed of Kentucky stated, "[T]he right to vote in such a primary for the nomination of candidates without discrimination by the State, like the right to vote in a general election, is a right secured by the Constitution. By the terms of the Fifteenth Amendment that right may not be abridged by any State on account of race." Justice Reed then examined Texas election laws and concluded, "We think this statutory system for the selection of party nominees for inclusion on the general election ballot makes the party which is supposed to follow these legislative laws an agency of the state insofar as it determines participants in a primary election. . . . this Court has freely exercised its power to re-examine the basis of its constitutional questions. . . . *Grovey v. Townsend* is overruled." The Court held that while the Democratic Party of Texas was a voluntary organization, it operated under state authority in the selection of county-level party leaders and in conducting elections and under state courts in resolving contested elections; therefore, there was sufficient "state action" to implicate the Fifteenth Amendment protections, and blacks had the right to vote in primaries.

With the *Smith* decision, the coffin of the white primary was finally sealed. However, South Carolina tried to resurrect the issue by repealing all state laws governing primaries and placing primary elections in the hands of political parties. The Democratic Party in South Carolina then outright barred blacks from participating. This scheme did not work and was rejected by the Fourth Circuit Court of Appeals. The final blow to the white primary came in the case of *Terry v. Adams*, 345 U.S. 461 (1953). The Court declared "the Jaybird" (a cross between a political party and a private club in Texas) primary election scheme unconstitutional and ruled that it violated the Fifteenth Amendment because it was the equivalent of a white primary.

See also Democratic Party and Affirmative Action; Equal Protection Clause; Fifteenth Amendment; Fourteenth Amendment; Marshall, Thurgood; National Association for the Advancement of Colored People; Republican Party and Affirmative Action; State Action Doctrine; Voting Rights Act of 1965.

FURTHER READING: Abraham, Henry J., and Barbara A. Perry, 1994, *Freedom and the Court: Civil Rights and Liberties in the United States*, 6th ed., New York: Oxford University Press; Miller, Loren, 1966, *The Petitioners: The Story of the Supreme Court of the United States and the Negro*, New York: Pantheon Books; Wasby, Stephen L., Anthony A. D'Amato, and Rosemary Metrailer, 1977, *Desegregation from Brown to Alexander*, Carbondale: Southern Illinois University Press.

NAOMI ROBERTSON

White Supremacy

The contemporary white supremacist movement has vociferously opposed affirmative action and has used this position to recruit members from the broader population also opposed to affirmative action. While there are approximately 600 white supremacist groups in the United States today, the movement is not a new phenomenon. The Ku Klux Klan, historically the most influential white supremacist organization in the United States, was founded in 1866. While it is difficult to estimate the membership of these groups, there are estimated to be approximately 20,000 to 30,000 activists and another 150,000 "armchair" supporters. The reach of the movement is expanding as a result of the Internet and the World Wide Web, and far more people read white supremacist publications and web sites than actually join the movement. The movement's use of the World Wide Web and Internet to reach a wider audience over the past decade makes it increasingly difficult to measure its audience and influence.

American society has experienced tremendous social change in recent decades, sparked by the civil rights movement, the women's movement, and the gay and lesbian movement. More recently, debates over affirmative action, multicultural curricula, welfare, and other contentious topics have been perceived by many white men as attacks against them, not only against their racial privilege, but their identity as men as well. Organizing against the advances fought for by the civil rights movement, especially affirmative action and desegregation, these organizations seek to roll back the advances of the past three decades and reassert white, male, heterosexual hegemony. While the tactics of the movement are extreme, especially its encouragement of violence, it is part of a broader cultural backlash to movements for equality.

The traditional conception of masculinity teaches men that they are to be in control, aggressive, strong, and the breadwinner of the family. White men have learned to see this as their entitlement. But what it means to be a white man is no longer secure, and white male privilege no longer proceeds unquestioned. Many feel under siege and vulnerable, facing a "crisis of masculinity." As a result of these social and cultural changes, as well as economic dislocations and insecurity, many white men believe that they are being denied the opportunity to achieve the American dream, which they see as their birthright.

The white supremacist movement draws upon historically mainstream views about race and gender and is most likely to flourish in communities that are most sympathetic to racist beliefs. Research reveals that many Americans share the views of white supremacists, even if they are not members of the movement. While less than 10 percent of hate crimes are committed by members of white supremacist organizations, their ideology reaches far beyond their membership. The presence of the movement serves to encourage hate-motivated violence, providing a voice, a community, and even a sense of legitimacy for a wider audience. As survey research reveals, the movement articulates the wider concerns shared by many Americans, as well as a comprehensive ideology that enables a broader audience to interpret their own experiences and concerns.

Members of white supremacist organizations resemble the general population in terms of education levels, occupation, and income. The organizations attract primarily men; however, many groups have recently targeted women for recruitment. Despite the growing numbers of women in the movement, it remains centrally concerned with preserving white male privilege. It is not only about hatred of others, but about defining identity for its members and maintaining white male power. This movement provides white men with an opportunity to perform and prove their masculinity. The movement has also recently focused efforts on recruiting young people via white power music and the web.

There is a wide variety of white supremacist organizations, ranging from neo-Nazis and Klan groups to Christian Identity adherents and skinheads. While some organizations are attempting to move into the political mainstream, others have become increasingly violent. The movement is united by a shared system of beliefs. White supremacists believe that racial and gender differences are essential and unchanging, given either by God or biology. Social inequality is seen as a reflection of the natural order. This naturalized hierarchy places white men securely on top. Jews, defined as a nonwhite race, are constructed as the ultimate enemy, trying to race-mix the white race into oblivion. People of color and women are defined as inferior to white men, and it is believed to be white men's duty to protect innocent white women and children from the brainwashing Jews who control the world and from the criminal, animal-like blacks and other people of color. For adherents, the only way to secure the future of the white race is through the creation of a racially pure homeland.

Race and gender identities are naturalized and seen as justifying inequality. These assumptions undergird the movement's critique of contemporary America: if things are falling apart all around us, it is because we are trying to change people's essential nature. White supremacist ideology thus offers itself as the antidote to America's current social problems by promising to empower men who feel that they no longer have any power. The movement seemingly offers white men the chance to prove their masculinity. White men are repeatedly attacked by the movement for becoming feminized (and unsettling the natural order) and are encouraged to become real men by standing up and protecting white women, reasserting their place in the natural hierarchy, and taking over the world. Furthermore, the movement's fear of white genocide leads to an obsession with controlling white women's sexuality and reproduction.

Resistance to affirmative action has been a central tenet of the contemporary movement, and its views toward affirmative action in many ways resemble the concerns of a much larger conservative backlash. Because white supremacists believe that it is now white men who are the victims of inequality in the United States, affirmative action is characterized as reverse racism. It is believed to be a part of the larger plot to eliminate the white race. White supremacists argue that white men by nature deserve to be in power, and that affirmative action is a form of social engineering that is going against God and nature.

See also Hate Crimes; Ku Klux Klan; Reverse Discrimination; Scapegoating/Displaced-Aggression Theories.

FURTHER READING: Blee, Kathleen M., 2002, *Inside Organized Racism: Women in the Hate Movement*, Berkeley: University of California Press; Feagin, Joe, 2000, *Racist America*, New York: Routledge; Feagin, Joe R., Hernan Vera, and Pinar Batur, 2001, *White Racism*, 2d ed., New York: Routledge; Ferber, Abby L., 1998, *White Man Falling: Race, Gender, and White Supremacy*, Lanham, MD: Rowman and Littlefield.

ABBY L. FERBER

Women and the Workplace

Affirmative action policies have enabled women to enter a variety of traditionally male occupations from which they had been excluded. Today, most young women plan to work outside of the home, and women are now found in every career field. Women have turned to the law during the past century to combat discrimination by employers; however, women still face gender inequities in the workplace. Indeed, one of the most significant developments in the workplace since 1900 is the tremendous increase in the number of women entering the paid labor market. In 1900, 21 percent of women were in the labor force; by 1995, that number had risen to 76 percent. In 1900, 4 percent of married women were working for pay; by 1960, that number reached 19 percent. Today, nearly 60 percent of married women with children under six work in the paid labor force. Most women would choose to work even if they did not have to; however, the reality is that women have to work, either because they are the sole support of themselves and their children, or because their family cannot survive on one income.

Since the American Civil War, women's wages have fluctuated between two-fifths and two-thirds of men's wages. The gap has narrowed more in the past decade, with women earning seventy-four cents for every dollar men earned in 1997. This is due to women's higher educational levels, increased years in the labor market, use of antidiscrimination law to enter higher-paying fields, and increased unionization in female occupations. However, more than two-thirds of the narrowing of the wage gap is due to the decrease in men's real earnings. Further, from 1995 to 2000, in a number of fields the pay gap widened, according to the General Accounting Office.

Job segregation is the most pervasive form of inequality in the workplace and one of the primary causes of the wage gap. Women and men are largely concentrated in different jobs and occupations, and occupations in which women predominate are lower paying than similar jobs performed by men. The gender composition of an occupation is a much better predictor of wages than any features of the job itself. The pay gap is not strictly due to job segregation, however. Women also make less money at the exact same jobs as men, even when they are working for the same employers. For example, not only do female educators make less than men, but female elementary-school teachers, secondary-school teachers, and professors all earn less than males. This holds true in the vast majority of jobs, even when controlling for all other factors, such as education and experience. A "glass ceiling" still prevents most women from being promoted equally with men: women hold only 7 percent of corporate board seats; 95 to 97 percent of senior managers are men; and of the 4,000 highest paid directors, officers, and CEOs in the United States, less than .5 percent are women. Women who do make it to top managerial positions are less likely than men to be married, generally earn less, and are more likely to work part-time.

In the 1970s, sexual harassment was first identified as a problem and litigated as a violation of Title VII of the 1964 Civil Rights Act. At least half of all working women in the United States will experience sexual harassment. Sexual harassment usually takes the form of either quid pro quo harassment, where sexual activity is expected in exchange for advancement or to avoid punishment, or in the form of a hostile or offensive work environment. Traditional gender ideologies reinforce inequality in the workplace. Historically, employers have assumed that women will be less committed to their jobs than men, and that they are less likely to need their salary to support a family. Additionally, many occupations are constructed around the image of male workers, so women are caught between being seen as too feminine or too aggressive. Additionally, workplaces have been structured around the assumption that workers have wives at home to attend to the children and household. Understanding women and the workplace requires a broad reconceptualization of work. When the understanding of work is limited to paid work, much of the work that women perform is erased from view. There is dramatic gender segregation of domestic labor. As increasing numbers of women have entered the paid labor force, men's participation in the home has changed little. Women who are married and employed full-time outside of the home still perform 70 percent of the housework and child care for their families.

The law has been particularly helpful in enabling women to gain access to all occupational fields. The 1963 Equal Pay Act mandates that employers must pay men and women equal wages for the same work; Title VII of the 1964 Civil Rights Act prohibits discrimination based on sex. In addition, comparable worth policies have been proposed to provide similar wages for roughly comparable jobs, so that jobs can be compared and evaluated and wages set more equitably. Interventionist strategies in hiring and promotion, such as affirmative action, have been particularly helpful for women, as well as family-friendly workplace policies, such as on-site child care, parental leave, and flextime, which directly benefit all employees.

See also Civil Rights Act of 1964; Equal Pay Act of 1963; Gender Norms; Gender Segregation in Employment; Gender Stratification; General Accounting Office; Glass Ceilings; Sex and Gender; Stereotypes, Gender; Title VII of the Civil Rights Act of 1964.

FURTHER READING: Bose, Christine, and Glenna Spitze, 1987, *Ingredients for Women's Employment Policy*, Albany: State University of New York Press; Goldin, Claudia, 1990, *Understanding the Gender Gap: An Economic History of American Women*, New York: Oxford University Press; Kanter, Rosabeth Moss, 1977, *Men and Women of the Corporation*, New York: Basic Books; Kimmel, Michael S., 2000, *The Gendered Society*, New York: Oxford University Press;

MacKinnon, Catherine, 1977, *Sexual Harassment of Working Women*, Cambridge, MA: Harvard University Press; Reskin, Barbara, ed., 1984, *Sex Segregation in the Workplace: Trends, Explanations, Remedies*, Washington, DC: National Academy Press; Reskin, Barbara, and Irene Padavic, 1995, *Women and Men at Work*, Thousand Oaks, CA: Pine Forge Press.

ABBY L. FERBER

Women's Education

Until recently, higher education for women in the United States was limited to the liberal arts and to the less prestigious levels of professional fields. Men studied to become doctors, whereas women studied to become nurses. As undergraduates, women majored in home economics or English, for example, and especially in education. Professions were sharply circumscribed by gender. Women taught kindergarten or perhaps in high school. Men practiced law or went into business. Until well into the twentieth century, some states forbade women to practice law, so there was no point in admitting women to law school. Today, in part as a result of the women's movement and civil rights legislation such as Title IX of the Education Amendments of 1972, women are entering law schools and medical schools in numbers comparable to those of men, and more and more women are studying in theological seminaries to become members of the clergy. As undergraduates, many more women are majoring in business fields. The ratio of women studying for an M.B.A., however, remains quite low, and men continue to dominate the technical fields such as engineering. Moreover, some argue that women remain subject to a "glass ceiling" in education.

Before the twentieth century, higher education for women was restricted to an elite few, and even these women were segregated for the most part on separate campuses in both the public and the private sector. Harvard University established Radcliffe in 1879, a separate college for women. In 1884, the state of Mississippi established the first public woman's college, the Mississippi Industrial Institute and College, which focused on the liberal arts and industrial technologies. Women were not trained to develop industrial technologies, however, or even to function as managers. The purpose of their education was to train women to enter the lower levels of the industrial workforce or to serve as cultured hostesses in their own homes. In 1920, the name of the institute was changed to the Mississippi State College for Women to reflect an expanded range of professional opportunities, albeit limited still to fields such as nursing and education. In 1974, the name of the college was changed once more, this time to Mississippi University for Women to reflect the expansion of graduate programs. The state of Texas followed a similar approach to women's education with the establishment in 1901 of the Girl's Industrial College in Denton. It was renamed the Texas State College for Women in 1934 to reflect an expanded curriculum that included health sciences and public school teacher training. Now named Texas Woman's University, this state institution grants doctoral degrees in a range of fields, but limited primarily to the health sciences. It does not have a medical school, however, or a law school, nor does it offer an M.B.A. or degrees in theology. To earn these kinds of degrees, women must attend coeducational institutions of higher education, and they are doing so in greater and greater numbers nationally.

Despite the increase in representation of women in some professional and graduate programs, other programs remain the domain of males for the most part. At the graduate level, as noted previously, men far outnumber women in M.B.A. programs, even though there are as many women as men in many other graduate programs. At the undergraduate level, the number of male students majoring in engineering and even in computer sciences is far greater than that of women. Some have accounted for these disparities within the context of stereotypical gender roles, both in the choice of professions and in the education of females at an early age, especially with respect to mathematics. Although women are no longer barred legally from pursuing any degree or profession, there remains, some argue, a "glass ceiling" for women, at least with respect to some professions. Even those women who have chosen to pursue traditionally male-dominated degrees and professions are subject to gender bias, some argue, in that most of the professors in these fields are male, and they tend to favor the development of the male students. Moreover, women are subject to sexual harassment far more often than men, both from faculty and from students of the opposite gender. Some advocates of women's education have asserted as well that women learn differently than men and that this difference poses a greater hardship for women than men, primarily because there are many more men than women teaching what are ostensibly co-educational courses.

Some of the solutions to these and other problems associated with women's education include a call for an aggressive, affirmative approach to the composition of the faculty, especially with respect to gender. A more radical, separatist approach is to maintain and even expand the role of predominantly women's institutions such as Mississippi University for Women and Texas Woman's University. The extension of the mission of these kinds of institutions would include law and medical schools for women, schools of engineering, and other graduate or professional programs either traditionally or perhaps even still dominated by males. Rather than expanding the scope, however, advocates of these kinds of women's universities are fighting to maintain the very existence of a segregated or at least predominantly female institution of higher learning. Critics charge that since women are now eligible to attend any public university and major in any degree program, there is no longer any need for women's institutions and that such institutions represent a form of reverse discrimination against men.

Another method of promoting women's education has been the establishment of women's studies programs. The purpose and scope of such programs varies from one campus to another. Typical of such programs, however, is the commitment to educating students, and especially female students, with respect to the roles that sexuality and gender play, both personally and institutionally, in maintaining the hegemony of males. For example, one goal might be to help women see that the choice to leave school to have a family is not a natural choice based on her biology as much as it is one of gender, based on stereotypes of the "normal" family structure, with the mother as homemaker and the father as breadwinner.

See also Gender Norms; Gender Segregation in Employment; Gender Stratification; Glass Ceilings; Minority Professionals and Affirmative Action; *Mississippi University for Women v. Hogan*; Stereotypes, Gender; Sex Discrimination; Title IX of the Civil Rights Act of 1964.

FURTHER READING: Bae, Yupin, 1997, *Women in Mathematics and Science*, Washington, DC: U.S. Government Printing Office; David, Miriam, 1998, *Negotiating the Glass Ceiling: Careers of Senior Women in the Academic World*, New York: Routledge; Davis, Sara, 1999, *Coming into Her Own: Educational Success in Girls and Women*, New York: John Wiley and Sons; Deak, Joann, 1998, *How Girls Thrive: An Essential Guide for Educators*, New York: National Association of Independent Schools; Eisenhardt, Margaret, 1990, *Educated in Romance: Women, Achievement, and College Culture*, Chicago: University of Chicago Press; Hayes, Elisabeth, and Daniele D. Flannery, 2000, *Women as Learners: The Significance of Gender in Adult Learning*, New York: John Wiley and Sons; Howe, Florence, 1988, *Women and Higher Education in American History*, New York: W.W. Norton; Sadker, David, 1994, *Failing in Fairness: How America's Schools Cheat Girls*, New York: Charles Scribner's Sons; Weiler, Jeanne, 2000, *Codes and Controls: Race, Gender Identity, and Schooling*, Albany: State University of New York Press.

MICHAEL D. QUIGLEY

Wygant v. Jackson Board of Education, 476 U.S. 267 (1986)

The 1986 Supreme Court case *Wygant v. Jackson Board of Education* addressed an important question of affirmative action policy, whether a preferential protection against layoffs for school employees who were hired because of their race or ethnicity was consistent with the Equal Protection Clause of the Fourteenth Amendment. In *Wygant*, the Court dealt with two important constitutional questions: first, whether racial classifications that burden whites should be considered inherently suspect in the same way that classifications that impact minorities are said to be suspect; and second, whether classifications that provide compensatory benefits to a group of people (blacks, for instance) should be subject to the same strict scrutiny standard as invidious (harmful) classifications. Ultimately, in a 5–4 decision, the Court held that it was unconstitutional for a school board to terminate a white teacher to preserve the jobs of blacks with less seniority. The Court held that such a scheme violated the white teacher's equal protection rights. The Court also rejected the "role model theory" as a constitutionally permissible justification for implementing an affirmative action plan.

In 1972, the Jackson Board of Education and the union representing the schoolteachers agreed to a new provision in their collective-bargaining arrangement. The provision known as Article XII stated that "in the event that it becomes necessary to reduce the number of teachers through layoff from employment, teachers with the most seniority shall be retained, except that at no time will there be a greater percentage of minority personnel laid off than the current percentage of minority personnel at the time of the layoff." The school board attempted to follow Article XII, and in 1976–1977 and 1981–1982, when nonminority teachers with more seniority were laid off, minority teachers with less seniority were kept in the system. The displaced white teachers brought suit in a federal district court, arguing that the layoff policy violated their rights under the Equal Protection Clause of the Fourteenth Amendment. The district court ruled against the white plaintiffs, insisting that racial preferences in layoff policies were consistent with the Fourteenth Amendment in an attempt to remedy societal discrimination and provide minority schoolchildren with more identifiable role models. The U.S.

Court of Appeals for the Sixth Circuit affirmed the lower court decision, and the nonminority teachers brought the case to the U.S. Supreme Court.

In a 5–4 decision, the Supreme Court overturned the lower court decision and ruled for the white plaintiffs. The justices insisted that the role model theory and past societal discrimination were insufficient goals to justify race-conscious state action. The current layoff policy would permit the board to continue discriminatory hiring and layoffs well beyond the necessary remedy. The compensatory remedy also bore no relationship to actual past discriminatory policies. Additionally, societal discrimination was simply too "amorphous" a concept to justify this particular affirmative action plan. Finally, the Court majority answered the constitutional questions mentioned previously: should racial classifications that burden whites be considered suspect, and should compensatory programs for minorities be examined under a doctrine of strict scrutiny? The Court answered affirmatively to both ideas by insisting that "the level of scrutiny does not change merely because the challenged classification operates against a group that historically has not been subject to governmental discrimination." Whites could be burdened, the Court implied, in the same way as blacks, and consequently the state's effort at remedial action had to be declared unconstitutional under a strict scrutiny test.

Justices Thurgood Marshall, William Brennan, and Harry Blackmun wrote a dissenting opinion and took a different perspective regarding the facts of the *Wygant* appeal. Marshall insisted that the Court majority spent little time assessing evidence of past discrimination in the Jackson school system. He cited, for example, that although the first black teacher had been hired in 1954, minority representation in the Jackson public schools had grown only to 3.9 percent by 1969. When, according to Justice Marshall, the Jackson branch of the NAACP filed a complaint with the Michigan Civil Rights Commission, the commission found substantive legitimacy in the charge of race-based discrimination. Marshall's point was a direct refutation of the Court majority's unwillingness to acknowledge past discrimination and the need for a preferential plan for hiring and layoffs. In defense of Jackson's affirmative action plan, Marshall argued, "I, too, believe that layoffs are unfair. But unfairness ought not be confused with constitutional injury."

Justice John Paul Stevens's dissenting opinion raised additional claims to those of Marshall, Brennan, and Blackmun. Stevens argued that the Court should not focus on whether Jackson's affirmative action plan was instituted to remedy past "sins," but rather should examine why the board felt that the plan advanced "the public interest in educating children for the future." For Stevens, the education of children by an integrated faculty should supersede any adverse effects felt by the disadvantaged group—in this case, the white teachers with greater seniority who suffered layoffs. In essence, for Justice Stevens in dissent, the role model theory should be a permissible justification for state-imposed affirmative action plans.

The *Wygant* decision was one of several during the 1980s and 1990s that challenged the legitimacy and scope of affirmative action in the United States. Conservative justices appointed by Republican presidents continued to argue that offering preferential treatment based on membership in a definable group was in direct opposition to the idea of equal protection under the law. Preferential treatment or reverse discrimination, as the justices referred to affirmative action policy, was an unconstitutional remedy for past incidents of discrimination. The *Wygant* decision, together with the Court's decisions in *City of Richmond v. J.A. Croson Co.*, 488 U.S. 469 (1989), and *Adarand Constructors, Inc. v. Peña*, 515 U.S. 200 (1995), would continue the trend of finding affirmative action plans unconstitutional under a strict scrutiny standard of the Fourteenth Amendment.

See also Adarand Constructors, Inc. v. Peña; Benign Discrimination; Blackmun, Harry Andrew; Brennan, William Joseph; *City of Richmond v. J.A. Croson Co.;* Equal Protection Clause, Fourteenth Amendment; Invidious Discrimination; Marshall, Thurgood; National Association for the Advancement of Colored People; Role Model Theory; Stevens, John Paul; Strict Scrutiny; Suspect Classification; *Taxman v. Piscataway Township Board of Education.*

FURTHER READING: Patterson, Katrina, 1999, "What May Have Become a New Title VII Precedent on Affirmative Action in the Workplace: *Piscataway Township Board of Education v. Taxman*—Permissible or Impermissible?" *New York Law School Journal of Human Rights* 15 (winter): 355–383; Spann, Girardeau A., 2000, *The Law of Affirmative Action: Twenty-five Years of Supreme Court Decisions on Race and Remedies,* New York: New York University Press.

JANIS JUDSON

X

Xenophobia

Xenophobia, which is a biological and psychological aversion to individuals or groups that are perceived to be strangers, has been a primary cause of racial conflict and oppression. Affirmative action programs are designed to reduce the impact of this oppression on racial minorities, but in doing so, they often increase racial conflict. Throughout much of history, people have gathered in groups to cooperatively provide for self-preservation and advancement. Sociobiologists attribute this trait, observed in humans and other mammals, to a biological response to predation from one's own or another species. Historically, isolated groups developed independent in-group verbal and nonverbal languages, cultural values, and group identities that differentiated them from members of out-groups, who represented a threat to their lives, identities, and economic resources.

The existence of this in-group/out-group rivalry does not always create conflict between differentiated groups. When economic, cultural, and identity resources are in abundance or secure, the rivalry manifests itself in competition, but when these resources become unstable or scarce, the rivalry can turn into open conflict, subjugation, and violence as ethnocentric members of in-groups pull together and cooperate to defeat out-groups that are illogically demonized. Xenophobic fears manifest themselves in governmental policy when portions of a polity's majority group feel that their cultural values, economic resources, and identity are threatened by out-groups. In U.S. history, there have been many instances in which majority groups have oppressed minority groups due to xenophobic fears or rhetoric. In the aftermath of the Civil War, former slaves and recent immigrants willing to accept low wages undercut wages for members of established majority groups who competed for similar jobs, causing a split in the labor market. Majority groups reacted by using their considerable political power to create laws and policies, including Jim Crow laws and civic restrictions on immigrants, to subjugate their competitors and remove them from labor markets. Gradually, formal subjugation was outlawed, but informal subjugation evidenced by de facto segregation and dramatic economic disparities between racial groups has persisted. To combat this oppression, governments under new political pressures have created affirmative action programs that attempt to ensure that minorities receive equal treatment in the marketplace. While these policies often relieve some of the effects of decades of oppression on minorities, they also reinforce in-group/out-group identity differences and exacerbate interracial conflict by rationing economic resources according to these differences.

See also Assimilation Theory; De Facto and De Jure Segregation; Discrimination; Ethnocentrism; Immigration Act of 1965; Integration; Jim Crow Laws; Split-Labor-Market Theory; *Yick Wo v. Hopkins.*

FURTHER READING: Bonacich, Edna, 1972, "A Theory of Ethnic Antagonism: The Split Labor Market," *American Sociological Review* 37, no. 5 (October): 547–559; Dennen, Johan M.G. van der, 1986, "Ethnocentrism and In-Group/Out-Group Differentiation: A Review and Interpretation of the Literature," in *The Sociobiology of Ethnocentrism: Evolutionary Dimensions of Xenophobia, Discrimination, Racism, and Nationalism,* edited by Vernon Reynolds, Vincent Falger and Ian Vine, Athens: University of Georgia Press; Falger, Vincent S.E., 1986, "From Xenophobia to Xenobiosis? Biological Aspects of the Foundation of International Relations," in *The Sociobiology of Ethnocentrism: Evolutionary Dimensions of Xenophobia, Discrimination, Racism, and Nationalism,* edited by Vernon Reynolds, Vincent Falger and Ian Vine, Athens: University of Georgia Press; Ross, Bernard H., and Myron A. Levine, 1996, *Urban Politics: Power in Metropolitan America,* 5th ed., Itasca, IL: F.E. Peacock.

MARK J. SENEDIAK

Y

Yick Wo v. Hopkins, 118 U.S. 356 (1886)

In *Yick Wo v. Hopkins,* the U.S. Supreme Court held that the Fourteenth Amendment's Equal Protection Clause applied equally to all persons, regardless of race or even citizenship or alien status. While the Court recognized the power of states to regulate safety and health practices pursuant to statutes, the Court made clear in *Yick Wo* that such state action in applying the statute must be done in a non-discriminatory and good-faith manner to the benefit of all individuals. In so holding, the Court recognized that even a statute that does not discriminate "on its face" (i.e., a statute that is facially neutral) could violate the Equal Protection Clause if the neutral statute was applied in a discriminatory manner. The *Yick Wo* case also represents one of the first major occasions in which the Court recognized the notion of "disparate treatment or impact" and allowed the use of statistical evidence to prove discrimination. The *Yick Wo* decision and *Strauder v. West Virginia,* 100 U.S. 303 (1879), were also two of the few major favorable decisions under the Fourteenth Amendment for minorities during this period of American history.

The facts of the *Yick Wo* case are briefly as follows: From 1820 to 1882 (the date the first Chinese Exclusion Act was passed by Congress), waves of Chinese immigrants came to California. The Chinese immigrants provided much of the labor needed to build the infrastructure and industries and to lay the tracks that connected the railroads in the western states. By 1880, the number of Chinese immigrants was estimated at 75,000, which amounted to roughly 10 percent of California's population at the time. Furthermore, nearly half of the Chinese population (approximately 30,000) was situated in the San Francisco area. As illustrated by the racist Chinese Exclusion Act of 1882, xenophobia against the Chinese immigrants was rampant, and many of the non-Chinese citizens of California viewed the Chinese immigrants in a very unfavorable light.

In the San Francisco area, many Chinese operated laundries as a way of earning a living, and, in fact, most laundries in San Francisco were operated by Chinese immigrants. As a way "to wipe out the Chinese laundry business" in San Francisco, the San Francisco Board of Supervisors adopted an ordinance that required all individuals who operated a laundry to obtain a laundry operating license (Wunder 1992, 948). The ordinance further exempted from its coverage laundries that operated in brick buildings, specifying that those wishing to operate laundries in wooden buildings must first obtain a permit. The arguable justification of the San Francisco Board of Supervisors in passing such an ordinance was the power to legislate for the general health and welfare of its citizenry and to protect residents from the danger of fire.

Of the approximately 200 Chinese who applied for permits, none were granted one. However, all but one of the non-Chinese who applied for permits were allowed to continue operating their laundry facilities. Countless Chinese who had not applied for a permit or had been rejected were fined and/or arrested for violating the ordinance. Yick Wo, the plaintiff in the case, was denied a license, despite the fact that he had operated a laundry in California for approximately twenty-two years. Yick Wo was also denied a license despite the fact that his facilities had been inspected and found safe a year before he was denied the permit. After he was denied his license, Yick Wo continued to operate his business and was subsequently arrested and held in jail for ten days.

Yick Wo filed suit in the California state court system, suing the local sheriff (Hopkins) who arrested him. In his case, Yick Wo's attorneys utilized statistical evidence to show that while the statute was nondiscriminatory on its face, it was being applied in a discriminatory fashion against Chinese immigrants. After the State Court loss, Yick Wo's case was appealed to the U.S. Supreme Court. In the Supreme Court's subsequent review, the Court indicated that it was under a duty to analyze the "real meaning of the ordinances in question." The Court then concluded that the state/governmental actors were being intentionally discriminatory in the implementation of the law. The Court famously described what would one day become the disparate impact theory of discrimination and affirmative action litigation: "Though the law itself be fair on its face and impartial in appearance, yet if it is applied and administered by public authority with an evil eye and an unequal hand, so as practically to make unjust and illegal discriminations between persons in similar circumstances, material to their rights, the denial of equal justice is still within the prohibition of the Constitution."

While the *Yick Wo* decision was groundbreaking, it did not gain instant recognition as a milestone case and was not utilized often by the Court in overturning other racially discriminatory practices involving facially neutral statutes. It was not until the mid-twentieth century that the Court began seriously building upon the *Yick Wo* precedent in the slow destruction of Jim Crow laws and segregation. Today, those utilizing the disparate impact/treatment theory may trace the lineage of this argument back to the famous case *Yick Wo v. Hopkins.*

See also Color-Blind Constitution; Disparate Treatment and Disparate Impact; Equal Protection Clause; Fourteenth Amendment; Immigration Act of 1965; Jim Crow Laws; Racism; Segregation; Statistical Proof of Discrimination; *Strauder v. West Virginia*; Xenophobia.

FURTHER READING: Tang, William, 1976, "The Legal Status of the Chinese in America," in *The Chinese in America*, edited by Paul K.T. Sih and Leonard Allen, New York: St. John's

University Center of Asian Studies; Wunder, John R., 1992, "*Yick Wo v. Hopkins*," in *The Oxford Companion to the Supreme Court of the United States*, edited by Kermit L. Hall, New York: Oxford University Press.

JAMES A. BECKMAN

Z

Zoning and Affirmative Action

Since shortly after land use zoning was introduced in 1904, exclusionary zoning practices have been used to segregate communities by race and wealth. However, coinciding with a series of cases in New Jersey from 1975 through 1983, many state and local governments have applied socioeconomic inclusionary affirmative action practices to their zoning ordinances to create more diverse new communities.

Zoning is the primary governmental control over land use in urban areas. State-delegated police powers grant local governments the power to enact and enforce zoning ordinances that divide land into distinct districts and apply different development and usage regulations to each district. While the history of land use regulations and legal challenges against them stretches back to the early 1800s, the first modern zoning regulations were enacted in 1904 by the city of Boston, which set different maximum heights for buildings in different districts of Boston. Shortly thereafter, the city of Los Angeles enacted a zoning ordinance segregating industrial and residential districts. In each of these cases, private landowners challenged the ordinances on the basis that the imposed regulations took away some of the value of their land without just compensation by reducing its usefulness. However, in each case, the ordinances were sustained due to the supremacy of the state's obligation to protect public health, safety, or commerce over the rights of private property owners.

In 1914, the city of Louisville, Kentucky, enacted a zoning ordinance segregating white and colored people into different residential blocks to promote the general welfare and preserve public peace by preventing racial conflict. Shortly after the ordinance took effect, Mr. Buchanan, who was black, and Mr. Warley, who was white, entered into a sales agreement transferring property owned by Warley in a primarily white block to Buchanan, who intended to erect a house for his residence. The contract was contingent on Buchanan's right to occupy the property under the laws of the state of Kentucky and the city of Louisville, but the zoning ordinance made it illegal for Buchanan to occupy the property on the basis of his color. Warley sued to enforce the contract on the basis that the ordinance was in conflict with the Fourteenth Amendment and therefore was no excuse for dissolving the sales contract. While state courts in Kentucky upheld the zoning ordinance nullifying the sale, the U.S. Supreme Court reversed them by ruling in *Buchanan v. Warley*, 245 U.S. 60 (1917), that the ordinance was not a legitimate use of state police powers and was in direct violation of the Fourteenth Amendment's Due Process Clause because public peace could not be preserved by denying the property rights of private landowners without due process of law as established by the federal Constitution.

While the judgment in *Buchanan v. Warley* made direct, racially based exclusionary zoning illegal across the country, many local governments introduced socioeconomic-based exclusionary zoning practices into their zoning ordinances that, when combined, have artificially inflated the value of new residential housing. This result has excluded less affluent individuals from entire communities and has had a disproportionate effect on minority groups. Examples of exclusionary practices include large-lot zoning, minimum house size requirements, prohibitions of multifamily housing, prohibitions of mobile homes, unnecessarily high subdivision requirements, and overburdensome administrative practices.

Exclusionary zoning practices have been challenged in state courts throughout the country, as exemplified by a series of New Jersey decisions that led to court-mandated affirmative action in zoning. In the 1975 case *Southern Burlington County NAACP v. Township of Mt. Laurel*, 336 A.2d 713 (N.J., 1975), the National Association for the Advancement of Colored People contended that the Mt. Laurel zoning ordinance, which limited all its residential areas to sizable single-family homes and set aside almost 30 percent of its land for light industrial purposes, was economically exclusionary. The New Jersey Supreme Court invalidated the ordinance, finding that its effect violated the New Jersey Constitution by not providing a realistic opportunity for the construction of the municipality's "fair share" of regional low- and moderately priced housing. Since the judgment in the Mt. Laurel case did not establish firm remedial action and removing exclusionary zoning practices alone did not generate the development of affordable housing, a series of additional cases arose during the next decade, including a reprise of the Mt. Laurel case. The result was a judicial declaration that established a constitutional doctrine forcing localities to amend their zoning ordinances to require new large-scale housing developments to either use state and federal housing subsidies or set aside proportions of their developments for price-controlled units. In exchange for meeting these new governmental regulations, developers would be provided with tax and regulatory incentives. If localities did not act, the court would invalidate entire zoning ordinances, restrict future development, or compel approval of low-income developments.

Whether by court mandate or legislative will, states and localities across the country are affirmatively introducing voluntary and involuntary practices of inclusion (as opposed to exclusion) into their zoning ordinances. Most zoning ordinances require developers to set aside specific portions of their developments to construct price-controlled housing affordable to low- and moderate-income individuals. In exchange for these often-mandatory requirements, developers are provided with just compensation in the form of incentives such as density bonuses, tax breaks, utility waivers, and relaxed regulatory requirements.

See also De Facto and De Jure Segregation; Fourteenth Amendment; Gentrification; Lending Practices and Affirmative Action.

FURTHER READING: *Buchanan v. Warley*, 245 U.S. 60 (1917); Fischer, Paul, and Jo Patton, 2001, "Ideas at Work: Expanding Housing Options through Inclusionary Zoning," *Campaign for Sensible Growth* 3 (June); Mandelker, Daniel R., Roger A. Cunningham, and John M. Payne, 1995, *Planning and Control of Land Development: Cases and Materials*, 4th ed., Charlottesville, VA: Michie Law Publishers; *Southern Burlington County NAACP v. Township of Mt. Laurel*, 336 A.2d 713 (N.J. 1975); Wolf, Peter, 1981, *Land in America: Its Value, Use, and Control*, New York: Pantheon Books.

MARK J. SENEDIAK

APPENDIX 1: FULL TEXT OF THE SUPREME COURT'S DECISION IN *GRATZ V. BOLLINGER*, JUNE 2003

Introduction

The landmark U.S. Supreme Court opinion in *Gratz v. Bollinger* addressed a reverse-discrimination challenge to the University of Michigan's undergraduate admissions program. The program awarded "underrepresented minority applicants," including African American, Hispanic, and Native American applicants, an automatic 20 points out of 100 points necessary to guarantee admission. The Court held that this aspect of the admissions program violated the Fourteenth Amendment to the U.S. Constitution and two federal statutes that prohibit race discrimination. The majority of the Court held that the mechanical formula of awarding 20 points to applicants solely because of their minority racial status had the effect of making race/ethnicity a determinative factor in admission decisions, thereby preventing the individualized consideration of each applicant. The plan also restricted the university's flexibility to consider other factors that could also contribute to educational diversity, such as traveling abroad, employment experience, and community service.

> NOTE: Where it is feasible, a syllabus (headnote) will be released, as is being done in connection with this case, at the time the opinion is issued. The syllabus constitutes no part of the opinion of the Court but has been prepared by the Reporter of Decisions for the convenience of the reader. See *United States* v. *Detroit Timber & Lumber Co.*, 200 U. S. 321, 337.

SUPREME COURT OF THE UNITED STATES

Syllabus

GRATZ ET AL. v. *BOLLINGER ET AL.*

CERTIORARI BEFORE JUDGMENT TO THE UNITED STATES COURT OF APPEALS FOR THE SIXTH CIRCUIT

No. 02–516. Argued April 1, 2003—Decided June 23, 2003

Petitioners Gratz and Hamacher, both of whom are Michigan residents and Caucasian, applied for admission to the University of Michigan's (University) College of Literature, Science, and the Arts (LSA) in 1995 and 1997, respectively. Although the LSA considered Gratz to be well qualified and Hamacher to be within the qualified range, both were denied early admission and were ultimately denied admission. In order to promote consistency in the review of the many applications received, the University's Office of Undergraduate Admissions (OUA) uses written guidelines for each academic year. The guidelines have changed a number of times during the period relevant to this litigation. The OUA considers a number of factors in making admissions decisions, including high school grades, standardized test scores, high school quality, curriculum strength, geography, alumni relationships, leadership, and race. During all relevant periods, the University has considered African-Americans, Hispanics, and Native Americans to be "underrepresented minorities," and it is undisputed that the University admits virtually every qualified applicant from these groups. The current guidelines use a selection method under which every applicant from an underrepresented racial or ethnic minority group is automatically awarded 20 points of the 100 needed to guarantee admission.

Petitioners filed this class action alleging that the University's use of racial preferences in undergraduate admissions violated the Equal Protection Clause of the Fourteenth Amendment, Title VI of the Civil Rights Act of 1964, and 42 U. S. C. §1981. They sought compensatory and punitive damages for past violations, declaratory relief finding that respondents violated their rights to nondiscriminatory treatment, an injunction prohibiting respondents from continuing to discriminate on the basis of race, and an order requiring the LSA to offer Hamacher admission as a transfer student. The District Court granted petitioners' motion to certify a class consisting of individuals who applied for and were denied admission to the LSA for academic year 1995 and forward and who are members of racial or ethnic groups that respondents treated less favorably on the basis of race. Hamacher, whose claim was found to challenge racial discrimination on a classwide basis, was designated as the class representative. On cross-motions for summary judgment, respondents relied on Justice Powell's principal opinion in *Regents of Univ. of Cal.* v. *Bakke*, 438 U. S. 265, 317, which expressed the view that the consideration of race as a factor in admissions might in some cases serve a compelling government interest. Respondents contended that the LSA has just such an interest in the educational benefits that result from having a racially and ethnically diverse student body and that its program is narrowly tailored to serve that interest. The court agreed with respondents as to the LSA's current admissions guidelines and granted them summary judgment in that respect. However, the court also found that the LSA's admissions guidelines for 1995 through 1998 operated as the functional equivalent of a quota running afoul of Justice Powell's *Bakke* opinion, and thus granted petitioners summary judgment with respect to respondents' admissions programs for those years. While interlocutory appeals were pending in the Sixth Circuit, that court issued an opinion in *Grutter* v. *Bollinger, post*, p. __, upholding the admissions program used by the University's Law School. This Court granted certiorari in both cases, even though the Sixth Circuit had not yet rendered judgment in this one.

Held:

1. Petitioners have standing to seek declaratory and injunctive relief. The Court rejects JUSTICE STEVENS' contention that, because Hamacher did not actually apply for admission as a transfer student, his future injury claim is at best conjectural or hypothetical rather than real and immediate. The "injury in fact" necessary to establish standing in this type of case is the denial of equal treatment resulting from the imposition of the barrier, not the ultimate inability to obtain the benefit. *Northeastern Fla. Chapter, Associated Gen. Contractors of America* v. *Jacksonville*, 508 U. S. 656, 666. In the face of such a barrier, to establish standing, a party need only demonstrate that it is able and ready to perform and that a discriminatory policy prevents it from doing so on an equal basis. *Ibid.* In bringing his equal protection challenge against the University's use of race in undergraduate admissions, Hamacher alleged that the University had denied him the opportunity to compete for admission on an equal basis. Hamacher was denied admission to the University as a freshman applicant even though an underrepresented minority applicant with his qualifications would have been admitted. After being denied admission, Hamacher demonstrated that he was "able and ready" to apply as a transfer student should the University cease to use race in undergraduate admissions. He therefore has standing to seek prospective relief with respect to the University's continued use of race. Also rejected is JUSTICE STEVENS' contention that such

use in undergraduate transfer admissions differs from the University's use of race in undergraduate freshman admissions, so that Hamacher lacks standing to represent absent class members challenging the latter. Each year the OUA produces a document setting forth guidelines for those seeking admission to the LSA, including freshman and transfer applicants. The transfer applicant guidelines specifically cross-reference factors and qualifications considered in assessing freshman applicants. In fact, the criteria used to determine whether a transfer applicant will contribute to diversity are *identical* to those used to evaluate freshman applicants. The *only* difference is that all underrepresented minority freshman applicants receive 20 points and "virtually" all who are minimally qualified are admitted, while "generally" all minimally qualified minority transfer applicants are admitted outright. While this difference might be relevant to a narrow tailoring analysis, it clearly has no effect on petitioners' standing to challenge the University's use of race in undergraduate admissions and its assertion that diversity is a compelling state interest justifying its consideration of the race of its undergraduate applicants. See *General Telephone Co. of Southwest* v. *Falcon*, 457 U. S. 147, 159; *Blum* v. *Yaretsky*, 457 U. S. 991, distinguished. The District Court's carefully considered decision to certify this class action is correct. Cf. *Coopers & Lybrand* v. *Livesay*, 437 U. S. 463, 469. Hamacher's personal stake, in view of both his past injury and the potential injury he faced at the time of certification, demonstrates that he may maintain the action. Pp. 11–20.

2. Because the University's use of race in its current freshman admissions policy is not narrowly tailored to achieve respondents' asserted interest in diversity, the policy violates the Equal Protection Clause. For the reasons set forth in *Grutter* v. *Bollinger*, *post*, at 15–21, the Court has today rejected petitioners' argument that diversity cannot constitute a compelling state interest. However, the Court finds that the University's current policy, which automatically distributes 20 points, or one-fifth of the points needed to guarantee admission, to every single "underrepresented minority" applicant solely because of race, is not narrowly tailored to achieve educational diversity. In *Bakke*, Justice Powell explained his view that it would be permissible for a university to employ an admissions program in which "race or ethnic background may be deemed a 'plus' in a particular applicant's file." 438 U. S., at 317. He emphasized, however, the importance of considering each particular applicant as an individual, assessing all of the qualities that individual possesses, and in turn, evaluating that individual's ability to contribute to the unique setting of higher education. The admissions program Justice Powell described did not contemplate that any single characteristic automatically ensured a specific and identifiable contribution to a university's diversity. See *id.*, at 315. The current LSA policy does not provide the individualized consideration Justice Powell contemplated. The only consideration that accompanies the 20-point automatic distribution to all applicants from underrepresented minorities is a factual review to determine whether an individual is a member of one of these minority groups. Moreover, unlike Justice Powell's example, where the race of a "particular black applicant" could be considered without being decisive, see *id.*, at 317, the LSA's 20-point distribution has the effect of making "the factor of race . . . decisive" for virtually every minimally qualified underrepresented minority applicant, *ibid.* The fact that the LSA has created the possibility of an applicant's file being flagged for individualized consideration only emphasizes the flaws of the University's system as a whole when compared to that described by Justice Powell. The record does not reveal precisely how many applications are flagged, but it is undisputed that such consideration is the exception and not the rule in the LSA's program. Also, this individualized review is only provided *after* admissions counselors automatically distribute the University's version of a "plus" that makes race a decisive factor for virtually every minimally qualified underrepresented minority applicant. The Court rejects respondents' contention that the volume of applications and the presentation of applicant information make it impractical for the LSA to use the admissions system upheld today in *Grutter*. The fact that the implementation of a program capable of providing individualized consideration might present administrative challenges does not render constitutional an otherwise prob-

lematic system. See, *e.g.*, *Richmond* v. *J. A. Croson Co.*, 488 U. S. 469, 508. Nothing in Justice Powell's *Bakke* opinion signaled that a university may employ whatever means it desires to achieve diversity without regard to the limits imposed by strict scrutiny. Pp. 20–27.

3. Because the University's use of race in its current freshman admissions policy violates the Equal Protection Clause, it also violates Title VI and §1981. See, *e.g.*, *Alexander* v. *Sandoval*, 532 U. S. 275, 281; *General Building Contractors Assn.* v. *Pennsylvania*, 458 U. S. 375, 389–390. Accordingly, the Court reverses that portion of the District Court's decision granting respondents summary judgment with respect to liability. Pp. 27–28.

Reversed in part and remanded.

REHNQUIST, C. J. delivered the opinion of the Court, in which O'CONNOR, SCALIA, KENNEDY, and THOMAS, JJ., joined. O'CONNOR, J., filed a concurring opinion, in which BREYER, J., joined in part. THOMAS, J., filed a concurring opinion. BREYER, J., filed an opinion concurring in the judgment. STEVENS, J., filed a dissenting opinion, in which SOUTER, J., joined. SOUTER, J., filed a dissenting opinion, in which GINSBURG, J., joined as to Part II. GINSBURG, J., filed a dissenting opinion, in which SOUTER, J., joined, and in which BREYER, J., joined as to Part I.

> NOTICE: This opinion is subject to formal revision before publication in the preliminary print of the United States Reports. Readers are requested to notify the Reporter of Decisions, Supreme Court of the United States, Washington, D. C. 20543, of any typographical or other formal errors, in order that corrections may be made before the preliminary print goes to press.

SUPREME COURT OF THE UNITED STATES

No. 02–516

JENNIFER GRATZ AND PATRICK HAMACHER, PETITIONERS v. *LEE BOLLINGER ET AL.*

ON WRIT OF CERTIORARI TO THE UNITED STATES COURT OF APPEALS FOR THE SIXTH CIRCUIT

[June 23, 2003]

CHIEF JUSTICE REHNQUIST delivered the opinion of the Court.

We granted certiorari in this case to decide whether "the University of Michigan's use of racial preferences in undergraduate admissions violate[s] the Equal Protection Clause of the Fourteenth Amendment, Title VI of the Civil Rights Act of 1964 (42 U. S. C. § 2000d), or 42 U. S. C. §1981." Brief for Petitioners i. Because we find that the manner in which the University considers the race of applicants in its undergraduate admissions guidelines violates these constitutional and statutory provisions, we reverse that portion of the District Court's decision upholding the guidelines.

I

A

Petitioners Jennifer Gratz and Patrick Hamacher both applied for admission to the University of Michigan's (University) College of Literature, Science, and the Arts (LSA) as residents of the State of Michigan. Both petitioners are Caucasian. Gratz, who applied for admission for the fall of 1995, was notified in January of that year that a final decision regarding her admission had been delayed until April. This delay was based upon the University's determination that, although Gratz was " 'well qualified,' " she was " 'less competitive than the students who ha[d] been admitted on first review.' " App. to Pet. for Cert. 109a. Gratz was notified in April that the LSA was unable to offer her admission. She enrolled in the University of Michigan at Dearborn, from which she graduated in the spring of 1999.

Hamacher applied for admission to the LSA for the fall of 1997. A final decision as to his application was also postponed because, though his " 'academic credentials [were] in the qualified range, they [were] not at the level needed for first review admission.' " *Ibid.* Hamacher's application was subsequently denied in April 1997, and he enrolled at Michigan State University.[1]

In October 1997, Gratz and Hamacher filed a lawsuit in the United States District Court for the Eastern District of Michigan against the University of Michigan, the LSA,[2] James Duderstadt, and Lee Bollinger.[3] Petitioners' complaint was a class-action suit alleging "violations and threatened violations of the rights of the plaintiffs and the class they represent to equal protection of the laws under the Fourteenth Amendment . . . , and for racial discrimination in violation of 42 U. S. C. §§1981, 1983, and 2000d *et seq.*" App. 33. Petitioners sought, *inter alia*, compensatory and punitive damages for past violations, declaratory relief finding that respondents violated petitioners' "rights to nondiscriminatory treatment," an injunction prohibiting respondents from "continuing to discriminate on the basis of race in violation of the Fourteenth Amendment," and an order requiring the LSA to offer Hamacher admission as a transfer student.[4] *Id.*, at 40.

The District Court granted petitioners' motion for class certification after determining that a class action was appropriate pursuant to Federal Rule of Civil Procedure 23(b)(2). The certified class consisted of "those individuals who applied for and were not granted admission to the College of Literature, Science and the Arts of the University of Michigan for all academic years from 1995 forward and who are members of those racial or ethnic groups, including Caucasian, that defendants treated less favorably on the basis of race in considering their application for admission." App. 70–71. And Hamacher, whose claim the District Court found to challenge a " 'practice of racial discrimination pervasively applied on a classwide basis,' " was designated as the class representative. *Id.*, at 67, 70. The court also granted petitioners' motion to bifurcate the proceedings into a liability and damages phase. *Id.*, at 71. The liability phase was to determine "whether [respondents'] use of race as a factor in admissions decisions violates the Equal Protection Clause of the Fourteenth Amendment to the Constitution." *Id.*, at 70.[5]

B

The University has changed its admissions guidelines a number of times during the period relevant to this litigation, and we summarize the most significant of these changes

---

[1]Although Hamacher indicated that he "intend[ed] to apply to transfer if the [LSA's] discriminatory admissions system [is] eliminated," he has since graduated from Michigan State University. App. 34.

[2]The University of Michigan Board of Regents was subsequently named as the proper defendant in place of the University and the LSA. See *id.*, at 17.

[3]Duderstadt was the president of the University during the time that Gratz's application was under consideration. He has been sued in his individual capacity. Bollinger was the president of the University when Hamacher applied for admission. He was originally sued in both his individual and official capacities, but he is no longer the president of the University. *Id.*, at 35.

[4]A group of African-American and Latino students who applied for, or intended to apply for, admission to the University, as well as the Citizens for Affirmative Action's Preservation, a nonprofit organization in Michigan, sought to intervene pursuant to Federal Rule of Civil Procedure 24. See App. 13–14. The District Court originally denied this request, see *id.*, at 14–15, but the Sixth Circuit reversed that decision. See *Gratz* v. *Bollinger*, 188 F. 3d 394 (1999).

[5]The District Court decided also to consider petitioners' request for injunctive and declaratory relief during the liability phase of the proceedings. App. 71.

briefly. The University's Office of Undergraduate Admissions (OUA) oversees the LSA admissions process.[6] In order to promote consistency in the review of the large number of applications received, the OUA uses written guidelines for each academic year. Admissions counselors make admissions decisions in accordance with these guidelines.

OUA considers a number of factors in making admissions decisions, including high school grades, standardized test scores, high school quality, curriculum strength, geography, alumni relationships, and leadership. OUA also considers race. During all periods relevant to this litigation, the University has considered African-Americans, Hispanics, and Native Americans to be "underrepresented minorities," and it is undisputed that the University admits "virtually every qualified . . . applicant" from these groups. App. to Pet. for Cert. 111a.

During 1995 and 1996, OUA counselors evaluated applications according to grade point average combined with what were referred to as the "SCUGA" factors. These factors included the quality of an applicant's high school (S), the strength of an applicant's high school curriculum (C), an applicant's unusual circumstances (U), an applicant's geographical residence (G), and an applicant's alumni relationships (A). After these scores were combined to produce an applicant's "GPA 2" score, the reviewing admissions counselors referenced a set of "Guidelines" tables, which listed GPA 2 ranges on the vertical axis, and American College Test/Scholastic Aptitude Test (ACT/SAT) scores on the horizontal axis. Each table was divided into cells that included one or more courses of action to be taken, including admit, reject, delay for additional information, or postpone for reconsideration.

In both years, applicants with the same GPA 2 score and ACT/SAT score were subject to different admissions outcomes based upon their racial or ethnic status.[7] For example, as a Caucasian in-state applicant, Gratz's GPA 2 score and ACT score placed her within a cell calling for a postponed decision on her application. An in-state or out-of-state minority applicant with Gratz's scores would have fallen within a cell calling for admission.

In 1997, the University modified its admissions procedure. Specifically, the formula for calculating an applicant's GPA 2 score was restructured to include additional point values under the "U" category in the SCUGA factors. Under this new system, applicants could receive points for underrepresented minority status, socioeconomic disadvantage, or attendance at a high school with a predominantly underrepresented minority population, or underrepresentation in the unit to which the student was applying (for example, men who sought to pursue a career in nursing). Under the 1997 procedures, Hamacher's GPA 2 score and ACT score placed him in a cell on the in-state applicant table calling for postponement of a final admissions decision. An underrepresented minority applicant placed in the same cell would generally have been admitted.

Beginning with the 1998 academic year, the OUA dispensed with the Guidelines tables and the SCUGA point system in favor of a "selection index," on which an applicant could score a maximum of 150 points. This index was divided linearly into ranges generally calling for admissions dispositions as follows: 100–150 (admit); 95–99 (admit or postpone); 90–94 (postpone or admit); 75–89 (delay or postpone); 74 and below (delay or reject).

Each application received points based on high school grade point average, standardized test scores, academic quality of an applicant's high school, strength or weakness of high school curriculum, in-state residency, alumni relationship, personal essay, and personal achievement or leadership. Of particular significance here, under a "miscellaneous" cate-

---

[6] Our description is taken, in large part, from the "Joint Proposed Summary of Undisputed Facts Regarding Admissions Process" filed by the parties in the District Court. App. to Pet. for Cert. 108a–117a.

[7] In 1995, counselors used four such tables for different groups of applicants: (1) in-state, nonminority applicants; (2) out-of-state, nonminority applicants; (3) in-state, minority applicants; and (4) out-of-state, minority applicants. In 1996, only two tables were used, one for in-state applicants and one for out-of-state applicants. But each cell on these two tables contained separate courses of action for minority applicants and nonminority applicants whose GPA 2 scores and ACT/SAT scores placed them in that cell.

gory, an applicant was entitled to 20 points based upon his or her membership in an underrepresented racial or ethnic minority group. The University explained that the " 'development of the selection index for admissions in 1998 changed only the mechanics, not the substance of how race and ethnicity were considered in admissions.' " App. to Pet. for Cert. 116a.

In all application years from 1995 to 1998, the guidelines provided that qualified applicants from underrepresented minority groups be admitted as soon as possible in light of the University's belief that such applicants were more likely to enroll if promptly notified of their admission. Also from 1995 through 1998, the University carefully managed its rolling admissions system to permit consideration of certain applications submitted later in the academic year through the use of "protected seats." Specific groups—including athletes, foreign students, ROTC candidates, and underrepresented minorities—were "protected categories" eligible for these seats. A committee called the Enrollment Working Group (EWG) projected how many applicants from each of these protected categories the University was likely to receive after a given date and then paced admissions decisions to permit full consideration of expected applications from these groups. If this space was not filled by qualified candidates from the designated groups toward the end of the admissions season, it was then used to admit qualified candidates remaining in the applicant pool, including those on the waiting list.

During 1999 and 2000, the OUA used the selection index, under which every applicant from an underrepresented racial or ethnic minority group was awarded 20 points. Starting in 1999, however, the University established an Admissions Review Committee (ARC), to provide an additional level of consideration for some applications. Under the new system, counselors may, in their discretion, "flag" an application for the ARC to review after determining that the applicant (1) is academically prepared to succeed at the University,[8] (2) has achieved a minimum selection index score, and (3) possesses a quality or characteristic important to the University's composition of its freshman class, such as high class rank, unique life experiences, challenges, circumstances, interests or talents, socioeconomic disadvantage, and underrepresented race, ethnicity, or geography. After reviewing "flagged" applications, the ARC determines whether to admit, defer, or deny each applicant.

C

The parties filed cross-motions for summary judgment with respect to liability. Petitioners asserted that the LSA's use of race as a factor in admissions violates Title VI of the Civil Rights Act of 1964, 78 Stat. 252, 42 U. S. C. §2000d, and the Equal Protection Clause of the Fourteenth Amendment. Respondents relied on Justice Powell's opinion in *Regents of Univ. of Cal. v. Bakke*, 438 U. S. 265 (1978), to respond to petitioners' arguments. As discussed in greater detail in the Court's opinion in *Grutter* v. *Bollinger, post*, at 10–13, Justice Powell, in *Bakke*, expressed the view that the consideration of race as a factor in admissions might in some cases serve a compelling government interest. See 438 U. S., at 317. Respondents contended that the LSA has just such an interest in the educational benefits that result from having a racially and ethnically diverse student body and that its program is narrowly tailored to serve that interest. Respondent-intervenors asserted that the LSA had a compelling interest in remedying the University's past and current discrimination against minorities.[9]

---

[8]LSA applicants who are Michigan residents must accumulate 80 points from the selection index criteria to be flagged, while out-of-state applicants need to accumulate 75 points to be eligible for such consideration. See App. 257.

[9]The District Court considered and rejected respondent-intervenors' arguments in a supplemental opinion and order. See 135 F. Supp. 2d 790 (ED Mich. 2001). The court explained that respondent-intervenors "failed to present any evidence that the discrimination alleged by them, or the continuing

The District Court began its analysis by reviewing this Court's decision in *Bakke*. See 122 F. Supp. 2d 811, 817 (ED Mich. 2001). Although the court acknowledged that no decision from this Court since *Bakke* has explicitly accepted the diversity rationale discussed by Justice Powell, see 122 F. Supp. 2d, at 820–821, it also concluded that this Court had not, in the years since *Bakke*, ruled out such a justification for the use of race. 122 F. Supp. 2d, at 820–821. The District Court concluded that respondents and their *amici curiae* had presented "solid evidence" that a racially and ethnically diverse student body produces significant educational benefits such that achieving such a student body constitutes a compelling governmental interest. See *id.*, at 822–824.

The court next considered whether the LSA's admissions guidelines were narrowly tailored to achieve that interest. See *id.*, at 824. Again relying on Justice Powell's opinion in *Bakke*, the District Court determined that the admissions program the LSA began using in 1999 is a narrowly tailored means of achieving the University's interest in the educational benefits that flow from a racially and ethnically diverse student body. See 122 F. Supp. 2d, at 827. The court emphasized that the LSA's current program does not utilize rigid quotas or seek to admit a predetermined number of minority students. See *ibid.* The award of 20 points for membership in an underrepresented minority group, in the District Court's view, was not the functional equivalent of a quota because minority candidates were not insulated from review by virtue of those points. See *id.*, at 828. Likewise, the court rejected the assertion that the LSA's program operates like the two-track system Justice Powell found objectionable in *Bakke* on the grounds that LSA applicants are not competing for different groups of seats. See 122 F. Supp. 2d, at 828–829. The court also dismissed petitioners' assertion that the LSA's current system is nothing more than a means by which to achieve racial balancing. See *id.*, at 831. The court explained that the LSA does not seek to achieve a certain proportion of minority students, let alone a proportion that represents the community. See *ibid.*

The District Court found the admissions guidelines the LSA used from 1995 through 1998 to be more problematic. In the court's view, the University's prior practice of "protecting" or "reserving" seats for underrepresented minority applicants effectively kept non-protected applicants from competing for those slots. See *id.*, at 832. This system, the court concluded, operated as the functional equivalent of a quota and ran afoul of Justice Powell's opinion in *Bakke*.[10] See 122 F. Supp. 2d, at 832.

Based on these findings, the court granted petitioners' motion for summary judgment with respect to the LSA's admissions programs in existence from 1995 through 1998, and respondents' motion with respect to the LSA's admissions programs for 1999 and 2000. See *id.*, at 833. Accordingly, the District Court denied petitioners' request for injunctive relief. See *id.*, at 814.

The District Court issued an order consistent with its rulings and certified two questions for interlocutory appeal to the Sixth Circuit pursuant to 28 U. S. C. §1292(b). Both parties appealed aspects of the District Court's rulings, and the Court of Appeals heard the case en banc on the same day as *Grutter* v. *Bollinger*. The Sixth Circuit later issued an opinion in *Grutter*, upholding the admissions program used by the University of Michigan Law School, and the petitioner in that case sought a writ of certiorari from this Court. Petitioners asked

---

effects of such discrimination, was the real justification for the LSA's race-conscious admissions programs." *Id.*, at 795. We agree, and to the extent respondent-intervenors reassert this justification, a justification the University has *never* asserted throughout the course of this litigation, we affirm the District Court's disposition of the issue.

[10]The District Court determined that respondents Bollinger and Duderstadt, who were sued in their individual capacities under Rev. Stat. §1979, 42 U. S. C. §1983, were entitled to summary judgment based on the doctrine of qualified immunity. See 122 F. Supp. 2d, at 833–834. Petitioners have not asked this Court to review this aspect of the District Court's decision. The District Court denied the Board of Regents' motion for summary judgment with respect to petitioners' Title VI claim on Eleventh Amendment immunity grounds. See *id.*, at 834–836. Respondents have not asked this Court to review this aspect of the District Court's decision.

this Court to grant certiorari in this case as well, despite the fact that the Court of Appeals had not yet rendered a judgment, so that this Court could address the constitutionality of the consideration of race in university admissions in a wider range of circumstances. We did so. See 537 U. S. 1044 (2002).

II

As they have throughout the course of this litigation, petitioners contend that the University's consideration of race in its undergraduate admissions decisions violates §1 of the Equal Protection Clause of the Fourteenth Amendment,[11] Title VI,[12] and 42 U. S. C. §1981.[13] We consider first whether petitioners have standing to seek declaratory and injunctive relief, and, finding that they do, we next consider the merits of their claims.

A

Although no party has raised the issue, JUSTICE STEVENS argues that petitioners lack Article III standing to seek injunctive relief with respect to the University's use of race in undergraduate admissions. He first contends that because Hamacher did not "actually appl[y] for admission as a transfer student[,] [h]is claim of future injury is at best 'conjectural or hypothetical' rather than 'real and immediate.' " *Post*, at 5 (dissenting opinion). But whether Hamacher "actually applied" for admission as a transfer student is not determinative of his ability to seek injunctive relief in this case. If Hamacher had submitted a transfer application and been rejected, he would still need to allege an intent to apply again in order to seek prospective relief. If JUSTICE STEVENS means that because Hamacher did not apply to transfer, he must never *really* have intended to do so, that conclusion directly conflicts with the finding of fact entered by the District Court that Hamacher "intends to transfer to the University of Michigan when defendants cease the use of race as an admission preference." App. 67.[14]

It is well established that intent may be relevant to standing in an Equal Protection challenge. In *Clements* v. *Fashing*, 457 U. S. 957 (1982), for example, we considered a challenge to a provision of the Texas Constitution requiring the immediate resignation of certain state officeholders upon their announcement of candidacy for another office. We concluded that the plaintiff officeholders had Article III standing because they had alleged that they *would have announced their candidacy* for other offices were it not for the "automatic resignation" provision they were challenging. *Id.*, at 962; accord, *Turner* v. *Fouche*, 396 U. S. 346, 361–362, n. 23 (1970) (plaintiff who did not own property had standing to challenge property ownership requirement for membership on school board even though there was no evidence that plaintiff had applied and been rejected); *Quinn* v. *Millsap*, 491 U. S. 95, 103, n. 8 (1989) (plaintiffs who did not own property had standing to challenge property ownership requirement for membership on government board even though they lacked standing to challenge the requirement "as applied"). Likewise, in *Northeastern Fla. Chapter, Associated Gen. Contractors of America* v. *Jacksonville*, 508 U. S. 656 (1993), we considered whether an association challenging an ordinance that gave preferential treatment to certain

---

[11]The Equal Protection Clause of the Fourteenth Amendment explains that "[n]o State shall . . . deny to any person within its jurisdiction the equal protection of the laws."

[12]Title VI provides that "[n]o person in the United States shall, on the ground of race, color, or national origin, be excluded from participation in, be denied the benefits of, or be subjected to discrimination under any program or activity receiving Federal financial assistance." 42 U. S. C. §2000d.

[13]Section 1981(a) provides that:

"All persons within the jurisdiction of the United States shall have the same right in every State and Territory to make and enforce contracts, . . . and to the full and equal benefit of all laws and proceedings for the security of persons and property as is enjoyed by white citizens."

[14]This finding is further corroborated by Hamacher's request that the District Court "[r]equir[e] the LSA College to offer [him] admission as a transfer student." App. 40.

minority-owned businesses in the award of city contracts needed to show that one of its members would have received a contract absent the ordinance in order to establish standing. In finding that no such showing was necessary, we explained that "[t]he 'injury in fact' in an equal protection case of this variety is the denial of equal treatment resulting from the imposition of the barrier, not the ultimate inability to obtain the benefit. . . . And in the context of a challenge to a set-aside program, the 'injury in fact' is the inability to compete on an equal footing in the bidding process, not the loss of contract." *Id.*, at 666. We concluded that in the face of such a barrier, "[t]o establish standing, a party challenging a set-aside program like Jacksonville's need only demonstrate that it is able and ready to bid on contracts and that a discriminatory policy prevents it from doing so on an equal basis." *Ibid.*

In bringing his equal protection challenge against the University's use of race in undergraduate admissions, Hamacher alleged that the University had denied him the opportunity to compete for admission on an equal basis. When Hamacher applied to the University as a freshman applicant, he was denied admission even though an underrepresented minority applicant with his qualifications would have been admitted. See App. to Pet. for Cert. 115a. After being denied admission, Hamacher demonstrated that he was "able and ready" to apply as a transfer student should the University cease to use race in undergraduate admissions. He therefore has standing to seek prospective relief with respect to the University's continued use of race in undergraduate admissions.

JUSTICE STEVENS raises a second argument as to standing. He contends that the University's use of race in undergraduate transfer admissions differs from its use of race in undergraduate freshman admissions, and that therefore Hamacher lacks standing to represent absent class members challenging the latter. *Post*, at 5 (dissenting opinion). As an initial matter, there is a question whether the relevance of this variation, if any, is a matter of Article III standing at all or whether it goes to the propriety of class certification pursuant to Federal Rule of Civil Procedure 23(a). The parties have not briefed the question of standing versus adequacy, however, and we need not resolve the question today: Regardless of whether the requirement is deemed one of adequacy or standing, it is clearly satisfied in this case.[15]

From the time petitioners filed their original complaint through their brief on the merits in this Court, they have consistently challenged the University's use of race in undergraduate admissions and its asserted justification of promoting "diversity." See, *e.g.*, App. 38; Brief for Petitioners 13. Consistent with this challenge, petitioners requested injunctive relief prohibiting respondent "from continuing to discriminate on the basis of race." App. 40. They sought to certify a class consisting of all individuals who were not members of an underrepresented minority group who either had applied for admission to the LSA and been rejected or who intended to apply for admission to the LSA, for all academic years from 1995 forward. *Id.*, at 35–36. The District Court determined that the proposed class satisfied the requirements of the Federal Rules of Civil Procedure, including the requirements of numerosity, commonality, and typicality. See Fed. Rule Civ. Proc. 23(a); App. 70. The court further concluded that Hamacher was an adequate representative for the class in the pursuit of compensatory and injunctive relief for purposes of Rule 23(a)(4), see App. 61–69, and found "the record utterly devoid of the presence of . . . antagonism between the interests of . . . Hamacher, and the members of the class which [he] seek[s] to

---

[15]Although we do not resolve here whether such an inquiry in this case is appropriately addressed under the rubric of standing or adequacy, we note that there is tension in our prior cases in this regard. See, *e.g.*, Burns, Standing and Mootness in Class Actions: A Search for Consistency, 22 U. C. D. L. Rev. 1239, 1240–1241 (1989); *General Telephone Co. of Southwest* v. *Falcon*, 457 U. S. 147, 149 (1982) (Mexican-American plaintiff alleging that he was passed over for a promotion because of race was not an adequate representative to "maintain a class action on behalf of Mexican-American applicants" who were not hired by the same employer); *Blum* v. *Yaretsky*, 457 U. S. 991 (1982) (class representatives who had been transferred to lower levels of medical care lacked standing to challenge transfers to higher levels of care).

represent," *id.*, at 61. Finally, the District Court concluded that petitioners' claim was appropriate for class treatment because the University's " 'practice of racial discrimination pervasively applied on a classwide basis.' " *Id.*, at 67. The court certified the class pursuant to Federal Rule of Civil Procedure 23(b)(2), and designated Hamacher as the class representative. App. 70.

JUSTICE STEVENS cites *Blum* v. *Yaretsky*, 457 U. S. 991 (1982), in arguing that the District Court erred. *Post*, at 8. In *Blum*, we considered a class action suit brought by Medicaid beneficiaries. The named representatives in *Blum* challenged decisions by the State's Medicaid Utilization Review Committee (URC) to transfer them to lower levels of care without, in their view, sufficient procedural safeguards. After a class was certified, the plaintiffs obtained an order expanding class certification to include challenges to URC decisions to transfer patients to *higher* levels of care as well. The defendants argued that the named representatives could not represent absent class members challenging transfers to higher levels of care because they had not been threatened with such transfers. We agreed. We noted that "[n]othing in the record . . . suggests that any of the individual respondents have been either transferred to more intensive care or threatened with such transfers." 457 U. S., at 1001. And we found that transfers to lower levels of care involved a number of fundamentally different concerns than did transfers to higher ones. *Id.*, at 1001–1002 (noting, for example, that transfers to lower levels of care implicated beneficiaries' property interests given the concomitant decrease in Medicaid benefits, while transfers to higher levels of care did not).

In the present case, the University's use of race in undergraduate transfer admissions does not implicate a significantly different set of concerns than does its use of race in undergraduate freshman admissions. Respondents challenged Hamacher's standing at the certification stage, but *never* did so on the grounds that the University's use of race in undergraduate transfer admissions involves a different set of concerns than does its use of race in freshman admissions. Respondents' failure to allege any such difference is simply consistent with the fact that no such difference exists. Each year the OUA produces a document entitled "COLLEGE OF LITERATURE SCIENCE AND THE ARTS GUIDELINES FOR ALL TERMS," which sets forth guidelines for all individuals seeking admission to the LSA, including freshman applicants, transfer applicants, international student applicants, and the like. See, *e.g.*, 2 App. in No. 01–1333 etc. (CA6), pp. 507–542. The guidelines used to evaluate transfer applicants specifically cross-reference factors and qualifications considered in assessing freshman applicants. In fact, the criteria used to determine whether a transfer applicant will contribute to the University's stated goal of diversity are *identical* to that used to evaluate freshman applicants. For example, in 1997, when the class was certified and the District Court found that Hamacher had standing to represent the class, the transfer guidelines contained a separate section entitled "CONTRIBUTION TO A DIVERSE STUDENT BODY." 2 *id.*, at 531. This section explained that any transfer applicant who could "*contribut[e] to a diverse student body*" should "generally be admitted" even with substantially lower qualifications than those required of other transfer applicants. *Ibid.* (emphasis added). To determine whether a transfer applicant was capable of "contribut[ing] to a diverse student body," admissions counselors were instructed to determine whether that transfer applicant met the "criteria as defined in Section IV of the 'U' category of [the] SCUGA" factors used to assess freshman applicants. *Ibid.* Section IV of the "U" category, entitled "Contribution to a Diverse Class," explained that "[t]he University is committed to a rich educational experience for its students. A diverse, as opposed to a homogenous, student population enhances the educational experience for all students. To insure a diverse class, significant weight will be given in the admissions process to indicators of students contribution to a diverse class." 1 *id.*, at 432. These indicators, used in evaluating freshman and transfer applicants alike, list being a member of an underrepresented minority group as establishing an applicant's contribution to diversity. See 3 *id.*, at 1133–1134, 1153–1154. Indeed, the *only* difference between the University's use of race in considering freshman and transfer applicants is that all underrepresented minority freshman applicants receive

20 points and "virtually" all who are minimally qualified are admitted, while "generally" all minimally qualified minority transfer applicants are admitted outright. While this difference might be relevant to a narrow tailoring analysis, it clearly has no effect on petitioners' standing to challenge the University's use of race in undergraduate admissions and its assertion that diversity is a compelling state interest that justifies its consideration of the race of its undergraduate applicants.[16]

Particularly instructive here is our statement in *General Telephone Co. of Southwest* v. *Falcon*, 457 U. S. 147 (1982), that "[i]f [defendant-employer] used a biased testing procedure to evaluate both applicants for employment and incumbent employees, a class action on behalf of every applicant or employee who might have been prejudiced by the test *clearly* would satisfy the . . . requirements of Rule 23(a)." *Id.*, at 159, n. 15 (emphasis added). Here, the District Court found that the sole rationale the University had provided for any of its race-based preferences in undergraduate admissions was the interest in "the educational benefits that result from having a diverse student body." App. to Pet. for Cert. 8a. And petitioners argue that an interest in "diversity" is not a compelling state interest that is *ever* capable of justifying the use of race in undergraduate admissions. See, *e.g.*, Brief for Petitioners 11–13. In sum, the same set of concerns is implicated by the University's use of race in evaluating all undergraduate admissions applications under the guidelines.[17] We therefore agree with the District Court's carefully considered decision to certify this class-action challenge to the University's consideration of race in undergraduate admissions. See App. 67 (" 'It is a singular policy . . . applied on a classwide basis' "); cf. *Coopers & Lybrand* v. *Livesay*, 437 U. S. 463, 469 (1978) ("[T]he class determination generally involves considerations that are enmeshed in the factual and legal issues comprising the plaintiff's cause of action" (internal quotation marks omitted)). Indeed, class action treatment was particularly important in this case because "the claims of the individual students run the risk of becoming moot" and the "[t]he class action vehicle . . . provides a mechanism for ensuring that a justiciable claim is before the Court." App. 69. Thus, we think it clear that Hamacher's personal stake, in view of both his past injury and the potential injury he faced at the time of certification, demonstrates that he may maintain this class-action challenge to the University's use of race in undergraduate admissions.

---

[16]Because the University's guidelines concededly use race in evaluating both freshman and transfer applications, and because petitioners have challenged *any* use of race by the University in undergraduate admissions, the transfer admissions policy is very much before this Court. Although petitioners did not raise a narrow tailoring challenge to the transfer policy, as counsel for petitioners repeatedly explained, the transfer policy is before this Court in that petitioners challenged any use of race by the University to promote diversity, including through the transfer policy. See Tr. of Oral Arg. 4 ("[T]he [transfer] policy is essentially the same with respect to the consideration of race"); *id.*, at 5 ("The transfer policy considers race"); *id.*, at 6 (same); *id.*, at 7 ("[T]he transfer policy and the [freshman] admissions policy are fundamentally the same in the respect that they both consider race in the admissions process in a way that is discriminatory"); *id.*, at 7–8 ("[T]he University considers race for a purpose to achieve a diversity that we believe is not compelling, and if that is struck down as a rationale, then the [result] would be [the] same with respect to the transfer policy as with respect to the [freshman] admissions policy, Your Honor").

[17]Indeed, as the litigation history of this case demonstrates, "the class-action device save[d] the resources of both the courts and the parties by permitting an issue potentially affecting every [class member] to be litigated in an economical fashion." *Califano* v. *Yamasaki*, 442 U. S. 682, 701 (1979). This case was therefore quite unlike *General Telephone Co. of Southwest* v. *Falcon*, 457 U. S. 147 (1982), in which we found that the named representative, who had been passed over for a promotion, was not an adequate representative for absent class members who were never hired in the first instance. As we explained, the plaintiff's "evidentiary approaches to the individual and class claims were entirely different. He attempted to sustain his individual claim by proving intentional discrimination. He tried to prove the class claims through statistical evidence of disparate impact. . . . It is clear that the maintenance of respondent's action as a class action did not advance 'the efficiency and economy of litigation which is a principal purpose of the procedure.' " *Id.*, at 159 (quoting *American Pipe & Constr. Co.* v. *Utah*, 414 U. S. 538, 553 (1974)).

B

Petitioners argue, first and foremost, that the University's use of race in undergraduate admissions violates the Fourteenth Amendment. Specifically, they contend that this Court has only sanctioned the use of racial classifications to remedy identified discrimination, a justification on which respondents have never relied. Brief for Petitioners 15–16. Petitioners further argue that "diversity as a basis for employing racial preferences is simply too open-ended, ill-defined, and indefinite to constitute a compelling interest capable of supporting narrowly-tailored means." *Id.*, at 17–18, 40–41. But for the reasons set forth today in *Grutter* v. *Bollinger, post*, at 15–21, the Court has rejected these arguments of petitioners.

Petitioners alternatively argue that even if the University's interest in diversity can constitute a compelling state interest, the District Court erroneously concluded that the University's use of race in its current freshman admissions policy is narrowly tailored to achieve such an interest. Petitioners argue that the guidelines the University began using in 1999 do not "remotely resemble the kind of consideration of race and ethnicity that Justice Powell endorsed in *Bakke*." Brief for Petitioners 18. Respondents reply that the University's current admissions program *is* narrowly tailored and avoids the problems of the Medical School of the University of California at Davis program (U. C. Davis) rejected by Justice Powell.[18] They claim that their program "hews closely" to both the admissions program described by Justice Powell as well as the Harvard College admissions program that he endorsed. Brief for Respondents 32. Specifically, respondents contend that the LSA's policy provides the individualized consideration that "Justice Powell considered a hallmark of a constitutionally appropriate admissions program." *Id.*, at 35. For the reasons set out below, we do not agree.

It is by now well established that "all racial classifications reviewable under the Equal Protection Clause must be strictly scrutinized." *Adarand Constructors, Inc.* v. *Peña*, 515 U. S. 200, 224 (1995). This " 'standard of review . . . is not dependent on the race of those burdened or benefited by a particular classification.' " *Ibid.* (quoting *Richmond* v. *J. A. Croson Co.*, 488 U. S. 469, 494 (1989) (plurality opinion)). Thus, "any person, of whatever race, has the right to demand that any governmental actor subject to the Constitution justify any racial classification subjecting that person to unequal treatment under the strictest of judicial scrutiny." *Adarand*, 515 U. S., at 224.

To withstand our strict scrutiny analysis, respondents must demonstrate that the University's use of race in its current admission program employs "narrowly tailored measures that further compelling governmental interests." *Id.*, at 227. Because "[r]acial classifications are simply too pernicious to permit any but the most exact connection between justification and classification," *Fullilove* v. *Klutznick*, 448 U. S. 448, 537 (1980) (STEVENS, J., dissenting), our review of whether such requirements have been met must entail " 'a most searching examination.' " *Adarand, supra*, at 223 (quoting *Wygant* v. *Jackson Bd. of Ed.*, 476 U. S. 267, 273 (1986) (plurality opinion of Powell, J.)). We find that the University's policy, which automatically distributes 20 points, or one-fifth of the points needed to guarantee admission, to every single "underrepresented minority" applicant solely because of race, is not narrowly

---

[18]U. C. Davis set aside 16 of the 100 seats available in its first year medical school program for "economically and/or educationally disadvantaged" applicants who were also members of designated "minority groups" as defined by the university. "To the extent that there existed a pool of at least minimally qualified minority applicants to fill the 16 special admissions seats, white applicants could compete only for 84 seats in the entering class, rather than the 100 open to minority applicants." *Regents of Univ. of Cal.* v. *Bakke*, 438 U. S. 265, 274, 289 (1978) (principal opinion). Justice Powell found that the program employed an impermissible two-track system that "disregard[ed] . . . individual rights as guaranteed by the Fourteenth Amendment." *Id.*, at 315. He reached this conclusion even though the university argued that "the reservation of a specified number of seats in each class for individuals from the preferred ethnic groups" was "the only effective means of serving the interest of diversity." *Ibid.* Justice Powell concluded that such arguments misunderstood the very nature of the diversity he found to be compelling. See *ibid.*

tailored to achieve the interest in educational diversity that respondents claim justifies their program.

In *Bakke*, Justice Powell reiterated that "[p]referring members of any one group for no reason other than race or ethnic origin is discrimination for its own sake." 438 U. S., at 307. He then explained, however, that in his view it would be permissible for a university to employ an admissions program in which "race or ethnic background may be deemed a 'plus' in a particular applicant's file." *Id.*, at 317. He explained that such a program might allow for "[t]he file of a particular black applicant [to] be examined for his potential contribution to diversity without the factor of race being decisive when compared, for example, with that of an applicant identified as an Italian-American if the latter is thought to exhibit qualities more likely to promote beneficial educational pluralism." *Ibid.* Such a system, in Justice Powell's view, would be "flexible enough to consider all pertinent elements of diversity in light of the particular qualifications of each applicant." *Ibid.*

Justice Powell's opinion in *Bakke* emphasized the importance of considering each particular applicant as an individual, assessing all of the qualities that individual possesses, and in turn, evaluating that individual's ability to contribute to the unique setting of higher education. The admissions program Justice Powell described, however, did not contemplate that any single characteristic automatically ensured a specific and identifiable contribution to a university's diversity. See *id.*, at 315. See also *Metro Broadcasting, Inc.* v. *FCC*, 497 U. S. 547, 618 (1990) (O'CONNOR, J., dissenting) (concluding that the FCC's policy, which "embodie[d] the related notions that a particular applicant, by virtue of race or ethnicity alone, is more valued than other applicants because [the applicant is] 'likely to provide [a] distinct perspective,' "impermissibly value[d] individuals" based on a presumption that "persons think in a manner associated with their race"). Instead, under the approach Justice Powell described, each characteristic of a particular applicant was to be considered in assessing the applicant's entire application. The current LSA policy does not provide such individualized consideration. The LSA's policy automatically distributes 20 points to every single applicant from an "underrepresented minority" group, as defined by the University. The only consideration that accompanies this distribution of points is a factual review of an application to determine whether an individual is a member of one of these minority groups. Moreover, unlike Justice Powell's example, where the race of a "particular black applicant" could be considered without being decisive, see *Bakke*, 438 U. S., at 317, the LSA's automatic distribution of 20 points has the effect of making "the factor of race . . . decisive" for virtually every minimally qualified underrepresented minority applicant. *Ibid.*[19]

Also instructive in our consideration of the LSA's system is the example provided in the description of the Harvard College Admissions Program, which Justice Powell both discussed in, and attached to, his opinion in *Bakke*. The example was included to "illustrate the kind of significance attached to race" under the Harvard College program. *Id.*, at 324. It provided as follows:

> "The Admissions Committee, with only a few places left to fill, might find itself forced to choose between A, the child of a successful black physician in an academic community with promise of superior academic performance, and B, a black who grew up in an inner-city ghetto of semi-literate parents whose academic achievement was lower but who had demonstrated energy and leadership as well as an apparently abiding interest in black power. If a good number of black students much like A but few like B had already been admitted, the Committee might prefer B; and vice versa. If C, a white student with extraordinary artistic talent, were also seeking one of the remaining places, his unique

---

[19]JUSTICE SOUTER recognizes that the LSA's use of race is decisive in practice, but he attempts to avoid that fact through unsupported speculation about the self-selection of minorities in the applicant pool. See *Post*, at 6 (dissenting opinion).

quality might give him an edge over both A and B. Thus, the critical criteria are often individual qualities or experience *not dependent upon race but sometimes associated with it." Ibid.* (emphasis added).

This example further demonstrates the problematic nature of the LSA's admissions system. Even if student C's "extraordinary artistic talent" rivaled that of Monet or Picasso, the applicant would receive, at most, five points under the LSA's system. See App. 234–235. At the same time, every single underrepresented minority applicant, including students A and B, would automatically receive 20 points for submitting an application. Clearly, the LSA's system does not offer applicants the individualized selection process described in Harvard's example. Instead of considering how the differing backgrounds, experiences, and characteristics of students A, B, and C might benefit the University, admissions counselors reviewing LSA applications would simply award both A and B 20 points because their applications indicate that they are African-American, and student C would receive up to 5 points for his "extraordinary talent."[20]

Respondents emphasize the fact that the LSA has created the possibility of an applicant's file being flagged for individualized consideration by the ARC. We think that the flagging program only emphasizes the flaws of the University's system as a whole when compared to that described by Justice Powell. Again, students A, B, and C illustrate the point. First, student A would never be flagged. This is because, as the University has conceded, the effect of automatically awarding 20 points is that virtually every qualified underrepresented minority applicant is admitted. Student A, an applicant "with promise of superior academic performance," would certainly fit this description. Thus, the result of the automatic distribution of 20 points is that the University would never consider student A's individual background, experiences, and characteristics to assess his individual "potential contribution to diversity," *Bakke, supra,* at 317. Instead, every applicant like student A would simply be admitted.

It is possible that students B and C would be flagged and considered as individuals. This assumes that student B was not already admitted because of the automatic 20-point distribution, and that student C could muster at least 70 additional points. But the fact that the "review committee can look at the applications individually and ignore the points," once an application is flagged, Tr. of Oral Arg. 42, is of little comfort under our strict scrutiny analysis. The record does not reveal precisely how many applications are flagged for this individualized consideration, but it is undisputed that such consideration is the exception and not the rule in the operation of the LSA's admissions program. See App. to Pet. for Cert. 117a ("The ARC reviews only a portion of all of the applications. The bulk of admissions decisions are executed based on selection index score parameters set by the EWG").[21] Additionally, this individualized review is only provided *after* admissions counselors automatically distribute the University's version of a "plus" that makes race a decisive factor for virtually every minimally qualified underrepresented minority applicant.

Respondents contend that "[t]he volume of applications and the presentation of applicant information make it impractical for [LSA] to use the . . . admissions system" upheld by

---

[20]Justice Souter is therefore wrong when he contends that "applicants to the undergraduate college are [not] denied individualized consideration." *Post,* at 6. As Justice O'Connor explains in her concurrence, the LSA's program "ensures that the diversity contributions of applicants cannot be individually assessed." *Post,* at 4.

[21]Justice Souter is mistaken in his assertion that the Court "take[s] it upon itself to apply a newly formulated legal standard to an undeveloped record." *Post,* at 7, n. 3. He ignores the fact that the respondents have told us all that is necessary to decide this case. As explained above, respondents concede that only a portion of the applications are reviewed by the ARC and that the "bulk of admissions decisions" are based on the point system. It should be readily apparent that the availability of this review, which comes *after* the automatic distribution of points, is far more limited than the individualized review given to the "large middle group of applicants" discussed by Justice Powell and described by the Harvard plan in *Bakke.* 438 U. S., at 316 (internal quotation marks omitted).

the Court today in *Grutter*. Brief for Respondents 6, n. 8. But the fact that the implementation of a program capable of providing individualized consideration might present administrative challenges does not render constitutional an otherwise problematic system. See *J. A. Croson Co.*, 488 U. S., at 508 (citing *Frontiero* v. *Richardson*, 411 U. S. 677, 690 (1973) (plurality opinion of Brennan, J.) (rejecting " 'administrative convenience' " as a determinant of constitutionality in the face of a suspect classification)). Nothing in Justice Powell's opinion in *Bakke* signaled that a university may employ whatever means it desires to achieve the stated goal of diversity without regard to the limits imposed by our strict scrutiny analysis.

We conclude, therefore, that because the University's use of race in its current freshman admissions policy is not narrowly tailored to achieve respondents' asserted compelling interest in diversity, the admissions policy violates the Equal Protection Clause of the Fourteenth Amendment.[22] We further find that the admissions policy also violates Title VI and 42 U. S. C. § 1981.[23] Accordingly, we reverse that portion of the District Court's decision granting respondents summary judgment with respect to liability and remand the case for proceedings consistent with this opinion.

It is so ordered.

SUPREME COURT OF THE UNITED STATES

No. 02–516

JENNIFER GRATZ AND PATRICK HAMACHER, PETITIONERS v. *LEE BOLLINGER ET AL.*

ON WRIT OF CERTIORARI TO THE UNITED STATES COURT OF APPEALS FOR THE SIXTH CIRCUIT

[June 23, 2003]

JUSTICE O'CONNOR, concurring.*

---

[22]JUSTICE GINSBURG in her dissent observes that "[o]ne can reasonably anticipate . . . that colleges and universities will seek to maintain their minority enrollment . . . whether or not they can do so in full candor through adoption of affirmative action plans of the kind here at issue." *Post*, at 7–8. She goes on to say that "[i]f honesty is the best policy, surely Michigan's accurately described, fully disclosed College affirmative action program is preferable to achieving similar numbers through winks, nods, and disguises." *Post*, at 8. These observations are remarkable for two reasons. First, they suggest that universities—to whose academic judgment we are told in *Grutter* v. *Bollinger*, *post*, at 16, we should defer—will pursue their affirmative-action programs whether or not they violate the United States Constitution. Second, they recommend that these violations should be dealt with, not by requiring the universities to obey the Constitution, but by changing the Constitution so that it conforms to the conduct of the universities.

[23]We have explained that discrimination that violates the Equal Protection Clause of the Fourteenth Amendment committed by an institution that accepts federal funds also constitutes a violation of Title VI. See *Alexander* v. *Sandoval*, 532 U. S. 275, 281 (2001); *United States* v. *Fordice*, 505 U. S. 717, 732, n. 7 (1992); *Alexander* v. *Choate*, 469 U. S. 287, 293 (1985). Likewise, with respect to §1981, we have explained that the provision was "meant, by its broad terms, to proscribe discrimination in the making or enforcement of contracts against, or in favor of, any race." *McDonald* v. *Santa Fe Trail Transp. Co.*, 427 U. S. 273, 295–296 (1976). Furthermore, we have explained that a contract for educational services is a "contract" for purposes of §1981. See *Runyon* v. *McCrary*, 427 U. S. 160, 172 (1976). Finally, purposeful discrimination that violates the Equal Protection Clause of the Fourteenth Amendment will also violate §1981. See *General Building Contractors Assn., Inc.* v. *Pennsylvania*, 458 U. S. 375, 389–390 (1982).

*JUSTICE BREYER joins this opinion, except for the last sentence.

I

Unlike the law school admissions policy the Court upholds today in *Grutter* v. *Bollinger*, *post*, p. 1, the procedures employed by the University of Michigan's (University) Office of Undergraduate Admissions do not provide for a meaningful individualized review of applicants. Cf. *Regents of Univ. of Cal.* v. *Bakke*, 438 U. S. 265 (1978) (principal opinion of Powell, J.). The law school considers the various diversity qualifications of each applicant, including race, on a case-by-case basis. See *Grutter* v. *Bollinger, post*, at 24. By contrast, the Office of Undergraduate Admissions relies on the selection index to assign *every* underrepresented minority applicant the same, *automatic* 20-point bonus without consideration of the particular background, experiences, or qualities of each individual applicant. Cf. *ante*, at 23, 25. And this mechanized selection index score, by and large, automatically determines the admissions decision for each applicant. The selection index thus precludes admissions counselors from conducting the type of individualized consideration the Court's opinion in *Grutter, supra*, at 25, requires: consideration of each applicant's individualized qualifications, including the contribution each individual's race or ethnic identity will make to the diversity of the student body, taking into account diversity within and among all racial and ethnic groups. Cf. *ante*, at 24 (citing *Bakke, supra*, at 324)).

On cross-motions for summary judgment, the District Court held that the admissions policy the University instituted in 1999 and continues to use today passed constitutional muster. See 122 F. Supp. 2d 811, 827 (ED Mich. 2001). In their proposed summary of undisputed facts, the parties jointly stipulated to the admission policy's mechanics. App. to Pet. for Cert. 116a–118a. When the university receives an application for admission to its incoming class, an admissions counselor turns to a Selection Index Worksheet to calculate the applicant's selection index score out of 150 maximum possible points—a procedure the University began using in 1998. App. 256. Applicants with a score of over 100 are automatically admitted; applicants with scores of 95 to 99 are categorized as "admit or postpone"; applicants with 90–94 points are postponed or admitted; applicants with 75–89 points are delayed or postponed; and applicants with 74 points or fewer are delayed or rejected. The Office of Undergraduate Admissions extends offers of admission on a rolling basis and acts upon the applications it has received through periodic "[m]ass [a]ction[s]." App. 256.

In calculating an applicant's selection index score, counselors assign numerical values to a broad range of academic factors, as well as to other variables the University considers important to assembling a diverse student body, including race. Up to 110 points can be assigned for academic performance, and up to 40 points can be assigned for the other, nonacademic factors. Michigan residents, for example, receive 10 points, and children of alumni receive 4. Counselors may assign an outstanding essay up to 3 points and may award up to 5 points for an applicant's personal achievement, leadership, or public service. Most importantly for this case, an applicant automatically receives a 20 point bonus if he or she possesses any one of the following "miscellaneous" factors: membership in an underrepresented minority group; attendance at a predominantly minority or disadvantaged high school; or recruitment for athletics.

In 1999, the University added another layer of review to its admissions process. After an admissions counselor has tabulated an applicant's selection index score, he or she may "flag" an application for further consideration by an Admissions Review Committee, which is composed of members of the Office of Undergraduate Admissions and the Office of the Provost. App. to Pet. for Cert. 117a. The review committee meets periodically to discuss the files of "flagged" applicants not already admitted based on the selection index parameters. App. 275. After discussing each flagged application, the committee decides whether to admit, defer, or deny the applicant. *Ibid.*

Counselors may flag an applicant for review by the committee if he or she is academically prepared, has a selection index score of at least 75 (for non-Michigan residents) or 80 (for Michigan residents), and possesses one of several qualities valued by the University. These qualities include "high class rank, unique life experiences, challenges, circumstances, interests or talents, socioeconomic disadvantage, and underrepresented race, ethnicity, or geography." App. to Pet. for Cert. 117a. Counselors also have the discretion to flag an application if, notwithstanding a high selection index score, something in the applicant's file suggests that the applicant may not be suitable for admission. App. 274. Finally, in "rare circumstances," an admissions counselor may flag an applicant with a selection index score below the designated levels if the counselor has reason to believe from reading the entire file that the score does not reflect the applicant's true promise. *Ibid.*

II

Although the Office of Undergraduate Admissions does assign 20 points to some "soft" variables other than race, the points available for other diversity contributions, such as leadership and service, personal achievement, and geographic diversity, are capped at much lower levels. Even the most outstanding national high school leader could never receive more than five points for his or her accomplishments—a mere quarter of the points automatically assigned to an underrepresented minority solely based on the fact of his or her race. Of course, as Justice Powell made clear in *Bakke*, a university need not "necessarily accor[d]" all diversity factors "the same weight," 438 U. S., at 317, and the "weight attributed to a particular quality may vary from year to year depending on the 'mix' both of the student body and the applicants for the incoming class," *id.*, at 317–318. But the selection index, by setting up automatic, predetermined point allocations for the soft variables, ensures that the diversity contributions of applicants cannot be individually assessed. This policy stands in sharp contrast to the law school's admissions plan, which enables admissions officers to make nuanced judgments with respect to the contributions each applicant is likely to make to the diversity of the incoming class. See *Grutter* v. *Bollinger, post*, at 22 ("[T]he Law School's race-conscious admissions program adequately ensures that all factors that may contribute to student body diversity are meaningfully considered alongside race in admissions decisions").

The only potential source of individualized consideration appears to be the Admissions Review Committee. The evidence in the record, however, reveals very little about how the review committee actually functions. And what evidence there is indicates that the committee is a kind of afterthought, rather than an integral component of a system of individualized review. As the Court points out, it is undisputed that the " '[committee] reviews only a portion of all the applications. The bulk of admissions decisions are executed based on selection index score parameters set by the [Enrollment Working Group].' " *Ante*, at 26 (quoting App. to Pet for Cert. 117a). Review by the committee thus represents a necessarily limited exception to the Office of Undergraduate Admissions' general reliance on the selection index. Indeed, the record does not reveal how many applications admissions counselors send to the review committee each year, and the University has not pointed to evidence demonstrating that a meaningful percentage of applicants receives this level of discretionary review. In addition, eligibility for consideration by the committee is itself based on automatic cut-off levels determined with reference to selection index scores. And there is no evidence of how the decisions are actually made—what type of individualized consideration is or is not used. Given these circumstances, the addition of the Admissions Review Committee to the admissions process cannot offset the apparent absence of individualized consideration from the Office of Undergraduate Admissions' general practices.

For these reasons, the record before us does not support the conclusion that the University of Michigan's admissions program for its College of Literature, Science, and the Arts—to the extent that it considers race—provides the necessary individualized consideration. The University, of course, remains free to modify its system so that it does so. Cf. *Grutter* v. *Bollinger, post*, p. 1. But the current system, as I understand it, is a nonindividualized, mechanical one. As a result, I join the Court's opinion reversing the decision of the District Court.

SUPREME COURT OF THE UNITED STATES

No. 02–516

JENNIFER GRATZ AND PATRICK HAMACHER, PETITIONERS v. LEE BOLLINGER ET AL.

ON WRIT OF CERTIORARI TO THE UNITED STATES COURT OF APPEALS FOR THE SIXTH CIRCUIT

[June 23, 2003]

JUSTICE THOMAS, concurring.

I join the Court's opinion because I believe it correctly applies our precedents, including today's decision in *Grutter* v. *Bollinger, post,* p. __. For similar reasons to those given in my separate opinion in that case, see *post,* p. (opinion concurring in part and dissenting in part), however, I would hold that a State's use of racial discrimination in higher education admissions is categorically prohibited by the Equal Protection Clause.

I make only one further observation. The University of Michigan's College of Literature, Science, and the Arts (LSA) admissions policy that the Court today invalidates does not suffer from the additional constitutional defect of allowing racial "discriminat[ion] among [the] groups" included within its definition of underrepresented minorities, *Grutter, post,* at 24 (opinion of the Court); *post,* at 27 (THOMAS, J., concurring in part and dissenting in part), because it awards all underrepresented minorities the same racial preference. The LSA policy falls, however, because it does not sufficiently allow for the consideration of nonracial distinctions among underrepresented minority applicants. Under today's decisions, a university may not racially discriminate between the groups constituting the critical mass. See *ibid.; Grutter, post,* at 17 (opinion of the Court) (stating that such "racial balancing . . . is patently unconstitutional"). An admissions policy, however, must allow for consideration of these nonracial distinctions among applicants on both sides of the single permitted racial classification. See *ante,* at 24 (opinion of the Court); *ante,* at 1–2 (O'CONNOR, J., concurring).

SUPREME COURT OF THE UNITED STATES

No. 02–516

JENNIFER GRATZ AND PATRICK HAMACHER, PETITIONERS v. LEE BOLLINGER ET AL.

ON WRIT OF CERTIORARI TO THE UNITED STATES COURT OF APPEALS FOR THE SIXTH CIRCUIT

[June 23, 2003]

JUSTICE BREYER, concurring in the judgment.

I concur in the judgment of the Court though I do not join its opinion. I join JUSTICE O'CONNOR's opinion except insofar as it joins that of the Court. I join Part I of JUSTICE GINSBURG's dissenting opinion, but I do not dissent from the Court's reversal of the District Court's decision. I agree with JUSTICE GINSBURG that, in implementing the Constitution's equality instruction, government decisionmakers may properly distinguish between policies of inclusion and exclusion, *post*, at 4, for the former are more likely to prove consistent with the basic constitutional obligation that the law respect each individual equally, see U. S. Const., Amdt. 14.

SUPREME COURT OF THE UNITED STATES

No. 02–516

JENNIFER GRATZ AND PATRICK HAMACHER, PETITIONERS v. *LEE BOLLINGER ET AL.*

ON WRIT OF CERTIORARI TO THE UNITED STATES COURT OF APPEALS FOR THE SIXTH CIRCUIT

[June 23, 2003]

JUSTICE STEVENS, with whom JUSTICE SOUTER joins, dissenting.

Petitioners seek forward-looking relief enjoining the University of Michigan from continuing to use its current race-conscious freshman admissions policy. Yet unlike the plaintiff in *Grutter* v. *Bollinger, post*, p. 1,[1] the petitioners in this case had already enrolled at other schools before they filed their class-action complaint in this case. Neither petitioner was in the process of reapplying to Michigan through the freshman admissions process at the time this suit was filed, and neither has done so since. There is a total absence of evidence that either petitioner would receive any benefit from the prospective relief sought by their lawyer. While some unidentified members of the class may very well have standing to seek prospective relief, it is clear that neither petitioner does. Our precedents therefore require dismissal of the action.

I

Petitioner Jennifer Gratz applied in 1994 for admission to the University of Michigan's (University) College of Literature, Science, and the Arts (LSA) as an undergraduate for the 1995–1996 freshman class. After the University delayed action on her application and then placed her name on an extended waiting list, Gratz decided to attend the University of Michigan at Dearborn instead; she graduated in 1999. Petitioner Patrick Hamacher applied for admission to LSA as an undergraduate for the 1997–1998 freshman class. After the University postponed decision on his application and then placed his name on an extended waiting list, he attended Michigan State University, graduating in 2001. In the complaint that petitioners filed on October 14, 1997, Hamacher alleged that "[h]e intends to apply to transfer [to the University of Michigan] if the discriminatory admissions system described herein is eliminated." App. 34.

At the class certification stage, petitioners sought to have Hamacher represent a class pursuant to Federal Rule Civil Procedure 23(b)(2).[2] See App. 71, n. 3. In response, Michigan contended that "Hamacher lacks standing to represent a class seeking declaratory and injunctive relief." *Id.*, at 63. Michigan submitted that Hamacher suffered " 'no threat of imminent future injury' " given that he had already enrolled at another undergraduate

---

[1]In challenging the use of race in admissions at Michigan's law school, Barbara Grutter alleged in her complaint that she "has not attended any other law school" and that she "still desires to attend the Law School and become a lawyer." App. in No. 02–241, p. 30.

[2]Petitioners did not seek to have Gratz represent the class pursuant to Federal Rule Civil Procedure 23(b)(2). See App. 71, n. 3.

institution.[3] *Id.*, at 64. The District Court rejected Michigan's contention, concluding that Hamacher had standing to seek injunctive relief because the complaint alleged that he intended to apply to Michigan as a transfer student. See *id.*, at 67 ("To the extent that plaintiff Hamacher reapplies to the University of Michigan, he will again face the same 'harm' in that race will continue to be a factor in admissions"). The District Court, accordingly, certified Hamacher as the sole class representative and limited the claims of the class to injunctive and declaratory relief. See *id.*, at 70–71.

In subsequent proceedings, the District Court held that the 1995–1998 admissions system, which was in effect when both petitioners' applications were denied, was unlawful but that Michigan's new 1999–2000 admissions system was lawful. When petitioners sought certiorari from this Court, Michigan did not cross-petition for review of the District Court's judgment concerning the admissions policies that Michigan had in place when Gratz and Hamacher applied for admission in 1994 and 1996 respectively. See Brief for Respondents 5, n. 7. Accordingly, we have before us only that portion of the District Court's judgment that upheld Michigan's new freshman admissions policy.

II

Both Hamacher and Gratz, of course, have standing to seek damages as compensation for the alleged wrongful denial of their respective applications under Michigan's old freshman admissions system. However, like the plaintiff in *Los Angeles* v. *Lyons*, 461 U. S. 95 (1983), who had standing to recover damages caused by "chokeholds" administered by the police in the past but had no standing to seek injunctive relief preventing future chokeholds, petitioners' past injuries do not give them standing to obtain injunctive relief to protect third parties from similar harms. See *id.*, at 102 ("[P]ast exposure to illegal conduct does not in itself show a present case or controversy regarding injunctive relief . . . if unaccompanied by any continuing, present adverse effects" (quoting *O'Shea* v. *Littleton*, 414 U. S. 488, 495–496 (1974))). To seek forward-looking, injunctive relief, petitioners must show that they face an imminent threat of future injury. See *Adarand Constructors, Inc.* v. *Peña*, 515 U. S. 200, 210–211 (1995). This they cannot do given that when this suit was filed, neither faced an impending threat of future injury based on Michigan's new freshman admissions policy.[4]

Even though there is not a scintilla of evidence that the freshman admissions program now being administered by respondents will ever have any impact on either Hamacher or Gratz, petitioners nonetheless argue that Hamacher has a personal stake in this suit because at the time the complaint was filed, Hamacher intended to apply to transfer to Michigan once certain admission policy changes occurred.[5] See App. 34; see also Tr. of Oral Arg. 4–5.

---

[3]In arguing that Hamacher lacked standing, Michigan also asserted that Hamacher "would need to achieve a 3.0 grade point average to attempt to transfer to the University of Michigan." *Id.*, at 64, n. 2. The District Court rejected this argument, concluding that "Hamacher's present grades are not a factor to be considered at this time." *Id.*, at 67.

[4]In responding to questions about petitioners' standing at oral argument, petitioners' counsel alluded to the fact that Michigan might continually change the details of its admissions policy. See Tr. of Oral Arg. 9. The change in Michigan's freshman admissions policy, however, is not the reason why petitioners cannot establish standing to seek prospective relief. Rather, the reason they lack standing to seek forward-looking relief is that when this suit was filed, neither faced a "real and immediate threat" of future injury under Michigan's freshman admissions policy given that they had both already enrolled at other institutions. *Adarand Constructors, Inc.* v. *Peña*, 515 U. S. 200, 210 (1995) (quoting *Los Angeles* v. *Lyons*, 461 U. S. 95, 105 (1983)). Their decision to obtain a college education elsewhere distinguishes this case from Allan Bakke's single-minded pursuit of a medical education from the University of California at Davis. See *Regents of Univ. of Cal.* v. *Bakke*, 438 U. S. 265 (1978); cf. *DeFunis* v. *Odegaard*, 416 U. S. 312 (1974) *(per curiam)*.

[5]Hamacher clearly can no longer claim an intent to transfer into Michigan's undergraduate program given that he graduated from college in 2001. However, this fact alone is not necessarily fatal to the instant class action because we have recognized that, if a named class representative has standing at

Petitioners' attempt to base Hamacher's standing in this suit on a hypothetical transfer application fails for several reasons. First, there is no evidence that Hamacher ever actually applied for admission as a transfer student at Michigan. His claim of future injury is at best "conjectural or hypothetical" rather than "real and immediate." *O'Shea* v. *Littleton*, 414 U. S., at 494 (internal quotation marks omitted); see also *Lujan* v. *Defenders of Wildlife*, 504 U. S. 555, 560 (1992).

Second, as petitioners' counsel conceded at oral argument, the transfer policy is not before this Court and was not addressed by the District Court. See Tr. of Oral Arg. 4–5 (admitting that "[t]he transfer admissions policy itself is not before you—the Court"). Unlike the University's freshman policy, which is detailed at great length in the Joint Appendix filed with this Court, the specifics of the transfer policy are conspicuously missing from the Joint Appendix filed with this Court. Furthermore, the transfer policy is not discussed anywhere in the parties' briefs. Nor is it ever even referenced in the District Court's Dec. 13, 2000, opinion that upheld Michigan's new freshman admissions policy and struck down Michigan's old policy. Nonetheless, evidence filed with the District Court by Michigan demonstrates that the criteria used to evaluate transfer applications at Michigan differ significantly from the criteria used to evaluate freshman undergraduate applications. Of special significance, Michigan's 2000 freshman admissions policy, for example, provides for 20 points to be added to the selection index scores of minority applicants. See *ante*, at 23. In contrast, Michigan does not use points in its transfer policy; some applicants, including minority and socioeconomically disadvantaged applicants, "will generally be admitted" if they possess certain qualifications, including a 2.5 undergraduate grade point average (GPA), sophomore standing, and a 3.0 high school GPA. 10 Record 16 (Exh. C). Because of these differences, Hamacher cannot base his right to complain about the *freshman* admissions policy on his hypothetical injury under a wholly separate *transfer* policy. For "[i]f the right to complain of *one* administrative deficiency automatically conferred the right to complain of *all* administrative deficiencies, any citizen aggrieved in one respect could bring the whole structure of state administration before the courts for review." *Lewis* v. *Casey*, 518 U. S. 343, 358–359, n. 6 (1996) (emphasis in original); see also *Blum* v. *Yaretsky*, 457 U. S. 991, 999 (1982) ("[A] plaintiff who has been subject to injurious conduct of one kind [does not] possess by virtue of that injury the necessary stake in litigating conduct of another kind, although similar").[6]

Third, the differences between the freshman and the transfer admissions policies make it extremely unlikely, at best, that an injunction requiring respondents to modify the freshman admissions program would have any impact on Michigan's transfer policy. See *Allen* v. *Wright*, 468 U. S. 737, 751 (1984) ("[R]elief from the injury must be 'likely' to follow from a favorable decision"); *Schlesinger* v. *Reservists Comm. to Stop the War*, 418 U. S. 208, 222 (1974) ("[T]he discrete factual context within which the concrete injury occurred or is threatened insures the framing of relief no broader than required by the precise facts to which the court's ruling would be applied"). This is especially true in light of petitioners' unequivocal disavowal of any request for equitable relief that would totally preclude the use of race in the processing of all admissions applications. See Tr. of Oral Arg. 14–15.

---

the time a suit is initiated, class actions may proceed in some instances following mootness of the named class representative's claim. See, *e.g.*, *Sosna* v. *Iowa*, 419 U. S. 393, 402 (1975) (holding that the requisite Article III "case or controversy" may exist "between a named defendant and a member of the class represented by the named plaintiff, even though the claim of the named plaintiff has become moot"); *Franks* v. *Bowman Transp. Co.*, 424 U. S. 747 (1976). The problem in this case is that neither Gratz nor Hamacher had standing to assert a forward-looking, injunctive claim in federal court at the time this suit was initiated.

[6]Under the majority's view of standing, there would be no end to Hamacher's ability to challenge any use of race by the University in a variety of programs. For if Hamacher's right to complain about the *transfer* policy gives him standing to challenge the *freshman* policy, presumably his ability to complain about the *transfer* policy likewise would enable him to challenge Michigan's *law school* admissions policy, as well as any other race-based admissions policy used by Michigan.

The majority asserts that petitioners "have challenged *any* use of race by the University in undergraduate admissions"—freshman and transfer alike. *Ante*, at 18, n. 16 (emphasis in original). Yet when questioned at oral argument about whether petitioners' challenge would impact both private and public universities, petitioners' counsel stated: "Your Honor, I want to be clear about what it is that we're arguing for here today. *We are not suggesting an absolute rule forbidding any use of race under any circumstances.* What we are arguing is that the interest asserted here by the University, this amorphous, ill-defined, unlimited interest in diversity is not a compelling interest." Tr. of Oral Arg. 14 (emphasis added). In addition, when asked whether petitioners took the position that the only permissible use of race is as a remedy for past discrimination, petitioners' lawyer stated: "I would not go that far. . . . [T]here may be other reasons. I think they would have to be extraordinary and rare. . . ." *Id.*, at 15. Consistent with these statements, petitioners' briefs filed with this Court attack the University's asserted interest in "diversity" but acknowledge that race could be considered for remedial reasons. See, *e.g.*, Brief for Petitioners 16–17.

Because Michigan's transfer policy was not challenged by petitioners and is not before this Court, see *supra*, at 5, we do not know whether Michigan would defend its transfer policy on diversity grounds, or whether it might try to justify its transfer policy on other grounds, such as a remedial interest. Petitioners' counsel was therefore incorrect in asserting at oral argument that if the University's asserted interest in "diversity" were to be "struck down as a rationale, then the law would be [the] same with respect to the transfer policy as with respect to the original [freshman admissions] policy." Tr. of Oral Arg. 7–8. And the majority is likewise mistaken in assuming that "the University's use of race in undergraduate transfer admissions does not implicate a significantly different set of concerns than does its use of race in undergraduate freshman admissions." *Ante*, at 16. Because the transfer policy has never been the subject of this suit, we simply do not know (1) whether Michigan would defend its transfer policy on "diversity" grounds or some other grounds, or (2) how the absence of a point system in the transfer policy might impact a narrow tailoring analysis of that policy.

At bottom, petitioners' interest in obtaining an injunction for the benefit of younger third parties is comparable to that of the unemancipated minor who had no standing to litigate on behalf of older women in *H. L.* v. *Matheson*, 450 U. S. 398, 406–407 (1981), or that of the Medicaid patients transferred to less intensive care who had no standing to litigate on behalf of patients objecting to transfers to more intensive care facilities in *Blum* v. *Yaretsky*, 457 U. S., at 1001. To have standing, it is elementary that the petitioners' own interests must be implicated. Because neither petitioner has a personal stake in this suit for prospective relief, neither has standing.

III

It is true that the petitioners' complaint was filed as a class action and that Hamacher has been certified as the representative of a class, some of whose members may well have standing to challenge the LSA freshman admissions program that is presently in effect. But the fact that "a suit may be a class action . . . adds nothing to the question of standing, for even named plaintiffs who represent a class 'must allege and show that they personally have been injured, not that injury has been suffered by other, unidentified members of the class to which they belong and which they purport to represent.' " *Simon* v. *Eastern Ky. Welfare Rights Organization*, 426 U. S. 26, 40, n. 20 (1976) (quoting *Warth* v. *Seldin*, 422 U. S. 490, 502 (1975)); see also 1 A. Conte & H. Newberg, Class Actions §2:5 (4th ed. 2002) ("[O]ne cannot acquire individual standing by virtue of bringing a class action").[7] Thus, in *Blum*, we squarely held that the interests of members of the class could not satisfy the requirement

---

[7] Of course, the injury to Hamacher would give him standing to claim damages for past harm on behalf of class members, but he was certified as the class representative for the limited purpose of seeking injunctive and declaratory relief.

that the class representatives have a personal interest in obtaining the particular equitable relief being sought. The class in *Blum* included patients who wanted a hearing before being transferred to facilities where they would receive more intensive care. The class representatives, however, were in the category of patients threatened with a transfer to less intensive care facilities. In explaining why the named class representatives could not base their standing to sue on the injury suffered by other members of the class, we stated:

> "Respondents suggest that members of the class they represent have been transferred to higher levels of care as a result of [utilization review committee] decisions. Respondents, however, 'must allege and show that they personally have been injured, not that injury has been suffered by other, unidentified members of the class to which they belong and which they purport to represent.' *Warth* v. *Seldin*, 422 U. S. 490, 502 (1975). Unless these individuals 'can thus demonstrate the requisite case or controversy between themselves personally and [petitioners], "none may seek relief on behalf of himself or any other member of the class." *O'Shea* v. *Littleton*, 414 U. S. 488, 494 (1974).' *Ibid*." 457 U. S., at 1001, n. 13.

Much like the class representatives in *Blum*, Hamacher—the sole class representative in this case—cannot meet Article III's threshold personal-stake requirement. While unidentified members of the class he represents may well have standing to challenge Michigan's current freshman admissions policy, Hamacher cannot base his standing to sue on injuries suffered by other members of the class.

IV

As this case comes to us, our precedents leave us no alternative but to dismiss the writ for lack of jurisdiction. Neither petitioner has a personal stake in the outcome of the case, and neither has standing to seek prospective relief on behalf of unidentified class members who may or may not have standing to litigate on behalf of themselves. Accordingly, I respectfully dissent.

SUPREME COURT OF THE UNITED STATES

No. 02–516

JENNIFER GRATZ AND PATRICK HAMACHER, PETITIONERS v. *LEE BOLLINGER ET AL.*

ON WRIT OF CERTIORARI TO THE UNITED STATES COURT OF APPEALS FOR THE SIXTH CIRCUIT

[June 23, 2003]

JUSTICE SOUTER, with whom JUSTICE GINSBURG joins as to Part II, dissenting.

I agree with JUSTICE STEVENS that Patrick Hamacher has no standing to seek declaratory or injunctive relief against a freshman admissions policy that will never cause him any harm. I write separately to note that even the Court's new gloss on the law of standing should not permit it to reach the issue it decides today. And because a majority of the Court has chosen to address the merits, I also add a word to say that even if the merits were reachable, I would dissent from the Court's judgment.

I

The Court's finding of Article III standing rests on two propositions: first, that both the University of Michigan's undergraduate college's transfer policy and its freshman admissions policy seek to achieve student body diversity through the "use of race," *ante*, at 12–20, and second, that Hamacher has standing to challenge the transfer policy on the grounds that diversity can never be a "compelling state interest" justifying the use of race in any admissions decision, freshman or transfer, *ante*, at 18. The Court concludes that, because Hamacher's argument, if successful, would seal the fate of both policies, his standing to challenge the transfer policy also allows him to attack the freshman admissions policy. *Ante*, at 18, n. 16 ("[P]etitioners challenged any use of race by the University to promote diversity, including through the transfer policy"); *ibid.* (" '[T]he University considers race for a purpose to achieve a diversity that we believe is not compelling, and if that is struck down as a rationale, then the [result] would be [the] same with respect to the transfer policy as with respect to the [freshman] admissions policy, Your Honor' " (quoting Tr. of Oral Arg. 7–8)). I agree with JUSTICE STEVENS's critique that the Court thus ignores the basic principle of Article III standing that a plaintiff cannot challenge a government program that does not apply to him. See *ante*, at 6, and n. 6 (dissenting opinion).[1]

But even on the Court's indulgent standing theory, the decision should not go beyond a recognition that diversity can serve as a compelling state interest justifying race-conscious decisions in education. *Ante*, at 20 (citing *Grutter* v. *Bollinger, post*, at 15–21). Since, as the Court says, "petitioners did not raise a narrow tailoring challenge to the transfer policy," *ante*, at 18, n. 16, our decision in *Grutter* is fatal to Hamacher's sole attack upon the transfer policy, which is the only policy before this Court that he claims aggrieved him. Hamacher's challenge to that policy having failed, his standing is presumably spent. The further question whether the freshman admissions plan is narrowly tailored to achieving student body diversity remains legally irrelevant to Hamacher and should await a plaintiff who is actually hurt by it.[2]

II

The cases now contain two pointers toward the line between the valid and the unconstitutional in race-conscious admissions schemes. *Grutter* reaffirms the permissibility of individualized consideration of race to achieve a diversity of students, at least where race is not assigned a preordained value in all cases. On the other hand, Justice Powell's opinion in *Regents of Univ. of Cal.* v. *Bakke*, 438 U. S. 265 (1978), rules out a racial quota or set-aside, in which race is the sole fact of eligibility for certain places in a class. Although the freshman admissions system here is subject to argument on the merits, I think it is closer to what *Grutter* approves than to what *Bakke* condemns, and should not be held unconstitutional on the current record.

The record does not describe a system with a quota like the one struck down in *Bakke*,

---

[1]The Court's holding arguably exposes a weakness in the rule of *Blum* v. *Yaretsky*, 457 U. S. 991 (1982), that Article III standing may not be satisfied by the unnamed members of a duly certified class. But no party has invited us to reconsider *Blum*, and I follow JUSTICE STEVENS in approaching the case on the assumption that *Blum* is settled law.

[2]For that matter, as the Court suggests, narrow tailoring challenges against the two policies could well have different outcomes. *Ante*, at 18. The record on the decisionmaking process for transfer applicants is understandably thin, given that petitioners never raised a narrow tailoring challenge against it. Most importantly, however, the transfer policy does not use a points-based "selection index" to evaluate transfer applicants, but rather considers race as one of many factors in making the general determination whether the applicant would make a " 'contribution to a diverse student body.' " *Ante*, at 17 (quoting 2 App. in No. 01–1333 etc. (CA6), p. 531 (capitalization omitted)). This limited glimpse into the transfer policy at least permits the inference that the University engages in a "holistic review" of transfer applications consistent with the program upheld today in *Grutter* v. *Bollinger, post*, at 25.

which "insulate[d]" all nonminority candidates from competition from certain seats. *Bakke, supra*, at 317 (opinion of Powell, J.); see also *Richmond* v. *J. A. Croson Co.*, 488 U. S. 469, 496 (1989) (plurality opinion) (stating that *Bakke* invalidated "a plan that completely eliminated nonminorities from consideration for a specified percentage of opportunities"). The *Bakke* plan "focused *solely* on ethnic diversity" and effectively told nonminority applicants that "[n]o matter how strong their qualifications, quantitative and extracurricular, including their own potential for contribution to educational diversity, they are never afforded the chance to compete with applicants from the preferred groups for the [set-aside] special admissions seats." *Bakke, supra*, at 315, 319 (opinion of Powell, J.) (emphasis in original).

The plan here, in contrast, lets all applicants compete for all places and values an applicant's offering for any place not only on grounds of race, but on grades, test scores, strength of high school, quality of course of study, residence, alumni relationships, leadership, personal character, socioeconomic disadvantage, athletic ability, and quality of a personal essay. *Ante*, at 6. A nonminority applicant who scores highly in these other categories can readily garner a selection index exceeding that of a minority applicant who gets the 20-point bonus. Cf. *Johnson* v. *Transportation Agency, Santa Clara Cty.*, 480 U. S. 616, 638 (1987) (upholding a program in which gender "was but one of numerous factors [taken] into account in arriving at [a] decision" because "[n]o persons are automatically excluded from consideration; all are able to have their qualifications weighed against those of other applicants" (emphasis deleted)).

Subject to one qualification to be taken up below, this scheme of considering, through the selection index system, all of the characteristics that the college thinks relevant to student diversity for every one of the student places to be filled fits Justice Powell's description of a constitutionally acceptable program: one that considers "all pertinent elements of diversity in light of the particular qualifications of each applicant" and places each element "on the same footing for consideration, although not necessarily according them the same weight." *Bakke, supra*, at 317. In the Court's own words, "each characteristic of a particular applicant [is] considered in assessing the applicant's entire application." *Ante*, at 23. An unsuccessful nonminority applicant cannot complain that he was rejected "simply because he was not the right color"; an applicant who is rejected because "his combined qualifications . . . did not outweigh those of the other applicant" has been given an opportunity to compete with all other applicants. *Bakke, supra*, at 318 (opinion of Powell, J.).

The one qualification to this description of the admissions process is that membership in an underrepresented minority is given a weight of 20 points on the 150-point scale. On the face of things, however, this assignment of specific points does not set race apart from all other weighted considerations. Nonminority students may receive 20 points for athletic ability, socioeconomic disadvantage, attendance at a socioeconomically disadvantaged or predominantly minority high school, or at the Provost's discretion; they may also receive 10 points for being residents of Michigan, 6 for residence in an underrepresented Michigan county, 5 for leadership and service, and so on.

The Court nonetheless finds fault with a scheme that "automatically" distributes 20 points to minority applicants because "[t]he only consideration that accompanies this distribution of points is a factual review of an application to determine whether an individual is a member of one of these minority groups." *Ante*, at 23. The objection goes to the use of points to quantify and compare characteristics, or to the number of points awarded due to race, but on either reading the objection is mistaken.

The very nature of a college's permissible practice of awarding value to racial diversity means that race must be considered in a way that increases some applicants' chances for admission. Since college admission is not left entirely to inarticulate intuition, it is hard to see what is inappropriate in assigning some stated value to a relevant characteristic, whether it be reasoning ability, writing style, running speed, or minority race. Justice Powell's plus factors necessarily are assigned some values. The college simply does by a numbered scale what the law school accomplishes in its "holistic review," *Grutter, post*, at 25; the distinction does not imply that applicants to the undergraduate college are denied individualized consideration or a fair chance to compete on the basis of all the various merits their applications may disclose.

Nor is it possible to say that the 20 points convert race into a decisive factor comparable to reserving minority places as in *Bakke*. Of course we can conceive of a point system in which the "plus" factor given to minority applicants would be so extreme as to guarantee every minority applicant a higher rank than every nonminority applicant in the university's admissions system, see 438 U. S., at 319, n. 53 (opinion of Powell, J.). But petitioners do not have a convincing argument that the freshman admissions system operates this way. The present record obviously shows that nonminority applicants may achieve higher selection point totals than minority applicants owing to characteristics other than race, and the fact that the university admits "virtually every qualified underrepresented minority applicant," App. to Pet. for Cert. 111a, may reflect nothing more than the likelihood that very few qualified minority applicants apply, Brief for Respondents Bollinger et al. 39, as well as the possibility that self-selection results in a strong minority applicant pool. It suffices for me, as it did for the District Court, that there are no *Bakke*-like set-asides and that consideration of an applicant's whole spectrum of ability is no more ruled out by giving 20 points for race than by giving the same points for athletic ability or socioeconomic disadvantage.

Any argument that the "tailoring" amounts to a set-aside, then, boils down to the claim that a plus factor of 20 points makes some observers suspicious, where a factor of 10 points might not. But suspicion does not carry petitioners' ultimate burden of persuasion in this constitutional challenge, *Wygant* v. *Jackson Bd. of Ed.*, 476 U. S. 267, 287–288 (1986) (plurality opinion of Powell, J.), and it surely does not warrant condemning the college's admissions scheme on this record. Because the District Court (correctly, in my view) did not believe that the specific point assignment was constitutionally troubling, it made only limited and general findings on other characteristics of the university's admissions practice, such as the conduct of individualized review by the Admissions Review Committee. 122 F. Supp. 2d 811, 829–830 (ED Mich. 2000). As the Court indicates, we know very little about the actual role of the review committee. *Ante*, at 26 ("The record does not reveal precisely how many applications are flagged for this individualized consideration [by the committee]"); see also *ante*, at 4 (O'CONNOR, J., concurring) ("The evidence in the record . . . reveals very little about how the review committee actually functions"). The point system cannot operate as a *de facto* set-aside if the greater admissions process, including review by the committee, results in individualized review sufficient to meet the Court's standards. Since the record is quiet, if not silent, on the case-by-case work of the committee, the Court would be on more defensible ground by vacating and remanding for evidence about the committee's specific determinations.[3]

Without knowing more about how the Admissions Review Committee actually functions, it seems especially unfair to treat the candor of the admissions plan as an Achilles' heel. In contrast to the college's forthrightness in saying just what plus factor it gives for membership in an underrepresented minority, it is worth considering the character of one alternative thrown up as preferable, because supposedly not based on race. Drawing on admissions systems used at public universities in California, Florida, and Texas, the United States contends that Michigan could get student diversity in satisfaction of its compelling interest by

---

[3]The Court surmises that the committee does not contribute meaningfully to the University's individualized review of applications. *Ante*, at 25–26. The Court should not take it upon itself to apply a newly-formulated legal standard to an undeveloped record. Given the District Court's statement that the committee may examine "any number of applicants, including applicants other than underrepresented minority applicants," 122 F. Supp. 2d 811, 830 (ED Mich. 2000), it is quite possible that further factual development would reveal the committee to be a "source of individualized consideration" sufficient to satisfy the Court's rule, *ante*, at 4 (O'CONNOR, J., concurring). Determination of that issue in the first instance is a job for the District Court, not for this Court on a record that is admittedly lacking.

guaranteeing admission to a fixed percentage of the top students from each high school in Michigan. Brief for United States as *Amicus Curiae* 18; Brief for United States as *Amicus Curiae* in *Grutter* v. *Bollinger*, O. T. 2002, No. 02–241, pp. 13–17.

While there is nothing unconstitutional about such a practice, it nonetheless suffers from a serious disadvantage.[4] It is the disadvantage of deliberate obfuscation. The "percentage plans" are just as race conscious as the point scheme (and fairly so), but they get their racially diverse results without saying directly what they are doing or why they are doing it. In contrast, Michigan states its purpose directly and, if this were a doubtful case for me, I would be tempted to give Michigan an extra point of its own for its frankness. Equal protection cannot become an exercise in which the winners are the ones who hide the ball.

III

If this plan were challenged by a plaintiff with proper standing under Article III, I would affirm the judgment of the District Court granting summary judgment to the college. As it is, I would vacate the judgment for lack of jurisdiction, and I respectfully dissent.

SUPREME COURT OF THE UNITED STATES

No. 02–516

JENNIFER GRATZ AND PATRICK HAMACHER, PETITIONERS v. *LEE BOLLINGER ET AL.*

ON WRIT OF CERTIORARI TO THE UNITED STATES COURT OF APPEALS FOR THE SIXTH CIRCUIT

[June 23, 2003]

JUSTICE GINSBURG, with whom JUSTICE SOUTER joins, dissenting.*

I

Educational institutions, the Court acknowledges, are not barred from any and all consideration of race when making admissions decisions. *Ante*, at 20; see *Grutter* v. *Bollinger, post*, at 13–21. But the Court once again maintains that the same standard of review controls judicial inspection of all official race classifications. *Ante*, at 21 (quoting *Adarand Constructors, Inc.* v. *Peña*, 515 U. S. 200, 224 (1995); *Richmond* v. *J. A. Croson Co.*, 488 U. S. 469, 494 (1989) (plurality opinion)). This insistence on "consistency," *Adarand*, 515 U. S., at 224, would be fitting were our Nation free of the vestiges of rank discrimination long reinforced by law, see *id.*, at 274–276, and n. 8 (GINSBURG, J., dissenting). But we are not far distant from an overtly discriminatory past, and the effects of centuries of law-sanctioned inequality remain painfully evident in our communities and schools.

In the wake "of a system of racial caste only recently ended," *id.*, at 273 (GINSBURG, J., dissenting), large disparities endure. Unemployment,[1] poverty,[2] and access to health

---

[4]Of course it might be pointless in the State of Michigan, where minorities are a much smaller fraction of the population than in California, Florida, or Texas. Brief for Respondents Bollinger et al. 48–49.

*JUSTICE BREYER joins Part I of this opinion.

[1]See, *e.g.*, U. S. Dept. of Commerce, Bureau of Census, Statistical Abstract of the United States: 2002, p. 368 (2002) (Table 562) (hereinafter Statistical Abstract) (unemployment rate among whites was 3.7% in 1999, 3.5% in 2000, and 4.2% in 2001; during those years, the unemployment rate among African-Americans was 8.0%, 7.6%, and 8.7%, respectively; among Hispanics, 6.4%, 5.7%, and 6.6%).

[2]See, *e.g.*, U. S. Dept of Commerce, Bureau of Census, Poverty in the United States: 2000, p. 291

care[3] vary disproportionately by race. Neighborhoods and schools remain racially divided.[4] African-American and Hispanic children are all too often educated in poverty-stricken and underperforming institutions.[5] Adult African-Americans and Hispanics generally earn less than whites with equivalent levels of education.[6] Equally credentialed job applicants receive different receptions depending on their race.[7] Irrational prejudice is still encountered in real estate markets[8] and consumer transactions.[9] "Bias both conscious and unconscious, reflecting traditional and unexamined habits of thought, keeps up barriers that must come down if equal opportunity and nondiscrimination are ever genuinely to become this country's law and practice." *Id.,* at 274 (GINSBURG, J., dissenting); see generally Krieger, Civil Rights Perestroika: Intergroup Relations After Affirmative Action, 86 Calif. L. Rev. 1251, 1276–1291 (1998).

The Constitution instructs all who act for the government that they may not "deny to any person . . . the equal protection of the laws." Amdt. 14, §1. In implementing this equality instruction, as I see it, government decisionmakers may properly distinguish between policies of exclusion and inclusion. See *Wygant* v. *Jackson Bd. of Ed.*, 476 U. S. 267, 316 (1986)

(2001) (Table A) (In 2000, 7.5% of non-Hispanic whites, 22.1% of African-Americans, 10.8% of Asian-Americans, and 21.2% of Hispanics were living in poverty); S. Staveteig & A. Wigton, Racial and Ethnic Disparities: Key Findings from the National Survey of America's Families 1 (Urban Institute Report B–5, 2000) ("Blacks, Hispanics, and Native Americans . . . each have poverty rates almost twice as high as Asians and almost three times as high as whites.").

[3]See, *e.g.*, U. S. Dept. of Commerce, Bureau of Census, Health Insurance Coverage: 2000, p. 391 (2001) (Table A) (In 2000, 9.7% of non-Hispanic whites were without health insurance, as compared to 18.5% of African-Americans, 18.0% of Asian-Americans, and 32.0% of Hispanics.); Waidmann & Rajan, Race and Ethnic Disparities in Health Care Access and Utilization: An Examination of State Variation, 57 Med. Care Res. and Rev. 55, 56 (2000) ("On average, Latinos and African Americans have both worse health and worse access to effective health care than do non-Hispanic whites. . . .").

[4]See, *e.g.*, U. S. Dept. of Commerce, Bureau of Census, Racial and Ethnic Residential Segregation in the United States: 1980–2000 (2002) (documenting residential segregation); E. Frankenberg, C. Lee, & G. Orfield, A Multiracial Society with Segregated Schools: Are We Losing the Dream? 4 (Jan. 2003), http://www.civilrightsproject.harvard.edu/research/reseg03/AreWeLosingtheDream.pdf (all Internet materials as visited June 2, 2003, and available in Clerk of Court's case file), ("[W]hites are the most segregated group in the nation's public schools; they attend schools, on average, where eighty percent of the student body is white."); *id.*, at 28 ("[A]lmost three-fourths of black and Latino students attend schools that are predominantly minority. . . . More than one in six black children attend a school that is 99–100% minority. . . . One in nine Latino students attend virtually all minority schools.").

[5]See, *e.g.*, Ryan, Schools, Race, and Money, 109 Yale L. J. 249, 273–274 (1999) ("Urban public schools are attended primarily by African-American and Hispanic students"; students who attend such schools are disproportionately poor, score poorly on standardized tests, and are far more likely to drop out than students who attend nonurban schools.).

[6]See, *e.g.*, Statistical Abstract 140 (Table 211).

[7]See, *e.g.*, Holzer, Career Advancement Prospects and Strategies for Low-Wage Minority Workers, in Low-Wage Workers in the New Economy 228 (R. Kazis & M. Miller eds. 2001) ("[I]n studies that have sent matched pairs of minority and white applicants with apparently equal credentials to apply for jobs, whites routinely get more interviews and job offers than either black or Hispanic applicants."); M. Bertrand & S. Mullainathan, Are Emily and Brendan More Employable than Lakisha and Jamal?: A Field Experiment on Labor Market Discrimination (Nov. 18, 2002), http://gsb.uchicago.edu/pdf/bertrand.pdf; Mincy, The Urban Institute Audit Studies: Their Research and Policy Context, in Clear and Convincing Evidence: Measurement of Discrimination in America 165–186 (M. Fix & R. Struyk eds. 1993).

[8]See, *e.g.*, M. Turner et al., Discrimination in Metropolitan Housing Markets: National Results from Phase I HDS 2000, pp. i, iii (Nov. 2002), http://www.huduser.org/Publications/pdf/Phase1_Report.pdf (paired testing in which "two individuals—one minority and the other white—pose as otherwise identical homeseekers, and visit real estate or rental agents to inquire about the availability of advertised housing units" revealed that "discrimination still persists in both rental and sales markets of large metropolitan areas nationwide"); M. Turner & F. Skidmore, Mortgage Lending Discrimination: A Review of Existing Evidence 2 (1999) (existing research evidence shows that minority homebuyers in the United States "face discrimination from mortgage lending institutions.").

[9]See, *e.g.*, Ayres, Further Evidence of Discrimination in New Car Negotiations and Estimates of its Cause, 94 Mich. L. Rev. 109, 109–110 (1995) (study in which 38 testers negotiated the purchase of more than 400 automobiles confirmed earlier finding "that dealers systematically offer lower prices to white males than to other tester types").

(STEVENS, J., dissenting). Actions designed to burden groups long denied full citizenship stature are not sensibly ranked with measures taken to hasten the day when entrenched discrimination and its after effects have been extirpated. See Carter, When Victims Happen To Be Black, 97 Yale L. J. 420, 433–434 (1988) ("[T]o say that two centuries of struggle for the most basic of civil rights have been mostly about freedom from racial categorization rather than freedom from racial oppressio[n] is to trivialize the lives and deaths of those who have suffered under racism. To pretend . . . that the issue presented in [*Regents of Univ. of Cal.* v. *Bakke*, 438 U. S. 265 (1978)] was the same as the issue in [*Brown* v. *Board of Education*, 347 U. S. 483 (1954)] is to pretend that history never happened and that the present doesn't exist.").

Our jurisprudence ranks race a "suspect" category, "not because [race] is inevitably an impermissible classification, but because it is one which usually, to our national shame, has been drawn for the purpose of maintaining racial inequality." *Norwalk Core* v. *Norwalk Redevelopment Agency*, 395 F. 2d 920, 931–932 (CA2 1968) (footnote omitted). But where race is considered "for the purpose of achieving equality," *id.*, at 932, no automatic proscription is in order. For, as insightfully explained, "[t]he Constitution is both color blind and color conscious. To avoid conflict with the equal protection clause, a classification that denies a benefit, causes harm, or imposes a burden must not be based on race. In that sense, the Constitution is color blind. But the Constitution is color conscious to prevent discrimination being perpetuated and to undo the effects of past discrimination." *United States* v. *Jefferson County Bd. of Ed.*, 372 F. 2d 836, 876 (CA5 1966) (Wisdom, J.); see Wechsler, The Nationalization Of Civil Liberties And Civil Rights, Supp. to 12 Tex. Q. 10, 23 (1968) (*Brown* may be seen as disallowing racial classifications that "impl[y] an invidious assessment" while allowing such classifications when "not invidious in implication" but advanced to "correct inequalities"). Contemporary human rights documents draw just this line; they distinguish between policies of oppression and measures designed to accelerate *de facto* equality. See *Grutter, post*, at 1 (GINSBURG, J., concurring) (citing the United Nations-initiated Conventions on the Elimination of All Forms of Racial Discrimination and on the Elimination of All Forms of Discrimination against Women).

The mere assertion of a laudable governmental purpose, of course, should not immunize a race-conscious measure from careful judicial inspection. See *Jefferson County*, 372 F. 2d, at 876 ("The criterion is the relevancy of color to a legitimate governmental purpose."). Close review is needed "to ferret out classifications in reality malign, but masquerading as benign," *Adarand*, 515 U. S., at 275 (GINSBURG, J., dissenting), and to "ensure that preferences are not so large as to trammel unduly upon the opportunities of others or interfere too harshly with legitimate expectations of persons in once-preferred groups," *id.*, at 276.

II

Examining in this light the admissions policy employed by the University of Michigan's College of Literature, Science, and the Arts (College), and for the reasons well stated by JUSTICE SOUTER, I see no constitutional infirmity. See *ante*, at 3–8 (dissenting opinion). Like other top-ranking institutions, the College has many more applicants for admission than it can accommodate in an entering class. App. to Pet. for Cert. 108a. Every applicant admitted under the current plan, petitioners do not here dispute, is qualified to attend the College. *Id.*, at 111a. The racial and ethnic groups to which the College accords special consideration (African-Americans, Hispanics, and Native-Americans) historically have been relegated to inferior status by law and social practice; their members continue to experience class-based discrimination to this day, see *supra*, at 1–4. There is no suggestion that the College adopted its current policy in order to limit or decrease enrollment by any particular racial or ethnic group, and no seats are reserved on the basis of race. See Brief for Respondents 10; Tr. of Oral Arg. 41–42 (in the range between 75 and 100 points, the review committee may look at applications individually and ignore the points). Nor has there been any demonstration that the College's program unduly constricts admissions opportunities for students who do not receive special consideration based on race. Cf. Liu, The Causation Fallacy: *Bakke* and the Basic Arithmetic of Selective Admissions, 100 Mich. L. Rev. 1045, 1049 (2002) ("In any admissions process where applicants greatly outnumber admittees, and where white applicants greatly outnumber minority applicants, substantial preferences for minority applicants will not significantly diminish the odds of admission facing white applicants.").[10]

The stain of generations of racial oppression is still visible in our society, see Krieger, 86 Calif. L. Rev., at 1253, and the determination to hasten its removal remains vital. One can reasonably anticipate, therefore, that colleges and universities will seek to maintain their minority enrollment—and the networks and opportunities thereby opened to minority graduates—whether or not they can do so in full candor through adoption of affirmative action plans of the kind here at issue. Without recourse to such plans, institutions of higher education may resort to camouflage. For example, schools may encourage applicants to write of their cultural traditions in the essays they submit, or to indicate whether English is their second language. Seeking to improve their chances for admission, applicants may highlight the minority group associations to which they belong, or the Hispanic surnames of their mothers or grandparents. In turn, teachers' recommendations may emphasize who a student is as much as what he or she has accomplished. See, *e.g.*, Steinberg, Using Synonyms for Race, College Strives for Diversity, N. Y. Times, Dec. 8, 2002, section 1, p. 1, col. 3 (describing admissions process at Rice University); cf. Brief for United States as *Amicus Curiae* 14–15 (suggesting institutions could consider, *inter alia*, "a history of overcoming disadvantage," "reputation and location of high school," and "individual outlook as reflected by essays"). If honesty is the best policy, surely Michigan's accurately described, fully disclosed College affirmative action program is preferable to achieving similar numbers through winks, nods, and disguises.[11]

* * *

For the reasons stated, I would affirm the judgment of the District Court.

---

[10]The United States points to the "percentage plans" used in California, Florida, and Texas as one example of a "race-neutral alternativ[e]" that would permit the College to enroll meaningful numbers of minority students. Brief for United States as *Amicus Curiae* 14; see Commission on Civil Rights, Beyond Percentage Plans: The Challenge of Equal Opportunity in Higher Education 1 (Nov. 2002), http://www.usccr.gov/pubs/percent2/percent2.pdf (percentage plans guarantee admission to state universities for a fixed percentage of the top students from high schools in the State). Calling such 10 or 20% plans "race-neutral" seems to me disingenuous, for they "unquestionably were adopted with the specific purpose of increasing representation of African-Americans and Hispanics in the public higher education system." Brief for Respondents 44; see C. Horn & S. Flores, Percent Plans in College Admissions: A Comparative Analysis of Three States' Experiences 14–19 (2003), http://www. civilrightsproject.harvard.edu/research/affirmativeaction/tristate.pdf. Percentage plans depend for their effectiveness on continued racial segregation at the secondary school level: They can ensure significant minority enrollment in universities only if the majority-minority high school population is large enough to guarantee that, in many schools, most of the students in the top 10 or 20% are minorities. Moreover, because such plans link college admission to a single criterion—high school class rank—they create perverse incentives. They encourage parents to keep their children in low-performing segregated schools, and discourage students from taking challenging classes that might lower their grade point averages. See Selingo, What States Aren't Saying About the 'X-Percent Solution,' Chronicle of Higher Education, June 2, 2000, p. A31. And even if percentage plans could boost the sheer numbers of minority enrollees at the undergraduate level, they do not touch enrollment in graduate and professional schools.

[11]Contrary to the Court's contention, I do not suggest "changing the Constitution so that it conforms to the conduct of the universities." *Ante*, at 27, n. 22. In my view, the Constitution, properly interpreted, permits government officials to respond openly to the continuing importance of race. See *supra*, at 4–5. Among constitutionally permissible options, those that candidly disclose their consideration of race seem to me preferable to those that conceal it.

APPENDIX 2: FULL TEXT OF THE SUPREME COURT'S DECISION IN *GRUTTER V. BOLLINGER*, JUNE 2003

Introduction

The landmark U.S. Supreme Court opinion in *Grutter v. Bollinger* addressed a reverse-discrimination challenge to the University of Michigan Law School's race-conscious admissions plan. One of the aims of the law school admissions program was to enroll a "critical mass" of underrepresented minority students to further the law school's interest in obtaining the educational benefits that student-body diversity provides to all students. To accomplish this, the law school considered the fact that an applicant was a member of a group that had historically been discriminated against, such as African Americans, Hispanics, or Native Americans, as a positive factor in determining whether the student would contribute to student-body diversity, and thus as a positive factor in the admissions process. A white female applicant who was denied admission brought suit alleging that the admissions plan discriminated against her on the basis of her race (Caucasian) in violation of the Equal Protection Clause of the Fourteenth Amendment to the U.S. Constitution and two federal statutes that prohibit race discrimination. In its opinion, a majority of the Court held that the law school's plan was lawful. It determined that universities can lawfully aim to assemble a student body that is diverse with respect to various qualifications and characteristics, including racial and ethnic diversity. The Court also held that the method used to achieve diversity was lawful because race could be considered only as a "plus" factor along with other factors contributing to diversity, such as one's athletic ability or musical talent. The law school's plan did not insulate any group from competition by considering minority racial status as a predominant factor for any applicant, and consideration of race did not interfere with the evaluation of each applicant as an individual. The Court held that the law school did not maintain illegal quotas or separate admissions tracks for certain racial or ethnic groups. Because it found the law school's plan constitutional, the Court also found that the plan did not violate the federal antidiscrimination statutes. Finally, the Court appeared to put a twenty-five-year limit on the law school's consideration of race in its admissions process to achieve student-body diversity.

> NOTE: Where it is feasible, a syllabus (headnote) will be released, as is being done in connection with this case, at the time the opinion is issued. The syllabus constitutes no part of the opinion of the Court but has been prepared by the Reporter of Decisions for the convenience of the reader. See *United States* v. *Detroit Timber & Lumber Co.*, 200 U. S. 321, 337.

SUPREME COURT OF THE UNITED STATES

Syllabus

CERTIORARI TO THE UNITED STATES COURT OF APPEALS FOR THE SIXTH CIRCUIT

No. 02–241. Argued April 1, 2003—Decided June 23, 2003

The University of Michigan Law School (Law School), one of the Nation's top law schools, follows an official admissions policy that seeks to achieve student body diversity through compliance with *Regents of Univ. of Cal.* v. *Bakke,* 438 U. S. 265. Focusing on students' academic ability coupled with a flexible assessment of their talents, experiences, and potential, the policy requires admissions officials to evaluate each applicant based on all the information available in the file, including a personal statement, letters of recommendation, an essay describing how the applicant will contribute to Law School life and diversity, and the applicant's undergraduate grade point average (GPA) and Law School Admissions Test (LSAT) score. Additionally, officials must look beyond grades and scores to so-called "soft variables," such as recommenders' enthusiasm, the quality of the undergraduate institution and the applicant's essay, and the areas and difficulty of undergraduate course selection. The policy does not define diversity solely in terms of racial and ethnic status and does not restrict the types of diversity contributions eligible for "substantial weight," but it does reaffirm the Law School's commitment to diversity with special reference to the inclusion of African-American, Hispanic, and Native-American students, who otherwise might not be represented in the student body in meaningful numbers. By enrolling a "critical mass" of underrepresented minority students, the policy seeks to ensure their ability to contribute to the Law School's character and to the legal profession.

When the Law School denied admission to petitioner Grutter, a white Michigan resident with a 3.8 GPA and 161 LSAT score, she filed this suit, alleging that respondents had discriminated against her on the basis of race in violation of the Fourteenth Amendment, Title VI of the Civil Rights Act of 1964, and 42 U. S. C. §1981; that she was rejected because the Law School uses race as a "predominant" factor, giving applicants belonging to certain minority groups a significantly greater chance of admission than students with similar credentials from disfavored racial groups; and that respondents had no compelling interest to justify that use of race. The District Court found the Law School's use of race as an admissions factor unlawful. The Sixth Circuit reversed, holding that Justice Powell's opinion in *Bakke* was binding precedent establishing diversity as a compelling state interest, and that the Law School's use of race was narrowly tailored because race was merely a "potential 'plus' factor" and because the Law School's program was virtually identical to the Harvard admissions program described approvingly by Justice Powell and appended to his *Bakke* opinion.

Held: The Law School's narrowly tailored use of race in admissions decisions to further a compelling interest in obtaining the educational benefits that flow from a diverse student body is not prohibited by the Equal Protection Clause, Title VI, or §1981. Pp. 9–32.

(a) In the landmark *Bakke* case, this Court reviewed a medical school's racial set-aside program that reserved 16 out of 100 seats for members of certain minority groups. The decision produced six separate opinions, none of which commanded a majority. Four Justices would have upheld the program on the ground that the government can use race to remedy disadvantages cast on minorities by past racial prejudice. 438 U. S., at 325. Four other Justices would have struck the program down on statutory grounds. *Id.*, at 408. Justice Powell, announcing the Court's judgment, provided a fifth vote not only for invalidating the program, but also for reversing the state court's injunction against any use of race whatsoever. In a part of his opinion that was joined by no other Justice, Justice Powell expressed his view that attaining a diverse student body was the only interest asserted by the university that survived scrutiny. *Id.*, at 311. Grounding his analysis in the academic freedom that "long has been viewed as a special concern of the First Amendment," *id.*, at 312, 314, Justice Powell emphasized that the " 'nation's future depends upon leaders trained through wide exposure' to the ideas and mores of students as diverse as this Nation." *Id.*, at 313. However, he also emphasized that "[i]t is not an interest in simple ethnic diversity, in which a specified percentage of the student body is in effect guaranteed to be members of selected ethnic groups," that can justify using race. *Id.*, at 315. Rather, "[t]he diversity that furthers a compelling state interest encompasses a far broader array of qualifications and characteristics of which racial or ethnic origin is but a single though important element." *Ibid.* Since *Bakke,* Justice Powell's opinion has been the touchstone for constitutional analysis of race-conscious admissions policies. Public and private universities across the Nation have modeled their own admissions programs on Justice Powell's views. Courts, however, have struggled to discern whether Justice Powell's diversity rationale is binding precedent. The Court finds it unnecessary to decide this issue because the Court endorses Justice Powell's view that student body diversity is a compelling state interest in the context of university admissions. Pp. 9–13.

(b) All government racial classifications must be analyzed by a reviewing court under strict scrutiny. *Adarand Constructors, Inc.* v. *Peña,* 515 U. S. 200, 227. But not all such uses are invalidated by strict scrutiny. Race-based action necessary to further a compelling governmental interest does not violate the Equal Protection Clause so long as it is narrowly tailored to further that interest. *E.g., Shaw* v. *Hunt,* 517 U. S. 899, 908. Context matters when reviewing such action. See *Gomillion* v. *Lightfoot,* 364 U. S. 339, 343–344. Not every decision influenced by race is equally objectionable, and strict scrutiny is designed to provide a framework for carefully examining the importance and the sincerity of the government's reasons for using race in a particular context. 13–15.

(c) The Court endorses Justice Powell's view that student body diversity is a compelling state interest that can justify using race in university admissions. The Court defers to the Law School's educational judgment that diversity is essential to its educational mission. The Court's scrutiny of that interest is no less strict for taking into account complex educational judgments in an area that lies primarily within the university's expertise. See, *e.g., Bakke,* 438 U. S., at 319, n. 53 (opinion of Powell, J.). Attaining a diverse student body is at the heart of the Law School's proper institutional mission, and its "good faith" is "presumed" absent "a showing to the contrary." *Id.,* at 318–319. Enrolling a "critical mass" of minority students simply to assure some specified percentage of a particular group merely because of its race or ethnic origin would be patently unconstitutional. *E.g., id.,* at 307. But the Law School defines its critical mass concept by reference to the substantial, important, and laudable educational benefits that diversity is designed to produce, including cross-racial understanding and the breaking down of racial stereotypes. The Law School's claim is further bolstered by numerous expert studies and reports showing that such diversity promotes learning outcomes and better prepares students for an increasingly diverse workforce, for society, and for the legal profession. Major American businesses have made clear that the skills needed in today's increasingly global marketplace can only be developed through exposure to widely diverse people, cultures, ideas, and viewpoints. High-ranking retired officers and civilian military leaders assert that a highly qualified, racially diverse officer corps is essential to national security. Moreover, because universities, and in particular, law schools, represent the training ground for a large number of the Nation's leaders, *Sweatt* v. *Painter,* 339 U. S. 629, 634, the path to leadership must be visibly open to talented and qualified individuals of every race and ethnicity. Thus, the Law School has a compelling interest in attaining a diverse student body. 15–21.

(d) The Law School's admissions program bears the hallmarks of a narrowly tailored plan. To be narrowly tailored, a race-conscious admissions program cannot "insulat[e] each category of applicants with certain desired qualifications from competition with all other applicants." *Bakke, supra,* at 315 (opinion of Powell, J.). Instead, it may consider race or ethnicity only as a " 'plus' in a particular applicant's file"; *i.e.,* it must be "flexible enough to consider all pertinent elements of diversity in light of the particular qualifications of each applicant, and to place them on the same footing for consideration, although not necessarily according them the same weight," *id.*, at 317. It follows that universities cannot establish quotas for members of certain racial or ethnic groups or put them on separate admissions tracks. See *id.*, at 315–316. The Law School's admissions program, like the Harvard plan approved by Justice Powell, satisfies these requirements. Moreover, the program is flexible enough to ensure that each applicant is evaluated as an individual and not in a way that makes race or ethnicity the defining feature of the application. See *Bakke, supra*, at 317 (opinion of Powell, J.). The Law School engages in a highly individualized, holistic review of each applicant's file, giving serious consideration to all the ways an applicant might contribute to a diverse educational environment. There is no policy, either *de jure* or *de facto*, of automatic acceptance or rejection based on any single "soft" variable. *Gratz v. Bollinger, ante*, p. __, distinguished. Also, the program adequately ensures that all factors that may contribute to diversity are meaningfully considered alongside race. Moreover, the Law School frequently accepts nonminority applicants with grades and test scores lower than underrepresented minority applicants (and other nonminority applicants) who are rejected. The Court rejects the argument that the Law School should have used other race-neutral means to obtain the educational benefits of student body diversity, *e.g.*, a lottery system or decreasing the emphasis on GPA and LSAT scores. Narrow tailoring does not require exhaustion of every conceivable race-neutral alternative or mandate that a university choose between maintaining a reputation for excellence or fulfilling a commitment to provide educational opportunities to members of all racial groups. See, *e.g.*, *Wygant* v. *Jackson Bd. of Ed.*, 476 U. S. 267, 280, n. 6. The Court is satisfied that the Law School adequately considered the available alternatives. The Court is also satisfied that, in the context of individualized consideration of the possible diversity contributions of each applicant, the Law School's race-conscious admissions program does not unduly harm nonminority applicants. Finally, race-conscious admissions policies must be limited in time. The Court takes the Law School at its word that it would like nothing better than to find a race-neutral admissions formula and will terminate its use of racial preferences as soon as practicable. The Court expects that 25 years from now, the use of racial preferences will no longer be necessary to further the interest approved today. Pp. 21–31.

(e) Because the Law School's use of race in admissions decisions is not prohibited by Equal Protection Clause, petitioner's statutory claims based on Title VI and §1981 also fail. See *Bakke, supra*, at 287 (opinion of Powell, J.); *General Building Contractors Assn., Inc.* v. *Pennsylvania*, 458 U. S. 375, 389–391. Pp. 31–32.

288 F. 3d 732, affirmed.

O'CONNOR, J., delivered the opinion of the Court, in which STEVENS, SOUTER, GINSBURG, and BREYER, JJ., joined, and in which SCALIA and THOMAS, JJ., joined in part insofar as it is consistent with the views expressed in Part VII of the opinion of THOMAS, J. GINSBURG, J., filed a concurring opinion, in which BREYER, J., joined. SCALIA, J., filed an opinion concurring in part and dissenting in part, in which THOMAS, J., joined. THOMAS, J., filed an opinion concurring in part and dissenting in part, in which SCALIA, J., joined as to Parts I–VII. REHNQUIST, C. J., filed a dissenting opinion, in which SCALIA, KENNEDY, and THOMAS, JJ., joined. KENNEDY, J., filed a dissenting opinion.

SUPREME COURT OF THE UNITED STATES

No. 02–241

BARBARA GRUTTER, PETITIONER v. LEE BOLLINGER ET AL.

ON WRIT OF CERTIORARI TO THE UNITED STATES COURT OF APPEALS FOR THE SIXTH CIRCUIT

[June 23, 2003]

JUSTICE O'CONNOR delivered the opinion of the Court.

This case requires us to decide whether the use of race as a factor in student admissions by the University of Michigan Law School (Law School) is unlawful.

I

A

The Law School ranks among the Nation's top law schools. It receives more than 3,500 applications each year for a class of around 350 students. Seeking to "admit a group of students who individually and collectively are among the most capable," the Law School looks for individuals with "substantial promise for success in law school" and "a strong likelihood of succeeding in the practice of law and contributing in diverse ways to the well-being of others." App. 110. More broadly, the Law School seeks "a mix of students with varying backgrounds and experiences who will respect and learn from each other." *Ibid.* In 1992, the dean of the Law School charged a faculty committee with crafting a written admissions policy to implement these goals. In particular, the Law School sought to ensure that its efforts to achieve student body diversity complied with this Court's most recent ruling on the use of race in university admissions. See *Regents of Univ. of Cal.* v. *Bakke*, 438 U. S. 265 (1978). Upon the unanimous adoption of the committee's report by the Law School faculty, it became the Law School's official admissions policy.

The hallmark of that policy is its focus on academic ability coupled with a flexible assessment of applicants' talents, experiences, and potential "to contribute to the learning of those around them." App. 111. The policy requires admissions officials to evaluate each applicant based on all the information available in the file, including a personal statement, letters of recommendation, and an essay describing the ways in which the applicant will contribute to the life and diversity of the Law School. *Id.*, at 83–84, 114–121. In reviewing an applicant's file, admissions officials must consider the applicant's undergraduate grade point average (GPA) and Law School Admissions Test (LSAT) score because they are important (if imperfect) predictors of academic success in law school. *Id.*, at 112. The policy stresses that "no applicant should be admitted unless we expect that applicant to do well enough to graduate with no serious academic problems." *Id.*, at 111.

The policy makes clear, however, that even the highest possible score does not guarantee admission to the Law School. *Id.*, at 113. Nor does a low score automatically disqualify an applicant. *Ibid.* Rather, the policy requires admissions officials to look beyond grades and test scores to other criteria that are important to the Law School's educational objectives. *Id.*, at 114. So-called " 'soft' variables" such as "the enthusiasm of recommenders, the quality of the undergraduate institution, the quality of the applicant's essay, and the areas and difficulty of undergraduate course selection" are all brought to bear in assessing an "applicant's likely contributions to the intellectual and social life of the institution." *Ibid.*

The policy aspires to "achieve that diversity which has the potential to enrich everyone's education and thus make a law school class stronger than the sum of its parts." *Id.*, at 118.

The policy does not restrict the types of diversity contributions eligible for "substantial weight" in the admissions process, but instead recognizes "many possible bases for diversity admissions." *Id.*, at 118, 120. The policy does, however, reaffirm the Law School's long-standing commitment to "one particular type of diversity," that is, "racial and ethnic diversity with special reference to the inclusion of students from groups which have been historically discriminated against, like African-Americans, Hispanics and Native Americans, who without this commitment might not be represented in our student body in meaningful numbers." *Id.*, at 120. By enrolling a " 'critical mass' of [underrepresented] minority students," the Law School seeks to "ensur[e] their ability to make unique contributions to the character of the Law School." *Id.*, at 120–121.

The policy does not define diversity "solely in terms of racial and ethnic status." *Id.*, at 121. Nor is the policy "insensitive to the competition among all students for admission to the [L]aw [S]chool." *Ibid.* Rather, the policy seeks to guide admissions officers in "producing classes both diverse and academically outstanding, classes made up of students who promise to continue the tradition of outstanding contribution by Michigan Graduates to the legal profession." *Ibid.*

B

Petitioner Barbara Grutter is a white Michigan resident who applied to the Law School in 1996 with a 3.8 grade point average and 161 LSAT score. The Law School initially placed petitioner on a waiting list, but subsequently rejected her application. In December 1997, petitioner filed suit in the United States District Court for the Eastern District of Michigan against the Law School, the Regents of the University of Michigan, Lee Bollinger (Dean of the Law School from 1987 to 1994, and President of the University of Michigan from 1996 to 2002), Jeffrey Lehman (Dean of the Law School), and Dennis Shields (Director of Admissions at the Law School from 1991 until 1998). Petitioner alleged that respondents discriminated against her on the basis of race in violation of the Fourteenth Amendment; Title VI of the Civil Rights Act of 1964, 78 Stat. 252, 42 U. S. C. §2000d; and Rev. Stat. §1977, as amended, 42 U. S. C. §1981.

Petitioner further alleged that her application was rejected because the Law School uses race as a "predominant" factor, giving applicants who belong to certain minority groups "a significantly greater chance of admission than students with similar credentials from disfavored racial groups." App. 33–34. Petitioner also alleged that respondents "had no compelling interest to justify their use of race in the admissions process." *Id.*, at 34. Petitioner requested compensatory and punitive damages, an order requiring the Law School to offer her admission, and an injunction prohibiting the Law School from continuing to discriminate on the basis of race. *Id.*, at 36. Petitioner clearly has standing to bring this lawsuit. *Northeastern Fla. Chapter, Associated Gen. Contractors of America* v. *Jacksonville*, 508 U. S. 656, 666 (1993).

The District Court granted petitioner's motion for class certification and for bifurcation of the trial into liability and damages phases. The class was defined as " 'all persons who (A) applied for and were not granted admission to the University of Michigan Law School for the academic years since (and including) 1995 until the time that judgment is entered herein; and (B) were members of those racial or ethnic groups, including Caucasian, that Defendants treated less favorably in considering their applications for admission to the Law School.' " App. to Pet. for Cert. 191a–192a.

The District Court heard oral argument on the parties' cross-motions for summary judgment on December 22, 2000. Taking the motions under advisement, the District Court indicated that it would decide as a matter of law whether the Law School's asserted interest in obtaining the educational benefits that flow from a diverse student body was compelling. The District Court also indicated that it would conduct a bench trial on the extent to which race was a factor in the Law School's admissions decisions, and whether the Law School's consideration of race in admissions decisions constituted a race-based double standard.

During the 15-day bench trial, the parties introduced extensive evidence concerning the Law School's use of race in the admissions process. Dennis Shields, Director of Admissions when petitioner applied to the Law School, testified that he did not direct his staff to admit a particular percentage or number of minority students, but rather to consider an applicant's race along with all other factors. *Id.*, at 206a. Shields testified that at the height of the admissions season, he would frequently consult the so-called "daily reports" that kept track of the racial and ethnic composition of the class (along with other information such as residency status and gender). *Id.*, at 207a. This was done, Shields testified, to ensure that a critical mass of underrepresented minority students would be reached so as to realize the educational benefits of a diverse student body. *Ibid.* Shields stressed, however, that he did not seek to admit any particular number or percentage of underrepresented minority students. *Ibid.*

Erica Munzel, who succeeded Shields as Director of Admissions, testified that " 'critical mass' " means " 'meaningful numbers' " or " 'meaningful representation,' " which she understood to mean a number that encourages underrepresented minority students to participate in the classroom and not feel isolated. *Id.*, at 208a–209a. Munzel stated there is no number, percentage, or range of numbers or percentages that constitute critical mass. *Id.*, at 209a. Munzel also asserted that she must consider the race of applicants because a critical mass of underrepresented minority students could not be enrolled if admissions decisions were based primarily on undergraduate GPAs and LSAT scores. *Ibid.*

The current Dean of the Law School, Jeffrey Lehman, also testified. Like the other Law School witnesses, Lehman did not quantify critical mass in terms of numbers or percentages. *Id.*, at 211a. He indicated that critical mass means numbers such that underrepresented minority students do not feel isolated or like spokespersons for their race. *Ibid.* When asked about the extent to which race is considered in admissions, Lehman testified that it varies from one applicant to another. *Ibid.* In some cases, according to Lehman's testimony, an applicant's race may play no role, while in others it may be a " 'determinative' " factor. *Ibid.*

The District Court heard extensive testimony from Professor Richard Lempert, who chaired the faculty committee that drafted the 1992 policy. Lempert emphasized that the Law School seeks students with diverse interests and backgrounds to enhance classroom discussion and the educational experience both inside and outside the classroom. *Id.*, at 213a. When asked about the policy's " 'commitment to racial and ethnic diversity with special reference to the inclusion of students from groups which have been historically discriminated against,' " Lempert explained that this language did not purport to remedy past discrimination, but rather to include students who may bring to the Law School a perspective different from that of members of groups which have not been the victims of such discrimination. *Ibid.* Lempert acknowledged that other groups, such as Asians and Jews, have experienced discrimination, but explained they were not mentioned in the policy because individuals who are members of those groups were already being admitted to the Law School in significant numbers. *Ibid.*

Kent Syverud was the final witness to testify about the Law School's use of race in admissions decisions. Syverud was a professor at the Law School when the 1992 admissions policy was adopted and is now Dean of Vanderbilt Law School. In addition to his testimony at trial, Syverud submitted several expert reports on the educational benefits of diversity. Syverud's testimony indicated that when a critical mass of underrepresented minority students is present, racial stereotypes lose their force because nonminority students learn there is no " 'minority viewpoint' " but rather a variety of viewpoints among minority students. *Id.*, at 215a.

In an attempt to quantify the extent to which the Law School actually considers race in making admissions decisions, the parties introduced voluminous evidence at trial. Relying on data obtained from the Law School, petitioner's expert, Dr. Kinley Larntz, generated and analyzed "admissions grids" for the years in question (1995–2000). These grids show the number of applicants and the number of admittees for all combinations of GPAs and LSAT scores. Dr. Larntz made " 'cell-by-cell' " comparisons between applicants of different races to determine whether a statistically significant relationship existed between race and admission rates. He concluded that membership in certain minority groups " 'is an extremely strong factor in the decision for acceptance,' " and that applicants from these minority groups " 'are given an extremely large allowance for admission' " as compared to applicants who are members of nonfavored groups. *Id.*, at 218a–220a. Dr. Larntz conceded, however, that race is not the predominant factor in the Law School's admissions calculus. 12 Tr. 11–13 (Feb. 10, 2001).

Dr. Stephen Raudenbush, the Law School's expert, focused on the predicted effect of eliminating race as a factor in the Law School's admission process. In Dr. Raudenbush's view, a race-blind admissions system would have a " 'very dramatic,' " negative effect on underrepresented minority admissions. App. to Pet. for Cert. 223a. He testified that in 2000, 35 percent of underrepresented minority applicants were admitted. *Ibid.* Dr. Raudenbush predicted that if race were not considered, only 10 percent of those applicants would have been admitted. *Ibid.* Under this scenario, underrepresented minority students would have comprised 4 percent of the entering class in 2000 instead of the actual figure of 14.5 percent. *Ibid.*

In the end, the District Court concluded that the Law School's use of race as a factor in admissions decisions was unlawful. Applying strict scrutiny, the District Court determined that the Law School's asserted interest in assembling a diverse student body was not compelling because "the attainment of a racially diverse class . . . was not recognized as such by *Bakke* and is not a remedy for past discrimination." *Id.*, at 246a. The District Court went on to hold that even if diversity were compelling, the Law School had not narrowly tailored its use of race to further that interest. The District Court granted petitioner's request for declaratory relief and enjoined the Law School from using race as a factor in its admissions decisions. The Court of Appeals entered a stay of the injunction pending appeal.

Sitting en banc, the Court of Appeals reversed the District Court's judgment and vacated the injunction. The Court of Appeals first held that Justice Powell's opinion in *Bakke* was binding precedent establishing diversity as a compelling state interest. According to the Court of Appeals, Justice Powell's opinion with respect to diversity comprised the controlling rationale for the judgment of this Court under the analysis set forth in *Marks* v. *United States*, 430 U. S. 188 (1977). The Court of Appeals also held that the Law School's use of race was narrowly tailored because race was merely a "potential 'plus' factor" and because the Law School's program was "virtually identical" to the Harvard admissions program described approvingly by Justice Powell and appended to his *Bakke* opinion. 288 F. 3d 732, 746, 749 (CA6 2002).

Four dissenting judges would have held the Law School's use of race unconstitutional. Three of the dissenters, rejecting the majority's *Marks* analysis, examined the Law School's interest in student body diversity on the merits and concluded it was not compelling. The fourth dissenter, writing separately, found it unnecessary to decide whether diversity was a compelling interest because, like the other dissenters, he believed that the Law School's use of race was not narrowly tailored to further that interest.

We granted certiorari, 537 U. S. 1043 (2002), to resolve the disagreement among the Courts of Appeals on a question of national importance: Whether diversity is a compelling interest that can justify the narrowly tailored use of race in selecting applicants for admission to public universities. Compare *Hopwood* v. *Texas*, 78 F. 3d 932 (CA5 1996) (*Hopwood I*) (holding that diversity is not a compelling state interest), with *Smith* v. *University of Wash. Law School*, 233 F. 3d 1188 (CA9 2000) (holding that it is).

II

A

We last addressed the use of race in public higher education over 25 years ago. In the landmark *Bakke* case, we reviewed a racial set-aside program that reserved 16 out of 100 seats in a medical school class for members of certain minority groups. 438 U. S. 265 (1978). The decision produced six separate opinions, none of which commanded a majority of the Court. Four Justices would have upheld the program against all attack on the ground that the government can use race to "remedy disadvantages cast on minorities by past racial prejudice." *Id.*, at 325 (joint opinion of Brennan, White, Marshall, and Blackmun, JJ., concurring in judgment in part and dissenting in part). Four other Justices avoided the constitutional question altogether and struck down the program on statutory grounds. *Id.*, at 408 (opinion of STEVENS, J., joined by Burger, C. J., and Stewart and REHNQUIST, JJ., concurring in judgment in part and dissenting in part). Justice Powell provided a fifth vote not only for invalidating the set-aside program, but also for reversing the state court's injunction against any use of race whatsoever. The only holding for the Court in *Bakke* was that a "State has a substantial interest that legitimately may be served by a properly devised admissions program involving the competitive consideration of race and ethnic origin." *Id.*, at 320. Thus, we reversed that part of the lower court's judgment that enjoined the university "from any consideration of the race of any applicant." *Ibid.*

Since this Court's splintered decision in *Bakke*, Justice Powell's opinion announcing the judgment of the Court has served as the touchstone for constitutional analysis of race-conscious admissions policies. Public and private universities across the Nation have modeled their own admissions programs on Justice Powell's views on permissible race-conscious policies. See, *e.g.*, Brief for Judith Areen et al. as *Amici Curiae* 12–13 (law school admissions programs employ "methods designed from and based on Justice Powell's opinion in *Bakke*"); Brief for Amherst College et al. as *Amici Curiae* 27 ("After *Bakke*, each of the *amici* (and undoubtedly other selective colleges and universities as well) reviewed their admissions procedures in light of Justice Powell's opinion . . . and set sail accordingly"). We therefore discuss Justice Powell's opinion in some detail.

Justice Powell began by stating that "[t]he guarantee of equal protection cannot mean one thing when applied to one individual and something else when applied to a person of another color. If both are not accorded the same protection, then it is not equal." *Bakke*, 438 U. S., at 289–290. In Justice Powell's view, when governmental decisions "touch upon an individual's race or ethnic background, he is entitled to a judicial determination that the burden he is asked to bear on that basis is precisely tailored to serve a compelling governmental interest." *Id.*, at 299. Under this exacting standard, only one of the interests asserted by the university survived Justice Powell's scrutiny.

First, Justice Powell rejected an interest in " 'reducing the historic deficit of traditionally disfavored minorities in medical schools and in the medical profession' " as an unlawful interest in racial balancing. *Id.*, at 306–307. Second, Justice Powell rejected an interest in remedying societal discrimination because such measures would risk placing unnecessary burdens on innocent third parties "who bear no responsibility for whatever harm the beneficiaries of the special admissions program are thought to have suffered." *Id.*, at 310. Third, Justice Powell rejected an interest in "increasing the number of physicians who will practice in communities currently underserved," concluding that even if such an interest could be compelling in some circumstances the program under review was not "geared to promote that goal." *Id.*, at 306, 310.

Justice Powell approved the university's use of race to further only one interest: "the attainment of a diverse student body." *Id.*, at 311. With the important proviso that "constitutional limitations protecting individual rights may not be disregarded," Justice Powell grounded his analysis in the academic freedom that "long has been viewed as a special concern of the First Amendment." *Id.*, at 312, 314. Justice Powell emphasized that nothing less than the " 'nation's future depends upon leaders trained through wide exposure' to the ideas and mores of students as diverse as this Nation of many peoples." *Id.*, at 313 (quoting *Keyishian* v. *Board of Regents of Univ. of State of N. Y.*, 385 U. S. 589, 603 (1967)). In seeking the "right to select those students who will contribute the most to the 'robust exchange of ideas,' " a university seeks "to achieve a goal that is of paramount importance in the fulfillment of its mission." 438 U. S., at 313. Both "tradition and experience lend support to the view that the contribution of diversity is substantial." *Ibid.*

Justice Powell was, however, careful to emphasize that in his view race "is only one element in a range of factors a university properly may consider in attaining the goal of a heterogeneous student body." *Id.*, at 314. For Justice Powell, "[i]t is not an interest in simple ethnic diversity, in which a specified percentage of the student body is in effect guaranteed to be members of selected ethnic groups," that can justify the use of race. *Id.*, at 315. Rather, "[t]he diversity that furthers a compelling state interest encompasses a far broader array of qualifications and characteristics of which racial or ethnic origin is but a single though important element." *Ibid.*

In the wake of our fractured decision in *Bakke*, courts have struggled to discern whether Justice Powell's diversity rationale, set forth in part of the opinion joined by no other Justice, is nonetheless binding precedent under *Marks*. In that case, we explained that "[w]hen a fragmented Court decides a case and no single rationale explaining the result enjoys the assent of five Justices, the holding of the Court may be viewed as that position taken by those Members who concurred in the judgments on the narrowest grounds." 430 U. S., at 193 (internal quotation marks and citation omitted). As the divergent opinions of the lower courts demonstrate, however, "[t]his test is more easily stated than applied to the various opinions supporting the result in [*Bakke*]." *Nichols* v. *United States*, 511 U. S. 738, 745–746 (1994). Compare, *e.g., Johnson* v. *Board of Regents of Univ. of Ga.*, 263 F. 3d 1234 (CA11 2001) (Justice Powell's diversity rationale was not the holding of the Court); *Hopwood* v. *Texas*, 236 F. 3d 256, 274–275 (CA5 2000) (*Hopwood II*) (same); *Hopwood I*, 78 F. 3d 932 (same), with *Smith* v. *University of Wash. Law School*, 233 F. 3d 1199 (Justice Powell's opinion, including the diversity rationale, is controlling under *Marks*).

We do not find it necessary to decide whether Justice Powell's opinion is binding under *Marks*. It does not seem "useful to pursue the *Marks* inquiry to the utmost logical possibility when it has so obviously baffled and divided the lower courts that have considered it." *Nichols* v. *United States, supra*, at 745–746. More important, for the reasons set out below, today we endorse Justice Powell's view that student body diversity is a compelling state interest that can justify the use of race in university admissions.

B

The Equal Protection Clause provides that no State shall "deny to any person within its jurisdiction the equal protection of the laws." U. S. Const., Amdt. 14, §2. Because the Fourteenth Amendment "protect[s] *persons*, not *groups*," all "governmental action based on race—a *group* classification long recognized as in most circumstances irrelevant and therefore prohibited—should be subjected to detailed judicial inquiry to ensure that the *personal* right to equal protection of the laws has not been infringed." *Adarand Constructors, Inc.* v. *Peña*, 515 U. S. 200, 227 (1995) (emphasis in original; internal quotation marks and citation omitted). We are a "free people whose institutions are founded upon the doctrine of equality." *Loving* v. *Virginia*, 388 U. S. 1, 11 (1967) (internal quotation marks and citation omitted). It follows from that principle that "government may treat people differently because of their race only for the most compelling reasons." *Adarand Constructors, Inc.* v. *Peña*, 515 U. S., at 227.

We have held that all racial classifications imposed by government "must be analyzed by a reviewing court under strict scrutiny." *Ibid.* This means that such classifications are constitutional only if they are narrowly tailored to further compelling governmental interests. "Absent searching judicial inquiry into the justification for such race-based measures," we have no way to determine what "classifications are 'benign' or 'remedial' and what classifications are in fact motivated by illegitimate notions of racial inferiority or simple racial politics." *Richmond* v. *J. A. Croson Co.*, 488 U. S. 469, 493 (1989) (plurality opinion). We apply strict scrutiny to all racial classifications to " 'smoke out' illegitimate uses of race by assuring that [government] is pursuing a goal important enough to warrant use of a highly suspect tool." *Ibid.*

Strict scrutiny is not "strict in theory, but fatal in fact." *Adarand Constructors, Inc.* v. *Peña, supra,* at 237 (internal quotation marks and citation omitted). Although all governmental uses of race are subject to strict scrutiny, not all are invalidated by it. As we have explained, "whenever the government treats any person unequally because of his or her race, that person has suffered an injury that falls squarely within the language and spirit of the Constitution's guarantee of equal protection." 515 U. S., at 229–230. But that observation "says nothing about the ultimate validity of any particular law; that determination is the job of the court applying strict scrutiny." *Id.,* at 230. When race-based action is necessary to further a compelling governmental interest, such action does not violate the constitutional guarantee of equal protection so long as the narrow-tailoring requirement is also satisfied.

Context matters when reviewing race-based governmental action under the Equal Protection Clause. See *Gomillion* v. *Lightfoot,* 364 U. S. 339, 343–344 (1960) (admonishing that, "in dealing with claims under broad provisions of the Constitution, which derive content by an interpretive process of inclusion and exclusion, it is imperative that generalizations, based on and qualified by the concrete situations that gave rise to them, must not be applied out of context in disregard of variant controlling facts"). In *Adarand Constructors, Inc.* v. *Peña,* we made clear that strict scrutiny must take " 'relevant differences' into account." 515 U. S., at 228. Indeed, as we explained, that is its "fundamental purpose." *Ibid.* Not every decision influenced by race is equally objectionable and strict scrutiny is designed to provide a framework for carefully examining the importance and the sincerity of the reasons advanced by the governmental decisionmaker for the use of race in that particular context.

III

A

With these principles in mind, we turn to the question whether the Law School's use of race is justified by a compelling state interest. Before this Court, as they have throughout this litigation, respondents assert only one justification for their use of race in the admissions process: obtaining "the educational benefits that flow from a diverse student body." Brief for Respondents Bollinger et al. i. In other words, the Law School asks us to recognize, in the context of higher education, a compelling state interest in student body diversity.

We first wish to dispel the notion that the Law School's argument has been foreclosed, either expressly or implicitly, by our affirmative-action cases decided since *Bakke.* It is true that some language in those opinions might be read to suggest that remedying past discrimination is the only permissible justification for race-based governmental action. See, *e.g., Richmond* v. *J. A. Croson Co., supra,* at 493 (plurality opinion) (stating that unless classifications based on race are "strictly reserved for remedial settings, they may in fact promote notions of racial inferiority and lead to a politics of racial hostility"). But we have never held that the only governmental use of race that can survive strict scrutiny is remedying past discrimination. Nor, since *Bakke,* have we directly addressed the use of race in the context of public higher education. Today, we hold that the Law School has a compelling interest in attaining a diverse student body.

The Law School's educational judgment that such diversity is essential to its educational mission is one to which we defer. The Law School's assessment that diversity will, in fact, yield educational benefits is substantiated by respondents and their *amici*. Our scrutiny of the interest asserted by the Law School is no less strict for taking into account complex educational judgments in an area that lies primarily within the expertise of the university. Our holding today is in keeping with our tradition of giving a degree of deference to a university's academic decisions, within constitutionally prescribed limits. See *Regents of Univ. of Mich.* v. *Ewing*, 474 U. S. 214, 225 (1985); *Board of Curators of Univ. of Mo.* v. *Horowitz*, 435 U. S. 78, 96, n. 6 (1978); *Bakke*, 438 U. S., at 319, n. 53 (opinion of Powell, J.).

We have long recognized that, given the important purpose of public education and the expansive freedoms of speech and thought associated with the university environment, universities occupy a special niche in our constitutional tradition. See, *e.g.*, *Wieman* v. *Updegraff*, 344 U. S. 183, 195 (1952) (Frankfurter, J., concurring); *Sweezy* v. *New Hampshire*, 354 U. S. 234, 250 (1957); *Shelton* v. *Tucker*, 364 U. S. 479, 487 (1960); *Keyishian* v. *Board of Regents of Univ. of State of N. Y.*, 385 U. S., at 603. In announcing the principle of student body diversity as a compelling state interest, Justice Powell invoked our cases recognizing a constitutional dimension, grounded in the First Amendment, of educational autonomy: "The freedom of a university to make its own judgments as to education includes the selection of its student body." *Bakke*, *supra*, at 312. From this premise, Justice Powell reasoned that by claiming "the right to select those students who will contribute the most to the 'robust exchange of ideas,' " a university "seek[s] to achieve a goal that is of paramount importance in the fulfillment of its mission." 438 U. S., at 313 (quoting *Keyishian* v. *Board of Regents of Univ. of State of N. Y.*, *supra*, at 603). Our conclusion that the Law School has a compelling interest in a diverse student body is informed by our view that attaining a diverse student body is at the heart of the Law School's proper institutional mission, and that "good faith" on the part of a university is "presumed" absent "a showing to the contrary." 438 U. S., at 318–319.

As part of its goal of "assembling a class that is both exceptionally academically qualified and broadly diverse," the Law School seeks to "enroll a 'critical mass' of minority students." Brief for Respondents Bollinger et al. 13. The Law School's interest is not simply "to assure within its student body some specified percentage of a particular group merely because of its race or ethnic origin." *Bakke*, 438 U. S., at 307 (opinion of Powell, J.). That would amount to outright racial balancing, which is patently unconstitutional. *Ibid.*; *Freeman* v. *Pitts*, 503 U. S. 467, 494 (1992) ("Racial balance is not to be achieved for its own sake"); *Richmond* v. *J. A. Croson Co.*, 488 U. S., at 507. Rather, the Law School's concept of critical mass is defined by reference to the educational benefits that diversity is designed to produce.

These benefits are substantial. As the District Court emphasized, the Law School's admissions policy promotes "cross-racial understanding," helps to break down racial stereotypes, and "enables [students] to better understand persons of different races." App. to Pet. for Cert. 246a. These benefits are "important and laudable," because "classroom discussion is livelier, more spirited, and simply more enlightening and interesting" when the students have "the greatest possible variety of backgrounds." *Id.*, at 246a, 244a.

The Law School's claim of a compelling interest is further bolstered by its *amici*, who point to the educational benefits that flow from student body diversity. In addition to the expert studies and reports entered into evidence at trial, numerous studies show that student body diversity promotes learning outcomes, and "better prepares students for an increasingly diverse workforce and society, and better prepares them as professionals." Brief for American Educational Research Association et al. as *Amici Curiae* 3; see, *e.g.*, W. Bowen & D. Bok, The Shape of the River (1998); Diversity Challenged: Evidence on the Impact of Affirmative Action (G. Orfield & M. Kurlaender eds. 2001); Compelling Interest: Examining the Evidence on Racial Dynamics in Colleges and Universities (M. Chang, D. Witt, J. Jones, & K. Hakuta eds. 2003).

These benefits are not theoretical but real, as major American businesses have made clear that the skills needed in today's increasingly global marketplace can only be developed through exposure to widely diverse people, cultures, ideas, and viewpoints. Brief for 3M et al. as *Amici Curiae* 5; Brief for General Motors Corp. as *Amicus Curiae* 3–4. What is more, high-ranking retired officers and civilian leaders of the United States military assert that, "[b]ased on [their] decades of experience," a "highly qualified, racially diverse officer corps . . . is essential to the military's ability to fulfill its principle mission to provide national security." Brief for Julius W. Becton, Jr. et al. as *Amici Curiae* 27. The primary sources for the Nation's officer corps are the service academies and the Reserve Officers Training Corps (ROTC), the latter comprising students already admitted to participating colleges and universities. *Id.*, at 5. At present, "the military cannot achieve an officer corps that is *both* highly qualified *and* racially diverse unless the service academies and the ROTC used limited race-conscious recruiting and admissions policies." *Ibid.* (emphasis in original). To fulfill its mission, the military "must be selective in admissions for training and education for the officer corps, *and* it must train and educate a highly qualified, racially diverse officer corps in a racially diverse setting." *Id.*, at 29 (emphasis in original). We agree that "[i]t requires only a small step from this analysis to conclude that our country's other most selective institutions must remain both diverse and selective." *Ibid.*

We have repeatedly acknowledged the overriding importance of preparing students for work and citizenship, describing education as pivotal to "sustaining our political and cultural heritage" with a fundamental role in maintaining the fabric of society. *Plyler* v. *Doe*, 457 U. S. 202, 221 (1982). This Court has long recognized that "education . . . is the very foundation of good citizenship." *Brown* v. *Board of Education*, 347 U.S. 483, 493 (1954). For this reason, the diffusion of knowledge and opportunity through public institutions of higher education must be accessible to all individuals regardless of race or ethnicity. The United States, as *amicus curiae*, affirms that "[e]nsuring that public institutions are open and available to all segments of American society, including people of all races and ethnicities, represents a paramount government objective." Brief for United States as *Amicus Curiae* 13. And, "[n]owhere is the importance of such openness more acute than in the context of higher education." *Ibid.* Effective participation by members of all racial and ethnic groups in the civic life of our Nation is essential if the dream of one Nation, indivisible, is to be realized.

Moreover, universities, and in particular, law schools, represent the training ground for a large number of our Nation's leaders. *Sweatt* v. *Painter*, 339 U.S. 629, 634 (1950) (describing law school as a "proving ground for legal learning and practice"). Individuals with law degrees occupy roughly half the state governorships, more than half the seats in the United States Senate, and more than a third of the seats in the United States House of Representatives. See Brief for Association of American Law Schools as *Amicus Curiae* 5–6. The pattern is even more striking when it comes to highly selective law schools. A handful of these schools accounts for 25 of the 100 United States Senators, 74 United States Courts of Appeals judges, and nearly 200 of the more than 600 United States District Court judges. *Id.*, at 6.

In order to cultivate a set of leaders with legitimacy in the eyes of the citizenry, it is necessary that the path to leadership be visibly open to talented and qualified individuals of every race and ethnicity. All members of our heterogeneous society must have confidence in the openness and integrity of the educational institutions that provide this training. As we have recognized, law schools "cannot be effective in isolation from the individuals and institutions with which the law interacts." See *Sweatt* v. *Painter, supra*, at 634. Access to legal education (and thus the legal profession) must be inclusive of talented and qualified individuals of every race and ethnicity, so that all members of our heterogeneous society may participate in the educational institutions that provide the training and education necessary to succeed in America.

The Law School does not premise its need for critical mass on "any belief that minority students always (or even consistently) express some characteristic minority viewpoint on any issue." Brief for Respondent Bollinger et al. 30. To the contrary, diminishing the force of such stereotypes is both a crucial part of the Law School's mission, and one that it cannot accomplish with only token numbers of minority students. Just as growing up in a particular region or having particular professional experiences is likely to affect an individual's views, so too is one's own, unique experience of being a racial minority in a society, like our own, in which race unfortunately still matters. The Law School has determined, based on its experience and expertise, that a "critical mass" of underrepresented minorities is necessary to further its compelling interest in securing the educational benefits of a diverse student body.

B

Even in the limited circumstance when drawing racial distinctions is permissible to further a compelling state interest, government is still "constrained in how it may pursue that end: [T]he means chosen to accomplish the [government's] asserted purpose must be specifically and narrowly framed to accomplish that purpose." *Shaw* v. *Hunt*, 517 U. S. 899, 908 (1996) (internal quotation marks and citation omitted). The purpose of the narrow tailoring requirement is to ensure that "the means chosen 'fit' . . . th[e] compelling goal so closely that there is little or no possibility that the motive for the classification was illegitimate racial prejudice or stereotype." *Richmond* v. *J. A. Croson Co.*, 488 U. S., at 493 (plurality opinion).

Since *Bakke*, we have had no occasion to define the contours of the narrow-tailoring inquiry with respect to race-conscious university admissions programs. That inquiry must be calibrated to fit the distinct issues raised by the use of race to achieve student body diversity in public higher education. Contrary to JUSTICE KENNEDY's assertions, we do not "abandon [ ] strict scrutiny," see *post*, at 8 (dissenting opinion). Rather, as we have already explained, *ante*, at 15, we adhere to *Adarand*'s teaching that the very purpose of strict scrutiny is to take such "relevant differences into account." 515 U. S., at 228 (internal quotation marks omitted).

To be narrowly tailored, a race-conscious admissions program cannot use a quota system—it cannot "insulat[e] each category of applicants with certain desired qualifications from competition with all other applicants." *Bakke, supra*, at 315 (opinion of Powell, J.). Instead, a university may consider race or ethnicity only as a " 'plus' in a particular applicant's file," without "insulat[ing] the individual from comparison with all other candidates for the available seats." *Id.*, at 317. In other words, an admissions program must be "flexible enough to consider all pertinent elements of diversity in light of the particular qualifications of each applicant, and to place them on the same footing for consideration, although not necessarily according them the same weight." *Ibid.*

We find that the Law School's admissions program bears the hallmarks of a narrowly tailored plan. As Justice Powell made clear in *Bakke*, truly individualized consideration demands that race be used in a flexible, nonmechanical way. It follows from this mandate that universities cannot establish quotas for members of certain racial groups or put members of those groups on separate admissions tracks. See *id.*, at 315–316. Nor can universities insulate applicants who belong to certain racial or ethnic groups from the competition for admission. *Ibid.* Universities can, however, consider race or ethnicity more flexibly as a "plus" factor in the context of individualized consideration of each and every applicant. *Ibid.*

We are satisfied that the Law School's admissions program, like the Harvard plan described by Justice Powell, does not operate as a quota. Properly understood, a "quota" is a program in which a certain fixed number or proportion of opportunities are "reserved exclusively for certain minority groups." *Richmond* v. *J. A. Croson Co., supra*, at 496 (plurality opinion). Quotas " 'impose a fixed number or percentage which must be attained, or which cannot be exceeded,' " *Sheet Metal Workers* v. *EEOC*, 478 U. S. 421, 495 (1986) (O'CONNOR, J., concurring in part and dissenting in part), and "insulate the individual from comparison with all other candidates for the available seats." *Bakke, supra*, at 317 (opinion of Powell, J.). In contrast, "a permissible goal . . . require[s] only a good-faith effort . . . to come within a range demarcated by the goal itself," *Sheet Metal Workers* v. *EEOC, supra*, at 495, and permits consideration of race as a "plus" factor in any given case while still ensuring that each candidate "compete[s] with all other qualified applicants," *Johnson* v. *Transportation Agency, Santa Clara Cty.*, 480 U. S. 616, 638 (1987).

Justice Powell's distinction between the medical school's rigid 16-seat quota and Harvard's flexible use of race as a "plus" factor is instructive. Harvard certainly had minimum *goals* for minority enrollment, even if it had no specific number firmly in mind. See *Bakke, supra,* at 323 (opinion of Powell, J.) ("10 or 20 black students could not begin to bring to their classmates and to each other the variety of points of view, backgrounds and experiences of blacks in the United States"). What is more, Justice Powell flatly rejected the argument that Harvard's program was "the functional equivalent of a quota" merely because it had some " 'plus' " for race, or gave greater "weight" to race than to some other factors, in order to achieve student body diversity. 438 U. S., at 317–318.

The Law School's goal of attaining a critical mass of underrepresented minority students does not transform its program into a quota. As the Harvard plan described by Justice Powell recognized, there is of course "some relationship between numbers and achieving the benefits to be derived from a diverse student body, and between numbers and providing a reasonable environment for those students admitted." *Id.,* at 323. "[S]ome attention to numbers," without more, does not transform a flexible admissions system into a rigid quota. *Ibid.* Nor, as JUSTICE KENNEDY posits, does the Law School's consultation of the "daily reports," which keep track of the racial and ethnic composition of the class (as well as of residency and gender), "suggest[ ] there was no further attempt at individual review save for race itself" during the final stages of the admissions process. See *post,* at 6 (dissenting opinion). To the contrary, the Law School's admissions officers testified without contradiction that they never gave race any more or less weight based on the information contained in these reports. Brief for Respondents Bollinger et al. 43, n. 70 (citing App. in Nos. 01–1447 and 01–1516 (CA6), p. 7336). Moreover, as JUSTICE KENNEDY concedes, see *post,* at 4, between 1993 and 2000, the number of African-American, Latino, and Native-American students in each class at the Law School varied from 13.5 to 20.1 percent, a range inconsistent with a quota.

THE CHIEF JUSTICE believes that the Law School's policy conceals an attempt to achieve racial balancing, and cites admissions data to contend that the Law School discriminates among different groups within the critical mass. *Post,* at 3–9 (dissenting opinion). But, as THE CHIEF JUSTICE concedes, the number of underrepresented minority students who ultimately enroll in the Law School differs substantially from their representation in the applicant pool and varies considerably for each group from year to year. See *post,* at 8 (dissenting opinion).

That a race-conscious admissions program does not operate as a quota does not, by itself, satisfy the requirement of individualized consideration. When using race as a "plus" factor in university admissions, a university's admissions program must remain flexible enough to ensure that each applicant is evaluated as an individual and not in a way that makes an applicant's race or ethnicity the defining feature of his or her application. The importance of this individualized consideration in the context of a race-conscious admissions program is paramount. See *Bakke, supra,* at 318, n. 52 (opinion of Powell, J.) (identifying the "denial . . . of th[e] right to individualized consideration" as the "principal evil" of the medical school's admissions program).

Here, the Law School engages in a highly individualized, holistic review of each applicant's file, giving serious consideration to all the ways an applicant might contribute to a diverse educational environment. The Law School affords this individualized consideration to applicants of all races. There is no policy, either *de jure* or *de facto,* of automatic acceptance or rejection based on any single "soft" variable. Unlike the program at issue in *Gratz* v. *Bollinger, ante,* the Law School awards no mechanical, predetermined diversity "bonuses" based on race or ethnicity. See *ante,* at 23 (distinguishing a race-conscious admissions program that automatically awards 20 points based on race from the Harvard plan, which considered race but "did not contemplate that any single characteristic automatically ensured a specific and identifiable contribution to a university's diversity"). Like the Harvard plan, the Law School's admissions policy "is flexible enough to consider all pertinent elements of diversity in light of the particular qualifications of each applicant, and to place them on the same footing for consideration, although not necessarily according them the same weight." *Bakke, supra*, at 317 (opinion of Powell, J.).

We also find that, like the Harvard plan Justice Powell referenced in *Bakke*, the Law School's race-conscious admissions program adequately ensures that all factors that may contribute to student body diversity are meaningfully considered alongside race in admissions decisions. With respect to the use of race itself, all underrepresented minority students admitted by the Law School have been deemed qualified. By virtue of our Nation's struggle with racial inequality, such students are both likely to have experiences of particular importance to the Law School's mission, and less likely to be admitted in meaningful numbers on criteria that ignore those experiences. See App. 120.

The Law School does not, however, limit in any way the broad range of qualities and experiences that may be considered valuable contributions to student body diversity. To the contrary, the 1992 policy makes clear "[t]here are many possible bases for diversity admissions," and provides examples of admittees who have lived or traveled widely abroad, are fluent in several languages, have overcome personal adversity and family hardship, have exceptional records of extensive community service, and have had successful careers in other fields. *Id.*, at 118–119. The Law School seriously considers each "applicant's promise of making a notable contribution to the class by way of a particular strength, attainment, or characteristic—*e.g.*, an unusual intellectual achievement, employment experience, non-academic performance, or personal background." *Id.*, at 83–84. All applicants have the opportunity to highlight their own potential diversity contributions through the submission of a personal statement, letters of recommendation, and an essay describing the ways in which the applicant will contribute to the life and diversity of the Law School.

What is more, the Law School actually gives substantial weight to diversity factors besides race. The Law School frequently accepts nonminority applicants with grades and test scores lower than underrepresented minority applicants (and other nonminority applicants) who are rejected. See Brief for Respondents Bollinger et al. 10; App. 121–122. This shows that the Law School seriously weighs many other diversity factors besides race that can make a real and dispositive difference for nonminority applicants as well. By this flexible approach, the Law School sufficiently takes into account, in practice as well as in theory, a wide variety of characteristics besides race and ethnicity that contribute to a diverse student body. JUSTICE KENNEDY speculates that "race is likely outcome determinative for many members of minority groups" who do not fall within the upper range of LSAT scores and grades. *Post*, at 3 (dissenting opinion). But the same could be said of the Harvard plan discussed approvingly by Justice Powell in *Bakke*, and indeed of any plan that uses race as one of many factors. See 438 U. S., at 316 (" 'When the Committee on Admissions reviews the large middle group of applicants who are "admissible" and deemed capable of doing good work in their courses, the race of an applicant may tip the balance in his favor' ").

Petitioner and the United States argue that the Law School's plan is not narrowly tailored because race-neutral means exist to obtain the educational benefits of student body diversity that the Law School seeks. We disagree. Narrow tailoring does not require exhaustion of every conceivable race-neutral alternative. Nor does it require a university to choose between maintaining a reputation for excellence or fulfilling a commitment to provide educational opportunities to members of all racial groups. See *Wygant* v. *Jackson Bd. of Ed.*, 476 U. S. 267, 280, n. 6 (1986) (alternatives must serve the interest " 'about as well' "); *Richmond* v. *J. A. Croson Co.*, 488 U. S., at 509–510 (plurality opinion) (city had a "whole array of race-neutral" alternatives because changing requirements "would have [had] little detrimental effect on the city's interests"). Narrow tailoring does, however, require serious, good faith consideration of workable race-neutral alternatives that will achieve the diversity the university seeks. See *id.*, at 507 (set-aside plan not narrowly tailored where "there does not appear to have been any consideration of the use of race-neutral means"); *Wygant* v. *Jackson Bd. of Ed.*, *supra*, at 280, n. 6 (narrow tailoring "require[s] consideration" of "lawful alternative and less restrictive means").

We agree with the Court of Appeals that the Law School sufficiently considered workable race-neutral alternatives. The District Court took the Law School to task for failing to consider race-neutral alternatives such as "using a lottery system" or "decreasing the emphasis for all applicants on undergraduate GPA and LSAT scores." App. to Pet. for Cert. 251a. But these alternatives would require a dramatic sacrifice of diversity, the academic quality of all admitted students, or both.

The Law School's current admissions program considers race as one factor among many, in an effort to assemble a student body that is diverse in ways broader than race. Because a lottery would make that kind of nuanced judgment impossible, it would effectively sacrifice all other educational values, not to mention every other kind of diversity. So too with the suggestion that the Law School simply lower admissions standards for all students, a drastic remedy that would require the Law School to become a much different institution and sacrifice a vital component of its educational mission. The United States advocates "percentage plans," recently adopted by public undergraduate institutions in Texas, Florida, and California to guarantee admission to all students above a certain class-rank threshold in every high school in the State. Brief for United States as *Amicus Curiae* 14–18. The United States does not, however, explain how such plans could work for graduate and professional schools. Moreover, even assuming such plans are race-neutral, they may preclude the university from conducting the individualized assessments necessary to assemble a student body that is not just racially diverse, but diverse along all the qualities valued by the university. We are satisfied that the Law School adequately considered race-neutral alternatives currently capable of producing a critical mass without forcing the Law School to abandon the academic selectivity that is the cornerstone of its educational mission.

We acknowledge that "there are serious problems of justice connected with the idea of preference itself." *Bakke*, 438 U. S., at 298 (opinion of Powell, J.). Narrow tailoring, therefore, requires that a raceconscious admissions program not unduly harm members of any racial group. Even remedial race-based governmental action generally "remains subject to continuing oversight to assure that it will work the least harm possible to other innocent persons competing for the benefit." *Id.*, at 308. To be narrowly tailored, a race-conscious admissions program must not "unduly burden individuals who are not members of the favored racial and ethnic groups." *Metro Broadcasting, Inc.* v. *FCC*, 497 U. S. 547, 630 (1990) (O'Connor, J., dissenting).

We are satisfied that the Law School's admissions program does not. Because the Law School considers "all pertinent elements of diversity," it can (and does) select nonminority applicants who have greater potential to enhance student body diversity over underrepresented minority applicants. See *Bakke, supra*, at 317 (opinion of Powell, J.). As Justice Powell recognized in *Bakke*, so long as a race-conscious admissions program uses race as a "plus" factor in the context of individualized consideration, a rejected applicant

> "will not have been foreclosed from all consideration for that seat simply because he was not the right color or had the wrong surname. . . . His qualifications would have been weighed fairly and competitively, and he would have no basis to complain of unequal treatment under the Fourteenth Amendment." 438 U. S., at 318.

We agree that, in the context of its individualized inquiry into the possible diversity contributions of all applicants, the Law School's race-conscious admissions program does not unduly harm nonminority applicants.

We are mindful, however, that "[a] core purpose of the Fourteenth Amendment was to do away with all governmentally imposed discrimination based on race." *Palmore* v. *Sidoti*, 466 U. S. 429, 432 (1984). Accordingly, race-conscious admissions policies must be limited in time. This requirement reflects that racial classifications, however compelling their goals, are potentially so dangerous that they may be employed no more broadly than the interest demands. Enshrining a permanent justification for racial preferences would offend this fundamental equal protection principle. We see no reason to exempt race-conscious admissions programs from the requirement that all governmental use of race must have a logical end point. The Law School, too, concedes that all "race-conscious programs must have reasonable durational limits." Brief for Respondents Bollinger et al. 32.

In the context of higher education, the durational requirement can be met by sunset provisions in race-conscious admissions policies and periodic reviews to determine whether racial preferences are still necessary to achieve student body diversity. Universities in California, Florida, and Washington State, where racial preferences in admissions are prohibited by state law, are currently engaged in experimenting with a wide variety of alternative approaches. Universities in other States can and should draw on the most promising aspects of these race-neutral alternatives as they develop. Cf. *United States* v. *Lopez*, 514 U. S. 549, 581 (1995) (KENNEDY, J., concurring) ("[T]he States may perform their role as laboratories for experimentation to devise various solutions where the best solution is far from clear").

The requirement that all race-conscious admissions programs have a termination point "assure[s] all citizens that the deviation from the norm of equal treatment of all racial and ethnic groups is a temporary matter, a measure taken in the service of the goal of equality itself." *Richmond* v. *J. A. Croson Co.*, 488 U. S., at 510 (plurality opinion); see also Nathanson & Bartnik, The Constitutionality of Preferential Treatment for Minority Applicants to Professional Schools, 58 Chicago Bar Rec. 282, 293 (May–June 1977) ("It would be a sad day indeed, were America to become a quota-ridden society, with each identifiable minority assigned proportional representation in every desirable walk of life. But that is not the rationale for programs of preferential treatment; the acid test of their justification will be their efficacy in eliminating the need for any racial or ethnic preferences at all").

We take the Law School at its word that it would "like nothing better than to find a race-neutral admissions formula" and will terminate its race-conscious admissions program as soon as practicable. See Brief for Respondents Bollinger et al. 34; *Bakke, supra*, at 317–318 (opinion of Powell, J.) (presuming good faith of university officials in the absence of a showing to the contrary). It has been 25 years since Justice Powell first approved the use of race to further an interest in student body diversity in the context of public higher education. Since that time, the number of minority applicants with high grades and test scores has indeed increased. See Tr. of Oral Arg. 43. We expect that 25 years from now, the use of racial preferences will no longer be necessary to further the interest approved today.

IV

In summary, the Equal Protection Clause does not prohibit the Law School's narrowly tailored use of race in admissions decisions to further a compelling interest in obtaining the educational benefits that flow from a diverse student body. Consequently, petitioner's statutory claims based on Title VI and 42 U. S. C. §1981 also fail. See *Bakke, supra*, at 287 (opinion of Powell, J.) ("Title VI . . . proscribe[s] only those racial classifications that would violate the Equal Protection Clause or the Fifth Amendment"); *General Building Contractors Assn., Inc.* v. *Pennsylvania*, 458 U. S. 375, 389–391 (1982) (the prohibition against discrimination in §1981 is coextensive with the Equal Protection Clause). The judgment of the Court of Appeals for the Sixth Circuit, accordingly, is affirmed.

It is so ordered.

SUPREME COURT OF THE UNITED STATES

No. 02–241

BARBARA GRUTTER, PETITIONER v. *LEE BOLLINGER ET AL.*

ON WRIT OF CERTIORARI TO THE UNITED STATES COURT OF APPEALS FOR THE SIXTH CIRCUIT

[June 23, 2003]

JUSTICE GINSBURG, with whom JUSTICE BREYER joins, concurring.

The Court's observation that race-conscious programs "must have a logical end point," *ante*, at 29, accords with the international understanding of the office of affirmative action. The International Convention on the Elimination of All Forms of Racial Discrimination, ratified by the United States in 1994, see State Dept., Treaties in Force 422–423 (June 1996), endorses "special and concrete measures to ensure the adequate development and protection of certain racial groups or individuals belonging to them, for the purpose of guaranteeing them the full and equal enjoyment of human rights and fundamental freedoms." Annex to G. A. Res. 2106, 20 U. N. GAOR Res. Supp. (No. 14) 47, U. N. Doc. A/6014, Art. 2(2) (1965). But such measures, the Convention instructs, "shall in no case entail as a consequence the maintenance of unequal or separate rights for different racial groups after the objectives for which they were taken have been achieved." *Ibid*; see also Art. 1(4) (similarly providing for temporally limited affirmative action); Convention on the Elimination of All Forms of Discrimination against Women, Annex to G. A. Res. 34/180, 34 U. N. GAOR Res. Supp. (No. 46) 194, U. N. Doc. A/34/46, Art. 4(1) (1979) (authorizing "temporary special measures aimed at accelerating *de facto* equality" that "shall be discontinued when the objectives of equality of opportunity and treatment have been achieved").

The Court further observes that "[i]t has been 25 years since Justice Powell [in *Regents of Univ. of Cal.* v. *Bakke*, 438 U. S. 265 (1978)] first approved the use of race to further an interest in student body diversity in the context of public higher education." *Ante*, at 31. For at least part of that time, however, the law could not fairly be described as "settled," and in some regions of the Nation, overtly race-conscious admissions policies have been proscribed. See *Hopwood* v. *Texas*, 78 F. 3d 932 (CA5 1996); cf. *Wessmann* v. *Gittens*, 160 F. 3d 790 (CA1 1998); *Tuttle* v. *Arlington Cty. School Bd.*, 195 F. 3d 698 (CA4 1999); *Johnson* v. *Board of Regents of Univ. of Ga.*, 263 F. 3d 1234 (CA11 2001). Moreover, it was only 25 years before *Bakke* that this Court declared public school segregation unconstitutional, a declaration that, after prolonged resistance, yielded an end to a law-enforced racial caste system, itself the legacy of centuries of slavery. See *Brown* v. *Board of Education*, 347 U. S. 483 (1954); cf. *Cooper* v. *Aaron*, 358 U. S. 1 (1958).

It is well documented that conscious and unconscious race bias, even rank discrimination based on race, remain alive in our land, impeding realization of our highest values and ideals. See, *e.g., Gratz* v. *Bollinger*, *ante*, at 1–4 (GINSBURG, J., dissenting); *Adarand Constructors, Inc.* v. *Peña*, 515 U. S. 200, 272–274 (1995) (GINSBURG, J., dissenting); Krieger, Civil Rights Perestroika: Intergroup Relations after Affirmative Action, 86 Calif. L. Rev. 1251, 1276–1291, 1303 (1998). As to public education, data for the years 2000–2001 show that 71.6% of African-American children and 76.3% of Hispanic children attended a school in which minorities made up a majority of the student body. See E. Frankenberg, C. Lee, & G. Orfield, A Multiracial Society with Segregated Schools: Are We Losing the Dream? p. 4 (Jan. 2003), http://www.civilrightsproject.harvard.edu/research/reseg03/AreWeLosingthe Dream.pdf (as visited June 16, 2003, and available in Clerk of Court's case file). And schools in predominantly minority communities lag far behind others measured by the educational resources available to them. See *id.*, at 11; Brief for National Urban League et al. as *Amici*

Curiae 11–12 (citing General Accounting Office, Per-Pupil Spending Differences Between Selected Inner City and Suburban Schools Varied by Metropolitan Area, 17 (2002)).

However strong the public's desire for improved education systems may be, see P. Hart & R. Teeter, A National Priority: Americans Speak on Teacher Quality 2, 11 (2002) (public opinion research conducted for Educational Testing Service); The No Child Left Behind Act of 2001, Pub. L. 107–110, 115 Stat. 1425, 20 U. S. C. A. §7231 (2003 Supp. Pamphlet), it remains the current reality that many minority students encounter markedly inadequate and unequal educational opportunities. Despite these inequalities, some minority students are able to meet the high threshold requirements set for admission to the country's finest undergraduate and graduate educational institutions. As lower school education in minority communities improves, an increase in the number of such students may be anticipated. From today's vantage point, one may hope, but not firmly forecast, that over the next generation's span, progress toward nondiscrimination and genuinely equal opportunity will make it safe to sunset affirmative action.*

SUPREME COURT OF THE UNITED STATES

No. 02–241

BARBARA GRUTTER, PETITIONER v. *LEE BOLLINGER ET AL.*

ON WRIT OF CERTIORARI TO THE UNITED STATES COURT OF APPEALS FOR THE SIXTH CIRCUIT

[June 23, 2003]

JUSTICE SCALIA, with whom JUSTICE THOMAS joins, concurring in part and dissenting in part.

I join the opinion of THE CHIEF JUSTICE. As he demonstrates, the University of Michigan Law School's mystical "critical mass" justification for its discrimination by race challenges even the most gullible mind. The admissions statistics show it to be a sham to cover a scheme of racially proportionate admissions.

I also join Parts I through VII of JUSTICE THOMAS's opinion.* I find particularly unanswerable his central point: that the allegedly "compelling state interest" at issue here is not the incremental "educational benefit" that emanates from the fabled "critical mass" of minority students, but rather Michigan's interest in maintaining a "prestige" law school whose normal admissions standards disproportionately exclude blacks and other minorities. If that is a compelling state interest, everything is.

I add the following: The "educational benefit" that the University of Michigan seeks to achieve by racial discrimination consists, according to the Court, of " 'cross-racial understanding,' " *ante*, at 18, and " 'better prepar[ation of] students for an increasingly diverse workforce and society,' " *ibid.*, all of which is necessary not only for work, but also for good "citizenship," *ante*, at 19. This is not, of course, an "educational benefit" on which students

---

*As the Court explains, the admissions policy challenged here survives review under the standards stated in *Adarand Constructors, Inc.* v. *Peña*, 515 U. S. 200 (1995), *Richmond* v. *J. A. Croson Co.*, 488 U. S. 469 (1989), and Justice Powell's opinion in *Regents of Univ. of Cal.* v. *Bakke*, 438 U. S. 265 (1978). This case therefore does not require the Court to revisit whether all governmental classifications by race, whether designed to benefit or to burden a historically disadvantaged group, should be subject to the same standard of judicial review. Cf. *Gratz, ante*, at 4–5 (GINSBURG, J., dissenting); *Adarand*, 515 U. S., at 274, n. 8 (GINSBURG, J., dissenting). Nor does this case necessitate reconsideration whether interests other than "student body diversity," *ante*, at 13, rank as sufficiently important to justify a race-conscious government program. Cf. *Gratz, ante*, at 5 (GINSBURG, J., dissenting); *Adarand*, 515 U. S., at 273–274 (GINSBURG, J., dissenting).

*Part VII of JUSTICE THOMAS's opinion describes those portions of the Court's opinion in which I concur. See *post*, at 27–31.

will be graded on their Law School transcript (Works and Plays Well with Others: B+) or tested by the bar examiners (Q: Describe in 500 words or less your cross-racial understanding). For it is a lesson of life rather than law—essentially the same lesson taught to (or rather learned by, for it cannot be "taught" in the usual sense) people three feet shorter and twenty years younger than the full-grown adults at the University of Michigan Law School, in institutions ranging from Boy Scout troops to public-school kindergartens. If properly considered an "educational benefit" at all, it is surely not one that is either uniquely relevant to law school or uniquely "teachable" in a formal educational setting. *And therefore:* If it is appropriate for the University of Michigan Law School to use racial discrimination for the purpose of putting together a "critical mass" that will convey generic lessons in socialization and good citizenship, surely it is no less appropriate—indeed, *particularly* appropriate—for the civil service system of the State of Michigan to do so. There, also, those exposed to "critical masses" of certain races will presumably become better Americans, better Michiganders, better civil servants. And surely private employers cannot be criticized—indeed, should be praised—if they also "teach" good citizenship to their adult employees through a patriotic, all-American system of racial discrimination in hiring. The nonminority individuals who are deprived of a legal education, a civil service job, or any job at all by reason of their skin color will surely understand.

Unlike a clear constitutional holding that racial preferences in state educational institutions are impermissible, or even a clear anticonstitutional holding that racial preferences in state educational institutions are OK, today's *Grutter-Gratz* split double header seems perversely designed to prolong the controversy and the litigation. Some future lawsuits will presumably focus on whether the discriminatory scheme in question contains enough evaluation of the applicant "as an individual," *ante*, at 24, and sufficiently avoids "separate admissions tracks" *ante*, at 22, to fall under *Grutter* rather than *Gratz*. Some will focus on whether a university has gone beyond the bounds of a " 'good faith effort' " and has so zealously pursued its "critical mass" as to make it an unconstitutional *de facto* quota system, rather than merely " 'a permissible goal.' " *Ante*, at 23 (quoting *Sheet Metal Workers* v. *EEOC*, 478 U. S. 421, 495 (1986) (O'CONNOR, J., concurring in part and dissenting in part)). Other lawsuits may focus on whether, in the particular setting at issue, any educational benefits flow from racial diversity. (That issue was not contested in *Grutter*, and while the opinion accords "a degree of deference to a university's academic decisions," *ante*, at 16, "deference does not imply abandonment or abdication of judicial review," *Miller-El* v. *Cockrell*, 537 U. S. 322, 340 (2003).) Still other suits may challenge the bona fides of the institution's expressed commitment to the educational benefits of diversity that immunize the discriminatory scheme in *Grutter*. (Tempting targets, one would suppose, will be those universities that talk the talk of multiculturalism and racial diversity in the courts but walk the walk of tribalism and racial segregation on their campuses—through minority-only student organizations, separate minority housing opportunities, separate minority student centers, even separate minority-only graduation ceremonies.) And still other suits may claim that the institution's racial preferences have gone below or above the mystical *Grutter*-approved "critical mass." Finally, litigation can be expected on behalf of minority groups intentionally short changed in the institution's composition of its generic minority "critical mass." I do not look forward to any of these cases. The Constitution proscribes government discrimination on the basis of race, and state-provided education is no exception.

SUPREME COURT OF THE UNITED STATES

No. 02–241

BARBARA GRUTTER, PETITIONER v. *LEE BOLLINGER ET AL.*

ON WRIT OF CERTIORARI TO THE UNITED STATES COURT OF APPEALS FOR THE SIXTH CIRCUIT

[June 23, 2003]

JUSTICE THOMAS, with whom JUSTICE SCALIA joins as to Parts I–VII, concurring in part and dissenting in part.

Frederick Douglass, speaking to a group of abolitionists almost 140 years ago, delivered a message lost on today's majority:

> "[I]n regard to the colored people, there is always more that is benevolent, I perceive, than just, manifested towards us. What I ask for the negro is not benevolence, not pity, not sympathy, but simply *justice*. The American people have always been anxious to know what they shall do with us. . . . I have had but one answer from the beginning. Do nothing with us! Your doing with us has already played the mischief with us. Do nothing with us! If the apples will not remain on the tree of their own strength, if they are worm-eaten at the core, if they are early ripe and disposed to fall, let them fall! . . . And if the negro cannot stand on his own legs, let him fall also. All I ask is, give him a chance to stand on his own legs! Let him alone! . . . [Y]our interference is doing him positive injury." What the Black Man Wants: An Address Delivered in Boston, Massachusetts, on 26 January 1865, reprinted in 4 The Frederick Douglass Papers 59, 68 (J. Blassingame & J. McKivigan eds. 1991) (emphasis in original).

Like Douglass, I believe blacks can achieve in every avenue of American life without the meddling of university administrators. Because I wish to see all students succeed whatever their color, I share, in some respect, the sympathies of those who sponsor the type of discrimination advanced by the University of Michigan Law School (Law School). The Constitution does not, however, tolerate institutional devotion to the status quo in admissions policies when such devotion ripens into racial discrimination. Nor does the Constitution countenance the unprecedented deference the Court gives to the Law School, an approach inconsistent with the very concept of "strict scrutiny."

No one would argue that a university could set up a lower general admission standard and then impose heightened requirements only on black applicants. Similarly, a university may not maintain a high admission standard and grant exemptions to favored races. The Law School, of its own choosing, and for its own purposes, maintains an exclusionary admissions system that it knows produces racially disproportionate results. Racial discrimination is not a permissible solution to the self-inflicted wounds of this elitist admissions policy.

The majority upholds the Law School's racial discrimination not by interpreting the people's Constitution, but by responding to a faddish slogan of the cognoscenti. Nevertheless, I concur in part in the Court's opinion. First, I agree with the Court insofar as its decision, which approves of only one racial classification, confirms that further use of race in admissions remains unlawful. Second, I agree with the Court's holding that racial discrimination in higher education admissions will be illegal in 25 years. See *ante*, at 31 (stating that racial discrimination will no longer be narrowly tailored, or "necessary to further" a compelling state interest, in 25 years). I respectfully dissent from the remainder of the Court's opinion and the judgment, however, because I believe that the Law School's current use of race violates the Equal Protection Clause and that the Constitution means the same thing today as it will in 300 months.

I

The majority agrees that the Law School's racial discrimination should be subjected to strict scrutiny. *Ante,* at 14. Before applying that standard to this case, I will briefly revisit the Court's treatment of racial classifications.

The strict scrutiny standard that the Court purports to apply in this case was first enunciated in *Korematsu* v. *United States,* 323 U. S. 214 (1944). There the Court held that "[p]ressing public necessity may sometimes justify the existence of [racial discrimination]; racial antagonism never can." *Id.,* at 216. This standard of "pressing public necessity" has more frequently been termed "compelling governmental interest,"[1] see, *e.g., Regents of Univ. of Cal.* v. *Bakke,* 438 U. S. 265, 299 (1978) (opinion of Powell, J.). A majority of the Court has validated only two circumstances where "pressing public necessity" or a "compelling state interest" can possibly justify racial discrimination by state actors. First, the lesson of *Korematsu* is that national security constitutes a "pressing public necessity," though the government's use of race to advance that objective must be narrowly tailored. Second, the Court has recognized as a compelling state interest a government's effort to remedy past discrimination for which it is responsible. *Richmond* v. *J. A. Croson Co.,* 488 U. S. 469, 504 (1989).

The contours of "pressing public necessity" can be further discerned from those interests the Court has rejected as bases for racial discrimination. For example, *Wygant* v. *Jackson Bd. of Ed.,* 476 U. S. 267 (1986), found unconstitutional a collective-bargaining agreement between a school board and a teachers' union that favored certain minority races. The school board defended the policy on the grounds that minority teachers provided "role models" for minority students and that a racially "diverse" faculty would improve the education of all students. See Brief for Respondents, O. T. 1984, No. 84–1340, pp. 27–28; 476 U. S., at 315 (STEVENS, J., dissenting) ("[A]n integrated faculty will be able to provide benefits to the student body that could not be provided by an all-white, or nearly all-white faculty"). Nevertheless, the Court found that the use of race violated the Equal Protection Clause, deeming both asserted state interests insufficiently compelling. *Id.,* at 275–276 (plurality opinion); *id.,* at 295 (White, J., concurring in judgment) ("None of the interests asserted by the [school board] . . . justify this racially discriminatory layoff policy").[2]

An even greater governmental interest involves the sensitive role of courts in child custody determinations. In *Palmore* v. *Sidoti,* 466 U. S. 429 (1984), the Court held that even the best interests of a child did not constitute a compelling state interest that would allow a state court to award custody to the father because the mother was in a mixed-race marriage. *Id.,* at 433 (finding the interest "substantial" but holding the custody decision could not be based on the race of the mother's new husband).

Finally, the Court has rejected an interest in remedying general societal discrimination as a justification for race discrimination. See *Wygant, supra,* at 276 (plurality opinion); *Croson,* 488 U. S., at 496–498 (plurality opinion); *id.,* at 520–521 (SCALIA, J., concurring in judgment). "Societal discrimination, without more, is too amorphous a basis for imposing a racially classified remedy" because a "court could uphold remedies that are ageless in their reach into the past, and timeless in their ability to affect the future." *Wygant, supra,* at 276 (plurality opinion). But see *Gratz* v. *Bollinger, ante,* p. __ (GINSBURG, J., dissenting).

Where the Court has accepted only national security, and rejected even the best interests

---

[1]Throughout I will use the two phrases interchangeably.

[2]The Court's refusal to address *Wygant*'s rejection of a state interest virtually indistinguishable from that presented by the Law School is perplexing. If the Court defers to the Law School's judgment that a racially mixed student body confers educational benefits to all, then why would the *Wygant* Court not defer to the school board's judgment with respect to the benefits a racially mixed faculty confers?

of a child, as a justification for racial discrimination, I conclude that only those measures the State must take to provide a bulwark against anarchy, or to prevent violence, will constitute a "pressing public necessity." Cf. *Lee* v. *Washington*, 390 U. S. 333, 334 (1968) *(per curiam)* (Black, J., concurring) (indicating that protecting prisoners from violence might justify narrowly tailored racial discrimination); *Croson, supra*, at 521 (SCALIA, J., concurring in judgment) ("At least where state or local action is at issue, only a social emergency rising to the level of imminent danger to life and limb . . . can justify [racial discrimination]").

The Constitution abhors classifications based on race, not only because those classifications can harm favored races or are based on illegitimate motives, but also because every time the government places citizens on racial registers and makes race relevant to the provision of burdens or benefits, it demeans us all. "Purchased at the price of immeasurable human suffering, the equal protection principle reflects our Nation's understanding that such classifications ultimately have a destructive impact on the individual and our society." *Adarand Construction, Inc.* v. *Peña,*, 515 U. S. 200, 240 (1995) (THOMAS, J., concurring in part and concurring in judgment).

II

Unlike the majority, I seek to define with precision the interest being asserted by the Law School before determining whether that interest is so compelling as to justify racial discrimination. The Law School maintains that it wishes to obtain "educational benefits that flow from student body diversity," Brief for Respondents Bollinger et al. 14. This statement must be evaluated carefully, because it implies that both "diversity" and "educational benefits" are components of the Law School's compelling state interest. Additionally, the Law School's refusal to entertain certain changes in its admissions process and status indicates that the compelling state interest it seeks to validate is actually broader than might appear at first glance.

Undoubtedly there are other ways to "better" the education of law students aside from ensuring that the student body contains a "critical mass" of underrepresented minority students. Attaining "diversity," whatever it means,[3] is the mechanism by which the Law School obtains educational benefits, not an end of itself. The Law School, however, apparently believes that only a racially mixed student body can lead to the educational benefits it seeks. How, then, is the Law School's interest in these allegedly unique educational "benefits" *not* simply the forbidden interest in "racial balancing," *ante,* at 17, that the majority expressly rejects?

A distinction between these two ideas (unique educational benefits based on racial aesthetics and race for its own sake) is purely sophistic—so much so that the majority uses them interchangeably. Compare *ante,* at 16 ("[T]he Law School has a compelling interest in attaining a diverse student body"), with *ante,* at 21 (referring to the "compelling interest in securing the *educational benefits* of a diverse student body" (emphasis added)). The Law School's argument, as facile as it is, can only be understood in one way: Classroom aesthetics

---

[3] "[D]iversity," for all of its devotees, is more a fashionable catchphrase than it is a useful term, especially when something as serious as racial discrimination is at issue. Because the Equal Protection Clause renders the color of one's skin constitutionally irrelevant to the Law School's mission, I refer to the Law School's interest as an "aesthetic." That is, the Law School wants to have a certain appearance, from the shape of the desks and tables in its classrooms to the color of the students sitting at them.

I also use the term "aesthetic" because I believe it underlines the ineffectiveness of racially discriminatory admissions in actually helping those who are truly underprivileged. Cf. *Orr* v. *Orr*, 440 U. S. 268, 283 (1979) (noting that suspect classifications are especially impermissible when "the choice made by the State appears to redound . . . to the benefit of those without need for special solicitude"). It must be remembered that the Law School's racial discrimination does nothing for those too poor or uneducated to participate in elite higher education and therefore presents only an illusory solution to the challenges facing our Nation.

yields educational benefits, racially discriminatory admissions policies are required to achieve the right racial mix, and therefore the policies are required to achieve the educational benefits. It is the *educational benefits* that are the end, or allegedly compelling state interest, not "diversity." But see *ante*, at 20 (citing the need for "openness and integrity of the educational institutions that provide [legal] training" without reference to any consequential educational benefits).

One must also consider the Law School's refusal to entertain changes to its current admissions system that might produce the same educational benefits. The Law School adamantly disclaims any race-neutral alternative that would reduce "academic selectivity," which would in turn "require the Law School to become a very different institution, and to sacrifice a core part of its educational mission." Brief for Respondents Bollinger et al. 33–36. In other words, the Law School seeks to improve marginally the education it offers without sacrificing too much of its exclusivity and elite status.[4]

The proffered interest that the majority vindicates today, then, is not simply "diversity." Instead the Court upholds the use of racial discrimination as a tool to advance the Law School's interest in offering a marginally superior education while maintaining an elite institution. Unless each constituent part of this state interest is of pressing public necessity, the Law School's use of race is unconstitutional. I find each of them to fall far short of this standard.

III

A

A close reading of the Court's opinion reveals that all of its legal work is done through one conclusory statement: The Law School has a "compelling interest in securing the educational benefits of a diverse student body." *Ante*, at 21. No serious effort is made to explain how these benefits fit with the state interests the Court has recognized (or rejected) as compelling, see Part I, *supra*, or to place any theoretical constraints on an enterprising court's desire to discover still more justifications for racial discrimination. In the absence of any explanation, one might expect the Court to fall back on the judicial policy of *stare decisis*. But the Court eschews even this weak defense of its holding, shunning an analysis of the extent to which Justice Powell's opinion in *Regents of Univ. of Cal.* v. *Bakke*, 438 U. S. 265 (1978), is binding, *ante*, at 13, in favor of an unfounded wholesale adoption of it.

Justice Powell's opinion in *Bakke* and the Court's decision today rest on the fundamentally flawed proposition that racial discrimination can be contextualized so that a goal, such as classroom aesthetics, can be compelling in one context but not in another. This "we know it when we see it" approach to evaluating state interests is not capable of judicial application. Today, the Court insists on radically expanding the range of permissible uses of race to something as trivial (by comparison) as the assembling of a law school class. I can only presume that the majority's failure to justify its decision by reference to any principle arises from the absence of any such principle. See Part VI, *infra*.

B

Under the proper standard, there is no pressing public necessity in maintaining a public law school at all and, it follows, certainly not an elite law school. Likewise, marginal improvements in legal education do not qualify as a compelling state interest.

---

[4]The Law School believes both that the educational benefits of a racially engineered student body are large and that adjusting its overall admissions standards to achieve the same racial mix would require it to sacrifice its elite status. If the Law School is correct that the educational benefits of "diversity" are so great, then achieving them by altering admissions standards should not compromise its elite status. The Law School's reluctance to do this suggests that the educational benefits it alleges are not significant or do not exist at all.

1

While legal education at a public university may be good policy or otherwise laudable, it is obviously not a pressing public necessity when the correct legal standard is applied. Additionally, circumstantial evidence as to whether a state activity is of pressing public necessity can be obtained by asking whether all States feel compelled to engage in that activity. Evidence that States, in general, engage in a certain activity by no means demonstrates that the activity constitutes a pressing public necessity, given the expansive role of government in today's society. The fact that some fraction of the States reject a particular enterprise, however, creates a presumption that the enterprise itself is not a compelling state interest. In this sense, the absence of a public, American Bar Association (ABA) accredited, law school in Alaska, Delaware, Massachusetts, New Hampshire, and Rhode Island, see ABA–LSAC Official Guide to ABA-Approved Law Schools (W. Margolis, B. Gordon, J. Puskarz, & D. Rosenlieb, eds. 2004) (hereinafter ABA–LSAC Guide), provides further evidence that Michigan's maintenance of the Law School does not constitute a compelling state interest.

2

As the foregoing makes clear, Michigan has no compelling interest in having a law school at all, much less an *elite* one. Still, even assuming that a State may, under appropriate circumstances, demonstrate a cognizable interest in having an elite law school, Michigan has failed to do so here.

This Court has limited the scope of equal protection review to interests and activities that occur within that State's jurisdiction. The Court held in *Missouri ex rel. Gaines* v. *Canada*, 305 U. S. 337 (1938), that Missouri could not satisfy the demands of "separate but equal" by paying for legal training of blacks at neighboring state law schools, while maintaining a segregated law school within the State. The equal protection

> "obligation is imposed by the Constitution upon the States severally as governmental entities—each responsible for its own laws establishing the rights and duties of persons within its borders. It is an obligation the burden of which cannot be cast by one State upon another, and no State can be excused from performance *by what another State may do or fail to do.* That separate responsibility of each State within its own sphere is of the essence of statehood maintained under our dual system." *Id.*, at 350 (emphasis added).

The Equal Protection Clause, as interpreted by the Court in *Gaines*, does not permit States to justify racial discrimination on the basis of what the rest of the Nation "may do or fail to do." The only interests that can satisfy the Equal Protection Clause's demands are those found within a State's jurisdiction.

The only cognizable state interests vindicated by operating a public law school are, therefore, the education of that State's citizens and the training of that State's lawyers. James Campbell's address at the opening of the Law Department at the University of Michigan on October 3, 1859, makes this clear:

> "It not only concerns *the State* that every one should have all reasonable facilities for preparing himself for any honest position in life to which he may aspire, but it also concerns *the community* that the Law should be taught and understood. . . . There is not an office *in the State* in which serious legal inquiries may not frequently arise. . . . In all these matters, public and private rights are constantly involved and discussed, and ignorance of the Law has frequently led to results deplorable and alarming. . . . [I]n the history of *this State*, in more than

one instance, that ignorance has led to unlawful violence, and the shedding of innocent blood." E. Brown, Legal Education at Michigan 1859–1959, pp. 404–406 (1959) (emphasis added).

The Law School today, however, does precious little training of those attorneys who will serve the citizens of Michigan. In 2002, graduates of the University of Michigan Law School made up less than 6% of applicants to the Michigan bar, Michigan Lawyers Weekly, available at http://www.michiganlawyersweekly.com/barpassers0202.cfm, barpassers0702.cfm (all Internet materials as visited June 13, 2003, and available in Clerk of Court's case file), even though the Law School's graduates constitute nearly 30% of all law students graduating in Michigan. *Ibid.* Less than 16% of the Law School's graduating class elects to stay in Michigan after law school. ABA–LSAC Guide 427. Thus, while a mere 27% of the Law School's 2002 entering class are from Michigan, see University of Michigan Law School Website, available at http://www.law.umich.edu/prospectivestudents/Admissions/index.htm, only half of these, it appears, will stay in Michigan.

In sum, the Law School trains few Michigan residents and overwhelmingly serves students, who, as lawyers, leave the State of Michigan. By contrast, Michigan's other public law school, Wayne State University Law School, sends 88% of its graduates on to serve the people of Michigan. ABA–LSAC Guide 775. It does not take a social scientist to conclude that it is precisely the Law School's status as an elite institution that causes it to be a waystation for the rest of the country's lawyers, rather than a training ground for those who will remain in Michigan. The Law School's decision to be an elite institution does little to advance the welfare of the people of Michigan or any cognizable interest of the State of Michigan.

Again, the fact that few States choose to maintain elite law schools raises a strong inference that there is nothing compelling about elite status. Arguably, only the public law schools of the University of Texas, the University of California, Berkeley (Boalt Hall), and the University of Virginia maintain the same reputation for excellence as the Law School.[5] Two of these States, Texas and California, are so large that they could reasonably be expected to provide elite legal training at a separate law school to students who will, in fact, stay in the State and provide legal services to its citizens. And these two schools far outshine the Law School in producing in-state lawyers. The University of Texas, for example, sends over three-fourths of its graduates on to work in the State of Texas, vindicating the State's interest (compelling or not) in training Texas' lawyers. *Id.*, at 691.

3

Finally, even if the Law School's racial tinkering produces tangible educational benefits, a marginal improvement in legal education cannot justify racial discrimination where the Law School has no compelling interest in either its existence or in its current educational and admissions policies.

IV

The interest in remaining elite and exclusive that the majority thinks so obviously critical requires the use of admissions "standards" that, in turn, create the Law School's "need" to discriminate on the basis of race. The Court validates these admissions standards by concluding that alternatives that would require "a dramatic sacrifice of . . . the academic quality of all admitted students," *ante,* at 27, need not be considered before racial discrimination

---

[5]Cf. U. S. News & World Report, America's Best Graduate Schools 28 (2004 ed.) (placing these schools in the uppermost 15 in the Nation).

can be employed.[6] In the majority's view, such methods are not required by the "narrow tailoring" prong of strict scrutiny because that inquiry demands, in this context, that any race-neutral alternative work " 'about as well.' " *Ante*, at 26–27 (quoting *Wygant*, 476 U. S., at 280, n. 6). The majority errs, however, because race-neutral alternatives must only be "workable," *ante*, at 27, and do "about as well" *in vindicating the compelling state interest.* The Court never explicitly holds that the Law School's desire to retain the status quo in "academic selectivity" is itself a compelling state interest, and, as I have demonstrated, it is not. See Part III–B, *supra*. Therefore, the Law School should be forced to choose between its classroom aesthetic and its exclusionary admissions system—it cannot have it both ways.

With the adoption of different admissions methods, such as accepting all students who meet minimum qualifications, see Brief for United States as *Amicus Curiae* 13–14, the Law School could achieve its vision of the racially aesthetic student body without the use of racial discrimination. The Law School concedes this, but the Court holds, implicitly and under the guise of narrow tailoring, that the Law School has a compelling state interest in doing what it wants to do. I cannot agree. First, under strict scrutiny, the Law School's assessment of the benefits of racial discrimination and devotion to the admissions status quo are not entitled to any sort of deference, grounded in the First Amendment or anywhere else. Second, even if its "academic selectivity" must be maintained at all costs along with racial discrimination, the Court ignores the fact that other top law schools have succeeded in meeting their aesthetic demands without racial discrimination.

A

The Court bases its unprecedented deference to the Law School—a deference antithetical to strict scrutiny—on an idea of "educational autonomy" grounded in the First Amendment. *Ante*, at 17. In my view, there is no basis for a right of public universities to do what would otherwise violate the Equal Protection Clause.

The constitutionalization of "academic freedom" began with the concurring opinion of Justice Frankfurter in *Sweezy* v. *New Hampshire*, 354 U. S. 234 (1957). Sweezy, a Marxist economist, was investigated by the Attorney General of New Hampshire on suspicion of being a subversive. The prosecution sought, *inter alia*, the contents of a lecture Sweezy had given at the University of New Hampshire. The Court held that the investigation violated due process. *Id.*, at 254.

Justice Frankfurter went further, however, reasoning that the First Amendment created a right of academic freedom that prohibited the investigation. *Id.*, at 256–267 (opinion concurring in result). Much of the rhetoric in Justice Frankfurter's opinion was devoted to the personal right of Sweezy to free speech. See, *e.g., id.*, at 265 ("For a citizen to be made to forgo even a part of so basic a liberty as his political autonomy, the subordinating interest of the State must be compelling"). Still, claiming that the United States Reports "need not be burdened with proof," Justice Frankfurter also asserted that a "free society" depends on "free universities" and "[t]his means the exclusion of governmental intervention in the intellectual life of a university." *Id.*, at 262. According to Justice Frankfurter: "[I]t is the business of a university to provide that atmosphere which is most conducive to speculation, experiment and creation. It is an atmosphere in which there prevail 'the four essential freedoms' of a university—to determine for itself on academic grounds who may teach, what may be taught, how it shall be taught, and who may be admitted to study.' " *Id.*, at 263 (citation omitted).

In my view, "[i]t is the business" of this Court to explain itself when it cites provisions of the Constitution to invent new doctrines—including the idea that the First Amendment authorizes a public university to do what would otherwise violate the Equal Protection

---

[6]The Court refers to this component of the Law School's compelling state interest variously as "academic quality," avoiding "sacrifice [of] a vital component of its educational mission," and "academic selectivity." *Ante*, at 27–28.

Clause. The majority fails in its summary effort to prove this point. The only source for the Court's conclusion that public universities are entitled to deference even within the confines of strict scrutiny is Justice Powell's opinion in *Bakke*. Justice Powell, for his part, relied only on Justice Frankfurter's opinion in *Sweezy* and the Court's decision in *Keyishian* v. *Board of Regents of Univ. of State of N. Y.*, 385 U. S. 589 (1967), to support his view that the First Amendment somehow protected a public university's use of race in admissions. *Bakke*, 438 U. S., at 312. *Keyishian* provides no answer to the question whether the Fourteenth Amendment's restrictions are relaxed when applied to public universities. In that case, the Court held that state statutes and regulations designed to prevent the "appointment or retention of 'subversive' persons in state employment," 385 U. S., at 592, violated the First Amendment for vagueness. The statutes covered all public employees and were not invalidated only as applied to university faculty members, although the Court appeared sympathetic to the notion of academic freedom, calling it a "special concern of the First Amendment." *Id.*, at 603. Again, however, the Court did not relax any independent constitutional restrictions on public universities.

I doubt that when Justice Frankfurter spoke of governmental intrusions into the independence of universities, he was thinking of the Constitution's ban on racial discrimination. The majority's broad deference to both the Law School's judgment that racial aesthetics leads to educational benefits and its stubborn refusal to alter the status quo in admissions methods finds no basis in the Constitution or decisions of this Court.

B

1

The Court's deference to the Law School's conclusion that its racial experimentation leads to educational benefits will, if adhered to, have serious collateral consequences. The Court relies heavily on social science evidence to justify its deference. See *ante*, at 18–20; but see also Rothman, Lipset, & Nevitte, Racial Diversity Reconsidered, 151 Public Interest 25 (2003) (finding that the racial mix of a student body produced by racial discrimination of the type practiced by the Law School in fact hinders students' perception of academic quality). The Court never acknowledges, however, the growing evidence that racial (and other sorts) of heterogeneity actually impairs learning among black students. See, *e.g.*, Flowers & Pascarella, Cognitive Effects of College Racial Composition on African American Students After 3 Years of College, 40 J. of College Student Development 669, 674 (1999) (concluding that black students experience superior cognitive development at Historically Black Colleges (HBCs) and that, even among blacks, "a substantial diversity moderates the cognitive effects of attending an HBC"); Allen, The Color of Success: African-American College Student Outcomes at Predominantly White and Historically Black Public Colleges and Universities, 62 Harv. Educ. Rev. 26, 35 (1992) (finding that black students attending HBCs report higher academic achievement than those attending predominantly white colleges).

At oral argument in *Gratz* v. *Bollinger*, *ante*, p. __, counsel for respondents stated that "most every single one of [the HBCs] do have diverse student bodies." Tr. of Oral Arg. in No. 02–516, p. 52. What precisely counsel meant by "diverse" is indeterminate, but it is reported that in 2000 at Morehouse College, one of the most distinguished HBC's in the Nation, only 0.1% of the student body was white, and only 0.2% was Hispanic. College Admissions Data Handbook 2002–2003, p. 613 (43d ed. 2002) (hereinafter College Admissions Data Handbook). And at Mississippi Valley State University, a public HBC, only 1.1% of the freshman class in 2001 was white. *Id.*, at 603. If there is a "critical mass" of whites at these institutions, then "critical mass" is indeed a very small proportion.

The majority grants deference to the Law School's "assessment that diversity will, in fact, yield educational benefits," *ante*, at 16. It follows, therefore, that an HBC's assessment that racial homogeneity will yield educational benefits would similarly be given deference.[7] An HBC's rejection of white applicants in order to maintain racial homogeneity seems permissible, therefore, under the majority's view of the Equal Protection Clause. But see *United States* v. *Fordice*, 505 U. S. 717, 748 (1992) (THOMAS, J., concurring) ("Obviously, a State cannot maintain . . . traditions by closing particular institutions, historically white or historically black, to particular racial groups"). Contained within today's majority opinion is the seed of a new constitutional justification for a concept I thought long and rightly rejected—racial segregation.

2

Moreover one would think, in light of the Court's decision in *United States* v. *Virginia*, 518 U. S. 515 (1996), that before being given license to use racial discrimination, the Law School would be required to radically reshape its admissions process, even to the point of sacrificing some elements of its character. In *Virginia*, a majority of the Court, without a word about academic freedom, accepted the all-male Virginia Military Institute's (VMI) representation that some changes in its "adversative" method of education would be required with the admission of women, *id.*, at 540, but did not defer to VMI's judgment that these changes would be too great. Instead, the Court concluded that they were "manageable." *Id.*, at 551, n. 19. That case involved sex discrimination, which is subjected to intermediate, not strict, scrutiny. *Id.*, at 533; *Craig* v. *Boren*, 429 U. S. 190, 197 (1976). So in *Virginia*, where the standard of review dictated that greater flexibility be granted to VMI's educational policies than the Law School deserves here, this Court gave no deference. Apparently where the status quo being defended is that of the elite establishment—here the Law School—rather than a less fashionable Southern military institution, the Court will defer without serious inquiry and without regard to the applicable legal standard.

C

Virginia is also notable for the fact that the Court relied on the "experience" of formerly single-sex institutions, such as the service academies, to conclude that admission of women to VMI would be "manageable." 518 U. S., at 544–545. Today, however, the majority ignores the "experience" of those institutions that have been forced to abandon explicit racial discrimination in admissions.

The sky has not fallen at Boalt Hall at the University of California, Berkeley, for example. Prior to Proposition 209's adoption of Cal. Const., Art. 1, §31(a), which bars the State from "grant[ing] preferential treatment . . . on the basis of race . . . in the operation of . . . public education,"[8] Boalt Hall enrolled 20 blacks and 28 Hispanics in its first-year class for 1996. In 2002, without deploying express racial discrimination in admissions, Boalt's entering class enrolled 14 blacks and 36 Hispanics.[9] University of California Law and Medical School Enrollments, available at http://www.ucop.edu/acadadv/datamgmt/lawmed/law-enrolls-eth2.html. Total underrepresented minority student enrollment at Boalt Hall now exceeds 1996 levels. Apparently the Law School cannot be counted on to be as resourceful. The

---

[7]For example, North Carolina A&T State University, which is currently 5.4% white, College Admissions Data Handbook 643, could seek to reduce the representation of whites in order to gain additional educational benefits.

[8]Cal. Const., Art. 1, §31(a), states in full:

"The state shall not discriminate against, or grant preferential treatment to, any individual or group on the basis of race, sex, color, ethnicity, or national origin in the operation of public employment, public education, or public contracting." See *Coalition for Economic Equity* v. *Wilson*, 122 F. 3d 692 (CA9 1997).

[9]Given the incredible deference the Law School receives from the Court, I think it appropriate to indulge in the presumption that Boalt Hall operates without violating California law.

Court is willfully blind to the very real experience in California and elsewhere, which raises the inference that institutions with "reputation[s] for excellence," *ante,* at 16, 26, rivaling the Law School's have satisfied their sense of mission without resorting to prohibited racial discrimination.

V

Putting aside the absence of any legal support for the majority's reflexive deference, there is much to be said for the view that the use of tests and other measures to "predict" academic performance is a poor substitute for a system that gives every applicant a chance to prove he can succeed in the study of law. The rallying cry that in the absence of racial discrimination in admissions there would be a true meritocracy ignores the fact that the entire process is poisoned by numerous exceptions to "merit." For example, in the national debate on racial discrimination in higher education admissions, much has been made of the fact that elite institutions utilize a so-called "legacy" preference to give the children of alumni an advantage in admissions. This, and other, exceptions to a "true" meritocracy give the lie to protestations that merit admissions are in fact the order of the day at the Nation's universities. The Equal Protection Clause does not, however, prohibit the use of unseemly legacy preferences or many other kinds of arbitrary admissions procedures. What the Equal Protection Clause does prohibit are classifications made on the basis of race. So while legacy preferences can stand under the Constitution, racial discrimination cannot.[10] I will not twist the Constitution to invalidate legacy preferences or otherwise impose my vision of higher education admissions on the Nation. The majority should similarly stay its impulse to validate faddish racial discrimination the Constitution clearly forbids.

In any event, there is nothing ancient, honorable, or constitutionally protected about "selective" admissions. The University of Michigan should be well aware that alternative methods have historically been used for the admission of students, for it brought to this country the German certificate system in the late-19th century. See H. Wechsler, The Qualified Student 16–39 (1977) (hereinafter Qualified Student). Under this system, a secondary school was certified by a university so that any graduate who completed the course offered by the school was offered admission to the university. The certification regime supplemented, and later virtually replaced (at least in the Midwest), the prior regime of rigorous subject-matter entrance examinations. *Id.,* at 57–58. The facially race-neutral "percent plans" now used in Texas, California, and Florida, see *ante,* at 28, are in many ways the descendents of the certificate system.

Certification was replaced by selective admissions in the beginning of the 20th century, as universities sought to exercise more control over the composition of their student bodies. Since its inception, selective admissions has been the vehicle for racial, ethnic, and religious tinkering and experimentation by university administrators. The initial driving force for the relocation of the selective function from the high school to the universities was the same desire to select racial winners and losers that the Law School exhibits today. Columbia, Harvard, and others infamously determined that they had "too many" Jews, just as today the Law School argues it would have "too many" whites if it could not discriminate in its admissions process. See Qualified Student 155–168 (Columbia); H. Broun & G. Britt, Christians Only: A Study in Prejudice 53–54 (1931) (Harvard).

Columbia employed intelligence tests precisely because Jewish applicants, who were predominantly immigrants, scored worse on such tests. Thus, Columbia could claim (falsely) that " '[w]e have not eliminated boys because they were Jews and do not propose to do so. We have honestly attempted to eliminate the lowest grade of applicant [through the use of intelligence testing] and it turns out that a good many of the low grade men are New York

---

[10]Were this Court to have the courage to forbid the use of racial discrimination in admissions, legacy preferences (and similar practices) might quickly become less popular—a possibility not lost, I am certain, on the elites (both individual and institutional) supporting the Law School in this case.

City Jews.' " Letter from Herbert E. Hawkes, dean of Columbia College, to E. B. Wilson, June 16, 1922 (reprinted in Qualified Student 160–161). In other words, the tests were adopted with full knowledge of their disparate impact. Cf. *DeFunis* v. *Odegaard*, 416 U. S. 312, 335 (1974) *(per curiam)* (Douglas, J., dissenting).

Similarly no modern law school can claim ignorance of the poor performance of blacks, relatively speaking, on the Law School Admissions Test (LSAT). Nevertheless, law schools continue to use the test and then attempt to "correct" for black underperformance by using racial discrimination in admissions so as to obtain their aesthetic student body. The Law School's continued adherence to measures it knows produce racially skewed results is not entitled to deference by this Court. See Part IV, *supra*. The Law School itself admits that the test is imperfect, as it must, given that it regularly admits students who score at or below 150 (the national median) on the test. See App. 156–203 (showing that, between 1995 and 2000, the Law School admitted 37 students—27 of whom were black; 31 of whom were "underrepresented minorities"—with LSAT scores of 150 or lower). And the Law School's *amici* cannot seem to agree on the fundamental question whether the test itself is useful. Compare Brief for Law School Admission Council as *Amicus Curiae* 12 ("LSAT scores . . . are an effective predictor of students' performance in law school") with Brief for Harvard Black Law Students Association et al. as *Amici Curiae* 27 ("Whether [the LSAT] measure[s] objective merit . . . is certainly questionable").

Having decided to use the LSAT, the Law School must accept the constitutional burdens that come with this decision. The Law School may freely continue to employ the LSAT and other allegedly merit-based standards in whatever fashion it likes. What the Equal Protection Clause forbids, but the Court today allows, is the use of these standards hand-in-hand with racial discrimination. An infinite variety of admissions methods are available to the Law School. Considering all of the radical thinking that has historically occurred at this country's universities, the Law School's intractable approach toward admissions is striking.

The Court will not even deign to make the Law School try other methods, however, preferring instead to grant a 25-year license to violate the Constitution. And the same Court that had the courage to order the desegregation of all public schools in the South now fears, on the basis of platitudes rather than principle, to force the Law School to abandon a decidedly imperfect admissions regime that provides the basis for racial discrimination.

VI

The absence of any articulated legal principle supporting the majority's principal holding suggests another rationale. I believe what lies beneath the Court's decision today are the benighted notions that one can tell when racial discrimination benefits (rather than hurts) minority groups, see *Adarand*, 515 U. S., at 239 (SCALIA, J., concurring in part and concurring in judgment), and that racial discrimination is necessary to remedy general societal ills. This Court's precedents supposedly settled both issues, but clearly the majority still cannot commit to the principle that racial classifications are *per se* harmful and that almost no amount of benefit in the eye of the beholder can justify such classifications.

Putting aside what I take to be the Court's implicit rejection of *Adarand's* holding that beneficial and burdensome racial classifications are equally invalid, I must contest the notion that the Law School's discrimination benefits those admitted as a result of it. The Court spends considerable time discussing the impressive display of *amicus* support for the Law School in this case from all corners of society. *Ante*, at 18–19. But nowhere in any of the filings in this Court is any evidence that the purported "beneficiaries" of this racial discrimination prove themselves by performing at (or even near) the same level as those students who receive no preferences. Cf. Thernstrom & Thernstrom, Reflections on the Shape of the River, 46 UCLA L. Rev. 1583, 1605–1608 (1999) (discussing the failure of defenders of racial discrimination in admissions to consider the fact that its "beneficiaries" are underperforming in the classroom).

The silence in this case is deafening to those of us who view higher education's purpose as imparting knowledge and skills to students, rather than a communal, rubber-stamp, credentialing process. The Law School is not looking for those students who, despite a lower LSAT score or undergraduate grade point average, will succeed in the study of law. The Law School seeks only a facade—it is sufficient that the class looks right, even if it does not perform right.

The Law School tantalizes unprepared students with the promise of a University of Michigan degree and all of the opportunities that it offers. These overmatched students take the bait, only to find that they cannot succeed in the cauldron of competition. And this mismatch crisis is not restricted to elite institutions. See T. Sowell, Race and Culture 176–177 (1994) ("Even if most minority students are able to meet the normal standards at the 'average' range of colleges and universities, the systematic mismatching of minority students begun at the top can mean that such students are generally overmatched throughout all levels of higher education"). Indeed, to cover the tracks of the aestheticists, this cruel farce of racial discrimination must continue—in selection for the Michigan Law Review, see University of Michigan Law School Student Handbook 2002–2003, pp. 39–40 (noting the presence of a "diversity plan" for admission to the review), and in hiring at law firms and for judicial clerkships—until the "beneficiaries" are no longer tolerated. While these students may graduate with law degrees, there is no evidence that they have received a qualitatively better legal education (or become better lawyers) than if they had gone to a less "elite" law school for which they were better prepared. And the aestheticists will never address the real problems facing "underrepresented minorities,"[11] instead continuing their social experiments on other people's children.

Beyond the harm the Law School's racial discrimination visits upon its test subjects, no social science has disproved the notion that this discrimination "engender[s] attitudes of superiority or, alternatively, provoke[s] resentment among those who believe that they have been wronged by the government's use of race." *Adarand*, 515 U. S., at 241 (THOMAS, J., concurring in part and concurring in judgment). "These programs stamp minorities with a badge of inferiority and may cause them to develop dependencies or to adopt an attitude that they are 'entitled' to preferences." *Ibid.*

It is uncontested that each year, the Law School admits a handful of blacks who would be admitted in the absence of racial discrimination. See Brief for Respondents Bollinger et al. 6. Who can differentiate between those who belong and those who do not? The majority of blacks are admitted to the Law School because of discrimination, and because of this policy all are tarred as undeserving. This problem of stigma does not depend on determinacy as to whether those stigmatized are actually the "beneficiaries" of racial discrimination. When blacks take positions in the highest places of government, industry, or academia, it is an open question today whether their skin color played a part in their advancement. The question itself is the stigma—because either racial discrimination did play a role, in which case the person may be deemed "otherwise unqualified," or it did not, in which case asking the question itself unfairly marks those blacks who would succeed without discrimination. Is this what the Court means by "visibly open"? *Ante*, at 20.

Finally, the Court's disturbing reference to the importance of the country's law schools as training grounds meant to cultivate "a set of leaders with legitimacy in the eyes of the citizenry," *ibid.*, through the use of racial discrimination deserves discussion. As noted earlier, the Court has soundly rejected the remedying of societal discrimination as a justification for governmental use of race. *Wygant*, 476 U. S., at 276 (plurality opinion); *Croson*, 488

---

[11]For example, there is no recognition by the Law School in this case that even with their racial discrimination in place, black *men* are "underrepresented" at the Law School. See ABA–LSAC Guide 426 (reporting that the Law School has 46 black women and 28 black men). Why does the Law School not also discriminate in favor of black men over black women, given this underrepresentation? The answer is, again, that all the Law School cares about is its own image among know-it-all elites, not solving real problems like the crisis of black male underperformance.

U. S., at 497 (plurality opinion); *id.*, at 520–521 (SCALIA, J., concurring in judgment). For those who believe that every racial disproportionality in our society is caused by some kind of racial discrimination, there can be no distinction between remedying societal discrimination and erasing racial disproportionalities in the country's leadership caste. And if the lack of proportional racial representation among our leaders is not caused by societal discrimination, then "fixing" it is even less of a pressing public necessity.

The Court's civics lesson presents yet another example of judicial selection of a theory of political representation based on skin color—an endeavor I have previously rejected. See *Holder* v. *Hall*, 512 U. S. 874, 899 (1994) (THOMAS, J., concurring in judgment). The majority appears to believe that broader utopian goals justify the Law School's use of race, but "[t]he Equal Protection Clause commands the elimination of racial barriers, not their creation in order to satisfy our theory as to how society ought to be organized." *DeFunis*, 416 U. S., at 342 (Douglas, J., dissenting).

VII

As the foregoing makes clear, I believe the Court's opinion to be, in most respects, erroneous. I do, however, find two points on which I agree.

A

First, I note that the issue of unconstitutional racial discrimination among the groups the Law School prefers is not presented in this case, because petitioner has never argued that the Law School engages in such a practice, and the Law School maintains that it does not. See Brief for Respondents Bollinger et al. 32, n. 50, and 6–7, n. 7. I join the Court's opinion insofar as it confirms that this type of racial discrimination remains unlawful. *Ante*, at 13–15. Under today's decision, it is still the case that racial discrimination that does not help a university to enroll an unspecified number, or "critical mass," of underrepresented minority students is unconstitutional. Thus, the Law School may not discriminate in admissions between similarly situated blacks and Hispanics, or between whites and Asians. This is so because preferring black to Hispanic applicants, for instance, does nothing to further the interest recognized by the majority today.[12] Indeed, the majority describes such racial balancing as "patently unconstitutional." *Ante*, at 17. Like the Court, *ante*, at 24, I express no opinion as to whether the Law School's current admissions program runs afoul of this prohibition.

B

The Court also holds that racial discrimination in admissions should be given another 25 years before it is deemed no longer narrowly tailored to the Law School's fabricated compelling state interest. *Ante*, at 30. While I agree that in 25 years the practices of the Law School will be illegal, they are, for the reasons I have given, illegal now. The majority does not and cannot rest its time limitation on any evidence that the gap in credentials between

---

[12]That interest depends on enrolling a "critical mass" of underrepresented minority students, as the majority repeatedly states. *Ante*, at 3, 5, 7, 17, 20, 21, 23, 28; cf. *ante*, at 21 (referring to the unique experience of being a "racial minority," as opposed to being black, or Native American); *ante*, at 24 (rejecting argument that the Law School maintains a disguised quota by referring to the total number of enrolled underrepresented minority students, not specific races). As it relates to the Law School's racial discrimination, the Court clearly approves of only one use of race—the distinction between underrepresented minority applicants and those of all other races. A relative preference awarded to a black applicant over, for example, a similarly situated Native American applicant, does not lead to the enrollment of even one more underrepresented minority student, but only balances the races within the "critical mass."

black and white students is shrinking or will be gone in that timeframe.[13] In recent years there has been virtually no change, for example, in the proportion of law school applicants with LSAT scores of 165 and higher who are black.[14] In 1993 blacks constituted 1.1% of law school applicants in that score range, though they represented 11.1% of all applicants. Law School Admission Council, National Statistical Report (1994) (hereinafter LSAC Statistical Report). In 2000 the comparable numbers were 1.0% and 11.3%. LSAC Statistical Report (2001). No one can seriously contend, and the Court does not, that the racial gap in academic credentials will disappear in 25 years. Nor is the Court's holding that racial discrimination will be unconstitutional in 25 years made contingent on the gap closing in that time.[15]

Indeed, the very existence of racial discrimination of the type practiced by the Law School may impede the narrowing of the LSAT testing gap. An applicant's LSAT score can improve dramatically with preparation, but such preparation is a cost, and there must be sufficient benefits attached to an improved score to justify additional study. Whites scoring between 163 and 167 on the LSAT are routinely rejected by the Law School, and thus whites aspiring to admission at the Law School have every incentive to improve their score to levels above that range. See App. 199 (showing that in 2000, 209 out of 422 white applicants were rejected in this scoring range). Blacks, on the other hand, are nearly guaranteed admission if they score above 155. *Id.*, at 198 (showing that 63 out of 77 black applicants are accepted with LSAT scores above 155). As admission prospects approach certainty, there is no incentive for the black applicant to continue to prepare for the LSAT once he is reasonably assured of achieving the requisite score. It is far from certain that the LSAT test-taker's behavior is responsive to the Law School's admissions policies.[16] Nevertheless, the possibility remains that this racial discrimination will help fulfill the bigot's prophecy about black underperformance—just as it confirms the conspiracy theorist's belief that "institutional racism" is at fault for every racial disparity in our society.

I therefore can understand the imposition of a 25-year time limit only as a holding that the deference the Court pays to the Law School's educational judgments and refusal to change its admissions policies will itself expire. At that point these policies will clearly have failed to " 'eliminat[e] the [perceived] need for any racial or ethnic' " discrimination because the academic credentials gap will still be there. *Ante*, at 30 (quoting Nathanson & Bartnika, The Constitutionality of Preferential Treatment for Minority Applicants to Professional Schools, 58 Chicago Bar Rec. 282, 293 (May–June 1977)). The Court defines this time limit in terms of narrow tailoring, see *ante*, at 30, but I believe this arises from its

---

[13]I agree with JUSTICE GINSBURG that the Court's holding that racial discrimination in admissions will be illegal in 25 years is not based upon a "forecast," *post*, at 3 (concurring opinion). I do not agree with JUSTICE GINSBURG's characterization of the Court's holding as an expression of "hope." *Ibid.*

[14]I use a score of 165 as the benchmark here because the Law School feels it is the relevant score range for applicant consideration (absent race discrimination). See Brief for Respondents Bollinger et al. 5; App. to Pet. for Cert. 309a (showing that the median LSAT score for all accepted applicants from 1995–1998 was 168); *id.*, at 310a–311a (showing the median LSAT score for accepted applicants was 167 for the years 1999 and 2000); University of Michigan Law School Website, available at http://www.law.umich.edu/prospectivestudents/Admissions/index.htm (showing that the median LSAT score for accepted applicants in 2002 was 166).

[15]The majority's non sequitur observation that since 1978 the number of blacks that have scored in these upper ranges on the LSAT has grown, *ante*, at 30, says nothing about current trends. First, black participation in the LSAT until the early 1990's lagged behind black representation in the general population. For instance, in 1984 only 7.3% of law school applicants were black, whereas in 2000 11.3% of law school applicants were black. See LSAC Statistical Reports (1984 and 2000). Today, however, unless blacks were to begin applying to law school in proportions greater than their representation in the general population, the growth in absolute numbers of high scoring blacks should be expected to plateau, and it has. In 1992, 63 black applicants to law school had LSAT scores above 165. In 2000, that number was 65. See LSAC Statistical Reports (1992 and 2000).

[16]I use the LSAT as an example, but the same incentive structure is in place for any admissions criteria, including undergraduate grades, on which minorities are consistently admitted at thresholds significantly lower than whites.

refusal to define rigorously the broad state interest vindicated today. Cf. Part II, *supra.* With these observations, I join the last sentence of Part III of the opinion of the Court.

* * *

For the immediate future, however, the majority has placed its *imprimatur* on a practice that can only weaken the principle of equality embodied in the Declaration of Independence and the Equal Protection Clause. "Our Constitution is color-blind, and neither knows nor tolerates classes among citizens." *Plessy* v. *Ferguson,* 163 U. S. 537, 559 (1896) (Harlan, J., dissenting). It has been nearly 140 years since Frederick Douglass asked the intellectual ancestors of the Law School to "[d]o nothing with us!" and the Nation adopted the Fourteenth Amendment. Now we must wait another 25 years to see this principle of equality vindicated. I therefore respectfully dissent from the remainder of the Court's opinion and the judgment.

SUPREME COURT OF THE UNITED STATES

No. 02–241

BARBARA GRUTTER, PETITIONER v. *LEE BOLLINGER ET AL.*

ON WRIT OF CERTIORARI TO THE UNITED STATES COURT OF APPEALS FOR THE SIXTH CIRCUIT

[June 23, 2003]

CHIEF JUSTICE REHNQUIST, with whom JUSTICE SCALIA, JUSTICE KENNEDY, and JUSTICE THOMAS join, dissenting.

I agree with the Court that, "in the limited circumstance when drawing racial distinctions is permissible," the government must ensure that its means are narrowly tailored to achieve a compelling state interest. *Ante,* at 21; see also *Fullilove* v. *Klutznick,* 448 U. S. 448, 498 (1980) (Powell, J., concurring) ("[E]ven if the government proffers a compelling interest to support reliance upon a suspect classification, the means selected must be narrowly drawn to fulfill the governmental purpose"). I do not believe, however, that the University of Michigan Law School's (Law School) means are narrowly tailored to the interest it asserts. The Law School claims it must take the steps it does to achieve a " 'critical mass' " of underrepresented minority students. Brief for Respondents Bollinger et al. 13. But its actual program bears no relation to this asserted goal. Stripped of its "critical mass" veil, the Law School's program is revealed as a naked effort to achieve racial balancing.

As we have explained many times, " ' "[a]ny preference based on racial or ethnic criteria must necessarily receive a most searching examination." ' " *Adarand Constructors, Inc.* v. *Peña,* 515 U. S. 200, 223 (1995) (quoting *Wygant* v. *Jackson Bd. of Ed.,* 476 U. S. 267, 273 (1986) (plurality opinion of Powell, J.)). Our cases establish that, in order to withstand this demanding inquiry, respondents must demonstrate that their methods of using race " 'fit' " a compelling state interest "with greater precision than any alternative means." *Id.,* at 280, n. 6; *Regents of Univ. of Cal.* v. *Bakke,* 438 U. S. 265, 299 (1978) (opinion of Powell, J.) ("When [political judgments] touch upon an individual's race or ethnic background, he is entitled to a judicial determination that the burden he is asked to bear on that basis is precisely tailored to serve a compelling governmental interest").

Before the Court's decision today, we consistently applied the same strict scrutiny analysis regardless of the government's purported reason for using race and regardless of the setting in which race was being used. We rejected calls to use more lenient review in the face of claims that race was being used in "good faith" because " '[m]ore than good motives should be required when government seeks to allocate its resources by way of an explicit racial classification system.' " *Adarand, supra,* at 226; *Fullilove, supra,* at 537 (STEVENS, J., dissenting) ("Racial classifications are simply too pernicious to permit any but the most exact connection between justification and classification"). We likewise rejected calls to apply more lenient review based on the particular setting in which race is being used. Indeed, even in the specific context of higher education, we emphasized that "constitutional limitations protecting individual rights may not be disregarded." *Bakke, supra,* at 314.

Although the Court recites the language of our strict scrutiny analysis, its application of that review is unprecedented in its deference.

Respondents' asserted justification for the Law School's use of race in the admissions process is "obtaining 'the educational benefits that flow from a diverse student body.' " *Ante,* at 15 (quoting Brief for Respondents Bollinger et al. i). They contend that a "critical mass" of underrepresented minorities is necessary to further that interest. *Ante,* at 17. Respondents and school administrators explain generally that "critical mass" means a sufficient number of underrepresented minority students to achieve several objectives: To ensure that these minority students do not feel isolated or like spokespersons for their race; to provide adequate opportunities for the type of interaction upon which the educational benefits of diversity depend; and to challenge all students to think critically and reexamine stereotypes. See App. to Pet. for Cert. 211a; Brief for Respondents Bollinger et al. 26. These objectives indicate that "critical mass" relates to the size of the student body. *Id.,* at 5 (claiming that the Law School has enrolled "critical mass," or "enough minority students to provide meaningful integration of its classrooms and residence halls"). Respondents further claim that the Law School is achieving "critical mass." *Id.,* at 4 (noting that the Law School's goals have been "greatly furthered by the presence of . . . a 'critical mass' of" minority students in the student body).

In practice, the Law School's program bears little or no relation to its asserted goal of achieving "critical mass." Respondents explain that the Law School seeks to accumulate a "critical mass" of *each* underrepresented minority group. See, *e.g., id.,* at 49, n. 79 ("The Law School's . . . current policy . . . provide[s] a special commitment to enrolling a 'critical mass' of 'Hispanics' "). But the record demonstrates that the Law School's admissions practices with respect to these groups differ dramatically and cannot be defended under any consistent use of the term "critical mass."

From 1995 through 2000, the Law School admitted between 1,130 and 1,310 students. Of those, between 13 and 19 were Native American, between 91 and 108 were African-Americans, and between 47 and 56 were Hispanic. If the Law School is admitting between 91 and 108 African-Americans in order to achieve "critical mass," thereby preventing African-American students from feeling "isolated or like spokespersons for their race," one would think that a number of the same order of magnitude would be necessary to accomplish the same purpose for Hispanics and Native Americans. Similarly, even if all of the Native American applicants admitted in a given year matriculate, which the record demonstrates is not at all the case,* how can this possibly constitute a "critical mass" of Native Americans in a class of over 350 students? In order for this pattern of admission to be consistent with the Law School's explanation of "critical mass," one would have to believe that the objectives of "critical mass" offered by respondents are achieved with only half the number of Hispanics and one-sixth the number of Native Americans as compared to African-Americans. But respondents offer no race-specific reasons for such disparities. Instead, they simply emphasize the importance of achieving "critical mass," without any explanation of why that concept is applied differently among the three underrepresented minority groups.

These different numbers, moreover, come only as a result of substantially different treatment among the three underrepresented minority groups, as is apparent in an example

---

*Indeed, during this 5-year time period, enrollment of Native American students dropped to as low as *three* such students. Any assertion that such a small group constituted a "critical mass" of Native Americans is simply absurd.

offered by the Law School and highlighted by the Court: The school asserts that it "frequently accepts nonminority applicants with grades and test scores lower than underrepresented minority applicants (and other nonminority applicants) who are rejected." *Ante*, at 26 (citing Brief for Respondents Bollinger et al. 10). Specifically, the Law School states that "[s]ixty-nine minority applicants were rejected between 1995 and 2000 with at least a 3.5 [Grade Point Average (GPA)] and a [score of] 159 or higher on the [Law School Admissions Test (LSAT)]" while a number of Caucasian and Asian-American applicants with similar or lower scores were admitted. Brief for Respondents Bollinger et al. 10.

Review of the record reveals only 67 such individuals. Of these 67 individuals, 56 were Hispanic, while only 6 were African-American, and only 5 were Native American. This discrepancy reflects a consistent practice. For example, in 2000, 12 Hispanics who scored between a 159–160 on the LSAT and earned a GPA of 3.00 or higher applied for admission and only 2 were admitted. App. 200–201. Meanwhile, 12 African-Americans in the same range of qualifications applied for admission and all 12 were admitted. *Id.*, at 198. Likewise, that same year, 16 Hispanics who scored between a 151–153 on the LSAT and earned a 3.00 or higher applied for admission and only 1 of those applicants was admitted. *Id.*, at 200–201. Twenty-three similarly qualified African-Americans applied for admission and 14 were admitted. *Id.*, at 198.

These statistics have a significant bearing on petitioner's case. Respondents have *never* offered any race-specific arguments explaining why significantly more individuals from one underrepresented minority group are needed in order to achieve "critical mass" or further student body diversity. They certainly have not explained why Hispanics, who they have said are among "the groups most isolated by racial barriers in our country," should have their admission capped out in this manner. Brief for Respondents Bollinger et al. 50. True, petitioner is neither Hispanic nor Native American. But the Law School's disparate admissions practices with respect to these minority groups demonstrate that its alleged goal of "critical mass" is simply a sham. Petitioner may use these statistics to expose this sham, which is the basis for the Law School's admission of less qualified underrepresented minorities in preference to her. Surely strict scrutiny cannot permit these sort of disparities without at least some explanation.

Only when the "critical mass" label is discarded does a likely explanation for these numbers emerge. The Court states that the Law School's goal of attaining a "critical mass" of underrepresented minority students is not an interest in merely " 'assur[ing] within its student body some specified percentage of a particular group merely because of its race or ethnic origin.' " *Ante*, at 17 (quoting *Bakke*, 438 U. S., at 307 (opinion of Powell, J.)). The Court recognizes that such an interest "would amount to outright racial balancing, which is patently unconstitutional." *Ante*, at 17. The Court concludes, however, that the Law School's use of race in admissions, consistent with Justice Powell's opinion in *Bakke*, only pays " '[s]ome attention to numbers.' " *Ante*, at 23 (quoting *Bakke*, *supra*, at 323).

But the correlation between the percentage of the Law School's pool of applicants who are members of the three minority groups and the percentage of the admitted applicants who are members of these same groups is far too precise to be dismissed as merely the result of the school paying "some attention to [the] numbers." As the tables below show, from 1995 through 2000 the percentage of admitted applicants who were members of these minority groups closely tracked the percentage of individuals in the school's applicant pool who were from the same groups.

For example, in 1995, when 9.7% of the applicant pool was African-American, 9.4% of the admitted class was African-American. By 2000, only 7.5% of the applicant pool was African-American, and 7.3% of the admitted class was African-American. This correlation is striking. Respondents themselves emphasize that the number of underrepresented minority students admitted to the Law School would be significantly smaller if the race of each applicant were not considered. See App. to Pet. for Cert. 223a; Brief for Respondents Bollinger et al. 6 (quoting App. to Pet. for Cert. of Bollinger et al. 299a). But, as the examples above illustrate, the measure of the decrease would differ dramatically among the groups.

Table 1						
Year	Number of law school applicants	Number of African-American applicants	% of applicants who were African-American	Number of applicants admitted by the law school	Number of African-American applicants admitted	% of admitted applicants who were African-American
1995	4147	404	*9.7%*	1130	106	*9.4%*
1996	3677	342	*9.3%*	1170	108	*9.2%*
1997	3429	320	*9.3%*	1218	101	*8.3%*
1998	3537	304	*8.6%*	1310	103	*7.9%*
1999	3400	247	*7.3%*	1280	91	*7.1%*
2000	3432	259	*7.5%*	1249	91	*7.3%*

Table 2						
Year	Number of law school applicants	Number of Hispanic applicants	% of applicants who were Hispanic	Number of applicants admitted by the law school	Number of Hispanic applicants admitted	% of admitted applicants who were Hispanic
1995	4147	213	*5.1%*	1130	56	*5.0%*
1996	3677	186	*5.1%*	1170	54	*4.6%*
1997	3429	163	*4.8%*	1218	47	*3.9%*
1998	3537	150	*4.2%*	1310	55	*4.2%*
1999	3400	152	*4.5%*	1280	48	*3.8%*
2000	3432	168	*4.9%*	1249	53	*4.2%*

Table 3						
Year	Number of law school applicants	Number of Native American applicants	% of applicants who were Native American	Number of applicants admitted by the law school	Number of Native American applicants admitted	% of admitted applicants who were Native American
1995	4147	45	*1.1%*	1130	14	*1.2%*
1996	3677	31	*0.8%*	1170	13	*1.1%*
1997	3429	37	*1.1%*	1218	19	*1.6%*
1998	3537	40	*1.1%*	1310	18	*1.4%*
1999	3400	25	*0.7%*	1280	13	*1.0%*
2000	3432	35	*1.0%*	1249	14	*1.1%*

The tight correlation between the percentage of applicants and admittees of a given race, therefore, must result from careful race based planning by the Law School. It suggests a formula for admission based on the aspirational assumption that all applicants are equally qualified academically, and therefore that the proportion of each group admitted should be the same as the proportion of that group in the applicant pool. See Brief for Respondents Bollinger et al. 43, n. 70 (discussing admissions officers' use of "periodic reports" to track "the racial composition of the developing class").

Not only do respondents fail to explain this phenomenon, they attempt to obscure it. See *id.*, at 32, n. 50 ("The Law School's minority enrollment percentages . . . diverged from the percentages in the applicant pool by as much as 17.7% from 1995–2000"). But the divergence between the percentages of underrepresented minorities in the applicant pool and in the *enrolled* classes is not the only relevant comparison. In fact, it may not be the most relevant comparison. The Law School cannot precisely control which of its admitted applicants decide to attend the university. But it can and, as the numbers demonstrate, clearly does employ racial preferences in extending offers of admission. Indeed, the ostensibly flexible nature of the Law School's admissions program that the Court finds appealing, see *ante*, at 24–26, appears to be, in practice, a carefully managed program designed to ensure proportionate representation of applicants from selected minority groups.

I do not believe that the Constitution gives the Law School such free rein in the use of race. The Law School has offered no explanation for its actual admissions practices and, unexplained, we are bound to conclude that the Law School has managed its admissions program, not to achieve a "critical mass," but to extend offers of admission to members of selected minority groups in proportion to their statistical representation in the applicant pool. But this is precisely the type of racial balancing that the Court itself calls "patently unconstitutional." *Ante*, at 17.

Finally, I believe that the Law School's program fails strict scrutiny because it is devoid of any reasonably precise time limit on the Law School's use of race in admissions. We have emphasized that we will consider "the planned duration of the remedy" in determining whether a race-conscious program is constitutional. *Fullilove*, 448 U. S., at 510 (Powell, J. concurring); see also *United States* v. *Paradise*, 480 U. S. 149, 171 (1987) ("In determining whether race-conscious remedies are appropriate, we look to several factors, including the . . . duration of the relief"). Our previous cases have required some limit on the duration of programs such as this because discrimination on the basis of race is invidious.

The Court suggests a possible 25-year limitation on the Law School's current program. See *ante*, at 30. Respondents, on the other hand, remain more ambiguous, explaining that "the Law School of course recognizes that race-conscious programs must have reasonable durational limits, and the Sixth Circuit properly found such a limit in the Law School's resolve to cease considering race when genuine race-neutral alternatives become available." Brief for Respondents Bollinger et al. 32. These discussions of a time limit are the vaguest of assurances. In truth, they permit the Law School's use of racial preferences on a seemingly permanent basis. Thus, an important component of strict scrutiny—that a program be limited in time—is casually subverted.

The Court, in an unprecedented display of deference under our strict scrutiny analysis, upholds the Law School's program despite its obvious flaws. We have said that when it comes to the use of race, the connection between the ends and the means used to attain them must be precise. But here the flaw is deeper than that; it is not merely a question of "fit" between ends and means. Here the means actually used are forbidden by the Equal Protection Clause of the Constitution.

SUPREME COURT OF THE UNITED STATES

No. 02–241

BARBARA GRUTTER, PETITIONER v. *LEE BOLLINGER ET AL.*

ON WRIT OF CERTIORARI TO THE UNITED STATES COURT OF APPEALS FOR THE SIXTH CIRCUIT

[June 23, 2003]

JUSTICE KENNEDY, dissenting.

The separate opinion by Justice Powell in *Regents of Univ. of Cal.* v. *Bakke* is based on the principle that a university admissions program may take account of race as one, nonpredominant factor in a system designed to consider each applicant as an individual, provided the program can meet the test of strict scrutiny by the judiciary. 438 U. S. 265, 289–291, 315–318 (1978). This is a unitary formulation. If strict scrutiny is abandoned or manipulated to distort its real and accepted meaning, the Court lacks authority to approve the use of race even in this modest, limited way. The opinion by Justice Powell, in my view, states the correct rule for resolving this case. The Court, however, does not apply strict scrutiny. By trying to say otherwise, it undermines both the test and its own controlling precedents.

Justice Powell's approval of the use of race in university admissions reflected a tradition, grounded in the First Amendment, of acknowledging a university's conception of its educational mission. *Bakke, supra,* at 312–314; *ante,* at 16–17. Our precedents provide a basis for the Court's acceptance of a university's considered judgment that racial diversity among students can further its educational task, when supported by empirical evidence. *Ante,* at 17–19.

It is unfortunate, however, that the Court takes the first part of Justice Powell's rule but abandons the second. Having approved the use of race as a factor in the admissions process, the majority proceeds to nullify the essential safeguard Justice Powell insisted upon as the precondition of the approval. The safeguard was rigorous judicial review, with strict scrutiny as the controlling standard. *Bakke, supra,* at 291 ("Racial and ethnic distinctions of any sort are inherently suspect and thus call for the most exacting judicial examination"). This Court has reaffirmed, subsequent to *Bakke,* the absolute necessity of strict scrutiny when the state uses race as an operative category. *Adarand Constructors, Inc.* v. *Peña,* 515 U. S. 200, 224 (1995) ("[A]ny person, of whatever race, has the right to demand that any governmental actor subject to the Constitution justify any racial classification subjecting that person to unequal treatment under the strictest judicial scrutiny"); *Richmond* v. *J. A. Croson Co.,* 488 U. S. 469, 493–494 (1989); see *id.,* at 519 (KENNEDY, J., concurring in part and concurring in judgment) ("[A]ny racial preference must face the most rigorous scrutiny by the courts"). The Court confuses deference to a university's definition of its educational objective with deference to the implementation of this goal. In the context of university admissions the objective of racial diversity can be accepted based on empirical data known to us, but deference is not to be given with respect to the methods by which it is pursued. Preferment by race, when resorted to by the State, can be the most divisive of all policies, containing within it the potential to destroy confidence in the Constitution and in the idea of equality. The majority today refuses to be faithful to the settled principle of strict review designed to reflect these concerns.

The Court, in a review that is nothing short of perfunctory, accepts the University of Michigan Law School's assurances that its admissions process meets with constitutional requirements. The majority fails to confront the reality of how the Law School's admissions policy is implemented. The dissenting opinion by THE CHIEF JUSTICE, which I join in full, demonstrates beyond question why the concept of critical mass is a delusion used by the Law School to mask its attempt to make race an automatic factor in most instances and to achieve numerical goals indistinguishable from quotas. An effort to achieve racial balance among the minorities the school seeks to attract is, by the Court's own admission, "patently unconstitutional." *Ante,* at 17; see also *Bakke,* 438 U. S, at 307 (opinion of Powell, J.). It remains to point out how critical mass becomes inconsistent with individual consideration in some more specific aspects of the admissions process.

About 80 to 85 percent of the places in the entering class are given to applicants in the upper range of Law School Admissions Test scores and grades. An applicant with these credentials likely will be admitted without consideration of race or ethnicity. With respect to the remaining 15 to 20 percent of the seats, race is likely outcome determinative for many members of minority groups. That is where the competition becomes tight and where any given applicant's chance of admission is far smaller if he or she lacks minority status. At this point the numerical concept of critical mass has the real potential to compromise individual review.

The Law School has not demonstrated how individual consideration is, or can be, preserved at this stage of the application process given the instruction to attain what it calls

Year	Percentage of enrolled minority students
1987	12.3%
1988	13.6%
1989	14.4%
1990	13.4%
1991	19.1%
1992	19.8%
1993	14.5%
1994	20.1%
1995	13.5%
1996	13.8%
1997	13.6%
1998	13.8%

critical mass. In fact the evidence shows otherwise. There was little deviation among admitted minority students during the years from 1995 to 1998. The percentage of enrolled minorities fluctuated only by 0.3%, from 13.5% to 13.8%. The number of minority students to whom offers were extended varied by just a slightly greater magnitude of 2.2%, from the high of 15.6% in 1995 to the low of 13.4% in 1998.

The District Court relied on this uncontested fact to draw an inference that the Law School's pursuit of critical mass mutated into the equivalent of a quota. 137 F. Supp. 2d 821, 851 (ED Mich. 2001). Admittedly, there were greater fluctuations among enrolled minorities in the preceding years, 1987–1994, by as much as 5 or 6%. The percentage of minority offers, however, at no point fell below 12%, historically defined by the Law School as the bottom of its critical mass range. The greater variance during the earlier years, in any event, does not dispel suspicion that the school engaged in racial balancing. The data would be consistent with an inference that the Law School modified its target only twice, in 1991 (from 13% to 19%), and then again in 1995 (back from 20% to 13%). The intervening year, 1993, when the percentage dropped to 14.5%, could be an aberration, caused by the school's miscalculation as to how many applicants with offers would accept or by its redefinition, made in April 1992, of which minority groups were entitled to race-based preference. See Brief for Respondents Bollinger et al. 49, n. 79.

The narrow fluctuation band raises an inference that the Law School subverted individual determination, and strict scrutiny requires the Law School to overcome the inference. Whether the objective of critical mass "is described as a quota or a goal, it is a line drawn on the basis of race and ethnic status," and so risks compromising individual assessment. *Bakke*, 438 U. S., at 289 (opinion of Powell, J.). In this respect the Law School program compares unfavorably with the experience of Little Ivy League colleges. *Amicus* Amherst College, for example, informs us that the offers it extended to students of African-American background during the period from 1993 to 2002 ranged between 81 and 125 out of 950 offers total, resulting in a fluctuation from 24 to 49 matriculated students in a class of about 425. See Brief for Amherst College et al. as *Amici Curiae* 10–11. The Law School insisted upon a much smaller fluctuation, both in the offers extended and in the students who eventually enrolled, despite having a comparable class size.

The Law School has the burden of proving, in conformance with the standard of strict scrutiny, that it did not utilize race in an unconstitutional way. *Adarand Constructors*, 515 U. S., at 224. At the very least, the constancy of admitted minority students and the close correlation between the racial breakdown of admitted minorities and the composition of the applicant pool, discussed by THE CHIEF JUSTICE, *ante*, at 3–9, require the Law School either to produce a convincing explanation or to show it has taken adequate steps to ensure individual assessment. The Law School does neither.

The obvious tension between the pursuit of critical mass and the requirement of individual review increased by the end of the admissions season. Most of the decisions where race may decide the outcome are made during this period. See *supra*, at 3. The admissions officers consulted the daily reports which indicated the composition of the incoming class along racial lines. As Dennis Shields, Director of Admissions from 1991 to 1996, stated, "the further [he] went into the [admissions] season the more frequently [he] would want to look at these [reports] and see the change from day-to-day." These reports would "track exactly where [the Law School] st[ood] at any given time in assembling the class," and so would tell the admissions personnel whether they were short of assembling a critical mass of minority students. Shields generated these reports because the Law School's admissions policy told him the racial make-up of the entering class was "something [he] need[ed] to be concerned about," and so he had "to find a way of tracking what's going on."

The consultation of daily reports during the last stages in the admissions process suggests there was no further attempt at individual review save for race itself. The admissions officers could use the reports to recalibrate the plus factor given to race depending on how close they were to achieving the Law School's goal of critical mass. The bonus factor of race would then become divorced from individual review; it would be premised instead on the numerical objective set by the Law School.

The Law School made no effort to guard against this danger. It provided no guidelines to its admissions personnel on how to reconcile individual assessment with the directive to admit a critical mass of minority students. The admissions program could have been structured to eliminate at least some of the risk that the promise of individual evaluation was not being kept. The daily consideration of racial breakdown of admitted students is not a feature of affirmative-action programs used by other institutions of higher learning. The Little Ivy League colleges, for instance, do not keep ongoing tallies of racial or ethnic composition of their entering students. See Brief for Amherst College et al. as *Amici Curiae* 10.

To be constitutional, a university's compelling interest in a diverse student body must be achieved by a system where individual assessment is safeguarded through the entire process. There is no constitutional objection to the goal of considering race as one modest factor among many others to achieve diversity, but an educational institution must ensure, through sufficient procedures, that each applicant receives individual consideration and that race does not become a predominant factor in the admissions decisionmaking. The Law School failed to comply with this requirement, and by no means has it carried its burden to show otherwise by the test of strict scrutiny.

The Court's refusal to apply meaningful strict scrutiny will lead to serious consequences. By deferring to the law schools' choice of minority admissions programs, the courts will lose the talents and resources of the faculties and administrators in devising new and fairer ways to ensure individual consideration. Constant and rigorous judicial review forces the law school faculties to undertake their responsibilities as state employees in this most sensitive of areas with utmost fidelity to the mandate of the Constitution. Dean Allan Stillwagon, who directed the Law School's Office of Admissions from 1979 to 1990, explained the difficulties he encountered in defining racial groups entitled to benefit under the School's affirmative action policy. He testified that faculty members were "breathtakingly cynical" in deciding who would qualify as a member of underrepresented minorities. An example he offered was faculty debate as to whether Cubans should be counted as Hispanics: One professor objected on the grounds that Cubans were Republicans. Many academics at other law schools who are "affirmative action's more forthright defenders readily concede that diversity is merely the current rationale of convenience for a policy that they prefer to justify on other grounds." Schuck, Affirmative Action: Past, Present, and Future, 20 Yale L. & Pol'y Rev. 1, 34 (2002) (citing Levinson, Diversity, 2 U. Pa. J. Const. L. 573, 577–578 (2000);

Rubenfeld, Affirmative Action, 107 Yale L. J. 427, 471 (1997)). This is not to suggest the faculty at Michigan or other law schools do not pursue aspirations they consider laudable and consistent with our constitutional traditions. It is but further evidence of the necessity for scrutiny that is real, not feigned, where the corrosive category of race is a factor in decisionmaking. Prospective students, the courts, and the public can demand that the State and its law schools prove their process is fair and constitutional in every phase of implementation.

It is difficult to assess the Court's pronouncement that race-conscious admissions programs will be unnecessary 25 years from now. *Ante*, at 30–31. If it is intended to mitigate the damage the Court does to the concept of strict scrutiny, neither petitioners nor other rejected law school applicants will find solace in knowing the basic protection put in place by Justice Powell will be suspended for a full quarter of a century. Deference is antithetical to strict scrutiny, not consistent with it.

As to the interpretation that the opinion contains its own self-destruct mechanism, the majority's abandonment of strict scrutiny undermines this objective. Were the courts to apply a searching standard to race-based admissions schemes, that would force educational institutions to seriously explore race-neutral alternatives. The Court, by contrast, is willing to be satisfied by the Law School's profession of its own good faith. The majority admits as much: "We take the Law School at its word that it would 'like nothing better than to find a race-neutral admissions formula' and will terminate its race-conscious admissions program as soon as practicable." *Ante*, at 30 (quoting Brief for Respondent Bollinger et al. 34).

If universities are given the latitude to administer programs that are tantamount to quotas, they will have few incentives to make the existing minority admissions schemes transparent and protective of individual review. The unhappy consequence will be to perpetuate the hostilities that proper consideration of race is designed to avoid. The perpetuation, of course, would be the worst of all outcomes. Other programs do exist which will be more effective in bringing about the harmony and mutual respect among all citizens that our constitutional tradition has always sought. They, and not the program under review here, should be the model, even if the Court defaults by not demanding it.

It is regrettable the Court's important holding allowing racial minorities to have their special circumstances considered in order to improve their educational opportunities is accompanied by a suspension of the strict scrutiny which was the predicate of allowing race to be considered in the first place. If the Court abdicates its constitutional duty to give strict scrutiny to the use of race in university admissions, it negates my authority to approve the use of race in pursuit of student diversity. The Constitution cannot confer the right to classify on the basis of race even in this special context absent searching judicial review. For these reasons, though I reiterate my approval of giving appropriate consideration to race in this one context, I must dissent in the present case.

SELECTED BIBLIOGRAPHY

Altschiller, Donald, ed. 1991. *Affirmative Action.* New York: H.W. Wilson.

Arthur, John, and Amy Shapiro, eds. 1995. *Campus Wars: Multiculturalism and the Politics of Difference.* Boulder, CO: Westview Press.

Ball, Howard. 2000. *The Bakke Case: Race, Education, and Affirmative Action.* Lawrence: University Press of Kansas.

Beckwith, Francis J., and Todd E. Jones, eds. 1997. *Affirmative Action: Social Justice or Reverse Discrimination?* Amherst, NY: Prometheus Books.

Bell, Derrick. 1987. *And We Are Not Saved: The Elusive Quest for Racial Justice.* New York: Basic Books.

Bell, Derrick. 1992. *Faces at the Bottom of the Well: The Permanence of Racism.* New York: Basic Books.

Belz, Herman. 1991. *Equality Transformed: A Quarter-Century of Affirmative Action.* Bowling Green, OH: Social Philosophy and Policy Center.

Bergmann, Barbara R. 1996. *In Defense of Affirmative Action.* New York: Basic Books.

Blanchard, Fletcher A., and Faye J. Crosby, eds. 1989. *Affirmative Action in Perspective.* New York: Springer-Verlag.

Bolick, Clint. 1996. *The Affirmative Action Fraud: Can We Restore the American Civil Rights Vision?* Washington, DC: Cato Institute.

Bowen, William G., and Derek Bok. 1998. *The Shape of the River.* Princeton, NJ: Princeton University Press.

Browne-Miller, Angela. 1996. *Shameful Admissions: The Losing Battle to Serve Everyone in Our Universities.* San Francisco: Jossey-Bass Publishers.

Cahn, Stephen M., ed. 1993. *Affirmative Action and the University: A Philosophical Inquiry.* Philadelphia: Temple University Press.

Carter, Stephen L. 1991. *Reflections of an Affirmative Action Baby.* New York: Basic Books.

Chavez, Lydia. 1998. *The Color Bind: California's Battle to End Affirmative Action.* Berkeley: University of California Press.

Clayton, Susan D., and Faye J. Crosby. 1992. *Justice, Gender, and Affirmative Action.* Ann Arbor: University of Michigan Press.

Cohen, Carl. 1995. *Naked Racial Preference.* Lanham, MD: Madison Books.

Crosby, Faye J., and Cheryl VanDeVeer, eds. 2000. *Sex, Race, and Merit: Debating Affirmative Action in Education and Employment.* Ann Arbor: University of Michigan Press.

Curry, George E., ed. 1996. *The Affirmative Action Debate*. Reading, MA: Perseus Books.

Drake, W. Avon, and Robert D. Holsworth. 1996. *Affirmative Action and the Stalled Quest for Black Progress*. Urbana: University of Illinois Press.

Dworaczek, Marian. 1988. *Affirmative Action and Minorities: A Bibliography*. Monticello, IL: Vance Bibliographies.

Eastland, Terry. 1996. *Ending Affirmative Action: The Case for Colorblind Justice*. New York: Basic Books.

Edley, Christopher, Jr. 1996. *Not All Black and White: Affirmative Action, Race, and American Values*. New York: Hill and Wang.

Ezorsky, Gertrude. 1991. *Racism and Justice: The Case for Affirmative Action*. Ithaca, NY: Cornell University Press.

Felkenes, George T., and Peter Charles Unsinger, eds. 1992. *Affirmative Action and Law Enforcement*. Springfield, IL: C.C. Thomas.

Fiscus, Ronald J. 1992. *The Constitutional Logic of Affirmative Action*. Durham, NC: Duke University Press.

Glazer, Nathan. 1975. *Affirmative Discrimination*. New York: Basic Books.

Graham, Hugh Davis. 2002. *Collision Course: The Strange Convergence of Affirmative Action and Immigration Policy in America*. New York: Oxford University Press.

Gray, W. Robert. 2001. *The Four Faces of Affirmative Action: Fundamental Answers and Actions*. Westport, CT: Greenwood Press.

Greene, Katherine W. 1989. *Affirmative Action and Principles of Justice*. New York: Greenwood Press.

Guinier, Lani, and Susan Sturm. 2001. *Who's Qualified?* Boston: Beacon Press.

Jones, Augustus J. 1991. *Affirmative Talk, Affirmative Action: A Comparative Study of the Politics of Affirmative Action*. New York: Praeger.

Kahlenberg, Richard D. 1996. *The Remedy: Class, Race, and Affirmative Action*. New York: Basic Books.

Kull, Andrew. 1992. *The Color-Blind Constitution*. Cambridge, MA: Harvard University Press.

Leiter, Samuel, and William M. Leiter. 2002. *Affirmative Action in Antidiscrimination Laws and Policy: An Overview and Synthesis*. Albany: State University of New York Press.

Lynch, Frederick R. 1991. *Invisible Victims: White Males and the Crisis of Affirmative Action*. New York: Praeger.

Mills, Nicolaus, ed. 1994. *Debating Affirmative Action: Race, Gender, Ethnicity, and the Politics of Inclusion*. New York: Dell Publishing.

Mosley, Albert G., and Nicholas Capaldi. 1996. *Affirmative Action*. Lanham, MD: Rowman and Littlefield.

Orfield, Gary, and Edward Miller, eds. 1998. *Chilling Admissions: The Affirmative Action Crisis and the Search for Alternatives*. Cambridge, MA: Harvard Education Publishing Group.

Orlans, Harold, and June O'Neill, eds. 1992. *Affirmative Action Revisited*. Newbury Park, CA: Sage.

Raza, M. Ali, A. Janell Anderson, and Harry Glynn Custred Jr. 1999. *The Ups and Downs of Affirmative Action Preferences*. Westport, CT: Praeger.

Reskin, Barbara F. 1998. *The Realities of Affirmative Action in Employment*. Washington, DC: American Sociological Association.

Roberts, Paul Craig, and Lawrence M. Stratton. 1995. *The New Color Line: How Quotas and Privilege Destroy Democracy*. Washington, DC: Regnery Publishers.

Rosenfeld, Michael. 1991. *Affirmative Action and Justice: A Philosophical and Constitutional Inquiry*. New Haven, CT: Yale University Press.

Rubio, Philip F. 2001. *A History of Affirmative Action, 1619–2000.* Jackson: University Press of Mississippi.

Simms, Margaret C., ed. 1995. *Economic Perspectives on Affirmative Action.* Washington, DC: Joint Center for Political and Economic Studies.

Skrentny, John David. 1996. *The Ironies of Affirmative Action: Politics, Culture, and Justice in America.* Chicago: University of Chicago Press.

Skrentny, John David. 2001. *Color Lines: Affirmative Action, Immigration, and Civil Rights Options for America.* Chicago: University of Chicago Press.

Sowell, Thomas. 1984. *Civil Rights: Rhetoric or Reality?* New York: William Morrow.

Sowell, Thomas. 1990. *Preferential Policies: An International Perspective.* New York: William Morrow.

Spann, Girardeau A. 2000. *The Law of Affirmative Action: Twenty-five Years of Supreme Court Decisions on Race and Remedies.* New York: New York University Press.

Steele, Shelby. 1990. *The Content of Our Character.* New York: St. Martin's Press.

Taylor, Bron Raymond. 1991. *Affirmative Action at Work: Law, Politics, and Ethics.* Pittsburgh: University of Pittsburgh Press.

Turner, Ronald. 1990. *The Past and Future of Affirmative Action: A Guide and Analysis for Human Resource Professionals and Corporate Counsel.* New York: Quorum Books.

Urofsky, Melvin I. 1991. *Conflict of Rights: The Supreme Court and Affirmative Action.* New York: Charles Scribner's Sons.

Wilkinson, J. Harvie, III. 1979. *From Brown to Bakke: The Supreme Court and School Integration. 1954–1978.* New York: Oxford University Press.

Yates, Steven. 1994. *Civil Wrongs: What Went Wrong with Affirmative Action.* San Francisco: Institute for Contemporary Studies.

INDEX

Page references in **bold** type indicate main entries in the encyclopedia.